DATE			

For Reference

Not to be taken from this room

INDEX
to
Black American
Literary Anthologies

INDEX
to
Black American
Literary Anthologies

Compiled
under the direction of
Jessamine S. Kallenbach
Assistant Humanities Librarian

Sponsored
by the
Center of Educational Resources
Eastern Michigan University
Ypsilanti, Michigan

G.K.HALL &CO.
70 Lincoln Street, Boston, Mass.

Library of Congress Cataloging in Publication Data
Kallenbach, Jessamine S   1915-
   Index to Black American literary anthologies.

   (Bibliographies and guides in Black studies)
   1. American literature — Afro-American authors — Indexes.
I. Eastern Michigan University. Center of Educational Resources.
II. Title.   III. Series.
Z1229.N39K34   [PS153.N5]   016.81′08′0896   78-13017
ISBN 0-8161-8186-1

MANUFACTURED IN THE UNITED STATES OF AMERICA
This publication is printed on permanent/durable acid-free paper

Contents

Preface   vii

Anthologies Indexed   ix

Index by Author   1

Index by Title   117

Preface

This "Index to Black American Literary Anthologies" is designed to aid students in locating Black American literature which has been published in collections. An effort has been made to include as many collections as we could identify and locate, which met our established criteria for inclusion. Whatever omissions there may be—and we are aware there are some—are due to our own inability to locate the titles. These omissions we hope will be corrected in any future editions.

The criteria established for inclusion in this index are as follows: the anthology must include more than two authors; it must be literary in quality, rather than solely political or social in purpose; it should be designed for an adult rather than a children's audience; it should be at least partly in English; it should include predominantly black authors; it should be longer than twenty-five pages; it may be limited to a single genre, or it may include a variety of genres; it may include excerpted or entire autobiographies, dramas, essays, fiction, narratives, poetry, short fiction, speeches, which will all be indexed; however, entire volumes of speeches and addresses have been excluded.

Section I of the *Index,* the main arrangement, is alphabetical by author. This section gives the fullest information, including birth and death dates (if known) of the author, the genres in which he writes, and citations to anthologies in which titles may be found. Under the author's name, the titles are listed by genre, alphabetically; and under genre, alphabetically by title. Section II, the "Title Index," must be supplemented by referral to the main author section.

It would be impossible to thank every individual who has contributed to creating this volume. Numerous clerical and student assistants in the Humanities Division of the Center of Educational Resources deserve mention for their aid. Special gratitude goes to Elizabeth Rebman, Music Librarian of the Humanities Division, who initiated the project in 1969; and to Hannelore Rader Delgado, Foreign Languages Librarian, who furthered it in 1970–71. My special OEO student assistant, Donna Marie Spitler, demonstrated indomitable perseverance in pushing it to completion this year.

Appreciation is also owing to Dr. Fred Blum, Director of the Center of Educational Resources of Eastern Michigan University for sponsoring the project; to Carol Selby, the Humanities Division Coordinator, for giving the project encouragement and impetus; to Donnetta Noland, Humanities Division Office Manager, for her loyal cooperation and tolerance; to Pamela Reeves, Associate Librarian, for helping with the business details; to Rita Bullard, CER Interlibrary Loan Assistant, who successfully brought many elusive titles to our hands; and to the many libraries throughout the United States which generously lent us their materials and services through the Interlibrary Loan System.

For any errors, omissions or inaccuracies I, myself, assume full responsibility.

J. K.

ANTHOLOGIES INDEXED

Adams   Adams, William, comp. *Afro-American Literature: Drama.* Boston: Houghton Mifflin, 1970.

Adams 2   Adams, William, comp. *Afro-American Literature: Fiction.* Boston: Houghton Mifflin, 1970.

Adams 3   Adams, William, comp. *Afro-American Literature: Poetry.* Boston: Houghton Mifflin, 1970.

Adams 4   Adams, William, comp. *Afro-American Literature: Essays.* Boston: Houghton Mifflin, 1970.

Adoff 4   Adoff, Arnold, ed. *Black on Black; Commentaries by Negro Americans.* New York: Macmillan, 1968.

Adoff   Adoff, Arnold, ed. *City in All Directions; an Anthology of Modern Poems.* New York: Macmillan, 1969.

Adoff 2   Adoff, Arnold, ed. *I Am The Darker Brother.* New York: Macmillan, 1968.

Adoff 3   Adoff, Arnold, ed. *Poetry of Black America: Anthology of the 20th Century.* New York: Harper and Row, 1973.

Alhamisi   Alhamisi, Ahmed and Harun Kofi Wangara, eds. *Black Arts; an Anthology of Black Creations.* Detroit: Black Arts Publications, 1969.

Baker   Baker, Houston A., Jr., ed. *Black Literature in America.* New York: McGraw-Hill, 1971.

Barksdale   Barksdale, Richard and K. Kinnamon, eds. *Black Writers of America.* New York: Macmillan, 1972.

Bell   Bell, Bernard W., ed. *Modern and Contemporary Afro-American Poetry.* Boston: Allyn and Bacon, 1972.

Bigsby   Bigsby, C.W.E., ed. *The Black American Writer.* Deland, Fla.: Everett/Edwards, 1969. Vol. I, Fiction; Vol. II, Poetry and Drama.

Black   *Black and Unknown Bards; a Collection of Negro Poetry* (Eric Walrond and Rosy Pool, eds.). Aldington, Kent: Hand and Flower Press, n.d.

Bontemps   Bontemps, Arna W., ed. *American Negro Poetry*. New York: Hill and Wang, 1963.

Bontemps 2   Bontemps, Arna W., ed. *American Negro Poetry*. Revised edition. New York: Hill and Wang, 1974.

Bontemps 3   Bontemps, Arna, ed. *Harlem Renaissance Remembered*. New York: Dodd, Mead, 1972.

Bookers   Bookers, The, eds. *Cry At Birth*. New York: McGraw-Hill, 1971.

Brasmer   Brasmer, William and Dominick Consolo, eds. *Black Drama, an Anthology*. Columbus, Ohio: Charles E. Merrill, 1970.

Brawley   Brawley, Benjamin, ed. *Early American Negro Writers*. Freeport, N.Y.: Books for Libraries Press, (©1935) 1968.

Breman   Breman, Paul, ed. *You Better Believe It; Black Verse in English from Africa, the West Indies and the United States*. Harmondsworth, England: Penguin Books, 1973.

Breman 2   Breman, Paul, ed. *Sixes and Sevens: an Anthology of New Poetry*. London: Paul Breman, 1962.

Brewer   Brewer, John Mason, ed. *Heralding Dawn; an Anthology of Verse*. Dallas: Superior Typesetting, ©1936.

Brooks   Brooks, Gwendolyn, ed. *Broadside Treasury*. Detroit: Broadside, 1971.

Brooks 2   Brooks, Gwendolyn, ed. *Jump Bad; a New Anthology*. Detroit: Broadside Press, 1971.

Brown, P.   Brown, Patricia, ed. *To Gwen With Love; an Anthology Dedicated to Gwendolyn Brooks*. Chicago: Johnson Publishing, 1971.

Brown   Brown, Sterling, ed. *The Negro Caravan*. New York: Citadel Press, 1941.

Bullins   Bullins, Ed, ed. *New Lafayette Theatre Presents Plays with Aesthetic Comments by 6 Black Playwrights*. Garden City, N.Y.: Anchor Press, Doubleday, 1974.

Bullins 2   Bullins, Ed, ed. *New Plays From the Black Theatre*. Des Plaines, Ill.: Bantam Books, 1969.

Burnett   Burnett, Whit, ed. *Black Hands on a White Face; a Timepiece of Experiences in a Black and White America*. New York: Dodd, Mead, 1971.

Caldwell   Caldwell, Ben, et al. *Black Quartet; Four New Black Plays by Ben Caldwell et al.* New York: New American Library, 1970.

Calverton   Calverton, V. F., ed. *Anthology of American Negro Literature*. Millwood, N. Y.: Kraus Reprint, (©1929) 1976.

Chambers   Chambers, Bradford and Rebecca Moon, eds. *Right on; an Anthology of Black Literature*. New York: New American Library, 1970.

Chapman   Chapman, Abraham, ed. *Black Voices*. New York: New American Library, 1968.

Chapman 2   Chapman, Abraham, ed. *New Black Voices; an Anthology of Contemporary Afro-American Literature*. New York: New American Library, 1972.

Clarke   Clarke, John H., ed. *American Negro Short Stories*. New York: Hill and Wang, 1966.

Clarke 2   Clarke, John H., ed. *William Styron's Nat Turner: Ten Black Writers Respond*. Boston: Beacon Press, 1968.

Clarke 3   Clarke, John Henrik, ed. *Harlem*. New York: New American Library, 1970.

Conference   Conference of Negro Writers, 1st., N. Y., 1959. *American Negro Writer and His Roots 1960*. New York: American Society of African Culture, 1960.

Coombs   Coombs, Orde, ed. *We Speak as Liberators: Young Black Poets*. New York: Dodd, Mead, 1970.

Coombs 2   Coombs, Orde, ed. *What We Must See. Young Black Storytellers*. New York: Dodd, Mead, 1971.

Couch   Couch, William, ed. *New Black Playwrights*. Baton Rouge: Louisiana State University Press, 1968.

Cromwell   Cromwell, Otelia, ed. *Readings from Negro Authors*. New York: Harcourt Brace, 1931.

Cullen   Cullen, Countee, ed. *Caroling Dusk; an Anthology of Verse by Negro Poets*. New York: Harper and Row, (©1927) 1974.

Cuney   Cuney, Waring, Langston Hughes and Bruce Wright, eds. *Centennial Anthology: Lincoln University Poets*. New York: Fine Editions Press, 1954.

Curry   Curry, Gladys J., ed. *Viewpoints from Black America*. New York: Prentice-Hall, 1970.

Davis   Davis, Arthur P. and Saunders Redding, eds. *Cavalcade; Negro American Writing from 1760 to the Present*. Boston: Houghton Mifflin, 1971.

Davis, C.   Davis, Charles T. and Daniel Walden, eds. *On Being Black; Writings by Afro-Americans from Frederick Douglass to the Present*. New York: Fawcett, 1970.

Demarest   Demarest, David P., and Lois S. Lamdin, eds. *The Ghetto Reader*. New York: Random House, 1970.

DeRohan   DeRohan, Pierre, ed. *Federal Theatre Plays*. New York: Random House, 1938.

Dreer   Dreer, Herman, ed. *American Literature by Negro Authors*. New York: Macmillan, 1950.

Emanuel Emanuel, James A. and Theodore Gross, eds. *Dark Symphony.* New York: Free Press, 1968.

Exum Exum, Pat Crutchfield, ed. *Keeping the Faith: Writings by Contemporary Black American Women.* Greenwich, Conn.: Fawcett, 1974.

Ford Ford, Nick Aaron, ed. *Black Insights: Significant Literature by Black Americans—1760 to the Present.* Waltham, Mass.: Ginn and Co., 1971.

Ford 2 Ford, Nick Aaron and H. Faggett, eds. (Baltimore Afro-American.) *Best Short Stories by Afro-American Writers (1925–1950).* New York: Kraus Reprint, (©1950) 1969.

Freedman Freedman, Frances S., ed. *The Black American Experience; a New Anthology of Black Literature.* New York: Bantam Books, 1970.

Gayle Gayle, Addison Jr., ed. *Bondage, Freedom and Beyond: The Prose of Black Americans.* Garden City, N. Y.: Zenith Books, 1971.

Gayle 2 Gayle, Addison, Jr., ed. *Black Expression; Essays by and About Black Americans in the Creative Arts.* New York: Weybright and Talley, 1969.

Gayle 3 Gayle, Addison, Jr. *The Black Aesthetic.* Garden City, N. Y.: Doubleday, 1971.

Gibson Gibson, Donald and C. Anselment, eds. *Black and White: Stories of American Life.* New York: Washington Square (©1971) 1973.

Gibson 2 Gibson, Donald B., ed. *Five Black Writers.* New York: New York University Press, 1970.

Gibson 3 Gibson, Donald, ed. *Modern Black Poets; a Collection of Critical Essays.* Englewood Cliffs, N. J.: Prentice-Hall, 1973.

Gross Gross, Seymour L. and J. E. Hardy, eds. *Images of the Negro in America.* Chicago: University of Chicago Press, 1966.

Haslam Haslam, Gerald W., ed. *Forgotten Pages of American Literature.* Boston: Houghton Mifflin, 1970.

Hatch Hatch, James V., ed. *Black Theater, U.S.A. Forty-Five Plays by Black Americans.* New York: Free Press, 1974.

Hayden Hayden, Robert, ed. *Afro-American Literature: an Introduction.* New York: Harcourt Brace Jovanovich, 1971.

Hayden 2 Hayden, Robert, ed. *Kaleidoscope.* Durham, N. C.: Moore Publishing, 1968.

Hemenway Hemenway, Robert, ed. *The Black Novelist.* Columbus, Ohio: Charles E. Merrill, 1970.

Henderson   Henderson, Stephen E., comp. *Understanding the New Black Poetry; Black Speech and Black Music as Poetic Reference.* New York: William Morrow, 1973.

Hill   Hill, Herbert, ed. *Anger and Beyond; The Negro Writer In the United States.* New York: Harper and Row, 1966.

Hill 2   Hill, Herbert, ed. *Soon, One Morning.* New York: Alfred A. Knopf, 1966.

Hollo   Hollo, Anselm. *Negro Verse.* London: Vista Books, 1964.

Hughes   Hughes, Langston, ed. *New Negro Poets USA.* Bloomington: Indiana University Press, 1964.

Hughes 2   Hughes, Langston and Arna Bontemps, eds. *Poetry of the Negro, 1746–1970.* Garden City, N. Y.: Doubleday, 1970.

Hughes 3   Hughes, Langston, ed. *Best Short Stories by Negro Writers.* . . . Boston: Little, Brown, 1967.

James   James, Charles L., ed. *From the Roots: Short Stories by Black Americans.* New York: Dodd, Mead, 1970.

Johnson, C.   Johnson, Charles S., ed. *Ebony and Topaz: a Collecteana.* Freeport, N. Y.: Books for Libraries Press, (©1927) 1971.

Johnson   Johnson, James Weldon, ed. *Book of American Negro Poetry.* New York: Harcourt Brace and World, 1958.

Jones   Jones, Leroy and Larry Neal, eds. *Black Fire.* New York: William Morrow, 1968.

Jordan   Jordan, June, ed. *Soulscript. Afro-American Poetry.* Garden City, N. Y.: Zenith, 1970.

Kearns   Kearns, Francis E., ed. *The Black Experience: an Anthology of American Literature for the 1970's.* New York: Viking, 1970.

Kearns 2   Kearns, Francis E., ed. *Black Identity: a Thematic Reader.* New York: Holt, Rinehart, and Winston, 1970.

Kendricks   Kendricks, Ralph and Claudette Levitt, eds. *Afro-American Voices, 1770's–1970's.* New York: Oxford Books, 1970.

Kerlin   Kerlin, Robert T., ed. *Negro Poets and Their Poems.* Washington, D. C.: Associated Publishers, 1935.

King   King, Woodie and Ron Milner, eds. *Black Drama Anthology.* New York: Columbia University Press, 1972.

King 2   King, Woodie, ed. *Black Short Story Anthology.* New York: Columbia University Press, 1972.

King 3   King, Woodie, ed. *Black Spirits; a Festival of New Black Poets in America.* New York: Random House, 1972.

Lane   Lane, Ronnie M., ed. *Face the Whirlwind; an Anthology of Black Michigan Poets.* Grand Rapids, Mi.: Pilot Press, 1973.

Locke Locke, Alain, ed. *Plays of Negro Life.* New York: Harper and Bros., 1927.

Locke 2 Locke, Alain, ed. *The New Negro: an Interpretation.* New York: Albert and Charles Boni, 1925.

Lomax Lomax, Alan, and Raoul Abdul, eds. *3000 Years of Black Poetry.* New York: Dodd, Mead, 1970.

Long Long, Richard A. and E. W. Collier, eds. *Afro-American Writing: an Anthology of Prose and Poetry.* New York: New York University Press, 1972. 2 vols.

Lowenfels Lowenfels, Walter, ed. *In a Time of Revolution.* New York: Random House, 1969.

✓ Major Major, Clarence, ed. *New Black Poetry.* New York: International Publishers, 1969.

Margolies Margolies, Edward, ed. *Native Sons Reader.* Philadelphia: Lippincott, 1970.

Miller, A. Miller, Adam David, ed. *Dices or Black Bones: Black Voices of the Seventies.* Boston: Houghton Mifflin, 1970.

Miller, R. Miller, Ruth, ed. *Blackamerican Literature, 1760–Present.* Beverley Hills, Calif.: Glencoe Press, 1971.

Murphy Murphy, Beatrice, ed. *Ebony Rhythm.* Freeport, N. Y.: Books for Libraries Press, 1968.

Murphy 2 Murphy, Beatrice M., ed. *Today's Negro Voices; an Anthology by Young Negro Poets.* New York: Julian Messner, 1970.

Murphy 3 Murphy, Beatrice M., ed. *Negro Voices: an Anthology of Contemporary Verse.* New York: Henry Harrison, 1938.

Oliver Oliver, Clinton F., ed. *Contemporary Black Drama.* New York: Scribners, 1971.

Patterson Patterson, Lindsay, comp. *Anthology of the American Negro in the Theatre: a Critical Approach.* Second revised edition. New York: Publishers' Co., 1969.

Patterson 2 Patterson, Lindsay, comp. *Black Theater; a 20th Century Collection of the Work of the Best Playwrights.* New York: New American Library, 1973.

✓ Patterson 3 Patterson, Lindsay, ed. *An Introduction to Black Literature in America from 1746 to the Present.* First edition. New York: Publishers' Co., 1968.

Patterson 4 Patterson, Lindsay, comp. *Rock Against the Wind; Black Love Poems.* New York: Dodd, Mead, 1973.

Pool Pool, Rosey E., ed. *Beyond the Blues.* London: Headley Bros., 1962.

Pool 2   Pool, Rosey, ed. *Ik Bin De Nieuwe Neger*. The Hague: Kees Nieuwen Huiyzen, 1965.

Porter   Porter, Dorothy, ed. *Early Negro Writing, 1760–1837*. Boston: Beacon Press, 1971.

Randall   Randall, Dudley, ed. *Black Poetry; a Supplement to Anthologies Which Exclude Black Poets*. Detroit: Broadside Press, 1969.

Randall 2   Randall, Dudley, ed. *The Black Poets*. New York: Bantam Books, 1971.

Reardon   Reardon, W. R. and Thomas D. Pawley, eds. *The Black Teacher and the Dramatic Arts; a Dialogue*. Westport, Conn.: Negro Universities Press, 1970.

Reed   Reed, Ishmael, ed. *Nineteen Necromancers from Now*. Garden City, N. Y.: Anchor Press, Doubleday, 1970.

Richardson   Richardson, Willis, ed. *Plays and Pageants from the Life of the Negro*. Washington, D. C.: Associated Publishers, 1930.

Richardson 2   Richardson, Willis and May Miller. *Negro History in Thirteen Plays*. Washington, D. C.: Associated Publishers, 1935.

Robinson   Robinson, William Henry, ed. *Early Black American Poets; Selections with Biographies and Critical Introductions*. Dubuque, Iowa: Wm. C. Brown, (©1969) 1971.

Robinson 2   Robinson, William Henry, ed. *Nommo: an Anthology of Modern Black African and Black American Literature*. New York: Macmillan, 1972.

Rose   Rose, Karel, ed. *Gift of the Spirit; Readings in Black Literature for Teachers*. New York: Holt, Rinehart and Winston, 1971.

Schulberg   Schulberg, Budd, ed. *From the Ashes*. Watts Writers' Workshop. New York: New American Library, 1967.

Shuman   Shuman, R. Baird, ed. *A Galaxy of Black Writing*. Durham, N. C.: Moore, 1970.

Shuman 2   Shuman, Robert B., ed. *Nine Black Poets*. Durham, N. C.: Moore, 1968.

Singh   Singh, R. K., and Peter Fellowes, eds. *Black Literature in America: a Casebook*. New York: Crowell, 1970.

Stadler   Stadler, Quandra Prettyman, ed. *Out of Our Lives: a Selection of Contemporary Black Fiction*. Washington, D. C.: Howard University Press, 1975.

Stanford   Stanford, Barbara Dodds, ed. *I, Too, Sing America*. Rochelle Park, N. J.: Hayden Book, 1971.

Takaki   Takaki, Ronald T., ed. *Violence in the Black Imagination, Essays and Documents*. New York: G. P. Putman's, 1972.

Ten   *Ten: An Anthology of Detroit Poets*. Fort Smith, Ark.:
                South & West, 1963.
Triad   *Triad: Poems by Helen C. Harris, Lucia Mae Pitts, Tomi*
                Carolyn Tinsley. Washington, D. C.: Privately pub-
                lished, 1945.
Troupe   Troupe, Quincy, ed. *Giant Talk; an Anthology of Third*
                World Writings. New York: Random House, 1975.
Troupe 2   Troupe, Quincy, ed. *Watts Poets: a Book of New Poetry and*
                Essays. House of Respect, 1968.
Turner   Turner, Darwin T., ed. *Black American Literature: Fic-*
                tion. Columbus, Ohio: Charles E. Merrill, 1969.
Turner 2   Turner, Darwin, ed. *Black American Literature: Essays*.
                Columbus, Ohio: Charles E. Merrill, 1969.
Turner 3   Turner, Darwin, ed. *Black American Literature: Essays,*
                Poetry, Fiction, Drama. Columbus, Ohio: Charles E.
                Merrill, 1970.
Turner 4   Turner, Darwin T., ed. *Black American Literature: Poetry*.
                Columbus, Ohio: Charles E. Merrill, 1969.
Turner 5   Turner, Darwin T., ed. *Black Drama in America; an An-*
                thology. Greenwich, Conn.: Fawcett, 1971.
Turner 6   Turner, Darwin T., and Jean M. Bright, eds. *Images of*
                the Negro in America. Boston: D. C. Heath, 1965.
Washington   Washington, Mary Helen, ed. *Black Eyed Susans; Classic*
                Stories by and about Black Women. Garden City,
                N. Y.: Anchor Press Doubleday, 1975.
Watkins   Watkins, Sylvestre C., ed. *Anthology of American Negro*
                Literature. New York: Modern Library, 1944.
Weisman   Weisman, Leonard and Elfreda S. Wright, eds. *Black*
                Poetry for All Americans. New York: Globe, 1971.
White   White, Ivey Newman, ed. *Anthology of Verse by American*
                Negroes. Folcroft, Pa.: Folcroft Press, 1924.
Wilentz   Wilentz, Ted and Tom Weatherly, eds. *Natural Process; an*
                Anthology of New Black Poetry. New York: Hill and
                Wang, 1970.
Williams   Williams, John A., ed. *Beyond the Angry Black*. New
                York: Cooper Square, 1966.
Witherspoon   Witherspoon, Jill, ed. *Broadside Annual 1972: Introducing*
                New Black Poets. Detroit: Broadside Press, 1972.
Witherspoon 2   Witherspoon, Jill, ed. *Broadside Annual, 1973*. Detroit:
                Broadside Press, 1973.

INDEX BY AUTHOR

ABAYOME, OJI. See **WAKEFIELD, JACQUES,** 1949- .

ABRAMS, ROBERT J., 1924- . Poet
Circles in Sand (fragment—poetry). Pool 35
For my unborn son (first line—poetry). Hughes 111
I Do Not Want to Turn Away (first line—poetry). Hughes 111

ABRAMSON, DOLORES. Poet
I Am (poetry). Patterson 4:83
To be . . . (poetry). Patterson 4:79

ABU ISHAK. See **HILL, ELTON.**

ACKERSON, JOHN. 1898- ?. Poet
Names on a Monument at Oberlin, Ohio (poetry). Pool 2:53

ADAMS, JEANETTE. Poet
For My Mama and Hers (poetry). Exum 51
Missed You (poetry). Exum 50
On the First Day of Summer in the Twenty-fifth Year of Our Lives (poetry). Exum 52
The Picture (poetry). Patterson 4:72
Portrait (poetry). Exum 49

ADDISON, LLOYD. 1931- . Poet
After MLK: The Marksman Marked Left-over Kill (poetry). Breman 268
Carpentry (poetry). Pool 37

ADOFF, ARNOLD. 1935- . Editor, Poet
Dry July (poetry). Adoff 47
Today is sun (poetry). Adoff 48

AI. Poet
Hangman (poetry). Troupe 122
The Anniversary (poetry). Troupe 121

AISHAH SAYYIDA MALI TOURE. See **SNELLINGS, ROLLAND.**

ALBA, NANINA, 1917-1968. Poet
Be Daedalus (poetry). Adoff 3:169, Hughes 2:329
For Malcolm X (poetry). Adoff 3:169

ALDRIDGE, AMANDA IRA, 1866-1956. Playwright
The Black Doctor (drama). Hatch 3

ALEE, LYCURGUS J., Poet
Upon Finding a False Friend (poetry). Murphy 3:9

ALEXANDER, LEWIS GRANDISON, 1900-1945. Poet, Critic
Africa (poetry). Cullen 123
The Dark Brother (poetry). Calverton 206, Cullen 124
Day and Night (poetry). Cromwell 46, Cullen 129
Dream Song (poetry). Adoff 3:59, Hughes 2:159, Murphy 3:10
Effigy (poetry). Johnson, C. 124
Enchantment (poetry). Adoff 3:58, Locke 2:149
Escape (poetry). Murphy 3:10
A Hokku Poem (poetry). Cromwell 47
Japanese Hokku (poetry). Cullen 127
My Epitaph (poetry). Murphy 3:9
Negro Woman (poetry). Adoff 3:58, Cullen 122
Nocturne Varial (poetry). Adoff 3:60, Hughes 2:158, Jordan 132, Murphy 3:11
Southland (poetry). Murphy 3:11
Tanka I-VIII (poetry). Cullen 125
Transformation (poetry). Cullen 124, Hughes 2:160, Murphy 3:12

ALEXANDER, MARGARET A. WALKER. See **WALKER, MARGARET ABIGAIL.**

ALEXANDRE, MARIE E. Poet
My Soul (poetry). Murphy 3:12

ALHAMISI, AHMED AKINWOLE, 1940- . Poet
Black Narrator (poetry). Randall 39
Look For Me, Dear Mother (poetry). Breman 425
Pome. For Weird. Hearts and All You Mothers (poetry). Jones 428
Sacrificial Ritual (poetry). Alhamisi 109
Spiritual Cleanliness (poetry). Brown, P. 8
Uhuru (poetry). Jones 424

1

ALLEN, ERNEST. See **MKALIMOTO, ERNIE.**

ALLEN, GEORGE LEONARD, 1905-1935. Poet
Pilate in Modern America (poetry). Brown 363
Portrait (poetry). Cullen 204
To Melody (poetry). Brown 364, Cullen 204, Kerlin 278

ALLEN, GEORGE R., 1816(?)- . Schoolboy
To the American Convention for promoting the Abolition of Slavery ... (essay). Porter 572

On Slavery (poetry). Porter 574

ALLEN, JUNIUS MORDECAI, (J. Mord) 1875-1906. Poet
Counting Out (poetry). Kerlin 48, White 131
The Devil and Sis' Viney (poetry). Robinson 250, White 117.
The Psalm of the Uplift (poetry). Kerlin 50, White 116.
Shine On, Mr. Sun (poetry). White 130
A Victim of Microbes (poetry). Kerlin 240
When the Fish Begin to Bite (poetry). White 128

ALLEN, RICHARD, 1760-1831. Poet, Narrator, Editor, Clergyman
Narrative of the Proceedings of the Black People During the Late Awful Calamity in Philadelphia (Essay, with Absalom Jones). Brawley 89, Miller, R. 23

Spiritual Song (poetry). Porter 559

An Address to the Public and People of Colour (Speech). Porter 414

ALLEN, SAMUEL W., 1917- . Poet, Critic, Editor
Négritude and its Relevance to the American Negro Writer (essay) Conference 8, Davis 617

Africa to Me (poetry). Davis 617, Miller, R. 412
American Gothic (or To Satch) (poetry). Adoff 2:55, Davis 616, Hayden 2:147, Hill 2:615, Jordan 58, Pool 2:81
Divestment (poetry). Breman 161
Dylan, Who Is Dead (poetry). Adoff 3:167, Pool 176
If the Stars Should Fall (poetry). Adoff 2:83, Adoff 3:168, Hughes 95
In My Father's House: A Reverie (poetry). Henderson 226, Robinson 2:213
Ivory Tusks (poetry). Henderson 227
Love Song (poetry). Hughes 18
A Moment Please (poetry). Adams 3:102, Adoff 2:22, Adoff 3:166, Barksdale 814, Black 36, Bontemps 2:138, Davis 615, Hayden 2:148, Hill 2:616, Miller, R. 410,

Patterson 3:220, Pool 177, Robinson 2:213
The Mules of Caesar (poetry). Miller, R. 411
My Friend (poetry). Robinson 2:215
Nat Turner (poetry). Barksdale 815
Springtime Ghetto, U.S.A. (poetry). Henderson 228
The Staircase (poetry). Adoff 3:167, Breman 160, Pool 175
That's Mighty Fine (poetry). Robinson 2:214
There Are No Tears (poetry). Miller, R. 413
To Chessman and Associates (poetry). Pool 178
To Satch (poetry). Adoff 3:167, Barksdale 815, Bontemps 140, Hayden 2:147, Henderson 226, Hughes 2:343, Lomax 244, Weisman 64.
View from the Corner (poetry). Adams 3:108, Brooks 159, Randall 27, Robinson 2:212
What Bright Pushbutton? (poetry). Hughes 2:344.
The Wreath (poetry). Brown, P. 11

ALLEN, WILLIAM G. Essayist
A Freeman's Flight from the South (essay). Patterson 3:46

Orators and Oratory (speech). Cromwell 246

ALLEN, WINSTON. Poet
The Black Violinist (poetry). Kerlin 262
Old Jim Crow (poetry). Kerlin 263

ALVAREZ, JULIA, 1950- . Poet
Lonely Tulip Grower (poetry). Jordan 11

AMERSON, RICH, 1927- . Poet
Black Woman (poetry). Henderson 108

AMES, RUSSELL. Essayist
Social Realism in Charles W. Chesnutt (essay). Hemenway 25

AMINI, JOHARI. See **LATIMORE, JEWEL CHRISTINE.**

ANDERSON, ALICE D. Poet
The Poet (poetry). Murphy 1

ANDERSON, ALSTON, Short Fiction Writer
The Checkerboard (short fiction). Hughes 3:207

ANDERSON, CHARLES, 1938- . Poet
Blow Man, Blow ... (poetry). Pool 41
Cracker Man (poetry). Pool 41
Finger Poppin' (poetry) Jones 189, Pool 39, Pool 2:201
I Know Jesus Heard Me (poetry). Pool 41
Prayer To The White Man's God (poetry). Jones 191
Question (poetry). Pool 39

(ANDERSON, CHARLES)
Street scene (poetry). Breman 2:94
What I Need, Is a Dark Woman (poetry),
Pool 41

ANDERSON, EDNA L. Poet
It Seems To Me (poetry). Murphy 1

ANDERSON, GARLAND, 1886-1939. Playwright
Appearances (drama). Hatch 100

ANDERSON, JOURDAN. Letter Writer
To My Old Master (letter). Freedman 97,
Gayle 37

ANDERSON, S. E., 1943- . Poet, Short
Fiction Writer, Essayist
Chain Waves (poetry). King 3:7
Elimination of the Blues (poetry). Alhamisi
122
Junglegrave (poetry). Adoff 3:441, Coombs
1
A New Dance (poetry). Major 23
The Red, the Black and the Green (poetry).
King 3:10
Soul—Smiles (poetry). Jones 357
Sound of Afro-American History, Chapter
1 (poetry). Adoff 3:440, Jones 359
Sound of Afro-American History, Chapter
II (poetry). Adoff 3:441
Sound of Afro-American Music (poetry).
King 3:6

Contraband (short fiction). Alhamisi 70,
King 2:321

ANDERSON, WILLIAM. Poet
The February Rain Is Falling (poetry). Miller, A. 81
The Huey Newton Trial (poetry). Miller,
A. 86
There's Not a Friend Like the Lowly
Jesus (poetry). Miller, A. 80

ANDREW, JOSEPH MAREE. Fiction Writer
And I passed by (fictionalized autobiography). Johnson, C. 158

ANGELOU, MAYA, 1928- . Poet, Short
Fiction Writer, Dramatist
I Know Why the Caged Bird Sings (excerpt—autobiography). Exum 123

All Day Long (short fiction). Clarke 3:189

ANTHONY, FLORENCE See AI.

ANTHONY, JAMES K. Poet
Window Washers (poetry). Weisman 53
Winter Weather Forecast (poetry). Weisman 65

ARNOLD, EDWARD, 1863- . Biographer
Some Personal Reminiscences of Paul Laurence Dunbar (excerpt—biography).
Brown 809

ARNOLD, WALTER G. Poet
Entreaty (poetry). Murphy 2
Interrogation (poetry). Murphy 3

ASKIA, MUHAMMAD TOURE See SNELLINGS, ROLLAND.

ATKINS, RUSSELL, 1926- . Poet, Playwright, Short Fiction Writer
At War (poetry). Bontemps 169
Christophe (poetry). Breman 208, Hughes
2:391
Editorial Poem on an Incident of Effects
Far Reaching (poetry). Major 24
Irritable Song (poetry). Bontemps 2:170
It's Here in the (poetry). Adoff 3:197, Bontemps 2:171, Jordan 98
Narrative (poetry). Adoff 3:198, Breman
207
Nigh) Th' cry, pt (poetry). Breman 2:78
Night and a Distant Church (poetry). Adoff
3:198, Breman 2:80
On the Fine Arts Garden, Cleveland (poetry). Adoff 3:197

ATTAWAY, WILLIAM, 1912 . Essayist,
Short Fiction Writer
Blood on the Forge (excerpt—fiction).
Margolies 93
Blood on the Forge (excerpt: Steel Mill
Rhythm—fiction). Brown 268

North to Hell (short fiction). Davis 378

AUBERT, ALVIN, 1930- . Poet, Critic
Blue (poetry). Witherspoon 11

AYERS, VIVIAN. Poet, Playwright
Instantaneous (poetry). Hughes 85

AZIKIWE, BEN N. Poet
To Lincoln (poetry). Cuney 1

BAILEY, WILLIAM EDGAR. Poet
The Slump (poetry). Kerlin 65

To a Wild Rose (prose-poem). Kerlin 229

BAKER, BARBARA ANNE. Poet
Grow in Hope and Grace (poetry). Murphy
2:16

BALAGON, KUWASI, 1947- . Poet
Beating hearts (first line—poetry). Jones
445
Children of the Cosmos (poetry). Jones 441
If You Love Them, Wouldn't You Like to
Se Them Better Off? (poetry). Jones 443
Untitle (poetry). Jones 445

BALDWIN, JAMES, 1924-... Fiction Writer,
Playwright, Autobiographer, Essayist
Notes of a Native Son (excerpts—autobiography). Adams 4:79, Emanuel 301,
Hayden 197, Stanford 183, Turner 6:63
Notes of a Native Son (excerpt: Autobio-

(BALDWIN, JAMES)
graphical notes—autobiography). Chapman 316

Notes of a Native Son (excerpt: Equal in Paris, autobiography). Kearns 2:87

Notes of a Native Son (excerpt: Many Thousands Gone, autobiography). Baker 310, Chapman 590, Gayle 2:325, Gibson 2:230

Notes of a Native Son (excerpt: Stranger in the Village, autobiography). Kearns 568

Amen Corner (drama). Hatch 514, Patterson 2:333

Blues for Mister Charlie (drama). Oliver 242

The Discovery of What It Means To Be an American (essay). Ford 194, Turner 2:113, Turner 3:113

Everybody's Protest Novel (essay). Barksdale 725, Hemenway 218

The Fire Next Time (excerpt—essays). Curry 79

Many Thousands Gone: Richard Wright's Native Son (essay). Gross 233

My Dungeon Shook (essay). Singh 162

Nobody Knows My Name (excerpt: Fifth Avenue Uptown: A Letter from Harlem—essay). Demarest 93, Freedman 221, Kendricks 290

Nobody Knows My Name (excerpt: A Letter from the South—essay). Long 621

Theatre: The Negro In And Out Of It (essay). Williams 3

Unnameable Objects, Unspeakable Crimes (essay) Adoff 4:94

Why I Left America (essay). Chapman 2:409

Another Country (excerpt—fiction). Troupe 8

Go Tell It on the Mountain (excerpt: Elizabeth's Prayer—fiction). Miller, R. 349

Go Tell It on the Mountain (excerpt: John's Conversion—fiction). Davis, C. 225, Rose 236

Go Tell It on the Mountain (excerpt: The Seventh Day—fiction). Hill 2:402

Go Tell It on the Mountain (excerpt: The Threshing Floor—fiction). Davis 572

Letter to My Nephew (letter). Davis 583

Letters From A Journey (letters). Hill 2:38

Journey to Atlanta (narrative). Patterson 3:212

Come Out the Wilderness (short fiction). James 249, King 2:277

Exodus (short fiction), Clarke 197

A Fly in Buttermilk (short fiction). Stanford 234

Gabriel's Prayer (short fiction). Ford 196

The Man Child (short ficton). Turner 104, Turner 3:394

The Outing (short fiction). Margolies 255

Previous Condition (short fiction). Gibson 21

The Rock Pile (short fiction). Adams 2:27, Haslam 332

Roy's Wound (short fiction). Clarke 3:114, Singh 113

Sonny's Blues (short fiction). Barksdale 729, Burnett 167, Emanuel 319, Hayden 70

This Morning, this Evening (short fiction). Hughes 3:213

BAMBARA, TONI CADE, 1939- . Editor, Critic, Fiction Writer, Essayist
Black Theatre (essay). Gayle 2:134

Blues Ain't No Mockin Bird (short fiction). Troupe 247

Gorilla, My Love (short fiction). Stadler 5

Mama Hazel Takes to Her Bed (short fiction). Exum 204

My Man Bovanne (short fiction). Washington 69

BANKS, BARBARA. Poet
Valediction (poetry). Exum 54

The Gypsies (short fiction). Exum 211

BANNEKER, BENJAMIN, 1731-1806. Scientist, Poet, Essayist
A Plan of Peace—Office for the United States (essay). Brawley 83, Patterson 3:17

Copy of a letter from Benjamin Banneker, to the Secretary of State, with his answer, 1792 (letter). Brawley 79, Porter 324

Letter from Benjamin Banneker to Thomas Jefferson, August 19, 1791 (letter). Barksdale 50, Kendricks 44, Stanford 14

Mathematical Problem in Verse (poetry). Barksdale 50

BARAKA, IMAMU AMIRI. See JONES, LE ROI.

BARBER, JOHN. Fiction Writer
Rites Fraternal (short fiction). Coombs 2:1

BARKSDALE, RICHARD K., 1915- . Critic, Editor
Humanistic Protest in Recent Black Poetry (essay). Gibson 3:157

BARLOW, GEORGE, 1948- . Poet
Catechism: Operation Homecoming, 1973 (poetry). Troupe 30

8 Ball (poetry). Shuman 250

In the Faculty Room (poetry). Shuman 251

Nigger (poetry). Shuman 251

Number Eight Apollo (poetry). Shuman 252

Sweet Diane (poetry). Shuman 252

Uncle Jesse (poetry). Shuman 254

BARNES, ALBERT C. Essayist
Negro Art and America (essay). Locke 2:19

BARNET, ————————.
Spell It With a Capital (editorial). Pool 2:213

BARNWELL, DESIREE A. Poet
Will The Real Black People Please Stand (poetry). Coombs 2

BARRAX, GERALD WILLIAM, 1933-
Poet
Black Narcissus (poetry). Adoff 3:223, Hayden 146, Hayden 2:203
Christmas 1959 et cetera (poetry). Hayden 2:200
Death of a Squirrel in McKinley Park (poetry). Hayden 2:202
The Dozens (poetry). Henderson 360
Efficiency Apartment (poetry). Adoff 3:217
For a Black Poet (poetry). Chapman 2:213, Henderson 358
For Malcolm: After Mecca (poetry) Adoff 3:224
Fourth Dance Poem (poetry). Adoff 3:225
The Old Glory (poetry). Chapman 2:211
Patroness (poetry). Hayden 2:201
The Sacrifice (poetry). Hayden 145, Hayden 2:199
The Scuba Diver Recovers The Body of a Drowned Child (poetry). Chapman 2:210
To a Woman Who Wants Darkness and Time (poetry). Adoff 3:222
Your Eyes Have Their Silence (poetry). Adoff 3:224

BARRETT, LINDSAY, 1941- . Essayist, Playwright, Poet, Journalist, Fiction Writer
In Finality Where to Go Is What to Do (essay). Alhamisi 95
The Tide Inside, It Rages (essay). Alhamisi 94, Jones 149

Rocks (poetry). Troupe 423

BASS, GEORGE HOUSTON, 1938- . Playwright, Poet, Script Writer
Games (drama). Patterson 3:268

BASS, KINGSLEY B. JR. Playwright (Pseudonym sometimes attributed to Ed Bullins)
We Righteous Bombers (drama). Bullins 2:22, Turner 3:543, Turner 5:557

BATES, DAISY. Autobiographer
She Walked Alone (autobiography). Freedman 244

BATES, MYRTLE. Poet
From the Sidelines (poetry). Exum 57
Tears (poetry). Exum 55
There Should Be Time (poetry). Exum 56

BAUMFREE, ISABELLA. See TRUTH, SOJOURNER.

BAYLEY, SOLOMON. Narrator
A Narrative of Some Remarkable Incidents, In the Life of Solomon Bayley 1825 (narrative). Porter 587

BECK, ROBERT, 1918- . Fiction Writer
Pimp: Story of My Life (excerpt—fiction). Robinson 2:135

BECKHAM, BARRY (1944- . Fiction Writer
Runner Mack (excerpt—fiction). Troupe 128

BEECHER, JOHN. Poet
Their Blood Cries Out (poetry). Pool 2:193

BEIER, ULLI. Poet
Your Presence (poetry). Patterson 4:16

BELL, GEORGE R., 1934- . Poet
And bury the dog that does not bark (poetry). Breman 2:51
If in reverse (poetry). Breman 2:57
Life centered by this last obsession (poetry). Breman 2:58
Linked between two obscurities (poetry). Breman 2:52
Pardon me while I pretend (poetry). Breman 2:56

BELL, JAMES MADISON, 1826-1902. Poet
The Day and the War (poetry). Brawley 279
Emancipation in the District of Columbia (April 16, 1862) (poetry). Brawley 288
Modern Moses, or 'My Policy' Man (poetry). Robinson 83
The Progress of Liberty (poetry). Calverton 176
The Progress of Liberty (excerpt—poetry). Kerlin 33
Song For the First of August (poetry). White 38

BELL, PHILIP. Orator
Resolutions of the People of Color, at a meeting held on the 25th of January, 1831. With an address to the Citizens of New York, 1831. In answer to those of the New York Colonization Society (speech). Porter 281

BENFORD, LAWRENCE, 1946- . Poet
The Beginning of a Long Poem on Why I Burned the City (poetry). Davis 763, Lomax 257, Major 26

BENITEZ, LILLIE KATE WALKER. Poet
Sectional Touchstone (poetry). Henderson 313

BENNETT, BOB, 1947- . Poet
The Girl with the Afro (first line—poetry). Jones 423
It Is Time for Action (poetry). Jones 420
Title (poetry). Jones 423

BENNETT, GWENDOLYN B., 1902- . Poet, Essayist, Short Fiction Writer
Advice (poetry). Cullen 156
Fantasy (poetry). Cullen 158
Hatred (poetry). Adoff 3:82, Bontemps 2:73, Cullen 160, Johnson 246, Patterson 4:113
He Came In Silvern Armour Trimmed In Black (poetry—Sonnet I). Bontemps 2:74, Cullen 160, Hughes 2:206, Patterson 3:218
Heritage (poetry). Adams 3:57, Adoff 3:81, Bontemps 2:73, Johnson 245, Weisman 14
Lines Written at the Grave of Alexander Dumas (poetry). Cullen 159, Hughes 2:208
Nocturne (poetry). Johnson 244
On a Birthday (poetry). Brewer 2
Quatrains (poetry). Cullen 155
Secret (poetry). Cullen 155
Some Things Are Very Dear To Me (poetry—Sonnet II). Adoff 3:82, Bontemps 75, Cullen 161, Hughes 2:206, Johnson 244, Patterson 3:218
Sonnet I (poetry—He Came In Silvern Armour Trimmed In Black). Bontemps 2:74, Cullen 160, Hughes 2:206, Patterson 3:218
Sonnet II (poetry—Some Things Are Very Dear To Me). Adoff 3:82, Bontemps 75, Cullen 161, Hughes 2:206, Johnson 244, Patterson 3:218
To a Dark Girl (poetry). Adams 3:38, Adoff 3:81, Black 24, Calverton 208, Cullen 157, Johnson 243, Kerlin 290
Your Songs (poetry). Black 24, Cullen 157

Tokens (short fiction). Johnson C., 149

BENNETT, LERONE, JR., 1928- . Poet Short Fiction Writer, Essayist
Introduction (essay). Brown, P. 1
Nat's Last White Man (essay). Clarke 2:3
The White Problem in America (essay). Adoff 4:102

Before the Mayflower: A History of Black America (excerpt: The African Past—history). Freedman 4

And Was Not Improved (poetry). Adoff 3:203
Blues and Bitterness (poetry). Adoff 3:202, Chapman 472, Hughes 53

The Convert (short fiction). Chambers 186, Clarke 282, King 2:151

BERNARD, C. JACKSON, 1927- . Playwright
Fly Blackbird (drama—with James Hatch). Hatch 671, Reardon 137

BERRY, CHANTAL SANDRE, 1948- . Poet
I-Hate-Love Poem N. 3 (poetry). Witherspoon 2:9

BERRY, FAITH, 1939- . Politician
Black Is Black: A Letter To Africa (essay). Davis 758

BERRY, JOSIE CRAIG. Poet
And Death Went Down (poetry). Murphy 3:13

BERTHA, GUS. Poet
A Voice Above the Wind (poetry). Brown, P. 13

BETHUNE, LEBERT, 1937- . Poet
Black Fire (poetry). Henderson 298
Blue Tanganyika (poetry). Adoff 3:311, Jones 383
Bwagamoyo (poetry). Adoff 3:310, Jones 384
Harlem Freeze Frame (poetry). Adoff 3:309, Jones 382
A Juju of My Own (poetry). Adoff 3:309, Henderson 297, Hughes 2:414, Jones 381
The Nature of . . . (poetry). Henderson 298
To Strike for Night (poetry). Major 27

The Burglar (short fiction). Hughes 3:458

BEVERLY, KATHERINE. Poet
Dreams Are So Pale (poetry). Murphy 4
Night Song (poetry). Murphy 3
Prayer for a Hill (poetry). Murphy 3:14
Resignation (poetry). Murphy 3:14
Temptation (poetry). Murphy 3:14

BEY, YILLIE. Poet
Making of a Militant (poetry). Murphy 2:18

BIBB, A. DENEE. Poet
Alma Mater (poetry). Cuney 2

BIBB, HENRY, 1815-? Essayist
Narrative of the Life and Adventures of Henry Bibb (excerpt—narrative). Miller, R. 62

BIBBS, HART LEROI, 1930- . Poet
Dirge for J. A. Rogers (poetry). Jones 320
Liveralissimo (poetry). Jones 319
Six Sunday (poetry). Major 28
Split Standard (poetry). Jones 318

BIGSBY, C. W. E. Essayist
Three Black Playwrights: Loften Mitchell, Ossie Davis, Douglas Turner Ward (essay). Washington 137

BISMILLAH-R-RAH-MANI-R-RAHIM   See **JACKMAN, MARVIN E.**

BLACK, AUSTIN, 1929- . Poet
Soul (poetry). Major 29

BLACK, ISAAC J. Poet
Racist Psychotherapy (poetry). Chapman 2:371

BLACK, LEWIS. Poet
Spanish Blues (poetry). Henderson 112

BLACKMAN, LOUISE. Poet
Miracle (poetry). Murphy 5
Rain Wish (poetry). Murphy 4

BLACKMAN, SHERRY. Poet
On Evergreen Street (poetry). Bookers 103

BLACKWELL, DOROTHY F. Poet
Crescendo (poetry). Murphy 6
Echo (poetry). Murphy 5
Nocturne (poetry). Murphy 6

BLAKELEY, NORA. Poet
Mama (poetry). Brown, P. 14

BLANTON, LORENZO D. Poet, Short Fiction Writer
I Wonder (poetry). Dreer 54

BLESSITT, BERNADINE. Poet
Little Boy's Prayer (poetry). Murphy 3:15

BLUE, CECIL A. Poet, Short Fiction Writer
The Flyer (short fiction). Brown 74

BOGGS, JAMES. Essayist
Black Power—A Scientific Concept Whose Time Has Come (essay). Jones 105

BOGLE, DONALD E. Poet
An Aristotelian Elegy (poetry). Murphy 2:21
Now (poetry). Murphy 2:23

BOHANON, MARY. Poet, Playwright
Find the Girl (drama). Shuman 38

Black Can Be Beautiful (poetry). Shuman 256
Bought and Paid For (poetry). Shuman 257
Complete Fulfillment (poetry). Shuman 257
Earth Bosom (poetry). Shuman 258
Fear Not (poetry). Shuman 258
Gone (poetry). Shuman 259
A Good God (poetry). Shuman 260
Know This Is True (poetry). Shuman 261
Naked (poetry). Shuman 262
A Plea (poetry). Shuman 263
Suspended (poetry). Shuman 263
Whut a Dawn (poetry). Shuman 264

Black Vignettes (short fiction). Shuman 28

BOHANON, OTTO LELAND. Poet
The Dawn's Awake (poetry). Cromwell 42, Johnson 203, Kerlin 277
The Washer-Woman (poetry). Cromwell 43, Johnson 204

BOLES, ROBERT, 1943- . Fiction Writer
The Engagement Party (short fiction). Hughes 3:479; Patterson 3:224

BOND, FREDERICK W. Poet, Playwwright, Essayist, Journalist
To a Whipporwill (poetry). Dreer 75

BOND, HORACE JULIAN, 1940- . Poet, Essayist
The Bishop of Atlanta: Ray Charles (poetry). Bontemps 2:184
Cambridge, Mass. (poetry). Pool 45
Habana (poetry). Hughes 86, Singh 36
I, Too, Hear America Singing (poetry). Lowenfels 11, Pool 44, Pool 2:110
Langston Hughes (poetry). Pool 2:164
Look At That Gal (poetry). Hughes 2:434, Lomax 253, Pool 45
Rotation (poetry). Hughes 67, Pool 44

BOND, HORACE MANN. 1904- . Essayist
A Negro Looks at His South (essay). Brown 1028

BONE, ROBERT S. Critic, Essayist
The Novels of James Baldwin (essay). Gross 265, Hemenway 111
Ralph Ellison and the Uses of Imagination (essay). Hill 86.
Zora Neale Hurston (essay). Hemenway 55

BONNER, MARITA, 1905- . Poet, Short Fiction Writer, Playwright
The Purple Flower (drama). Hatch 201

BONTEMPS, ARNA W., 1902-1973. Poet, Fiction Writer, Dramatist
Rock, Church, Rock! (biography). Watkins 425

Saint Louis Woman (drama—with C. Cullen). Patterson 2:3

The Awakening: a Memoir (essay). Bontemps 3:1
Harlem, the Beautiful Years (essay). Gayle 75
Introduction from The Book of Negro Folklore (essay). Gayle 2:29, Turner 6:80
Negro Poets, Then and Now (essay). Gayle 2:82
The Negro Renaissance: Jean Toomer and the Harlem Writers of the 1920's (essay). Hemenway 150, Hill 20, Patterson 3:126
Ole Sis Goose (essay). Conference 51
Why I Returned (essay). Chapman 321

Black Thunder (excerpt: Conspirators—fiction). Brown 254
Black Thunder (excerpt: The Trial—fiction). Brown 258
Drums at Dusk (excerpt—fiction). Dreer 269

Letter to My Nephew (letter). Davis 583

A Black Man Talks of Reaping (poetry). Adams 3:91, Adoff 2:76, Adoff 3:85, Barksdale 630, Bell 43, Bontemps 2:75,

(BONTEMPS, ARNA W.)
Breman 85, Brown 381, Chapman 424, Cullen 165, Davis 332, Hayden 2:83, Hughes 2:209, Johnson 262, Kearns 391, Kearns 2:245, Miller, R. 389, Patterson 3:161, Randall 2:94, Stanford 147, Turner 2:387
Blight (poetry). Cullen 170, Johnson 264
Close Your Eyes (poetry). Adoff 3:86, Bontemps 2:76, Cullen 171, Cunard 259, Hayden 118, Hayden 2:79, Hughes 2:218
Day-breakers (poetry). Adams, 3:5, Adoff 2:66, Adoff 3:84, Bontemps 76, Chapman 424, Cullen 171, Dreer 84, Hughes 2.223, Kearns 391, Randall 10
Gethsemane (poetry). Chapman 421, Cullen 169
God Give To Men (poetry). Cullen 172, Hughes 2:225, Johnson 267, Randall 2:92
Golgotha Is a Mountain (poetry). Bontemps 77, Cullen 173, Hughes 2:219
Here Is the Sea (poetry). Cromwell 27
Homing (poetry). Cullen 172, Dreer 83
Idolatry (poetry). Bontemps 79, Hughes 2:217, Johnson, C. :66, Patterson 3:161
Lancelot (poetry). Cullen 169
Length of Moon (poetry). Cullen 168, Hughes 2:213, Pool 49
Miracles (poetry). Davis 333, Emanuel 479, Hughes 2:209
My Heart Has Known Its Winter (poetry). Bell 45, Chapman 422
Nocturne at Bethesda (poetry). Baker 215, Barksdale 631, Bell 43, Bontemps 81, Brown 379, Chapman 422, Cromwell 28, Cullen 166, Davis 333, Hughes 2:210, Johnson 265, Kerlin 284, Long 441, Miller, R 387, Pool 47, Turner 2:230, Turner 4:74
Nocturne of the Wharves (poetry). Hughes 2:224, Johnson 263, Randall 2:93
A Note of Humility (poetry). Bell 46, Chapman 421, Hughes 2:222
Reconnaissance (poetry). Baker 217, Barksdale 630, Bontemps 80, Emanuel 480, Hayden 2:81, Randall 2:92.
The Return (poetry). Adoff 3:84, Cullen 163, Davis 335, Dreer 82, Hughes 2:215, Johnson, C. 152, Kerlin 286
Southern Mansion (poetry). Adams 3:69, Adoff 2:25, Adoff 3:83, Baker 217, Barksdale 631, Bell 45, Bontemps 80, Breman 84, Chapman 422, Davis 335, Emanuel 479, Freedman 59, Hayden 118, Hayden 2:80, Hughes 2:213, Johnson 263, Kearns 391, Lomax 224, Patterson 3:161, Pool 49, Turner 3:229, Turner 4:73
To a Young Girl Leaving the Hill Country (poetry). Cullen 165, Hayden 2:82
A Tree Design (poetry). Cullen 170

A Summer Tragedy (short fiction). Baker 208, Chapman 88, Clarke 54, Davis, C. 149, Ford 81, Freedman 129, Gibson 206, Hughes 3:60, James 128, Singh 48, Stanford 139, Watkins 77

Reflections on Richard Wright: a Symposium on an Exiled Native Son (symposium). Gibson 2:58

BOOKER, SIMEON, JR. Short Fiction Writer
She Never Knew? (short fiction). Ford 2:83

BOOKER, SUE. Poet, Playwright
The Flags (drama). Bookers 139

He Keeps Company with What He Knows (poetry). Bookers 57
Love Is a Purple Toothpick (poetry). Bookers 79
The Stamper of Life (poetry). Bookers 95

BOONE, IDA. See SHARON

BOURKE, SHARON. Poet
I Know She Will Pray For Me (poetry). Henderson 375
I Remember That Day (poetry). Henderson 374
People of Gleaming Cities, and of The Lion's and the Leopard's Brood (poetry). Henderson 374
Sopranosound, Memory of John (poetry). Henderson 376

BOWEN, ROBERT. Poet
Y'all Forgit (poetry). Troupe 2:86

BOYD, FRANCIS A., 1844-1872. Poet
Canto IV (excerpt: The Soliloquy—poetry). Robinson 77
Canto V (excerpt: The Dream—poetry). Robinson 79

BOYD, JOHN. Poet
Ocean (poetry). Robinson 163
Sketch of a Varying Evening Sky (poetry). Robinson 162
The Vision/a Poem in Blank Verse (poetry). Robinson 158

BOYD, SAMUEL E. Poet
And So Tomorrow (poetry). Murphy 8
Dance Finale (poetry). Murphy 7
Rebel (poetry). Murphy 7
Tomorrow's Winds (poetry). Murphy 8

BOYER, JILL WITHERSPOON. See WITHERSPOON, JILL.

BRADFORD, FRED. Poet
Death of a Nigger (poetry). Breman 433

BRADFORD, WALTER, 1937- . Poet, Essayist
A Black Social Statement on the Occasion of . . . (essay). Brooks 2:50

(BRADFORD, WALTER)
Confessions of Nat Turner (essay). Brooks 2:51
Sketches of a Trip Home (essay). Brooks 2:47

Gwen; words pretty or precise (first line—poetry). Brown, P. 15
T. C. (poetry). Brooks 177
Untitled (poetry). Brown, P. 15

BRAGG, LINDA BROWN See BROWN, LINDA.

BRAITHWAITE, EDWARD. Poet
Cherries (poetry). Troupe 222
Prelude (poetry). Kearns 2:43

BRAITHWAITE, WILLIAM STANLEY BEAUMONT, 1878-1962. Poet, Critic, Fiction Writer, Autobiographer
House Under Arcturus (excerpt—autobiography). Watkins 402
House Under Arcturus (excerpt: Search for Employment—autobiography). Brown 773

The Negro In American Literature (essay). Gayle 2:169, Locke 2:29, Long 269
Novels of Jessie Fauset (essay). Hemenway 48

Autumn Sadness (poetry). Kerlin 108
The Book of Love (poetry). Patterson 4:5
By an Inland Lake (poetry). White 136
Del Cascar (poetry). Cullen 33, Davis 225, Johnson 103
The Eternal Self (To Vere Goldthwaite) (poetry). Dreer 43, White 141
Foscati (poetry). Kerlin 108
From The Crowd (poetry). White 137
Golden Moonrise (poetry). Adoff 3:14, White 142
Gray Dawn (poetry). Cromwell 30
House of Falling Leaves (poetry). Hughes 2:47
Hymn for the Slain in Battle (poetry). Turner 3:191, Turner 4:35
If I Could Touch (poetry). Patterson 4:158, Turner 3:190, Turner 4:34
In a Graveyard (poetry). Adoff 3:13, White 136
Ironic: LLD (poetry). Johnson 104
It's a Long Way (poetry). Kerlin 106
A Little Song (poetry). White 135
The Mystery (poetry). White 144
New England Spinster (excerpts—poetry). Kerlin 106
October XXIX, 1795 (poetry). Cullen 32
Quiet Has a Hidden Sound (poetry). Davis 227
Rhapsody (poetry). Barksdale 453, Bontemps 15, Cromwell 31, Johnson 106, Long 269, Turner 3:189, Turner 4:33
Rye Bread (poetry). Cullen 31
Sandy Star (poetry). Barksdale 454, Brown 319, Johnson 100, Kerlin 106, White 144

Scintilla (poetry). Barksdale 453, Bontemps 2:15, Calverton 198, Cullen 31, Davis 226, Johnson 105
Sic Vita (poetry). Cromwell 31, Davis 225, Johnson 105, White 142
Song of a Syrian Lace Seller (poetry). White 138
A Song of Living (poetry). White 139
Song: Today and Tomorrow (poetry). Dreer 43, White 137
Thanking God (poetry). Kerlin 109
Thanksgiving (poetry). Kerlin 316
This Is My Life (poetry). White 143
To— (poetry). Adoff 3:13, Turner 3:90
To the Sea (poetry). White 145
Turn Me to My Yellow Leaves (poetry). Davis 225, Johnson 103
Two Questions (poetry). Turner 3:191, Turner 4:35
The Watchers (poetry). Barksdale 454, Brown 318, Davis 226, Hughes 2:48, Long 268
White Magic: An Ode (poetry). Hughes 2:49
A White Road (poetry): Cromwell 30

BRANCH, WILLIAM BLACKWELL. 1927- . Critic, Playwright
In Splendid Error (drama). Hatch 587, Patterson 2:93
A Medal for Willie (drama). King 439

Marketing the Products of American Negro Writers (essay). Conference 46

BRAWLEY, BENJAMIN GRIFFITH 1882-1939. Literary Historian, Poet, Essayist
The Lower Rungs of the Ladder (excerpt—autobiography). Brown 757

Introduction to Negro Biography (excerpt: John Jasper: The Sun Do Move—biography). Brown 793

Negro Builders and Heroes (excerpts—essay). Turner 6:47
The Negro in Literature (excerpt: The Negro in American Fiction—essay). Baker 128, Calverton 237, Gayle 2:182, Watkins 108
The Writing of Essays (essay). Cromwell 222

Ballade of One That Died Before His Time (poetry). White 159
The Bells of Notre Dame (poetry). White 158
Chaucer (poetry). Johnson 151, White 158
My Hero (poetry). Cromwell 45, Hughes 2:59, Johnson 150
The Plan (poetry). White 157

BRAZIEL, ARTHUR. Poet
Virgin Field (poetry). Murphy 9

BRESSACK, GORDON. Poet
The End (poetry). Bookers 119
The Last Thing of Beauty (poetry). Bookers 119

BREWER, J. MASON, 1896- . Editor,
Essayist, Poet
American Folk Literature (essay). Gayle
2:19

Apostolic (poetry). Brewer 6
Deep Ellum and Central Track (poetry).
Brewer 4
Dew (poetry). Brewer 4
Secon' Pickin' (poetry). Brewer 5

BREWSTER, TOWNSEND T. Poet
Black Is Beautiful (poetry). Murphy 2:25

BRIERRE, JEAN. Poet
Areytos (poetry). Murphy 9
Harlem (poetry). Murphy 11
To Paul Robeson (poetry). Murphy 12

BRISTER, IOLA M. Poet
Epigram (poetry). Murphy 13
A Negro Speaks of Night (poetry). Murphy
14
Night Club Entrance (poetry). Murphy 3:16
Thoughts of the Girl He Left Behind
(poetry). Murphy 3:17

BROOKS, EDWIN. Poet
Tulips from Their Blood (poetry). Major 30

BROOKS, GWENDOLYN, 1917- . Poet, Fic-
tion Writer
Maud Martha (excerpt: At the Burns-
Coopers—fiction). Adams 2:97
Maud Martha (excerpt: Helen—fiction).
Hill 2:320
Maud Martha (excerpt: If You're Light
And Have Long Hair—fiction). Wash-
ington 37
Maud Martha (excerpt: Self Solace—fic-
tion). Adams 2:93, Washington 45
Maud Martha (excerpt: We're the Only
Colored People Here—fiction). Patter-
son 3:205
Maud Martha (excerpt: You're Being So
Good, So Kind—fiction). Adams 2:91

Artists' and Models' Ball (poetry). Chap-
man 461
An Aspect of Love, Alive in the Ice and
Fire (poetry). Randall 2:179
The ballad of chocolate Mabbie (poetry).
Ford 224
The Ballad of Rudolph Read (poetry).
Jordan 46, Robinson 2:209
Bean Eaters (poetry). Adoff 3:154, Bell
81, Hayden 2:159, Jordan 23, Kearns
546, Lomax 245, Patterson 3:217, Rob-
inson 2:209, Singh 19
Beverly Hills, Chicago (poetry). Robin-
son 2:207
Birth in a Narrow Room (poetry). Hughes
2:35, Singh 16
Blackstone Rangers (poetry). Adoff 59,
Adoff 3:159, Turner 3:260, Turner 4:104
Boy Breaking Glass (poetry). Robinson
2:211

Bronzeville Man with a Belt in the Back
(poetry). Adoff 2:16, Adoff 3:157, Freed-
man 180, Hayden 143, Patterson 3:217
Bronzeville Mother (poetry). Baker 331
But Can See Better There, And Laughing
There (poetry). Hayden 2:157
The Chicago Defender Sends a Man to
Little Rock, Fall, 1957 (poetry). Adoff
3:155, Barksdale 718, Bell 82, Bontemps
2:142, Chapman 466, Davis 521, Hay-
den 141, Kearns 546, Kearns 2:121,
Long 581, Singh 17, Stanford 242
The Chicago Picasso (poetry). Davis, C.
382, Randall 2:169
Children of the Poor (poetry). Barksdale
717, Bell 80, Chapman 463, Emanuel 500
Children of the Poor (excerpt—poetry).
Stanford 201
The Crazy Woman (poetry). Adams 3:115
DeWitt Williams on His Way to Lincoln
Cemetery (poetry). Barksdale 716, Davis
516
Do Not Be Afraid of No (poetry). Barks-
dale 717
Egg-boiler (poetry). Adoff 3:154, Emanuel
501
The Empty Woman (poetry). Haslam 329
First Fight, Then Fiddle (poetry). Hughes
2:337, Randall 22
Flags (poetry). Bontemps 2:141
Hunchback Girl: She Thinks of Heaven
(poetry). Hayden 2:51, Patterson 3:217
I Love Those Little Booths at Benvenuti's
(poetry). Henderson 174
In the Mecca (poetry). Miller, R. 413
Intermission (poetry). Davis 525, Hill 2:565
Jessie Michell's Mother (poetry). Breman
164
Kitchenette Building (poetry). Adams 3:80,
Ford 224, Hughes 2:334, Randall 2:166,
Stanford 200, Turner 3:257, Turner 4:101
Langston Hughes (poetry). Singh 20
Last Quatrain of the Ballad of Emmett Till
(poetry). Adoff 3:155
Life for My Child Is Simple (poetry). Long
583
Life of Lincoln West (poetry). Troupe 211
A Little Poem (poetry). Pool 54
Loam Norton (poetry). Barksdale 721, Ran-
dall 22
Love Note (poetry). Dreer 89
A Lovely Love (poetry). Randall 2:167
The Lovers of the Poor (poetry). Bell 82,
Ford 226, Stanford 245
Malcolm X (poetry). Adoff 3:158, Breman
165, Davis 523, Haslam 330, Kearns
2:145, Lomax 246, Randall 24, Turner
3:262, Turner 4:106
Martin Luther King (poetry). Adoff 3:159,
Brooks 167
Medger Evers (poetry). Adams 3:29, Adoff
3:158, Haslam 330, Kearns 548, Williams
11
Mentors (poetry). Barksdale 717, Hay-
den 2:156

(BROOKS, GWENDOLYN)
The Mother (poetry). Barksdale 715, Bell 79, Hill 2:577, Randall 2:165
Negro Hero (poetry). Ford 225, Hayden 2:152, Robinson 2:206
Old Laughter (poetry). Black 42
Old-Marrieds (poetry). Adoff 3:154, Bontemps 2:141
Paul Robeson (poetry). Adoff 3:165, Brooks 38
People Who Have No Children Can Be Hard (poetry). Kearns 545
Piano After War (poetry). Barksdale 716, Bontemps 142, Hayden 2:155, Patterson 3:217
The Preacher: Ruminates Behind the Sermon (poetry). Bell 80, Chapman 462, Henderson 169, Kearns 545
Pygmies Are Pygmies Still, Though Percht on Alps (poetry). Hughes 2:336
Riders to the Blood-Red Wrath (poetry). Barksdale 719
Riot (poetry). Adoff 3:164, Chapman 2:201, Exum 60, Randall 26, Randall 2:175
Rites for Cousin Vit (poetry). Davis 520, Randall 2:167
Rudolph Is Tired of the City (poetry). Weisman 43
Sadie and Maud (poetry). Hayden 144
Second Sermon on the Warpland (poetry). Adoff 3:163, Baker 335, Randall 2:171
Sermon on the Warpland (poetry). Adoff 3:163, Randall 2:170
A Song in the Front Yard (poetry). Adoff 2:11, Adoff 3:153, Ford 224, Hill 2:558
The Sonnet-Ballad (poetry). Black 42
Speech to the Young . . . (poetry). Troupe 329
Strong Men, Riding Horses (poetry). Adoff 3:157, Hayden 2:158
Sundays of Satin-legs Smith (poetry). Davis 516, Henderson 169, Hill 2:560, Margolies 178
Takes Time (poetry). Long 584
Third Sermon on the Warpland (poetry). Randall 2:176
To Be in Love (poetry). Patterson 4:11
Truth (poetry). Robinson 2:208
Two Dedications (excerpt—poetry). Adoff 3:161
The Vacant Lot (poetry). Singh 19
The Wall (poetry). Barksdale 721, Davis 524, Hughes 2:338, Randall 24
Way-out Morgan (poetry). Barksdale 720, Randall 23
We Real Cool (poetry). Adams 3:105, Adoff 2:5, Adoff 3:157, Barksdale 718, Bell 81, Chambers 118, Chapman 465, Davis 521, Henderson 176, Lomax 245, Long 580, Margolies 217, Patterson 3:217, Pool 51, Robinson 2:209, Stanford 206
What Shall I Give My Children (poetry). Randall 2:166
When You Have Forgotten Sunday: The Love Story (poetry). Hill 2:559, Randall 2:168

The White Troops Had Their Orders But The Negroes Looked Like Men (poetry). Kearns 2:85
The Womanhood (poetry). Davis, C. 379, Turner 3:258, Turner 4:102
Young Africans (poetry). Brooks 37
Young Heroes (poetry). Randall 2:172

Life of Lincoln West (short fiction). Brooks 33, Gibson 3, Hill 2:316
We're the Only Colored People Here (short fiction). Hughes 3:202, Stanford 251

BROOKS, HELEN MORGAN. Poet
Plans (poetry). Hughes 109, Hughes 2:274
Words (poetry). Hughes 104, Hughes 2:278, Patterson 4:149
A Young David: Birmingham (poetry). Hughes 2:276

BROOKS, JONATHAN HENDERSON, 1904-1945. Poet
And One Shall Live In Two (poetry). Hughes 2:239, Johnson, C. 72
Depression (poetry). Cunard 259
The Last Quarter Moon of the Dying Year (poetry). Brown 365, Cullen 195
Muse in Late November (poetry). Hughes 2:240
My Angel (poetry). Hughes 2:238
Paean (poetry). Cullen 195
The Poet (poetry). Cunard 259
The Resurrection (poetry). Bontemps 2:95, Brown 364, Cullen 193, Hughes 2:236
She Said . . . (poetry). Hughes 2:241
A Student I Know (poetry). Johnson, C. 156

BROOKS, ROSA PAUL. Poet
Not Wanted (poetry). Dreer 91
Winter's Morn (poetry). Dreer 91

BROOKS, WILLIAM F. Poet
Our Mission (poetry). Cuney 3

BROONZY, BIG BILL, 1893-1958. Poet
Hollerin' the Blues (poetry). Henderson 110

BROWN, BENJAMIN A. Fiction Writer
Thunder At Dawn (excerpt—fiction, unpublished). Hill 2:503

BROWN, CECIL, 1937- . Fiction Writer, Short Fiction Writer, Playwright, Critic
Life and Loves of Mr. Jiveass Nigger (excerpt: Black Mass—fiction). Reed 3.
The Life and Loves of Mr. Jiveass Nigger (excerpt: Prologue—fiction). Chapman 2

BROWN, CLAUDE, 1937- . Fiction Writer
Manchild In a Promised Land (excerpt—fiction, autobiographical). Adams 4:51, Davis 724, Demarest 145, Ford 311
Manchild In a Promised Land (excerpt: Harlem, My Harlem—fiction, autobiographical). Freedman 172

(BROWN, CLAUDE)
Manchild In a Promised Land (excerpt: Harlem Revisited—fiction, autobiographical). Burnett 335

BROWN, DARYL. Poet
Jumpstreet for a Black Man (poetry). Bookers 108

BROWN, DELORES A. Poet
Upon Looking at Love (poetry). Murphy 15

BROWN, ELAINE. Poet
The End of Silence (poetry). Troupe 2:50
The Meeting (poetry). Troupe 2:54
Poppa's Come Home (poetry). Troupe 2:52
Very Black Man (poetry). Troupe 2:53

BROWN, FANNIE CAROLE, 1942- . Poet
Lullaby, My Son (poetry). Schulberg 181
The Realization of a Dream Deferred (poetry). Schulberg 181

BROWN, FRANK LONDON, 1927-1962. Fiction Writer, Short Fiction Writer, Critic, Poet
Jazz (poetry). Hughes 2:395

The Dougal (short fiction). Chapman 202, Margolies 287
A Matter of Time (short fiction). Clarke 245
Singing Dinah's Song (short fiction). Adams 2:107, Hill 2:348, Hughes 3:295

BROWN, HENRY "BOX," 1816-?. Autobiographer, Poet, Narrator
Narrative of the Life of Henry "Box" Brown (excerpt—autobiography). Miller, R. 57

Hymn of Thanksgiving (poetry). Miller, R. 61

BROWN, H. "RAP." Poet, Civil Rights Worker
Rap's Poem (poetry). Henderson 187

BROWN, ISABELLA MARIA, 1917- . Poet
Another Day (poetry). Hughes 2:342
Prayer (poetry). Hughes 61, Hughes 2:341

BROWN, JAMES, Poet
Say It Loud, I'm Black and I'm Proud (poetry). Demarest 314

BROWN, JOE C. Poet
Rustic Love (poetry). Murphy 16
Signs of Sleep (poetry). Murphy 15

BROWN, JOHN. Narrator
Slave Life in Georgia (excerpt—narrative). Rose 47

BROWN, JOSEPHINE, Letter Writer
Letters to Samuel May, Jr. (letter). Gayle 19

We Had To Occupy a Seat Apart (letter). Gayle 19

BROWN, LANDA LORETTA. Poet
The Hell-bound Train (poetry). Bookers 104

BROWN, LILLIAN. Poet
Disillusion (poetry). Johnson, C. 151

BROWN, LINDA 1939- . Poet
A Little Poem (poetry). Pool 54
Precocious Curiosity (poetry). Pool 54

BROWN, MARTHA. Short Fiction Writer
The Red Hat (short fiction). Ford 2:54

BROWN, RUBY BERKELEY. Poet
Song of the Awakened Negro (poetry). Weisman 76

BROWN, STERLING A., 1901- . Poet, Critic, Teacher, Editor
American Race Problem as Reflected in American Literature (essay). Baker 221
Century of Negro Portraiture in American Literature (essay). Chapman 564, Ford 66, Hayden 249
Contemporary Negro Poetry: 1914-1936 (essay). Patterson 3:146, Watkins 243
The Federal Theatre (essay). Patterson 101
Negro Character As Seen By White Authors (essay). Emanuel 139
Negro Folk Expression (essay). Gayle 2:3
Roland Hayes (essay). Cromwell 234

After Winter (poetry). Adoff 3:65, Bell 30, Hughes 2:165, Jordan 50, Pool 58
Ballad of Joe Meek (poetry). Bell 31, Chapman 414
Break of Day (poetry). Brown 389
Cabaret (poetry). Henderson 130
Challenge (poetry). Cullen 138, Patterson 3:161
Children of the Mississippi (poetry). Cunard 259
Children's Children (poetry). Henderson 142
Crispus Attucks McCoy (poetry). Pool 2:197, Randall 2:115
Effie (poetry). Johnson 261
Foreclosure (poetry). Adoff 3:64, Hughes 2:170, Johnson, C. 36
He Was a Man (poetry). Kerlin 259
Home (poetry). Kerlin 251
Long Gone (poetry). Brown 381, Calverton 209, Cullen 134, Johnson 254, Long 468, Randall 2:112, Turner 3:235, Turner 4:79
Ma Rainey (poetry). Henderson 134, Pool 59, Pool 2:85
Maumee Ruth (poetry). Cullen 133, Henderson 133
Memphis Blues (poetry). Black 14, Chapman 405, Cunard 259, Davis 405, Johnson 252
Mose (poetry). Hayden 2:70

(BROWN, STERLING A.)
Odyssey of Big Boy (poetry). Cullen 130, Davis 400, Johnson 248
Old Lem (poetry). Adams 3:77, Adoff 2:68, Adoff 3:69, Barksdale 633, Breman 66, Brown 387, Davis 402, Hughes 2:167, Lomax 221, Randall 2:109, Stanford 148
An Old Woman Remembers (poetry). Adoff 3:68, Breman 68
Remembering Nat Turner (poetry). Adams 3:67, Adoff 3:63, Bell 35, Chapman 410, Davis 408, Hughes 2:172, Pool 2:73
Return (poetry). Cullen 139, Dreer 62, Patterson 3:161, Turner 3:236, Turner 4:80
Revelations (poetry). Hayden 2:74
Salutamus (poetry). Cullen 138
Sister Lou (poetry). Adoff 3:66, Baker 218, Bontemps 2:53, Chapman 404, Davis 404, Hughes 2:174, Long 479, Pool 56
Slim Greer (poetry). Black 16, Henderson 136, Johnson 256, Turner 3:233, Turner 4:77
Slim in Atlanta (poetry). Davis 407
Slim in Hell (poetry). Brown 383, Chapman 407, Henderson 138, Long 469, Randall 2:105
Southern Cop (poetry). Adams 3:109, Chapman 413
Southern Road (poetry). Adoff 3:67, Bell 29, Brown 386, Chapman 412, Dreer 61, Johnson 250, Long 474, Randall 2:111, Troupe 283, Turner 3:237, Turner 4:81
Sporting Beasley (poetry). Davis, C., 261, Hayden 2:76, Miller, R. 223
Strange Legacies (poetry). Adoff 3:62, Davis, C. 260, Hayden 2:72, Lomax 218
Strong Men (poetry). Adams 3:27, Adoff 3:60, Barksdale 634, Brown 390, Chambers 230, Chapman 419, Cunard 259, Hayden 112, Johnson 258, Kerlin 256, Lomax 219, Long 475, Randall 113, Troupe 281
Thoughts of Death (poetry). Cromwell 42, Dreer 62
To a Certain Lady in Her Garden (poetry). Cullen 136
When De Saints Go Ma'ching Home (poetry). Bontemps 2:55, Davis, C. 255, Kerlin 251, Miller, R. 219
The Young Ones (poetry). Chapman 413

And/or (short fiction). Clarke 131, James 228

BROWN, WILLIAM. Poet
Enough (poetry). Murphy 3:18
Forest Park (poetry). Murphy 3:18
Rain (poetry). Murphy 3:18
Shadow and Sun (poetry). Murphy 3:21
Whimsey (poetry). Murphy 3:21
Why (poetry). Murphy 3:21

BROWN, WILLIAM WELLS, 1815-1884. Lecturer, Historian, Anthropologist, Fiction Writer, Playwright, Essayist, Autobiographer

The Escape (drama). Hatch 34
The Escape; Or A Leap for Freedom (excerpt—drama). Kendricks 84

Crispus Attucks (essay). Patterson 3:54
A Day in the British Museum (essay). Cromwell 181
Letter XI (essay). Turner 2:9, Turner 3:9
My Southern Home (excerpt: Stud Negro—essay). Davis 63
The Negro in the American Rebellion: His Heroism and His Fidelity (essay). Barksdale 254
The New Negro in Literature (essay). Davis 410
Visit of a Fugitive Slave To The Grave of Wilberforce (essay). Barksdale 186, Brawley 170

Clotel: a Tale of the Southern States (fiction). Takaki 231
Clotel: a Tale of the Southern States (excerpts—fiction). Barksdale 181, Davis 58, Long 48, Miller, R. 95, Patterson 3:73
Clotel: A Tale of the Southern States (excerpt: Ch. 10-14—fiction). Kendricks 94
Clotel (excerpt: Clotel in Slavery—fiction). Patterson 3:73
Clotel (excerpt: Quadroon: Octoroon—fiction). Brown 149
Clotel (excerpt: Speculating in Slaves—fiction). Brown 145

Letters to Garrison (letters). Brown 625

BROWNE, GEORGE B. Poet
The Train Ride (poetry). Murphy 16

BROWNE, ROSCOE LEE, 1924- . Poet
Pellets of May 2, 1960 (poetry). Pool 62
10-9-8-7-6-5-4-3-2-1 Death (poetry). Pool 63

BROWNE, THEODORE. Playwright, Fiction Writer
Natural Man (drama). Hatch 360

BROWNE, WILLIAM, 1930- . Poet
And Once Again: Pain (poetry). Pool 64
Harlem Sounds: Hallelujah Corner (poetry). Bontemps 173, Pool 65
Saturday Night in Harlem (poetry). Pool 66

BRUCE, RICHARD, 1906- . Playwright, Poet
Shadji, an African Ballet (drama). Locke 387

Cavalier (poetry). Cullen 207
Shadow (poetry). Black 33, Cullen 206

BRYANT, FREDERICK JAMES, JR., 1942- . Poet, Playwright
A Bird in the City (poetry). Brown, P. 16
Black Orpheus (poetry). Jones 397
Cathexis (poetry). Adoff 3:406, Chapman 2:216

(BRYANT, FREDERICK JAMES, JR.)
The Languages We Are (poetry). Major 32
Nothing Lovely As a Tree (poetry). Jones 396
Patience of a People (poetry). Breman 460

BUDBELL, DAVID. Poet
New York In The Spring (poetry). Adoff 3

BUFORD, NAOMI, E. Poet
Heritage (poetry). Murphy 16

BULLINS, ED, 1935- . Playwright, Editor, Critic, Fiction Writer
Clara's Ole Man (drama). Davis 658, Haslam 353
The Corner (drama). King 77
Electronic Nigger (drama). Robinson 2:158
The Fabulous Miss Marie (drama). Bullins 7
Gentleman Caller (drama). Caldwell 117, Oliver 370
Goin' a Buffalo (drama), Couch 155, Hatch 826
How Do You Do (drama). Jones 595
In New England Winter (drama). Couch 130
In the Wine Time (drama). Patterson 2:379
You Gonna Let Me Take You Out Tonight, Baby? (drama). Alhamisi 45

The So-Called Western Avant-Garde Drama (essay). Gayle 2:143

Seventh Avenue Poem (poetry). King 3:36
Spirit Enchantment (poetry). King 3:38
When Slavery Seems Sweet (poetry). Breman 340, Major 32

Dandy, or Astride the Funky Finger of Lust (short fiction). King 2:59

BULLOCK, DORIS POWERS. Essayist
In Defense of the Negro Male (essay). Shuman 58

BULLOCK, RALPH W. Biographer
In Spite of Handicaps (excerpt: Charles Clinton Spaulding—biography). Dreer 130

BUNCHE, RALPH J. 1904- . Educator, Statesman
Disfranchisement of the Negro (essay). Brown 925

BUNTON, FREDERICA KATHERYNE. Poet
You Taught Me Love (poetry). Murphy 17

BURBRIDGE, EDWARD DEJOIE. Poet
Dreams Are Fragile (poetry). Murphy 3:22
The Heart Toasts (poetry). Murphy 3:22
The Letter (poetry). Murphy 3:23
Remembrance (poetry). Murphy 3:22

BURKE, INEZ M. Playwright
Two Races (drama). Richardson 295

BURRELL, BENJAMIN EBENEZER, 1892- . Poet
To a Negro Mother (poetry). Kerlin 303

BURRILL, MARY, 1919- . Playwright
They That Sit In Darkness (drama). Hatch 178

BURROUGHS, MARGARET TAYLOR GOSS, 1917- Editor, Essayist, Poet, Short Fiction Writer
She'll Speak To Generations Yet To Come (essay). Brown, P. 129

Because I have Wandered Long (poetry). Brooks 147
I Have Spent My Life (poetry). Chapman 2:340
It Is Again (poetry). Chapman 2:341
Moving Deep (poetry). Chapman 2:341
My Love When This Is Past (poetry). Brooks 148, Randall 2:332
What marked the river's flow (poetry). Chapman 2:339
Who Collects the Pain (poetry). Brooks 149, Chapman 2:240
Who Is Not a Stranger Still (poetry). Brooks 148, Randall 2:331
You Are Instantly Enfolded (poetry). Brooks 147

BURTON, JOHN W. Poet
Black Cameo on Pink Quartz (poetry). Murphy 18
Fogged (poetry). Murphy 3:25
Hope (poetry). Murphy 3:25
Life's Like the Wind (poetry). Murphy 3:23
Pride (poetry). Murphy 20
Rain (poetry). Murphy 3:26
Snowflakes (poetry). Murphy 3:25
Suicide (poetry). Murphy 3:26
Tid Bit (poetry). Murphy 3:26
Vignette (poetry). Murphy 19

BURVICK, KAREN. Poet
Happiness (poetry). Bookers 64

BUSH, JOSEPH BEVANS, ?-1968. Poet, Essayist
The Alienated Richard Wright: a Native Son Remembered (essay). Shuman 63

Ambıvalence (poetry). Shuman 266
Indictment (poetry). Shuman 67
Nittygritty (poetry). Coombs 4
Orange Soda and Chocolate Cupcakes (poetry). Alhamisi 128
Saint Is a Soul Brother (poetry). Shuman 267

BUTCHER, JAMES W. JR., Playwright
The Seer (drama). Brown 520

BUTCHER, MARGARET JUST. Essayist, Historian
The Negro As Artist And In American Art (essay). Curry 163

BUTCHER, PHILIP, 1918- . Critic, Poet, Essayist
Emerson and the South (essay). Emanuel 529

BUTLER, HOOD C. Poet
Ebony Rhythm (poetry). Murphy 22

BUTLER, JAMES ALPHEUS, 1905- . Editor, Poet
Maid and Violinist (poetry). Murphy 21
Portrait of a Poet (poetry). Murphy 21
Primrose and Thistle (poetry). Murphy 20
Things Too Beautiful (poetry). Murphy 3:27

BUTLER, REGINALD. Poet
Something to Think about and Dig Jazz (poetry). Henderson 189

BUYSON, CLARENCE F. Poet
The Soudan (poetry). Johnson, C. 151

CADE, TONI. See **BAMBARA, TONI CADE.**

CAIN, RICHARD H. Orator
Against Segregation in Schools (speech). Freedman 114

CALDWELL, BEN Playwright
All White Cast (drama). King 389
The Job (drama). Demarest 308, Kearns 2:137, Robinson 2:423
The King of Soul, or, The Devil and Otis Reading (drama). Bullins 2:176
Prayer Meeting, or, the First Militant Minister (drama). Caldwell 27, Jones 589

CALVERTON, VIRGIL F. Historian, Editor
The Growth of Negro Literature (essay). Calverton 1, Cunard 78

CAMPBELL, E. SIMMS, 1906- . Essayist
Early Jam (essay). Brown 983

CAMPBELL, FRANK. Short Fiction Writer
The Slum (short fiction). Bookers 14

CAMPBELL, JAMES EDWIN, 1867-1895. Poet
Compensation (poetry). Johnson 70
De Cunjah Man (poetry). Johnson 65, Long 232, Robinson 266
Negro Serenade (poetry). Johnson 65, Patterson 3:94
Ol' Doc' Hyar (poetry). Barksdale 451, Brown 316, Johnson 67, Long 233, Robinson 263

Sciplinin' Sister Brown (poetry). Long 235, Robinson 267
Uncle Eph-Epicure (poetry). Robinson 265
Uncle Eph's Banjo Song (poetry). Johnson 67
When Ol' Sis' Judy Pray (poetry). Barksdale 451, Brown 317, Johnson 69

CAMPBELL, JOSIE. Poet
My Street Is Kind of Dead (poetry). Bookers 19

CANADAY, NICHOLAS, JR. Essayist
Major Themes in the Poetry of Countee Cullen (essay). Bontemps 3:103

CANNON, DAVID WADSWORTH, JR., 1911-1938. Poet
Boston Tea (poetry). Murphy 24
Dark Love (poetry). Murphy 26
Freedom in Mah Soul (poetry). Hughes 2:281
Insight (poetry). Murphy 26
Mountains (poetry). Murphy 23
To Nita (poetry). Murphy 24
Western Town (poetry). Hughes 2:281
World Weariness (poetry). Murphy 25

CANNON, STEVE, 1935- . Essayist, Fiction Writer
Groove, Bang and Jive Around (excerpt—fiction). Reed 13

Robin's Strange Assignment (short fiction). Troupe 257

CANTONI, LOUIS J. Poet
Bright Moment (poetry). Ten 30
Double Harvest (poetry). Ten 27
Essence (poetry). Ten 27
Juncos (poetry). Ten 30
Old Lecture Notes (poetry). Ten 30
Poetic Themes (poetry). Ten 29
Social Worker (poetry). Ten 28
Sunsets (poetry). Ten 29
To A Stolen Flute (poetry). Ten 28
When Summer Comes (poetry). Ten 30

CAREW, JAN. Poet
Africa-Guyana (poetry). Breman 189

CARMICHAEL. STOKELY. Essayist
Black Is Good (essay). Demarest 354
Black Power (excerpt—essay—with C. V. Hamilton). Adoff 4:207
Power and Racism (essay). Curry 223
Toward Black Liberation (essay). Jones 119

CARMICHAEL, WAVERLY TURNER. Poet
It's All Through Life (poetry). Kerlin 53
Keep Me, Jesus, Keep Me (poetry). Johnson 162
Mammy's Baby Scared (poetry). Kerlin 235
Winter Is Coming (poetry). Johnson 163

CARPENTER, HOWARD. Poet
Solar Flight (poetry). Murphy 27

CARR, CLARENCE F., 1880- . Poet
The Encampment Choir (poetry). Brewer 9

CARROTHERS, JAMES D. Poet
An Indignation Dinner (poetry). Singh 4
Der Rabbit's Foot (poetry). Robinson 275

CARSKADON, T. R. Fiction Writer
Nigger Schoolhouse (short fiction). Burnett
79

CARTER, HERMAN, J. D. Poet
Mountain in a Storm (poetry). Murphy 29
Negro Audience (poetry). Murphy 29
A Poetess (poetry). Murphy 28
The Voice of the Hill (poetry). Murphy 27

CARTER, JIMMIE. Poet
The Dream of a Southern Governor (poetry). Bookers 149

CARTER, KARL, 1944- . Poet
Heroes (poetry). Henderson 311
Roots (poetry). Henderson 312

CARTER, LOLETA. Poet
Black Reflections (poetry). Bookers 7
The Outcast (poetry). Bookers 6

CATER, CATHERINE, 1917- . Poet
Here and Now (poetry). Bontemps 2:140,
Hughes 2:340

CAUTION, ETHEL. Poet
Sunset (poetry). Cromwell 52

CAYTON, HORACE R., 1903- . Essayist,
Sociologist, Autobiographer
Ideological Forces in the Work of the
Negro Writer (essay). Hill 37
A Picnic with Sinclair Lewis (essay).
Hill 2:22

Reflections on Richard Wright: a Symposium on an Exiled Native Son (symposium). Gibson 2:58

CESAIRE, AIME. Poet
Son of lightning (poetry). Hollo 18
Tom-tom (poetry). Hollo 18

CHANDLER, LEN, 1935- . Poet
From 21A (poetry). Lowenfels 15
I Would Be a Painter Most of All (poetry). Major 34

CHAPMAN, NELL. Poet
Bread on the Water (poetry). Murphy 29
Requiem (poetry). Murphy 30

CHAPPELL, HELEN F. Poet
Flood Song (poetry). Murphy 3:28
For the Lips of One Grown Weary (poetry). Murphy 3:28

Sophisticated Postscript for a Five-Page
Letter (poetry). Murphy 3:29

CHARLES, MARTE. See **CHARLES, MARTHA EVANS.**

CHARLES, MARTHA EVANS. Playwright
Black Cycle (drama). King 525
Job Security (drama). Hatch 765

CHENAULT, JOHN. Poet
To Gwen Brooks (poetry). Brown, E. 17

CHESNUTT, CHARLES WADDELL, 1858-
1932. Essayist, Poet, Fiction Writer
The Marrow of Tradition (excerpt: The
Storm Breaks—fiction). Brown 161

Baxter's Procrustes (short fiction). Chapman 50
The Bouquet (short fiction). Baker 117
The Goophered Grapevine (short fiction).
Barksdale 329, Calverton 27, Clarke 11,
Davis 169, Emanuel 27, James 5,
Kearns 2:55, Long 202, Patterson 3:87,
Singh 37, Watkins 39
The Gray Wolf's Ha'nt (short fiction).
James 17
Hot-Foot Hannibal (short fiction). Cromwell 59
A Matter of Principle (short fiction).
Kearns 2:179
The Passing of Grandison (short fiction).
Barksdale 340, Kearns 293
Po' Sandy (short fiction). Kearns 282,
Margolies 43, Turner 8, Turner 3:298
The Sheriff's Children (short fiction).
Brown 27, Chambers 168, Haslam 256,
Hughes 3:1, Kendricks 170, Rose 122
The Wife of His Youth (short fiction).
Barksdale 335, Cromwell 72, Davis 179,
Davis, C. 53, Dreer 230, Ford 50, Miller, R. 161, Rose 112, Stanford 78

CHESTER, ALFRED. Interviewer
Interview with Ralph Ellison (interview;
with Vilma Howard). Patterson 3:291

CHEW, BIRDELL. See **MOORE, BIRDELL
CHEW.**

CHILDRESS, ALICE. Playwright, Essayist,
Short Fiction Writer
Trouble in Mind (drama). Patterson 2:135
Wine in the Wilderness (drama). Hatch
737

The Negro Women in American Literature
(panel discussion). Exum 26

The Pocketbook Game (short fiction).
Hughes 3:205, Rose 249, Stanford 254

CHITTICK, CONRAD. Poet
Spain (poetry). Murphy 3:31
Torches (poetry). Murphy 3:31

CHRISTIAN, BARBARA. Essayist
Ralph Ellison: a Critical Study (essay).
Gayle 2:353

CHRISTIAN, MARCUS BRUCE, 1900-
Poet, Essayist
The Craftsman (poetry). Hughes 2:156,
Murphy 35
Dark Heritage (poetry). Murphy 31
Dialect Quatrain (poetry). Bontemps 2:53
Go Down, Moses! (poetry). Murphy 34
Humoresque (poetry). Murphy 3:33
McDonogh Day in New Orleans (poetry).
Bontemps 2:52, Hughes 2:157
Selassie at Geneva (poetry). Murphy 34
Song of Hannibal (poetry). Murphy 3:33
Spring in the South (poetry). Murphy 3:34

CHRISTMAS, EDWARD. Poet
Light, Light, Light (poetry). Brown, P. 7

CHRISTOPHER, JAMES (NAKISAKI).
Poet
Lullaby to a Dream (poetry). Murphy 35

CLARK, BENJAMIN P. Poet
Do They Miss Me? (poetry). Robinson
191
The Emigrant (poetry). Robinson 187
Love (poetry). Robinson 192
No Enemies (poetry). Robinson 193
The Pauper's Grave (poetry). Robinson
190
Requiescat in Pace (poetry). Robinson 190
The Seminole (poetry). Robinson 187
What Is a Slave? (poetry). Robinson 188

CLARK, CARL. 1932- . Poet
Allegory in Black (poetry). Brooks 2:81
Conundrum (poetry). Brooks 2:80
No More (poetry). Brooks 2:80
Ode to a Beautiful Woman (poetry).
Brooks 2:84
The Second Coming (poetry). Brooks 2:86

CLARK, JOHN PEPPER. Playwright
Song of a Goat (excerpt—drama). Robinson 2:360

CLARK, KENNETH B. 1941- . Fiction
Writer, Essayist
Dark Ghetto (excerpts—essay). Adoff 4:218

CLARK, PETER WELLINGTON. Poet
Deserted Village (poetry). Murphy 38
Historic Episodes (poetry). Murphy 39
Paradox (poetry). Murphy 36
Reality (poetry). Murphy 37

CLARKE, AUSTIN. Fiction Writer
Four Stations in His Circle (short fiction).
Troupe 184

CLARKE, HELEN F. Poet
Shadows (poetry). Murphy 40
You Are Black (poetry). Murphy 41

CLARKE, JOHN HENRIK, 1915- . Poet,
Essayist, Critic, Editor, Short Fiction
Writer
The Alienation of James Baldwin (essay).
Gayle 2:350
Origin and Growth of Afro-American Literature (essay). Chapman 632, Hayden
283
Reclaiming the Lost African Heritage (essay). Conference 21, Jones 11, Patterson
3:277

America (poetry). Murphy 44
Bombardment and Aftermath (poetry).
Murphy 44
Confession (poetry). Pool 2:112
Determination (poetry). Adoff 3:144
Inquiry (poetry). Murphy 43
Love (poetry). Weisman 65
Meditations of a European Farmer (poetry).
Murphy 43
No Tears (poetry). Murphy 44
Question (poetry). Weisman 57
Sing Me a New Song (poetry). Adoff 3:143,
Murphy 42
Truth (poetry). Weisman 66

The Boy Who Painted Christ Black (short
fiction). Chambers 258, Clarke 108,
Gibson 199, Rose 266, Singh 94
Revolt of the Angels (short fiction). Clarke
3:123
Santa Claus Is a White Man (short fiction). Hughes 3:181, Jones 172

CLARKE, LEROY. Poet
Inquiry (poetry). Troupe 512

CLARKE, MILTON, c. 1817-?. Autobiographer
Narratives of the Sufferings of Lewis and
Milton Clarke . . . (excerpt: Abolitionist Rescue—autobiographical narrative).
Brown 704

CLEAGE, PEARL. See **LOMAX, PEARL CLEAGE**

CLEAVER, ELDRIDGE, 1935- . Essayist,
Orator, Short Fiction Writer
Domestic Law and International Order
(essay). Demarest 346
The Muhammad Ali-Patterson Fight (essay). Kearns 2:105
Notes on a Native Son (essay). Davis, C.
313, Gayle 2:339, Hemenway 233
On Becoming (essay). Ford 347, Haslam
372, Hayden 230, Kearns 630
Primeval Mitosis (essay). Margolies 340.
Psychology: The Black Bible (essay). Chapman 2:474
Soul Food (essay). Kearns 630
Soul on Ice (excerpts—essay). Davis 843,
Kearns 628, Long 701, Patterson 2:377,
Rose 252
Soul on Ice (excerpt: Initial Reaction on
the Assassination of Malcolm X—essay).
Kendricks 331

(CLEAVER, ELDRIDGE)
Soul on Ice (excerpt: on Watts—essay). Kearns 628
To All Black Women from All Black Men (essay). Barksdale 884, Patterson 2:377, Singh 170
The White Race and Its Heroes (essay). Adams 4:165, Ford 352, Miller, R. 177, Stanford 286, Turner 2:139, Turner 3:140

CLEAVES, MARY WILKERSON. Poet
April Longing (poetry). Murphy 46
Black Soldier (poetry). Murphy 45
Why Do I Love This Country (poetry). Murphy 46

CLEMMONS, CAROLE GREGORY, 1945- . Poet
Area (poetry). Shuman 2:84
Black Children (poetry). Brown, P. 20
Black Eurydice (poetry). Shuman 2:86
A Black Poet to Saint Exupery (poetry). Shuman 269
The Bull (poetry). Shuman 2:87
Conjugation (poetry). Shuman 2:88
Cosmic Attack on Poets (poetry). Shuman 2:84
David (poetry). Shuman 270, Shuman 2:81
For Dr. Coffin Who Loves (poetry). Shuman 2:89
Ghetto Love-Song-Migration (poetry). Major 56, Shuman 2:82
I'm Just a Stranger Here, Heaven Is My Home (poetry). Adoff 3:489
Long Distance (poetry). Shuman 2:85
Love from My Father (poetry). Adoff 3:489, Shuman 2:85
Love Has Two (poetry). Shuman 2:88
Love Poem (poetry). Shuman 2:83
Migration (poetry). Adams 3:87, Adoff 3:489, Troupe 147
Nina Simone (poetry). Shuman 270
NYC Love Poem (poetry). Shuman 2:83
On Snobbery (poetry). Shuman 2:88
People (poetry). Shuman 2:87
A Response to the Visiting Poet's Name (poetry). Shuman 2:86
Spring (poetry). Adoff 3.488
To Koala, Who Will Be Extinct (poetry). Shuman 2:86
What Order (poetry). Shuman 2:89

Porky (short fiction). Shuman 68

CLEMMONS, FRANCOIS, 1945- . Poet
The Cross (poetry). Shuman 272
Dedicated to the Living Memory of Miss Gwendolyn Brooks (poetry). Brown, P. 21
The Miracle (poetry). Shuman 272
Mother (poetry). Shuman 273
My Aunt Clara (poetry). Shuman 274
Sons (poetry). Shuman 274
Thanksgiving (poetry). Shuman 274
To Maria Callas (poetry). Shuman 275
Warren (poetry). Shuman 275

CLIFFORD, CARRIE WILLIAMS. Poet
The Black Draftee from Dixie (poetry). Cunard 261
An Easter Message (poetry). Kerlin 272

CLIFTON, LUCILLE, 1936- . Poet, Essayist
Admonitions (poetry). Davis, C. 55, Randall 2:251
After Kent State (poetry). Bell 142
Apology (To the Panthers) (poetry). Exum 67
being property once myself (poetry). Exum 65
Ca'line's Prayer (poetry). Bell 141, Miller, A. 54
The 1st (poetry). Miller, A. 51
For de Lawd (poetry). Adoff 3:306, Miller, A. 53, Troupe 204
Good Times (poetry). Adoff 3:306, Bell 140, Bontemps 2:196, Hayden 150, Miller, A., 52, Randall 2:250
If I Stand in My Window (poetry). Miller, A. 54, Randall 2:251
In the Inner City (poetry). Bell 139, Miller, A. 52
The Kind of Man He Is (poetry). Exum 68
later i'll say (poetry). Exum 66
Listen, Children (poetry). Adoff 3:308, Troupe 244
The lost baby poem (poetry). Bell 141
Love Rejected (poetry). Randall 2:250
Mary (poetry). Troupe 441
The Meeting after the Saviour Gone (poetry). Miller, A. 50
Miss Rosie (poetry). Adoff 3:307, Bell 139, Miller, A. 51
My Mama Moved Among the Days (poetry). Adoff 3:308, Bell 139, Miller, A. 50
Those Boys that Ran Together (poetry). Adoff 3:307, Miller, A. 53
To Bobby Seale (poetry). Adoff 3:308

CLINTON, DOLORES. Poet
Heritage (poetry). Murphy 47

CLOROX. Essayist, Poet
Searching (essay). Brooks 67

Rejoice (poetry). Bookers 19
Why (poetry). Bookers 147

COBB, BESSIE A. Poet
Change (poetry). Murphy 3:35

COBB, CHARLIE, 1944- . Poet, Essayist
Ain't that a Groove (literary collage). Jones 519

Containing Communism (poetry). Adoff 3:472
For Sammy Younge (poetry). Adoff 3:471
L.A.: the order of Things (poetry). Breman 500
Nation (poetry). Adoff 3:468, Lowenfels 17
To Vietnam (poetry). Adoff 3:471

COBB, W. MONTAGUE. Essayist
Daniel Hale Williams—Pioneer and Innovator (biography). Dreer 126

COGGINS, FRANK. Short Fiction Writer
The Killer (short fiction). Ford 2:288

COLE, JOHN. Essayist
Culture: Negro, Black and Nigger (essay).
Chapman 2:491

COLEMAN, ANITA SCOTT. Poet, Short Fic-
tion Writer
American Negro (poetry). Murphy 48
Black Faces (poetry). Murphy 51
The Colorist (poetry). Murphy 50
Hands (poetry). Murphy 50
Humility (poetry). Murphy 51
Theme with Variations (poetry). Murphy
3:36

COLEMAN, ETHEL. Poet
Voodoo (poetry). Murphy 3:39

COLEMAN, HORACE WENDELL, 1943- .
Poet, Critic, Short Fiction Writer
A Downed Black Pilot Learns How to
Fly (poetry). Troupe 374
Nanette Neely/wherever you are (poetry).
Troupe 246

COLEMAN, JAMYE H. Poet
Impossibility (poetry). Murphy 52
The Swing of Life (poetry). Murphy 52

COLLAZO, JAMIE. Poet
The Awakening (poetry). Bookers 156
Shoe, Tell Me What You Know (poetry).
Bookers 99

COLLIER, EUGENIA N., 1928- . Critic,
Editor, Poet, Short Fiction Writer
I Do Not Marvel, Countee Cullen (es-
say). Gibson 3:69

COLLINS, DURWARD, JR., 1937- . Poet
Temperate Belt (poetry). Pool 68

COLLINS, HELEN ARMSTEAD JOHNSON,
1918- . Poet
Affirmation (poetry). Bontemps 2:194
Philodendron (poetry). Bontemps 2:194
To An Avenue Sport (poetry). Hughes
2:346

COLLINS, LESLIE MORGAN, 1914- .
Poet
Creole Girl (poetry). Black 43, Hughes
2:297
Soliloqui (poetry). Pool 70, Pool 2:37
Stevedore (poetry). Bontemps 2:127, Pool
73

COLTER, CYRUS, 1910- . Poet, Fiction
Writer
The Beach Umbrella (short fiction). Adams
2:139, Hill 2:530, Hughes 3:107

Black for Dinner (short fiction). Stadler
238
Mary's Convent (short fiction). Chapman
2:70

CONLEY, CYNTHIA M. Poet
Praise Due to Gwen Brooks (poetry).
Brown, P. 22

CONLEY, MALCOLM CHRISTIAN. Poet
American Ideals (poetry). Brewer 13
For Mother in Paradise (poetry). Brewer
12
Four Walls (poetry). Brewer 13

CONNER, CHARLES H., 1864- . Preacher,
Poet
The Life of the Spirit in the Natural
World (poetry). Kerlin 226

CONYUS, 1942- . Poet
Black Moses, Black Moses Black Moses
Black (poetry). Wilentz 1
Confession to Malcolm (poetry). Chap-
man 2:230
A Day in the Life of . . . (poetry). Wilentz
5
December 26, 1968 (poetry). Wilentz 7
For Che (poetry). Wilentz 7
A Gold Watch Hung in the Sky (poetry).
Miller, A. 48
The Great Santa Barbara Oil Disaster
OR: (poetry). Chapman 2:218
He's Doing Natural Life (poetry). Adoff
3:403, Wilentz 4
i rode with geronimo (poetry). Chapman
2:228, Miller, A. 45
Mama Too Tight (poetry). Wilentz 11
On Gossip Behind My Back (poetry).
Miller, A. 47
Requiem for Tomorrow (poetry). Wilentz
10
san francisco county jail cell b-6 (poetry).
Adoff 3:400
six ten sixty-nine (poetry). Adoff 3:401
untitled: requiem for tomorrow (poetry).
Adoff 3:402
Upon leaving the parole board hearing
(poetry). Adoff 3:401, Miller, A. 48

COOK, GWENDOLYN. Poet
To (poetry). Brooks 82

COOK, JOHN FRANCIS. Orator
Remarks on the subject of Temperance, delivered before the American Moral Reform Society, in St. Thomas' Church,
Pa. Aug. 16th, 1837 (speech). Porter 241

COOK, MIKE, 1939- . Poet, Short Fiction
Writer
Bootie Black and the Seven Giants (po-
etry). Brooks 2:19

If I Knock You Down, Don't You Blame
It On Me (short fiction). Brooks 2.21

COOLEY, KATHERINE. Poet
The Negro's Plea (poetry). Weisman 70

COOPER, CHARLES B., 1948- . Poet, Playwright
Companions (poetry). Shuman 2:37
Damn Equal Shit (poetry). Shuman 2:40
Doorway at 12 Midnight (poetry). Shuman 280
Dreams (poetry). Adoff 3:505, Shuman 2:31
Fo' Want a dat Pot a' Gold (poetry). Shuman 2:34
Honkey (poetry). Adoff 3:504, Shuman 2:39
Hope (poetry). Shuman 2:33
Hypocrisy in Black (poetry). Shuman 2:28
Idle Chatter (poetry). Shuman 2:35
Love (poetry). Shuman 2:38
Mary, May I (poetry). Shuman 2:29
Nation's Blood (poetry). Shuman 276, Shuman 2:32
Native Ascension (poetry). Shuman 277
Polarity (poetry). Shuman 2:25
Rubin (poetry). Adoff 3:504, Shuman 2:27
Sixteen (poetry). Shuman 2:26
Skillet Love on Flame (poetry). Shuman 277
Slave Days (poetry). Shuman 278
Soul of Christ (poetry). Shuman 278
This Damn Earth (poetry). Shuman 2:41
Thoughts from a Fillmore (poetry). Shuman 280
Thoughts of a Lawyer Out of Work (poetry). Shuman 2:36
To Be On . . . (poetry). Shuman 282, Shuman 2:25
To End Nuttery (poetry). Shuman 2:30
Where To (poetry). Shuman 2:42
Yessuh (poetry). Shuman 2:33

COOPER, CLARENCE L., JR. Fiction Writer
Not We Many (short fiction). King 2:209

CORBIN, LLOYD, 1949- . Poet
Ali (poetry). Adoff 3:511
Dedication to the Final Confrontation (poetry). Adoff 3:512, Jordan 12

CORNISH, SAM, 1938- . Poet, Editor
A Black Man (poetry). Adoff 3:298
Courting (poetry). Wilentz 16
Cross over the River (poetry). Wilentz 17
Death of Dr. King (poetry). Adoff 3:296
Frederick Douglass (poetry). Adoff 3:294, Wilentz 19
Harriet Tubman (poetry). Breman 409
Lord (poetry). Wilentz 17
Lord, While I Sow Earth (poetry). Breman 409.
Montgomery (poetry). Adoff 3:293, Wilentz 14
One-eyed Black Man in Nebraska (poetry). Adoff 3:294, Wilentz 15
Other Nat Turners (poetry). Wilentz 18
Panther (poetry). Adoff 3:297

Promenade (poetry). Jones 398
The River (poetry). Adoff 3:292
Sam's World (poetry). Wilentz 14
To a Single Shadow without Pity (poetry). Adoff 3:294, Major 39
Turk (poetry). Jones 399

CORR, JOSEPH M. (REV). Clergyman, Orator
Address delivered before the Humane Mechanics' Society, on the 4th of July, 1834 (speech). Porter 146

CORROTHERS, JAMES DAVID, 1869-1917. Autobiographer, Fiction Writer, Poet
At the Closed Gate of Justice (poetry). Black 7, Calverton 179, Davis 189, Johnson 73, Kerlin 88
The Black Man's Soul (poetry). Kendricks 197
Der Rabbit's Foot (poetry). Robinson 275
The Dream and the Song (poetry). Johnson 79, Kerlin 85, White 167
In the Matter of Two Men (poetry). Johnson 76
An Indignation Dinner (poetry). Hughes 2:27, Johnson 77, White 164
The Negro Singer (poetry). Davis 190, Johnson 74, Kerlin 89, White 165
Paul Lawrence Dunbar (poetry). Davis 190, Hughes 2:25, Johnson 73, Kerlin 37, White 166
The Road to The Bow (poetry). Johnson 75
Sweeten 'Tatahs (poetry). Robinson 270

CORSO, GREGORY. Poet
Birthplace Revisited (poetry). Adoff 63

CORTEZ, JAYNE, 1936- . Poet
Bull Shit (poetry). Coombs 18
Consultation (poetry). Troupe 454
For Real (poetry). Adoff 3:344, Coombs 16
How Long Has Trane Been Gone? (poetry). Coombs 13
I would like to be Serene (poetry). Patterson 4:63
I'm A Worker (poetry). Chapman 2:234
Initiation (poetry). Adoff 3:345
Lead (poetry). Adoff 3:343
Lonely Woman (poetry). Chapman 2:233
Pray For The Lovers (poetry). Patterson 4:120
The Rising (poetry). Chapman 2:236
Solo (poetry). Exum 69
Song for Kwame (poetry). Troupe 296
Suppression (poetry). Chapman 2:236

COTTER, JOSEPH SEAMON, SR., 1861-1949. Poet, Playwright
Caleb the Degenerate (drama). Hatch 61

Answer to Dunbar's "A Choice" (poetry). Robinson 202
Answer to Dunbar's After a Visit (poetry). Robinson 199
The Book's Creed (poetry). Kerlin 77

(COTTER, JOSEPH SEAMON, SR.)
Contradiction (poetry). Robinson 196
Destiny (poetry). White 147
The Don't-Care Negro (poetry). Kerlin 236
Emerson (poetry). Robinson 201
The flowers take the tears (first line—poetry). Kerlin 76
Frederick Douglass (poetry). Robinson 195
I will suppose that fate is just (first line—poetry). Kerlin 52
Let None Ignobly Halt (poetry). Robinson 202
My Poverty and Wealth (poetry). Robinson 202
The Nation's Neglected Child (excerpt—poetry). Kerlin 77
The Negro Child (poetry). Kerlin 302
The Negro's Educational Creed (poetry) White 147
Oh, my way and thy way (first line—poetry). Kerlin 81
Oliver Wendell Holmes (poetry). Robinson 201
On a Proud Man (poetry). White 147
On Hearing James W. Riley Read (poetry). Robinson 200
Poet (poetry). Robinson 197
Prologue to a Supposed Play (poetry). Robinson 197
Sequel to the Pied Piper of Hamlin (excerpt—poetry). Kerlin 78
The Threshing Floor (poetry). Kerlin 75
The Tragedy of Pete (poetry). Brown 343, Cullen 11
The Wayside Well (poetry). Cullen 15, Hughes 2:18
What deeds have sprung from plow and pick (first line —poetry). Kerlin 80

The Boy and the Ideal (short fiction). Kerlin 74

COTTER, JOSEPH SEAMON, Jr., 1895-1919. Poet
And What Shall You Say (poetry). Adams 3:6, Adoff 3:35, Brown 346, Cullen 103, Hughes 2:135, Johnson 186, White 182
An April Day (poetry). Cullen 102
The Band of Gideon (poetry). Calverton 178, Cullen 103, Johnson 187, Kerlin 83
Compensation (poetry). Kerlin 82
The Deserter (poetry). Cullen 102
The Goal (poetry). White 181
Is It Because I Am Black? (poetry) Johnson 186
The Mulatto to His Critics (poetry). Kerlin 67
A Prayer (poetry). Johnson 185
Rain Music (poetry). Brown 346, Cullen 100, Johnson 188, Kerlin 81, White 181
Sonnet to Negro Soldiers (poetry). Adoff 3:35, White 182
Supplication (poetry). Cullen 101, Hughes 2:134, Johnson 189

COURLANDER, HAROLD. Poet, Fiction Writer
The African (excerpt: The Voyage—fiction). Freedman 25

COUSINS, LINDA. Poet
i can luv Blkman (first line—poetry). Patterson 4:27
Portrait in Black Soul (poetry). Bookers 159

COUSINS, WILLIAM. Poet
Black Gauntlet (poetry). Murphy 53
The House of Time (poetry). Murphy 53
Ultimatum (poetry). Murphy 53

COWDERY, MAE V. Poet
Dusk (poetry). Johnson, C. 26

COX, OLLIE H. Critic, Poet
Debt (poetry). Shuman 283
The Old Order (poetry). Shuman 283

COX, SANDRA, 1949- . Poet
Middle Passage (poetry). Witherspoon 2:9

COX, THELMA PARKER. Poet
Evolution (poetry). Murphy 2:28
Frustration, a Heritage (poetry). Murphy 2:29

COX, WALTER, 1952- . Poet
Rosedale Street (poetry). Witherspoon 2:11

CRAVAT, JOHN A., 1831-1897. Soldier, Letter-writer
Letters (letters). Barksdale 265

CRAYTON, PEARL. Short Fiction Writer
The Day the World almost Came to an End (short fiction). Hughes 3:325
The Goldfish Monster (short fiction). Stadler 286

CREWS, STELLA LOUISE, (1950- . Poet
Black and Full (poetry). Lane 13
Brother Rat (poetry). Witherspoon 11
Dream (poetry). Lane 18
Feel Eyes (poetry). Lane 17
For Don and Donna (poetry). Lane 16
It Is in Shadows (poetry). Lane 16
Nura (poetry). Lane 17
Poem For E. J. Summer '71 (poetry). Lane 20
Portrait Number One (poetry). Lane 14
Portrait Number Two (poetry). Lane 15
Sometimes I Wonder If You (poetry). Lane 19

CROMWELL, JOHN W. Educator, Historian
The Negro in American History (excerpt: Benjamin Banneker—biography). Dreer 107

CROUCH, STANLEY, 1945- . Poet, Journalist, Critic
After The Rain (poetry). Coombs 25
Albert Tyler: Eulogy for a Decomposed Saxaphone Player (poetry). Adoff 3:486, King 3:42
All Praise (poetry). Coombs 22
Blackie Speaks on Campus: a Valentine for Vachel Lindsay (poetry). Jones 393, Troupe 2:69
Blackie Thinks of His Brothers (poetry). Adoff 3:484, Jones 392
Blues, For Sallie (poetry). Coombs 23
Chops Are Flying (poetry). Major 42
Hot Lunch (poetry). Troupe 330
Lady Leo: Miss T. (poetry). Troupe 2:76
No New Music (poetry). Adoff 3:484
Noah: a Cold Cold Man (poetry). Troup 331
Pimp's Last March: Death REQuest (poetry). King 3:40
The Revelation (poetry). Coombs 25
Riding Across John Lee's Finger (poetry). Adoff 3:485, Coombs 20
Right Now (Martin, Medgar, Malcolm) (poetry). Troupe 2:78
Sallie Jewel (poetry). Coombs 24
Three Up None Down (poetry). Troupe 2:74
To a Note from a Rainy Day (poetry). Troupe 2:72
Up on the Spoon (poetry). Breman 507, Troupe 2:80

CRUMMELL, ALEXANDER, 1819-1898, Orator, Essayist
The Attitude of the American Mind Toward the Negro Intellect (essay). Long 119
The Black Woman of the South: Her Neglects and Her Needs (essay). Patterson 3:56
The Negro Race Not Under a Curse (essay). Turner 2:25, Turner 3:26
Relations and Duties of Free Colored Men in America to Africa (letter). Barksdale 104
Hope for Africa (sermon). Brawley 301
Right-Mindedness (speech). Cromwell 258

CRUSE, HAROLD. Critic, Essayist, Historian
Crisis of the Negro Intellectual (excerpt: Postscript on Black Power—the Dialogue Between Shadow and Substance—essay). Davis 853
Revolutionary Nationalism and the Afro-American (essay). Jones 39

CRUZ, VICTOR HERNANDEZ, 1949- . Poet, Fiction Writer
Rhythm Section/Part One (excerpt—fiction). Reed 57
Bring the Soul Blocks (poetry). Adoff 60
Bronxomania (poetry). Troupe 193

Carmen (poetry). Adoff 61, Adoff 3:506
The Electric Cop (poetry). Adoff 3:507, Miller, A. 38
Energy (poetry). Adoff 3:507
First Claims Poem (poetry). Chapman 2:238
The Land (poetry). Lowenfels 26
Mellow (poetry). Miller, A. 36
O. K. (poetry). Jones 436
Poetry Lesson (poetry). Miller, A. 39
The Secrets II (excerpt—poetry). Troupe 487
Spirits (poetry). Adoff 3:509
The Story of the Zeros (poetry). Adoff 3:510, Miller, A. 37
Today is a day of great joy (poetry). Lomax 260
Two Way (poetry). Breman 516
Urban Dream (poetry). Chapman 2:239, Major 45
White Powder (poetry). Jones 437

CUESTAS, KATHERINE L., 1944- . Poet
I Seek (poetry). Pool 76
Mea Culpa (poetry). Pool 76
Poem (poetry). Jordan 85, Pool 75

CUFFEE, PAUL, 1759-1817. Orator
A Brief Account of the Settlement and Present Situation of the Colony of Sierra Leone, in Africa, 1812 (essay). Porter 256

CUGLAR, LOIS AUGUSTA. Poet
Consecration (poetry). Johnson, C. 114

CULBERTSON, ERNEST H. Playwright
Packey (drama). Locke 51

CULLEN, COUNTEE PORTER, 1903-1946. Playwright, Essayist, Editor, Fiction Writer, Poet
Saint Louis Woman (drama—with Arna Bontemps). Patterson 2:3
One Way To Heaven (excerpt—fiction). Clarke 3:34
One Way To Heaven (excerpt: Ch. 6—fiction). Dreer 263
Any Human to Another (poetry.) Weisman 38
Atlantic City Waiter (poetry). Kerlin 292
Black Magdalens (poetry). Baker 158, Ford 79, Johnson 230, Kerlin 291
Black Majesty (poetry). Adoff 3:92, Barksdale 537, Dreer 70, Kearns 388, Weisman 31
Brown Boy to Brown Girl (poetry). Adoff 3:93
A Brown Girl Dead (poetry). Barksdale 531, Bown 362, Chapman 384, Hayden 2:96, Locke 2:131, Randall 11
Caprice (poetry). Breman 94
Cor Cordium (poetry). Pool 80
Counter Mood (poetry). Emanuel 182
Epitaph for a Lady I Know (poetry). Adams 3:106, Black 29

(CULLEN, COUNTEE PORTER)
Epitaphs (poetry). Stanford 110
Extenuation to Certain Critics (poetry).
Johnson, C. 58
For a Lady I Know (poetry). Adoff 3:84,
Chapman 386, Cunard 261, Davis 326,
Hayden 2:100, Hughes 2:231, Singh 12
For a Mouthy Woman (poetry). Adoff 3:92
For a Pessimist (poetry). Emanuel 180
For a Poet (poetry). Emanuel 180, Ford
80, Hughes 2:229, Lomax 234
For John Keats, Apostle of Beauty (poetry).
Barksdale 533, Davis 329, Emanuel 180,
Hayden 2:101
For My Grandmother (poetry). Chapman
386
For Paul Lawrence Dunbar (poetry). Barks-
dale 533, Chapman 386, Emanuel 181,
Hayden 2:102, Kearns 2:71, Turner 3:222,
Turner 4:66
Four epitaphs (poetry). Adoff 3:91, Bon-
temps 2:88, Cullen 186
From the Dark Tower (poetry). Adams
3:4, Adoff 2:77, Adoff, 3:87, Barksdale
534, Bell 51, Black 25, Brown 362,
Chapman 384, Cromwell 16, Cullen 183,
Cunard 261, Hayden 119, Hayden 2:103,
Hughes 2:235, Johnson 228, Jordan 133,
Kearns 388, Long 420, Miller, R. 210,
Randall 2:100, Turner 3:221, Turner
4:65
Fruit of the Flower (poetry). Davis, C. 170,
Jordan 20, Locke 2:132
Harlem Wine (poetry). Locke 2:130
Heritage (poetry). Adams 3:53, Adoff 3:88,
Baker 154, Barksdale 531, Bell 47, Black
25, Bontemps 83, Breman 90, Brown 357,
Calverton 192, Davis 326, Davis, C. 171,
Hayden 120, Henderson 120, Johnson
221, Kearns 384, Locke 2:250, Lomax
230, Margolies 6, Randall 2:95, Turner
3:218, Turner 4:62
Heritage for Harold Jackman (poetry).
Bontemps 2:83, Emanuel 176
I Have a Rendezvous with Life (poetry).
Cullen 180
If Love Be Staunch (poetry). Cromwell
13
In Memory of Colonel Charles Young
(poetry). Adoff 3:86, Calverton 198,
Cromwell 14, Ford 80, Locke 2:133
Incident (poetry). Adams 3:96, Adoff 2:85,
Adoff 3:91, Barksdale 531, Bell 51, Black
25, Brown 361, Chambers 88, Chapman
384, Cullen 187, Cunard 261, Davis 324,
Ford 79, Freedman 154, Hayden 124,
Hughes 2:232, Jordan 107, Kearns 384,
Kendricks 235, Patterson 3:158, Pool 79,
Randall 2:98, Singh 12, Stanford 109
Judas Iscariot (poetry). Kerlin 293
Leaves (poetry). Cromwell 12
Lines to Our Elders (poetry). Cullen 179
The Litany of the Dark People (poetry).
Miller, R. 210
Little Sonnet to Little Friends (poetry).
Barksdale 536

Love's Way (poetry). Dreer 71
Magnets (poetry). Barksdale 538, Emanuel
184, Turner 3:222, Turner 4:66
Mood (poetry). Kearns 2:243
Negro Mother's Lullaby (poetry). Barks-
dale 538
Nocturne (poetry). Cromwell 16, Patter-
son 4:159
Nothing Endures (poetry). Barksdale 537,
Emanuel 183
One Day We Played a Game (Yolande:
Her Poem) (poetry). Dreer 72
Pagan Prayer (poetry). Davis 325
Poem to American Poets (poetry). Chap-
man 385, Emanuel 186
The Poet (poetry). Cromwell 14
Protest (poetry). Cullen 181
Red (poetry). Adams 3:40
Saturday's Child (poetry). Adoff 3:86,
Baker 157, Hayden 2:98
Scotsboro, Too, Is Worth Its Song (po-
etry). Adoff 3:93, Bell 52, Emanuel 186,
Miller, R. 211
Self-Criticism (poetry). Johnson, C. 58
She of the Dancing Feet Sings (poetry).
Barksdale 533, Emanuel 184, Locke 2:131
Simon the Cyrenian Speaks (poetry).
Adams 3:50, Bontemps 2:89, Kearns
2:242, Kerlin 292, Lomax 235, Patterson
3:158, Randall 2:99
Song in Spite of Myself (poetry). Eman-
uel 182, Turner 3:221, Turner 4:65
A Song No Gentleman Would Sing to Any
Lady (poetry). Johnson, C. 58
A Song of Praise (poetry). Baker 158,
Chapman 383, Kearns 383, Kearns 2:173
Song of Sour Grapes (poetry). Barksdale
536, Patterson 4:114
Sonnet: These Are No Wind Blown Ru-
mors (poetry). Emanuel 185
Sonnet: What Am I Saying Now (poetry).
Emanuel 184
Tableau (poetry). Adoff 3:92, Calverton
197, Hayden 2:97, Johnson 231, Locke
2:130
That Bright Chimeric Beast (poetry). Barks-
dale 536, Bontemps 2:86
There Must Be Words (poetry). Patter-
son 4:146
Therefore, Adieu (poetry). Barksdale 537
A Thorn Forever in the Breast (poetry).
Freedman 257
Thoughts in a Zoo (poetry). Cromwell 15
Threnody for a Brown Girl (poetry).
Barksdale 534
Timid Lover (poetry). Johnson 228
To a Brown Boy (poetry). Calverton 197,
Ford 79, Locke 2:129
To a Brown Girl (poetry). Calverton
196, Locke 2:129
To Certain Critics (poetry). Davis 331,
Randall 2:101
To Endymion (poetry). Pool 79
To France (poetry). Emanuel 186
To John Keats, Poet, At Springtime (po-
etry). Barksdale 533, Black 29, Brown

(CULLEN, COUNTEE PORTER)

360, Calverton 191, Cullen 184, Johnson 226, Long 418

To Lovers of Earth: Fair Warning (poetry). Cullen 182

To You Who Read My Book (poetry). Calverton 187, Dreer 67

The Touch (poetry). White 210

Tribute (poetry). Davis 326

Two Who Crossed a Line (She Crosses) (poetry). Ford 80

Uncle Jim (poetry). Johnson 229

Variations on a Theme (poetry). Barksdale 535

What is Africa to me: (first line—poetry). Freedman 4

Wisdom Cometh With the Years (poetry). Hayden 2:99

The Wise (poetry). Hughes 2:230

Yet Do I Marvel (poetry). Adams 3:97, Adoff 2:88, Adoff 3:87, Baker 153, Barksdale 531, Bell 50, Black 30, Bontemps 2:88 Chapman 383, Cullen 182, Davis 324, Davis, C. 169, Emanuel 176, Ford 80, Henderson 120, Hughes 233, Johnson 231, Jordan 128, Kearns 383, Kearns 2:241, Kendricks 235, Lomax 235, Long 421, Miller, R. 209, Patterson 3:158, Pool 78, Pool 2:111, Randall 11, Randall 2:100, Rose 135, Stanford 109, Troupe 143

Youth Sings a Song of Rosebuds (poetry). Brown 362, Hughes 2.234, Johnson 226

CUMBERBATCH, LAWRENCE S. Poet

Again the Summoning (poetry). Coombs 28

Fake-Out (poetry). Coombs 30

I Swear to You, That Ship Never Sunk in Middle-Passage! (poetry). Coombs 28

In the Early Morning Breeze (poetry). Coombs 29

CUMBO, KATTIE M., 1938- . Essayist, Poet

For My People's Children (essay). Shuman 76

African Beauty Rose (poetry). Shuman 2:44

Age (poetry). Shuman 286, Shuman 2:45

All Hung Up (poetry). Shuman 2:46

Anatomy of Frustration (poetry). Shuman 287

Another Time, Another Place (poetry). Shuman 2:47

Bahamas I (poetry). Shuman 2:48

Bahamas II (poetry). Shuman 2:48

Black Future (poetry). Shuman 288

Black Goddess (poetry). Shuman 2:49

Black Sister (poetry). Shuman 2:66

A Call for Black Unity (poetry). Shuman 289

Consumed (For Brother Leroi) (poetry). Shuman 2:51

Dark People (poetry). Shuman 2:52

Domestics (poetry). Shuman 2:47

Indifference (poetry). Shuman 290

Is That Really What Little Girls Are Made Of? (poetry). Shuman 2:54

It's Time (Repatriation . . . Africa?) (poetry). Shuman 2:53

Malcolm (poetry). Shuman 2:65

The Night (poetry). Shuman 2:55

Nocturnal Sounds (poetry). Shuman 2:57

Not Blue (poetry). Shuman 2:56

November/December (Echoing Voices of Remembrances) (poetry). Shuman 2:58

Now I Understand (poetry). Shuman 2:59

Ring-around-the-Rosy (poetry). Shuman 2:54

Song from Brooklyn (poetry). Shuman 285, Shuman 2:60

That's a Summer Storm (poetry). Shuman 2:61

This Island Now (Jamaica) (poetry). Shuman 2:62

Three Poems for Nat Nakasa (poetry). Shuman 2:64

Unknowns (poetry). Shuman 2:63

Was That Rreally How Her Garden Grew? (poetry). Shuman 2:54

Washiri Poet (poetry). Shuman 2:44

Boy (short fiction). Shuman 72

CUNEY, WARING, 1906- . Critic, Editor, Poet, Songwriter

The Alley Cat Brushed His Whiskers (poetry). Cuney 7

Ballad of the Lame Man and the Blind Man (poetry). Cuney 14

Beale Street (poetry). Davis 375, Pool 2:84

Burial of the Young Love (poetry). Johnson 285

Carry Me Back (poetry). Black 31

Charles Parker, 1925-1955, (poetry). Pool 83, Pool 2:103

Colored (poetry). Davis 374

Conception (poetry). Johnson 284

Couples (poetry). Cuney 13

Crucifixion (poetry). Johnson 285

The Death Bed (poetry), Brown 374, Cullen 208

Dust (poetry). Cullen 210, Kerlin 204

Earth-quake (poetry). Pool 82

Finis (poetry). Bontemps 100, Johnson 287, Patterson 3:160

Girl from Oklahoma (poetry). Davis 376

Guitar Music (poetry). Cuney 7, Pool 2:112

Hard Time Blues (poetry). Breman 100, Brown 375, Cuney 10

I Think I See Him There (poetry). Cullen 210

I Thought of My True Love (poetry). Cuney 12

Lame Man and the Blind Man (poetry). Black 32, Weisman 58

The Mothers (poetry). Cuney 8, Weisman 62

My Lord, What a Morning (poetry). Lomax 236, Pool 81, Pool 2:81

(CUNEY, WARING)

The Neighbors Stood on The Corner (poetry). Cuney 9

No Images (poetry). Black 31, Bontemps 2:98, Breman 100, Brown 375, Cromwell 51, Cullen 212, Cuney 9, Davis 377, Johnson 283, Kerlin 204, Lomax 237, Weisman 42

Oh My, Oh Yes (poetry). Pool 82

Old Workman (poetry). Davis 374

Old Workman's Song (poetry). Pool 83

Play a Blues for Louise (poetry). Cromwell 51

Prayer (poetry). Cuney 16

The Radical (poetry). Cullen 212

Summer (poetry). Pool 85

Sunset Thoughts (poetry). Cuney 13

Threnody (poetry). Bontemps 2:99, Johnson 283, Patterson 3:160

A Triviality (poetry). Cullen 209

Troubled Jesus (poetry). Johnson 284

True Love (poetry). Cullen 213

Two Quartets (poetry). Pool 2:10/

Wake Cry (poetry). Johnson 285

White Mice at the Parcel Post Window (poetry). Cuney 15

Women and Kitchens (poetry). Davis 376, Cuney 15

CUNEY-HARE, MAUD, 1874-1936. Playwright, Critic, Essayist, Poet, Songwriter

Antar of Araby (drama)). Richardson 29

Musical Comedy (essay). Patterson 37

CUNNINGHAM, JAMES, 1936- . Critic, Poet, Essayist

Hemlock for the Artist: Karenga Style (essay). Chapman 2:483

Incest for Brothers: a Criticism (essay). Brooks 2:151

Brooks and Stones (poetry). Brown, P. 23

City Rises (poetry). Brooks 2:128

The Covenant (poetry). Brooks 2:143

Fishing (poetry). Brown, P. 23

Footnote to a Gray Bird's Pause (poetry). Brooks 2:144

For Cal (poetry). Brooks 2:131

From a Brother Dreaming in the Rye (poetry). Brooks 2:142

From the Narrator's Trance (poetry). Brooks 2:136

Happy Day (poetry). Brooks 2:148

High-cool/2 (poetry). Brooks 2:149

Incidental Pieces to a Walk: For Conrad (poetry). Brooks 2:130

Lee-ers of Hew (poetry). Brooks 2:135

Legacy of a Blue Capricorn (poetry). Brooks 2:147

Plea to My Sister Carolyn Cunningham: the Artist (poetry). Brooks 2:139

Rapping along with Rhonda Davis (poetry). Brooks 2:132

Rippling Shadows (poetry). Brown, P. 24

River Voices (poetry). Brown, P. 25

St. Julien's Eve: for Dennis Cross (poetry). Brooks 2:129

Slow Riff for Billy (poetry). Brooks 2:138

Solitary Visions of a Kaufmanoid (poetry). Brooks 2:134

A Street in Kaufman-ville (poetry). Brooks 2:133

Tambourine (poetry). Brooks 2:150

Welcome for Etheridge (poetry). Brooks 2:128

While Cecil Snores: Mom Drinks Cold Milk (poetry). Brooks 2:145

CURRY, GLADYS J. Essayist

Black Politics: a Brief Summary Beginning the New Revolution in the 1950's (essay). Curry 215

CURRY, LINDA, 1953- . Poet

No Way Out (poetry). Jordan 8

CURTWRIGHT, WESLEY, 1910- . Poet

The Close of Day (poetry). Cullen 225

Heart at the Woods (poetry). Hughes 2:280

Summer's End (poetry). Murphy 3:42

What Do I Care? (poetry). Murphy 3:42

DABNEY, WENDELL PHILLIPS, 1865-1952. Essayist

Duncanson (essay). Johnson, C. 128

Visit to Dunbar's Tomb (essay). Brown 1001

DALCOUR, PIERRE, 18??-? Poet

Verse Written in the Album of Mademoiselle (poetry). Hughes 2:16

DAMU. See STOKES, HERBERT.

DANCY, WALTER, 1946- . Poet

Chinese River Prophet Song (poetry). Henderson 300

Jazz Coltrane Sings (poetry). Coombs 31

Metaphorical Egress (poetry). Henderson 301

This the Poet as I See (poetry). Henderson 302

DANDRIDGE, RAYMOND GARFIELD, 1882-1930. Poet

Days (poetry). White 191

De Drum Majah (poetry). Johnson 193

De Innah Part (poetry). Kerlin 237

Eternity (poetry). Kerlin 172

Facts (poetry). Kerlin 172

'Ittle Touzle Head (poetry). Johnson 191

The Poet (poetry). Kerlin 170

Sprin' Fevah (poetry). Johnson 192

Time to Die (poetry). Adoff 3:18, Breman 48, Johnson 109, Kerlin 171

Tired (poetry). Breman 50

To— (poetry). Kerlin 170

Tracin' Tales (poetry). White 192

Yes, I am lynched. Is it that I (first line— poetry). Kerlin 54

Zalka Peetruza (poetry). Adoff 3:19, Johnson 192, Kerlin 130, White 192

DANIEL, PORTIA BIRD. Poet
God Gave Me a Son (poetry). Murphy
3:43
Lament (poetry). Murphy 3:44

DANIELS, IONIE. Poet
Old Jonah (poetry). Murphy 3:44

DANNER, DEBORAH. Short Fiction Writer,
Poet
Loving Blues (poetry). Bookers 86

The Slum (short fiction). Bookers 15

DANNER, JAMES. Poet
My Brother (poetry). Jones 271
The Singer (poetry). Jones 269

DANNER, MARGARET, 1915- . Poet
And Through the Caribbean Sea (poetry).
Long 638, Randall 2:152
As Critic (poetry). Brown, P. 29
Best Loved of Africa (poetry). Adoff 3:137,
Hughes 2:162
The Convert (poetry). Brooks 40, Ran-
dall 2:149
Dance of the Abakweta (poetry). Bell 88,
Hughes 2:163, Kerlin 30, Long 634
The Elevator Man Adheres to Form (po-
etry). Adoff 3:137, Bell 87, Davis 764,
Hughes 2:161, Pool 86
Etta Morten's Attic (poetry). Bell 90,
Brooks 39
Far From Africa: Four Poems (poetry).
Adoff 3:134, Barksdale 816, Bell 88,
Bontemps 2:153, Kerlin 29
Garnishing the Aviary (poetry). Bell 88-90,
Henderson 229, Kerlin 29, Randall 20,
Randall 2:149
Gold Is the Shade Esperanto (poetry).
Long 637
Goodby David Tamunoemi West (poetry).
Pool 2:117, Randall 2:153
I'll Walk the Tightrope (poetry). Bell 87,
Hayden 2:125, Patterson 3:219, Pool 87,
Randall 21
My Birthright, Too (poetry). Henderson
231
The Painted Lady (poetry). Randall 2:152
Passive Resistance (poetry). Henderson 231
Sadie's Playhouse (poetry). Adoff 3:138,
Hayden 2:128, Pool 87, Pool 2:117
Slave and the Iron Lace (poetry). Bon-
temps 2:157, Breman 103, Henderson 229,
Randall 2:154
The Small Bells of Benin (poetry). Brooks
39
A Sparrow Is a Bird (poetry). Weisman 46
These Beasts and the Benin Bronze (po-
etry). Hayden 126
This Is an African Worm (poetry). Hen-
derson 230, Randall 2:151
Through the Varied Patterned Lace (po-
etry). Hayden 140, Hayden 2:129
To a cold caucasion on a bus (poetry).
Pool 2:133

Visit of the Professor of Aesthetics (poetry). Bell 89, Kerlin 31, Long 635

DANTE. See **GRAHAM, DONALD L.**

DAVIDSON, JOHN ALLEN, JR. Fiction
Writer
Black Sons of Bitches (short fiction). Bur-
nett 206

DAVIDSON, NORBERT R., JR., 1940- .
Playwright
El Hajj Malik (drama). Couch 202

DAVIS. See **JOYCE, JOHN**

DAVIS, ALLISON, 1902- . Essayist
Color, Caste, and Economic Relations in
the Deep South (essay). Watkins 278
A Glorious Company (essay). Brown 1024,
Johnson, C. 156

What Does Negro Youth Think of Present-
Day Negro Leaders? (speech). Cromwell
307

DAVIS, ARTHUR P., 1904- . Autobiographer, Critic, Editor, Essayist, Literary
Historian, Short Fiction Writer
Autobiography (excerpt: Growing up in
the New Negro Renaissance—autobiography). Davis 428

The Harlem of Langston Hughes' Poetry
(essay). Gross 194, Singh 201
Integration and Race Literature (essay).
Conference 34, Jones 605
The New Poetry of Black Hate (essay).
Gibson 3:147
The Tragic Mulatto Theme in Six Works
of Langston Hughes (essay). Gibson
2:167
Trends in Negro American Literature
(1940-1965) (essay). Emanuel 519

How John Boscoe Outsung the Devil
(short fiction). Clarke 156, Gibson 107

DAVIS, CHARLES T. Essayist
Robert Hayden's Use of History (essay).
Gibson 3:96

DAVIS, DANIEL WEBSTER, 1862-1913.
Poet, Essayist, Historian
Aunt Chloe's Lullaby (poetry). Robinson
270
Hog Meat (poetry). Johnson 83, White 100
Miss Liza's Banjer (poetry). Robinson 268
Night of the Ol' Plantashun (poetry).
White 9
Pomp's Case Argued (poetry). White 103
Stickin' To de Hoe (poetry). White 101
Weh Down Souf (poetry). Johnson 81

DAVIS, FRANK MARSHALL, 1905- . Poet,
Essayist
Statement on Poetics (essay). Bell 175,
Gibson 3:175

(DAVIS, FRANK MARSHALL)
Arthur Ridgewood, M.D. (poetry). Bell 53, Brown 397, Hayden 2:106, Randall 2:121
Black Weariness (poetry). Ford 160
Creation (poetry). Ford 163
Dreams (poetry). Weisman 79
Egotistic Runt (poetry). Murphy 3:45
Flowers of Darkness (poetry). Adoff 2:12, Adoff 3:95, Bell 55, Bontemps 2:96, Hughes 2:255
Four Glimpses of Night (poetry). Adoff 3:97, Bell 54, Bontemps 2:97, Chapman 433, Hughes 2:250, Murphy 3:47
Frank Marshall Davis: Writer (poetry). Ford 157
Giles Johnson, Ph.D. (poetry). Adoff 3:96, Bell 53, Brown 397, Hayden 2:107, Randall 2:122, Turner 2:217
Hands of a Brown Woman (poetry). Ford 161
I Sing No New Songs (poetry). Adoff 3:98, Chapman 434, Hughes 252
Jazz Band (poetry). Henderson 144
Mental Man (poetry). Murphy 3:49
Miss Samantha Wilson (poetry). Murphy 57
Mojo Mike's Beer Garden (poetry). Miller, R. 215
Moses Mitchell (poetry). Miller, R. 217
Only My Words (poetry). Ford 163
Peace Is a Fragile Cup (poetry). Murphy 54
Race (poetry). Weisman 47
Robert Whitmore (poetry). Adams 3:32, Adoff 3:96, Bell 53, Brown 397, Chapman 435, Hayden 2:105, Hughes 2:254, Miller, R. 217, Randall 2:121
Roosevelt Smith (poetry). Ford 162, Henderson 146
Snapshots of the Cotton South (poetry). Adoff 3:98, Brown 391
Snapshots of the Cotton South (excerpt—poetry). Kerlin 323
South State Street Profile (poetry). Ford 163
Spinster: Old (poetry). Murphy 3:49
Tenement Room: Chicago (poetry). Freedman 166, Murphy 3:51
What do you want, America? (poetry). Ford 158

DAVIS, GENE. Short Fiction Writer
Amateur Night in Harlem (short fiction). Ford 2:225

DAVIS, GLORIA. Poet, Short Fiction Writer
Dreams (poetry). Pool 2:113
Epitaph For Jimmy (poetry). Ten 37
My Face (poetry). Ten 38
To Egypt (a Tale to be Told) (poetry). Major 46, Pool 2:219, Ten 39
Your Promise (poetry). Pool 2:114

Like a Piece of Blues (short fiction). King 2:339

DAVIS, JOHN PRESTON, 1905- . Editor, Short Fiction Writer, Journalist
The Overcoat (short fiction). Clarke 36
Verisimilitude (short fiction). Clarke 3:15, Johnson, C. 137

DAVIS, OSSIE, 1917- . Playwright, Poet, Critic, Essayist
Curtain Call, Mr. Aldridge, Sir (drama). Reardon 235
Purlie Victorious (drama). Adams 177, Davis 627, Oliver 127, Patterson 2:277, Turner 3:473, Turner 5:465

Malcolm Was a Man (essay). Freedman 267
Why I Eulogized Malcolm X (essay). Adoff 4:170
The Wonderful World of Law and Order (essay). Hill 154

To a Brown Girl (poetry). Hill: 2:607, Hughes 2:378

DAVIS, ROBERT A., 1917- . Poet
Dust Bowl (poetry). Adoff 2:31

DAVIS, RONDA MARIE, 1940- . Poet
Debra . . . An Africanese Name . . . (poetry). King 3:56
I Am Here to Announce (poetry). King 3:48
Invitation (poetry). Brooks 2:58
Parasitosis (poetry). Brooks 2:61
Personality Sketch: Bill (poetry). Brooks 2:62
Poems About Playmates (poetry). Brooks 2:59
Rip-off (poetry). Brooks 181
Spacin' (poetry). Brooks 2:60

DAWLEY, JACK H. Poet
I'll Remember Lincoln (poetry). Cuney 18

DAY, CAROLINE BOND. Short Fiction Writer
A Fairy Story (short fiction). Cromwell 124

DEAN, PHILIP HAYES. Playwright
The Owl Killer (drama). King 301

DE ANDA, PETER. Playwright
Ladies In Waiting (drama). King 475

DEBROSSES, NELSON. Poet
Le Retour au Village aux Perles (poetry). Robinson 173
Le Retour au Village aux Perles (English version) (poetry). Robinson 174

DE GRASSE, ISAIAH G. Essayist
Essay, 1828 (essay). Porter 576

DELANY, CLARISSA SCOTT, 1901-1927. Poet, Playwright
A Golden Afternoon in Germany (essay). Cromwell 239

(DELANY, CLARISSA SCOTT)
Interim (poetry). Cullen 142, Hughes 2:181,
Kerlin 279
Joy (poetry). Cullen 140, Hughes 2:180
The Mask (poetry). Cromwell 43, Cullen
143, Hughes 2:177, Kerlin 279
Solace (poetry). Adoff 3:71, Bontemps
2:59, Cromwell 44, Cullen 141, Hughes
2:178

DELANY, MARTIN R., 1812-1885. Ethnolo-
gist, Editor, Physician, Orator, Essayist,
Fiction Writer
Condition, Elevation and Destiny of the
Colored People of the United States,
Politically Considered (essay). Barksdale
194, Brawley 220
Condition of Free Negroes (essay). Brown
634

Blake; or the Huts of America (fiction).
Takaki 103
Blake or the Huts of America (excerpts—
fiction). Davis 66
Blake, or The Huts of America (excerpt:
Conspiracy—fiction). Brown 152

DELEGALL, WALTER, 1936- . Poet
Elegy for a Lady (poetry). Jones 280, Pool
88
Elegy for a Lady (excerpt—poetry). Pool
2:91
Psalm for Sonny Rollens (poetry). Henderson 202, Jones 278

DEMBY, WILLIAM, 1922- . Fiction Writer
Beetlecreek (excerpts—fiction). Davis 489,
Hill 2:452, Miller, R. 310
The Catacombs (excerpt: Doris and the
Count [title supplied by editor] fiction).
Margolis 330
Love Story Black (excerpt—fiction). Troupe
319

Table of Wishes Come True (short fiction).
Barksdale 769

DENNIS, R. M. Poet
To Gwendolyn Brooks (poetry). Brown,
P. 30

DENT, THOMAS C. (Poet, Playwright,
Critic, Editor
Come Visit My Garden (poetry). Kerlin
80, Patterson 3:274
For Walter Washington (poetry). Chap-
man 2:372
Love (poetry). Hughes 71
A Message for Langston (poetry). Chap-
man 2:380
Ray Charles at Mississippi State (poetry).
Chapman 2:372

DE SAAVEDRA, GUADALUPE, 1936- .
Essayist, Poet
To Save a Tear (essay). Schulberg 89

Brief Thought Before Dawn (poetry).
Schulberg 90

Existence (poetry). Schulberg 93
Jealousy (poetry). Schulberg 89
The Jewel (poetry). Schulberg 93
The Law (poetry). Schulberg 90
The Shoe Shine (poetry). Schulberg 91
Suppression (poetry). Schulberg 92
What Is (poetry). Schulberg 91

DETT, ROBERT NATHANIEL, 1882-1943.
Poet, Musician
At Niagara (poetry). Kerlin 232
The Rubinstein Staccato Etude (poetry).
Johnson 196

DICKERSON, JUANITA M. Poet
Pulkha (poetry). Murphy 3:52

DICKINSON, BLANCHE TAYLOR, 1896- .
Poet
Four Walls (poetry). Cullen 110
Poem. Cullen 107, Patterson 4:148
Revelation (poetry). Cullen 107
That Hill (poetry). Cullen 109
Things Said When He Was Gone (poetry).
Johnson, C. 51
To an Icicle (poetry). Cullen 110
The Walls of Jericho (poetry). Cullen 106

DIGGS, ALFRED. Poet
Black Lady's Inspiration (poetry). Brown,
P. 31

DINGANE. See GONCALVES, JOE.

DINKINS, REV. CHARLES R. Poet,
Preacher
Invocation (poetry). White 105
Thy Works Shall Praise Thee (poetry).
White 113
We Are Black But We Are Men (poetry).
White 111

DIOP, DAVID. See BEIER, ULLI.

DISMOND, HENRY BINGA, 1891- . Poet
At Early Morn (poetry). Hughes 2:94
The Dominicaine (poetry). Murphy 58
Revolt in the South (poetry). Murphy 58
Status Quo (poetry). Adams 3:7, Hughes
2:93
To the Men of the Soviet Army (poetry).
Murphy 58
We Who Would Die (excerpt—poetry).
Kerlin 327

DIXON, EDWINA S. Short Fiction Writer
Pa Sees Again (short fiction). Ford 2:235

DJANGA TOLALUM. See CORBIN,
LLOYD.

DODSON, OWEN, 1914- . Poet, Critic, Es-
sayist, Fiction Writer, Playwright
Bayou Legend (drama). Turner 5:205
Divine Comedy (drama). Hatch 320
Divine Comedy (excerpt—drama). Brown
543

(DODSON, OWEN)
Boy at the Window (excerpt: Train Ride—fiction). Davis 396

Black Mother Praying (poetry). Chambers 95, Chapman 451, Henderson 177
Circle One (poetry). Hayden 2:119
The Confession Stone (poetry). Hayden 2:123, Lomax 238, Pool 93
Conversation on V. (poetry). Hayden 121
Countee Cullen (1903-1946) (poetry). Henderson 180, Pool 2:162
Counterpoint (poetry). Baker 260, Hughes 2:30, Jordan 59
Cradle Song (poetry). Brown 403, Long 556
The Decision (poetry). Hughes 2:302
Drunken Lover (poetry). Bontemps 2:123, Chapman 454
Epitaph for a Negro Woman (poetry). Hughes 2:301
For Edwin R. Embrée (poetry). Adams 3:8, Breman 145
For My Brother (poetry). Turner 3:251, Turner 4:95
Guitar (poetry). Chapman 450
Hymn Written After Jeremiah Preached to Me in a Dream (poetry). Bontemps 2:124, Davis, C. 287, Hayden 2:122
I Break the Sky (poetry). Adoff 3:133
Jonathan's Song (poetry). Chapman 455
Lament (poetry). Black 37
Mary Passed this Morning (poetry). Adoff 3:127
Miss Packard and Miss Giles (poetry). Brown 404, Davis 394
Open Letter (poetry). Turner 3:252, Turner 4:96
Poem for Pearl Primus' Dancers (poetry). Pool 2:77
Poems for My Brother Kenneth, VII (poetry). Adoff 2:101, Adoff 3:131, Hughes 2:304
Rag Doll and Summer Birds (poetry). Baker 259, Hughes 299
The Reunion (poetry). Chapman 454, Long 557
Sailors on Leave (poetry). Bontemps 2:126, Chapman 457
Sickle Pears (For Glidden Parker) (poetry). Bontemps 2:124
Six O'Clock (poetry). Hughes 2:298
Sorrow Is the Only Faithful One (poetry). Adoff 2:82, Adoff 3:132, Barksdale 812, Bontemps 2:122, Hayden 135, Jordan 123, Miller, R., 286, Turner 3:253, Turner 4:97
Tell Rachel, He Whispered (poetry). Davis 395, Pool 91
When I Am Dead (poetry). Davis, C. 285, Hayden 2:120, Kerlin 331
Widow Walk (poetry). Pool 92
Yardbird's Skull (For Charlie Parker) (poetry). Adoff 2:58, Adoff 3:132, Barksdale 813, Bontemps 2:125, Chapman 456, Long 558

Come Home Early, Chile (short fiction). Hill 2:338, Hughes 3:171

DOLAN, HARRY, 1927- . Short Fiction Writer, Essayist, Playwright
Losers Weepers (drama). Schulberg 45

Can an Angry Black Man Write of Laughter and Love? (essay). Ford 296
Will There Be Another Riot in Watts? (essay). Schulberg 34

I Remember Papa (short fiction). Schulberg 27
Nigger Crazy (short fiction). Schulberg 40
The Sand-Clock Day (short fiction). Schulberg 36

DOMINGO, W. A. Essayist
Gift of the Black Tropics (essay). Locke 2:341

DONALDSON, ULYSSES S. Orator
George Washington and the Negro (speech). Dreer 197

DONEGAN, Pamela. Poet
A Blue Day for a Black Woman (poetry). Troupe 2:83

DOOLEY, THOMAS, 1942- . Poet
Easter Bunny Blues or All I Want for Christmas Is the Loop (poetry). Adoff 3:436
Presidential Press Parley (poetry). Henderson 351
The Prophet's Warning or Shoot to Kill (poetry). Adoff 3:434, Henderson 349
Query (poetry). Adoff 3:435
To Our First Born (poetry). Brooks 160, Randall 46
Wednesday Night Prayer Meeting or Rappin' to My Boy (poetry). Henderson 350

DORSETT, VINCENT. Poet
Walk Down My Street (poetry). Bookers 18

DORSEY, DAVID. Poet
Reflection of a Peace Marcher (poetry). Bookers 155

DOUGLAS, ELROY. Poet
This Day (poetry). Murphy 59

DOUGLAS, EMERY. Essayist
On Revolutionary Culture (essay). Chapman 2:489

DOUGLASS, FREDERICK, c. 1817-1895. Abolitionist Writer, Lecturer, Autobiographer, Orator, Historian
Life and Times of Frederick Douglass (excerpt—autobiography). Adoff 4:9, Stanford 18, Turner 6:2

(DOUGLASS, FREDERICK)
Life and Times of Frederick Douglass (excerpt: A Child's Reasoning—autobiography). Emanuel 14
Life and Times of Frederick Douglass (excerpt: Ch. X: How a Slave Was Made a Man—autobiography). Chambers 159
Life and Times of Frederick Douglass (excerpt: Escape from Slavery—autobiography). Dreer 116
Life and Times of Frederick Douglass (excerpt: My First Acquaintance with Abolitionists—autobiography). Davis 83
Life and Times of Frederick Douglass (excerpt: Treatment of Slaves on Lloyd's Plantation—autobiography). Brown 720
My Bondage and My Freedom (excerpt: Ch. 4: A General Survey of the Slave Plantation—autobiography). Long 70
My Bondage and My Freedom (excerpt: Ch. 19: The Runaway Plot—autobiography). Calverton 447
My Bondage and My Freedom (excerpt: Ch. 22—autobiography). Brawley 179
My Bondage and My Freedom (excerpt: Ch. 23—autobiography). Brawley 196
My Bondage and My Freedom (excerpt: Lecture in England on the Horrors of Slavery—autobiography). Kendricks 62
My Bondage and My Freedom (excerpt: Liberty Attained—autobiography). Brawley 179
Narrative of the Life of Frederick Douglass (excerpt—autobiography). Adams 4:3, Baker 66, Davis, C. 45, Miller, R. 47, Rose 49
Narrative of the Life of Frederick Douglass (excerpt: In the City—autobiography). Freedman 60
Narrative of the Life of Frederick Douglass, an American Slave (excerpt: Ch. 1—autobiography). Chapman 232
Narrative of the Life of Frederick Douglass, an American Slave (excerpt: Ch. 6—autobiography). Chapman 236
Narrative of the Life of Frederick Douglass, an American Slave (excerpt: Ch. 7—autobiography). Chapman 239
Narrative of the Life of Frederick Douglass, an American Slave (excerpt: Ch. 10—autobiography). Barksdale 69, Chapman 244

Editorial from the North Star, Vol –, No. 1 (ediorial). Freedman 82

The Future of the Negro (essay). Patterson 3:64
The Inhumanity of Slavery (essay). Takaki 51
Nemesis (essay). Long 81
The Right to Criticize American Institutions (essay). Long 61
Women Suffrage Movement (essay). Long 83

Letter to His Master (Thomas Auld) (letter). Brown 608, Emanuel 20

A Letter to Mrs. Stowe, 3/8/1853 (letter). Dreer 95, Turner 2:17, Turner 3:18
The Heroic Slave (short fiction). Takaki 37
The Heroic Slave (excerpt—short fiction). Brown 10

American Slavery (speech). Brawley 202
Lecture on Slavery No. 2 delivered in Corinthian Hall, Rochester, on Sunday evening, Dec. 8, 1850 (speech). Gayle 21
Oration Delivered in Corinthian Hall, Rochester, July 5, 1852 (speech). Barksdale 89, Miller, R. 81
Oration Delivered in Corinthian Hall, Rochester, July 5, 1852 (excerpt—speech). Adoff 4:1, Dreer 188, Ford 6, Rose 109
Speech at a reception for Mr. Douglass in England 1846 (excerpt—speech). Adoff 4:6
Speech in Faneuil Hall, June 8, 1849 (speech). Brown 612
Speech on the Death of William Lloyd Garrison (speech). Cromwell 251
West India Emancipation Speech (Aug. 1857) (excerpt—speech). Adoff 4:1
What The Black Man Wants (speech) [Delivered 1865 at Annual Meeting of the Massachusetts Anti-Slavery Society, Boston]. Brawley 208

DOUGLAS, RUDOLPH. Essayist
What I Am Really Like Inside (essay). Bookers 62

DRAKE, JOHN GIBBS ST. CLAIR, JR. Essayist, Sociologist
Hide My Face? On Pan-Africanism and Negritude (essay). Hill 2:77

DRAYTON, RONALD. Playwright
Nocturne on the Rhine (drama). Jones 570
Notes from a Savage God (drama). Jones 566

DUBOIS, WILLIAM EDWARD BURGHARDT, 1868-1963. Critic, Playwright, Editor, Essayist, Poet, Fiction Writer, Historian, Reviewer
Autobiography (excerpts—autobiography). Adams 4:17, Barksdale 383, Davis 237, Watkins 311
Dusk of Dawn (excerpt: the DuBois Washington Controversy — autobiography. Brown 764
Dusk of Dawn (excerpt: Revolution—autobiography). Adoff 4:31

Haiti (drama). DeRohan 123

The Negro and World War II (editorial). Freedman 168

An ABC of Color (excerpt—essay). Curry 10
Business and Philanthropy (essay). Cromwell 196
Crime and Lynching (essay). Long 169

(DUBOIS, WILLIAM E. B.)

Darkwater (excerpt: The Souls of White Folk—essay). Long 171

Declaration of Principles of the Niagara Movement (excerpt—essay). Kendricks 166

The Freedmen's Bureau (essay). Watkins 174

Immediate Program of the American Negro (1915) (essay). Barksdale 380

In Black (1920) (essay). Barksdale 382

The Negro Mind Reaches Out (essay). Locke 2:385

Of Alexander Crummell (essay). Cromwell 187, Turner 2:57, Turner 3:57

Of Course We Will Not Accept One Jot or Tittle Less Than Full Manhood Rights (essay). Gayle 63

Resolutions at Harper's Ferry, 1906 (essay). Barksdale 377

The Souls of Black Folk (excerpt: Ch. 1: Of Our Spiritual Strivings—essay). Chapman 494, Davis, C. 75, Freedman 145, Kearns 333, Margolies 12

The Souls of the Black Folk (excerpt: Ch. 3: Of Mr. Booker T. Washington and Others—essay). Baker 96, Kearns 2:227, Stanford 65, Turner 6:17

The Souls of Black Folk (excerpt: Ch. V; Of the Wings of Atlanta—essay). Barksdale 369

The Souls of Black Folk (excerpt: Ch. IX; Of the Sons of Master and Man—essay). Emanuel 45, Turner 6:21

The Souls of Black Folk (excerpt: Ch. 14; Of the Sorrow Songs—essay). Barksdale 373, Brown 975, Chapman 501, Ford 39, Gayle 2:37, Long 159

The Souls of Black Folk (excerpt: The Black Belt—essay). Adoff 4:25

The Souls of Black Folk (excerpt: Booker T. Washington's Program: A Critique—essay). Kendricks 150

The Souls of Black Folk (excerpt: Of the Coming of John—essay). Ford 33, Miller, R. 145

The Souls of Black Folk (excerpt: Of the Faith of the Fathers—essay). Dreer 145

The Souls of Black Folk (excerpt: Of the Passing of the First-Born—essay). Chambers 44, Davis, C. 83, Turner 2:51, Turner 3:52

To a Schoolgirl, 1905 (essay). Adoff 4:22

Twenty-fifth Birthday, 1893 (essay). Adoff 4:21

Two (essay). Hemenway 148

The Dark Princess (excerpt—fiction). Calverton 80

The Negro Problem (excerpt: The Talented Tenth—history). Kendricks 156

Letter in 'Crisis,' March, 1928, to Roland A. Barton (letter). Adoff 4:24

Darkwater (excerpt: The Comet—poetry). Long 180

Ghana Calls (1960) (poetry). Pool 2:153

Last Message to the World (poetry). Pool 2:152

A Litany at Atlanta (poetry). Barksdale 378, Brown 321, Chapman 360, Cullen 26, Davis, C. 93, Hughes 2:20, Johnson 90, Kerlin 218, Long 155, Margolies 305

Prayers of God (1918) (poetry). Pool 99

Riddle of the Sphinx (poetry). Baker 126

Song of the Smoke (poetry). Adoff 3:1, Breman 29, Chapman 359, Davis, C. 91, Emanuel 44, Kearns 331, Long 153

Dreams (short fiction). Patterson 3:110

On Being Crazy (short fiction). Adams 2:101, Clarke 8, James 43, Singh 46, Stanford 74.

St. Francis of Assisi (speech). Cromwell 273

DUBONEE, YLESSA Poet

Departure (poetry). Murphy 60

Nocturne (poetry). Murphy 61

DU CILLE, ANN, 1949- . Poet

From the Bone, From the Blood, the Rib (poetry). Exum 72

Lady in Waiting (poetry). Exum 71

Song (poetry). Exum 70

DUCKETT, ALFRED A., 1918- . Poet, Essayist

Portrait Philippines (poetry). Hughes 2:358

Sonnet (Where Are We to Go When This Is Done?) (poetry). Adoff 3:172, Bontemps 2:145, Hughes 2:359, Jordan 80

Where Are We to Go When This Is Done? (sonnet—poetry). Adoff 3:172, Bontemps 2:145, Hughes 2:359, Jordan 80

DUMAS, HENRY L. 1934-1968. Poet, Essayist, Short Fiction Writer

America (poetry). Adoff 3:267

Black Star Line (poetry). Adoff 3:269

Black Trumpeter (poetry). Adoff 3:267, Shuman 292

Buffalo (poetry). Adoff 3:267

Chase (poetry). Shuman 293

Epiphany (poetry). Shuman 293

Genesis on an Endless Mosaic (poetry). Henderson 366

I Laugh Talk Joke (poetry). Henderson 369

Keep the Faith Blues (poetry). Henderson 370

Knock on Wood (poetry). Adoff 3:268, Breman 320

Machines Can Do It Too (poetry). Shuman 294

Ngoma (poetry). Troupe 298

The Puppets Have a New King (poetry). Shuman 294

Sanctuary (poetry). Shuman 295

Song (poetry). Shuman 295

Ark of Bones (short fiction). Troupe 270

Cuttin' Down To Size (short fiction). Jones 349

(DUMAS, HENRY L.)
Fon (short fiction). Jones 455
Knock on Wood (short fiction). Jones 347
Mosaic Harlem (short fiction). Jones 345

DUNBAR, PAUL LAURENCE, 1872-1906. Poet, Playwright, Essayist, Fiction Writer, Song Writer
Negro Life in Washington (essay). Turner 2:45, Turner 3:46

The Uncalled (excerpt: Ch. 9—fiction). Kendricks 184

Accountability (poetry). Kearns 265
After the Quarrel (poetry). Cullen 5
Angelina (poetry). White 72
An Ante-Bellum Sermon (poetry). Breman 37, Davis 206, Long 216, Randall 2:44, Stanford 88, Turner 3:183, Turner 4:27
At Candle-Lightin' Time (poetry). Brown 309, Kearns 272
Banjo Song (poetry). White 68
Black Samson of Brandywine (poetry). Ford 47, Kearns 274
By Rugged Ways (poetry). White 66
Choice (poetry). White 87
Chrismus on the Plantation (poetry). Davis 212, Kearns 271, Kearns 2:35
Christmas Folk Song (poetry). Brown 314
Colored Band (poetry). Kearns 273
Colored Soldiers (poetry). Barksdale 353, Kearns 266
Compensation (poetry). Barksdale 361, Bontemps 2:5, Ford 48, Hughes 2:45, Kearns 279, Patterson 4:163, Randall 2:56, White 90
The Crisis (poetry). White 55
Dawn (poetry). Barksdale 355, Bontemps 2:5, Davis, C. 90, Dreer 34, Ford 48, Hughes 2:35
Day (poetry). Cromwell 7
A Death Song (poetry). Barksdale 360, Brown 316, Chapman 356, Cullen 4, Ford 49, Hughes 2:42, Johnson 62, White 91
The Debt (poetry). Bontemps 2:5, Brown 312, Cullen 9, Hayden 2:24, Johnson 58
Deserted Plantation (poetry). White 71
Dreamin' Town (poetry). Cromwell 9
Dreams (1) (poetry). White 56
Dreams (2) (poetry) White 57
End of the Chapter (poetry). White 57
Ere Sleep Comes Down to Soothe the Weary Eyes (poetry). Barksdale 354, Brown 303, Cullen 2, Ford 45, Hughes 2:43, Johnson 54, Kerlin 41, Long 221, Patterson 3:96, Turner 3:182, Turner 4:26, White 59
Expectation (poetry). White 74
Forever (poetry). Brown 311, Ford 45
Frederick Douglass (poetry). Adoff 3:9, Ford 47, Kendricks 192, Turner 3:180, Turner 4:47
A Frolic (poetry). White 75
Harriet Beecher-Stowe (poetry). Brown 312, Hayden 2:18, Pool 2:147, Randall 2:47

The Haunted Oak (poetry). Breman 40, Hayden 2:21, Johnson 58, Miller, R. 174
How Lucy Backslid (poetry). White 76
A Hymn (poetry). White 61
In the Morning (poetry). Barksdale 360, Henderson 92, Randall 51
Itching Heels (poetry). Brown 315
Jealous (poetry). Baker 111
Life (poetry). Bontemps 2:6, Cromwell 11, Cullen 5, Ford 46, Kerlin 43, White 89
Life's Tragedy (poetry). White 90
Lincoln (poetry). Ford 46
Little Brown Baby (poetry). Dreer 34, Haslam 272, Hughes 2:40, Johnson 53, Stanford 91
Love Despoiled (poetry). White 61
Lovers' Lane (poetry). Johnson 56
Love's Phases (poetry). White 62
Misapprehension (poetry). Randall 2:46
Mortality (poetry). White 88
My Sort o' Man (poetry). Bontemps 2:6
A Negro Love Song (poetry). Barksdale 357, Chapman 357, Cromwell 10, Hughes 2:36, Johnson 52
The News (poetry). Kearns 270
Night (poetry). White 64
Not They Who Soar (poetry). Baker 112, Stanford 92
Ode to Ethiopia (poetry). Calverton 181, Davis 208, Dreer 28, Kerlin 44, Turner 3:180, Turner 4:24, White 64
On the Dedication of Dorothy Hall (poetry). Kearns 276
The Paradox (poetry). Adoff 3:11, Hayden 2:16
The Party (poetry). Barksdale 355, Bontemps 2:8, Brown 305, Emanuel 38
Philosophy (poetry). Baker 111, Randall 2:55
The Poet (poetry). Barksdale 360, Cromwell 11, Ford 48, Hayden 2:20, Henderson 96, Long 220, Randall 2:52
The Poet and the Baby (poetry). White 89
Possum (poetry). White 82
Puzzle (poetry). White 67
The Real Question (poetry). Baker 117
The Rivals (poetry). Dreer 30
Robert Gould Shaw (poetry). Brown 311, Calverton 180, Hayden 2:25
Scamp (poetry). Baker 115, Henderson 91
Ships that Pass in the Night (poetry). Barksdale 354, Cromwell 11, Cullen 7, Dreer 35, Ford 48, Johnson 56, Patterson 3:95
Signs of the Times (poetry). Brown 313, Davis 211
Slow through the Dark (poetry). Baker 112, Ford 48, White 66
Soliloquy of a Turkey (poetry). Barksdale 359, Randall 2:47
Song (poetry). Bontemps 2:13, Brown 312, Dreer 28, Emanuel 40, Ford 46
Speakin' at de Cou'thouse (poetry). Miller, R. 173

(DUNBAR, PAUL LAURENCE)
A Spiritual (poetry). Randall 2:53
Spirituals (poetry). Patterson 3:97
The Sun (poetry). White 88
Sunset (poetry). Dreer 27
Sympathy (poetry). Adoff 2:81, Adoff 3:8,
Barksdale 358, Bontemps 2:13, Brown
310, Chambers 184, Chapman 356, Cullen
8, Ford 46, Hughes 2:34, Kearns 270,
Kendricks 194, Miller, R. 173, Patterson
3:96, Singh 6, Weisman 8
Temptation (poetry). White 83
To a Captious Critic (poetry). Hayden 2:19,
Randall 2:50
To the South (poetry). Kearns 277
Two Little Boots (poetry). Cromwell 8
The Unsung Heroes (poetry). Randall 2:54
Warrior's Prayer (poetry). White 63
De Way T'ings Come (poetry). Kendricks
195
We Wear the Mask (poetry). Adams 3:114,
Adoff 2:86, Adoff 3:8, Baker 116, Barks-
dale 352, Bontemps 2:14, Breman 43,
Brown 310, Chapman 355, Cullen 8,
Davis 212, Davis, C. 89, Emanuel 41,
Ford 46, Haslam 274, Jordan 134, Kearns
268, Kearns 2:64, Kendricks 194, Kerlin
47, Lomax 208, Long 219, Miller, R.
176, Patterson 3:95, Rose 139, Stanford
88, Turner 6:1, Weisman 51
When a Feller's Itchin' to Be Spanked
(poetry). Turner 3:186, Turner 4:30
When All Is Done (poetry). Dreer 36
When de Co'n Pone's Hot (poetry). John-
son 61
When Dey 'Listed Colored Soldiers (po-
etry). Randall 2:48
When Malindy Sings (poetry). Adoff 3:10,
Baker 113, Barksdale 357, Black 11, Cal-
verton 182, Ford 49, Henderson 94,
Hughes 2:37, Margolies 283, White 85
Why Fades a Dream? (poetry). Baker
116, Kearns 269
With the Lark (poetry). Kerlin 46
The Wooing (poetry). Dreer 32

Anner' Lizer's Stumblin' Block (short fic-
tion). Davis 213
The Colonel's Awakening (short fiction).
Cromwell 85
The Ingrate (short fiction). James 45,
Stanford 93
Jim's Probation (short fiction). James 30
Jimsella (short fiction). Barksdale 361
Lynching of Jube Benson (short fiction).
Clarke 1, Freedman 118, Long 223
Mr. Cornelius Johnson, Office Seeker
(short fiction). Turner 27, Turner 3:317
The Mortification of the Flesh (short fic-
tion). Turner 20, Turner 3:310
Scape goat (short fiction). Hughes 3:17,
Patterson 3:103
The Strength of Gideon (short fiction).
Dreer 218`
The Wisdom of Silence (short fiction).
James 36

DUNBAR-NELSON, ALICE RUTH MOORE,
1875-1935. Poet, Fiction Writer, Essayist
Mine Eyes Have Seen (drama). Hatch 173

April Is On the Way (poetry). Cromwell
32, Johnson, C. 52
I Had No Thought of Violets of Late
(sonnet: first line—poetry). Adoff 3:12,
Cullen 72, Hughes 2:46, Johnson 164
I Sit and Sew (poetry). Cullen 73, Kerlin
145
The Lights at Carney's Point (poetry).
Kerlin 146
Snow in October (poetry). Cullen 71
Sonnet: I Had No Thought of Violets of
Late (poetry). Adoff 3:12, Cromwell 32,
Cullen 72, Hughes 2:46, Johnson 164
Violets (poetry). Kerlin 55

DUNCAN, THELMA MYRTLE. Dramatist
The Death Dance (drama). Locke 321
Sacrifice (drama). Richardson 5

DUNGEE, ROSCOE RILEY. Poet
Ode to Booker T. Washington (excerpt—
poetry). Kerlin 58

DUNHAM, KATHERINE, 1912- . Autobiog-
rapher, Essayist, Poet
A Touch of Innocence (excerpt: The
Creek—autobiography). Hill 2:255

The Negro Dance (excerpt—essay). Brown
991

The Babies of Biafra (poetry). Shuman 297
The Lesson (poetry). Shuman 299
Mathematics (poetry). Shuman 300

Afternoon into Night (short fiction).
Hughes 3:145

DUREM, RAY, 1915-1963. Poet
Apology (poetry). Breman 2:14
Award (poetry). Adams 3:98, Adoff 2:90,
Adoff 3:152, Kerlin 33, Lomax 243, Ran-
dall 19, Randall 2:164, Singh 21
Basic (poetry). Hughes 2:331
Broadminded (poetry). Breman 151
Dark little mother mistress (poetry).
Breman 2:17
Friends (poetry). Adoff 3:150
I Know I'm Not Sufficiently Obscure
(poetry). Adoff 3:151, Black 38, Jordan
122, Pool 103, Randall 2:163
Now, All You Children (poetry). Jordan
106, Pool 104
Prisons, prisons (poetry). Breman 2:15
Problem in Social Geometry—the Inverted
Square (poetry). Adoff 3:151, Major 47
The Saddest Tears (poetry). Breman 150,
Breman 2:18
Sympthy (poetry). Adams 3:107, Breman
2:12
To All the Nice White People (poetry).
Breman 149, Breman 2:11
To the Pale Poets (poetry). Adams 3:118,
Breman 2:16

(DUREM, RAY)
Ultimate Equality (poetry). Hughes 2:330
Vet's Rehabilitation (poetry). Adoff 3:150
White People got Trouble, Too (poetry).
    Breman 2:13
You know, Joe (poetry). Pool 104, Pool
    2:146

EAGANS, PETER MALACHI. Orator
Oration on the Abolition of the Slave
    Trade (Jan. 1st, 1813) (speech). Porter
    374

EARLEY, JACQUELINE, 1939- . Essayist,
    Poet
The Gospel Truth (poetry). King 3:62,
    Patterson 4:31
One Thousand Nine Hundred and Sixty-
    Eight Winters . . . (poetry). Jordan 127,
    King 3:65
. . . to be a woman (poetry). Coombs 33,
    Patterson 4:53

EBON. See DOOLEY, THOMAS.

ECHOLS, CARL. Poet
Men (poetry). Murphy 3:53
Not for Gold (poetry). Murphy 3:53
Thought (poetry). Murphy 3:53

ECKELS, JON B. Poet
Hell, Mary (poetry). Brooks 43
To Gwen with Love (poetry). Brown, P.
    32

ECKFORD, ELIZABETH. Narrator
Narrative of the first schoolday (narra-
    tion). Pool 2:128

EDMONDS, RANDOLPH, 1900- . Critic,
    Essayist, Playwright
Bad Man (drama). Brown 507, Hatch 241
Earth and Stars (drama). Turner 5:377
Nat Turner (drama). Richardson 2:189,
    Turner 3:455
Old Man Pete (drama). Dreer 310

Brown Girl (poetry). Murphy 3:55
Some Day (poetry). Murphy 3:56
Southern Colonel (poetry). Murphy 3:56

EDWARD, H. F. V. Playwright
Job Hunters (drama). Hatch 255

EDWARDS, ELI. See MC KAY, CLAUDE.

EDWARDS, HARRY, 1942- . Poet
How to Change the USA (poetry). Cham-
    bers 219, Major 48

EDWARDS, JUNIUS, 1929- . Fiction Writer
If We Must Die (excerpt—fiction). Adams
    2:39

Duel with the Clock (short fiction).
    Hughes 3:301
Liars Don't Qualify (short fiction). King
    2:327

Mother Dear and Daddy (short fiction).
    Adams 2:78, Margolies 205, Stadler 223,
    Williams 13

EDWARDS, SOLOMON, 1932- . Poet
Brothers (poetry). Hughes 70
Dream (poetry). Hughes 75, Hughes 2:402
Shoplifter (poetry). Hughes 82

ELDER, LONNE III. Playwright, Essayist
Ceremonies in Dark Old Men (drama).
    Couch 71, Patterson 2:451
Charades on East Fourth Street (drama).
    King 147

ELLIS, ALFRED B. Short Fiction Writer
The Maiden Who Always Refused (short
    fiction). Kendricks 9
The Poor Wife and the Rich Wife (short
    fiction). Kendricks 7
The Tortoise and the Elephant (short fic-
    tion). Kendricks 5
Twelve Proverbs of the Ewe (short fiction).
    Kendricks 10
Twelve Proverbs of the Yoruba (short
    fiction). Kendricks 11

ELLISON, RALPH WALDO, 1914- . Fic-
    tion Writer, Essayist, Critic
Beating That Boy (essay). Curry 103
Brave Words for a Startling Occasion (es-
    say). Ford 185, Long 603
Change the Joke and Slip the Yoke (essay).
    Singh 228
The Golden Age. Time Past (essay). Mar-
    golies 290
Hidden Name and Complex Fate (essay).
    Davis 550, Emanuel 279
Invisible Man: Prologue (Power Line
    Tapped) (essay). Burnett 229, Davis, C.
    213, Kendricks 272, Patterson 3:172
Living With Music (essay). Takaki 151
On Becoming a Writer (essay). Turner
    2:103, Turner 3:103
Remarks at the American Academy of Arts
    and Sciences Conference on the Negro
    American, 1965 (essay). Chapman 2:402
Richard Wright's Blues (essay). Barksdale
    686, Ford 186, Gayle 2:311, Haslam 313
Twentieth-Century Fiction and the Black
    Mask of Humanity (essay). Gross 115
The World and the Jug (essay). Davis, C.
    241, Gibson 2:271

Invisible Man (excerpts—fiction). Burnett
    230, Chapman 192, Davis 533, Demarest
    84, 150, Ford 178, 182, Hill 2:242, Long
    589, Margolies 184, Miller, R. 321, Rose
    152, Troupe 163

The Art of Fiction (interview). Hemenway
    205, Kearns 552
For Paris Review 'Writer at Work' (ex-
    cerpt—interview). Adoff 4:89

And Hickman Arrives (short fiction).
    Barksdale 693

(ELLISON, RALPH WALDO)
At the Golden Day (short fiction). Davis 533
A Coupla Scalped Indians (short fiction). Baker 321, King 2:263
Death of a Grandfather (short fiction). Demarest 150
Did You Ever Dream Lucky (short fiction). Singh 82
Dispossession (short fiction). Demarest 84
Flying Home (short fiction). Adams 2:57, Emanuel 254, Gibson 75, Hughes 3:151, James 218, Kearns 2:277, Stanford 159
King of the Bingo Game (short fiction). Adams 2:128, Emanuel 271, Hayden 61
Mister Toussan (short fiction). Turner 96, Turner 3:386
Son, You Really Can't Laugh about It. (short fiction). Gayle 93

ELLISTON, MAXINE HALL. Poet
For Gwen (poetry). Brown, P. 33

EMANUEL, JAMES A., SR., 1921- . Poet Editor, Critic
Blackness Can: A Quest for Aesthetics (essay). Gayle 3:182
Christ in Alabama: Religion In The Poetry of Langston Hughes (essay). Gibson 3:57
Future of Negro Poetry (essay). Gayle 2:100

After the Record Is Broken (poetry). Emanuel 505
Black humor (poetry). Breman 181
Black Man, 13th Floor (poetry). Chapman 2:241
Black Muslim Boy in a Hospital (poetry). Hughes 2:375
Church Burning: Mississippi (poetry). Adoff 3:178, Hughes 2:374
A Clown at Ten (poetry). Emanuel 504
Defeat (poetry). Murphy 61
Emmett Till (poetry). Adoff 3:179, Emanuel 504, Henderson 235
The Fisherman (poetry). Brooks 45, Randall 28
For Malcolm, U.S.A. (poetry). Henderson 235, Weisman 33
For Mr. Dudley, a Black Spy (poetry). Chapman 2:242, Randall 2:191
Freedom Rider: Washout (poetry). Brooks 44, Henderson 237, Stanford 268, Weisman 30
Get up, Blues (poetry). Adoff 3:179, Bontemps 2:175
I Touched the hand of a soldier dead (poetry). Breman 2:75
Negritude (poetry). Randall 2:189
The Negro (poetry). Brooks 44, Hayden 2:171, Randall 2:188, Stanford 216
Nightmare (poetry). Randall 2:188
Old Black Men Say (poetry). Adoff 3:180
Panther Man (poetry). Chapman 2:243, Randall 2:192
A Pause for a Fine Phrase (poetry). Emanuel 506

Sixteen, Yeah (poetry). Brooks 46
Son (poetry). Hughes 2:376
Sonnet for a writer (poetry). Breman 2:76
To a Negro Preacher (poetry). Henderson 236
Treehouse (poetry). Adoff 3:178, Bontemps 2:174, Brooks 45, Hughes 21, Randall 2:190, Weisman 48
Voyage of Jimmy Poo (poetry). Bontemps 174, Breman 2:74, Hughes 97
Wedding Procession, from a Window (poetry). Hayden 2:170, Hughes 81
Whitey, Baby (poetry). Brooks 47, Chapman 2:240
The Young Ones, Flip Side (poetry). Hayden 2:169, Weisman 69

EMMONS, RONALD, 1948- . Poet
This Man Is Full (poetry). Witherspoon 17

ENGEL, TIM. Short Fiction Writer
On Broadway (short fiction). Bookers 125

ENGLAND, JAY RAYMOND. Poet
Rebel (poetry). Murphy 3:57

ENNALS, SAMUEL, Orator
Resolutions of the people of Color, at a Meeting held on the 25th of January, 1831, With an address to the Citizens of New York, 1831 In answer to those of the New York Colonization Society (speech). Porter 281

EQUIANO, OLAUDAH. See VASSA, GUSTAVUS.

ESEOGHENE. See BARRETT, LINDSAY.

ESTE, CHARLES H. Poet
The Child Is Found (excerpt—poetry). Kerlin 57

EVANS, EMMERY, JR., 1943- . Poet
Falstaff (poetry). Troupe 2:68
God Bless Our Home (poetry). Troupe 2:64
Love of Life (poetry). Schulberg 197
The Lovely Red Color of Feelings (poetry). Troupe 2:67
The Question Is (poetry). Troupe 2:66

EVANS, MARI, 1923- . Poet, Critic
The Alarm Clock (poetry). Emanuel 509, Pool 2: 170, Stanford 249
And the Old Women Gathered (poetry). Adoff 3:187, Emanuel 510, Hayden 79, Hayden 2:175, Miller, R. 434
Black Jam for Dr. Negro (poetry). Adoff 3:188, Barksdale 818, Chapman 481, Emanuel 512, Henderson 250, Long 683, Margolies 319, Randall 2:183
Brother . . . The Twilight (poetry). King 3:72
Conditional (poetry). Pool 2:179
Coventry (poetry). Chapman 478

(EVANS, MARI)

Emancipation of Georg-Hector (a Colored Turtle) (poetry). Bontemps 2:165, Chapman 480, Pool 105

Flames (poetry). Miller, R. 434

Freedom rider (poetry). Pool 2:180

A Good Assassination Should Be Quiet (poetry). King 3:70

The Great Civil Rights Law (poetry). Exum 75

Here—Hold My Hand (poetry). Patterson 4:89

I Am a Black Woman (poetry). Baker 349, Exum 74

I Am Not Lazy . . . (poetry). Coombs 38

If There Be Sorrow (poetry). Hayden 2:174, Hughes 22, Hughes 2:308, Miller, R. 434

In the Name of God (poetry). Schulberg 198

Into Blackness Softly (poetry). Adoff 3:191

Marrow of My Bone (poetry). Randall 2:187

My Man Let Me Pull Your Coat (poetry). Chapman 480

Point of No Return (poetry). Hughes 19

Princeling (poetry). King 3:71

The Rebel (poetry). Adoff 2:4, Adoff 3:187, Bontemps 2:163, Chambers 201, Weisman 50

A Serpent Smiles (poetry). Schulberg 197

Shrine To What Should Be (poetry). Hughes 77

Speak the Truth to the People (poetry). Coombs 39, Henderson 253

Spectrum (poetry). Randall 2:186

Status Symbol (poetry). Adoff 2:92, Baker 348, Chapman 479, Freedman 219, Long 682, Pool 2:43, Stanford 248, Weisman 40

Take four (poetry). Pool 2:185

This Ain't No Mass Thing (poetry). Pool 2:215

To Mother and Steve (poetry). Adoff 3:191, Henderson 251, Patterson 4:146, Randall 2:185

Vive Noir! (poetry). Adoff 3:188, Chapman 2:245, Coombs 35, Davis 765, Henderson 247, Long 684, Miller, R. 435

When in Rome (poetry). Barksdale 818, Bontemps 2:164, Emanuel 510, Patterson 3:274, Pool 105

Where Have You Gone (poetry). Hughes 105, Hughes 2:307, King 3:68, Lomax 254, Patterson 3:274, Patterson 4:105, Randall 2:186

The World I See (poetry). Hayden 2:173

EXUM, PAT CRUTCHFIELD. Poet

3 Serendipitous Poems (poetry). Exum 76

EZELL, DORIS AMURR. Poet

The Little Things of Life (poetry). Bookers 97

'Til the End of the World (poetry). Bookers 83

FABIO, SARAH WEBSTER, 1928- . Poet, Playwright, Critic

Tripping With Black Writing (essay). Gayle 3:173

Who Speaks Negro? (essay). Gayle 2:115

All Day We've Longed for Night (poetry). Miller, A. 29

Back into the Garden (poetry). Miller, A. 31

Black Man's Feast (poetry). Adoff 3:203, Hughes 2:393

Bronzeville Breakthrough (poetry). Brown, P. 37

Evil Is No Black Thing (poetry). Adoff 3:205, Henderson 241, Miller, A. 27

Live Celebration (poetry). Brown, P. 34

Race Results, U. S. A. 1966 (poetry). Brooks 171

To Turn from Love (poetry). Miller, A. 30

Tribute to Duke (poetry). Henderson 243

Work It Out (poetry). Miller, A. 32

FAGGETT, H. L. Editor, Short Fiction Writer

Chatter-stick Sermon (short fiction). Ford 2:119

Cupid Wags His Tail (short fiction). Ford 2:292

Goldfish Bowl (short fiction). Ford 2:214

FAIR, RONALD L., 1932- . Playwright, Fiction Writer

We Can't Breathe (excerpt: Part One of a Two-Part Prologue—fiction). Reed 77

Life With Red Top (short fiction). Jones 500

Miss Luhester Gives a Party (short fiction). Hughes 3:403

We Who Came After (short fiction). Chapman 2:107

FAIRBAIRN, ANN, 1920- . Fiction Writer

Five Smooth Stones (excerpt: He Ain't Nothin' but a Chile—fiction). Kendricks 281

FANITA. Poet

Brown Sugar Is Not Sweet (poetry). Troupe 2:13

FARIS, ELLSWORTH. Essayist

Natural History of Race Prejudice (essay). Johnson, C. 89

FARMER, JAMES, 1920- . Essayist, Civil Rights Leader

A Southern Tale (essay). Adams 4:117

FARUK. Interviewer

Islam and the Black Arts: an Interview with Amiri Baraka (interview). Alhamisi 141

FAUSET, ARTHUR HUFF, 1899- . Essayist, Short Fiction Writer, Critic

Sojourner Truth (excerpt—biography). Brown 798

(FAUSET, ARTHUR HUFF)
American Negro Folk Literature (essay).
Gayle 2:14, Locke 2:238

B'Rer Rabbit Fools Buzzard (folk literature). Locke 2:248
T'Appin (Terrapin) (folk literature). Locke
2:245

Jumby (short fiction). Johnson, C. 15

FAUSET, JESSIE REDMOND, 1886-1961.
Playwright, Fiction Writer, Poet, Essay-
ist, Songwriter
The Gift of Laughter (essay). Gayle 2:159,
Long 2:161
Henry Ossawa Tanner (essay). Cromwell
212

The Chinaberry Tree (excerpt: Ch. 33; The
Meal—fiction). Kendricks 216
The Chinaberry Tree (excerpt: Christmas
Time—fiction). Dreer 255
Comedy American Style (excerpt: Color-
struck—fiction). Brown 189
There Is Confusion (excerpt: Class—fic-
tion). Calverton 92, Davis 354

Christmas Eve in France (poetry). John-
son 206
Dead Fires (poetry). Hughes 2:68, John-
son 207
Divine Afflatus (poetry). Johnson, C. 27
Enigma (poetry). Hughes 2:66, Patterson
4:118
Fragment (poetry). Cullen 70
Noblesse Oblige (poetry). Cromwell 38,
Cullen 67
Oblivion (poetry). Hughes 2:69, Johnson
208
Oriflamme (poetry). Adoff 3:18, Johnson
207, Kerlin 162, White 194
Rencontre (poetry). Cullen 70
The Return (poetry). Cullen 70
Rondeau (poetry). Cromwell 38
This Way to the Flea Market (poetry).
Cromwell 216
Touché (poetry). Cullen 66
La Vie C'est La Vie (poetry). Calverton
206, Cullen 69, Hughes 2:67, Johnson
206
Words! Words! (poetry). Cullen 65

FELTON, B., 1934- . Poet
Ghetto Waif (poetry). Brooks 173

FENNER, JOHN J., JR. Poet
Rise! Young Negro—Rise! (poetry). Kerlin 299

FENNER, LANON A., JR. Poet
A Sweet Thing/Last Thoughts (poetry).
Coombs 41

FENTRESS, JOHN W. Poet
Abraham Lincoln (poetry). Murphy 63
Booker T. Washington (poetry). Murphy 62

FERDINAND, VAL, 1947- . Critic, Playwright, Poet, Short Fiction Writer
Blk Love Song (drama). Hatch 864

BLKARTSOUTH Get on up (essay). Chapman 2:468

The Blues (in two parts) (poetry). Chapman 2:375
Food for Thought (poetry). Chapman 2:378
2 B BLK (poetry). Chapman 2:377
Whi/te boys gone (poetry). Chapman 2:374

Second Line/Cutting the Body Loose (short
fiction). Coombs 2:21

FERNANDEZ, RENALDO. Poet
legacy of a brother (poetry). Chapman
2:380

FERNANDIS, SARAH COLLINS, 1863- .
Poet
A Vision (poetry). White 212

FIELDS, HERMAN E. Poet
To a Mocking Bird (poetry). Johnson, C.
135

FIELDS, JULIA, 1938- . Poet, Short Fiction
Writer
Statement on Poetics (essay). Bell 177

Aardvark (poetry). Shuman 2:75
Accident: Edgecomb General Hospital, May
16, 1968 (poetry). Shuman 310, Shuman
2:71
Alabama (poetry). Adoff 3:319, Hughes
2:420
Ambrosia (poetry). Shuman 301
And Beauty's All Around (poetry). Shu-
man 2:72
Big Momma (poetry). Exum 80
Birmingham (poetry). Adoff 3:320, Hughes
2:418
Black Students (poetry). Major 49
Boats in Winter (poetry). Shuman 2:69
Chopin Deciphered (poetry). Shuman 2:73
Dancer (poetry). Shuman 301
Death in Autumn (poetry). Shuman 2:78
Death of Kennedy (poetry). Pool 2:204
Eulogy for Philosophers (poetry). Shuman
2:77
Execution (poetry). Pool 2:140
Flowers (poetry). Shuman 303
For Malcolm X (poetry). Bremen 398
Generations (poetry). Shuman 311, Shuman
2:74
Harlem in January (poetry). Adoff 33
High on the Hog (poetry). Bell 154, Troupe
371
I Heard a Young Man Saying (poetry).
Bell 149, Hughes 110, Pool 107
I, Woman (poetry). Miller, R. 522, Pat-
terson 4:51
If Love Dies (poetry). Shuman 309, Shu-
man 2:70
In The End Let All White Racists Thank
the Holy Jackass (poetry). Shuman 2:76
Langston Hughes (poetry). Shuman 2:79

(FIELDS, JULIA)
Madness one Monday evening (poetry).
Bell 150, Hayden 2:221, Hughes 78, Patterson 3:275, Pool 108, Pool 2:113
Masks (poetry). Shuman 304
Moths (poetry). Hughes 2:417
No Time for Poetry (poetry). Bell 149, Bontemps 2:183, Patterson 3:275
Pastels (poetry). Shuman 306
A Poem for Heroes (poetry). Shuman 2:68
Poem: Let us Poets put away our pens (poetry). Bell 151
Poems: Birmingham 1962-1964 (poetry). Adoff 3:320
Poems for two cities (poetry). Pool 2:181
The Policeman (poetry). Exum 82
Seizin (poetry). Exum 79
Shelter (poetry). Pool 2:142
Strange (poetry). Shuman 307
Testimonials (poetry). Miller, R. 530

Not Your Singing, Dancing Spade (short fiction). Jones 479, King 2:167

FINCH, LINDA. Poet
Chill of the Night (poetry). Bookers 61

FINLEY, CATHERINE L. Poet
Icicles on Trees (poetry). Murphy 63
Perception (poetry). Murphy 64

FISHBERG, LAWRENCE. Poet
Social Comment (poetry). Bookers 124

FISHER, LELAND MILTON, 1875-c. 1905.
Poet
For You, Sweetheart (poetry). Kerlin 189

FISHER, RUDOLPH, 1897-1934. Fiction Writer, Playwright, Physician
The Walls of Jericho (excerpt—fiction). Calverton 136
Walls of Jericho (excerpt: Miss Cramp And The Function—fiction). Brown 208
Walls of Jericho (excerpt: Shine and the Sheba—fiction). Brown 203

Blades of Steel (short fiction). Calverton 53, Cromwell 90
The City of Refuge (short fiction). Baker 169, Barksdale 591, Clarke 21, James 71, Locke 2:57, Watkins 49
Common Meter (short fiction). Chapman 74, Ford 2:195
High Yaller (short fiction). Davis 337
Miss Cynthie (short fiction). Brown 54, Clarke 3:40, Davis, C. 135, Emanuel 112, Hughes 3:35, Long 404, Patterson 2:102
Vestiges; Harlem Sketches (short fiction). Locke 2:75

FLEMING, RAY, 1945- . Poet
For Le Roi Jones (poetry). Witherspoon 20

FLETCHER, BOB, 1938- . Poet
A Love Dirge to the Whitehouse (or: it Soots You Right) (poetry). Major 50

FLETCHER, T. THOMAS FORTUNE. Poet
For a Certain PH.D I know (poetry). Cunard 261
Night (poetry). Johnson, C. 143
That Other Golgotha (poetry). Cunard 261
White God (poetry). Johnson, C. 143
Youth of Twenty Contemplates Suicide (poetry). Johnson, C. 115

FLYNN, JAVITA G. Essayist
"Reach Out" (essay). Bookers 44

FOLLY, DENNIS WILSON, 1954- . Poet
I Am Mother's Gentle Pet (poetry). Witherspoon 2:13
I'm Going To Make Time My Master (poetry). Witherspoon 2:13

FORBES, CALVIN, 1945- . Poet
Europe (poetry). Chapman 2:248
Lullaby for Ann-Lucian (poetry). Adoff 3:490, Chapman 2:249
Reading Walt Whitman (poetry). Adoff 3:490, Chapman 2:248

FORD, GREGORY J. Poet
Bits and Pieces (poetry). Murphy 2:31

FORD, HEYWOOD. Short Fiction Writer
Red-Bone Hound (short fiction). Margolies 54

FORD, NICK AARON, 1904- . Essayist, Short Fiction Writer, Critic, Poet
Blueprint for Negro Authors (essay). Gayle 2:276
Cultural Integration Through Literature (essay). Ford 128
The Ordeal of Richard Wright (essay). Ford 123, Gibson 2:26

Song of the Negro (poetry). Murphy 3:58

Let the Church Roll on (short fiction). Ford 132, Ford 2:25
The Majesty of the Law (short fiction). Ford 2:113
No Room in the Inn (short fiction). Ford 2:19
One Way to Victory (short fiction). Ford 133, Ford 2:30

FORD, WALLACE. Poet
Dry Wishing Well (poetry). Coombs 42
Sunrise on the Sunset (poetry). Coombs 42
Termination (poetry). Bookers 96

FOREMAN, KENT. Poet
Judgement Day (poetry). Brooks 26

FORREST, LEON. Short Fiction Writer
There Is a Tree More Ancient than Egypt (short fiction). Troupe 299

FORTEN, CHARLOTTE L., 1838-1914. Poet, Autobiographer
Journal of Charlotte Forten (excerpts—autobiography). Barksdale 277, Davis 109

Life on the Sea Islands (essay). Brown 649

FORTEN, JAMES, JR., 1766-1842. Orator, Letter Writer
Letter addressed to the Honourable George Thatcher, Member of Congress 1799 (letter). Porter 333
Letter from a Man of Color: on a late Bill before the Senate of Pennsylvania (letter). Patterson 3:35

An address delivered before the American Moral Reform Society, Philadelphia, Aug. 17th, 1837 (speech). Porter 225
To the Humane and Benevolent Inhabitants of the city and County of Philadelphia, Address delivered Dec. 10, 1818 (speech). Porter 265

FORTUNE, MICHAEL. Poet, Composer
Anthems and Hymns, 1808-1814 (poetry). Porter 562
New Year's Anthem (poetry). Miller, R. 41, Porter 563

FORTUNE, TIMOTHY THOMAS, 1856-1928. Essayist, Poet
Black and White . . . (excerpt: Land and Labor in the South—essay). Brown 880
Black and White (excerpt: The Negro and the Nation—essay). Long 125

Byron's Oak at Newstead Abbey (poetry). Robinson 255
Every Man a King (poetry). Robinson 254
Lincoln (poetry). White 115
The Savage Dreamer (poetry). Robinson 256
Tell Me, Ye Sad Winds (poetry). Robinson 256
We Know No More (poetry). Robinson 254, White 115

FOSTER, FRANCIS M. Poet
Hunger (poetry). Murphy 64
A Lover's Lament (poetry). Murphy 64

FRANKLIN, CHARLES. Poet
Another Man Has Died (poetry). Bookers 102
War Babies (poetry). Bookers 120

FRANKLIN, CLARENCE, 1932- . Poet, Playwright
Death of Days and Nights of Life (poetry). Jones 361, Patterson 4:45
Two Dreams (for M. L. K.'s One) (poetry). Jones 364
Visions . . . Leaders . . . Shaky Leaders . . . Parasitical Leaders . . . (poetry). Jones 362

FRANKLIN, J. E. Playwright, Short Fiction Writer
The Enemy (short fiction). King 2:349

FRANKLIN, JOHN HOPE , 1915- . Essayist, Historian
The Dilemma of the American Negro Scholar (essay). Curry 22, Hill 2:60

FRASER, W. ALFRED. Poet, Political Scientist, Historian
To the J. F. K. Quintet (poetry). Jones 272

FRAZIER, E. FRANKLIN, 1894-1962. Essayist
Black Bourgeoisie (excerpt—essay). Demarest 253
Black Bourgeoisie (excerpt: Ch. 5: The Break With the Traditional Background; Part 2: The Renaissance That Failed—Essay). Turner 6:68
Black Bourgeoisie (excerpt: Ch. 10: Behind the Masks—essay). Turner 6:70
Durham: Capital of the Black Middle Class (essay). Locke 2:333
The Negro Family in the United States (essay). Watkins 202
Pathology of Race Prejudice (essay). Brown 904
Racial Self-Expression (essay). Johnson, C. 119

FREEMAN, CAROL S., 1941- . Poet. Playwright
The Suicide (drama). Jones 631

Christmas Morning: I (poetry). Adoff 3:397, Jones 329, Lomax 255, Miller, R. 525
Do Not Think (poetry). Miller, R. 526
Gift (poetry). Hughes 2:435
I Saw Them Lynch (poetry). Adoff 3:397, Jones 330
When My Uncle Willie Saw (poetry). Jones 331, Miller, R. 525

FREEMAN, LORRAINE. Short Fiction Writer
Harlem Teacher (short fiction). Clarke 3:185

FRENCH, JAMES EDGAR. Poet
Dunbar and Cotter (poetry). Kerlin 307

FULLER, CHARLES H. JR., 1939- . Critic, Playwright, Essayist, Short Fiction Writer
The Rise (drama). Bullins 2:248

Love Song for Seven Little Boys Called; Sam (short fiction). Chambers 220, Jones 467
Love Song for Willa Mae (short fiction). Alhamisi 75
A Love Song for Wing (short fiction). King 2:141

FULLER, HOYT W., 1927- . Short Fiction Writer, Essayist, Critic, Poet
Dinner at Diop's (essay). Long 668
The New Black Literature: Protest or Affirmation (essay). Gayle 3:327
Role of the Negro Writer in an Era of Struggle (essay). Baker 389
Towards a Black Aesthetic (essay). Demarest 301, Gayle 2:263, Gayle 3:3

Lost Moment (poetry). Adoff 3:201, Brown, P. 44
Serraveza (poetry). Adoff 3:200

The Apostle (short fiction). Williams 24
The Senegalese (short fiction). Clarke 226

FULLER, NIEMA. See **RASHIDD, NIEMA.**

FULLER, STEPHANY, 1947- . Poet.
In The Silence (poetry). Randall 2:330
Let Me Be Held When The Longing Comes (poetry). Randall 2:332
That We Head Towards (poetry). Randall 2:333

GADSDEN, JANICE MARIE. Poet
Everything (poetry). Coombs 45
We Don't Need No Music (poetry). Coombs 44

GAINES, ERNEST J., 1933- . Fiction Writer
What If It Had Turned Up Heads (drama). Bullins 71

Autobiography of Miss Jane Pittman (excerpt—fiction). Troupe 225

Just Like a Tree (poetry). Davis 704, King 2:185

Anne-Marie Duvall (short fiction). Davis 716
Aunt Clo (short fiction). Davis 714
Aunt Lou (short fiction). Davis 721
Ben O (short fiction). Davis 712
Chris (short fiction). Davis 715
Chuckie (short fiction). Davis 705
Emile (short fiction). Davis 706
Etienne (short fiction). Davis 719
James (short fiction). Davis 710
Leola (short fiction). Davis 708
A Long Day in November (short fiction). Hughes 3:359, James 302
The Sky Is Gray (short fiction). Barksdale 782, Clarke 321, Emanuel 429, Long 744, Singh 136
Three Men (short fiction). Chapman 2:86, Stadler 162

GAINS-SHELTON, RUTH, 1873- . Playwright
The Church Fight (drama). Hatch 188

GANT, LISBETH A., 1948- . Bibliographer, Critic, Essayist, Short Fiction Writer
Etta's Mind (short fiction). Coombs 2:29

GARDNER, BENJAMIN FRANKLIN. Poet
Night (poetry). Murphy 3:60

GARDNER, CARL. Poet, Playwright, Fiction Writer
Angling up from the wheeling feet of fire (first line—poetry). Pool 109
The Dead Man Dragged from the Sea (poetry). Adoff 3:216, Lowenfels 37
Dowager's Death (poetry). Pool 109
Reflections (poetry). Adoff 3:217, Hughes 98
Untitled (Angling up from the wheeling feet of fire) (poetry). Pool 109

GARNET, HENRY HIGHLAND, 1815-1882. Clergyman, Abolitionist, Orator, Letter Writer
Address to the Slaves of the United States of America (speech). Barksdale 176, Brown 601, Gayle 3, Kendricks 73, Long 32
Memorial Discourse Delivered in the Hall of the House of Representatives, Feb. 12, 1865 (speech). Barksdale 268

GARRETT, JIMMY, 1947?- . Playwright
We Own the Night—A Play of Blackness (drama). Chambers 233, Jones 527, Singh 185

GARVEY, MARCUS, 1887-1940. Orator, Pamphleteer, Letter Writer
Message from the Atlanta Prison (essay). Long 369
The New Negro (essay). Gayle 67
Philosophy and Opinions of Marcus Garvey (excerpt: The Negro's Place in World Reorganization—essay). Brown 677
Philosophy and Opinions of Marcus Garvey or Africa for the Africans (excerpts—essay). Miller, R. 192
The Principles of the Universal Negro Improvement Association (essay). Long 357

An Appeal to the Conscience of the Black Race to See Itself (speech). Long 365

GATES, BETTY. Poet
Mamma Settles the Drop-out Problem (poetry). Henderson 309

GAYLE, ADDISON, JR., 1932- . Biographer, Critic, Essayist, Editor, Short Fiction Writer
Cultural Strangulation: Black Literature and the White Aesthetic (essay). Baker 369, Gayle 3:38
The Function of Black Literature at the Present Time (essay). Gayle 3:383
Perhaps Not So Soon One Morning (essay). Gayle 2:280
The Son of My Father (essay). Chapman 2:525

(GAYLE, ADDISON, JR.)
I Have Always Wanted Black Power (letter). Gayle 128
Letter To a White Colleague (letter). Gayle 129

GEARY, BRUCE C., 1942- . Poet
And the Heart Speaks (poetry). Patterson 4:93, Witherspoon 13

GEE, LETHONIA. Poet
Black Music Man (poetry). Jones 222, Patterson 4:24
By Glistening, Dancing Seas (poetry). Jones 221

GEORGAKAS, DAN. Critic
James Baldwin . . . in Conversation (interview). Chapman 660

GERALD, CAROLYN FOWLER, 1937- . Critic, Essayist, Poet
The Black Writer and His Role (essay). Exum 40, Gayle 3:349

GERAN, JULIANA. Poet
His Hera Mourned (poetry). Ten 32
In Need Of A Catullus To Adore (poetry). Ten 32
Monody (poetry). Ten 33
Rays (poetry). Ten 33
Virginalis (poetry). Ten 34
Wintry Child-Burial (poetry). Ten 32
Zion (poetry). Ten 31

GIBSON, DONALD B., 1933- . Critic
From Poetry by Black Writers to Black Poetry: a Brief History (essay). Gibson 3:1
The Good Black Poet and the Good Gray Poet: The Poetry of Hughes and Whitman (essay). Gibson 3:43
The Melting Pot (essay). Shuman 79
The Negro: An Essay on Definition (essay). Shuman 90

GIDDINGS, PAULA. Critic, Poet
Death Motion (poetry). Coombs 48
Rebirth (poetry). Coombs 49, Patterson 4:66
Resurrection (poetry). Coombs 50

GILBERT, L. ZACK, 1925- . Poet
For Angela (poetry). Adoff 3:196
For Gwendolyn Brooks (poetry). Brown, P. 46
For Stephen Dixon (poetry). Adoff 3:195
In Spite of All This Much Needed Thunder (poetry). Hughes 2:390
The Long, Black Line (poetry). Murphy 65
My Own Hallelujahs (poetry). Adoff 3:194
When I Heard Dat White Man Say (poetry). Adoff 3:195, Brown, P. 47

GILBERT, WILLIE. Essayist
Inner-city Slums (essay). Bookers 20

GILLISON, LENORA. Poet
Supremacy (poetry). Murphy 66

GILPIN, PATRICK J. Essayist
Charles S. Johnson: Entrepreneur of the Harlem Renaissance (essay). Bontemps 3:215

GIOVANNI, NIKKI, 1943- . Critic, Editor, Essayist, Poet, Short Fiction Writer, Autobiographer
Adulthood (poetry). Bell 169, Long 772, Wilentz 23
Alone (poetry). Brooks 65
Atrocities (poetry). Exum 83
Balance (poetry). Bell 171
Beautiful Black Men (poetry). Brooks 57, Randall 2:320
Black Judgment (poetry). Murphy 2:33
Black Judgements (poetry). Brooks 60
Black Power (poetry). Brooks 53
The Black revolution is passing you by (poem: no name no. 3) (first line— poetry). Brooks 50, Miller, R. 533
Concerning One Responsible Negro with New Power (poetry). Randall 2:323
Dreams (poetry). Adoff 3:454
For a Lady of Pleasure Now Retired (poetry). Brooks 67
For Gwendolyn Brooks (poetry). Brown, P. 48
For Saundra (poetry). Barksdale 823, Brooks 57, Lomax 256, Murphy 2:34, Randall 2:321, Wilentz 28
For Theresa (poetry). Bell 172
Funeral of Martin Luther King, Jr. (poetry). Bontemps 2:206, Brooks 54, Murphy 2:37, Randall 2:323
Game of Game (poetry). Brooks 65
The Geni in the jar (poetry). Breman 478
The Great Pax Whitie (poetry). Coombs 51
Housecleaning (poetry). Patterson 4:117
I'd Rapp (poetry). Brooks 68
• I'm Not Lonely (poetry). Brooks 52
Kidnap Poem (poetry). Bontemps 2:206, Brooks 66, Randall 2:326
Knoxville, Tennessee (poetry). Adoff 3:450, Bontemps 2:205, Brooks 55, Randall 2:322, Wilentz 21
My House (poetry). Troupe 439
My Poem (poetry). Adoff 3:453, Bontemps 2:202, Breman 476, Brooks 58, Chapman 2:250, Miller, R. 534, Murphy 2:35, Randall 2:319, Wilentz 29
Nikki-Rosa (poetry). Adoff 20, Adoff 3:451, Bell 169, Bontemps 2:204, Breman 475, Chambers 300, Freedman 230, Jordan 22, Major 53, Randall 48, Stanford 208, Wilentz 22
No Reservations (poetry). Brooks 64
Poem for Aretha (poetry). Adoff 3:454, Brooks 61, Randall 2:326
•Poem for Black Boys (poetry). Randall 2:325

(GIOVANNI, NIKKI)
Poem for B. M. C. No. 1 (poetry). Brooks 48
Poem for Flora (poetry). Adoff 3:456
Poem of Angela Yvonne Davis (poetry). Adoff 3:458, King 3:74
Poem (The Black Revolution Is Passing You By—No Name No. 3) (poetry). Brooks 50, Coombs 54, Miller, R. 533
Reflections on April 4, 1968 (poetry). Henderson 279
Revolutionary Music (poetry). Brooks 55, Henderson 280
A Robin's Poem (poetry). Bontemps 2:207, Brooks 68
Seduction (poetry). Brooks 54, Patterson 4:125, Wilentz 25
Toy Poem (poetry). Brooks 69
True Import of Present Dialogue; Black vs. Negro (poetry). Adoff 3:451, Alhamisi 117, Brooks 48, Randall 2:318
12 Gates to the City (poetry). Adoff 3:457
Wilmington, Delaware (poetry). Brooks 51, Wilentz 26
Word Poem (poetry). Adoff 3:450

A Revolutionary Tale (short fiction). King 2:19

GIPSON, EDNA, 1946- . Essayist
A Deep Blue Feeling (essay). Schulberg 189

GLICKSBERG, CHARLES I. Essayist
The Alienation of Negro Literature (essay). Singh 238

GLOSTER, HUGH MORRIS, 1911- . Critic, Editor, Essayist, Educator
Charles W. Chesnutt, Pioneer in The Fiction of Negro Life (essay). Watkins 295
Race and the Negro Writer (essay). Gayle 2:255
Sutton E. Griggs: Novelist of the New Negro (essay). Hemenway 11

GOLDEN, BERNETTE. Poet
Morning (poetry). Murphy 2:39
Paying Dues (poetry). Exum 85
There Are Seeds to Sow (poetry). Murphy 2:40
Words (poetry). Murphy 2:41

GONCALVES, JOE, 1937- . Poet, Editor, Critic, Essayist
Natural Black Beauty (essay). Alhamisi 19

Now the Time Is Ripe To Be (poetry). Jones 265
Sister Brother (poetry). Jones 266
The Way It Is (poetry). Jones 267
Words (poetry). Brown, P. 49

GOODE, MICHAEL, 1954- . Poet
April 4, 1968 (poetry). Jordan 6
I Am Waiting (poetry). Jordan 5

GOODEN, LAURETTA HOLMAN. Poet
A Dream of Revenge (poetry). Brewer 15
Question to a Mob (poetry). Brewer 16

GOODWIN, LE ROY. Poet
The Day a Dancer Learned to Sing of Dreamless Escapades (poetry). Jones 416

GOODWIN, RUBY BERKLEY, 1903- . Poet
Anxiety (poetry). Murphy 3:61
Guilty (poetry). Murphy 68
I Dream Alone Again (poetry). Murphy 3:61
I Sing (poetry). Murphy 3:62
If This Be Good-bye (poetry). Murphy 67
New Year's Prayer (poetry). Murphy 67
Race Prejudice in America (poetry). Murphy 3:63
Rendezvous with God (poetry). Murphy 3:63
We Launched a Ship (poetry). Murphy 69

GORDON, BAREFIELD. Poet
To Lincoln University 1923-1924 (poetry). Cuney 19

GORDON, CHARLES F. 1943- . Playwright, Poet
Breakout (drama). King 407
His First Step (drama). Bullins 133
The Long Night Home (poetry). Major 54

GORDON, EDYTHE MAE. Poet
Buried Deep (poetry). Murphy 3:66
Sonnet for June (poetry). Murphy 3:65

GORDONE, CHARLES, 1925- . Playwright, Poet
No Place to Be Somebody (drama). Oliver 394, Patterson 2:407

A Quiet Talk with Myself (essay). Ford 327

GORHAM, MYRTLE CAMPBELL. Poet
Service, Please (poetry). Murphy 71

GOSS, CLAY, 1946- . Playwright, Poet
On Being Hit (drama). Bullins 117

And If I Die Before I Wake (poetry). Coombs 56

GOSS, LINDA. Poet
Revolution Man Black (poetry). Coombs 61, Patterson 4:23

GOSS, WILLIAM THOMPSON. Poet
Man To Man (poetry). Murphy 72
Variety (poetry). Murphy 72

GOVAN, DONALD D., 1945- . Poet
Recollection (poetry). Major 55

GOVAN, OSWALD. Poet
The Lynching (poetry). Henderson 196

LE GRAHAM. See ALHAMISI, AHMED AKINWOLE.

GRAHAM, DONALD L., 1944-1970. Poet
April 5th (poetry). Henderson 320
The Clown (poetry). Jones 434
Poem for Eric Dolphy (poetry). Henderson 321
Portrait of Johnny Doller (poetry). Breman 503, Jones 432
Remember: When the door closes you in (first line; Untitled—poetry). Henderson 324
Soul (poetry). Adams 3:43, Adoff 3:482, Hayden 2:231, Henderson 322
Tony get the boys (poetry). Adoff 3:480
Untitled (poetry). (Remember: When the door closes you in) (first line—poetry). Henderson 324
. . . We Ain't Got No Time (poetry). Henderson 323
West Ridge Is Menthol-Cool (poetry). Adoff 3:481, Jones 430

GRAHAM, ERNESTINE. Essayist
A Pretender (essay). Bookers 71

GRAHAM, LINDA B., 1958- . Poet
The Blackbird (poetry). Shuman 313
Lilies (poetry). Shuman 313
Orange (poetry). Shuman 314
Purple (poetry). Shuman 313

GRAHAM, RUBY BEE, 1947- . Poet
Learning To Dance (poetry). Jones 377
A Lynching for Skip James (poetry). Jones 374
Memorandum (poetry). Hughes 2:441

GRANT, MICKI. Poet
Rude Awakening (poetry). Pool 2:123

GRANT, OTTO. Poet
Untitled Poem (poetry). Brooks 66

GRANT, RICHARD E., 1949- . Poet
Broken Heart, Broken Machine (poetry). Adoff 3:505

GRAVES, CONRAD, Poet
This Place (poetry). Bookers 71

GRAVES, MILFORD. Musician
Black Music: New Black Revolutionary Art (essay). Alhamisi 40

GRAY, DARRELL M., 1950- . Poet, Short Fiction Writer
A Change of Heart (short fiction). Shuman 100
A Harsh Greeting (short fiction). Shuman 104, Stadler 1

GRAY, JOCELYN. Poet
I Love You, What More Can I Say? (poetry). Bookers 85

GRAYSON, WILLIAM JOHN. Poet
The Hireling and the Slave (excerpts—poetry). Kearns 2:23

GREAVES, DONALD. 1943- . Playwright
The Marriage (drama). King 253

GREEN, DONALD. Poet
Growing Clean (poetry). Coombs 63
Making It, or Black Corruption (poetry). Coombs 63
Truth (poetry). Coombs 62

GREEN, JOHNSON. Autobiographer
The Life and Confession of Johnson Green, who is to be executed this day, Aug. 17th, 1786 for the Atrocious Crime of Burglary; Together with his last and dying words, a broadside (excerpt—autobiography). Porter 405

GREEN, PAUL 1894- . Playwright
In Abraham's Bosom (drama). Locke 139
Native Son (drama). Brasner 69
The No 'Count Boy (drama). Locke 69
On the Road One Day, Lord (drama). Johnson, C. 23
White Dresses (drama). Locke 117

GREENE, CARL H., 1945- . Poet
The Excuse (poetry). Chapman 2:253
Hear Those Tambourines (poetry). Shuman 315
I Killed One (poetry). Shuman 315
Many Sing Songs (poetry). Shuman 316
The Metal Was Stuck Deep (poetry). Shuman 316
On Apathy (poetry). Shuman 317
Poems Modern (poetry). Witherspoon 9
The Realist (poetry). Chapman 2:253
Something Old, Something New (poetry). Chapman 2:252
Walking Among the Benches (poetry). Shuman 317

GREENE, EMILY JANE. Poet
He's Coming Home At Last (poetry). Murphy 73

GREENE, LORENZO JOHNSTON. Essayist, Editor, Historian
The Negro in Colonial New England, 1620-1776 (excerpt: The Slave Family—history). Dreer 157
The Negro in Colonial New England, 1620-1776 (excerpt: Slave Occupations—history). Dreer 155

GREENER, RICHARD T., 1844-1922. Essayist
The Black Man Must Leave the South (essay). Gayle 40

GREENLEE, SAM, 1930- . Critic, Poet, Fiction Writer
Myth (poetry). Patterson 4:119

(GREENLEE, SAM)
Sonny's Not Blue (short fiction). King 2:91

GREER, ROSLYN. Poet
Triangle (poetry). Murphy 2:44

GREGORY, CAROLE. See CLEMMONS, CAROLE GREGORY.

GREGORY, DICK, 1932- . Essayist, Civil Rights Worker, Autobiographer
Nigger (excerpt—autobiography). Adoff 4:111
Nigger (excerpt: Not Poor, Just Broke—autobiography). Adams 4:23, Chambers 295

GREGORY, MONTGOMERY. Essayist
Drama of Negro Life (essay). Gayle 2:128, Locke 2:153, Patterson 25

GREGORY, YVONNE, 1919- . Poet
Christmas Lullaby for a New-Born Child (poetry). Bontemps 2:153

GRIFFIN, AMOS J. Poet
Salute to the Tan Yanks (poetry). Murphy 74

GRIGGS, SUTTON ELBERT, 1872-1930. Essayist, Fiction Writer
The Hindered Hand (excerpt: The Blaze—fiction). Davis 164

GRIMKE, ANGELINA WELD, 1880-1958. Biographer, Playwright, Essayist, Poet
Biographical Sketch of Archibald H. Grimké (excerpt—biography). Brown 804

Rachel (drama). Hatch 137

At the Spring Dawn (poetry). Kerlin 154
El Beso (poetry). Kerlin 154
The Black Finger (poetry). Adoff 3:15, Bontemps 2:17, Chambers 267, Locke 2:148
Dawn (poetry). Cromwell, 24, Kerlin 153
Dusk (poetry). Cullen 46
The Eyes of My Regret (poetry). Cullen 37
For the Candle Light (poetry). Calverton 187, Cullen 45, Hughes 2:55
Grass Fingers (poetry). Barksdale 627, Cromwell 24, Cullen 38
Greenness (poetry). Cullen 36
Hushed by the Hands of Sleep (poetry). Brown 341, Cullen 36
I Weep (poetry). Cullen 45, Patterson 4:115
A June Song (excerpt—poetry). Kerlin 156
A Mona Lisa (poetry). Barksdale 627, Cullen 42
Paradox (poetry). Cullen 43
Puppet-Player (poetry). Cullen 46, Kerlin 153
Surrender (poetry). Brown 342, Cromwell 25, Cullen 38

Tenebris (poetry). Adams 3:10, Adoff 3:15, Cullen 40, Hughes 2:58
To Clarissa Scott Delany (poetry). Bontemps 2:15, Johnson, C. 67
To Keep the Memory of Charlotte Forten Grimké (poetry). Kerlin 155
To the Dunbar High School—A Sonnet (poetry). Cromwell 24
The Want of You (poetry). Kerlin 154
The Ways of Men (poetry). Cullen 39
When the Green Lies over the Earth (poetry). Brown 342, Cullen 41, Hughes 2:56
A Winter Twilight (poetry). Adoff 3:16, Brown 343, Cullen 46, Hughes 2:54, Kerlin 153
Your Hands (poetry). Adoff 3:16, Cromwell 25, Cullen 44, Patterson 4:3

GRIMKE, CHARLOTTE (MRS. FRANCIS). See FORTEN, CHARLOTTE L.

GRIT, BRUCE, Poet
Black Man's Burden (poetry). Breman 45

GROSS, THEODORE. Editor, Essayist
The Negro in the Literature of the Reconstruction (essay). Gross 71
Stereotype to Archetype: The Negro in American Literary Criticism (essay). Gross 1

GROSVENOR, VERTA MAE, 1938- . Poet, Autobiographer, Short Fiction Writer
Black Is (poetry). King 3:104
Circles (poetry). King 3:105
What's Happening to the Heroes (poetry). King 3:106

GROVER, WAYNE. Fiction Writer
Finer Points (short fiction). Burnett 118

GUERARD, VERA E., 1944-1967. Poet
At Sea (poetry). Murphy 2:46
Spring of Joy (poetry). Murphy 2:47

GUIDON, HENRY. Autobiographer
Well, After Freedom (autobiography). Gayle 29

GUILLEN, NICHOLAS. Poet
Guadalupe W. I. (poetry). Hollo 19
Madrigal (poetry). Hollo 19

GUINN, DOROTHY. Playwright
Out of the Dark (drama). Richardson 305

GUINN, I. E. Bishop
Arise, Ye Garvey Nation (poetry). Pool 2:188

GULLINS, D. EDNA. Poet
If Winter Comes (poetry). Murphy 3:66
Soul Suffering (poetry). Murphy 3:67

GUNNER, FRANCES. Playwright
The Light of the Women (drama). Richardson 333

HADLIN, WARRINGTON. Essayist
The Renaissance Re-examined (essay). Bontemps 3:268

HAIRSTON, LOYLE, 1926- . Critic, Short Fiction Writer, Essayist
William Styron's Nat Turner—Rogue—Nigger (essay). Clarke 2:66

Harlem on the Rocks (short fiction). Clarke 3:211
Winds of Change (short fiction). Clarke 297, Gibson 130

HALL, CARLYLE B. Poet
I Wake Up Screaming (poetry). Murphy 76
Malevolence (poetry). Murphy 76
Solitude (poetry). Murphy 77

HALL, DOUGLAS. Short Fiction Writer
Foggy (short fiction). Ford 2:265

HALL, JOHN E., 1943- . Poet
Dark Shadows (poetry). Major 57
Justice (poetry). Murphy 3:69

HALL, KIRKWOOD M., 1944- . Poet
blackgoldblueswoman (poetry). Chapman 2:254
Illusions (poetry). Jones 336
Impressions (poetry). Jones 335
Song of Tom (poetry). Jones 332
today is not like they said . . . (poetry). Chapman 2:255
Wig (poetry). Jones 334

HALL, PRINCE, 1748?-1807. Speaker
A Charge Delivered to the Brethren of the African Lodge on the 25th of June, 1792 (speech). Porter 63
A Charge delivered to the African Lodge, June 24, 1797, at Menotomy (speech). Porter 70
A Charge delivered to the African Lodge, June 24, 1797 at Menotomy (excerpt—speech). Brawley 97

HALSEY, WILLIAM. Poet
Dear Brother (letter). Bookers 55

Like Me (poetry). Bookers 33
Made (poetry). Bookers 57

HAMER, MARTIN J., 1931- . Poet, Short Fiction Writer
Sarah (short fiction). Clarke 311, Freedman 199, Patterson 3:238, Stadler 135

HAMILTON, BOBB, 1928- . Poet, Short Fiction Writer, Sculptor
Brother Harlem Bedford Watts Tells Mr. Charlie Where It's At (poetry). Breman 233, Jones 447
A Child's Nightmare (poetry). Brooks 168
A Father Tells His Son About the Status of Liberty (poetry). Alhamisi 123

Poem to a Nigger Cop (poetry). Jones 452, Lomax 255
Pygmalion (poetry). Pool 110

HAMILTON, CHARLES V. Essayist
Our Nat Turner and William Styron's Creation (essay). Clarke 2:73, Kearns 2:47

HAMILTON, RICHARD T., 1869- . Poet, Physician
A Negro's Prayer (poetry). Brewer 20
Sister Mandy Attends the Business League (poetry). Brewer 18

HAMILTON, ROLAND T. Short Fiction Writer
Symbol of Courage (short fiction). Ford 2:127

HAMILTON, WILLIAM. Composer, Orator
Anthems and Hymns, 1808-1814 (poetry). Porter 562

An Address to the New York African Society, for Mutual Relief (speech). Porter 33
An oration delivered in the African Zion Church on July 4, 1827, in Commemoration of the Abolition of Domestic Slavery in this State, 1827 (speech). Porter 96
An oration on the Abolition of the Slave Trade, Delivered in the Episcopal Asbury African Church, in Elizabeth St., N. Y. Jan. 2, 1815 (speech). Porter 391

HAMMON, BRITON. Autobiographer, Essayist, (First Published Negro American, 1760)
A Narrative of the Uncommon Sufferings and Surprising Deliverance of Briton Hammon, Negro Man Servant to General Winslow of Marshfield, in New England, 1760 (autobiography). Patterson 3:5, Porter 522

HAMMON, JUPITER, 1720?-1800?. Poet, Essayist
An Address to Miss Phillis Wheatley, Ethiopian Poetess (poetry). Barksdale 47, Long 20, Porter 535, Robinson 9
A Dialogue Entitled The Kind Master and The Dutiful Servant (poetry). Brawley 26, Miller, R. 7
A Dialogue Entitled The Kind Master and The Dutiful Servant (excerpts—poetry). Kerlin 22
An Evening Thought (poetry). Brawley 23, Hughes 2:4, Patterson 3:27, Porter 529, Robinson 7
An Evening Thought (excerpts—poetry). Barksdale 46, Kerlin 21
A Poem for Children, with Thoughts on Death (excerpt—poetry). Kerlin 22

An Address to the Negroes in the State of N. Y. 1787 (speech). Porter 313
An Address to the Negroes of the State of New York (excerpts—speech). Kendricks 30

HAMMOND, MRS. J. W. Poet
The Optimist (poetry). Kerlin 143
To My Neghbor Boy (poetry). Kerlin 143

HAND, Q. R., 1937- . Poet
And I can remember still your first lies
America (first line, untitled—poetry).
Jones 256
I Wonder (poetry). Jones 261
Untitled Poem (And I Can Remember still
your first lies America) (first line—
poetry). Jones 256

HANDY, W. C. Autobiographer
St. Louis Blues and Solvent Bank (excerpt—autobiography). Watkins 357

HANKINS, PAULA. Short Fiction Writer
Testimonial (short fiction). King 2:97

HANNAH, GEORGE. Short Fiction Writer
I Died One Night (short fiction). Bookers
61

HANNIBAL, GREGOR. Poet
Untitled (You Walk Like Bells: first line—
poetry). Henderson 317
You Walk Like Bells (first line, untitled—
poetry). Henderson 317

HANSBERRY, LORRAINE, 1930-1965. Auto-
biographer, Critic, Playwright, Essayist,
Poet
The Drinking Gourd (drama). Hatch 713
A Raisin in the Sun (drama). Adams 1,
Ford 279, Oliver 33, Patterson 2:221
A Raisin in the Sun (excerpts—drama).
Chambers 268, Kendricks 339, Rose 73,
98, 172

HARDING, VINCENT, 1931- . Essayist
You've Taken My Nat and Gone (essay).
Clarke 2:23

HARDNETT, LINDA G., 1950- . Poet,
Short Fiction Writer
If Hair Makes Me Black, I Must Be Pur-
ple (poetry). Shuman 319
To You (poetry). Shuman 320

Black Tornado (short fiction). Shuman
107

HARE, NATHAN, 1934- . Editor, Essayist,
Journalist, Poet
Brainwashing of Black Men's Minds (es-
say). Jones 178
The Challenge of a Black Scholar (essay).
Barksdale 837
The Exiles (essay). Curry 73

Algiers 1969: A Report on the Pan-
American Cultural Festival (poetry).
Chapman 2:426

HARMON, FLORENCE MARION. Short
Fiction Writer
Attic Romance (short fiction). Cromwell
121

HARPER, FRANCES ELLEN WATKINS,
1825-1911. Essayist, Poet, Fiction
Writer
The Colored People in America (essay).
Kendricks 80

Advice To The Girls (poetry). Kendricks
82, Patterson 4:92
Bury Me in a Free Land (poetry). Black
6, Brawley 292, Brown 296, Davis 103,
Long 98, Randall 2:40, Robinson 36,
White 42
Death of the Old Sea King (poetry). Rob-
inson 29
Double Standard (poetry). Davis 104, Pat-
terson 4:58, Robinson 27
Dying Bondman (poetry). Davis 102, Pat-
terson 3:93
Eliza Harris (poetry). Brown 293, Ken-
dricks 82
Ethiopia (poetry). Brawley 293
Fifteenth Amendment (poetry). Brawley
297
Go Work in My Vineyard (excerpt—po-
etry). Kerlin 27
It shall flash through coming ages (first
line—poetry). Kerlin 26
Learning to Read (poetry). Davis 106, Rob-
inson 37
Let the Light Enter (poetry). Brown 296,
Hughes 2:15
Make me a grave wher'er you will (first
line—poetry). Kerlin 26
Nothing and Something (poetry). Robin-
son 32
Poem Addressed to Women (poetry). Cal-
verton 176
President Lincoln's Proclamation of Free-
dom (poetry). Brawley 296
Report (poetry). Patterson 4:90
Slave Auction (poetry). Adams 3:62,
Brown 295, Chambers 41, Davis 105,
Hayden 2:13, Hughes 2:14, Kendricks
81, Lomax 205, Long 96, Randall 2:39,
Robinson 32
Slave Mother (poetry). Long 97, Robin-
son 31, White 41
Songs for the People (poetry). Robinson 30
Truth (poetry). Kerlin 28
Vashti (poetry). Brawley 294, Kerlin 30,
Robinson 34

The Two Offers (short fiction). Patterson
3:81

HARPER, MICHAEL S., 1938- . Editor,
Poet
Aftermath (poetry). Wilentz 37
American History (poetry). Randall 2:291
Another Season (poetry). Wilentz 40
Barricades (poetry). Adoff 3:316
The Black Angel (poetry). Wilentz 38
Black Study (poetry). Wilentz 33
Blue Ruth: America (poetry). Adoff 3:317
Come Back Blues (poetry). Adoff 3:314
Dear John, Dear Coltrane (poetry). Hen-
derson 238

(HARPER, MICHAEL S.)
Deathwatch (poetry). Adoff 3:317
Effendi (poetry). Adoff 3:318, Troupe 233, Wilentz 33
Elvin's Blues (poetry). Randall 2:290
The Guerrilla-Cong (poetry). Chapman 2:258
Here Where Coltrane Is (poetry). Adoff 3:313
High Modes: Vision As Ritual: Confirmation (poetry). Chapman 2:257
Madimba: Gwendolyn Brooks (poetry). Brown, P. 50
Martin's Blues (poetry). Adoff 3:312
A Mother Speaks: the Algiers Motel Incident, Detroit (poetry). Chapman 2:256, Randall 2:291
New Season (poetry). Wilentz 41
Newsletter from My Mother (poetry). Adoff 3:315
Ode to Lonachtitlan (poetry). Wilentz 33
Photographs: a Vision of Massacre (poetry). Adoff 3:313
Proposition 15 (poetry). Wilentz 32
To James Brown (poetry). Henderson 240
We Assume (poetry). Wilentz 39
Where Is My Woman Now (poetry). Wilentz 36
Zocalo (poetry). Chapman 2:258

HARRELL, DENNIS, 1949- . Poet
Ballad of Uncle Tom (poetry). Shuman 322
I'm Just a Little Penny (poetry). Shuman 326

HARRIS, ABRAM L., 1899- . Essayist
Economics of the Founding Fathers (essay). Brown 910
The Prospects of Black Bourgeoisie (essay). Johnson, C. 131

HARRIS, ERNESTINE. Essayist
Negro History Week (esay). Bookers 44

HARRIS, HELEN C. Poet
Autumn Rain (poetry). Triad 19
Cities (poetry). Triad 28
Comparison (poetry). Triad 30
Conviction (poetry). Triad 20
Cure (poetry). Triad 23
Deepest, Darkest Turn (poetry). Triad 24
Divers (poetry). Triad 26
Evening (poetry). Triad 4
Hunger (poetry). Triad 18
I Heard Your Heart's Soft Tears (poetry). Murphy 78, Triad 5
I Share Your Presence (poetry). Triad 14
Measurements (poetry). Triad 31
Message (poetry). Triad 11
Moonlight (poetry). Triad 17
Nexus (poetry). Triad 13
Of Love (poetry). Triad 12
Opus 7 (poetry). Triad 8
Plea (poetry). Triad 15
Question (poetry). Triad 9
Rose Petals (poetry). Triad 29
Round Trip Ticket (poetry). Triad 21

Spin Me a Dream (poetry). Murphy 78, Triad 10
Sudden Flight (poetry). Triad 7
These Words (poetry). Triad 22
To Lovers (poetry). Triad 6
To the Men in 350th Hdg Co. (poetry). Triad 25
To the Muse (poetry). Triad 3
To the Singer (poetry). Murphy 79
Young Hermit Speaks (poetry). Triad 27

HARRIS, HELEN WEBB. Dramatist
Genifrede (drama). Richardson 2:219

HARRIS, HOWARD. Poet
Sad and Blue (poetry). Bookers 81

HARRIS, JESSIE REDMOND. See FAUSET, JESSIE REDMOND.

HARRIS, LEON R., 1886- . Editor, Fiction Writer, Poet
The Steel Makers (poetry). Kerlin 182
We travel a common road, Brother (first line—poetry). Kerlin 63

HARRIS, MARLA V. Poet
Away (poetry). Bookers 13

HARRIS, WILLIAM J., 1942- . Essayist, Poet
An Ad in the Times (poetry). Shuman 330, Shuman 2:111
Beautiful Bathtub (poetry). Shuman 2:110
Bent-back Jim (poetry). Shuman 2:95
Can I Write You an Anthem (poetry). Wilentz 51
Catwoman or the Lament of Bruce Wayne (poetry). Shuman 2:113
Cut in Half (poetry). Shuman 2:108
A Daddy Poem (poetry). Chapman 2:262
For Bill Hawkins, a Black Militant (poetry). Adoff 3:439, Wilentz 48
For Janet (poetry). Shuman 2:111
For Janice (poetry). Shuman 2:102
Frightened Flower (poetry). Shuman 2:106
A Grandfather Poem (poetry). Adoff 3:439
Habitual (poetry). Wilentz 50
An Historic Moment (poetry). Shuman 2:108
I, Satan (poetry). Wilentz 48
I See You Standing, Toothpick Lady (poetry). Shuman 2:100
I'm No Martian (poetry). Shuman 2:95
Jill Made It With a Goat (poetry). Shuman 2:93
Letter to Thomas Becket . . . (poetry). Shuman 328, Shuman 2:105
Loneliness Is a Movie Theatre (poetry). Shuman 2:114
My baby (poetry). Chapman 2:260
My Blue Angel (poetry). Shuman 109, Shuman 2:115
My Friend, Wendell Berry (poetry). Wilentz 44
My Girl Wants To Leave Ohio (poetry). Shuman 2:91

(HARRIS, WILLIAM J.)
. . . Nor Do I Expect (poetry). Shuman 2:98
Oh Banana Man (poetry). Shuman 2:104
On Wearing Ears (poetry). Shuman 2:114
Persecuted, Betrayal, Volkswagon Blues (poetry). Shuman 2:112
Practical Concerns (poetry). Adoff 3:440
Samantha Is My Negro Cat (poetry). Davis 767, Shuman 2:92, Wilentz 49
Strange (poetry). Shuman 2:99
Student (poetry). Shuman 2:101
Sweet Dreams of Comradeship (poetry). Shuman 2:94
Symbiosis (poetry). Shuman 2:109
To Be the Invisible Man (poetry). Shuman 2:97
Truth Is Quite Messy (poetry). Shuman 330, Shuman 2:98
An Unofficial Eulogy (poetry). Shuman 327, Shuman 2:103
We Live in a Cage (poetry). Adoff 3:438, Wilentz 47
Why Would I Want to Be in the Distant Hills? (poetry). Adoff 3:439, Shuman 2:108
A Winter Song (poetry). Wilentz 51
With My Napalm Six Shooters (poetry). Shuman 2:96, Wilentz 45
You Tell Me (poetry). Shuman 2:110
You Wear Black Plastic Sunglasses (poetry). Shuman 2:107

HARRISON, DE LEON, 1941- . Poet
A Collage for Richard Davis—Two Short Forms (poetry). Adoff 3:396, Miller, A. 25
Dream #6 (poetry). Miller, A. 19
Excursion on a Wobbly Rail (poetry). Miller, A. 20
Last Night I Died (poetry). Miller, A. 22
Poem for Herbie Nichols (poetry). Miller, A. 24
The Room (poetry). Adoff 3:394, Miller, A. 18
Seed of Nimrod (poetry). Adoff 3:394, Miller, A. 18
Some Days! Out Walking Above (poetry). Adoff 3:396, Miller, A. 21
Some Pseudo Philanthropist (poetry). Miller, A. 22
Yellow (poetry). Adoff 3:395, Miller, A. 26

HARRISON, DELORIS. Short Fiction Writer
A Friend For a Season (short fiction). Stadler 52

HARRISON, EDNA L. Poet
First Lady (poetry). Murphy 79

HASLAM, GERALD W. Essayist
The Awakening of American Negro Literature, 1619-1900 (essay). Bigsby 41

HASSON, UMAR ABD ROHIM, 1945- .
See RUTHERFORD, TONY.

HATCH, JAMES V., 1928- . Playwright
Fly Blackbird (drama with Jackson, C. Bernard). Hatch 671, Reardon 137

HAWKINS, DARNELLE, 1946- . Poet
Olduvai Gorge: Homo Sacrificus (poetry). Witherspoon 2:14

HAWKINS, WALTER EVERETTE, 1886- . Poet
Ask Me Why I Love You (poetry). Kerlin 125
Credo (poetry). Kerlin 119
The Death of Justice (poetry). Adoff 3:20, Kerlin 123, White 150
A Festival in Christendom (excerpt—poetry). Kerlin 266
Hero of the Road (poetry). Kerlin 122
In Spite of Death (poetry). Kerlin 62
The man who complains (first line—poetry). Kerlin 123
A Spade Is Just a Spade (poetry). Adoff 3:19, White 149
Thus Speaks Africa (poetry). Cunard 262
To Prometheus (poetry). Cunard 262
Wrong's Reward (poetry). White 148

HAYDEN, ROBERT EARL, 1913- . Poet
Statement on Poetics (essay). Bell 175

Approximations (poetry). Lane 23
Aunt Jemima of the Ocean Waves (poetry). Adoff 3:125
Bacchanal (poetry). Brown 408
Baha'u'llah in Garden of Ridivan (poetry). Adoff 3:122, Miller, R. 397
Ballad of Nat Turner (poetry). Breman 132, Henderson 154, Randall 2:133, Turner 3:248, Turner 4:92
Ballad of Remembrance (poetry). Adoff 2:32, Adoff 3:115, Baker 252, Barksdale 679, Bontemps 2:109, Breman 124, Hayden 133, Hughes 2:291, Randall 2:131, Robinson 2:201
The Ballad of Sue Ellen Westerfield (poetry). Hayden 2:113
Ballad Of The True Beast (poetry). Lane 22
Belsen, Liberation Day (for Rosey) (poetry). Pool 2:139
Dance the Orange (poetry). Lane 25
The Diver (poetry). Bell 66, Davis 385, Emanuel 483, Hayden 2:109, Long 572, Pool 112, Randall 2:136
The Dream (1863) (poetry). Chapman 2:203
El-Hajj Malik El-Shabazz (poetry). Adoff 3:123, Brooks 20, Troupe 55
Figure (poetry). Chapman 440
Frederick Douglass (poetry). Adams 3:26, Adoff 2:45, Adoff 3:120, Barksdale 667, Bell 56, Bontemps 2:119, Breman 135, Chapman 449, Davis 392, Davis, C. 371, Emanuel 485, Freedman 84, Hayden 2:117, Henderson 159, Hughes 2:296, Jordan 41, Lomax 237, Patterson 3:220, Pool 2:56, Stanford 34, Weisman 28

(HAYDEN, ROBERT EARL)
Full Moon (poetry). Hayden 2:112, Hill 2:581, Miller, R. 398, Pool 111, Randall 2:135
Gabriel—Hanged for leading a slave revolt (poetry). Brown 405, Pool 2:49
Homage to the Empress of the Blues (poetry). Adoff 3:117, Barksdale 678, Bell 64, Chapman 433, Davis 387, Hughes 2:290, Margolies 286
In Light Half Nightmare and Half Vision (poetry). Chapman 441
In the Mourning Time (poetry). Randall 2:138
Incense of the Lucky Virgin (poetry). Robinson 2:202
Kid (poetry). Adoff 68
Locus (poetry). Breman 123
Market (poetry). Bell 65, Chapman 442
Middle Passage (poetry). Adams 3:44, Adoff 2:34, Adoff 3:110, Baker 254, Barksdale 680, Bell 56, Bontemps 2:113, Breman 126, Chapman 444, Davis 388, Davis, C. 372, Freedman 42, Hayden 124, Kearns 2:15, Long 563, Margolies 23, Miller, R. 390, Randall 2:123, Stanford 6
The Mirages (poetry). Lane 26
Morning Poem for the Queen of Sunday (poetry). Adoff 3:117, Barksdale 680, Chapman 443, Henderson 153
Mountains (poetry). Lane 23
O Daedalus, Fly Away Home (poetry). Adoff 2:26, Adoff 3:116, Davis 393, Hughes 2:288, Jordan 120
Obituary (poetry). Brown 407
On the Coast of Maine (poetry). Chapman 439
Prophecy (poetry). Brown 404
The Rabbi (poetry). Patterson 3:219
Richard Hunt's Arachne (poetry). Lane 24
Runagate Runagate (poetry). Adams 3:71, Adoff 2:46, Adoff 3:120, Barksdale 677, Bell 61, Black 33, Chambers 165, Emanuel 485, Hayden 130, Henderson 157, Hughes 2:293, Jordon 38, Kearns 623, Pool 2:61, Randall 12, Randall 2:128, Robinson 2:203, Stanford 49, Turner 3:246, Turner 4:90
School integration riot (poetry). Pool 114, Pool 2:132
Smelt Fishing (poetry). Lane 25
Soledad (poetry). Lane 21
Speech (poetry). Brown 406, Kerlin 326
Summertime and the Living (poetry). Adoff 3:118, Hayden 2:115, Randall 2:103, Robinson 2:202
Those Winter Sundays (poetry). Adoff 2:10, Adoff 3:19, Jordan 21, Randall 15
Tour 5 (poetry). Adams 3:70, Barksdale 680, Bell 64, Chapman 439, Kearns 622, Long 569
Travelling Through Fog (poetry). Lane 24
Veracruz (poetry). Bontemps 2:119, Hill 2:578, Long 570
The Wheel (poetry). Randall 2:137

The Whipping (poetry). Adoff 2:8, Adoff 3:119, Randall 14, Weisman 44
Witch Doctor (poetry). Bontemps 2:110, Henderson 151, Miller, R. 395

HAYES, DONALD JEFFREY, 1904- . Poet
After All (poetry). Cullen 191
Alien (poetry). Bontemps 2:93
Appoggiatura (poetry). Adoff 3:94, Bontemps 2:90, Cunard 262, Hughes 2:246
Auf Wiedersehen (poetry). Cullen 189
Benediction (poetry). Bontemps 2:91, Hughes 2:248
Confession (poetry). Cullen 190
Haven (poetry). Bontemps 2:92, Hughes 2:245
Inscription (poetry). Cullen 188
Night (poetry). Cullen 189
Nocturne (poetry). Cullen 190
Pastourelle (poetry). Bontemps 2:94
Poet (poetry). Bontemps 2:92, Hughes 2:242
Prescience (poetry). Hughes 2:243, Patterson 4:164
This Place (poetry). Johnson, C. 57
Threnody (poetry). Bontemps 2:93

HAYFORD, GLADYS MAY CASELY, 1904- . Poet
Baby Cobina (poetry). Cullen 200
Nativity (poetry). Cullen 197
The Palm Wine Seller (poetry). Kerlin 288
Rainy Season Love Song (poetry). Cullen 198
The Serving Girl (poetry). Cullen 200

HAYNES, ALBERT E., JR., Poet
Eclipse (poetry). Jones 406, Major 58
The Law (poetry). Major 58

HAYNES, LEMUEL B., 1753-1833. Preacher
Universal Salvation—A Very Ancient Doctrine (sermon). Barksdale 227, Porter 448

HAYNES, SAMUEL A. Poet
The Challenge (poetry). Murphy 82
Warning (poetry). Murphy 80

HAYWOOD, CLARA H. Poet
Garden Ghosts (poetry). Murphy 3:69
I Am Too Much Loved (poetry). Murphy 3:70
I Saw Beauty (poetry). Murphy 3:70
Late Lesson (poetry). Murphy 3:70
Pity Me (poetry). Murphy 3:71

HEARD, NATHAN C., 1936- . Fiction Writer
Howard Street (excerpt—fiction). Robinson 2:143

HEATH, GORDON, 194?- . Poet
Two Songs of Love (poetry). Pool 115, Pool 2:115

HEMENWAY, ROBERT. Critic, Essayist
Zora Neale Hurston and the Eatonville Anthropology (essay). Bontemps 3:190

HENDERSON, DAVID. 1942- . Critic, Essayist, Poet
The Man Who Cried I Am: a Critique (essay). Gayle 2:365
Sly and the Family Stone (essay). Reed 97

Bopping (poetry). Miller, A. 102
Boston Road Blues (poetry). Davis, C. 364, Jones 233, Miller, A. 96
Do Nothing Till You Hear from Me (poetry). Adoff 3:419
Downtown-Boy Uptown (poetry). Hughes 99, Hughes 2:437, Singh 32
Elvin Jones Gretsch Freak (poetry). Henderson 264, Lowenfels 45
Felix of the Silent Forest (poetry). Miller, A. 95
Five Winters Ago (poetry). Jordan 27
Fork of the West River (5) (poetry). Miller, A. 103
4th Dimension (poetry). King 3:87
Hanging Out in the Music (poetry). King 3:85
Harlem Anthropology (poetry). Troupe 196
Keep on Pushing (poetry). Adoff 3:408, Davis, C. 359, Jones 239, Miller, R. 518
The Louisiana Weekly #4 (poetry). Adoff 3:421, Jordan 103
Neon Diaspora (poetry). Jones 230
Number 5—December (poetry). Jordan 84
Pentecostal Sunday/A Song of Power (poetry). Breman 463, Henderson 267
Poem for Painters (poetry). Wilentz 51
Psychedelic Fieman (poetry). Major 60
Riot Laugh and I Talk (poetry). Jordan 109
Sketches of Harlem (poetry). Hayden 2:223, Hughes 76, Hughes 2:437, Patterson 3:273
So We Went to Harlem (poetry). Miller, A. 104
They Are Killing All the Young Men (poetry). Adoff 3:414
Walk with de Mayor of Harlem (poetry). Adoff 3:412, King 3:82
White people (poetry). Adoff 3:420

HENDERSON, ELLIOT B. Poet
Git on Board, Chillun (poetry). Robinson 277
Trussey's Visit (poetry). Robinson 279
Uncle Ned an' de Mockin' Bird (poetry). Robinson 278

HENDERSON, GEORGE WYLIE, 1904- . Fiction Writer
Ollie Miss (excerpt: Dance—fiction). Brown 230

HENDERSON, MAE GWENDOLYN. Essayist
Portrait of Wallace Thurman (essay). Bontemps 3:147

HENDERSON, SHARON, Poet
Blue Jean Wearin Women??? (poetry). Exum 87

HENRY, LOIS-ALLISON. Autobiographer
Africa: Return and Turnabout (autobiography). Exum 144

HENSON, JOSIAH, 1789-1881. Autobiographer
Autobiography (excerpt: Home at Dawn—autobiography). Brown 711
The Life of Josiah Henson (excerpt: A Slave's Dilemma—autobiography). Freedman 69
Truth Stranger than Fiction (excerpt: Ch. VI—autobiography). Brawley 162

HERNDON, ANGELO, 1913- . Autobiographer
Let Me Live (excerpt: Georgia Trial—autobiography). Brown 777

HERNTON, CALVIN C., 1932- . Critic, Essayist, Poet, Short Fiction Writer
Dynamite Growing out of Their Skulls (essay). Jones 78

Scarecrow People (excerpt—fiction). Reed 109

A Being Exit in the World (poetry). Breman 2:28, Pool 118
A Black Stick with a Ball of Cotton for a Head and a Running Machine for a Mouth (poetry). Jones 210
Blues Spiritual (poetry). Breman 2:23
The Coming of Chronos to the House of Nightsong (excerpt—poetry). Breman 274
The Cosmic Age (poetry). Jones 219
D Blues (poetry). Adoff 3:244
The Distant Drum (poetry). Breman 2:26, Hughes 101, Jordan 97, Lomax 250, Miller, A. 34, Pool 117
Elements of Grammar (poetry). Major 64
Fall Down (poetry). Adoff 3:244, Miller, A. 34
Jitterbugging in the Streets (poetry). Adoff 3:240, Jones 205, Lowenfels 49
Madhouse (poetry). Adoff 2:17, Hayden 2:197, Hughes 102, Hughes 2:403, Jordan 81, Patterson 3:276
The Patient: Rockland County Sanitarium (poetry). Adoff 3:238
Remigrant (poetry). Breman 2:22
Thespian (poetry). Pool 117
Thief (poetry). Breman 2:27
The Underlying Strife (poetry). Breman 2:24
An Unexpurgated communiqué to David Henderson: London—1966 (poetry). Breman 272
West at bay (poetry). Breman 2:25
Young Negro Poet (poetry). Bontemps 2:193, Breman 2:21, Hayden 2:195

HERSKOVITS, MELVILLE, J. Essayist
The Negro's Americanism (essay). Locke 2:353

HIGGINS, DEWEY. Poet
Love (poetry). Bookers 78

HILL, ABRAM, 1911- . Playwright
Walk Hard (drama). Hatch 437

HILL, EDNA WHITE. Poet
Plea (poetry). Murphy 3:72

HILL, ELTON, 1950- . Poet
Theme Brown Girl (poetry). Major 71
To My Contemporaries in the Great American Universities (poetry). Alhamisi 110

HILL, ERROL, 1921- . Playwright, Editor, Essayist, Professor
Strictly Matrimony (drama). King 553

HILL, HERBERT, Editor
Reflections on Richard Wright: A Symposium on an Exiled Native Son (symposium). Gibson 2:58

HILL, JAMES H. Short Fiction Writer
A Captain Returns (short fiction). Ford 2:146
Comfort and Joy (short fiction). Ford 2:279
A Gust of Wind (short fiction). Ford 2:273

HILL, LESLIE PINCKNEY, 1880-1960. Playwright, Poet
Armageddon (poetry). Kerlin 135
Christmas at Melrose (poetry). Johnson 153, White 200
L'Envoi (poetry). Cromwell 35
Freedom (poetry). Dreer 49, White 197
I Have a Song (poetry). Kerlin 133
Lines on Leadership (poetry). Cromwell 35
Mater Dolorosa (poetry). Kerlin 134
My life were lost if I should keep (first line—poetry). Kerlin 52
Self-determination (The Philosophy of the American Negro) (poetry). Kerlin 137, White 198
So Quietly (poetry). Adams 3:66, Adoff 2:65, Adoff 3:14, Brown 338, Freedman 127, Johnson 156, White 197
Spring (poetry). White 203
Summer Magic (poetry). Dreer 49, Johnson 155
The Symphony (poetry). White 202
The Teacher (poetry). Dreer 50, Hughes 2:52, Johnson 156
To a Caged Canary in a Negro Restaurant (poetry). Kerlin 136
To a Nobly-gifted Singer (poetry). Kerlin 137
To the Smartweed (poetry). White 199
Tuskegee (poetry). Brown 339, Hughes 2:53, Johnson 153, White 196
Wings of Oppression (excerpts—poetry). Kerlin 133, White 195

HILL, PAMELA WOODRUFF. Poet
Untitled (To Smell the stink of rotting brownstones) (first line—poetry). Henderson 318

HILL, QUENTIN, 1950- . Poet
Time Poem (poetry). Major 68

HILL, TIMOTHY ARNOLD, 1888-1947. Essayist
Phantom Color Lines (essay). Johnson, C. 100

HILL, WILLIAM ALLYN. Poet
Autumn Song (poetry). Cuney 22
Comprehension (poetry). Cuney 21
Confession (poetry). Cuney 22
Night Walks Down the Mountain (poetry). Cuney 20
To a Young Suicide (poetry). Cuney 21
To an Ecclesiast I Know (poetry). Cuney 22

HIMES, CHESTER, 1909- . Autobiographer, Critic, Fiction Writer
Dilemma of the Negro Novelist in the U. S. (essay). Chapman 2:394, Williams 51
Lonely Crusade (excerpt—fiction). Hill 2:210
Pink Toes (excerpt: Excursion in Paradox—fiction). Kearns 594, Miller, R. 449
Third Generation (excerpt: Rape—fiction). Davis 481
Mama's Missionary Money (short fiction). Clarke 170
Marihuana and a Pistol (short fiction). Chambers 115, Hughes 3:104
The Morning After (short fiction). Margolies 323
The Night's For Cryin' (short fiction). Brown 101
Salute to the Passing (short fiction). Barksdale 620
So Softly Smiling (short fiction). Clarke 3:99

HINER, EDNA. Poet
The Paper Boy (poetry). Bookers 124

HINES, CARL WENDELL, JR., 1940- . Poet
Jazz poem (poetry). Chambers 293
Now that he is safely dead (poetry). Breman 431
Two Jazz Poems (poetry). Bontemps 2:184, Hayden 2:227

HITE, VERNOY E. Poet
Malcolm X (poetry). Murphy 2:49
Trapped (poetry). Murphy 2:50

HOAGLAND, EVERETT, 1942- . Poet
The Anti-Semanticist (poetry). Chapman 2:263, Randall 2:314
For Ann (poetry). Troupe 245
Georgia—It's the Gospel Truth (poetry). Brooks 71
Hokku (poetry). Troupe 330

(HOAGLAND, EVERETT)
It's a Terrible Thing! (poetry). Randall 2:315
love child—a black aesthetic (poetry). Randall 2:312
My Spring Thing (poetry). Randall 2:313
Night Interpreted (poetry). Major 70
Prologue (poetry). Brooks 70

HOLLOWAY, JOHN WESLEY, 1865-1935. Poet
Black Mammies (poetry). Johnson 138
Calling the Doctor (poetry). Johnson 135, White 186
The Corn Song (poetry). Johnson 136, White 187
Discouraged (poetry). White 184
Miss Melerlee (poetry). Hughes 2:19, Johnson 134
Plowin' Cane (poetry). White 185

HOLLOWAY, LUCY ARIEL WILLIAMS, 1905- . Poet
Northboun' (poetry). Black 30, Brown 377, Cullen 201, Johnson 288.

HOLMAN, MOSES CARL, 1919- . Playwright, Poet
An Afternoon of a Young Poet (essay). Hill 138

And on This Shore (poetry). Adoff 3:175, Bontemps 2:148, Hughes 2:364
Intoxication (poetry). Murphy 3:72
Judas Iscariot (poetry). Murphy 3:73
Letter across Doubt and Distance (poetry). Bontemps 2:150, Hughes 2:363
Mr. Z (poetry). Adams 3:30, Hayden 2:166, Hill 2:586
Notes for a Movie Script (poetry). Adoff 3:174, Bontemps 2:151, Hayden 2:163, Hughes 2:362
Picnic: The Liberated (poetry). Adams 3:74, Adoff 3:176, Freedman 197, Hill 2:582, Hughes 2:367
Song (poetry). Bontemps 2:152, Hayden 2:164, Hughes 2:361, Jordan 86
Three Brown Girls Singing (poetry). Hayden 2:165, Hill 2:585

HOLMES, ETHLYNNE E. Poet
Butterfly (poetry). Murphy 3:75
Happiness (poetry). Murphy 3:75

HOLMES, GLEN. Poet
The Golden Stool (poetry). Murphy 83

HOLMES, R. ERNEST, 1943- . Poet, Short Fiction Writer
Black Lady in an Afro Hairdo Cheers for Cassius (poetry). Coombs 65
Black Woman (poetry). Coombs 66
Two From the Country (poetry). Coombs 67

Cheesy, Baby (short fiction). Coombs 2:41

HOLOWAY, L. A. W. Poet. See HOLLOWAY, LUCY ARIEL WILLIAMS

HOLTZCLAW, WILLIAM H. Autobiographer
The Black Man's Burden (excerpt—autobiography). Freedman 107

HONIGMAN, ROBERT. Poet
Green Pears (poetry). Ten 35
I Hear The Soul Of A Murderer Tonight (poetry). Ten 36
Three Poems On War (poetry). Ten 36

HOPE, LEZLI. Poet
His Own Maniac Self (poetry). Exum 90
Lovesigns (poetry). Exum 88
Music Screams in the Mind (poetry). Exum 91
Ode (poetry). Exum 89

HORNE, FRANK M., 1899- . Poet, Critic, Autobiographer, Short Fiction Writer
Arabesque (poetry). Johnson, C. 99
Balm in Gilead—a Christmas jingle, played with trumpets and muffled drums (poetry). Pool 2:209
I never saw him before—a Mississippi Folk Song (poetry). Pool 2:120
Immortality (poetry). Johnson 278
Kid Stuff (poetry). Adoff 3:56, Bontemps 41, Chapman 401, Hayden 2:67, Hughes 2:148, Patterson 3:157, Pool 119
Letters Found Near a Suicide (poetry). Cullen 114, Hayden 2:65, Hughes 2:151, Pool 120, Randall 2:71
Letters Found Near a Suicide (excerpt: To James—poetry). Hayden 2:65, Randall 2:73
Mama (poetry). Randall 2:76
More Letters Found Near a Suicide (poetry). Johnson 270
Nigger (poetry). Brown 378, Calverton 207, Chapman 402, Cullen 120, Johnson 268, Kerlin 207
Notes Found Near a Suicide (poetry). Adoff 3:48, Bontemps 2:42
On Seeing Two Brown Boys in a Catholic Church (poetry). Adoff 3:55, Black 13, Cullen 112, Hughes 2:146, Johnson 276, Kerlin 206, Lomax 212
Patience (poetry). Randall 2:77
Resurrection (poetry). Adoff 3:56
Symphony (poetry). Bontemps 2:51
To a Persistent Phantom (poetry). Bontemps 2:50, Cullen 113, Johnson 277
To Chick (poetry). Randall 2:71
To You (poetry). Randall 2:72
Toast (poetry). Hughes 2:150, Johnson 277
Walk (poetry). Randall 2:75
Youth (poetry). Johnson, C. 129

HORTON, GEORGE MOSES, 1797-1883. Poet
Hope of Liberty (excerpt: Explanation—essay). Brawley 112

(HORTON, GEORGE MOSES)
An Acrostic for Julia Shepard (poetry). Davis 35
Art of a Poet (poetry). Long 43, Robinson 24
Creditor to his Proud Debtor (poetry). Davis 35
Eye of Love (poetry). Turner 3:176, Turner 4:20
George Moses Horton, Myself (poetry). Brawley 122, Brown 287, Hayden 2:9, Miller, R. 103
The Hope of Liberty (excerpts—poetry). Porter 581
Jefferson in a Tight Place (poetry). Davis 39
Letter to Mr. Horace Greeley (poetry). Davis 40
Like Brothers We Meet (poetry). Davis 40
Love (poetry). Brawley 120, Davis 36, Miller, R. 101
Lover's Farewell (poetry). Robinson 19
Meditation on a Cold, Dark and Rainy Night (poetry). White 34
On Hearing of the Intention of a Gentleman to Purchase the Poet's Freedom (poetry). Barksdale 221, Brawley 117, Robinson 23
On Liberty and Slavery (poetry). Brawley 114, Breman 24, Brown 288, Davis 37, Hayden 2:10, Hughes 2:11, Miller, R. 102, Patterson 3:93
On Spring (poetry). Brawley 118
On the Truth of the Savior (poetry). Brawley 120
Poem by a Slave (excerpt—poetry). Kerlin 26
The Poet's Fable Petition (poetry). Breman 26
Powers of Love (poetry). Turner 3:174, Turner 4:18
Praise of Creation (poetry). White 35
The Setting Sun (poetry). Turner 3:176, Turner 4:20
Slavery (poetry). Barksdale 220, Long 44, Robinson 21
Slave's Complaint (poetry). Barksdale 221, Brawley 116, Robinson 22
The Swan-Vain Pleasures (poetry). Turner 3:173, Turner 4:17
To a Departing Favorite (poetry). Turner 3:175, Turner 4:19
To Eliza (poetry). Brown 290, Davis 38, Long 42, Robinson 20

HOUSE, EDDIE "SON." Poet
Dry Spell Blues (poetry). Henderson 113

HOUSE, G. L. Poet
Poem (They Already Dance to Our Drums) (first line—poetry). Alhamisi 113
They already dance to our drums (first line—poetry). Alhamisi 113
Woman (poetry). Alhamisi 112

HOUSTON, VIRGINIA. Poet
Couplet (poetry). Murphy 3:76

For H. M. G. (poetry). Murphy 3:76
Fugit Amor (poetry). Murphy 3:77
Interim (poetry). Murphy 3:77
Query (poetry). Murphy 3:78
Recapitulation (poetry). Murphy 3:78

HOWARD, FLORETTA. Poet, Playwright
On a Colored Doll (poetry). Dreer 53
'Round the Nedghborhood (poetry). Dreer 53

HOWARD, VANESSA, 1955- . Poet, Short Fiction Writer
Monument in Black (poetry). Jordan 3
Reflections (poetry). Jordan 2

HOWARD, VILMA. Poet
Interview with Ralph Ellison (Interview; with Alfred Chester). Patterson 3:291
The Citizen (poetry). Hughes 58

HUFF, WILLIAM HENRY. Poet
Graduating (poetry). Weisman 78

HUGHES, JAMES C. Poet
Apology for Wayward Jim (poetry—excerpt). Kerlin 188
Aspiration (poetry). Kerlin 188

HUGHES, LANGSTON, 1902-1967. Poet, Playwright, Fiction Writer, Critic, Editor, Autobiographer
The Big Sea (excerpt—autobiography). Adoff 4:44
The Big Sea (excerpt: Harlem Literati—autobiography). Barksdale 524, Kendricks 202
The Big Sea (excerpt: I've Known Rivers—autobiography). Barksdale 522
The Big Sea (excerpt: Salvation—autobiography). Patterson 3:142, Shuman 111
I Wonder As I Wander (excerpt: Moscow Movie—autobiography). Hill 2:106

Don't You Want to Be Free? (drama). Hatch 262
Emperor of Haiti (drama). Turner 5:48
Limitations of Life (drama). Hatch 655
Little Ham (drama). Hatch 775
Mother and Child (drama). King 399
Simply Heavenly (drama). Patterson 2:175
Soul Gone Home (drama). Miller, R. 255

Fooling Our White Folks (essay). Turner 2:81, Turner 3:82
Go South, Young Man, Go South (essay). Gayle 105
In Love With Harlem (essay). Adoff 4:41
Making Poetry Pay (essay). Ford 148
The Negro Artist and the Racial Mountain (essay). Davis, C. 159, Gayle 2:258, Gayle 3:167, Gibson 2:225
What the Negro Wants (essay). Watkins 262
Writers: Black and White (essay). Chapman 618, Conference 41, Patterson 3:281

Not Without Laughter (excerpt: Guitar—fiction). Brown 224

(HUGHES, LANGSTON)
Simple's Uncle Sam (excerpt: Census—fiction). Rose 178
Simples' Uncle Sam (excerpt: Color Problems—fiction). Patterson 3:144
African question mark (poetry). Hollo 21
Afro-American Fragment (poetry). Chapman 425, Stanford 4
Always The Same (poetry). Cunard 263
American Heartbreak (poetry). Randall 2:87
Angola Question Mark (poetry). Lomax 230, Pool 127, Randall 2:89
As I Grew Older (poetry). Adams 3:12, Chapman 426, Ford 142, Johnson 240, Weisman 4
Ask Your Mama (poetry). Hill 2:589, Pool 2:95
Aunt Sue's Stories (poetry). Cromwell 18
Azikiwe in Jail (poetry). Cuney 29
Backlash Blues (poetry). Davis, C. 267, Randall 2:90, Robinson 2:197
Ballad of a Man that's Gone (poetry). Black 21
Ballad of the Landlord (poetry). Adams 3:83, Barksdale 521, Chapman 432
Birmingham Sunday (poetry). Davis, C. 268, Hughes 2:200
Black Panther (poetry). Kearns 2:147
Blues in Stereo (poetry). Hill 2:587
Border Line (poetry). Patterson 3:160
Bound No'th Blues (poetry). Barksdale 520, Bontemps 2:65, Davis 308
Brass Spittoons (poetry). Baker 197, Barksdale 520, Bontemps 2:61, Ford 141, Johnson 234
Cabaret (poetry). Cromwell 20
Cat and the Saxophone (poetry). Davis 303
Children's Rhymes (poetry). Adams 3:104, Chapman 428, Hill 2:596, Randall 2:86
Christ in Alabama (poetry). Adoff 3:73
College Formal: Renaissance Casino (poetry). Cuney 25, Turner 3:227, Turner 4:71
Corner Meeting (poetry). Adoff 31
Cross (poetry). Adoff 2:6, Adoff 3:73, Barksdale 519, Bell 39, Bontemps 2:62, Davis 304, Johnson 236, Weisman 60
Crowns and Garlands (poetry). Adams 3:35
Cultural Exchange (poetry). Adoff 3:76, Hughes 2:203, Randall 2:83
Daybreak in Alabama (poetry). Chapman 427, Davis, C. 268, Ford 141, Kearns 533
Death in Yorkville (poetry). Adoff 3:79
Desert (poetry). Hayden 2:91
Desire (poetry). Murphy 3:79
Dinner Guest: Me (poetry). Kearns 2:103, Randall 2:78
Dive (poetry). Adoff 51
The dove (poetry). Hollo 21
Draftees (poetry). Cuney 25
Dream Boogie (poetry). Barksdale 522, Chapman 428, Ford 142, Hill 2:593
A Dream Deferred (poetry). Adoff 3:76, Ford 142

A Dream Deferred (excerpts—poetry). Miller, R. 382
Dream Variation (poetry). Adams 3:41, Adoff 2:100, Adoff 3:74, Baker 196, Barksdale 518, Bontemps 2:66, Chapman 427, Cromwell 19, Cullen 149, Davis, C. 181, Hollo 21, Hughes 2:183, Jordan 129, Locke 2:143, Long 428, Turner 3:224, Turner 4:68
The Dreamer (poetry). Johnson, C. 36
Dreams (poetry). Dreer 55, Weisman 84
An Earth Song (poetry). Locke 2:142
Epilogue (poetry). Turner '3:225, Turner 4:69
Esthete in Harlem (poetry). Johnson 239, Randall 2:57
Evenin' Air Blues (poetry). Emanuel 207
Fantasy in Purple (poetry). Cullen 148, Johnson 242
Feet o' Jesus (poetry). Patterson 3:159
Final Call (poetry). Robinson 2:199
Florida Road Workers (poetry). Cunard 263
For Billie Holiday (poetry). Murphy 87
Frederick Douglass: 1817-1895 (poetry). Randall 2:87
Freedom (poetry). Adoff 3:78
Freedom ride (poetry). Pool 2:180
Freedom Train (poetry). Adams 3:92
From Selma (poetry). Murphy 88
Good Morning (poetry). Baker 199
Goodbye, Christ (poetry). Cunard 264
Grandma (poetry). Pool 126
Hard Daddy (poetry). Johnson 238
Harlem (poetry). Adoff 32, Bell 42, Chapman 430, Demarest 360, Hill 2:600, Hughes 2:199, Kearns 537, Margolies 183, Patterson 3:158, Robinson 2:196, Stanford 200, Troupe 147
Harlem Sweeties (poetry). Hughes 2:190, Lomax 227
Havana Dreams (poetry). Hughes 2:189
Heaven (poetry). Cuney 24, Weisman 80
High to Low (poetry). Davis 310, Kearns 536
Homesick Blues (poetry). Cullen 147
A House in Taos (poetry). Cullen 152, Cuney 30
House in the World (poetry). Cunard 263
I Dream a World (poetry). Bontemps 2:71, Randall 10, Weisman 72
I Thought It Was Tangiers I Wanted (poetry). Hughes 2:196
I, Too, Sing America (poetry). Adoff 2:75, Adoff 3:75, Baker 194, Barksdale 519, Bell 40, Bontemps 2:64, Calverton 210, Cullen 145, Freedman 143, Hayden 117, Hayden 2:86, Hughes 2:182, Kendricks 236, Kerlin 203, Locke 2:145, Patterson 3:160, Singh 8, Stanford 103, Weisman 71
Impasse (poetry). Adams 3:116, Stanford 216
Island (poetry). Baker 201
Jazz Band in a Parisian Cabaret (poetry). Johnson 239
Jazzonia (poetry). Baker 198, Barksdale

(HUGHES, LANGSTON)
518, Bontemps 2:63, Davis, C. 181, Hayden 2:87, Henderson 128, Johnson 236, Locke 2:226

Jazztet Muted (poetry). Hill 2:592

Joy (poetry). Dreer 55

Juke Box Love Song (poetry). Adoff 2:14, Adoff 3:74, Cuney 26, Demarest 101, Kearns 2:9

Junior Addict (poetry). Breman 81, Randall 2:85

Justice (poetry). Randall 2:87

Ku Klux (poetry). Randall 2:81

Late Corner (poetry). Hayden 2:93

Laughers (poetry). Henderson 125

Lennox Avenue Bar (poetry). Kearns 543

Lennox Avenue Mural (poetry). Bontemps 2:67, Breman 77, Chambers 153, Davis, C. 263

Lennox Avenue Mural (excerpt: Good Morning—poetry). Rose 234

Lennox Avenue Mural (excerpt: Harlem—poetry). Black 21, Rose 233

Lennox Avenue Mural (excerpt: Same in Blues—poetry). Rose 234

Let America Be America Again (excerpt—poetry). Brown 370, Hughes 2:193, Kerlin 321-2

Letter (poetry). Baker 200

Life Is Fine (poetry). Randall 9

Lincoln University 1954 (poetry). Cuney 24

Little Song on Housing (poetry). Robinson 2:199

Low to High (poetry). Davis 309

Lumumba's Grave (poetry). Troupe 58

Madam and Her Madam (poetry). Turner 3:228, Turner 4:72

Me and the Mule (poetry). Adoff 2:3, Haslam 283, Stanford 268

Mellow (poetry). Kearns 2:177

Merry-Go-Round (poetry). Adams 3:95, Black 20, Hughes 2:192, Patterson 3:158, Weisman 61

Militant (poetry). Adoff 3:80

Minstrel Man (poetry). Brown 370, Davis, C. 180, Locke 2:144

Montmartre (poetry). Baker 198, Hayden 2:90

Moscow (poetry). Murphy 3:79

Mother to Son (poetry). Barksdale 518, Bell 38, Black 19, Bontemps 2:67, Cromwell 19, Cullen 151, Cuney 32, Davis 306, Dreer 57, Ford 141, Henderson 126, Hughes 2:186, Jordan 19, Lomax 225, Patterson 3:160, Weisman 82

Motto (poetry). Adams 3:42, Adoff 3:75, Davis 309, Hughes 2:202, Jordan 118, Stanford 206

Mulatto (poetry). Calverton 211, Emanuel 204, Kerlin 249

My People (poetry). Breman 75, Jordan 18, Patterson 3:159

The Negro (poetry). Kerlin 202

Negro Dancers (poetry). Davis 303

The Negro Mother (poetry). Demarest 149, Emanuel 206

The Negro Speaks of Rivers (poetry). Adams 3:52, Adoff 2:24, Adoff 3:72, Baker 193, Barksdale 517, Bell 38, Black 20, Bontemps 2:63, Breman 76, Brown 366, Cullen 149, Cuney 33, Davis 307, Emanuel 204, Ford 141, Freedman 3, Hayden 116, Henderson 129, Hughes 2:187, Johnson 241, Kendricks 236, Kerlin 201, Locke 2:141, Lomax 225, Margolies 5, Patterson 3:159, Randall 2:78, Weisman 3

Night and Morn (poetry). Dreer 56

Night Funeral in Harlem (poetry). Hill 2:598

Nude Young Dancers (poetry). Davis, C. 182, Locke 2:227

October 16 (poetry). Adoff 3:78, Murphy 3:80

One-Way Ticket (poetry). Baker 196, Patterson 3:159

Oppression (poetry). Cuney 28

Our Land (poetry). Davis, C. 179, Locke 2:144

Pain in One (poetry). Pool 126

Parade (poetry). Hill 2:594

Passing (poetry). Singh 9

Pattern (poetry). Murphy 3:79

Peace (poetry). Randall 2:82

Pennsylvania Station (poetry). Bontemps 2:71, Hayden 2:88

Personal (poetry). Bontemps 2:66, Hughes 2:188

Po' Boy Blues (poetry). Bell 41, Johnson 237, Kerlin 247

Poem: The night is beautiful (poetry). Cromwell 17, Cullen 150

Poem (We Have Tomorrow). (poetry). Cromwell 17, Kerlin 246, Locke 2:142

Poet to Bigot (poetry). Cuney 29

Prayer (poetry). Cullen 146

Prime (poetry). Adoff 3:76, Robinson 2:196

Puzzled (poetry). Davis 308

Question and Answer (poetry). Randall 2:89

Railroad Avenue (poetry). Kearns 534

Refugee in America (poetry). Baker 194

Roland Hayes Beaten (Georgia 1942) (poetry). Kearns 534, Pool 2:163

Ruby Brown (poetry). Davis 304

Same in Blues (poetry). Baker 199, Chambers 154, Chapman 431, Ford 143, Hill 2:431

Sea Charm (poetry). Cromwell 17

Silhouette (poetry). Baker 195, Kearns 2:115

Slum Dreams (poetry). Ford 142

Song (poetry). Locke 2:143

Song for a Banjo Dance (poetry). Henderson 127

Song for a Dark Girl (poetry). Adams 3:65, Adoff 2:67, Adoff 3:73, Barksdale 5:20, Brown 639, Calverton 211, Cullen 147, Kerlin 250

(HUGHES, LANGSTON)

Song for a Negro Wash-woman (poetry). Brown 373, Long 426

Song for a Suicide (poetry). Hughes 2:198

Special Bulletin (poetry). Adoff 3:80

Spirituals (poetry). Singh 11

Still Hue (poetry). Randall 2:83, Robinson 2:198

Subway Rush Hour (poetry). Kearns 537

Suicide (poetry). Kerlin 247

Suicide's Note (poetry). Cullen 151

Sylvester's Dying Bed (poetry). Barksdale 521

Theme for English B (poetry). Chapman 429, Davis 305, Demarest 171, Hayden 114, Kearns 535, Turner 3:226, Turner 4:70

Third Degree (poetry). Randall 2:80

To Cerain Negro Leaders (poetry). Cunard 263

To Midnight Nan at Leroy's (poetry). Brown 368

Troubled Woman (poetry). Baker 195, Cromwell 18, Patterson 3:159

Trumpet Player—52nd Street (poetry). Cuney 27, Lomax 226, Pool 124, Pool 2:105, Singh 10

Two Somewhat Different Epigrams (poetry). Hayden 2:89

Un-American Investigators (poetry). Randall 2:79

Undertow (poetry). Baker 201

Variation (poetry). Bontemps 66

Warning (poetry). Randall 2:91

The Weary Blues (poetry). Barksdale 519, Bell 39, Black 18, Brown 367, Calverton 213, Dreer 56, Hughes 2:184, Turner 3:225, Turner 4:69

When Sue Wears Red (poetry). Black 20, Henderson 126, Lomax 228, Patterson 3:158, Patterson 4:48, Pool 125

Where, When, Which? (poetry). Hayden 2:92, Randall 2:88

Who But the Lord (poetry). Randall 2:81, Robinson 2:198

Wisdom and War (poetry). Murphy 88

Without Benefit of Declaration (poetry). Bontemps 2:72, Lomax 229

Words Like Freedom (poetry). Randall 2:87, Robinson 2:198

Young Gal's Blues (poetry). Brown 369, Long 425

Youth (poetry). Cuney 33, Freedman 235, Locke 2:142, Weisman 68

The Best of Simple (excerpt: Minnie Again—short fiction). Long 433

Bombs in Barcelona (short fiction). Davis 318

Bop (short fiction). Chapman 103

Census (short fiction). Chapman 105

Christmas Song (short fiction). Turner 68, Turner 3:358

Coffee Break (short fiction). Chapman 106

Cora Unashamed (short fiction). James 120

Cracker Prayer (short fiction). Chapman 108

Dear Mr. Butts (short fiction). Barksdale 521, Emanuel 214, Stanford 282

Early Autumn (short fiction). King 2:183

Feet Live Their Own Life (short fiction). Chapman 99

Gumption (short fiction). Stanford 154

Jazz, Jive and Jam (short fiction). Emanuel 217, Haslam 283

Last Whipping (short fiction). Turner 65, Turner 3:355

Little Dog (short fiction). Gibson 12

Name In Print (short fiction). Kearns 2:297, Williams 59

Not Without Laughter (excerpt: The Doors of Life—short fiction). Long 429

On the Road (short fiction). Adams 2:115, Emanuel 209, Stanford 150

On the Way Home (short fiction). Burnett 158

One Friday Morning (short fiction). Clarke 114, Rose 274, Watkins 30

Picture for Her Dresser (short fiction). Davis 314

Promulgations (short fiction). Chapman 110

Rock, Church (short fiction). Hill 2:231, Margolies 244

Simple Prays a Prayer (short fiction). Ford 146

Simple Stakes a Claim (excerpt: Big Round World—short fiction). Turner 6:77

Slave on the Block (short fiction). Brown 89

Soul Food (short fiction). Freedman 212, Hayden 13

Tales of Simple (excerpt: Coffee Break—short fiction). Rose 179

Temptation (short fiction). Chapman 101, Kearns 541

Thank you, M'am (short fiction). Chambers 253, Hughes 3:70, Singh 57, Stanford 203, Turner 62, Turner 3:352

A Toast to Harlem (short fiction). Kearns 538

Tragedy at Hampton (short fiction). Ford 147

Trouble with the Angels (short fiction). Ford 143

Who's Passing for Who? (short fiction). Clarke 3:109, Davis 311, Stanford 105

Why, You Reckon? (short fiction). James 184

Epigram. Poem by Armand Lanusse, translated by L. Hughes (translation). Hill 2:603

Flute Players. Poem by Jean Joseph Rabearivels (Madagascar), Translated by L. Hughes (translation). Hill 2:605

She Left Herself One Evening. Poem by Leon Damas (French Guiana), translated by L. Hughes (translation). Hill 2:604

HUGHES, LOIS ROYAL. Poet

I Could Not Know (poetry). Murphy 90

Let There Be Three of Us (poetry). Murphy 3:80

(HUGHES, LOIS ROYAL)
Like Unto a Rose (poetry). Murphy 89
Rendezvous (poetry). Murphy 89
To Death (poetry). Murphy 3:82
The Veil (poetry). Murphy 3:81

HUNT, TED. Poet
I Am a Man (poetry). Henderson 319

HUNTER, ELEANOR C. Poet
Frustration (poetry). Murphy 3:83

HUNTER, KRISTIN, 1931- . Fiction Writer
Debut (short fiction). Turner 131, Turner 3:421
An Interesting Social Study (short fiction). Hughes 3:332

HUNTLEY, ELIZABETH MADDOX. Dramatist
Legion, the Demoniac (drama). Dreer 306

HURSTON, ZORA NEAL, 1903-1960. Fiction Writer, Playwright, Autobiographer
Dust Tracks on a Road (excerpt: Backstage and the Railroad—autobiography). Dreer 132
Dust Tracks on a Road (excerpt: Wandering—autobiography). Long 448

Lawrence of the River (biography). Watkins 433

The First One (drama). Johnson, C. 53

Their Eyes Were Watching God (excerpt: Hurricane—fiction). Brown 244
Their Eyes Were Watching God (excerpt: The Return—fiction). Patterson 3:138

Drenched in Light (short fiction). Cromwell 112
Folk Tales (short fiction). Davis 454
The Gilded Six-Bits (short fiction). Barksdale 613, Burnett 129, Clarke 63, Hughes 3:74, Watkins 65
Spunk (short fiction). James 86, Locke 2:105
Sweat (short fiction). Turner 50, Turner 3:340

HURT, MISSISSIPPI JOHN. Poet
Stack O'Lee Blues (poetry). Henderson 106

HYDE, EVANS. Short Fiction Writer
How He Went (short fiction). Bookers 108

HYMAN, MARK. Short Fiction Writer
The Shepherd (short fiction). Ford 2:49

ICEBERG SLIM. See BECK, ROBERT.

IFETAYO, FEMI FUMNI. See MICOU, REGINA.

IMAMU AMIRI BARAKA. See JONES, LE ROI

IMAN, KASISI YUSEF. Poet, Playwright, Singer, Actor
Love Your Enemy (poetry). Jones 387, Lomax 258, Randall 2:293
Show Me, Lord, Show Me (poetry). Jones 386

ISHAK, ELTON HILL-ABU. See HILL, ELTON.

JACKMAN, MARVIN E. Poet, Playwright, Essayist
The Black Bird (drama). Bullins 2:110
Flowers for the Trashman (drama). Jones 541

Islam and Black Art—An Interview with Ameer Baraka (interview). Alhamisi 141

Al asil suddi—the origin of blackness (poetry). Breman 498
Al Fitnah Mukajri (poetry). Alhamisi 138
Blues For Lucifer (poetry). Lowenfels 57
Burn, Baby, Burn (poetry). Jones 269
Did You Vote Nigger (poetry). Alhamisi 139
Proverbs (poetry). Brooks 155
Soul on ice (poetry). Breman 497
That Old Time Religion (poetry). Jones 268
Till the Sun Goes Down (poetry). Brooks 155

JACKSON, BLYDEN, 1910- . Critic, Essayist, Editor
The Negro's Image of the Universe as Reflected in His Fiction (excerpt—essay). Chapman 623, Turner 6:85
The Negro's Negro in Negro Literature (essay). Singh 299
A Word About Simple (essay). Gibson 2:183

JACKSON, C. BERNARD, 1927- . Playwright
Fly Blackbird (drama with Hatch, James). Hatch 671, Reardon 137

JACKSON, ELAINE. Playwright
Toe Jam (drama). King 641

JACKSON, GERALD. Poet
Poem to Americans (poetry). Lowenfels 58
The Song (for Kevin) (poetry). Breman 381

JACKSON, JAMES THOMAS. Essayist, Poet, Short Fiction Writer
Some Notes on Frederick Douglass . . . (essay). Schulberg 171

Shade of Darkness (excerpt—fiction). Schulberg 156

Jean (poetry). Schulberg 169

Reveille (short fiction). Schulberg 149

JACKSON, KATHERINE. Poet
Congenital (poetry). Johnson, C. 135

JACKSON, MAE, 1946- . Poet, Short Fiction Writer
The Blues Today (poetry). Adoff 3:496
For Some Poets (poetry). Adoff 3:497
i remember (poetry). Adoff 3:498
i used to wrap my white doll up in (poetry). Adoff 3:498
January 3, 1970 (poetry). Adoff 3:499
Just One in a Series (poetry). Exum 93
Night (poetry). Exum 92
Please (poetry). King 3:90
Poems for the Lonely (poetry). King 3:91
reincarnation (poetry). Adoff 3:498
(To Someone I Met on 125th Street, 1966) (poetry). Exum 93

JACKSON MARSHA ANN. Poet
In Between Time (Transience) (poetry). Murphy 2:52
Tears and a Dream (poetry). Murphy 2:53

JACKSON, MAURICE SHELLEY. Poet
No End to the Limit (poetry). Bookers 98
Old Lang Hughes (poetry). Bookers 101

JACOBUS, LEE A. Critic
Imamu Amiri Baraka: the Quest for Moral Order (essay). Gibson 3:112

JAMESON, GLADYS M. Poet
Idyll (poetry). Johnson, C. 135

JAMISON, ROSCOE CONKLING,. 1888-1918. Poet
Castles in the Air (poetry). Kerlin 193
The Edict (poetry). Kerlin 194
Hopelessness (poetry). Kerlin 195
The Negro Soldiers (poetry). Johnson 195
A Song (poetry). Kerlin 193

JASPER, JOHN J. 1812-1893. Preacher
De Sun Do Move (sermon). Miller, R. 128

JEFFERS, LANCE, 1919- . Poet, Short Fiction Writer, Essayist, Critic
Afroamerican literature: the Conscience of Man (essay). Chapman 2:506

Witherspoon (excerpt—fiction). Shuman 132

Awakened by a Woman's Cedared Thighs (poetry). Shuman 2:135
Black Bourgeoisie (poetry). Shuman 2:139
The Black Folk Arrest Their Blackness (poetry). Shuman 2:134
Black Soul of the Land (poetry). Henderson 199, Jones 275, Troupe 2:34
Blue Eyes Were the Foundry (poetry). Shuman 2:143
Bombs on Asian Flesh Descending (poetry). Shuman 2:124
Breath in My Nostrils (poetry). Henderson 201
Children and a Fetus (poetry). Shuman 2:144
Cruelty (poetry). Shuman 2:140

A Dark and Sudden Beauty (poetry). Adams 3:39, Shuman 2:126
De La Beckwith and the Bombers (poetry). Shuman 2:131
The Fire That Laid Her Mad (poetry). Shuman 332
Gift of Horses (poetry). Shuman 2:135
Grief Streams Down My Chest (poetry). Adoff 3:173, Chapman 474
How High the Moon (poetry). Adoff 3:172, Henderson 200, Pool 130
How Many Poets Scrub the River's Back? (poetry). Shuman 332
Human Life (poetry). Shuman 2:132
Humiliation (poetry). Shuman 2:121
I Am the Record of Man (poetry). Shuman 2:117
I do not know the power of my hand (poetry). Chapman 2:266
I Make a Nation (poetry). Shuman 335, Shuman 2:122
I Sing My People (poetry). Shuman 2:136, Troupe 2:32
I Spread These Flaps of Flesh and Fly (poetry). Henderson 201
I Strongly Sweep (poetry). Shuman 2:117
I Touch the Past (poetry). Shuman 334
Let My Last Breath Be Immortal (poetry). Shuman 336, Shuman 2:134
Listening to Bach (poetry). Shuman 2:141
Loneliness and Madness (poetry). Shuman 2:130
Man with a Furnace in his Hand (poetry). Jones 276, Troupe 2:35
My Blackness Is the Beauty of This Land (poetry). Adoff 3:173, Henderson 198, Jones 273, Major 72, Troupe 2:33
My Father (poetry). Shuman 333
My Music, My Music! (poetry). Shuman 2:142
My Storm-Shook Belly Must Hide a Prodigy (poetry). Shuman 2:143
Myself (poetry). Breman 178, Troupe 2:31
A Negro Girl: Echo of that Older Mother's Moan (poetry). Shuman 2:127
The Night Rains Hot Tar (poetry). Chapman 473, Shuman 2:141
Old Love Butchered (Colorado Springs and Huachuca) (poetry). Chapman 2:265
On Listening to the Spirituals (poetry). Adoff 3:173, Chapman 474, Davis 769, Shuman 2:118
Prison (poetry). Shuman 2:120
The Quarrel (poetry). Shuman 2:137
Sandals (poetry). Shuman 336
She Wears a Dress (poetry). Shuman 2:128
Sitinner (poetry). Shuman 2:119
So Deep in Rivers of That Stromsberg Time (poetry). Shuman 2:125
Song (poetry). Shuman 2:129
The Strong-Backed Whore (poetry). Shuman 2:124
Tearsplotches for My Children (poetry). Shuman 2:144
There is a nation (poetry). Chapman 2:267

(JEFFERS, LANCE)
To Crack That Nut Were a Seeker Task (poetry). Shuman 2:142
Trellie (poetry). Chapman 2:265
The Unknown (poetry). Chapman 475, Shuman 2:123
Vietnam: I Need More Than This Crust of Salt (poetry). Brooks 72
What Moor Has Placed His Body in My Throat (poetry). Shuman 2:140
When I Have Wrung the Last Tear (poetry). Shuman 2:138
When She Spoke of God (poetry). Brooks 72, Shuman 2:139

The Dawn Swings In (short fiction). Shuman 114
Williebelle (short fiction). Shuman 137

JEFFERSON, RICHARD. Poet
Life (poetry). Johnson, C. 143
Poem: You Went Away (poetry). Johnson, C. 115, 143

JEFFREY, MAURINE L., 1900- . Poet
My Rainy Day (poetry). Brewer 23
Pappy's Last Song (poetry). Brewer 24

JEFFREY, ROBERT. Poet
Black Proclamation (poetry). Bookers 3

JEMMOTT, CLAUDIA E., 1949- . Poet
City Park (poetry). Shuman 352
Falling (poetry). Shuman 353
There Are Times (poetry). Shuman 354

JENNINGS, KEVIN. Poet
Love (poetry). Bookers 78

JESSYE, EVA ALBERTA, 1897- . Essayist, Poet
The Singer (poetry). Kerlin 69
Spring with the Teacher (poetry). Kerlin 139
To a Rosebud (poetry). Kerlin 141

JOANS, TED, 1928- . Biographer, Poet, Short Fiction Writer
Afrique Accidentale (excerpt—poetry). Hollo 28
For Me Again (poetry). Bell 100
In Homage to Heavy Loaded Trane, J. C. (poetry). Baker 388
It Is Time (poetry). Hayden 2:192, Hughes 34
It's Curtains (poetry). Adoff 3:206, Lomax 248
Jazz Must be a Woman (poetry). Henderson 221, Pool 2:109
Je Suis un homme (poetry). Breman 229
Lester Young (poetry). Bell 101, Bontemps 2:171, Patterson 3:273
Love Light (poetry). Patterson 4:9
Miles' Delight (poetry). Hughes 2:396
My Ace of Spades (poetry). Brooks 17
Nice Colored Man (poetry). Henderson 223
O Great Black Mosque (poetry). Bell 104

The Protective Grigri (poetry). Adoff 3:207
S. C. Threw S. C. into the Railroad Yard (poetry). Henderson 220
Santa Claws (poetry). Henderson 223
Scenery (poetry). Adoff 3:206
Think Twice and Be Nice (poetry). Pool 131
The 38 (poetry). Bell 102, Hughes 83
The Truth (poetry). Bell 100, Lomax 247
The Ubiquitous Lions (poetry). Baker 387
Voice in the Crowd (poetry). Bontemps 2:172, Hayden 2:191, Weisman 52
Why Try (poetry). Bell 101, Pool 132

JOHNS, VERNON S. Educator, Minister
Civilized Interiors (sermon). Dreer 210

JOHNSON, ALICIA LOY, 1944- . Poet
Black Art Spirits (poetry). Alhamisi 101
Black Lotus/a Prayer (poetry). Major 74
A Black Poetry Day (poetry). Shuman 341, Shuman 2:149
Blue/Black Poems (poetry). Shuman 338, Shuman 2:146
A Day of Peace, a Day of Peace (poetry). Shuman 2:159
Enemy of Man (poetry). Shuman 2:155
A Gathering of Artists (poetry). Brown, P. 52
The Long March (poetry). Shuman 342, Shuman 2:150
Monologue (poetry). Coombs 69
On My Blk/ness (poetry). Davis 769, Shuman 340, Shuman 2:148
Our Days Are Numbered (poetry). Brooks 176
Some Smooth Lyrics for a Natural People (poetry). Brown, P. 55

JOHNSON, BRADLON. Playwright
All Behind the Line Is Mine (drama). Bookers 131

JOHNSON, CHARLES BERTRAM, 1880- . Poet
crossed legs (poetry). Coombs 73
Lacrimae Aethiopiae (excerpt—poetry). Kerlin 192
A Little Cabin (poetry). Johnson 198
My people laugh and sing (first line—poetry). Kerlin 63
Negro Poets (poetry). Johnson 199
Old Friends (poetry). Kerlin 97
Old Things (poetry). White 190
the parking lot world of sergeant pepper (poetry). Coombs 74
A Rain Song (poetry). Kerlin 99, White 189
So Much (poetry). Kerlin 98
Soul and Star (poetry). Kerlin 96
We have fashioned laughter (first line—poetry). Kerlin 52

JOHNSON, CHARLES S., 1893- Essayist
Introduction (essay). Johnson, C. 11
The New Frontage on American Life (essay). Locke 2:278

(JOHNSON, CHARLES S.)
Shadow of the Plantation (excerpt—essay).
Brown 896
Striking the Economic Balance (essay).
Watkins 192

JOHNSON, CLIFFORD VINCENT, 1936- .
Short Fiction Writer
Old Blues Singers Never Die (short fiction). Hughes 3:414, Patterson 3:250

JOHNSON, DON ALLEN, 1942- . Poet
Brainwashing Dramatized (poetry). Hughes 2:436
O White Mistress (poetry). Hughes 40, Singh 32

JOHNSON, DOROTHY VENA, ?-1970. Poet
Crystal Shreds (poetry). Murphy 3:85
Epitaph for a Bigot (poetry). Hughes 2:226, Murphy 91
Green Valley (poetry). Hughes 2:227
Jerked to God (poetry). Murphy 3:85
Ode to Justice (poetry). Murphy 3:83
Post War Ballad (poetry). Murphy 91
Road to Anywhere (poetry). Murphy 92
Success (poetry). Murphy 92

JOHNSON, FENTON, 1888-1958. Poet
Aunt Jane Allen (poetry). Adoff 2:7, Adoff 3:24, Chapman 371, Hughes 2:89, Long 285
The Banjo Player (poetry). Chapman 369, Hayden 2:43, Hughes 2:86, Johnson 145, Miller, R. 214, Patterson 3:207, Pool 2:80
Children of the Sun (poetry). Johnson 141
Counting (poetry). Bontemps 2:27
Daily Grind (poetry). Bontemps 2:25, Chapman 367
Death of Love (poetry). White 161
Ethiopia (poetry). Robinson 148
I Played on David's Harp (poetry). Kerlin 64
In the Evening (poetry). White 161
Lonely Mother (poetry). Hughes 2:91
Long de Cool o' Night (poetry). Robinson 148
Love's Good-Night (poetry). White 160
The Marathon Runner (poetry). Cullen 64
The Minister (poetry). Hayden 2:42
The Mulatto's Song (poetry). Kerlin 101
Negro Peddler's Song (poetry). Bontemps 26, Chapman 368
The New Day (poetry). Calverton 184, Johnson 142, Kerlin 102, Miller, R. 212
The Old Repair Man (poetry). Bontemps 27, Chapman 369, Long 286, Patterson 3:218
The Plaint of the Factory Child (poetry). Kerlin 101
Puck Goes to Court (poetry). Cullen 63
Rome Is Dying (poetry). Robinson 146
Rulers (poetry). Chambers 257, Hughes 2:85, Miller, R. 215, Stanford 116
Scarlet Woman (poetry). Adoff 3:24, Baker 126, Barksdale 456, Brown 348, Chap-

man 370, Hughes 2:87, Johnson 145, Long 284, Robinson 154
Soldiers of the Dusk (poetry). Robinson 147
These Are My People (poetry). Kerlin 100
Tired (poetry). Adoff 2:80, Adoff 3:24, Baker 125, Barksdale 456, Brown 347, Chapman 370, Hayden 2:41, Hughes 2:88, Johnson 144, Lomax 210, Miller, R. 214, Robinson 154, Stanford 116
The Vision of Lazarus (excerpt—poetry). Johnson 146
When I Die (poetry). Cullen 62, Hughes 2:90, Miller, R. 212, White 162
Who Is That A-Walking in the Corn? (poetry). Hughes 2:92
The World Is a Mighty Ogre (poetry). Bontemps 26, Chapman 368

JOHNSON, FRED, 1940- . Poet
Arabesque (poetry). Adoff 3:393
Fire, Hair, Meat and Bone (poetry). Adoff 3:391

JOHNSON, GEORGIA DOUGLAS, 1886-1966. Playwright, Poet
Frederick Douglas (drama). Richardson 2:143
Plumes (drama). Calverton 147, Locke 287
A Sunday Morning in the South (drama). Hatch 211
William and Ellen Craft (drama). Richardson 2:164

Armour (poetry). Patterson 4:136
Black Recruit (poetry). Murphy 94
Black Woman (poetry). Turner 3:199, Turner 4:43
Common Dust (poetry). Adoff 3:22, Bontemps 20, Lomax 209, Patterson 3:155
Conquest (poetry). Bontemps 24
Credo (poetry). Adoff 3:23, Turner 3:200, Turner 4:44
Delusion (poetry). Patterson 4:116
The Dreams of the Dreamer (poetry). Cullen 80
Escape (poetry). Adoff 3:22, Locke 2:147
Foregather (poetry). Dreer 73
Good-bye (poetry). Dreer 74, Patterson 4:96
The Heart of a Woman (poetry). Brown 339, Cromwell 26, Cullen 81, Dreer 74, Hughes 2:73, Johnson 181
The Heart of a Woman (excerpts—poetry). Kerlin 148
Hope (poetry). Cullen 75
I Closed My Shutters Fast Last Night (poetry). Brown 340, Hughes 2:79
I Want to Die While You Love Me (poetry). Bontemps 22, Brown 340, Calverton 186, Cullen 78, Hayden 2:39, Johnson 183, Patterson 3:155, Patterson 4:151
Interracial (poetry). Hughes 2:78, Lomax 210, Murphy 93, Patterson 4:90
Isolation (poetry). White 208
I've Learned to Sing (poetry). Murphy 93
Lethe (poetry). Cullen 77

(JOHNSON, GEORGIA DOUGLAS)
Little Son (poetry). Cullen 76, White 209
Lost Illusions (poetry). Johnson 182
Lovelight (poetry). Bontemps 23
The Mother (poetry). Kerlin 303
My Little Dreams (poetry). Cullen 79, Hughes 2:81, Johnson 184
The Octoroon (poetry). Kerlin 151, White 209
Old Black Men (poetry). Adoff 3:21, Cullen 77, Hughes 2:77, Weisman 4
The Ordeal (poetry). Locke 2:146
Peace (poetry). Kerlin 61
The Poet Speaks (poetry). Bontemps 2:22
Prejudice (poetry). Adoff 3:23, Bontemps 2:24
Proving (poetry). Cullen 77, Patterson 4:10
Recessional (poetry). Cullen 79, Hughes 2:80
Remember (poetry). Hughes 2:75
Requiem (poetry). Johnson, C. 35
Retrospection (poetry). Cromwell 27
The Riddle (poetry). Adoff 3:23, Locke 2:147
Service (poetry). Cullen 75
Smothered Fires (poetry). Kerlin 150
The Suppliant (poetry). Adoff 3:23, Brown 340, Cullen 76, Hughes 2:76, Turner 3:200, Turner 4:44
Taps (poetry). White 209
To My Son (poetry). Kerlin 264
To Samuel Coleridge Taylor, Upon Hearing His (Song) (poetry). Locke 2:146
To William Stanley Braithwaite (poetry). Turner 3:200, Turner 4:44
Trifle (poetry). Bontemps 2:21
Values (poetry). Cromwell 26
Welt (poetry). Johnson 183
What Need Have I for Memory? (poetry). Cullen 80
When I Am Dead (poetry). Cullen 80
Your World (poetry). Bontemps 2:23
Youth (poetry). Hughes 2:74, Johnson 182

JOHNSON, GUY B. Fiction Writer, Essayist
John Henry, a Negro Legend (essay). Johnson, C. 47

JOHNSON, HELEN ARMSTEAD. See COLLINS, HELEN ARMSTEAD JOHNSON

JOHNSON, HELEN AURELIA. Poet
Roaring Third (poetry). Murphy 3:87

JOHNSON, HELENE HUBBELL, 1907- . Poet
Bottled (poetry). Adoff 3:104, Cullen 221, Kerlin 280
Fulfillment (poetry). Cullen 219, Hughes 2:262, Patterson 4:162
Invocation (poetry). Bontemps 2:102, Hughes 2:265, Johnson 282, Patterson 4:161
Magalu (poetry). Adoff 3:103, Cullen 223, Hughes 2:263
Metamorphism (poetry). Cromwell 50

Poem: Little Brown Boy (poetry). Adoff 3:103, Bontemps 2:100, Cullen 218, Johnson 279
Remember Not (poetry). Hughes 2:264, Johnson 281, Patterson 4:95
The Road (poetry). Bontemps 2:101, Cromwell 50, Cullen 221, Hughes 2:266, Johnson 280
Sonnet to a Negro in Harlem (poetry). Adams 3:86, Bontemps 102, Cullen 217, Johnson 281, Johnson, C. 148, Kerlin 280
Summer Matures (poetry). Cullen 217, Hughes 2:261
What Do I Care For Morning (poetry). Cullen 216

JOHNSON, HERBERT CLARK, 1911- . Poet
A Boy's Need (poetry). Hughes 2:283
Crossing a Creek (poetry). Hughes 2:284
On Calvary's Lonely Hill (poetry). Hughes 2:286
Willow Bend and Weep (poetry). Hughes 2:285

JOHNSON, HERSCHELL, 1948- . Poet
Hegira (poetry). Bookers 95
Sound Flowers (poetry). Bookers 80
To Mareta (poetry). Coombs 77, Patterson 4:17
Us (poetry). Bookers 58
"We Are Not Mantan" (poetry). Coombs 79

JOHNSON, JAMES WELDON, 1871-1938. Editor, Essayist, Fiction Writer, Poet, Songwriter, Autobiographer
Along This Way (excerpts—autobiography). Chapman 270, Watkins 370
Autobiography of an Ex-colored Man (excerpt—autobiography). Calverton 497
Autobiography of an Ex-colored Man (excerpt: Camp Meeting—autobiography). Brown 168
Autobiography of an Ex-colored Man (excerpt: Childhood of an Ex-colored Man—autobiography). Patterson 3:113
The Autobiography of an Ex-coloured Man (excerpt: Ch. 10; Race and Money—autobiography). Kendricks 222

Black Manhattan (excerpt—essay). Davis 258
Black Manhattan (excerpt: Early Negro Shows—essay). Brown 968
Black Manhattan (excerpt: Marcus Garvey—essay). Dreer 173
Book of American Negro Poetry, 1st ed., Preface (essay). Baker 181, Barksdale 483
Detroit (essay). Turner 2:73, Turner 3:74
Harlem: The Cultural Capital (essay). Locke 2:301, Long 322
The History of the Spiritual (essay). Watkins 117

(JOHNSON, JAMES WELDON)

Answer to Prayer (poetry). White 178

De Ballet of de Boll Weevil (poetry). Patterson 3:121

The Black Mammy (poetry). Baker 135, Kerlin 268

Brothers (poetry). Brown 326, Johnson 127

Cala Vendor's Cry (poetry). Patterson 3:125

Crab Man (poetry). Patterson 3:125

The Creation (poetry). Adoff 3:3, Black 7, Calverton 199, Chapman 364, Cullen 19, Ford 64, Haslam 279, Hayden 105, Johnson 116, Jordan 60, Locke 2:138, Margolies 241, Patterson 3:120, Stanford 111, Turner 3:194, Turner 4:38, Weisman 10

Fifty Years (poetry). Barksdale 485, Johnson 130, Kendricks 231, White 172

Fragment (poetry). Barksdale 487

From the German of Uhland (poetry). Cullen 17

The Glory of the Day Was in Her Face (poetry). Adoff 2:15, Adoff 3:5, Cullen 18, Johnson 127, Kerlin 93, Patterson 4:147

Go Down, Death (A Funeral Sermon) (poetry). Adoff 3:6, Baker 191, Barksdale 488, Bontemps 2:2, Brown 331, Davis, C. 97, Kearns 371

God's Trombones (excerpt: The Crucifixion—poetry). Miller, R. 200

God's Trombones (excerpt: The Judgment Day—poetry). Miller, R. 202

Good Mornin' Blues (poetry). Patterson 3:124

Good Morning, Captain (poetry). Patterson 3:121

How long Blues (poetry). Patterson 3:124

John Henry (poetry). Patterson 3:122

The Judgment Day (poetry). Henderson 81, Kerlin 213

Lazy (poetry). Singh 5, White 177

Lift every voice and sing (Negro National Anthem, Words & Music). Dreer 41, Hughes 2:32, Kerlin 234, Patterson 3:119, Pool 2:186, Weisman 35

Listen Lord—A Prayer (poetry). Ford 65, Johnson 125, Randall 2:41

Mother Night (poetry). Johnson 83, White 179

My City (poetry). Cullen 25, Hughes 2:31, Johnson 125, Weisman 56

My Lady's Lips Am Like De Honey (poetry). Kerlin 242

O Black and Unknown Bards (poetry). Adoff 3:2, Baker 136, Barksdale 486, Black 10, Bontemps 2:1 Brown 324, Cromwell 36, Dreer 37, Emanuel 71, Ford 64, Freedman 67, Hughes 2:29, Johnson 123, Kearns 369, Kearns 2:239, Kendricks 112, Lomax 206, Patterson 3:119, Randall 2:42, White 175

O Southland! (poetry). Dreer 39, Johnson 84, Kerlin 92

Oyster Man's Cry (poetry). Patterson 3:125

Pick a Bale of Cotton (poetry). Patterson 3:121

The Prodigal Son (poetry). Brown 328, Davis 254, Long 313

Saint Peter Relates an Incident of the Resurrection Day (poetry). Brown 333, Hayden 2:26, Kendricks 226, Long 317

Sence You Went Away (poetry). Barksdale 484, Brown 328, Emanuel 72, Johnson 122, Turner 3:194, Turner 4:38

Southern blues (poetry). Patterson 3:124

Sweet Potato Man (poetry). Patterson 3:125

To America (poetry). Kerlin 53

Tunk (poetry). Dreer 40

Watermelon Vendor's Cry (poetry). Patterson 3:125

The White Witch (poetry). Barksdale 487, Breman 33, Cullen 22, Johnson 120

The Young Warrior (poetry). Kerlin 94

JOHNSON, JOE, 1940- . Essayist, Fiction Writer, Poet

If I Ride This Train (poetry). Adoff 3:384, Lowenfels 59

Judeebug's Country (poetry). Adoff 3:383

Yes, Jesus Loves Me (short fiction). Troupe 284

JOHNSON, LEANNA F. Poet

Joy or Sorrow (poetry). Murphy 95

Supremacy (poetry). Murphy 95

JOHNSON, LEMUEL. Poet

Covenant (poetry). Troupe 441

JOHNSON, MAE SMITH, 1890- . Poet

To My Grandmother (poetry). Kerlin 305

To My Grandmother (excerpt—poetry). Kerlin 57

JOHNSON, MORDECAI WYATT, 1890- . Orator, Pamphleteer, Letter Writer

Faith of the American Negro (essay). Brown 681

JOHNSON, RAY. Poet

Walking East on 125th Street (spring 1959) (poetry). Jones 418

JOHNSON, RUTH BROWNLEE. Poet, Short Fiction Writer

Chained (poetry). Murphy 97

Cords (poetry). Murphy 96

Cross Buns for Friday (short fiction). Ford 2:35

JOHNSON, YVETTE. Poet

Ghetto (poetry). Murphy 2:55

Reality (poetry). Murphy 2:56

Sapling (poetry). Murphy 2:57

This Is the City (poetry). Murphy 2:58

JOHNSTON, PERCY EDWARD, 1930- . Playwright, Editor, Essayist, Poet

Apology to Leopold Sedar Senghor (poetry). Henderson 191

(JOHNSTON, PERCY EDWARD)
Canto #4 (poetry). Lowenfels 60
Concerto for Girl and Convertible (poetry).
Pool 133
Number Five Cooper Square (poetry). Henderson 191
'Round 'Bout Midnight, Opus 17 (poetry).
Henderson 192
To Paul Robeson, Opus No. 3 (poetry).
Breman 2:86, Davis 771

JONES, ABSALOM, 1746-1818. Preacher
The Life Experience and Gospel Labors of
The Rt. Reverend Richard Allen (excerpt: a Narrative of the Proceedings of
the Colored People during the Awful Calamity in Philadelphia in the year
1793 . . .—narrative with Richard Allen).
Brawley 89, Miller, R. 23, Patterson 3:22

The Petition of the People of Colour, Free
Men, within the city and suburbs of
Philadelphia. To the President, Senate
and House of Representatives, December
30, 1799 (petition). Porter 330

A Thanksgiving Sermon (sermon). Miller,
R. 34, Porter 335

JONES, ALICE H. Poet
For Sapphire, My Sister (poetry). Breman
435, Coombs 81, Patterson 4:61

JONES, BARBARA. See ODARO.

JONES, EDWARD SMYTH, 1881- . Poet
Cell No. 40, East Cambridge Jail, Cambridge, Massachusetts, July 26, 1910
excerpt—poetry). Kerlin 164
Flag of the Free (poetry). Kerlin 167
A Song of Thanks (poetry). Johnson 148,
White 154

JONES, EUGENE KINCKLE. Essayist
Some Observations on the American Race
Problem (essay). Johnson, C. 96

JONES, EVERETT LE ROI. See JONES,
LE ROI.

JONES, GAYLE, 1949- . Poet, Short Fiction Writer
Many Die Here (poetry). Jordan 14
Salvation (poetry). Exum 94
Satori (poetry). Jordan 15
Tripart (poetry). Jordan 13

White Rat (short fiction). Troupe 287

JONES, GEORGIA HOLLOWAY. Poet
Enchantment (poetry). Murphy 98
To James Weldon Johnson (poetry). Murphy 98

JONES, HOWARD, 1941- . Poet
Fall To (poetry). Major 77

JONES, JAMES ARLINGTON, 1936- . Poet
America (poetry). Shuman 347
Anonymous (poetry). Shuman 2:169
Another Consumes (poetry). Shuman 2:172
An Answer (poetry). Shuman 347
At Will (poetry). Shuman 2:172
The Battle (poetry). Shuman 2:166
But for One (poetry). Shuman 2:181
Cold War (poetry). Shuman 2:185
Come Dusk (poetry). Shuman 348
Come Wednesdays (poetry). Shuman 348
Contentment (poetry). Shuman 2:171
Count Down (poetry). Shuman 2:182
Courtyard Level (poetry). Shuman 2:168
Day (poetry). Shuman 2:173
Day Dreaming (poetry). Shuman 2:168
Eugene McCarthy (poetry). Shuman 2:173
Exposition (poetry). Shuman 2:179
Face to Face (poetry). Shuman 2:179
Fellow Travelers (poetry). Shuman 2:174
For the Defense (poetry). Shuman 2:164
From Dawn to Dusk (poetry). Shuman 349
From the Bleachers (poetry) Shuman 2:167
Gossip (poetry). Shuman 349
Gratitude (poetry). Shuman 2:171
Guiding Light (poetry). Shuman 2:178
However Small a Deed (poetry). Shuman
2:177
In a Lifetime (poetry). Shuman 2:166
Life (poetry). Shuman 349
Matter of Fact (poetry). Shuman 2:170
A Moment in the White (poetry). Shuman
2:164
Mother Nature (poetry). Shuman 2:182
Now and Then (poetry). Shuman 2:177
Once Upon a Time (poetry). Shuman 2:180
Party Solicitor (poetry). Shuman 2:170
Peut-être (poetry). Shuman 2:175
Reward Ungiven (poetry). Shuman 2:176
Speak Neither of Turning Memory around,
— — — (first line—poetry). Shuman
2:169
Spring (poetry). Shuman 2:181
Suicides (poetry). Shuman 350
Survivor: One (poetry). Shuman 2:180
Sweat (poetry). Shuman 2:167
Sweet Digestion (poetry). Shuman 2:183
Time (poetry). Shuman 2:174
Timely Message (poetry). Shuman 2:165
Undefeated (poetry). Shuman 2:169
Unrewarded (poetry). Shuman 2:184
Unveiled (poetry). Shuman 2:165
Vanity (poetry). Shuman 2:175
Welcomed Exit (poetry). Shuman 2:183
Where Else? (poetry). Shuman 350

JONES, JOSHUA HENRY, JR., 1876- .
Fiction Writer, Poet
Brothers (poetry). Kerlin 118
Excerpt (poetry). Kerlin 266
Goodbye Old Year (poetry). Kerlin 310
The Heart of the World (poetry). Kerlin
117
A Southern Love Song (poetry). Kerlin 115
They've lynched a man in Dixie (excerpt—
first line—poetry). Kerlin 266

(JONES, JOSHUA HENRY, JR.)
To a Skull (poetry). Johnson 201
Turn Out the Light (poetry). Kerlin 114

JONES, JYMI, 1940- . Poet, Editor, Publisher
He Said She Said She Said He Said (poetry). Kendricks 347

JONES, LE ROI, 1934- . Critic, Playwright, Editor, Essayist, Fiction Writer, Poet
Bloodrites (drama). Alhamisi 115, Brasmer 25
The Death of Malcolm X (drama). Bullins 2:2
Dutchman (drama). Oliver 215, Patterson 2:319
Great Goodness of Life (drama). Caldwell 139
Junkies Are Full of (Shhh . . .) (drama). King 11
Madheart (drama). Jones 574, Robinson 2:172
The Slave (drama). Hatch 812
The Toilet (drama). Turner 5:535

City of Harlem (essay). Turner 2:131, Turner 3:131
Classic Blues (essay). Curry 138
Cold Hurt and Sorrow (essay). Turner 2:136, Turner 3:136
The Dempsey-Liston Fight (essay). Singh 166
Last Days of the American Empire (Including Some Instruction for Black People) (essay). Barksdale 751
Legacy of Malcolm X and the Coming Black Nation (essay). Chapman 2:458
Leroi jones talking (essay). Ford 323
Mythe of a Negro Literature (essay). Curry 109, Davis 651, Davis, C. 293, Demarest 294, Gayle 2:190, Singh 308
Nationalism vs. Pimp Art (essay). Barksdale 759
Philistinism and the Negro Writer (essay). Hill 51
The Revolutionary Theatre (essay). Hayden 295
Soul Food (essay). Curry 85, Demarest 286
Statement on Poetics (essay). Bell 176
Tokenism: 300 Years for Five Cents (essay). Adams 4:153

System of Dante's Hell (excerpt: The Christians—fiction). Hill 2:324
System of Dante's Hell (excerpt: The Rape—fiction). Hill 2:329
Tales (excerpt: Answers on Progress—fiction). Reed 141

Islam and Black Arts: an Interview with Amiri Baraka (interview). Alhamisi 141

Home (excerpt—narration). Adoff 4:202

African Love History (poetry). King 3:30
An Agony as Now (poetry). Barksdale 749, Jordan 124, Randall 2:211, Turner 3:276, Turner 4:120

As a Possible Lover (poetry). Bontemps 2:180, Jordan 78
Audubon Drafted (poetry). Hayden 2:213, Lomax 250
Babylon Revisited (poetry). Randall 2:214
Ballad of the Morning Street (poetry). Weisman 85
Beautiful Black Women (poetry). Breman 332, Randall 2:213
Biography (poetry). Troupe 221
Black Art (poetry). Baker 396, Bell 119, Henderson 213, Jones 302, Randall 33, Randall 2:223, Robinson 2:444
Black Bourgeoisie (poetry). Randall 2:223
Black Dada Nihilism (poetry). Davis 648
Black People (poetry). Baker 397, Barksdale 750, Randall 2:226, Robinson 2:445
Bludoo Baby, Want Money, and Got Alligator to Give (poetry). Jones 299
The Bridge (poetry). Chapman 491
Bumi (poetry). Adoff 3:256
Charlie Parker: The Human Condition (poetry). Hill 2:609
Cold Term (poetry). Randall 2:220
A Contract for the Destruction and Rebuilding of Paterson (poetry). Kearns 2:135
Crow Jane in High Society (poetry). Davis 647
The Dance (poetry). Hayden 148
The Death of Nick Charles (poetry). Chapman 488, Davis, C. 353
Drowned Love (poetry). Pool 137
Each Morning (poetry). Adoff 2:21, Adoff 3:250, Haslam 351, Hughes 74, Stanford 4
Election Day (Newark, New Jersey) (poetry). Jones 296
The End of Man Is His Beauty (poetry). Bontemps 2:181, Jordan 76, Pool 135, Turner 3:277, Turner 4:121
Epistrophe (poetry). Adoff 107, Hayden 2:210, Hughes 2:407, Kerlin 73, Patterson 3:272
For Tom Postell, dead black poet (poetry). Breman 333
Genealogy (poetry). Margolies 11
A Guerrilla Handbook (poetry). Adoff 3:256
I Am Speaking of Future Good-ness and Social Philosophy (poetry). Henderson 216
I Substitute for the Dead Lecturer (poetry). Baker 393, Breman 331, Jordan 110
In One battle (poetry). Randall 2:221
The Insidious Dr. Fu Man Chu (poetry). Hill 2:611
The Invention of Comics (poetry). Adoff 3:251, Bontemps 2:179, Chapman 484, Davis 647
Jitterbugs (poetry). Emanuel 516
Ka Ba (poetry). Chapman 2:207, Kendricks 346, Randall 2:213
Lead Belly Gives an Autograph (poetry). Troupe 422
Legacy (poetry). Adoff 3:253

(JONES, LE ROI)

leroy (poetry). Adoff 3:255, Barksdale 750, Randall 2:215

Letter to E. Franklin Frazier (poetry). Adoff 3:253, Randall 2:217

Lines to Garcia Lorca (poetry). Hughes 55, Patterson 3:272

Look for You Yesterday, Here You Come Today (poetry). Bell 113, Chapman 485, Singh 28

Move (poetry). King 3:24

The Nation Is Like Ourselves (poetry). King 3:19

The New Sheriff (poetry). Hill 2:612, Singh 25

Notes for a Speech (poetry). Breman 328, Hollo 26, Kearns 591, Singh 25

Numbers, Letters (poetry). Randall 2:218

Ostriches and Grandmothers (poetry). Kearns 587, Singh 27

A Poem for Black Hearts (poetry). Adoff 2:52, Adoff 3:255, Barksdale 749, Bell 118, Brooks 28, Emanuel 515, Hayden 147, Henderson 211, Kearns 592, Long 696, Miller, R. 522, Randall 32, Robinson 2:443, Rose 251, Stanford 280

A Poem for Democrats (poetry). Pool 136

A Poem Some People Will Have to Understand (poetry). Breman 330, Hollo 26, Randall 2:216

Poems for Half White College Students (poetry). Bell 118, Randall 2:225

The Politics of Rich Painters (poetry). Baker 394, Bell 116

Preface to a 20 Volume Suicide Note (poetry). Adams 3:90, Adoff 3:250, Baker 392, Barksdale 748, Bontemps 2:178, Chapman 483, Emanuel 515, Ford 326, Hayden 2:211, Hughes 96, Hughes 2:406, Jordan 33, Kearns 587, Lomax 251, Long 695, Patterson 3:272, Stanford 280

The Pressures (poetry). Randall 2:212

Return of the Native (poetry). Randall 2:222

Sacred Chant for the Return of Black Spirit and Power (poetry). Chapman 2:209

Snake Eyes (poetry). Hayden 2:212

Somebody's Slow Is Another Body's Fast (poetry). King 3:14

SOS (poetry). Adoff 3:257, Henderson 212, Randall 2:181

The Spirit of Creation Is Blackness (poetry). King 3:27

State/Ment (poetry). Long 697

Study Peace (poetry). Adoff 3:258, Alhamisi 115, Henderson 218

Three Movements and a Coda (poetry). Henderson 214, Jones 294, Miller, R. 523

The Turncoat (poetry). Hill 2:613

Vice (poetry). Singh 23

W. W. (poetry). Adoff 3:254, Chambers 274, Major 78, Robinson 2:445

Way Out West (poetry). Adoff 3:252, Kearns 589

We Own the Night (poetry). Adoff 3:257

World Is Full of Remarkable Things (poetry). Jones 292, Randall 34

Young Soul (poetry). Randall 2:220

The Alternative (short fiction). King 2:117

The Screamers (short fiction). Clarke 304, Demarest 288, Stadler 69

Uncle Tom's Cabin—Alternate Ending (short fiction). James 341, Patterson 3:265

Unfinished (short fiction). Clarke 3:153

JONES, MARTE. Poet

A Flame Within (poetry). Exum 95

You Are Stolen Kisses in My Unsuspecting Sleep (poetry). Exum 96

JONES, PAMELA. Poet

Sleep Is a Blanket over the Eye (poetry). Bookers 99

JONES, PAULETTE. Poet

Tree Poem (poetry). Brown, P. 58

JONES, TILFORD. Poet

Sympathy (excerpt—poetry). Kerlin 264

JONES-QUARTEY, H. A. B. Poet

The Chameleon Is Everywhere (poetry). Cuney 37

Fragment (poetry). Cuney 35

In Memoriam (poetry). Cuney 35

Lyrics to the Well-Beloved (poetry). Cuney 36

We've Got To Live before We Die (poetry). Cuney 36

JORDAN, JUNE MEYER, 1936- . Critic, Editor, Essayist, Poet

All The World Moved (poetry). Adoff 3:303, Major 89

Cameo No. II (poetry). Randall 2:243

Getting Down to Get Over (poetry). Exum 99

If You Saw a Negro Lady (poetry). Jordan 54, Lowenfels 92

In Memoriam: Rev. Martin Luther King, Jr. (poetry). Adoff 3:305, Jordan 115

My Sadness Sits Around Me (poetry). Randall 2:248

The New Pietà: for the Mothers and Children of Detroit (poetry). Adoff 3:303

No Poem Because Time Is Not a Name (poetry). Exum 98

Nobody Rides the Roads Today (poetry). Randall 2:249

of faith: confessional (poetry). Jordan 70

Okay Negroes (poetry). Randall 2:243

Poem for my family: Hazel Griffin and Victor Hernandez Cruz (poetry). Randall 2:245

Poem from the Empire State (poetry). Randall 2:248

Poem: On My Happy/Matrimonial Condition (poetry). Exum 97

Then It Was (poetry). Patterson 4:7

(JORDAN, JUNE MEYER)
These Poems (poetry). Troupe 455
Uncle Bull-boy (poetry). Adoff 3:304,
Jordan 28
What Happens (poetry). Randall 2:249

JORDAN, NORMAN, 1938- . Playwright,
Poet
August 2 (poetry). Adoff 3:323
Be You (poetry). Chapman 2:270, Troupe
244
Black Warrior (poetry). Adoff 3:322,
Breman 404, Jones 389
Brothers, The Struggle Must Go On (Mem-
bers don't git weary) (poetry). King
3:95
Cities and Seas (poetry). Hughes 2:422
Clairvoyance (poetry). King 3:96
Ending (poetry). Hughes 2:423
Feeding the Lions (poetry). Adoff 3:322,
Chambers 114, Major 78
I Have Seen Them (poetry). Chapman
2:269
July 27 (poetry). Chapman 2:272
July 31 (poetry). Adoff 3:323
Light (poetry). Alhamisi 130
Mind and Soul After Dark (poetry). King
3:97
The Poet and Dreamer (poetry). Chapman
2:272
Popsicle Cold (poetry). King 3:94
The Sacrifice (poetry). Jones 391
The Second Plane (poetry). Alhamisi 130,
Breman 403
The Silent Prophet (poetry). Chapman
2:271
Sinner (poetry). Jones 390
When a Woman Gets Blue (poetry). Chap-
man 2:270

JORDAN, W. CLARENCE. Poet
What Is the Negro Doing? (poetry). Kerlin 190

JORDON, WINIFRED VIRGINIA. Poet
Loneliness (poetry). Kerlin 56

JOSEPH, RAYMOND A. Poet
Our Meeting (poetry). Brown, P. 59

JOSEPH, STEPHEN M., ed. Poet
The Me Nobody Knows: Children's Voices
from the Ghetto (excerpt—poetry). Rose
254

JOYCE, JOHN. Essayist
Confessions of John Joyce, alias Davis, who
was executed . . . (essay). Porter 414

KAIN, GYLAN, Playwright, Poet
Song of Ditta (poetry). King 3:100

KAISER, ERNEST, 1915- . Critic, Editor,
Essayist
The Failure of William Styron (essay).
Clarke 2:50
The Literature of Harlem (essay). Gayle
2:239, Shuman 6

KALAMU YA SALAAM. See FERDINAND,
VAL.

KALI. See GROSVENOR, VERTA MAE.

KARENGA, MAULANA RON. Critic, Essay-
ist
Black Art: Mute Matter Given Force and
Function (essay). Chapman 2:477
Black Cultural Nationalism (essay). Gayle
3:31

KARIUKI, JOSEPH. Poet
Come Away, My Love (poetry). Patterson
4:99

KATIBU, SULTANI. See MILLER, LARRY
A.

KAUFMAN, BOB, 1925- . Poet
African Dream (poetry). Adoff 3:263, Bell
129, Bontemps 2:188
Afterwards They Shall Dance (poetry).
Hughes 2:409
Battle Report (poetry). Adoff 93, Bon-
temps 2:189, Lomax 252
Believe, Believe (poetry). Miller, R. 516
Benediction (poetry). Bell 132, Hughes
2:412
Blues Note (poetry). Adoff 3:263, Bell 131,
Henderson 209, Jordan 36, Robinson
2:461
Camus: I Want To Know (poetry). Troupe
333
Cincophrenicpoet (poetry). Hughes 2:411
Cocoa Morning (poetry). Bontemps 2:187
Falling (poetry). Adoff 3:266, Troupe 491
Forget to Not (poetry). Bontemps 2:190
Geneology (poetry). Chapman 2:275
Heavy Water Blues (poetry). Breman 199,
Chapman 2:274
High on Life (poetry). Bell 132
I Have Folded My Sorrows (poetry).
Adoff 3:264, Bell 129, Bontemps 2:187,
Henderson 207
I, Too, Know What I Am Not (poetry).
Major 79
Letter to the Chronicle (poetry). Hender-
son 206
Mingus (poetry). Adoff 3:262, Bell 131
Night Sung Sailor's Prayer (poetry). Miller,
R. 517
O-Jazz-O (poetry). Henderson 208
October 5th, 1963 (poetry). Robinson 2:462
Patriotic Ode on the Fourteenth Anni-
versary of the Persecution of Charlie
Chaplin (poetry). Adoff 3:264
Perhaps (poetry). Hayden 2:217
Response (poetry). Hayden 2:219
To My Son Parker, Asleep in the Next
Room (poetry). Adoff 3:265, Hayden
2:215, Jordan 30
Unhistorical events (poetry). Breman 201
Unholy Missions (poetry). Lomax 253
Walking Parker Home (poetry). Adoff
3:265, Bell 130, Henderson 208, Troupe
256

(KAUFMAN, BOB)
When We Hear the Eye Open (poetry).
Troupe 150
Who Has Seen the Wind? (poetry). Hayden 2:218

KECKLEY, ELIZABETH, 1825-1905. Autobiographer
Behind the Scenes (excerpts—autobiography). Barksdale 307
Behind the Scenes, or Thirty Years a Slave (excerpt: Death of Lincoln—autobiography). Brown 728
Behind the Scenes; or Thirty Years a Slave (excerpt: The Secret History of Mrs. Lincoln's Wardrobe—autobiography). Davis 132

KELLEY, WILLIAM MELVIN, (1937- .
Critic, Essayist, Fiction Writer
A Different Drummer (excerpt—fiction).
Miller, R. 438
A Different Drummer (excerpt: Harry Leland—fiction). Kendricks 298
Dunsfords Travels Everywhere excerpt:
Jest Like Sam—fiction). Reed 149

The African (short fiction). Margolies 29
Brother Carlyle (short fiction). Stanford 209
Cry for Me (short fiction). Baker 374, Chambers 276, Clarke 248, Emanuel 456, Long 716
The Dentist's Wife (short fiction). Barksdale 797
Enemy Territory (short fiction). Ford 220
A Good Long Sidewalk (short fiction).
Chapman 2:125, Clarke 3:128
Harlem Quest (short fiction). Davis 693
The Life You Save (short fiction). Margolies 218
The Only Man on Liberty Street (short fiction). Davis 686, Davis, C. 303, Hughes 3:428, Kearns 351, Turner 121, Turner 3:1411
Poker Party (short fiction). Adams 2:15, King 2:311
Saint Paul and the Monkeys (short fiction). James 286

KELLOGG, PAUL U. Essayist
The Negro Pioneers (essay). Locke 2:271

KELLUM-ROSE, MATTHEW, 1934- . Artist, Poet
America (poetry). Shuman 356
The Beauty of Living (poetry). Shuman 356
Black Tuesday (poetry). Shuman 357
Conversation of Letting (poetry). Shuman 359
Getting Things Together (poetry). Shuman 360
The Hunters (poetry). Shuman 361
The Negro (poetry). Shuman 363
To Nancy (poetry). Shuman 363
Walu, the Antelope (poetry). Shuman 364

KEMP, ARNOLD. Poet, Playwright, Fiction Writer
A Black Cop's Communion (poetry).
Coombs 83
The End of the World (poetry). Coombs 87
Guilt Redeemed (poetry). Coombs 84
Hello Blackness (poetry). Coombs 84
How to Succeed (poetry). Coombs 84
Love Me Black Woman (poetry). Coombs 90

The Blue of Madness (short fiction).
Coombs 2:55

KENDRICK, DELORES. Poet
Three Poems for Gwendolyn Brooks (poetry). Brown, P. 60

KENNEDY, ADRIENNE, 1931- . Playwright
Funnyhouse of a Negro (drama). Brasmer 247, Oliver 192, Patterson 281
The Owl Answer (drama). Hatch 756
A Rat's Mass (drama). Couch 61

KENNEDY, VALLEJO RYAN, 1947- .
Poet
Another Day (poetry). Schulberg 139
Love of a Woman (poetry). Schulberg 140
My Black Man's Togetherness Was Called
Revolt (poetry). Schulberg 141

KENNER, PEGGY SUSBERRY, 1937- .
Poet, Short Fiction Writer
Black Taffy (poetry). Brooks 2:100
Comments (poetry). Brooks 2:98
Image in the Mirror (poetry). Brooks 2:92
No Bargains Today (poetry). Brooks 2:94
Round Table (poetry). Brooks 2:99

Life in My Own Dust (short fiction).
Brooks 2:105
Memories of the Long Seat (short fiction).
Brooks 2:104

KENT, GEORGE E., 1920- . Critic, Short
Fiction Writer
Baldwin and the Problem of Being (essay).
Gibson 2:148
Ethnic Impact in American Literature (essay). Chapman 691
Patterns of the Harlem Renaissance (essay). Bontemps 3:27

KGOSITSILE, KEORAPETSE WILLIAM,
1938- . Critic, Editor, Essayist, Poet,
Short Fiction Writer
Amandla (essay). Alhamisi 118
Paths to the Future (essay). Gayle 3:234
Towards our Theatre: a Definitive Act (essay). Gayle 2:146

The Awakening (poetry). Jones 227
Brother Malcolm's Echo (poetry). Bell 146, Brooks 27, Robinson 2:218
The Elegance of Memory (poetry). Bell 147
Elegy for David Diop (poetry). Brooks 75

(KGOSITSILE, KEORAPETSE WILLIAM)
For Eusi, Ahy Kwei and Gwen Brooks (poetry). Adoff 3:325, Brown, P. 62
For Leroi Jones (April 1965) (poetry). Alhamisi 119
Ivory Musks in Orbit (poetry). Adoff 3:324, Brooks 76, Jones 224
Like the tide: Cloudward (poetry). Breman 406
Lumumba Section (poetry). Robinson 2:217
Mandela's Sermon (poetry). Bell 146, Brooks 75, Robinson 2:218
My Name Is Afrika (poetry). Adoff 3:326, Alhamisi 121, Henderson 307, King 3:112
My people no longer sing (poetry). Breman 407
New Dawn (poetry). Alhamisi 121
Origins (for Melba) (poetry). Adoff 3:324, Henderson 308
Point of Departure: Fire Dance Fire Song (poetry). King 3:108, Troupe 477
Song for Aimé Césaire (poetry). Bell 146
Spirits Unchained (poetry). Adoff 3:325, Robinson 2:217
To Fanon (poetry). Brooks 77, Robinson 2:216
Towards a Walk in the Sun (poetry). Jones 228
Victor or Legacy (poetry). Henderson 307
When Brown is Black (poetry). Brooks 73

KHAJIU KA. See MIZELL, DON A.

KILLEBREW, CAROL. Poet
The Squared Circle (poetry). Brooks 175

KILLENS, JOHN OLIVER, 1916- . Critic, Playwright, Editor, Essayist, Fiction Writer
Black Man's Burden (excerpt—essay). Adoff 4:135
The Black Psyche (essay). Long 609, Turner 2:121, Turner 3:121
The Black Writer Vis-á-Vis His Country (essay). Gayle 3:357
The Confessions of Willie Styron (essay). Clarke 2:34
Explanation of the Black Psyche (essay). Adoff 4:137
Negroes Have a Right to Fight Back (essay). Adams 4:135
Opportunities for Development of Negro Talent (essay). Conference 64
The Smoking Sixties (essay). King 2:xi

And Then We Heard the Thunder (excerpt—fiction). Troupe 39
'Sippi (excerpt: Malcolm X Is Dead—fiction). Patterson 3:207

The Cotillion (foreword—short fiction). Chapman 2:58
God Bless America (short fiction). Adams 2:49, Baker 339, Chambers 89, Clarke 204, Ford 320
Rough Diamond (short fiction). Clarke 3:169

The Stick Up (short fiction). Hughes 3:188, Singh 109
A White Loaf of Bread (short fiction). Brown, P. 105

KILONFE, OBA, 1940- . See PENNY, ROB.

KING, HELEN H., 1931- . Poet
For Gwendolyn Brooks (poetry). Brown, P. 63

KING, LEYLAND. Poet
"Didn't it come like a tidal wave" (poetry). Coombs 94
"I could never ask you" (poetry). Coombs 92

KING, MARTIN LUTHER, JR., 1929-1968. Essayist, Minister, Orator, Civil Rights Leader
Answer to a Perplexing Question (essay). Curry 197
Essay in Political Philosophy (excerpt: Stride Toward Freedom—essay). Barksdale 843, Pool 2:171
Racism and the White Blacklash (essay). Ford 227
Why We Can't Wait (excerpts—essays). Turner 6:106
Why We Can't Wait (excerpt: Letter from Birmingham Jail—essay). Adoff 4:174, Barksdale 863, Miller, R. 458, Stanford 219
World House (essay). Davis 779

Facing the Challenge of a New Age (speech). Long 641
I Have a Dream (speech). Adams 4:103, Barksdale 871, Demarest 336, Freedman 251, Stanford 230
I Have a Dream (excerpt—speech). Gayle 142, Lomax 249

KING, WOODIE, JR., 1937- . Critic, Playwright, Editor, Short Fiction Writer
Beautiful Light and Black Our Dreams (short fiction). Hughes 3:438
The Game (short fiction). King 2:301

KNIGHT, ETHERIDGE, 1931- . Editor, Poet, Short Fiction Writer
Apology for Apostasy? (poetry). Bell 111
As You Leave Me (poetry). Bell 110, Brooks 80, Demarest 152, Randall 30
Belly Song (poetry). Troupe 306
Cell Song (poetry). Adoff 3:228, Miller, A. 79
Crazy Pigeon (poetry). Chapman 2:217, Miller, A. 71
Dark Prophesy: I Sing of Shine (poetry). Henderson 330
For Black Poets Who Think of Suicide (poetry). Adoff 3:233, Alhamisi 131, Bell 112, Breman 309, Brooks 161, Randall 31
For Freckled-Face Gerald (poetry). Randall 2:205

(KNIGHT, ETHERIDGE)
For Langston Hughes (poetry). Chapman 2:279, Henderson 329, Miller, A. 79
For Malcolm, a Year After (poetry). Miller, A. 77, Robinson 2:460
Haiku (poetry). Randall 2:206
Hard Rock Returns to Prison from the Hospital for the Criminal Insane (poetry). Baker 422, Brooks 78, Henderson 327, Miller, A. 72, Randall 29
He Sees Through Stone (poetry). Adoff 3:231, Bell 109, Breman 307, Major 80, Miller, A. 73, Troupe 206, Turner 3:280, Turner 4:124
I Sing of Shine (poetry). Randall 2:209
The Idea of Ancestry (poetry). Adoff 3:229, Barksdale 819, Bell 108, Breman 306, Brooks 79, Demarest 47, Henderson 326, Miller, A. 74, Randall 2:203, Turner 3:279, Turner 4:123
It Was a Funky Deal (poetry). Adoff 3:231, Baker 425, Brooks 83, Chapman 2:278, Miller, A., 78, Randall 2:207, Robinson 2:460
A Love Poem (poetry). Bell 110
A Nickle Bet (poetry). Adoff 43
On Universalism (poetry). Henderson 330, Miller, A. 76
Portrait of Malcolm X (poetry). Adoff 3:232
The Sun Came (poetry). Adoff 3:229, Brooks 84, Brown, P. 64
Sweethearts in a Mulberry Tree (poetry). Demarest 48
To Dinah Washington (poetry). Adoff 3:230, Henderson 329
To Gwendolyn Brooks (poetry). Brown, P. 65
To Make a Poem in Prison (poetry). Miller, A. 70
Two Poems for Black Relocation Centers (poetry). Barksdale 820, Brooks 82
The Violent Space (poetry). Baker 423, Brooks 81, Miller, A. 75, Randall 2:208
The Warden Said to Me the Other Day (poetry). Chapman 2:277, Miller, A. 71
A WASP Woman Visits a Black Junkie in Prison (poetry). Chapman 2:277

A Time to Mourn (short fiction). Chapman 2:120

KORNWEIBEL, THEODORE, JR. Essayist
Theophilus Lewis and The Theatre of the Harlem Renaissance (essay). Bontemps 3:171

KOSTELANETZ, RICHARD. Critic
The Politics of Ellison's Booker: Invisible Man As Symbolic History (essay). Hemenway 88

KOVEN, DIVA GOODFRIEND. Poet
Untitled Poem (poetry). Bookers 59

KUSH. See DENT, THOMAS C.

KWARTHER, STEPHEN, 1950-   Poet
Epilogue: bewildered souls i've looked upon condemned (poetry). Jordan 4

LABRIE, PETER. Essayist, Political Scientist, City Planner
The New Breed (essay). Jones 64

LACY, ED. Short Fiction Writer
The Right Thing (short fiction). Ford 2:184

LACY, LESLIE ALEXANDER. Essayist, Political Scientist
African Responses to Malcolm X (essay). Jones 19

LACY, MARCH. Short Fiction Writer
The Fighting Finnish (short fiction). Ford 2:140
No Fools, No Fun (short fiction). Ford 2:284

LADELLE X. See POWELL, LESLIE.

LA GRONE, OLIVER, 1915-   . Poet
Bathed Is My Blood (poetry). Hughes 38
Break Now This Silence (poetry). Ten 40
Dawn Is Eternally (poetry). Ten 41
For Lionel Hampton (poetry). Pool 139
Lines to the Black Oak (poetry). Chapman 2:282
My America (poetry). Hughes 36
Of Bread and Wine (poetry). Pool 139
Remnant Ghosts at Dawn (poetry). Chapman 2:281
Suncoming (poetry). Chapman 2:280
This Hour (poetry). Hughes 37, Hughes 2:327
Time In The City (poetry). Ten 42

LALANDE, ATHELSTAN R. Poet
Friendship (poetry). Murphy 3:90

LAMBERT, CALVIN S. Poet
Loch Lomond (poetry). Murphy 3:91
Love, The Exotic Maiden (poetry). Murphy 3:92
Release (poetry). Murphy 3:92
La Trinidad (poetry). Murphy 3:91

LA MARRE, HAZEL L., 1917-1973. Poet
Time and Tide (poetry). Hughes 2:360

LANE, PINKIE GORDON, 1923-   . Editor, Poet
His Body Is an Eloquence (poetry). Brown, P. 66

LANGSTON, CHARLES, 1817-1892. Speech Writer, Pamphleteer, Letter Writer
Speech before Sentence (speech). Brown 642

LANGSTON, JOHN MERCER, 1829-1897. Speech Writer, Pamphleteer, Letter Writer

(LANGSTON, JOHN MERCER)
The Exodus (excerpt—autobiography).
Brown 667

LANKIN, MATTIE T., 1917- . Teacher,
Poet
Realization (poetry). Shuman 366

LANUSSE, ARMAND, 1812-1867. Editor,
Essayist, Poet
Epigram (poetry). Hill 2:603, Hughes 2:13,
Singh 3
Un Frère au Tombeau de son Frère (po-
etry). Robinson 167
Un Frère au Tombeau de Son Frère
(English version) (poetry). Robinson
168

LARSEN, NELLA, 1893-1963. Fiction Writer
Quicksand (excerpt—fiction). Calverton
121

LATIMER, BETTE DARCIE, 1927- . Poet
For William Edward Burghardt DuBois on
His Eightieth Birthday (poetry). Adoff
3:199, Hughes 2:392

LATIMORE, JEWEL CHRISTINE, 1935- .
Poet
Before/and After (poetry). Brooks 2:167
Brother (poetry). Brooks 2:166
Childhood (poetry). Brooks 2:165
A Folk Fabel: The Third World Had Hung
the un/Humans (poetry). Alhamisi 104
For Gwendolyn Brooks—a Whole and Beau-
tiful Spirit (poetry). Brown, P. 12
(for Nigareens) (poetry). Robinson 2:459
Identity (poetry). Henderson 352
Masque (poetry). Coombs 95
positives (poetry). Adoff 3:291
Saint Malcolm (poetry). Randall 2:230
Signals (poetry). Adoff 3:242, King 3:2,
Patterson 4:28
A Sun Heals (poetry). Brooks 2:168
to a poet i knew (poetry). Adoff 3:291
To A Wite Boy (poetry). Robinson 2:460
Untitled (We Will Be No Generashuns to
Cum) (poetry). Brooks 2:169, King 3:4
Upon Being Black One Friday Night in
July (poetry). Henderson 354
Utopia (poetry). Coombs 95, Randall 2:230

Cromlech: a Tale (short fiction). Brooks
2:157

LAWRENCE, GEORGE. Orator
Oration on the Abolition of the Slave Trade,
Delivered on the First Day of January,
1813 in the African Methodist-Episcopal
Church, 1813 (speech). Porter 374

LAWRENCE, HAROLD G., 1928- . Poet,
Teacher, Critic, Short Fiction Writer
Sidi' Ahmed Bada: Portrait of a Black
Intellectual (essay). Alhamisi 23

LAWRENCE, JOYCE WHITSITT, 1938- .
Poet
For Malcolm (poetry). Brooks 23
For Me Who Don't Read Classics (poetry).
Alhamisi 114
From a Bus (poetry). Chambers 265, Major
130
Give Them Grace (poetry). Ten 51
Revelation (poetry). Ten 52
Still (poetry). Ten 51
When Night Comes (poetry). Ten 50

LAWRENCE, MRS. LLOYD.· See FIELDS,
JULIA.

LAWS, CLARENCE A. Poet
Evening Reverie (poetry). Murphy 3:93

LAWSON, EDWARD. Short Fiction Writer
The Ebony Elephant (short fiction). Ford
2:107

LEAKS, Sylvester. Short Fiction Writer
The Blues Begins (short fiction). Hughes
3:275

LEDBETTER, HUDDIE. Poet
Titanic (poetry). Henderson 101

LEE, AUDREY. Poet, Fiction Writer
The Maudlin Mist of Morning (poetry).
Exum 106
Nostalgia (poetry). Exum 106

Waiting for Her Train (short fiction).
Coombs 2:85

LEE, DON L., 1942- . Critic, Editor, Essay-
ist, Poet
Black Critic (essay). Brooks 2:30
Black Writing (essay). Brooks 2:37
Introduction (essay). Ford 358
Statement on Black Arts (essay). Alhamisi
95
Statement on Poetics (essay). Bell 177,
Gibson 3:177
Think Black (introduction—essay). Baker
420
Toward a Definition: Black Poetry of the
Sixties (after Le Roi Jones) (essay).
Gayle 3:222

An Afterword: for Gwen Brooks (poetry).
Brooks 2:42, Brown, P. 135
Assassination (poetry). Adoff 3:423, Baker
422, Barksdale 821, Bontemps 2:200,
Brooks 97, Randall 43
Awareness (poetry). Adoff 3:421, Brooks
85
Back Again, Home (poetry). Baker 419,
Demarest 259, Ford 359, Randall 2:295,
Turner 3:282, Turner 4:126
Big Momma (poetry). Breman 457, Randall
2:304
Blackman/an unfinished history (poetry).
Bell 161
Black Music/A Beginning (poetry). Brooks
101

(LEE, DON L.)

Blackwoman (poetry). Brooks 102, King 3:116, Robinson 2:451

Bloodsmiles (poetry). Long 792

But He Was Cool (or: He Even Stopped for a Green Light—poetry). Adoff 3.426, Alhamisi 97, Bell 160, Bontemps 2:199, Brooks 92, King 3:114, Long 785, Randall 41, Randall 2:299

Change Is Not Always Progress (poetry). Bell 163, Brooks 111

Change-up (poetry). Adoff 3:428

Communication in Whi-te (poetry). Randall 2:299

The Cure All (poetry). Adoff 30, Brooks 85

The Death Dance (poetry). Brooks 90

Don't Cry, Scream (poetry). Brooks 93, Henderson 336

Education (poetry). Bontemps 2:201, Ford 359, Turner 3:281, Turner 4:125

For Black People (poetry). Brooks 112

Gwendolyn Brooks (poetry). Brown, P. 68

History of the Poet As a Whore (poetry). Alhamisi 98

i ain't seen no poems stop a .38 (poetry). Brooks 86, Ford 359, Henderson 332

In the Interest of Black Salvation (poetry). Brooks 88, Coombs 97, Henderson 332, Randall 42, Robinson 2:446

last week my mother died (poetry). Brooks 86, Ford 359, Henderson 332

The Mainstream of Society (poetry). Demarest 49

Malcolm Spoke/Who Listened? (poetry). Brooks 98

Man Thinking About Woman (poetry). Patterson 4:43

A Message All Black People Can Dig (poetry). Brooks 106, Robinson 2:451

Mixed Sketches (poetry). Brooks 108, Long 793, Randall 2:306

Move Un-Noticed to Be Noticed: a Nationhood Poem (poetry). Bell 166, Brooks 117, Henderson 340

Mwilu/or Poem for the Living (poetry). Brooks 2:40

The Negro (a pure product of Americanism) (poetry). Bell 157

The New Integrationist (poetry). Brooks 86, Robinson 2:446

Nigerian Unity, or: Little Niggers Killing Little Niggers (poetry). Breman 451, Long 786

No More Marching (poetry). Robinson 2:449

On Seeing Diana Go MaDDDDDDDDD (poetry). Brooks 109

One Sided Shoot-Out (poetry). Adoff 3:423, Chapman 2:284, Randall 2:302

The Only One (poetry). Demarest 258

Pains With a Light Touch (poetry). Brooks 87

Poem for a Poet (poetry). Adoff 3:425, Brooks 110

A Poem for Black Minds (poetry). Baker 421

A Poem Looking for a Reader (poetry). Barksdale 822, Brooks 105, Jordan 92, King 3:117, Randall 44

A Poem to Complement Other Poems (poetry). Bell 158, Brooks 99, Chapman 2:286, Randall 2:300

Positive for Sterling Plumpp (poetry). Adoff 3:427, Brooks 2:45

The Primitive (poetry). Ford 360, Randall 2:297

Re-Act for Action (poetry). Coombs 96, Major 82, Randall 2:296

Reflections on a Lost Love (poetry). Brooks 103, Patterson 4:125

The Revolutionary Screw (poetry). Brooks 102

The Self-Hatred of Don L. Lee (poetry). Davis 777, Ford 360, Randall 2:297

Stereo (poetry). Bontemps 2:202, Brooks 85

To Be Quicker (for Black Political Prisoners . . .) (poetry). Breman 456, Brooks 2:44

The Traitor (poetry). Robinson 2:448

Two Poems (poetry). Brooks 86, Ford 359, Henderson 332

Wake-Up Niggers (poetry). Adoff 3:422

The Wall (poetry). Brooks 89, Henderson 334, Robinson 2:447

We Walk the Way of the New World (poetry). Adoff 3:428, Bell 164, Randall 2:307

With All Deliberate Speed (poetry). Brooks 2:43

You Finished It (I Loved, I love) (poetry). Patterson 4:4

LEE, ED. Poet

Blend (poetry). Murphy 99

Freedom's Snare (poetry). Murphy 99

Man (poetry). Murphy 99

Southern Justice (poetry). Murphy 100

Tragedy (poetry). Murphy 100

LEE, GEORGE WASHINGTON, 1894- . Fiction Writer

River George (excerpt: Sharecropping—fiction). Brown 235

LEE, JARENA, 1783-?. Autobiographer

Life and Religious Experience of Jarena Lee . . . 1836 (autobiography). Porter 494

LEE, MARY EFFIE. Poet

Sunset (poetry). Kerlin 56

LEE, ROGER B. Essayist

"Invisible People" (essay). Bookers 53

LEE, ULYSSES, 1914-1969. Lecturer, Editor

The Draft and the Negro (essay). Davis 587

LEGALL, WALTER DE. See DE LEGALL, WALTER.

LENIHAN, ANDREW. Poet
A Breath of Life (poetry). Bookers 39
Defiance of Lunch Rules (poetry). Bookers 43

LENNON, FLORENCE BECKER. Poet
Little white school house blues (poetry). Pool 2:122

LESLIE, CY, 1921- . Poet
On Riots (poetry). Major 83

LESTER, JULIUS, 1939- . Editor, Essayist, Poet, Short Fiction Writer
Black Pawns in a White Game (essay). Adams 4:143
Search for a new land (excerpt: The Mud of Vietnam—essay). Burnett 384

In the Time of Revolution (excerpt—poetry). Adoff 3:354, Lowenfels 75
lxuxii (poetry). Jordan 70
Mud in Vietnam (poetry). Jordan 66
On the Birth of My Son, Malcolm Coltrane (poetry). Adoff 3:356, Breman 417, Jordan 24
Poems (poetry). Hayden 2:225
Us (poetry). Adoff 3:357

LEVINSON, NICK. Short Fiction Writer
The Door (short fiction). Bookers 121

LEWIS, ANGELO, 1950- . Poet
America Bleeds (poetry). Adoff 3:513
Clear (poetry). Adoff 3:513

LEWIS, CORINNE E. Poet
Christmas Cheer (poetry). Kerlin 309

LEWIS, DIO. Poet
The Malcontents (poetry). Murphy 101
Time (poetry). Murphy 102

LEWIS, ETHYL. Poet
The Optimist (excerpt—poetry). Kerlin 60

LEWIS, HARRY WYTHE, JR. Poet
Rainy Day (poetry). Murphy 3:95

LEWIS, JACEYLIN, 1950- . Poet
Michael (poetry). Witherspoon 2:15

LEWIS, LEIGHLA. Poet
Chrysis (poetry). Murphy 3:96
Incidentally (poetry). Murphy 3:95
My Hate (poetry). Murphy 3:96

LEWIS, LILLIAN TUCKER. Poet
Longing (poetry). Brewer 27

LEWIS, ROSCOE E., 1904- . Historian
The Negro In Virginia (excerpt: The Narrators—history). Brown 847
The Negro in Virginia (excerpt: Slave Row—history). Brown 855

LEWIS, THEOPHILUS, 1891- . Critic
The Negro Actor's Deficit (essay). Johnson, C. 125

LILLY, OCTAVE, JR. Poet
The Worker (poetry). Murphy 3:97

LINCOLN, ABBEY. Critic
The Negro Woman in American Literature (panel discussion). Exum 22

LINO. Poet
Soul (poetry). Troupe 2:82

LINYATTA. Short Fiction Writer, Poet
Fragment Reflection I (poetry). Brooks 2:77
Reckoning A. M. Thursday After an Encounter (poetry). Brooks 2:77

3 Units Single Cycle (short fiction). Brooks, 2:64

LITTLE, MALCOLM, 1925-1965. Autobiographer, Civil Rights Leader
Autobiography of Malcolm X (excerpt: Ch. 1: Nightmare—autobiography). Barksdale 874, Chambers 98, Chapman 333, Kearns 2:125, Kendricks 312
Autobiography of Malcolm X (excerpt: Ch. 2: Mascot—autobiography). Adams 4:35, Kendricks 312, Rose 282
Autobiography of Malcolm X (excerpt: Ch. 11: Saved—autobiography). Davis 740
Autobiography of Malcolm X (excerpt: Ch. 19—autobiography). Baker 401, Ford 333
Autobiography of Malcolm X (excerpt: detroit red—autobiography). Demarest 240
Autobiography of Malcolm X (excerpt: Icarus—autobiography). Adoff 4:153
Autobiography of Malcolm X (excerpt: 1965—autobiography). Adoff 4:165, Hayden 214
Autobiography of Malcolm X (excerpt: Out—autobiography). Adoff 4:160

Basic Unity Program, Organization of Afro-American Unity (essay). Chapman 2:564
Declaration of Independence (essay). Gayle 116
Leverett House Forum (excerpt—essay). Stanford 269
Message to the Grass Roots (excerpt—essay). Long 655
Statement on Basic Aims and Objectives of the Organization of Afro-American Unity (essay). Chapman 2:558

Homeboy (short fiction). Demarest 75

Harvard Law School Forum Speech of March 24, 1961 (speech). Curry 191
To Mississippi Youth (speech). Freedman 258, Haslam 343, Margolies 310

LITTLEJOHN, DAVID. Essayist
Black on White (excerpt—essay). Singh 316

LIVINGSTON, MYRTLE SMITH, 1901- .
Playwright
For Unborn Children (drama). Hatch 184

LLORENS, DAVID, 1939-1973. Critic, Essayist, Poet
The Fellah, the Chosen Ones, the Guardian (essay). Jones 169

Of a Woman Who Turns Rivers (poetry). Brown, P. 70
One Year Ago (poetry). Brooks 22
A Resonant Silence (poetry). Murphy 2:60
A Wayward Child (poetry). Murphy 2:61

LOCKE, ALAIN LEROY, 1886-1954. Biographer, Critic, Editor
Apropos of Africa (essay). Long 335
The Drama of Negro Life (essay). Gayle 2:123
Jazz and the Jazz Age: 1918-1926 (essay). Curry 143
The Legacy of the Ancestral Arts (essay). Locke 2:254
The Negro and the American Stage (essay). Patterson 21
The Negro and the American Theatre (1927) (essay). Gayle 3:249
The Negro in American Culture (essay). Calverton 248, Chapman 523, Watkins 155
Negro Youth Speaks (essay). Gayle 3:16, Hayden 243, Locke 2:47
The Negro's Contribution (essay). Davis, C. 105
The New Negro, An Interpretation (excerpt: The Negro Spirituals—essay). Gayle 2:47, Locke 2:199, Long 343, Turner 6:35
The New Negro, An Interpretation (excerpt: The New Negro—essay). Baker 144, Barksdale 575, Brown 948, Chapman 512, Davis 274, Dreer 168, Emanuel 74, Locke 2:3, Miller, R. 180, Turner 6:35
Our Little Renaissance (essay). Cromwell 206, Johnson, C. 117
The Sorrow Songs: The Spirituals (essay). Curry 131
Sterling Brown: The New Negro Folk-Poet (essay). Cunard 88

LOCKETT, REGINALD, 1947- . Poet, Short Fiction Writer
Death of the Moonshine Superman (poetry). Jones 352
Die Black Pervert (poetry). Jones 354
This Poem for Black Women (poetry). Jones 351

LOCKETT, TENA L. Poet
The Almost Revolutionist (poetry). Coombs 99

LOFTIN, ELOUISE, 1950- . Poet
Bassy (poetry). Witherspoon 2:17

Sunni's Unveiling (poetry). Exum 109, Witherspoon 2:16
Virginia (poetry). Adoff 3:514
Weeksville Women (poetry). Adoff 3:515, Troupe 374
Woman (poetry). Adoff 3:514, Exum 108

LOFTY, PAUL. Fiction Writer
Untitled Novel (excerpt: Ch. X—fiction). Reed 157

LOGAN, RAYFORD W., 1897- . Essayist
Confessions of an Unwilling Nordic (essay). Brown 1043

LOGUEN, JERMAIN W., 1814-1871. Orator, Pamphleteer, Letter Writer
Reply to His Old Mistress (letter). Brown 647

LOMAX, LOUIS EMANUEL, 1922- . Journalist, Essayist
The Nation of Islam—Is This a True Religion? (essay). Curry 180
The Negro Revolt (excerpts—essay). Turner 6:100

LOMAX, PEARL CLEAGE, 1948- . Playwright, Essayist, Poet
Baptism (poetry). Bookers 31
Benediction (poetry). Bookers 32
Call to Worship (poetry). Bookers 27
Communion (poetry). Bookers 31
Confession (poetry). Coombs 7
Feelings of a Very Light Negro as the Confrontation Approaches (poetry). Coombs 11
For Death by Choice (poetry). Coombs 10
Glimpse (poetry). Adoff 3:503, Coombs 7
Hymn (poetry). Bookers 29
Morning Meditation (poetry). Bookers 29
Offertory (poetry). Bookers 30
Poem: "You said . don't write me a love poem . . . " (poetry). Patterson 4:29
Processional (poetry). Bookers 27
Reading from the Record (poetry). Bookers 30
Responsive Reading (poetry). Bookers 28, Coombs 6
Retrospect (poetry). Bookers 89, Coombs 8
Schemin' (poetry). Patterson 4:108
Untitled (poetry). Coombs 9

LONG, DOC. See **LONG, DOUGHTRY.**

LONG, DOUGHTRY, 1942- . Poet
Africa II (poetry). Troupe 483
Gingerbread Mama (poetry). Adoff 3:404, Randall 2:310
Negro Dreams (poetry). Adoff 3:405
#4 (Where My Grandmother lived) (poetry). Murphy 2:63
#20 (From the Window) (poetry). Murphy 2:64
#25 (If 'Trane had only seen her body) (poetry). Murphy 2:65

(LONG, DOUGHTRY)
#28 (Black people) (poetry). Murphy 2:66
One Time Henry Dreamed the Number 47
(poetry). Adoff 3:405, Brooks 161, Patterson 4:8, Randall 47, Randall 2:310

LONG, NAOMI CORNELIA. See **MADGETT, NAOMI CORNELIA LONG WITHERSPOON.**

LONG, RICHARD A., 1927- . Playwright,
Critic, Editor, Essayist, Poet
Black Studies: International Dimensions
(essay). Chapman 2:420

Hearing James Brown at the Café des Nattes
(poetry). Bontemps 2:190
Juan de Pareja (poetry). Bontemps 2:191

LONG, WORTH, 1936- . Poet
Arson and Cold Lace (poetry). Major 84
Safari (poetry). Lowenfels 83

LORDE, AUDRE, 1934- . Poet
The American Cancer Society or There Is
More Than One Way to Skin a Coon
(poetry). Wilentz 71
And Fall Shall Sit In Judgment (poetry).
Hughes 20
And What about the Children (poetry)..
Adoff 3:247, Wilentz 68
Bloodbirth (poetry). Wilentz 70
Coal (poetry). Adoff 3:244, Bell 121,
Breman 313, Chapman 2:291, Henderson
284, Jordan 95, Pool 141
Fantasy and Conversation (poetry). Wilentz
66
Father, Son, and Holy Ghost (poetry).
Adoff 3:248, Bell 121, Breman 2:47,
Henderson 285, Pool 140
Father the Year Is Fallen (poetry). Adoff
3:246, Breman 2:48
Generation (poetry). Chapman 2:288
How can I love . . . (poetry). Breman
2:44
If You Come Softly (poetry). Bontemps
2:192
Moon-minded The Sun . . . (poetry).
Breman 2:46
Naturally (poetry). Bell 122, Henderson
283, Jordan 87, Wilentz 65
New York City 1970 (poetry). Chapman
2:289
Now That I Am Forever with Child (poetry). Adoff 3:246
Nymph (poetry). Breman 2:43
Oaxaca (poetry). Breman 2:41
Pirouette (poetry). Hughes 106, Margolies
339
A Poem for a Poet (poetry). Wilentz 72
Rites of Passage (poetry). Adoff 3:249,
Wilentz 69
Suffer the Children (poetry). Adoff 3:248
Summer Oracle (poetry). Adoff 3:245,
Bell 123, Jordan 88
Suspension (poetry). Breman 2:45

To a girl who knew what side her bread
was buttered on (poetry). Breman 2:42
What My Child Learns of the Sea (poetry). Adoff 3:247, Major 85
The Woman Thing (poetry). Wilentz 67

LOVE, GEORGE. Poet
The Noonday April Sun (poetry). Adoff
2:103, Hughes 69

LOVE, J. AUSTIN. Poet
Down Fish Trap Lane (poefry). Brewer 30
Out in the Still Wet Night (poetry).
Brewer 29

LOVELACE, C. C. Preacher, Poet
The Wounds of Jesus (sermon). Miller, R.
119

LUCAS, JAMES R. Poet
The Beat (poetry). Coombs 100

LUCIANO, FELIPE, 1947- . Poet
Hot Blood/Bad Blood (poetry). King 3:124
You're Nothing but a Spanish Colored
Kid (poetry). Adoff 3:501, King 3:122

LUKE, ALLEN. Short Fiction Writer
At Life's End (short fiction). Bookers 68

LUPER, LUTHER GEORGE, JR. Poet
Sonnet Spiritual (poetry). Murphy 102

LYLE, K. CURTIS, 1944- . Playwright,
Poet
Cadence (poetry). Troupe 312
Ebony (poetry). Troupe 2:49
I Can Get It For You Wholesale (poetry).
Troupe 2:44
Lacrimas or There Is a Need to Scream
(poetry). Adoff 3:466, Chapman 2:295
Sometimes I Go to Camarillo and Sit in
the Lounge (poetry). Adoff 3:464, Chapman 2:293
Songs for the Cisco Kid #2 (poetry).
Adoff 3:462
Tampa Red's Contemporary Blues (poetry).
Troupe 231
Terra Cotta (poetry). Troupe 500

LYMAN, JAMES C. Short Fiction Writer
The Two Worlds (short fiction). James
270

LYNCH, CHARLES HENRY, 1943- . Poet
If We Cannot Live as People (poetry).
Adoff 3:461
Memo (poetry). Adoff 3:461

LYONS, LEONA. Poet
Faith (poetry). Murphy 3:99

LYONS, MARTHA E. Poet
A Thing Born of Darkness (poetry). Murphy 103

LYTLE, CORINNE. Poet
Behold the Bride (poetry). Murphy 3:103

MC BAIN, BARBARA MAHONE, 1944- .
Poet
Colors for Mama (poetry). Adoff 3:473
a poem for positive thinkers (poetry).
Adoff 3:473
Sugarfields (poetry). Adoff 3:473

MC BROWN, GERTRUDE PARTHENIA.
Playwright, Poet
Bronze Queen (poetry). Murphy 104
Happy Fairies (poetry). Cromwell 53
Jack Frost (poetry). Cromwell 54
Lilacs (poetry). Murphy 104
The Painter (poetry). Cromwell 54
They Are Calling Me (poetry). Cromwell 54

MC CALL, JAMES EDWARD, 1880- . Poet
The New Negro (poetry). Breman 46, Cul-
len 34, Kerlin 278, Pool 2:137
Tribute to Countee Cullen, 1928 (poetry).
Pool 143

MC CLELLAN, GEORGE MARION, 1860-
1934. Poet, Short Fiction Writer
The April of Alabama (poetry). Long 239,
Robinson 125
A Belated Oriole (poetry). White 97
A Butterfly in Church (poetry). Johnson
97
The Color Bane (poetry). Robinson 122
Daybreak (poetry). Kerlin 300, Robinson
126
A Decoration Day (poetry). Long 240,
Robinson 129
Dogwood Blossoms (poetry). Johnson 96
The Ephemera (poetry). White 95
Eternity (poetry). Long 238, Robinson 123
The Feet of Judas (poetry). Hughes 2:17,
Johnson 97, Kerlin 177, White 96
The Hills of Sewanee (poetry). Johnson 95,
Kerlin 176
I will hide my soul and its mighty love
(first line—poetry). Kerlin 54
In Memory of Kate Reynolds, Dying (po-
etry). Kerlin 178
In The Heart of a Rose (poetry). Robin-
son 124
A January Dandelion (poetry). Robinson
122
The Legend of Tannhauser and Elizabeth
(excerpt—poetry). Robinson 130
Love Is a Flame (poetry). Robinson 124
The Path of Dreams (poetry). White 92
The Path of Dreams (excerpts—poetry).
Kerlin 173
A September Night (poetry). Robinson 124
Spring Dawn (poetry). Cromwell 53
The Sun Went Down in Beauty (poetry).
Robinson 128
To Hollyhocks (poetry). Kerlin 176, White
94

MC CLUSKEY, JOHN, 1944- . Poet, Short
Fiction Writer
The Pilgrims (short fiction). Coombs 2:93

MC COO, EDWARD J. Playwright
Ethiopia at the Bar of Justice (drama).
Richardson 345

MC COY, FLEETWOOD M., JR. Poet
Underway (poetry). Murphy 105

MC CRAE, NETTIE. See SALIMU.

MC CURINE, WILLIAM. Poet
Kinds of Blue (poetry). Bookers 24

MC DOUGALD, ELISE JOHNSON. Essayist
The Task of Negro Womanhood (essay).
Locke 2:369

MC DUFFIE, ELEANOR. Poet
If You Forget (poetry). Murphy 3:103

MC FARLANE, MILTON. Essayist
To Join or Not to Join (essay). Troupe 2:1

MC GAUGH, LAWRENCE, 1940- . Poet
To Children (poetry). Adoff 3:377
Two Mornings (poetry). Adoff 3:376
Young Trainings (poetry). Adoff 3:376

MC GRIFF, (MISS) T. P. Poet
A Ghetto-torn Fantasy (poetry). Bookers 17

MACK, L. V. Poet
Biafra (poetry). Adoff 3:499, Wilentz 77
Death Songs (poetry). Adoff 3:499, Wilentz
79
Jungle Fever (poetry). Wilentz 81
Mad Man's Blues (poetry). Wilentz 76
Over a Glass of Wine (poetry). Wilentz 77
Piece (poetry). Wilentz 78
Zeus in August (poetry). Wilentz 78

MC KAY, CLAUDE, 1890-1948. Autobiog-
rapher, Essayist, Poet, Fiction Writer
A Long Way from Home (excerpt: The
New Negro in Paris—autobiography).
Long 380
Home to Harlem (excerpt—fiction). Calver-
ton 128
Home to Harlem (excerpt: Ch. 2; Arrival—
fiction). Barksdale 498
Home to Harlem (excerpt: The Treeing of
the Chief—fiction). Brown 196
Absence (poetry). Cullen 91, Dreer 46,
White 207
Africa (poetry). Pool 146, Turner 3:204,
Turner 4:48
After the Winter (poetry). Adoff 2:104,
Adoff 3:28, Cromwell 20, Ford 156,
Hughes 2:96, Johnson 138
America (poetry). Adoff 3:26, Baker 166,
Barksdale 496, Bell 15, Brown 349, Chap-
man 374, Cromwell 23, Cullen 83, Davis
294, Dreer 45, Emanuel 89, Ford 155,
Hughes 2:100, Kearns 379, Margolies 309,
Stanford 114, Turner 3:205, Turner 4:49
Baptism (poetry). Brown 348, Chapman

(MC KAY, CLAUDE)

372, Emanuel 93, Ford 155, Henderson 116, Hughes 2:103, Kearns 376, Locke 2:133, White 206

The Barrier (poetry). Johnson 141, Kearns 2:175

The City's Love (poetry). Baker 166

Desolate (poetry). Cullen 88

Desolate City (poetry). Barksdale 495

The Easter Flower (poetry). White 204

Enslaved (poetry). Randall 2:62, Turner 3:204, Turner 4:48

Exhortation: Summer, 1919 (poetry). Cullen 84

Flame Heart (poetry). Barksdale 493, Bontemps 2:30, Brown 351, Cullen 85, Ford 156, Hughes 2:104, Johnson 143, Long 379, Patterson 3:156, Turner 3:206, Turner 4:50

Flower of Love (poetry). Barksdale 497, Turner 3:207, Turner 4:51

The Harlem Dancer (poetry). Baker 167, Barksdale 496, Breman 54, Calverton 204, Emanuel 90, Ford 156, Johnson 136, Kerlin 128, Randall 2:59, Stanford 104, Turner 3:207, Turner 4:51

Harlem Shadows (poetry). Barksdale 496, Davis 293, Emanuel 91, Ford 156, Henderson 115, Hughes 2:99, Johnson 137, Kearns 379, White 205

Heritage (poetry). Bell 13

Home Thoughts (poetry). Baker 168, Kearns 376

Homing Swallows (poetry). Cromwell 21

I Know My Soul (poetry). Randall 2:65

If We Must Die (poetry). Adoff 2:63, Adoff 3:25, Baker 165, Barksdale 493, Bell 13, Black 13, Bontemps 2:31, Brown 350, Calverton 203, Chambers 245, Chapman 372, Davis 294, Davis, C. 167, Emanuel 94, Ford 155, Freedman 243, Hayden 105, Hayden 2:48, Henderson 117, Hughes 2:102, Jordan 135, Kearns 377, Kearns 2:133, Kendricks 237, Kerlin 273, Miller, R. 206, Randall 5, Randall 2:63, Rose 190, Stanford 114, Troupe 39 Turner 3:206, Turner 4:50

In Bondage (poetry). Adams 3:11, Adoff 3:26, Emanuel 91, Kerlin 129, White 205

Jasmine (poetry). Baker 167

Like a Strong Tree (poetry). Barksdale 494, Locke 2:134

The Lynching (poetry). Adoff 2:64, Adoff 3:27, Baker 166, Barksdale 494, Bell 13, Brown 350, Calverton 205, Johnson 133, Kearns 377, Kearns 2:113, Kerlin 128, Long 378, Miller, R. 207, Singh 7, Turner 3:205, Turner 4:49, White 206

Memorial (poetry). Barksdale 498

Memory of June (poetry). Barksdale 497

My House (poetry). Cullen 92

My Mother (poetry). Barksdale 492

The Negro (poetry). Kerlin 298

Negro Dancers (poetry). Locke 2:214

Negroes' Tragedy (poetry). Baker 167,

Chapman 373, Kearns 378, Pool 145, Randall 2:63

The New Negro (poetry). Pool 142

North and South (poetry). Emanuel 93, Henderson 115

The Outcast (poetry). Adoff 3:25, Bell 14, Bontemps 2:28, Breman 54, Chapman 373, Hayden 109, Kearns 378, Patterson 3:156, Randall 5, Turner 3:203, Turner 4:47

The Pagan Isms (poetry). Randall 2:64

Romance (poetry). Miller, R. 207, Patterson 4:15

Russian Cathedral (poetry). Cullen 87, Locke 2:135

St. Isaac's Church, Petrograd (poetry). Adoff 3:27, Barksdale 497, Bell 15, Bontemps 2:29, Hayden 2:49, Miller, R. 208

Song of the Moon (poetry). Hughes 2:98

Spring in New Hampshire (poetry). Barksdale 492, Calverton 205, Davis 293, Hayden 2:46, Hughes 2:97, Johnson 139, Kerlin 127, Randall 2:59

Subway Wind (poetry). Weisman 49

Summer Morn in New Hampshire (poetry). Kearns 375

The Tiger (poetry). Baker 168, Barksdale 494, Randall 2:62

The Tired Worker (poetry). Dreer 45, Johnson 140, Miller, R. 207, Randall 2:60

To a Poet (poetry). Cromwell 21

To O. E. A. (poetry). Dreer 46, Johnson 142, Randall 2:60

To the White Friends (poetry). Adoff 3:27, Johnson 135

Tropics in New York (poetry). Adams 3:88, Adoff 3:25, Barksdale 493, Bontemps 2:28, Breman 53, Davis, C. 165, Hayden 2:47, Locke 2:135, Pool 145, White 204

Truth (poetry). Pool 144, Randall 2:64

Two-an'-Six (poetry). Johnson 145

When Dawn Comes to the City (poetry). Cromwell 22

The White City (poetry). Chapman 374, Emanuel 92, Randall 2:61

White Horses (poetry). Bell 15, Hughes 2:101

The White House (poetry). Adams 3:113, Adoff 3:28, Barksdale 497, Bontemps 2:31, Chapman 375, Davis 294, Davis, C. 166, Emanuel 89, Jordan 119, Kearns 380, Rose 189

White Houses (poetry). Brown 349, Locke 2:134, Patterson 3:156

The Wild Goat (poetry). Cullen 87

Zalka Peetruza (poetry). Kerlin 130

He Also Loved (short fiction). James 104

Home to Harlem (short fiction). Clarke 3:27

Myrtle Avenue (short fiction). Davis 295

Truant (short fiction). Clarke 41, Watkins 16

MC KELLER, SONORA. Essayist

Watts—Little Rome (essay). Schulberg 213

MACKEY, WILLIAM WELLINGTON. Playwright
Family Meeting (drama). Couch 217
Requiem for Brother X (drama). King 325

MC LEAN, ELDON GEORGE. Poet
Bitterness (poetry). Murphy 106
Experience (poetry). Murphy 107
Gutter Rats (poetry). Murphy 106
The Inevitable Road (poetry). Murphy 107
Retrospection (poetry). Murphy 107

MC LEMORE, JAMES H. Poet
Come Not into My Presence (poetry). Bookers 155

MC LLELAN, GEORGE MARION. See MC CLELLAN, GEORGE MARION.

MC MILLAN, HERMAN L. Poet
Equality (poetry). Murphy 2:73
Looking for Equality (poetry). Murphy 2:74
Lost Love (poetry). Murphy 2:75
Nocturnal (poetry). Murphy 2:76

MC MILLAN, JOSEPH. Poet
Death Scene (poetry). Brewer 32

MC NEIL, DEE DEE, 1943- . Poet
The Doorway That We Hide Behind (poetry). Patterson 4:131, Witherspoon 19

MC PHERSON, JAMES ALAN, 1943- . Short Fiction Writer, Essayist
An Act of Prostitution (short fiction). Robinson 2:103
Gold Coast (short fiction). Ford 240
A Matter of Vocabulary (short fiction). James 346
On Trains (short fiction). Hayden 97
A Solo Song: for Doc (short fiction). Chapman 2:151, Davis, C. 327

MC WRIGHT, BRUCE MC M. Poet
To Be Dazzled by the Racing of Her Blood (poetry). Singh 20

MADGETT, NAOMI CORNELIA LONG WITHERSPOON 1923- . Poet
Statement on Poetics (essay). Gibson 3:175, Hayden 175

After (poetry). Pool 147
Alabama Centennial (for Rosey) (poetry). Ford 120, Pool 2:222, Randall 2:197, Turner 3:267, Turner 4:111
Beginning And End (poetry). Lane 34, Ten 23
Black Woman (poetry). Adoff 3:183
Brothers at the Bar (poetry). Chapman 2:296
City Thought (poetry). Dreer 87
Dedication (poetry). Lane 31
Destiny (poetry). Ten 24
Dream Sequence, Part 9 (poetry). Randall 2:195

For a Child (poetry). Chambers 50, Davis 772, Pool 148
From Generation to Generation (poetry). Lane 28
Her Story (poetry). Adoff 3:183, Chapman 476, Ford 121
If Not In Summer (poetry). Lane 29
Late (poetry). Lane 33
Life (poetry). Weisman 29
Midway (poetry). Bell 93, Ford 121, Hughes 39, Hughes 2:381, Jordan 126, Randall 2:197
Morality (poetry). Adoff 3:182, Bell 92, Ford 122, Hughes 23, Hughes 2:382, Ten 24
Native (poetry). Bell 92, Chapman 476, Lane 30
Night Rider (poetry). Lane 34
Nocturne (poetry). Lane 30, Long 690, Turner 3:267, Turner 4:111
Not I Alone (poetry). Dreer 86
Out of Heaven (poetry). Lane 31
Pavlov (poetry). Randall 2:196
The Poet Deserts His Ivory Tower (poetry). Dreer 85
Poor Renaldo (poetry). Pool 148
Quest (poetry). Dreer 84, Randall 2:194
The Race Question (poetry). Bell 93, Chapman 477, Ford 120, Long 691, Randall 2:196
The Reckoning (poetry). Hayden 2:177
Refugee (poetry). Hughes 2:379, Ten 25
Sally: Twelfth Street (poetry). Chapman 2:296
Simple (poetry). Adoff 3:182
Souvenir (poetry). Chapman 2:297
Star Journey (poetry). Randall 2:195
Sunny (poetry). Brooks 169, Ten 26
Tree of Heaven (poetry). Ford 120, Lane 32, Ten 25
The Twenty Grand (poetry). Chapman 2:297, Lane 27
Two Poems from 'Trinity: a Dream Sequence' (poetry). Hayden 2:178
White Cross (poetry). Ford 122
Woman with Flower (poetry). Bontemps 2:195, Randall 29, Ten 24

MADHUBUTI, HAKI R. See LEE, DON L.

MAHONE, BARBARA. See MC BANE, BARBARA MAHONE.

MAHONEY, WILLIAM, 1941- . Essayist, Fiction Writer
Travels in the South: a Cold Night in Alabama (short fiction). Jones 144

MAJOR, CLARENCE, 1936- . Critic, Editor, Essayist, Poet, Fiction Writer
Black Criterion (essay). Chapman 698
Statement on Poetics (essay). Bell 177

All Night Visitors (excerpt: Gypsy—fiction). Reed 183
All Night Visitors (excerpt: We Is Grunts—fiction). Reed 177

(MAJOR, CLARENCE)

Air (poetry). Jordan 96
American Setup (poetry). Lowenfels 85
Author of an Attitude (poetry). Breman 388
Being Different (poetry). King 3:132
Blind and Deaf Old Woman (poetry). Jordan 49
Blind Old Woman (poetry). Adoff 3:300
Brother Malcolm (poetry). Randall 38
Celebrated Return (poetry). Bell 143, Bontemps 182
Design (poetry). Adoff 3:300
Dismal Moment, Passing (poetry). Bell 144, Miller, A. 123
Down Wind, Against the Highest Peaks (poetry). Major 86
Dynamite Transported from Canada to New York City (poetry). Wilentz 89
Flesh Line, the Space (poetry). Bell 143, Miller, A. 124
For her, the design (poetry). Breman 385
Guadalajara (poetry). Wilentz 85
Holyghost Woman (poetry). Jordan 52
How to Describe Fall from Now on (poetry). Wilentz 90
In Chapala, Jal (poetry). Wilentz 84
Instant Revolution (poetry). King 3:128
Iron Years: for Money (poetry). Jordan 89
Is Natural, Takes Me In (poetry). Wilentz 85
Longlegs (poetry). Bell 144, Miller, A. 121
Moonlight, Moonlight (poetry). Jordan 94
Pictures (poetry). Wilentz 88
Self World (poetry). Chapman 2:299
Swallow the Lake (poetry). Adoff 3:302
This Temple (poetry). Miller, A. 118
Tud (poetry). Miller, A. 119
Vietnam #4 (poetry). Adoff 3:298, Chapman 2:299
Weak Dynamite (poetry). Wilentz 86
Widow (poetry). King 3:131

MAJOR, JOSEPH, 1948- . Poet
Poems for Thel—The Very Tops of Trees (poetry). Major 88

MALCOLM X. See **LITTLE, MALCOLM.**

MALCOLM, BARBARA. Poet
Bedtime Story (poetry). Breman 437, Chapman 2:382
Black Woman Throws a Tantrum (poetry). Chapman 2:383
Easy Way Out (poetry). Chapman 2:385
First time I was sweet sixteen (poetry). Chapman 2:384
I watched little black boys (poetry). Chapman 2:384
The Men Are All Away (poetry). Breman 438

MANNING, PAMELA. Poet
Am I a Man? (poetry). Bookers 59

MANNIX, DANIEL P. Historian
Black Cargoes (excerpt: The Middle Passage—history with Malcom Cowley). Freedman 38

MANNS, WILLIAM II. See **BEY, YILLIE.**

MARGETSON, GEORGE REGINALD, 1877- . Essayist, Poet
The Fledgling Bard and the Poetry Society (excerpt—poetry). Johnson 108
The Light of Victory (poetry). Kerlin 110
Prayer (poetry). White 169
Resurrection (poetry). White 170
Time (poetry). White 169

MARRANT, JOHN, 1755- . Narrator, Essayist, Preacher
A Narrative of the Lord's Wonderful Dealings with John Marrant, a Black, 1802 (autobiography). Porter 427

The Conversion of a Young Musician (essay). Patterson 3:19

MARSHALL, BARBARA. Poet
Colonized Mind (poetry). Murphy 2:68
Little Black Boy (poetry). Murphy 2:69
On Philosophy (poetry). Murphy 2:70
On Request (poetry). Murphy 2:71

MARSHALL, LEE. Playwright, Poet
I Gotta Keep Butting My Head against the Wall and Hoping Maybe the Wall Will Break before I Bust My Brains Out (drama). Bookers 127

Irving (poetry). Bookers 148
On Philosophy (poetry). Bookers 56
On the Ledge (poetry). Bookers 125
Suppression (poetry). Bookers 157
Yesterday's Hero (poetry). Bookers 123

MARSHALL, PAULE, 1929- . Fiction Writer, Critic
The Negro Woman in American Literature (Panel Discussion). Exum 33

Brooklyn (short fiction). Davis 598, Ford 111
Reena (short fiction). Clarke 264, Washington 114
Some Get Wasted (short fiction). Clarke 3:136
Soul Clap Hands and Sing (excerpt: Barbados—short fiction). Baker 358, Barksdale 774, Ford 104, Hughes 3:309, Patterson 3:196
Soul Clap Hands and Sing (excerpt: Brazil—short fiction). Emanuel 400
To Da-duh, in Memoriam (short fiction). Chapman 205, Long 732

MARSHBURN, EVERETT LEE. See **MARSHALL, LEE.**

MARTIN, HERBERT WOODWARD, 1933- . Playwright, Poet
Antigone I (poetry). Adoff 3:226

(MARTIN, HERBERT WOODWARD)
Antigone VI (poetry). Adoff 3:226
Antigone XI (poetry). Lane 41
Antigone XII (poetry). Lane 42
Antigone XV (poetry). Lane 42
Contrapuntal No. 6 (poetry). Lane 41
Contrapuntal No. 7 (poetry). Lane 35
Durer (poetry). Lane 35
Grand Central Station (poetry). Lane 38
I Dream You Harlem (poetry). Lane 39
Lines (poetry). Adoff 3:227
Man Woman (poetry). Lane 40
A Negro Soldier's Vietnam Diary (poetry).
Adoff 3:227, Hayden 146
New York the Nine Million (poetry).
Lane 36

MARTIN, J. SELLA, c. 1837-c. 1900. Clergyman, Editor
Address to the Paris Antislavery Conference (1867) (speech). Kendricks 134

MARTINEZ, CARMEN. Poet
Denizen of Hell (poetry). Bookers 102

MARTINEZ, JOE. Short Fiction Writer
Rehabilitation and Treatment (short fiction). Chapman 2:197

MARTINEZ, LYDIA. Poet
I'm Just an Idealist (poetry). Bookers 40
Poetry (poetry). Bookers 86
While at Good Old Cornell (poetry).
Bookers 37
While Sitting Here in Class (poetry).
Bookers 37

MARTINEZ, MAURICE, 1934- . Poet
Suburbia (poetry). Hughes 2:408

MARVIN X. See JACKMAN, MARVIN E.

MASON, CLIFFORD, 1932- . Critic, Playwright, Essayist
Gabriel (drama). King 167

MASON, LEO J., 1947- . Poet
It Was a Hot Day (poetry). Henderson 362

MATHEUS, JOHN FREDERICK, 1887- .
Critic, Playwright, Editor, Essayist, Poet,
Short Fiction Writer
'Cruiter (drama). Calverton 157, Crom-
well 162, Hatch 225, Locke 187, Miller,
R. 225

Some Aspects of the Negro in Contemporary Literature (essay). Cunard 83

Requiem (poetry). Cullen 61, Patterson
4:160

Fog (short fiction). Brown 65, Locke 2:85
General Drums (short fiction). Johnson,
C. 29
Swamp Moccasin (short fiction). Crom-
well 106

MATTHEWS, JOHN. Playwright
Ti Yette (drama). Richardson 77

MATTHEWS, RALPH. Short Fiction Writer
Fisherman's Luck (short fiction). Ford
2:299

MAXEY, BOB. Poet
blues (poetry). Coombs 105
The City Enscriber (poetry). Coombs 109
Moses Miles (poetry). Coombs 101

MAYFIELD, JULIAN, 1928- . Critic, Play-
wright, Editor, Essayist, Fiction Writer
Into the Mainstream and Oblivion (essay).
Baker 415, Conference 29, Emanuel 557,
Gayle 2:271
You Touch My Black Aesthetic And I'll
Touch Yours (essay). Gayle 3:23

MAYHAND, ERNEST A., JR. Poet
Life, a Gamble (poetry). Schulberg 145

MAYS, CLYDE E. Poet
A Time In The Bosom Of Scar (poetry).
Troupe 2:11

MBEMBE. Poet
Pool Hall (poetry). Witherspoon 2:19

MEADDOUGH, RAY J., III, 1935- . Short
Fiction Writer, Critic
Death of Tommy Grimes (short fiction).
Gibson 169, Hughes 3:408
The Other Side of Christmas (short fic-
tion). Clarke 3:159
Poppa's Story (short fiction). Stadler 151

MEANS, STERLING M. Poet
The Old Deserted Cabin (poetry). Kerlin
239
The Old Plantation Grave (poetry). Kerlin 238

MEBANE, MARY ELIZABETH. Essayist,
Short Fiction Writer
Martin County, North Carolina (essay).
Shuman 151
Progress (essay). Shuman 156
The Regal (essay). Shuman 154

MENKEN, ADAH ISAAKS, 1835-1868. Poet
Infelicia (excerpt—poetry). Robinson 237
My Heritage (poetry). Robinson 240
Pro Patria America, 1861 (poetry). Robin-
son 242

MERIWETHER, LOUISE M. Critic, Essay-
ist, Fiction Writer
Daddy Was a Number Runner (short fic-
tion). Clarke 3:198, Stadler 32
A Happening in Barbados (short fiction).
King 2:173, Washington 51

MERRIAM, EVE. Poet
Ballad of the students' sit-ins (poetry).
Pool 2:176

(MERRIAM, EVE)
Montgomery, Alabama (December 5th, 1955) (poetry). Pool 2:164

MERRIWEATHER, ANGELA, 1951- . Short Fiction Writer
The Worms (short fiction). Shuman 158

MESCHI, HOWARD. Short Fiction Writer
If We Could See (short fiction). Ford 2:78

MEYER, JUNE. See JORDAN, JUNE MEYER.

MICOU, REGINA, 1954- . Poet
We The Black Woman (poetry). Patterson 4:76

MILLER, ADAM DAVID, 1922- . Critic, Editor, Poet, Essayist
It's a Long Way to Saint Louis (essay). Curry 171
Some Observations on a Black Aesthetic (essay). Gayle 3:374

The Africa Thing (poetry). Chapman 2:301, Miller, A. 113
Crack in the Wall Holds Flowers (poetry). Adoff 3:181, Miller, A. 112
Hungry Black Child (poetry). Adoff 3:181, Chapman 2:303, Miller, A. 112
The Middle Passage and After (poetry). Chapman 2:305
Mulch (poetry). Chapman 2:304
The Pruning (poetry). Chapman 2:304

MILLER, CLIFFORD LEONARD, 192?- . Playwright, Poet
Springtime (poetry). Murphy 108
The Wonder of the Modern Age (poetry). Pool 150
The World Wonders (poetry). Pool 150

MILLER, JEANETTE V. Poet
Church Lets Out (poetry). Murphy 3:104

MILLER, JORDAN H. Critic
Lorraine Hansberry (essay). Bigsby 157

MILLER, KELLY, 1863-1939. Essayist, Educator, Poet, Short Fiction Writer
The Farm—the Negro's Best Chance (essay). Dreer 159
Frederick Douglass (essay). Turner 2:65, Turner 3:65
Howard: The National Negro University (essay). Locke 2:312
Negro Patriotism and Devotion (essay). Cromwell 199
The People Did Not Choose Mr. Washington as a Leader (essay). Gayle 52
Radicals and Conservatives (essay). Ford 18
Woodrow Wilson and the Negro (essay). Davis 202

As to the Leopard's Spots (letter). Ford 23

An Open Letter to Thomas Dixon, Jr. (letter). Brown 885, Davis 192, Long 245

I See and Am Satisfied (poetry). Cromwell 39, Kerlin 223

MILLER, LARRY A., 1949- . Poet
Peace (poetry). Alhamisi 116

MILLER, MAY. Playwright, Editor, Poet, Short Fiction Writer
Christophe's Daughters (drama). Richardson 2:241
Graven Images (drama). Hatch 353, Richardson 109
Harriet Tubman (drama). Richardson 2:265
Riding the Goat (drama). Richardson 141
Samory (drama). Richardson 2:289
Sojourner Truth (drama). Richardson 313

Calway Way (poetry). Pool 151
Gift from Kenya (poetry). Davis 359
The Last Warehouse (poetry). Pool 152
Procession (poetry). Davis 360
Tally (poetry). Davis 361
The Wrong Side of the Morning (poetry). Pool 152

MILNER, RONALD, 1938- . Critic, Playwright, Editor, Essayist, Short Fiction Writer
The Monster (drama). Alhamisi 52, Robinson 2:428
The Warning—A Theme for Linda (drama). Caldwell 37
Who's Got His Own (drama). King 89

Black Magic, Black Art (essay). Gibson 2:296
Black Theater—Go Home (essay). Gayle 3:288

The Flogging (short fiction). King 2:371
Junkee-Joe Had Some Money (short fiction). Gibson 164, Hughes 3:465
The Ray (short fiction). King 2:105

MIMS, HARLEY, 1925- . Fiction Writer
Memoirs of a Shoeshine Boy (excerpt—fiction). Schulberg 221

MITCHELL, LOFTEN, 1919- . Critic, Playwright, Essayist, Fiction Writer, Screenplay Writer
A Land Beyond the River (drama). Adams 101, Reardon 303
Star of the Morning (drama). Hatch 618, King 575
Tell Pharoh (drama). Reardon 257

Black Drama (excerpt—essay). Adoff 4:85
I Work Here to Please You (essay). Gayle 3:275
The Negro Theatre and the Harlem Community (essay). Gayle 2:148
The Negro Writer and His Materials (essay). Conference 55, Patterson 3:284
On the Emerging Playwright (essay). Bigsby 129

MITCHELL, MATTHEW. Poet
Prayer to the Muse of Song (poetry). Murphy 3:105
These Things I Love (poetry). Murphy 3:105

MIZELL, DON A. Poet
Hope was faced alone (poetry). Coombs 114, Patterson 4:13
"I Want You To Hear Me" (poetry). Coombs 113

MKALIMOTO, ERNIE, 1942- . Critic, Poet
Energy For a New Thing (poetry). Major 90

MOLETTE, BARBARA J., 1940- . Playwright
Rosalie Pritchett (drama with Carlton W. Molette). Barksdale 825

MOLETTE, CARLTON W., 1939- . Critic, Playwright
Rosalie Pritchett (drama with Barbara J. Molette). Barksdale 825

MOMADAY, N. SCOTT. Fiction Writer
House Made of Dawn (short fiction). Troupe 445

MONN, ALBERT. Short Fiction Writer
The Award (short fiction). Ford 2:44
Our Country (short fiction). Ford 2:134

MONROE, ISABELLE H. Poet
To—— (poetry). Murphy 3:106

MOODY, ANNE. Autobiographer
Coming of Age in Mississippi (excerpt—Autobiography). Exum 166
Coming of Age in Mississippi (excerpt: The Movement—autobiography). Adams 4:109

MOODY, DAVID REESE, 1933- . Essayist, Short Fiction Writer
Consequence (short fiction). Schulberg 185

MOORE, ALICE RUTH. See DUNBAR-NELSON, ALICE RUTH MOORE.

MOORE, BIRDELL CHEW, 1913- . Short Fiction Writer
A Black Mother's Plea (essay). Schulberg 243
The Promise of Strangers (short fiction). Schulberg 244

MOORE, DAVID. Poet
The Coming of John (poetry). King 3:142
Poem to the Hip Generation (poetry). King 3:134

MOORE, GERALD. Essayist
Poetry in the Harlem Renaissance (essay). Bigsby 67

MOORE, JOHN P. Short Fiction Writer
Beauty and The Diamond Ring (short fiction). Ford 2:254

MOORE, WILLARD, 1917- . Poet
In between (poetry). Breman 2:70
The job (poetry). Breman 2:71
Spring (poetry). Breman 2:72

MOORE, WILLIAM H. A. Poet
As the Old Year Passed (poetry). Kerlin 112
Dusk Song (poetry). Johnson 85
Expectancy (poetry). Kerlin 112
It Was Not Fate (poetry). Johnson 87

MOR, AMUS. See MOORE, DAVID.

MORELAND, CHARLES KING, JR., 1945- . Poet, Short Fiction Writer
Assassination (poetry). Troupe 2:30
Drums of Africa (poetry). Shuman 367
Eloise (poetry). Shuman 369
For Cousin L. B., in Noxapater, Mississippi (poetry). Shuman 370
Ode to Leslie Parham (poetry). Shuman 371
On the Rainstorm After Sonia Sanchez (poetry). Shuman 373
paper route (poetry). Troupe 2:27
shorty blue (poetry). Troupe 2:29

MOORELAND, WAYNE, 1948- . Poet
Sunday Morning (poetry). Adoff 3:502

MORRIS, JAMES CLIFTONNE, 1920- . Poet, Short Fiction Writer
The Blues (poetry). Pool 2:83, Pool 154
Peace (poetry). Pool 155
Ruby-Jane, Mother-Wife (poetry). Brown, P. 71
The Street (poetry). Weisman 55

MORRIS, MYRA ESTELLE. Poet
Man and Maid (poetry). Murphy 3:106
What Is Love? (poetry). Murphy 3:107
White Collar Job (poetry). Murphy 3:108
Women in Politics (poetry). Murphy 3:108

MORRIS, STANLEY, JR., 1944- . Poet
Admonition (poetry). Pool 156

MORRISON, ALLAN. Essayist
A New Surge in Literature (essay). Patterson 3:221

MORRISON, TONI, 1931- . Fiction Writer
The Bluest Eye (excerpt—fiction). Exum 215
The Bluest Eye (excerpt: The Coming of Maureen Peal—fiction). Washington 23
The Bluest Eye (excerpt: See Mother-Mother Isborgnice—fiction). Washington 93
Sula (excerpt—fiction). Troupe 470

MORRISON, WILLIAM LORENZO. Poet
Eternal Desire (poetry). Murphy 109

MORROW, GLORIA. Poet
Bus Stop (poetry). Bookers 103

MORSE, GEORGE CHESTER, 1904- .
Essayist, Poet, Short Fiction Writer
Confession to the Eternal She (poetry).
Cuney 40
To a Young Poet (poetry). Johnson, C. 134

MORYCK, BRENDA RAY. Autobiographer
I—(autobiography). Johnson C. 153

MOSLEY, JOSEPH M., JR., 1935- . Poet
Black Church On Sunday (poetry). Major
91

MOTLEY, DENNIS, 1950- . Poet
The Death of a Dream (poetry). Shuman
376

MOTLEY, WILLARD, 1912-1965. Fiction
Writer
The Almost White Boy (short fiction).
Hill 2:389, Hughes 3:134, Patterson
3:186, Singh 72, Stanford 256

MOTEN, CORA BALL. Poet
Dream Market (poetry). Murphy 3:111
Lullaby (poetry). Murphy 3:111
Sight (poetry). Murphy 3:111

MOTON, ROBERT RUSSA, 1867-1940.
Autobiographer
Finding a Way Out (excerpt: War Activi-
ties—autobiography). Brown 746

Hampton-Tuskegee: Missioners of the Mass
(essay). Locke 2:323

MPHAHLELE, EZEKIAL, 1919- . Autobiographer, Fiction Writer, Poet
Death (poetry). Breman 172

MTU WEUSI. See **WALTON, BRUCE.**

EL MUHAJIR. See **JACKMAN, MARVIN.**

MULLER-THYM, THOMAS, 1948- . Short
Fiction Writer
A Word About Justice (short fiction).
Coombs 2:107

MUNGEN, HORACE, 1941- . Poet
Welfare (poetry). Robinson 2:458
White (poetry). Robinson 2:458

MURAPA, RUKUDZO. Essayist, Poet
Gwen Brooks—Our Inspirer (poetry).
Brown, P. 72

MURPHY, BEATRICE M., 1908- . Editor,
Poet
Anniversary (poetry). Murphy 3:113
Evicted (poetry). Murphy 2:140

The Guest (poetry). Murphy 3:115
Hatred (poetry). Murphy 3:114
The Letter (poetry). Hughes 2:287
Release (poetry). Murphy 3:114
Safeguard (poetry). Murphy 3:115
Trivia (poetry). Murphy 2:141
Waste (poetry). Murphy 3:117
We Pass (poetry). Murphy 2:139

MURRAY, ALBERT, 1916- . Critic, Essayist, Short Fiction Writer
Something Different, Something More (essay). Hill 112

Stonewall Jackson's Waterloo (short fic-
tion). Margolies 76, Stadler 14
Train Whistle Guitar (short fiction).
Clarke 209, Emanuel 376

MURRAY, PAULI, 1910- . Essayist, Poet
Proud Shoes (excerpt: A Black Soldier in
the Civil War—biography). Freedman 87
Proud Shoes (excerpt: Memoir—biography). Hill 2:291

Dark Testament (poetry). Bontemps 2:107
Death of a Friend (poetry). Adoff 3:110
For Mack C. Parker (poetry). Adoff 3:110
Harlem Riot, 1943 (poetry). Adoff 3:109
Mr. Roosevelt Regrets (poetry). Adoff
3:109
Without Name (poetry). Adoff 3:108, Bon-
temps 2:106, Hughes 2:279, Patterson
4:14

MUSGRAVE, MARIAN E. Educator, Essayist
Teaching English as a Foreign Language to
Students with Sub-Standard Dialect (essay). Curry 119

MUSTAFA, MUKKTARR. See **JOHNSON,
DON ALLEN.**

MUSU BER. Poet
Peaches (poetry). Breman 519

MYERS, WALTER D., 1937- . Short Fic-
tion Writer, Essayist
The Fare to Crown Point (short fiction).
Coombs 2:113

MYLES, GLEN, 1933- . Poet
Express Rider (poetry). Miller, A. 125
Percy (poetry). Miller, A. 128
Percy/68 (poetry). Major 92
A Poem for Jill/68 (poetry). Miller, A. 126
When New Green Tales (poetry). Miller,
A. 127

NAYO. See **MALCOLM, BARBARA.**

NAZZAM AL FITNAH. See **JACKMAN,
MARVIN E.**

NAZZAM AL SUDAN. Poet
Al Fitnah Muhajir (poetry). Major 127

NEAL, GASTON, 1934- . Poet
Personal Jihad (poetry). Jones 414
Today (poetry). Jones 413

NEAL, LARRY, 1937- . Critic, Playwright, Editor, Essayist, Poet, Short Fiction Writer
And Shine Swam On (essay). Jones 637
The Black Arts Movement (essay). Bigsby 187, Davis 797, Gayle 3:257, Gibson 2:215, Singh 325
Black Writing (essay). Alhamisi 124
The Negro Genius (excerpt: the Negro and the Arts—essay). Turner 6:51
Some Reflections on the Black Aesthetic (essay). Gayle 3:12

Baroness and the Black Musician (poetry). Jones 309
Don't Say Goodbye to the Pork-Pie Hat (poetry). Henderson 290
For Our Women (poetry). Jones 310
Garvey's Ghost (poetry). Baker 400
Ghost Poem I (poetry). Troupe 369
Ghost Poem 3 (poetry). Troupe 370
Harlem Gallery: From the Inside (poetry). Chapman 2:306, Randall 2:268
Holy Days (poetry). King 3:148
James Powell on Imagination (poetry). Randall 2:269
Kunter (poetry). Henderson 294, Miller, R. 529
Lady's Days (poetry). Chapman 2:307
A Live Eschatology (poetry). Brown, P. 74
Love Song in Middle Passage (poetry). Baker 398
Malcolm X—an Autobiography (poetry). Bontemps 2:196, Breman 394, Brooks 17, Jones 315, Jordan 42, Randall 2:269
Morning Raga for Malcolm (poetry). Brooks 19, Henderson 296
Narrative of the Black Magicians (poetry). Jones 312, Miller, R. 526
One Spark Can Light a Prairie Fire (poetry). Alhamisi 125
Orishas (poetry). Major 92
Rhythm Is a Groove (#2) (poetry). Jordan 105
The Summer After Malcolm (poetry). Breman 393
The Way It Went Down (poetry). King 3:149

Sinner Man, Where You Gonna Run To? (short fiction). Jones 510, Robinson 2:408

NEGRO NATIONAL ANTHEM. See **JOHNSON, J. W.,** Lift Every Voice and Sing.

NELL, WILLIAM COOPER, 1816-1874. Orator, Letter Writer
Colored American Patriots (essay). Patterson 3:53

Letter to Garrison (letter). Brown 639

NELSON, ALICE RUTH MOORE DUNBAR. See **DUNBAR-NELSON, ALICE RUTH MOORE.**

NELSON, DAVID. Poet, Fiction Writer
Essie Mae (poetry). King 3:154

NEWSOME, E. MARIE. Poet
Freedom (poetry). Patterson 4:150
! ! ! He ! ! ! (poetry). Patterson 4:130

NEWSOME, MARY EFFIE LEE, 1885- . Poet
Arctic Tern in a Museum (poetry). Hughes 2:71
The Baker's Boy (poetry). Cullen 58
Little Birches (poetry). Hughes 2:72
Morning Light (poetry). Adoff 3:21, Bontemps 2:19, Cullen 55, Hughes 2:70
Pansy (poetry). Cullen 56
The Quilt (poetry). Cullen 58
Quoits (poetry). Cullen 59
Sassafras Tea (poetry). Cullen 56
Sky Pictures (poetry). Cullen 57
Wild Roses (poetry). Cullen 59

NICHOLAS, A. X. Poet
(For Lee) (poetry). Coombs 116
(For Mack) (poetry). Coombs 116
(For Poki) (poetry). Coombs 118
This Baptism with Fire . . . (poetry). Coombs 115

NICHOLAS, MICHAEL, 1941- . Poet
Today: The Idea Market (poetry). Major 94

NICHOLS, CONSTANCE. Poet
Baby Hair (poetry). Murphy 110
Civil Service (poetry). Murphy 109
Desire (poetry). Murphy 110

NICHOLS, ELEANOR GRAHAM. Poet
Black Boy Singing (poetry). Kerlin 296

NORTHUP, SOLOMON, 1808-?. Autobiographer
Twelve Years a Slave (excerpts—autobiography). Freedman 51
Twelve Years a Slave (excerpt: Christmas on Bayou Boeuf—autobiography). Brown 714

NOTTINGHAM, PAT. Poet
Carnevale (poetry). Exum 110
Entries: 13, 14, 15, 21 (poetry). Exum 111

NUGENT, BRUCE. Short Fiction Writer
Sahdji (short fiction). Locke 2:113

OBLIVIOUS. See **WOOTEN, CHARLES R.**

OCCOMY, MARITA BONNER. See **BONNER, MARITA.**

O'DANIEL, THERMAN B., 1908- . Essayist
The Image of Man as Portrayed by Ralph Ellison (essay). Gibson 2:102

ODARO, 1946- . Poet
Alafia (poetry). Jones 356

ODEN, GLORIA CATHERINE, 1923- . Poet, Critic, Essayist
As When Emotion Too Far Exceeds Its Cause (poetry). Bell 96, Bontemps 2:160, Hayden 2:183, Patterson 4:143
The Carousel (poetry). Adoff 3:185, Bell 95, Bontemps 2:159, Hayden 2:181
Man White, Brown Girl, etc. (poetry). Adoff 3:186, Williams 143
The Map (poetry). Bell 97, Bontemps 2:161, Hughes 47, Hughes 2:385
Private Letter to Brazil (poetry). Bontemps 2:158, Hayden 2:185, Hughes 91, Hughes 2:383, Patterson 3:275
Review from Staten Island (poetry). Adoff 3:184, Bell 95, Hayden 2:182, Hughes 90, Patterson 3:275
Riven Quarry (poetry). Adoff 3:185

O'DONNELL, E. P. Short Fiction Writer
Arrangement in Black (short fiction). Burnett 88

OFFORD, CARL RUTHVEN, 1910- . Short Fiction Writer
So Peaceful in the Country (short fiction). Burnett 144

OGILVIE, D. T. Poet
Black Thoughts (poetry). Breman 515
Last Letter to the Western Civilization (poetry). Major 95

OGLETREE, CAROLYN J., 1948- . Essayist, Poet
Formula (poetry). Murphy 2:78
Life Is the Art of Drawing (poetry). Murphy 2:79

O'HIGGINS, MYRON, 1918- . Poet
Blues for Bessie (poetry). Hughes 2:347, Pool 2:88
Sunset Horn (poetry). Bontemps 2:146, Hughes 2:352
Two Lean Cats (poetry). Adoff 3:170, Hughes 2:350
Vaticide (poetry). Adoff 2:51, Adoff 3:171, Breman 167, Hayden 2:161
Young Poet (poetry). Adoff 3:170, Hughes 2:351

OJENKE. See SAXON, ALVIN A.

OLIVER, DIANE ALENE, 1943-1966. Short Fiction Writer
Neighbors (short fiction). Chambers 202, Margolies 58

OLIVER, GEORGIANA. Poet
Blind Street (poetry). Murphy 3:118
Lifetime (poetry). Murphy 3:118
Poem (poetry). Murphy 3:117

OLOGBONI, TEJUMOLA, 1945- . Poet
Black Henry (poetry). Chapman 2:311
Changed Mind (or the day i woke up) (poetry). Chapman 2:309
I Wonta Thank Ya (poetry). Chapman 2:312
To Gwen (poetry). Brown P. 77

OLSEN, PAUL. Short Fiction Writer
Line of Duty (short fiction). Williams 145

OLUMO. See CUNNINGHAM, JAMES.

O'NEAL, JOHN, 1940- . Critic, Playwright, Poet
Black Arts: Notebook (essay). Gayle 3:46
Shades of Pharoh Sanders Blues for My Baby (poetry). Chapman 2:386

OSLO, JO TENJFORD. Poet
Some Children Are . . . (poetry). Weisman 73

OTTLEY, ROY, 1906- . Essayist
The Negro Press Today (essay). Watkins 89

OVERBY, BEATRIS. Poet
Dust (poetry). Murphy 3:119
Hands (poetry). Murphy 3:119

OVERTON, SHARLET. Poet
Burn, Baby, Burn (poetry). Bookers 160

OWEN, DANIEL WALTER, 1948- . Playwright, Poet
Borne (poetry). Murphy 2:82

OWENS, I. L. Poet
We're Still a Proud Race (poetry). Bookers 8

OWENS, (REV.) JOHN HENRY. Poet
The Alternative (poetry). Murphy 112
The Answer (poetry). Murphy 111

OXLEY, LLOYD G. Poet
Death Sows a Seed (poetry). Murphy 3:121
The Suttee (poetry). Murphy 3:122

OYAMO. See GORDON, CHARLES F.

PAGE, DAPHNE DIANE. Poet
Untitled (I Take/My War Machine) (poetry). Henderson 316
Untitled (So/I've found me/at last) (poetry). Henderson 316

PALEY, GRACE. Short Fiction Writer
Th Loudest Voice (short fiction). Demarest 166

PALMER, R. RODERICK. Essayist
The Poetry of Three Revolutionists: Don
L. Lee, Sonia Sanchez, and Nikki Gio-
vanni (essay). Gibson 3:135

PARKER, GLADYS MARIE. Poet
The Dream (poetry). Murphy 112

PARKER, PATRICIA. Poet
Assassination (poetry). Miller, A. 110
A Family Tree (poetry). Miller, A. 111
From Cavities of Bones (poetry). Miller, A.
108
I Followed a Path (poetry). Miller, A. 109
Sometimes My Husband (poetry). Miller,
A. 111

PARKER, THOMAS L. Poet
Dissertation (poetry). Bookers 138
Life as Reflected off an Onyx Stone (po-
etry). Bookers 5
Soft Birmingham Sunday (poetry). Bookers
139

PARKS, GORDON, 1912- . Autobiographer,
Essayist, Poet, Fiction Writer
A Choice of Weapons (excerpt—narra-
tion). Adoff 4:74

PARKS, HENRIETTA C. Poet
(My Life) (poetry). Murphy 2:84
Uncertainty (poetry). Murphy 2:85

PARKS, VALERIE. Poet
Love (poetry). Murphy 3:123
Southern Negro Heart Cry (poetry). Mur-
phy 3:124

PARRISH, DOROTHY. Poet
etc etc etc (poetry). Murphy 2:87
Hush Now (poetry). Murphy 2:88
Indictment (poetry). Murphy 2:89
Soliloquy (poetry). Murphy 2:90

PARROTT, RUSSELL. Orator
An oration on the abolition of the slave
trade delivered on the first of January,
1814, at the African Church of St.
Thomas (speech). Porter 383
To the Humane and Benevolent Inhabitants of the City and County of Philadelphia, Address delivered December 10,
1818 (speech). Porter 265

PATTERSON, CHARLES, 1941- . .Play-
wright, Poet
Black Ice (drama). Jones 559
Legacy (drama). Reed 191

Listen (poetry). Major 98

PATTERSON, JESSIE F. Poet
Grill Room (poetry). Murphy 114
War (poetry). Murphy 113

PATTERSON, LINDSAY. Critic, Editor, Es-
sayist, Screenplaywright, Short Fiction
Writer
At Long Last (poetry). Patterson 4:34

Miss Nora (short fiction). Coombs 2:129
Red Bonnet (short fiction). Gibson 216,
Hughes 3:448, Patterson 3:244

PATTERSON, RAYMOND RICHARD,
1929- . Poet
The Accident (poetry). Adoff 102
At that Moment (poetry). Adoff 3:210,
Brooks 29, Jordan 37, Robinson 2:453,
Troupe 99
Birmingham 1963 (poetry). Adoff 3:209
Black All Day (poetry). Adoff 3:212,
Breman 2:84, Pool 157
Black Power (poetry). Chapman 2:316
Envoi (poetry). Pool 158
The Forgotten (poetry). Pool 157
In Time of Crisis (poetry). Adoff 2:102,
Jordan 45, Weisman 63
Invitation (poetry). Coombs 120
I've Got a Home in that Rock (poetry).
Adoff 3:209, Hughes 2:398
Letter in Winter (poetry). Adoff 3:211
Martin Luther King (poetry). Weisman 34
Night Piece (poetry). Adoff 103, Adoff
3:211
Riot Rimes: U. S. A. (excerpt—poetry).
Jordan 108, Robinson 2:454
Schwerner, Chaney, Goodman (poetry).
Chapman 2:318
Second Avenue Encounter (poetry). Jor-
dan 53
This Age (poetry). Chapman 2:318, Jor-
dan 79
Three views of dawn (poetry). Breman
2:82
TLa TLa (poetry). Breman 2:83
Twenty Six Ways of Looking at a Black-
man (excerpt—poetry). Jordan 109
What We Know (poetry). Chapman 2:315,
Robinson 2:453
When I Awoke (poetry). Adoff 3:208,
Chapman 2:317, Hughes 113
A Word To The Wise Is Enough (poetry).
Chapman 2:315
You are the Brave (poetry). Adoff 3:209,
Major 99, Pool 158, Pool 2:215

PATTERSON, THOMAS C. Short Fiction
Writer
Special Assignment (short fiction). Ford
2:101

PAUL, NATHANIEL, c. 1775-1839. Minister, Abolitionist, Orator
An Address Delivered on the Celebration
of the Abolition of Slavery in the State
of New York, July 5, 1827 (excerpt—
speech). Kendricks 47
Speech delivered at the Anti-Colonization
Meeting, London, 1833 (speech). Porter 286

PAUL, THOMAS, Preacher
Letter Relative to Conditions in Hayti, July 1, 1824, Written to the Editor of the Columbian Sentinel (letter). Porter 279

PAWLEY, THOMAS D., JR., 1917- . Editor, Playwright, Poet
Jedgement Day (drama). Brown 534
The Tumult and the Shouting (drama). Hatch 475

PAYNE, ANTOINETTE T. Poet
Oh, Lord (poetry). Murphy 2:92

PAYNE, (REV.) DANIEL A., 1811-1893. Autobiographer, Essayist, Poet
Recollections of Seventy Years (excerpts— autobiography). Brown 733

May I Not Love (poetry). Robinson 58
The Mournful Lute (or The Perceptor's Farewell) (poetry). Brawley 151, Robinson 51
The Pleasures (excerpts—poetry). Robinson 55
Poem Composed for the Soirée of the Vigilant Committee of Philadelphia (poetry). Brawley 157

PAZ, OCTAVIO. Poet
Wind from all Compass Points (poetry). Troupe 461

PEACE, ERNEST E., 1890- . Poet
Night (poetry). Murphy 3:125

PEACE, JERRY. Poet
And Where, My Love, Are You? (poetry). Bookers 80
Greetings (poetry). Bookers 120
The Lynching Tree (poetry). Bookers 138

PEARSON, BERNARD. Essayist, Poet
Negro: The Word and the Meaning (essay). Bookers 51
Number Please? (poetry). Bookers 77

PENNY, ROB, 1940-?. Poet
And we conquered (poetry). Adoff 3:391
be cool, baby (poetry). Adoff 3:390
Black and Lyrical (poetry). Demarest 153
For Nubian Dudes Steeped Deep in Negritude (poetry). Demarest 361
i remember how she sang (poetry). Adoff 3:389
The real people loves one another (poetry). Adoff 3:388
Square Business (poetry). Patterson 4:38

PERKINS, EUGENE, 1932- . Critic, Editor, Essayist, Playwright, Poet
Bronzeville Poet (poetry). Brown, P. 78
Diary of a Bronzeville Boy (poetry). Breman 300
Heart of Black Ghetto (poetry). Alhamisi 99

PERRY, JULIANNE, 1952- . Poet
no dawns (poetry). Adoff 3:516
to L. (poetry). Adoff 3:516

PERRY, PEGGY. Poet
Justice (poetry). Bookers 147

PERRY, ROBERT N., JR. Poet
Frank (poetry). Murphy 3:125
The Funeral (poetry). Murphy 3:127
Inevitability (poetry). Murphy 116
Jim (poetry). Murphy 3:126
Of Dictators (poetry). Murphy 116
The Seasons (poetry). Murphy 114
Storm at Evening (poetry). Murphy 3:126

PETERKIN, JULIA. Essayist
Gullah (essay). Johnson, C. 35

PETERSON, DOROTHY. Essayist
The Negro of the Jazz Band (essay). Johnson, C. 63

PETERSON, LOUIS, 1922- . Playwright
Take a Giant Step (drama). Ford 247, Hatch 547, Patterson 2:43, Turner 5:297
Take a Giant Step (excerpt—drama). Freedman 181

PETRY, ANN LANE, 1911- . Autobiographer, Critic, Essayist, Fiction Writer
The Street (excerpt—fiction). Adams 2:3
The Street (excerpt: Bub and Ben Franklin—fiction). Demarest 247
The Street (excerpt: Dead End Street— fiction). Davis 500

In Darkness and Confusion (short fiction). Chambers 119, Chapman 161, Clarke 3:66
Like a Winding Sheet (short fiction). Baker 262, Barksdale 763, James 233
Miss Muriel (short fiction). Hill 2:166
The New Mirror (short fiction). Stadler 79
Solo on the Drums (short fiction). Clarke 165

PFISTER, ARTHUR, 1949- . Poet
The Funny Company (or Why Ain't him and his girls on T. O.?) (poetry). King 3:160
Granny Black Poet (in Pastel) (poetry). Brooks 179
If Beer Cans Were Bullets (poetry). Coombs 126
If She Bees (poetry). Coombs 123
Ode To The Idiots (poetry). Coombs 127
Poem and ½ for Blackwoman (poetry). King 3:162
The Poet's Guilt (poetry). Coombs 122

PHARR, ROBERT DEAN, 1916- . Fiction Writer
The Numbers Writer (short fiction). Chapman 2:60

PHILLIPS, FRANK LAMONT, 1953- .
Poet
Genealogy (poetry). Bontemps 2:208,
Witherspoon 2:18
Maryuma (poetry). Bontemps 2:209
No Smiles (poetry). Bontemps 2:208

PHILLIPS, LOUIS. Essayist
Le Roi Jones and Contemporary Black
Drama (essay). Bigsby 203

PICKENS, WILLIAM, 1881-1954. Autobiographer, Essayist, Short Fiction Writer
Bursting Bonds (excerpt: Arkansas Trav-
eler—autobiography). Long 258
Bursting Bonds (excerpt: A Christion Missionary College—autobiography). Brown
754

Alexander Hamilton (essay). Cromwell 224
Suffrage (essay). Johnson, C. 111

PICKETT, HERBERT. Poet
Signs of Spring (poetry). Johnson, C. 151

PIERCY, MARGE. Poet
On Visiting a Dead Man on a Summer
Day (poetry). Lowenfels 102

PITCHER, OLIVER, 1924- . Playwright,
Poet
The One (drama). King 243

Harlem; Sidewalk Icons (poetry). Davis
773, Pool 160
The Pale Blue Casket (poetry). Adoff
3:194, Hughes 114, Lomax 247
Raison d'etre (poetry). Bontemps 166, Hay-
den 2:189, Hughes 115
Salute (poetry). Adoff 3:193, Hayden 2:187,
Pool 161

PITTS, HERBERT LEE. Poet
Reality (poetry). Coombs 130
We Must Lead (poetry). Coombs 130

PITTS, LUCIA MAE. Playwright, Poet
Afternoon off (poetry). Murphy 121, Triad
49
And Now Irrevocably (poetry). Triad 52
Bury the Dead (poetry). Triad 38
Challenge (poetry). Murphy 3:128
Declaration (poetry). Murphy 3:128
First Kiss (poetry). Triad 36
Franklin Delano Roosevelt (poetry). Triad
35
I Offer You Wine (poetry). Triad 51
If Ever You Should Walk Away (poetry).
Murphy 121
Let the Book Close (poetry). Triad 41
Let Them Come to Us (poetry). Murphy
117, Triad 46
Little Café (poetry). Triad 54
Moment in Paradise (poetry). Murphy
3:129
Never, Never, Never (poetry). Murphy 120
One April (poetry). Murphy 120

One Day (poetry). Triad 45
Poets (poetry). Murphy 122
Promise (poetry). Murphy 3:131
Punctuation Suite (11 parts) (poetry).
Triad 55
Requiem (poetry). Murphy 3:133
Strange Ways (poetry). Triad 50
This Is My Vow (poetry). Murphy 3:133
This Is The Thing We Ask (poetry).
Triad 39
Transient (poetry). Triad 42
Warwick Castle (poetry). Triad 43
Weeds in My Garden (poetry). Triad 37

PLATO, ANN. Poet, Short Fiction Writer
Forget Me Not (poetry). Robinson 116
The Natives of America (poetry). Robinson 118
Reflections Written on Visiting the Grave
of a Venerated Friend (poetry). Robinson 115
To the First of August (poetry). Robinson
117

PLUMPP, STERLING DOMINIC, 1940- .
Essayist, Poet
Beyond the Nigger (poetry). Adoff 3:387
Black Angel Child (poetry). Brown, P. 81
Half Black, Half Blacker (poetry). Adoff
3:385
I Told Jesus (poetry). Adoff 3:385
The Living Truth (poetry). Adoff 3:388

POLITE, ALLEN. Poet
Am Driven Mad (poetry). Hughes 103
I will sit now (poetry). Breman 2:90
IT was Knife (poetry). Breman 2:92
Stopped (poetry). Hughes 72
A Talk with George (poetry). Breman 2:91

POLITE, CARLENE HATCHER, 1932- .
Essayist, Fiction Writer
The Flagellants (excerpt—fiction). Robin-
son 2:127

POOLE, TOM, 1938- . Poet
I/Wonder . . . (poetry). Major 100

POPEL, ESTHER, Poet
Little Grey Leaves (poetry). Cromwell 48
Symphonies (poetry). Cromwell 49
Theft (poetry). Cromwell 47

PORTER, JAMES A., 1905- . Essayist
Henry Ossawa Tanner (essay). Brown
959

PORTER, KENNETH W. Poet
The Slave Raid (poetry). Kerlin 289

PORTER, LINDA. Poet
As a Basic (poetry). Bookers 7
In Reverse (poetry). Bookers 139
My Mother Was a Black Woman (poetry).
Bookers 4

PORTER, TIMOTHY L. Poet
Now in the black (poetry). Coombs 138

POSTON, TED R., 1906-1974. Autobiographer, Essayist, Short Fiction Writer
The Revolt of the Evil Fairies (excerpt—autobiography). Adoff 4:69, Hughes 3:86, Patterson 3:178, Rose 271, Watkins 417

The Making of Mamma Harris (short fiction). Brown 96
Rat Joiner Routs the Klan (short fiction). Hill 2:378

POUSSAINT, ALVIN F. Essayist
The Confessions of Nat Turner and the Dilemma of William Styron (essay). Clarke 2:17

POWE, BLOSSOM, 1929- . Poet, Short Fiction Writer
Black Phoenix (poetry). Schulberg 203
It Was Here (poetry). Troupe 2:25
To A Young Blood (poetry). Troupe 2:23
Tomorrow (poetry). Schulberg 205
What Can I Say? (poetry). Schulberg 204, Troupe 2:24

Christmas in the Ghetto (short fiction). Schulberg 206

POWELL, LESLIE. Poet
O-o-oo-ld Miss Liza (poetry). Henderson 356

POWELL, WILLIAM I. Poet
Blue Melody (poetry). Murphy 122

PRETTYMAN, QUANDRA. Poet
The Mood (poetry). Adoff 3:260
Photograph (poetry). Adoff 3:258
Still Life: Lady with Birds (poetry). Adoff 50, Adoff 3:259
When Mahalia Sings (poetry). Adams 3:33, Adoff 2:56, Adoff 3:260

PRIESTLY, ERIC JOHN, 1943- . Poet, Short Fiction Writer
Can You Dig Where I'm Commin' From (poetry). Troupe 2:15
Poetry (poetry). Coombs 143
Recreation (poetry). Coombs 145

The Seed of a Slum's Eternity (short fiction). Coombs 2:137

PRIMEAU, RONALD. Essayist
Frank Horne and the Second Echelon Poets of the Harlem Renaissance (essay). Bontemps 3:247

PRINGLE, RONALD J. Playwright
The Finger Meal (drama). Reed 237

PRITCHARD, NORMAN HENRY, II, 1939- . Poet, Short Fiction Writer
: (poetry). Miller, A. 67
(poetry). Adoff 3:360, Miller, A. 65

.—.—.—. (poetry). Miller, A. 68
Alcoved Agonies (poetry). Miller, A. 66
As (poetry). Miller, A. 63
Aswelay (poetry). Adoff 3:538, Miller, A. 64
Concrete Poems (poetry). Wilentz 92
Gyre's Galax (poetry). Adoff 3:359, Lowenfels 105
Love (poetry). Adoff 3:361
Metagnomy (poetry). Major 100
O (poetry). Breman 419
Ovo (poetry). Miller, A. 69
Parcy Jutridge (poetry). Miller, A. 69
Passage (poetry). Chapman 2:321
Self (poetry). Adoff 3:359
The Signs (poetry). Chapman 2:320

PRITCHARD, SHEILA. Poet
At The Inn (poetry). Ten 47
Daquiries At Needlepoint (poetry). Ten 49
The Florida Cock (poetry). Ten 45
For Free (poetry). Ten 46
How To See Angels (poetry). Ten 47
In All The Days Of The Dunes (poetry). Ten 47
Maine Morning (poetry). Ten 44
Mirage (poetry). Ten 48
Up Alone And Late (poetry). Ten 45

PROPES, ARTHUR. Short Fiction Writer
All that Glitters (short fiction). Ford 2:189

PURVIS, ROBERT, 1810-1898. Civil Rights Leader, Historian
Appeal of Forty Thousand Citizens, Threatened With Disenfranchisement, to the People of Pennsylvania (speech). Barksdale 143

PYNE, A. WARNYENEH. Essayist
Living through the Senses Is Living in Love (essay). Bookers 87

QUIGLESS, HELEN, 1944- . Poet
At the Ebony Circle (poetry). Murphy 2:94
Circled by a Horsefly (poetry). Murphy 2:96
Concert (poetry). Major 102
Lip Service (poetry). Murphy 97

QUINN, WILLIAM PAUL, 1788-1873. Essayist
The Origin, Horrors and Results of Slavery, 1834— (essay). Porter 614

RAGLAND, J. FARLEY, 1904- . Poet
Black and Tan (poetry). Murphy 124
Divorce (poetry). Murphy 3:134
Gittin' Happy (poetry). Murphy 3:135
I Wonder (poetry). Pool 164
Sid down Chillun (poetry). Pool 163, Pool 2:173
Strictly Speaking (poetry). Murphy 124
Uncle Tom (poetry). Murphy 123

RAHMAN, YUSEF. Poet
Transcendental Blues (poetry). Jones 369

RAINEY, GERTRUDE ("MA"), 1886-1959. Poet, Blues Singer
Sweet Rough Man (poetry). Henderson 111

RANDALL, DUDLEY, 1914- . Critic, Editor, Essayist, Poet, Short Fiction Writer
The Black Aesthetic in the Thirties, Forties and Fifties (essay). Gayle 3:212, Gibson 3:34
Black Poetry (essay). Gayle 2:109
Statement on Poetics (essay). Bell 175

Abu (poetry). Randall 2:147
After the Killing (poetry). Troupe 67
Analysands (poetry). Randall 2:139
Ancestors (poetry). Randall 2:148
And Why The Softness? (poetry). Patterson 4:49
Ballad of Birmingham (poetry). Baker 337, Bell 71, Brooks 124, Henderson 233, Pool 2:183, Randall 2:143
Black Magic (poetry). Adoff 3:140, Lane 45
Black Poet, White Critic (poetry). Ford 318, Henderson 234, Randall 2:33
Blackberry Sweet (poetry). Chambers 252, Major 103
Booker T. and W. E. B. (poetry). Adams 3:27, Barksdale 813, Bell 69, Brooks 127, Chapman 470, Davis 774, Emanuel 491, Hayden 2:131, Kearns 2:295, Pool 165, Pool 2:159, Randall 16, Stanford 76, Ten 22, Weisman 17
A Different Image (poetry). Randall 2:142
The Flight (poetry). Lane 44
George (poetry). Brooks 126, Hayden 136, Hayden 2:133, Randall 17, Randall 2:145, Ten 20
Good to be in you (poetry). Lane 47, Patterson 4:129
Green Apples (poetry). Patterson 4:107
Hail, Dionysus (poetry). Brooks 123, Randall 2:140
Hymn (poetry). Ten 19
I Loved You Once (From the Russian of Alexander Pushkin) (poetry). Bontemps 2:122
The Idiot (poetry). Chapman 471, Randall 2:144
The Intellectuals (poetry). Adoff 3:142, Alhamisi 112
The Leaders (poetry). Alhamisi 111
Legacy: My South (poetry). Adoff 3:138, Barksdale 814, Bell 71, Chapman 469, Hughes 43, Hughes 2:306, Pool 166
Literary Poetry (poetry). Randall 2:33
Love Poem (poetry). Lane 46
Melting Pot (poetry). Chapman 2:323, Ford 318, Randall 2:141, Turner 3:264, Turner 4:108
Memorial Wreath (poetry). Adoff 2:50, Adoff 3:140, Freedman 95, Hughes 59, Hughes 2:305
My Childhood (poetry). Brooks 133
Old Witherington (poetry). Chapman 2:324, Ten 20
On Getting a Natural (poetry). Adoff 3:141

On Getting an Afro (poetry). Brown, P. 82
On Having a Young Mistress (poetry). Lane 48
Perspectives (poetry). Barksdale 814, Bontemps 2:121
Primitives (poetry). Baker 338, Brooks 122, Chapman 2:322, Ford 318, Randall 2:139, Ten 18, Turner 3:263, Turner 4:107
The Profile on the Pillow (poetry). Adoff 3:141, Brooks 128, Hayden 137, Lane 47, Patterson 4:128, Randall 18, Randall 2:147
The Rite (poetry). Ford 318, Ten 21
Roses and Revolutions (poetry). Adoff 3:142, Brooks 121, Randall 2:142
Sanctuary (poetry). Lane 44
Seascape (poetry). Brooks 132
Southern Road (poetry). Adoff 3:139, Bell 70, Breman 143, Brooks 125, Chapman 468, Emanuel 490, Hughes 41
Souvenirs (poetry). Hayden 2:135, Lane 43, Patterson 4:139, Randall 2:146, Ten 17
Thunder Storm (poetry). Lane 45
To the Mercy Killers (poetry). Emanuel 492
The Trouble With Intellectuals (poetry). Ten 18
Vacant Lot (poetry). Pool 167

RANDALL, JAMES A., JR., 1938- . Essayist, Poet
Bloodsonnet XVI (poetry). Lane 50
Bloodsonnet XXI (poetry). Lane 50
Bloodsonnet XXXV (ah papa, in Whitey's World War II, You fought) (poetry). Lane 57
Bloodsonnet XLIX (But how to get rid of it, pain?) (poetry). Lane 57
Bloodsonnet LIV (Big, bad, and bluesy, Black Harry) (poetry). Lane 58
Don't Ask Me Who I Am (poetry). Lane 49, Randall 2:274
Execution (poetry). Brooks 129, Lane 52, Randall 2:277
In Memory of Martin Luther King (poetry). Lane 54
Jew (poetry). Pool 2:138, Randall 2:278
Seascape (poetry). Lane 58
Untitled (Why should I be eaten by love?) (poetry). Randall 2:273
A Visit (poetry). Lane 56
When Something Happens (poetry). Randall 2:275
Who Shall Die? (Poetry). Brooks 131, Randall 2:272
A Winter Death (poetry). Lane 51

RANDALL, JON, 1942- . Poet
And Where Can I Go Now Except Away (poetry). Lane 63
Because Is Why (poetry). Lane 64, Witherspoon 9
Black Seasons—Haiku (poetry). Lane 59
Blacksinging (poetry). Lane 62

(RANDALL, JON)
DE-troit Summerscene (poetry). Lane 63, Witherspoon 12
For My Brother * * A Big Apple Poet (poetry). Lane 61
I Knew You Better (poetry). Lane 64
It Has Come To Black Beauty (poetry). Lane 64
Revolution?/ Illusion? (poetry). Lane 62
When the Black Mule Kicked (poetry). Lane 60

RANDOLPH, A. PHILIP. Essayist
The Reasons for This State of Mind (essay). Gayle 71
Why Should We March? (essay). Watkins 274

RANSOM, BIRDELLE WYCOFF, 1914- . Poet
Night (poetry). Brewer 34

RAPHAEL, LENNOX, 1940- . Critic Essayist, Playwright, Poet, Fiction Writer
Tales of Poor Ulysses (excerpt—fiction). Reed 283

Infants of Summer (poetry). Major 104
Mike 65 (poetry). Adoff 3:377, Wilentz 99
Nighttime (poetry). Wilentz 109
Sidewalk Blues (poetry). Lowenfels 108

RASHIDD, AMIR, 1943- . Poet
Eclipse (poetry). Major 105
That House (poetry). Troupe 283

RASHIDD, NIEMA. Critic, Poet
Warriors Prancing (poetry). Major 107

RAULLERSON, CALVIN H. Poet
The Cycle (poetry). Cuney 41

RAVEN, JOHN, 1936- . Poet
Assailant (poetry). Brooks 134, Randall 2:258
An Inconvenience (poetry). Brooks 135, Randall 2:258
Reptile (poetry). Brooks 134
The Roach (poetry). Brooks 134, Randall 2:259

RAY, HENRIETTA CORDELIA, 1850-1916. Essayist, Poet
Antigone and Oedipus (poetry). Robinson 141
The Dawn of Love (poetry). Robinson 142
Dawn's Carol (poetry). White 152
Idyl (poetry). Robinson 142
Milton (poetry). Robinson 139
The Months (poetry). Kerlin 311
Our Task (poetry). White 152
Robert G. Shaw (poetry). Robinson 140
Shakespeare (poetry). Robinson 140
To My Father (poetry). Robinson 139
The Triple Benison (poetry). White 153

RAY, IRVIN. Poet
The Panther (poetry). Bookers 155

RAYE, JESSE ANDREW. Short Fiction Writer
. . . Cry at Birth . . . (short fiction). Bookers 21

RAZAFKERIEFO, ANDREA, 1895- . Poet
Equality (poetry). Kerlin 274
The Negro Church (poetry). Kerlin 199
The Negro Woman (poetry). Kerlin 301
Rainy Days (poetry). Kerlin 317

REASON, ARTHUR W. Poet
Ma Honey (poetry). Dreer 60
Why Worry? (poetry). Dreer 59

REASON, CHARLES L., 1818-1898. Essayist, Poet
Freedom (poetry). Brawley 252, White 44
Freedom (excerpt—poetry). Kerlin 24
The Spirit Voice (poetry). Brawley 257, Robinson 73

REDDING, JAY SAUNDERS, 1906- . Critic, Fiction Writer
No Day of Triumph (excerpt—autobiography). Watkins 342
No Day of Triumph (excerpt—Ch. 1, Sect. 1, 5, 7—autobiography). Chapman 300

The Alien Land of Richard Wright (essay). Gibson 2:3, Hill 2:50.
American Negro Literature (essay). Gayle 2:229, Hayden 273, Turner 2:91, Turner 3:91
The Forerunners (essay). Gayle 2:59
The Negro Writer and American Literature (essay). Henderson 91, Hill 1, Long 548
The Negro Writer and His Relationship To His Roots (essay). Baker 350, Chapman 612, Conference 1, Davis 438, Patterson 3:287
The Negro Writer—Shadow and Substance essay). Hemenway 191
The New Negro Poet in the Twenties (essay). Gibson 3:18
On Being Negro in America (excerpts— essay). Curry 65, Turner 6:57
Lonesome Road (excerpt: Mr. Smith Goes to Washington—history). Ford 135

It's All Complicated Up (short fiction). Gayle 98

Reflections on Richard Wright; a Symposium on an exiled Native Son (symposium). Gibson 2:58

REDDY, T. J., 1945- . Poet
For God's Sake (poetry). Shuman 377
From Sleep, Dark Settles in the Eye (poetry). Shuman 379
Land of Make Believe (poetry). Shuman 377
Peace, the Lot Left Over from Justice (poetry). Shuman 378
Synonym for Selective History (poetry). Shuman 379
To the Bright Bystanders (poetry). Shuman 379

REDMOND, EUGENE B., 1937- . Critic, Editor, Playwright, Poet
All the Rain Long It Was Daying (poetry). Shuman 381
The Assassin (poetry). Shuman 382
Autumn God (poetry). Shuman 383
Barbecued Cong: Or We Laid Mai Lai Low (poetry). Troupe 99
City Night Storm (poetry). Shuman 384
Definition of Nature (poetry). Adoff 3:311, Chapman 2:328, Henderson 373
Dragons at Noon (poetry). Shuman 384
1831: For Vincent Terrell (poetry). Shuman 385
Evanescent Love (poetry). Murphy 2:99
Gods in Vietnam (poetry). Adoff 3:312, Major 108
Growing Up (poetry). Shuman 386
Parapoetics (poetry). Chapman 2:325, Henderson 371
Poetic Reflections Enroute to and during the Funeral and Burial of Henry Dumas, Poet (poetry). Shuman 386
Rivers of Bones and Flesh and Blood (Mississippi) (poetry). Shuman 392, Troupe 456
Rush City—The Hale (poetry). Murphy 2:100
Spearo's Blues (or: Ode to a Grecian Yearn) (poetry). Chapman 2:327
Spring in the Jungle (poetry). Murphy 2:102
The Still Soaring Black Angel (poetry). Shuman 394
Sun Ritual (poetry). Shuman 395
Wind Goddess: Sound of Sculpture (poetry). Henderson 372

REED, CLARENCE. Poet
Cosa Nostra Economics (poetry). King 3:171
Harlem '67 (poetry). Jones 404
In a Harlem Storefront Church (poetry). Jones 403
The Invaders (poetry). Jones 400
Lemme Tell You What My Black Is All About (poetry). King 3:168
Lord, Girl She Dance, She Dance (poetry). King 3:170
My Brother and Me (poetry). Jones 402
'Trane (poetry). King 3:172

REED, ISHMAEL, 1938- . Critic, Editor, Poet, Fiction Writer
Can a Metronome Know the Thunder or Summon a God? (essay). Gayle 3:381
19 Necromancers from Now (Introduction) (essay). Chapman 2:513
When State Magicians Fail (essay). Ford 305

Free-Lance Pallbearers (excerpt—fiction). Robinson 2:414
Mumbo Jumbo (excerpt: Cal Calloway Stands In for the Moon—fiction). Reed 293

Badman of the Guest Professor (poetry). Miller, A. 131, Randall 2:284
Beware: Do Not Read This Poem (poetry). Adoff 3:328, Jordan 64, Miller, A. 135, Randall 2:288
black power poem (poetry). Randall 2:288
Catechism of a Neo-American hoodoo Church (poetry). Breman 401, Chapman 2:329
Dragon's Blood (poetry). Troupe 331
dress rehearsal paranoia #2 (poetry). Troupe 332
The Feral Pioneers—for Dancer (poetry). Adoff 3:335, Hughes 2:415
Gangster's Death (poetry). Adoff 3:331
I Am a Cowboy in the Boat of Ra (poetry). Adoff 3:330, Ford 310, Hayden 151, Major 109, Miller, A. 129, Troupe 279
Instructions to a Princess (poetry). Adoff 3:336
The Jackal-Headed Cowboy (poetry). Lowenfels 114
Off d pig (poetry). Jordan 90
Rain Rain on the Splintered Girl (poetry). Adoff 3:327
Sermonette (poetry). Adoff 3:328
White hope (poetry). Troupe 331

REEDBURG, ROBERT. Poet
Epitaph to a Man (poetry). Murphy 2:104
Yesterday's Child (poetry). Murphy 2:108

REESE, SARAH CAROLYN. Poet
Letter from a Wife (poetry). Brooks 170, Hughes 2:413, Patterson 4:152

REID, IRA DE AUGUSTINE, 1901-1968. Essayist
Mrs. Bailey Pays the Rent (essay). Brown 1017, Johnson, C. 145

REMOND, CHARLES LENOX. Essayist, Orator
Every Slave Has the Right to Be Free (speech). Gayle 14

REUTER, E. B. Essayist
The Changing Status of the Mulatto (essay). Johnson, C. 107

REYNOLDS, B. A. Poet
To Gwendolyn Brooks the Creator in the Beginning—Words (poetry). Brown, P. 83

RICE, ALBERT. Poet
The Black Madonna (poetry). Cullen 177, Kerlin 209

RICE, JO NELL. Poet
De Dicshonary (poetry). Bookers 137
You and Me (poetry). Bookers 8

RICHARDS, EDWARD (1915 or 16- . Poet
Fear (poetry). Murphy 125

RICHARDS, ELIZABETH DAVIS. Poet
Dreams (poetry). Weisman 67

RICHARDS, NATHAN A. Poet
Cranes of Wrath and Other Tragedies (poetry). Henderson 204

RICHARDS, STANLEY, 1918- . Playwright
District of Columbia (drama). Hatch 432

RICHARDSON, ALICE I. Fiction Writer
A Right Proper Burial (short fiction). Coombs 2:149

RICHARDSON, WILLIS, 1889- . Dramatist, Essayist
Antonio Maceo (drama). Richardson 2:3
Attucks, The Martyr (drama). Richardson 2:29
The Black Horseman (drama). Richardson 179
Broken Banjo (drama). Barksdale 639, Cromwell 133, Locke 301
The Chip Woman's Fortune (drama). Patterson 89, Turner 5:25
Compromise, a Folk Play (drama). Locke 2:168
The Elder Dumas (drama). Richardson 2:63
Flight of the Natives (drama). Hatch 382, Locke 97
The House of Sham (drama). Dreer 284, Richardson 241
The Idle Head (drama). Hatch 233
In Menelek's Court (drama). Richardson 2:109
The King's Dilemma (drama). Richardson 219
Mortgaged (drama). Cromwell 147
Near Calvary (drama). Richardson 2:95

RIDHIANA. Poet
On Contemporary Issues (poetry). Troupe 2:83
Tricked Again (poetry). Major 111

RILEY, CLAYTON, 1935- . Essayist, Short Fiction Writer
On Black Theater (essay). Gayle 3: 295

Now that Henry Is Gone (short fiction). Clarke 3:146

RILEY, CONSTANTIA, E. Poet
Adieu (poetry). Murphy 126

RILEY, EDWIN GARNETT. Poet
A Nation's Greatness (poetry). Kerlin 316

RIQUET, NICOLE, 19th century. Creole Poet
Rondeau Redoublé (poetry). Robinson 174
Rondeau Redoublé (English version) (poetry). Robinson 175

RIVE, RICHARD. Short Fiction Writer
The Bench (short fiction). Freedman 236

RIVERA, EDWARD. Short Fiction Writer
In Black Turf (short fiction). Burnett 242

RIVERS, CONRAD KENT, 1933-1968. Poet
Statement on Poetics (essay). Bell 175

Africa (poetry). Baker 357
The Death of a Negro Poet (poetry). Breman 2:34, Randall 2:201
For All Things Black and Beautiful (poetry). Henderson 257
For Richard Wright (poetry). Breman 312
Four Sheets to the Wind and a One-Way Ticket to France (poetry). Adoff 2:105, Adoff 3:234, Baker 356, Bontemps 176, Breman 2:38, Hughes 107, Hughes 2:404, Randall 2:199
If Blood Is Black, Then Spirit Neglects My Unborn Son (poetry). Adoff 3:236, Brooks 24
In Defense of Black Poet (poetry). Henderson 255, Randall 2:200
The Invisible Man (poetry). Bell 105, Hayden 2:205, Pool 168
A Mourning Letter from Paris (poetry). Henderson 256, Randall 2:199
On Passing Two Negroes on a Dark Country Road Somewhere in Georgia (poetry). Adoff 2:78, Hughes 42
On the Death of William Edward Burghardt Dubois by African Moonlight and Forgotten Shores (poetry). Adoff 3:235, Barksdale 821, Major 113
Orison (poetry). Breman 2:36
Postscript (poetry). Breman 2:32
Prelude (poetry). Adoff 3:233, Bell 107
Prelude for Dixie (poetry). Breman 2:35
The Still Voice of Harlem (poetry). Adoff 2:99, Adoff 3:237, Bell 107, Breman 311, Breman 2:37, Hayden 2:206, Hughes 44, Singh 22
The Subway (poetry). Bell 106, Hayden 2:207
To Richard Wright (poetry). Adoff 2:54, Adoff 3:234, Barksdale 820, Bell 105, Bontemps 177, Breman 2:31
The Train Runs Late to Harlem (poetry). Adams 3:85, Adoff 2:89, Adoff 3:237
Underground (poetry). Henderson 257
Watts (poetry). Adoff 3:233, Breman 311, Henderson 256

Mother to Son (short fiction). Hughes 3:356

ROBERSON, CHARLES EDWIN, 1939- . Poet
blue horses (poetry). Adoff 3:351
eclipse (poetry). Hughes 2:431
18,000 feet (poetry). Hughes 2:430
Four Lines of a Black Love Letter Between Teachers (poetry). Chapman 2:334
if the black frog will not ring (poetry). Adoff 3:353
Mayday (poetry). Adoff 3:350
othello jones dresses for dinner (poetry). Adoff 3:349, Hughes 2:429

(ROBERSON, CHARLES EDWIN)
poll (poetry). Adoff 3:350
seventh son (poetry). Adoff 3:352
when thy king is a boy (excerpt—poetry).
Adoff 3:351

ROBERTS, WALTER ADOLPHE, 1886-
1965. Poet
San Francisco (poetry). Hughes 2:82
Vieux Carré (poetry). Hughes 2:84
Villanelle of Washington Square (poetry).
Hughes 2:83

ROBESON, ESLANDA GOODE, 1896- .
Biographer, Essayist
Paul Robeson and the Provincetowners
(biography). Brown 815
Paul Robeson, Negro (excerpt—biography).
Brown 815

We Have Passed The Point of No Return
(essay). Gayle 111

ROBINSON, ETHOLIA ARTHUR. Poet
What Is God? (poetry). Murphy 127

ROBINSON, OPHELIA, 1897-? Poet
Black Boy (poetry). Dreer 52
Nat Turner (Prologue) (poetry). Dreer 51

ROBINSON, T. L. Poet
Twang (poetry). Coombs 147

RODANICHE, ARCADEO. Poet
Premonition (poetry). Johnson, C. 118

RODGERS, CAROLYN M. Critic, Poet,
Short Fiction Writer
All the Clacks (poetry). King 3:184
And While We Are Waiting (poetry).
Brooks 2:127
Breakthrough (poetry). Randall 2:263
C. C. Rider (poetry). Wilentz 115
Eulogy (poetry). Coombs 152
5 Winos (poetry). Henderson 344
for h. w. fuller (poetry). Randall 2:262
For O.—Two Hung-up (poetry). King
3:182, Patterson 4:103
how i got ovah (poetry). Troupe 387
In this House There Shall Be No Idols
(poetry). Brooks 2:110
It Is Deep (poetry). Long 780
Jazz (poetry). Brooks 2:113
Jesus Was Crucified or: It Must Be Deep
(poetry). Breman 481, Coombs 155,
Wilentz 118
Jump Bad (poetry). Brooks 2:109
The Last M. F. (poetry). Henderson 346
Look at My Face, a collage (poetry).
Brooks 2:122
Me, In Kulu Se & Karma (poetry). Adoff
3:432, Henderson 345
Missing Beat (poetry). Brooks 2:116
My Lai as Related to No. Vietnam Ala-
bama (poetry). Long 776
Newark, For Now (68) (poetry). Adoff
3:430, Coombs 150

A Non Poem about Vietnam or (Try
Black) (poetry). Coombs 151
Now Ain't that Love? (poetry). Brooks
180, Patterson 4:6, Randall 2:260
One (poetry). Randall 2:261
Phoenix (poetry). Brooks 2:112
Plagiarism for a Trite Love Poem (po-
etry). Patterson 4:26, Wilentz 117
Poem/Ditty-Bop (poetry). Brooks 2:126
Poems for Malcolm (poetry). Henderson
347
Portrait (poetry). Wilentz 111
Portrait of a White Nigger (poetry). Al-
hamisi 108, Long 777
Proclamation/From Sleep Arise (poetry).
Brooks 2:117
The Rain Is in Our Heads (poetry). Long
778, Wilentz 113
Remember Times For Sandy (poetry).
Brooks 2:117
Robobuchinary X-mas/Eastuh julie 4/etc
etc etc etc (poetry). Brooks 2:114
Setting/Slow Drag (poetry). Brooks 2:122
Somebody Call (for help) (poetry). Brooks
2:119
Story/Riff (poetry). Brooks 2:125
Testimony (poetry). Randall 2:261
Tired Poem/Slightly Negative/More Posi-
tive! (poetry). King 3:178
To Gwen, mo luve (poetry). Brown, P. 84
Together (poetry). King 3:176
U Name This One (poetry). Adoff 3:430,
Coombs 154, Murphy 2:112, Wilentz 117
Voodoo On the Un-assing of janis joplin
(poetry). Brooks 2:115
We Dance Like Ella Riffs (poetry). Adoff
3:431, Murphy 2:113, Wilentz 112
What Color Is Lonely? (poetry). Randall
2:265
Written for Love of an Ascension—Col-
trane (poetry). Robinson 2:457
Yuh Lookin' Good (poetry). Randall 2:266

RODGERS, LORETTA. Poet
Beautiful Black Me (poetry). Patterson
4:78
To the Sisters (poetry). Patterson 4:81

RODGERS, PETER T. Poet
Blues Chorus (poetry). Pool 2:83

ROGERS, ALEX. Playwright, Poet
The Rain Song (poetry). Johnson 159
Why Adam Sinned (poetry). Johnson 158

ROGERS, ELYMAS PAYSON. Poet
On the Fugivite Slave Law (poetry). Rob-
inson 60
The Repeal of the Missouri Compromise
Considered (poetry). Robinson 64

ROGERS, JOEL AUGUSTUS, 1883-1966.
Essayist, Fiction Writer
Jazz at Home (essay). Locke 2:216

From Superman to Man (excerpt: The
Porter Debates the Senator—fiction).
Brown 173

ROGERS, JOHN W., JR. Playwright
Judge Lynch (drama). Locke 215

ROKER, MYNTORA J. Poet
Until (poetry). Murphy 3:137

ROOT, E. MERRILL. Poet
The Dunes (poetry). Johnson, C. 36

ROPER, MOSES, 1816-?. Autobiographer
Narrative of the Adventures and Escape
of Moses Roper from American Slavery
(excerpt—autobiography). Barksdale 210,
Miller, R. 66
A Final Escape from American Slavery
(autobiography). Patterson 3:40

ROYSTER, SANDRA H. 1942- . Poet
Love Ain't Hip (poetry). Patterson 4:97,
Witherspoon 18
On Seeing an Old Friend (poetry). Pat-
terson 4:75, Witherspoon 14

RUGGLES, DAVID, ?-1849. Essayist
The Abrogation of the Seventh Command-
ment, by the American Churches, 1835.
Signed—a Puritan (essay). Porter 478
Appeal to the Colored Citizens of New
York and Elsewhere in Behalf of the
Press, 1835 (essay). Porter 637
Extinguisher Extinguished (excerpt: Extin-
guishing an Extinguisher—essay). Brown
595

RUSAN, FRANCILLE. Poet
Black Comedy (poetry). Bookers 147
Boredom '67 (poetry). Bookers 71
How Are You Gonna Keep 'Em from the
Fiery Pits after They've Seen Me Toe-
tap? (poetry). Bookers 101
If I Tell You That (poetry). Bookers 87
A Note for Music Lovers (poetry). Bookers
79

RUSSELL, BILL. Autobiographer
Go Up For Glory (excerpt—autobiography).
Adoff 4:124

RUSSELL, CHARLES L., 1932- . Short
Fiction Writer
Klactoviedsedstene (short fiction). Adams
2:121
Quietus (short fiction). Hughes 3:347

RUSSWORM, JOHN BROWNE, 1799-1851.
Orator
Condition and Prospects of Haiti (essay).
Barksdale 190

RUTHERFORD, TONY, 1945- . Poet
Black and White (poetry). Brooks 174

ST. JOHN, PRIMUS, 1939- . Poet
Benign Neglect/Mississippi, 1970 (poetry).
Adoff 3:346
Elephant Rock (poetry). Adoff 3:347

Lynching and Burning (poetry). Adoff
3:349
Morning Star (poetry). Adoff 3:346
Tyson's Corner (poetry). Adoff 3:345

SALAAM, KALAMU YA. See FERDINAND,
VAL

SALGADO, LIONEL, 1928- . Poet
Fool's Voice (poetry). Shuman 397
Golgotha Nihilist (poetry). Shuman 397
Late Dream (poetry). Shuman 398

SALIMU. Playwright
Growin' Into Blackness (drama). Bullins
2:196

SANCHEZ, SONIA, 1934- . Editor, Play-
wright, Poet, Short Fiction Writer
The Bronx Is Next (drama). Davis 811
Sister Son/ji (drama). Bullins 2:98
Uh, Uh; But How Do It Free Us? (drama).
Bullins 165

Statement on Poetics (essay). Bell 177

—answer to yr question of am i not yr
woman even if u went on shit again
(poetry). Patterson 4:55, Randall 2:238,
Wilentz 129
A Ballad for Stirling Street (poetry). Brooks
146
Black Magic (poetry). Brooks 137, Patterson 4:30, Randall 2:232
blk/Rhtoric (poetry). Bell 137, Wilentz
128
The Blues (poetry). Jones 254
A chant for young/brothas & sistuhs (poetry). Randall 2:240
A/Coltrane/Poem (poetry). Henderson 274
definition for blk/children (poetry). Adoff
3:288
Don't Wanna Be (poetry). King 3:191
For Our Lady (poetry). Wilentz 125
homecoming (poetry). Adoff 3:286
hospital/poem (poetry). Adoff 3:289, Ran-
dall 2:236
indianapolis/summer/1969/poem (poetry).
Breman 365, Wilentz 131
last poem i'm gonna write about us (po-
etry). Bell 136, Patterson 4:135
Let Us Begin the Real Work (poetry).
Brooks 145
liberation/poem (poetry). Bell 135, Chap-
man 2:337
Life (poetry) Brooks 142
Listen to the Big Black at S. F. State (po-
etry). Randall 2:235
Malcolm (poetry). Bell 134, Brooks 25,
Exum 113, Randall 37
A Needed Poem for My Salvation (poetry).
Brooks 140
Nigger (poetry). Randall 2:232, Robinson
2:456
Now poem. for us (poetry). Adoff 3:290
On Watching a World Series Game (po-
etry). Chapman 2:338

(SANCHEZ, SONIA)
Poem at Thirty (poetry). Adoff 3:286, Brooks 136, Henderson 271, Jones 250, Randall 2:231
Poem (for d c's 8th graders—1966-67) (poetry). Adoff 3:288, Alhamisi 132
poem for ethridge (poetry). Randall 2:239
Poem for My Children (poetry). Alhamisi 132
A Poem for My Father (poetry). Brooks 139, Randall 2:236
present (poetry). Troupe 427
Queens of the Universe (poetry). King 3:186
Right on: White America (poetry). Adoff 3:286, Bell 135, Coombs 158, Jordan 104, Wilentz 124
Small Comment (poetry). Barksdale 822, Exum 115, Major 114
So This Is Our Revolution (poetry). Brooks 144, Wilentz 127
Summary (poetry). Brooks 138, Jones 252, Lowenfels 118, Randall 2:233
Summer Words for a Sistuh Addict (poetry). Randall 2:237, Wilentz 126
Sunday Evening at Gwen's (poetry). Brown, P. 86
To All Brothers (poetry). Brooks 136, Patterson 4:65, Randall 2:231
To All Sisters (poetry). Adoff 3:290, Jones 255
To Anita (poetry). King 3:190
To Blk/Record/Buyers (poetry). Henderson 272, Robinson 2:456
To Chuck (poetry). Henderson 273
To Morani/Munger (poetry). King 3:188
We a Ba-a-d People (poetry). Brooks 141, Brown, P. 87
After Saturday Night Comes Sunday (short fiction). Coombs 2:159

SANCHEZ, THOMAS. Fiction Writer.
Rabbit Boss (excerpt—fiction). Troupe 67

SANDERS, GLENN C. Poet
Contradictions (poetry). Bookers 88
The Master of a Slave (poetry). Bookers 106

SANDERS, STANLEY, 1942- . Autobiographer
I'll Never Escape the Ghetto (autobiography). Chapman 347

SARVER, RUTH E. J. Poet
The Compensation (poetry). Murphy 128
Dream Love (poetry). Murphy 128

SATO, HIROKO. Essayist
Under the Harlem Shadow: a Study of Jessie Fauset & Nella Larsen (essay). Bontemps 3:63

SAUNDERS, PRINCE, 1807-1840. Orator
An address delivered at Bethel Church, Pennsylvania; on the 30th of September, 1818. Before the Pennsylvania Augustine Society, for the education of People of Colour (speech). Porter 87
A Memoir Presented to the American Convention for Promoting the Abolition of Slavery, and Improving the Condition of the African Race, December 11, 1818 (speech). Porter 269

SAUNDERS, RUBY CONSTANCE X, 1939- . Playwright, Poet, Essayist
Auditions (poetry). Coombs 165
Ballad for the Brother (poetry). Patterson 4:109
Be Natural, Baby (poetry). Coombs 162
Don't Pay (poetry). Coombs 161
The Generation Gap (poetry). Coombs 163
Lawd, Dese Colored Chillum (poetry). Coombs 160
My Man Was Here Today (poetry). Coombs 165, Patterson 4:84

SAXON, ALVIN A. Poet
Black Power (poetry). Adoff 3:493, Schulberg 62
Indictment (poetry). Schulberg 61
Legacy of the Word (poetry). Troupe 169, Troupe 2:17
Morality (poetry). Schulberg 61
A Poem for Integration (poetry). Adoff 3:495
Sukardri (poetry). Troupe 2:21
To Mr. Charles and Sister Annie (poetry). Schulberg 63
Watts (poetry). Adoff 3:494, Schulberg 65

SAXON, DAN. Poet
Atman (poetry). Lowenfels 123

SCARBOROUGH, DOROTHY. Essayist, Teacher
New Lights on an Old Song (essay). Johnson, C. 59

SCARBOROUGH, W. S. Orator
The Educated Negro and His Mission (speech). Cromwell 291

SCHOMBERG, ARTHUR A., 1874-1938. Scholar, Editor, Essayist
Juan Latino, Magister Latinus (essay). Johnson, C. 69
The Negro Digs Up His Past (essay). Locke 2:231, Watkins 101
Racial Integrity (essay). Cunard 74

SCHUYLER, GEORGE SAMUEL, 1895- . Autobiographer, Critic, Essayist, Poet, Short Fiction Writer
Dr. Jekyll and Mr. Hyde, and the Negro (essay). Watkins 266
Our Greatest Gift to America (essay). Johnson, C. 122
What the Negro Thinks of the South (essay). Turner 2:87, Turner 3:87

(SCHUYLER, GEORGE SAMUEL)
Black No More (excerpt: Ch. 8—fiction).
Long 458, Miller, R. 244
Black No More (excerpt: a World-Shaking
Discovery—fiction). Brown 213

Black Warriors (excerpt—short fiction).
Brown 86

SCOTT, CALVIN. Poet
Black Am I Like the Night (poetry). Haslam 384
Come Soft in the Waking Hours of Morning (poetry). Haslam 383

SCOTT, DENNIS. Poet
Bird of Passage (poetry). Troupe 486

SCOTT, EDDIE, JR. Poet
Birth (poetry). Bookers 5
Rape of a Man (poetry). Bookers 68
Reflection (poetry). Bookers 162
The Second Unveiling (poetry). Bookers 136
Winter (poetry). Bookers 100

SCOTT, JOHNIE, 1946- . Poet, Essayist
What Poetry is for Me (essay). Coombs
169

Alan Paton Will Die (poetry). Schulberg
129
The American Dream (poetry). Major 115
Attention (poetry). Schulberg 123
Bad News (poetry). Schulberg 212
Black Consciousness (poetry). Schulberg
128
Chaos in a Ghetto Alley (poetry). Breman
513, Schulberg 127
The Fist Party (poetry). Schulberg 123
Hush (poetry). Schulberg 120
India (poetry). Schulberg 117
Intent (poetry). Schulberg 125
Jeremy (poetry). Schulberg 124
Long Live the Peace Corps of America
(poetry). Schulberg 130
Poem: A Negro in Two Parts (poetry).
Pool 2:144
Poem for Joyce (poetry). Coombs 170,
Patterson 4:39
A Short Poem for Frustrated Poets (po-
etry). Coombs 166
The Suicide Note (poetry). Schulberg 118
Watts, 1966 (poetry). Schulberg 132

The Coming of the Hoodlum (short fiction). Schulberg 97

SCOTT, NATHAN ALEXANDER, JR.,
1925- . Critic, Editor, Essayist, Theo-
logian
The Dark and Haunted Tower of Richard
Wright (essay). Gayle 2:296, Gibson
2:12, Hemenway 72
Judgment Marked by a Cellar: The American Negro Writer and the Dialect of
Despair (essay). Davis 821

Society and Self in Recent American Literature,—for Ralph Ellison (essay).
Emanuel 539

SCOTT, SHARON, 1951- . Poet
Between Me and Anyone Who Can Under-
stand (poetry). Brooks 2:174
Come on Home (poetry). Brooks 2:175
Discovering (poetry). Brooks 2:172
For both of Us at Fisk (poetry). Brooks
2:180
For Gwen (poetry). Brown, P. 89
Just Taking Note (poetry). Brooks 2:172
A Little More about the Brothers and
Sisters (poetry). Brooks 2:171
Mama Knows (poetry). Brooks 2:175
Oh, Yeah! (poetry). Brooks 2:176
OKay (poetry). Brooks 2:173
On My Strand (poetry). Brooks 2:173
Our Lives (poetry). Brooks 2:174
Sharon Will Be No/Where on Nobody's
Best Selling List (poetry). Brooks 2:177
Untitled (fish is) (poetry). Brooks 2:179
Untitled (Hi Ronda) (poetry). Brooks
2:178

SEBREE, CHARLES, 1914- . Playwright
Dry August (drama). Hatch 658

SEESE, ETHEL GRAY. Poet
The Beat (poetry). Ten 13
Communication (poetry). Ten 13
De-Ho-Cho (poetry). Ten 16
English Sparrows (poetry). Ten 13
The Fallen (poetry). Ten 13
Intimacy (poetry). Ten 14
A Loop In The Day (poetry). Ten 13
The Man With The Horn Is Not Just
Blowing (poetry). Ten 10
To Martin Luther King, Jr. (poetry).
Ten 9
Westward Flight (poetry). Ten 15
You Ask (poetry). Ten 14

SEJOUR, VICTOR, 1817-1874. Playwright,
Poet
The Brown Overcoat (drama). Hatch 25
Le Retour de Napoleon (poetry). Robinson
169
Le Retour de Napoléon (English version)
(poetry). Robinson 172

SENNA, CARL, 1944- . Critic, Editor
Short Fiction Writer
A Chill Morning (short fiction). Shu-
man 164

SEXTON, WILL. Poet
The Bomb Thrower (poetry). Kerlin 198
The New Negro (poetry). Kerlin 198
To My Lost Child (poetry). Kerlin 265

SHABAZZ, SAYIF. See **GEARY, BRUCE C.**

SHACKLEFORD, THEODORE HENRY,
1887-1923. Poet
The Big Bell In Zion (poetry). Johnson 209

SHAED, DOROTHY LEE LOUISE. Poet
Before Autumn Leaves Turn Gold (poetry). Murphy 3:139
For a Discontented Soul (poetry). Murphy 3:139
On a Letter I Received (poetry). Murphy 3:139
Reprobate (poetry). Murphy 3:139
Snow (poetry). Murphy 3:140

SHARON. Poet
Why Me? (poetry). Bookers 38
You Because (poetry). Bookers 38

SHARP, SAUNDRA, 1942- . Poet
New Blues from a Brown Baby (poetry). Patterson 4:67
Reaching Back (poetry). Coombs 174, Patterson 4:137
A Seeing Eye-Dog (poetry). Coombs 175, Patterson 4:64
Sundays Are Special (poetry). Patterson 4:69

SHAW, DORIS ANN, 1943- . Poet
Emotions of the Blacks (poetry). Shuman 400

SHAW, EDNA. Poet
Little Helper (poetry). Murphy 3:140

SHAW, MARGARET ADELAIDE. Poet
Closed Doors (poetry). Kerlin 233

SHEPHERD, GERALD. Essayist
Living in a Slum—What Slums Need (essay). Bookers 16

SHEPP, ARCHIE, 1937- . Playwright
Junebug Graduates Tonight (drama). King 33

SHEPPERD, WALT. Essayist
An Interview with Clarence Major and Victor Hernandez Cruz (essay). Chapman 2:545

SHERMAN, JIMMIE. Playwright, Poet
As Bald as She Could Be (poetry). Schulberg 82
I'm Here (poetry). Schulberg 83
My Beard (poetry). Schulberg 83
Negro History (poetry). Schulberg 84
Race Compliments (poetry). Schulberg 86
Sammy Lee (poetry). Schulberg 84
This Is the Home of My Fathers (poetry). Schulberg 85
The Workin' Machine (poetry). Schulberg 81
The World Is Ready to Explode (poetry). Schulberg 81

SHINE, TED, 1936- . Editor, Playwright
Herbert III (drama). Hatch 854
Morning, Noon and Night (drama). Reardon 399

SHOCKLEY, ANN ALLEN. Autobiographer, Critic, Editor, Fiction Writer
The Funeral (short fiction). Stadler 274

SHORTER, LYNN, 1946- . Poet
domo's mirror (poetry). Hayden 156
Ibe (poetry). Hayden 155

SIDNEY, JOSEPH, Orator
An Oration Commemorative of the Abolition of the Slave Trade; Delivered Before the Wilberforce Philanthropic Association, January, 1809 (speech). Porter 355

SIDNEY, ROBERT Y. Songwriter
Anthems and Hymns 1808-1814 (poetry). Porter 562

SIDNEY, THOMAS S. Poet
On Freedom, 1828 (poetry). Porter 574

SILBER, FRED. Poet
Sunglasses (poetry). Lowenfels 125

SILVERA, EDWARD S., 1906-1937. Poet
Forgotten Dreams (poetry). Cuney 42, Hughes 2:259
Jungle Taste (poetry). Adams 3:58, Cullen 214, Kerlin 210, Weisman 32
Old Maid (poetry). Johnson, C. 127
On the Death of a Child (poetry). Cuney 44, Hughes 2:260
South Street (poetry). Cullen 214, Cuney 43
To Lincoln at Graduation (poetry). Cuney 42
The Unknown Soldier (poetry). Johnson, C. 127
You (poetry). Cuney 43

SIMMONS, BARBARA. Poet
Soul (poetry). Jones 304

SIMMONS, CARMEL. Poet
My Mother's Child (poetry). Pool 2:127

SIMMONS, DAN. Poet
Nationalism (poetry). Coombs 177

SIMMONS, GERALD L., JR., 1944- . Poet
Take Tools Our Strength (poetry). Major 119

SIMMONS, HERBERT ALFRED, 1930- . Fiction Writer, Poet
Ascendency (poetry). Major 120, Troupe 2:39
Contemplation for Lovers, 1968 (poetry). Troupe 2:38
Martyrs (February 21, 1965) (poetry). Troupe 2:41
Martyrs (April 4, 1968) (poetry). Troupe 2:43
Ode to a Dying Sun (poetry). Troupe 2:38

SIMMONS, JUDY DOTHARD, 1944-   . Poet
The Answer (poetry). Henderson 365
Generations (poetry). Troupe 206
Poem for Larry Ridley (poetry). Henderson 364

SIMPSON, JUANITA. Poet
The Leviathan (poetry). Bookers 157
We Are an Embryo People (poetry). Bookers 161

SIMS, CLEVELAND. Poet
Birthday Song to Cleveland (poetry). Troupe 2:84

SIMS, LEFTY. Poet
An Angel's Prayer (poetry). Jones 379

SINCLAIR, JOHN, 1941-   . Poet
Breakthrough (poetry). Major 122

SIPKINS, HENRY, 1788-1838. Orator
An Oration on the Abolition of the Slave Trade; Delivered in the African Church, in the City of N. Y., January 2, 1809 (speech). Porter 365

SIRRAH, LEUMAS, 1947-   . Poet
Day Off the Street (poetry). Breman 511, Troupe 2:43
Infinite (poetry). Schulberg 233
Insanity, the Question (poetry). Schulberg 236
Me—I'm black (poetry). Breman 510, Schulberg 233
One, Two, Three (poetry)). Schulberg 235
Who's Life? (poetry). Schulberg 234
Who's the Man Asleep? (poetry). Schulberg 236
You and I (poetry). Schulberg 234

SISTER BERNADINE. Poet
The Sermon (Revelations) (poetry). Exum 58

SKEETER, SHARYN JEANNE, 1945-   . Critic, Poet
Self (poetry). Exum 116
Summer Street (poetry). Exum 116

SLAY, JOHNNIE BEA. Short Fiction Writer
The Last Mile (short fiction). Shuman 168

SMALLWOOD, WILL. Poet
Come, Beloved (poetry). Murphy 129
Forgiveness (poetry). Murphy 130
I Own a Dream (poetry). Murphy 129
Pledge (poetry). Murphy 130

SMART, ALICE MC GEE. Poet
Pa (poetry). Dreer 64
The Street Called Petticoat Lane (poetry). Dreer 63

SMITH, ABRAM G. F. Poet
Alpha and Omega (poetry). Murphy 3:142
I Pass (poetry). Murphy 3:141

SMITH, G. T. Poet
Watermelon (poetry). Brewer 38

SMITH, JAMES EDGAR. Poet
Fragility (poetry). Murphy 130
Shadows (poetry). Murphy 131

SMITH, JAMES MC CUNE, 1813-1865. Essayist
The German Invasion (essay). Patterson 3:49

SMITH, JEAN WHEELER, 1942-   . Critic, Short Fiction Writer
Frankie Mae (short fiction). King 2:35, Washington 3
That She Would Dance No More (short fiction). Jones 486

SMITH, JOHN CASWELL, 1907-   . Essayist, Short Fiction Writer
Fighter (short fiction). Clarke 135

SMITH, JULES WYNN. Poet
A Quoi Bon? (poetry). Murphy 31

SMITH, LAURA E. Poet
Exitus (poetry). Murphy 3:143
Wings (poetry). Murphy 3:143

SMITH, LINWOOD D. Poet
Dawn Song (poetry). Murphy 2:116
Free Wine on Communion Day (poetry). Murphy 2:117
Pride and Prejudice (poetry). Murphy 2:118
This Is For You (poetry). Brown, P. 90
What Good Are Words (poetry). Murphy 2:119

SMITH, LUCY. Poet
Face of Poverty (poetry). Hughes 45, Hughes 2:267, Singh 34

SMITH, MARY CARTER, 1924-   . Poet
Clubwoman (poetry). Hughes 2:388
Jungle (poetry). Hughes 2:389

SMITH, MILTON. See **MBEMBE.**

SMITH, NANNIE TRAVIS, 1893-   . Poet
Dark Hands (poetry). Murphy 142
White Fear (poetry). Murphy 143

SMITH, VENTURE, 1729-1805. Narrator
A Narrative of the Life and Adventures of Venture, A Native of Africa: But Resident above sixty years in the United States of America, 1798 (narrative). Porter 538

SMITH, WELTON, 1940-   . Playwright, Poet
The Beast Section (poetry). Adoff 3:374, Jones 290
A Folding and Unfolding (poetry). Hughes 2:372

(SMITH, WELTON)
Interlude (poetry). Adoff 3:374, Jones 287
Malcolm (poetry). Jones 203, Randall 2:280
The Nigga Section (poetry). Jones 285, Randall 2:282
A Sequence from the Roach Rider, a play (poetry). King 3:149
Special Section for Niggas on the Lower East Side or: Divert the Division and Multiply (poetry). Jones 287
Strategies (poetry). Adoff 3:375, Major 124

SMITH, WILLIAM GARDNER, 1926- . Critic, Essayist, Fiction Writer
The Negro Writer—Pitfalls and Compensations (essay). Gayle 2:288, Hemenway 198

SMITH, WILLIAM JAY. Poet
The Park in Milan (poetry). Adoff 52

SNELLINGS, ROLLAND, 1938- . Essayist
Crisis in Black Culture (essay). Alhamisi 29
The Sound of Allah's Horn (essay). Alhamisi 135
What is to be done: The role of an Authentic Black Intelligensia (essay). Alhamisi 34

Blacklove | East (poetry). Troupe 255
Crisis (poetry). Alhamisi 37
Dago Red (a Harlem Snow Song) (poetry). King 3:223
Earth (poetry). Brooks 172, Jones 327
Extension (poetry). Henderson 304
Floodtide (poetry). Adoff 3:336, Hughes 2:424
For Love to Survive (poetry). Patterson 4:169
JuJu (poetry). Adoff 3:340, Wilentz 134
Mississippi Concerto (poetry). Jones 324
Notes from a Guerilla Diary (poetry). King 3:220
Pome for Dionne Warwick aboard the aircraft carrier U. S. S. Enterprise (poetry). Wilentz 138
The Song of Fire (poetry). Jones 325
Sunrise (poetry). Jones 322
Tauhid (poetry). Adoff 3:339, Wilentz 139

SNYDER, THURMOND L. Poet
Beale Streat, Memphis (poetry). Hughes 54
The Beast With Chrome Teeth (poetry). Hughes 87
Seeds (poetry). Hughes 88

SOLOMON, PHILIP, 1954- . Poet
Foxey Lady (poetry). Jordan 4

SPELLMAN, ALFRED B., 1935- . Essayist, Poet
Not Just Whistling Dixie (essay). Jones 159

The beautiful day (poetry). Hollo 23
The Beautiful Day #2 (poetry). Jones 245, Miller, A. 56

Did John's Music Kill Him? (poetry). Henderson 261
For My Unborn and Wretched Children (poetry). Adoff 3:283, Miller, A. 57
Friends I Am Like You Tied (poetry). Bell 126, Jones 248
I Looked and Saw History Caught (poetry). Major 126
in orangeburg my brothers did (poetry). Adoff 3:285, Henderson 262, Miller, A. 62, Randall 2:229
Jelly Wrote (poetry). Bell 125, Miller, A. 60
The Joel blues (poetry). Henderson 262, Hollo 23, Miller, A. 58
John Coltrane/an impartial review (poetry). Adoff 3:283, Bell 125, Hughes 57, Miller, A. 60
1½ Seasons (poetry). Miller, A. 56
Sequel to the Above (For My Unborn and Wretched Children) (poetry). Miller, A. 57
Song for the Sisters (poetry). Brown, P. 91
A Thrift of Wishes (poetry). Pool 170
Tomorrow the Heroes (poetry). Adoff 3:285, Jones 247
Untitled (poetry). Breman 324
Untitled (in orangeburg my brothers did) (poetry). Henderson 262
What Is It (poetry). Pool 169
When black people are (poetry). Adoff 3:284, Bell 127, Miller, A. 61, Randall 2:228
Zapata and the Landlord (poetry). Adoff 3:282, Hughes 60

SPENCE, EULALIE, 1894- . Playwright.
The Starter (drama). Locke 205
Undertow (drama). Hatch 192

SPENCER, ANNE, 1882-?. Poet
At the Carnival (poetry). Brown 352, Cullen 53, Davis 271, Hayden 2:35, Hughes 2:62, Johnson 215, Kerlin 188
Before the Feast of Shushan (poetry). Brown 353, Davis 269, Johnson 213
Creed (poetry). Cullen 51
Dunbar (poetry). Cullen 50, Dreer 47, Hayden 2:37, Johnson 218
For Jim, Easter Eve (poetry). Bontemps 2:17, Hughes 2:65
I Have a Friend (poetry). Cullen 47
Innocence (poetry). Cullen 51
Lady, Lady (poetry). Adoff 3:17, Locke 2:148
Letter to My Sister (poetry). Adoff 3:16, Barksdale 628, Bontemps 2:19, Davis 270, Hughes 2:61, Patterson 3:155
Life-long, Poor Browning (poetry). Brown 351, Cullen 49, Hughes 2:60
Lines to a Nasturtium (A lover muses) (poetry). Barksdale 627, Bontemps 2:18, Brown 354, Cullen 52, Davis 272, Dreer 47, Hughes 2:64, Patterson 3:155
Neighbors (poetry). Cullen 47

(SPENCER, ANNE)
Questing (poetry). Cullen 48
Substitution (poetry). Cullen 48
Sybil Warns Her Sister (poetry). Johnson, C. 94
Translation (poetry). Johnson 218
The Wife-Woman (poetry). Johnson 216

SPENCER, GILMORE. Short Fiction Writer
Mulatto Flair (short fiction). Ford 2:87

SPENCER, WADE. Short Fiction Writer
The Cherrybomb Command (short fiction). Bookers 60

SPRIGGS, EDWARD S., 1934- . Poet
Black Power (poetry). Alhamisi 128
Every Harlem Face is Afromanism Surviving (poetry). Jones 341
For black Newark: 1968 (poetry). Breman 336
For Brother Malcolm (poetry). Adoff 62, Brooks 30
For the Truth (Because it is necessary) (poetry). Brooks 162, Jones 339, Randall 36
My Beige Mom (poetry). Jones 342
Pending Solemnization (poetry). Breman 337
Sassafras Memories (poetry). Jones 343
Some Hop-Scotching (poetry). Alhamisi 126
We Waiting on You (poetry). Jones 337

STALLWORTH, ROBERT. Poet
God's Gift to the Woman (poetry). Bookers 89

STANFORD, THEODORE. Poet
That Vengeance Gathers (poetry). Murphy 132

STAPLES, SHIRLEY. Poet
"Getting It Together" (poetry). Coombs 178
A Sister Speaks of Rapping (poetry). Coombs 179

STATEMAN, NORMAN HILLS. Poet
Aren't We All? (poetry). Murphy 133

STEPHANY. See FULLER, STEPHANY.

STERN, RICHARD G., 1928- . Essayist, Interviewer
That Same Pain, That Same Pleasure: an Interview with Ralph Ellison (essay). Chapman 645

STEVENS, RUBY. Poet
The Hill (poetry). Murphy 3:146
A Murderer Awaiting Sentence (poetry). Murphy 3:145
Passing (poetry). Murphy 3:145
To You (poetry). Murphy 3:147

STEVENS, SANDRA E., 1950- . Poet
Black Is . . . (poetry). Shuman 401

STEVENSON, C. LEIGH. Short Fiction Writer
Over the Line (short fiction). Ford 2:60

STEVENSON, J. C. Poet
A Day's Recreation (poetry). Brewer 36

STEWARD, AUSTIN, 1794- . Autobiographer
Slave Narrative (excerpt—autobiography). Miller, R. 51

STEWART, CHARLES. Poet
This Is for Freedom, My Son (poetry). Murphy 2:121

STEWART, JAMES T., 1926- . Critic, Playwright, Poet
The Development of the Black Revolutionary Artist (essay). Hemenway 136, Jones 3

Announcement (poetry). Jones 202
Don't You Forget It (poetry). Alhamisi 133
Poem: A Piece (poetry). Jones 201
Poem (We drank Thunderbird all night). Alhamisi 134, Jones 203

STEWART, JOHN. Orator
An Address to the Wyandotte Nation and Accompanying Letter to William Walker dated May 25, 1817 (speech). Porter 455

STEWART, MARIE, 1803- . Essayist
Religion and the Pure Principles of Morality, the Sure Foundation on Which We Must Build, Oct. 1831 (essay). Porter 460

STEWART, OLLIE. Essayist, Short Fiction Writer
End of a Dream (short fiction). Ford 2:242
I Shall Not Be Moved (short fiction). Ford 2:72
Leg Man (short fiction). Ford 2:172
No Greater Love (short fiction). Ford 2:166
Soft Boiled (short fiction). Ford 2:66

STILL, WILLIAM, 1821-1902. Essayist, Biographer, Narrator
Underground Railroad. A Record (excerpts —biography). Brown 785
Underground Railroad. A Record (excerpt: William and Ellen Craft—biography). Davis 126

STOJF, MICHAEL B. Essayist
Claude McKay And The Cult of Primitivism (essay). Bontemps 3:126

STOKES, DEBORAH. Poet
Salt Water (poetry). Weisman 81

STOKES, GLENN. Poet
Blue Texarkana (poetry). Coombs 182

STOKES, HERBERT. Playwright
The Man Who Trusted the Devil Twice
(drama). Bullins 2:120

STONE, LEROY, 1926- . Essayist, Poet
Calypso (poetry). Pool 171
Flamenco Sketches (poetry). Henderson 194

STONE, RONALD. See **RAHMAN, YUSEF.**

STRICKLAND, WILLIAM. Essayist
Where Do We Go From Here? (essay).
Gayle 119

STUCKEY, STERLING, 1932- . Critic, Essayist, Poet
Frank London Brown (essay). Chapman
669
Through the Prism of Folklore: The Black
Ethos in Slavery (essay). Chapman 2:439

SUN RA. Poet
The Cosmic Age (poetry). Jones 219
The Image Reach (poetry). Jones 218
Nothing Is (poetry). Adoff 3:207, Jones 216
Of the Cosmic-Blueprints (poetry). Jones
214
The Plane: Earth (poetry). Adoff 3:207
Primary Lesson: the Second Class Citizen
(poetry). Adoff 3:208
Saga of Resistance (poetry). Jones 212
To the Peoples of Earth (poetry). Jones
217
The Visitation (poetry). Breman 266, Jones
213
Would I For All That Were (poetry).
Jones 215

SYE, ROBERT J. Poet
Why I Rebel (poetry). Murphy 2:124

TANNENBAUM, SHELDON. Short Fiction
Writer
The Huge Dull Night Under the Stars (short
fiction). Gibson 6

TARVER, VALERIE. Poet
Differences (poetry). Murphy 2:127
Explanation (poetry). Murphy 2:128
I Pledge Allegiance (poetry). Murphy 2:129
To the White Man (poetry). Murphy 2:130

TATE, ELEANORA E., 1948- . Essayist,
Poet
African Madness (poetry). Witherspoon 16

TATUM, LAWRENCE CARLYLE, 1893- .
Poet
Choicy (poetry). Brewer 40

TAYLOR, ALRUTHEUS AMBUSH. Historian, Essayist, Educator
to his children, 12/25/1945 (letter). Dreer
100

TAYLOR, CLYDE. Essayist
Baraka as Poet (essay). Gibson 3:127

TAYLOR, D. Poet
Personal Prayer of Millions (poetry).
Murphy 3:147
We The People (poetry). Murphy 3:148

TAYLOR, ISABELLE MCCLELLAN. Poet
In Some Time Hence (poetry). Murphy 136
Loving Beauty is Loving God (poetry).
Murphy 134
The Lynching (poetry). Murphy 135
Peace and Principle (poetry). Murphy 136

TAYLOR, JEANNE A., 1934- . Essayist,
Playwright, Short Fiction Writer
Listen, America, Ebony Middle-Class Is
Talking (essay). Schulberg 69

A House Divided (short fiction). Chapman
2:173
The House on Mettler Street (short fiction). Schulberg 71
The Stake-Out (short fiction). Schulberg 74

TAYLOR, JERRY. Poet
It May Be Bad (poetry). Bookers 18

TAYLOR, MERVYN. Poet
Calypso (poetry). Troupe 454
You're The One (poetry). Patterson 4:151

TAYLOR, PATRICIA E. Essayist
Langston Hughes and the Harlem Renaissance, 1921-1931: Major Events & Publications (essay). Bontemps 3:90

TAYLOR, PRENTISS, JR., 1951- . Essayist, Poet
From an Eighteen Year old poet with a
raggedy face (poetry). Brown, P. 93
Portrait: Jimmy Mack (poetry). Witherspoon 10

TAYLOR, ROCKIE D. See **OLOGBONI,
TEJUMOLA.**

TAYLOR, SANDRA. Essayist
Sweet Home (essay). Burnett 154

TEAGUE, BOB, 1929- . Playwright, Letter Writer
Fallout: a Letter to a Black Boy (letter).
Burnett 295
Letters to a Black Boy (excerpt—letters).
Adams 4:59, Stanford 277

TEMPLE, GEORGE HANNIBAL. Poet
Crispus Attucks (poetry). White 104

TERRELL, ROBERT L. Poet
For Frantz Fanon (poetry). Coombs 184

TERRY, LUCY, 1730-1821. Poet
Bars Fight (August 28, 1746) (poetry).
Hughes 2:3, Patterson 3:27, Randall 2:37,
Robinson 4

THELWELL, MIKE, 1938- . Critic, Short Fiction Writer
Back With the Wind: Mr. Styron and the Reverend Turner (essay). Clarke 2:79

Bright and Mownin' Star (short fiction). Chapman 2:132, Gibson 226, Stadler 202
Direct Action (short fiction). Hughes 3:470, Patterson 3:230
The Organizer (short fiction). Burnett 301

THIGPEN, WILLIAM A., JR. 1948-1971. Poet.
Peaches (poetry). Witherspoon 12
Wintertime in the Ghetto (poetry). Witherspoon 15

THOMAS, BEVERLY, 1948- . Poet
i (poetry). Witherspoon 16

THOMAS, CHARLES CYRUS, 1909- . Poet
In Search of a God (poetry). Coombs 185
Ode to the Smiths: Bessie, Mamie, Laura, Clara and Trixie (poetry). Coombs 187

THOMAS, D. GATEWOOD. Poet
I Think I Thought a Lie (poetry). Murphy 137

THOMAS, EDWARD. Poet
The Streets Are Small (poetry). Bookers 18

THOMAS, JOYCE CAROL. Poet
I Know a Lady (poetry). Troupe 62

THOMAS, LORENZO, 1944- . Poet
Inauguration (poetry). Chapman 2:342
Onion Bucket (poetry). Adoff 3:483, Jones 410
Subway Witnesses (poetry). Adoff 3:482
Twelve Gates (poetry). Jones 411

THOMAS, RAMBLIN'. Poet
Poor Boy Blues (poetry). Margolies 91

THOMAS, RICHARD W., 1939- . Essayist, Poet
Amen (poetry). Adoff 3:372, Jones 192
April Crucifix, To: Dr. Martin Luther King (poetry). Shuman 2:232
August 10, 1969 (poetry). Lane 75
Calling (poetry). Shuman 2:206
The Day the Old Man Joined the Church (poetry). Shuman 402
Edith Mother of Man (poetry). Shuman 2:209
Ethnography of a Downtown Joint (poetry). Shuman 2:210
Evicted Worlds (poetry). Lane 68
Fall/1968 (poetry). Shuman 403
The Fisherman (poetry). Lane 75
The Glass Stomach (poetry). King 3:203
Her Wedding Day (poetry). Shuman 2:211
The Hole (poetry). Shuman 2:224
How We Must Teach The Children (poetry). Witherspoon 2:22

Index to a Black Catharsis (poetry). Jones 194
It (poetry). Shuman 2:199
Jazzy Vanity (poetry). Jones 197, Patterson 4:145
Just Making It (Blood for Sale) (poetry). Hughes 2:432
Kids (poetry). Shuman 404
Last Evening with a Lady (poetry). Shuman 2:194
Life after Death (poetry). Adoff 3:373, Shuman 2:204
Little Dark Girl (poetry). Shuman 405
Lonely, Thou (poetry). Shuman 2:230
Low Wages (poetry). Shuman 2:228
Martyrdom (poetry). Adoff 3:370, Shuman 2:197
Monday (poetry). Shuman 2:229
My Plant and I (poetry). Shuman 2:190
The Ninth Savior (poetry). Shuman 2:191
Philosophy for Street Folk (poetry). Shuman 2:223
Prayer/15 (poetry). Shuman 2:207
The Reformer (poetry). Shuman 2:188
Revolution (poetry). Jones 196
Riots and Rituals (poetry). Adoff 3:371, Shuman 2:218
2nd Solo (2/10/67) (poetry). Shuman 2:231
Sept. 26, 1967 (poetry). Shuman 2:227
Sermon From the Thirteenth Floor of a Tomb (poetry). Lane 70
Shopping for Light (poetry). Shuman 2:225
A Sister Crosses Over (poetry). Lane 67
Sitting on the Side of the Bed With My Underwear on . . . Thinking (poetry). Shuman 2:198
6:00 A.M., 12/16/66 (poetry). Shuman 2:208
That Hunger Beyond Our Physical Shapes (poetry). Lane 65
Tina (poetry). Shuman 2:193
To Lovers (poetry). Shuman 2:187
To the New Annex to the Detroit County Jail (poetry). Adoff 3:373, Shuman 2:203
To the Singular Arrival of Chris and Julie Ruke (poetry). Shuman 2:202
To the Survivor of Hiroshima and Nagasaki (poetry). King 3:200
Tombs (poetry). Shuman 2:212
War (poetry). Shuman 2:200
Warning to Brothers (for Kunle Adejumo) (poetry). Shuman 2:226
Wasted (poetry). Shuman 2:216
We Are No One (poetry). Witherspoon 2:21
We Used To Really/Be Up-tight (poetry). Lane 66
When I'm Alone (poetry). Witherspoon 2:20
The Woman (poetry). Shuman 2:205
The Worker (poetry). Adoff 3:370, Hughes 2:433, Jones 193, Shuman 2:189

THOMPSON, CHARLES H., 1896- . Orator
Education of the Negro in the United States (speech). Brown 937

THOMPSON, CLARA ANN. Poet
His Answer (poetry). White 133
Mrs. Johnson Objects (poetry). White 133

THOMPSON, GLEN, 1955- . Poet
The Air is Dirty (poetry). Jordan 10
Hands (poetry). Jordan 9

THOMPSON, JAMES W., 1935- . Poet,
Short Fiction Writer
And There Are Those (poetry). King 3:210
Arms & Exit (poetry). Coombs 190
Beauty Then Is Being (poetry). Coombs
197
A Constant Labor (poetry). Breman 2:61,
Randall 2:253
Fading cadence (poetry). Breman 2:64
The Greek Roman (poetry). Pool 174,
Randall 2:254
Journey from the night (poetry). Breman
2:62
Mock Pop Forsooth: a Tale of life and
death (poetry). Coombs 198
The Plight—Theme variation fugue and
coda (poetry). Pool 2:220, Randall 2:256
Silent music (poetry). Breman 2:63
The spawn of slums (poetry). Pool 2:149,
Randall 2:254
Tableau vivant (poetry). Breman 2:65
Tomorrow's for remembering (poetry).
Breman 2:66
The Yellow Bird (poetry). Adoff 3:271,
Breman 2:68
You Are Alms (poetry). Adoff 3:270,
Breman 370, King 3:208

See What Tomorrow Brings (short fiction).
King 2:225

THOMPSON, LARRY, 1950- . Playwright,
Poet, Essayist
Jean Toomer: As Modern Man (essay).
Bontemps 3:51

Black Is Best (poetry). Adoff 3:512

THURMAN, HOWARD, 1899- . Poet, Essayist
Good News for the Underprivileged (essay). Brown 686
The Luminous Darkness (excerpt—essay).
Curry 207

THURMAN, I. M. Poet
Easter (poetry). Murphy 3:149

THURMAN, WALLACE, 1902-1934. Playwright, Critic, Essayist, Fiction Writer
Negro Poets and Their Poetry (essay).
Gayle 2:70

The Blacker the Berry (excerpt—fiction).
Calverton 107
Infants of the Spring (excerpt: Niggeratti
Manor—fiction). Brown 220
Cordelia the Crude (short fiction). Turner 43, Turner 3:333
Grist in the Mill (short fiction). Barksdale
606

TIGHLMAN, CHIEF JUSTICE. Justice,
Orator
An Address on the Condemnation of John
Joyce (speech). Porter 414

TINSLEY, TOMI CAROLYN. Poet
Anticipation (poetry). Triad 80
Blueprint (poetry). Triad 86
Classified Ad (poetry). Murphy 142
Cynic (poetry). Murphy 141, Triad 85
Elegy (poetry). Triad 84
Entry (poetry). Triad 75
Fear (poetry). Triad 91
For You (poetry). Triad 77
Fragments (poetry). Triad 90
Ghost Writer (poetry). Triad 83
I Am Man (poetry). Murphy 140, Triad 94
Incurable (poetry). Triad 93
Knowledge (poetry). Triad 76
Late Visitor (poetry). Triad 69
Mockery (poetry). Triad 88
Move Up (poetry). Triad 89
My Portion (poetry). Triad 70
On Reaching My Twenty-fourth Year (poetry). Triad 95
Our Love Was a War Baby (poetry).
Triad 74
Perchance (poetry). Triad 81
Raindrop (poetry). Triad 82
Retaliation (poetry). Murphy 142
Seasonal (poetry). Triad 92
Song to X and Son Yet to Be Born
(poetry). Triad 71
Still with Me, Ghost? (poetry). Triad 87
This Night of Peace (poetry). Triad 78
We Have a Tryst (poetry). Triad 79

TODD, ELLA. Poet
Forever (poetry). Bookers 95

TODD, JOE. Poet
A Significant Other (poetry). Brown, P.
94

TOLSON, MELVIN BEAUNORUS, 1900-
1966. Playwright, Poet
A Poet's Odyssey (essay). Gibson 3:84,
Hill 181

Abraham Lincoln of Rock Spring Farm
(poetry). Hill 2:572
African China (poetry). Adoff 3:45, Cuney
49, Davis, C. 280, Hayden 2:58, Miller,
R. 404
The Auction (poetry). Murphy 3:152
The Birth of John Henry (poetry). Randall
2:118
Damascus Blade (poetry). Cuney 48
Dark Symphony (poetry). Adams 14, Baker
239, Barksdale 670, Bell 20, Bontemps
2:37, Brown 398, Chapman 388, Ford
100, Hughes 2:136, Kearns 501, Kearns
2:273, Long 536, Miller, R. 400, Rose
60, Stanford 175, Turner 3:240, Turner
4:84
Dark Symphony (excerpts—poetry). Kerlin
324

(TOLSON, MELVIN BEAUNORUS)
Do (poetry). Hughes 2:143
An Ex-Judge at the Bar (poetry). Chapman 387
The Gallows (poetry). Cuney 45
Gamma (poetry). Troupe 376
A Hamlet Rives Us (poetry). Patterson 3:218
Harlem Gallery (excerpt—poetry). Breman 59, Davis, C. 275, Hayden 2:63, Lomax 213, Long 541, Rose 80
Harlem Gallery (excerpt: Na section—poetry). Emanual 473
Harlem Gallery (excerpt: Psi—poetry). Adoff 3:36, Baker 242, Barksdale 671, Chapman 392, Davis 364
Harlem Gallery (excerpt: The Sea Turtle and the Shark—poetry). Rose 250
I Have Seen Black Hand (excerpt—poetry). Kerlin 325
John Henry in Harlem (poetry). Adams 3:81
Lamda (poetry). Bell 24, Henderson 148, Hughes 2:141
Legend of Versailles (poetry). Randall 2:118
Libretto for the Republic of Liberia (excerpt—poetry). Ford 102, Robinson 2:189
My Soul and I (poetry). Cuney 48
A Primer for Today (poetry). Cuney 45
Roland Hayes (poetry). Murphy 3:151
Satchmo (poetry). Randall 2:119
A Scholar Looks at an Oak (poetry). Cuney 46
The Sea-Turtle and the Shark (poetry). Adoff 3:44, Hayden 111, Randall 8, Rose 250
The Town Fathers (poetry). Cuney 47
The Wine of Ecstacy (poetry). Murphy 3:153

TOOMER, JEAN, 1894-1967. Autobiographer, Essayist, Poet, Fiction Writer
Balo (drama). Hatch 218, Locke 269

At sea (poetry). Turner 3:215, Turner 4:59
Banking Coal (poetry). Hughes 2:106
Beehive (poetry). Adoff 2:79, Adoff 3:29, Bontemps 17, Lomax 211
Blue Meridian (poetry). Barksdale 507, Hughes 2:107, Turner 4:54
The Blue Meridian (excerpt—poetry). Turner 3:210
Brown River, Smile (poetry). Adoff 3:31, Bontemps 2:34, Chapman 378, Jordan 72
Carma (excerpt—poetry). Hayden 2:53
Conversion (poetry). Bell 17, Margolies 10, Miller, R. 242, Patterson 3:157
Cotton Song (poetry). Chapman 377, Cullen 97, Davis 286, Davis, C. 177, Randall 2:68
Evening Song (poetry). Cullen 94, Dreer 81, Miller, R., 237, Randall 2:70
Face (poetry). Cullen 98
Five Vignettes (poetry). Adoff 3:34, Turner 3:214, Turner 4:58

Georgia Dusk (poetry). Adoff 3:29, Baker 163, Bell 17, Bontemps 2:32, Brown 356, Calverton 202, Cullen 95, Davis, C. 176, Dreer 80, Hayden 2:55, Henderson 119, Jordan 102, Kerlin 283, Locke 2:136, Randall 7, Randall 2:69
Harvest Song (poetry). Chapman 375, Long 396, Patterson 3:156, Troupe 234
Lost Dancer (poetry). Adoff 3:34, Turner 3:214, Turner 4:58
November Cotton Flower (poetry). Breman 57, Cullen 99, Dreer 80, Jordan 121
Nullo (poetry). Miller, R. 236
Portrait in Georgia (poetry). Barksdale 506, Margolies 57
Prayer (poetry). Davis, C., 178, Patterson 3:157
The Reapers (poetry). Adams 3:117, Adoff 3:29, Breman 56, Cullen 94, Hayden 2.52, Jordan 63, Randall 2:68
Song of the Son (poetry). Adoff 3:30, Baker 164, Barksdale 504, Bell 18, Bontemps 2:33, Brown 355, Calverton 203, Chapman 377, Cullen 96, Davis 285, Davis, C. 175, Hayden 110, Hayden 2:54, Henderson 118, Jordan 32, Kerlin 282, Locke 2:137, Long 395, Randall 6
Storm Ending (poetry). Baker 165

Avey (short fiction). Baker 159, Brown 49, Emanuel 104, Long 397
Blood-Burning Moon (short fiction). Brown 41, Chapman 66, Ford 150, Hayden 5, James 63, Kendricks 208
Carma (short fiction). Locke 2:96
Esther (short fiction). Davis 287, Emanuel 99, Miller, R. 237, Patterson 3:134
Fern (short fiction). Barksdale 504, Calverton 21, Hughes 3:30, Kearns 406, Locke 2:99, Turner 38, Turner 3:328
Kabnis (short fiction). Davis, C. 111
Karintha (short fiction). Barksdale 503, Chambers 249, Chapman 64, Haslam 275, Hayden 2:51, Randall 2:66
Seventh Street (short fiction). Barksdale 506

TORREGIAN, SOTERE, 1941- . Poet
The Newark Public Library Reading Room (poetry). Chapman 2:344
Poem for the Birthday of Huey Newton (poetry). Chapman 2:343
Travois of the Nameless (poetry). Chapman 2:345

TORRENCE, RIDGLEY, Playwright
The Danse Calinda (drama). Locke 373
Granny Maumee (drama). Locke 235
The Rider of Dreams (drama). Locke 25

TOURE, AISHAH SAYYIDA MALI. See SNELLINGS, ROLLAND.

TRAVIS, NANNIE M. See SMITH, NANNIE TRAVIS.

TROTTER, WILLIAM MONROE, 1872-
1934. Essayist
Why Be Silent (essay). Long 195

TROUP, CORNELIUS V., 1902- . Editor,
Poet
The Bitter Cup (poetry). Murphy 3:155
Traffic Signs (poetry). Murphy 144

TROUPE, QUINCY, 1943- . Editor, Fiction Writer, Poet
After Hearing a Radio Announcement . . .
(poetry). Troupe 375
Conversation Overheard the Way They
Saw It (poetry). King 3:238
A Day in the Life of a Poet (poetry).
Chapman 2:347, Coombs 203
Dirge (poetry). Adoff 3:442, Coombs 207
Embryo (poetry). Troupe 465
Flies on Shit (poetry). Coombs 205
For Malcolm Who Walks in the Eyes of
Our Children (poetry). Adoff 3:444
Impressions of Chicago: For Howlin' Wolf
(poetry). Chapman 2:348
In Texas Grass (poetry). Adoff 3:443
In The Line Of Duty (poetry). Troupe
2:62
Ode to John Coltrane (poetry). King 3:230,
Troupe 2:55
Poem for Friends (poetry). Adoff 3:445
A Sense of Coolness (poetry). Adoff 3:442
South African Bloodstone (poetry). Troupe
217
A Splib Odyssey (poetry). Coombs 200
Streetscene (poetry). Troupe 2:60
The Syntax of the Mind Grips (poetry).
Chapman 2:350
Transformation (poetry). Patterson 4:100
The Wait (poetry). Coombs 206
White Weekend (poetry). Major 128
You come to me (poetry). Chapman 2:349,
Patterson 4:35

TRUTH, SOJOURNER, 1797-1883. Speaker
And Aren't I a Woman? (speech). Davis
79

TUCKER, KHARLOS. See **WIMBERLI, SIGMONDE.**

TURNER, CLAIRE. Poet
The Creation (poetry). Murphy 3:156
Misfit (poetry). Murphy 3:156
A Poet Questions His Immortality (poetry).
Murphy 3:156
To F. S. 1. (poetry). Murphy 3:155
To Some Who Are Prone to Criticize (poetry). Murphy 3:156

TURNER, DARWIN T., 1931- . Critic, Editor, Essayist, Poet
Afro-American Literary Critics: An Introduction (essay). Gayle 3:57
The Afro-American Playwright in the New
York Professional Theatre, 1923-1959
(essay). Turner 3:435

The Black Playwright in the Professional
Theatre of the United States of America
1859-1959 (essay). Bigsby 113
Frank Yerby as Debunker (essay). Hemenway 62
The Negro Dramatist's Image of the Universe, 1920-1960 (essay). Patterson 65
The Negro Dramatists' Image of the Universe, 1920-1960 (excerpt—essay). Chapman 677, Turner 6:91
Paul Laurence Dunbar: The Rejected Symbol (essay). Hemenway 35
The Teaching of Afro-American Literature
(essay). Chapman 2:506

Death (poetry). Turner 3:270, Turner 4:114
Finale (poetry). Turner 3:272, Turner
4:116
Guest Lecturer (poetry). Turner 3:272,
Turner 4:116
Love (poetry). Patterson 4:106, Turner
3:271, Turner 4:115
Night Slivers (poetry). Major 129
One Last Word (poetry). Shuman 407
The Sit-In (poetry). Turner 3:269, Turner
4:113
Sonnet Sequence I (poetry). Turner 3:271,
Turner 4:115
To Vanity (poetry). Hughes 2:401

TURNER, DORIS. See **LINYATTA**

TURNER, EZRA W. Poet, Educator
Tell Yo' Ma I Said So (poetry). Dreer 76

TURNER, JOHN ADOLPH. Poet
Rain (poetry). Dreer 58

TURNER, LUCY MAE. Poet
A Bird Is Singing (poetry). Murphy 3:157

TURNER, NAT, 1800-1831. Autobiographer
Nat Turner's Confession (excerpt—autobiography). Barksdale 163, Freedman 75

TURNER, RAYMOND. Poet
Buttons (poetry). Coombs 209
Find a Role, Define a Role (poetry).
Coombs 209

TURPIN, WATERS EDWARD, 1910-1968.
Critic, Fiction Writer
These Low Grounds (excerpt: Ch. 40-42—
fiction). Ford 86
These Low Grounds (excerpt: Oystering—
fiction). Brown 263

TWITT, NATHANIEL I. Poet
Dream About Me (poetry). Murphy 145

TWITTY, COUNTESS W. Poet
Dali Fantasy (poetry). Murphy 148
Defeat (poetry). Murphy 146
Dusk Thoughts (poetry). Murphy 148
High Tide (poetry). Murphy 146
Quo Vadis (poetry). Murphy 149
Subterfuge (poetry). Murphy 147
Unrepentant (poetry). Murphy 147

UNDERHILL, IRVIN W., 1868-?. Poet
To Our Boys (poetry). Kerlin 185

UNDERWOOD, EDNA WORTHLEY. Short
Fiction Writer
La Perla Negra (short fiction). Johnson,
C. 60

VAL, FERDINAND. See **FERDINAND, VAL.**

VALE, COSTON. Poet
Flight (poetry). Murphy 3:159
Toleration (poetry). Murphy 3:159

VALENTINE, CHRISTOPHER. Essayist
Darkness of Terror (essay). Bookers 63

VALLEJO. Poet
Locust of Satan (poetry). Troupe 2:36

VAN DYKE, HENRY, 1928- . Fiction
Writer
Ruth's Story (short fiction). Patterson
3:258

VASHON, GEORGE B., 1820?-1878. Essay-
ist, Poet
A Life-Day (poetry). Brawley 274
Vincent Ogé (poetry). Brawley 263
Vincent Ogé (excerpt—poetry). Robinson
177

VASSA, GUSTAVUS, 1745-1801. Autobiog-
rapher, Abolitionist, Essayist, Orator,
Poet
Autobiography (excerpts—autobiography).
Davis 18, Miller, R. 13
The Interesting Narrative of the Life of
Olaudah Equiano, or Gustavus Vassa
the African. Written by Himself (ex-
cerpt: Slave of Black Men, Slave of
White Men—autobiography). Kendricks
13, Rose 40
The Interesting Narrative . . . (excerpt:
Ch. II: Kidnapping and Enslavement—
autobiography). Brawley 57, Patterson
3:9
Autobiography (excerpts: miscellaneous
verses—poetry). Barksdale 29, Robinson
14

VAUGHN, GEORGE L., ?-1949. Essayist,
Historian
The Negro's Armageddon (speech). Dreer
200

VAUGHN, JAMES P., 1929- . Poet
Four Questions Addressed to His Excel-
lency the Prime Minister (poetry). Bon-
temps 2:167
Movie Queen (poetry). Hughes 62
So? (poetry). Bontemps 2:168
Three Kings (poetry). Hughes 24, Hughes
2:399
Two Ladies Bidding us 'Good Morning'
(poetry). Hughes 63

VAUGHN, NAOMI EVANS. Poet
Barred (poetry). Murphy 150
Camouflage (poetry). Murphy 3:160
Mistakes (poetry) Murphy 149
Retrospection of a Black Woman (poetry).
Murphy 3:160
Souls of Black Men (poetry). Murphy 3:161

VERANO, MAAMI. Poet
Grass Man (poetry). Patterson 4:153

VESEY, PAUL. See **ALLEN, SAMUEL W.**

VROMAN, MARY ELIZABETH, 1923-1967.
Essayist, Poet, Fiction Writer, Screen
Playwright
See How They Run (short fiction). Clarke
176, Hughes 3:253

WAKEFIELD, JACQUES, 1949- . Poet
. . . Days Prior To (poetry). Jones 439
"it ain't no jive" (poetry). Coombs 211
"our world is" (poetry). Coombs 211
A Shit a Riot (poetry). Jones 440
We Exist Living Dead (poetry). Jones 438
"well well" (poetry). Coombs 212

WALCOTT, DEREK. Poet, Short Fiction
Writer
The royal palms (poetry). Hollo 16
The Volcano (poetry). Troupe 3

WALKER, ALICE, 1944- . Critic, Essayist,
Poet, Fiction Writer
Hymn (poetry). Hayden 153
In These Dissenting Times (poetry). Adoff
3:475
Once (excerpt—poetry). Adoff 3:474
So We've Come At Last To Freud (po-
etry). Patterson 4:87
Everyday Use (short fiction). Washington
78
Her Sweet Jerome (short fiction). Troupe
116
Strong Horse Tea (short fiction). King
2:133
A Sudden Trip Home In the Spring (short
fiction). Washington 141
To Hell With Dying (short fiction). Gib-
son 190, Hughes 3:490, Stadler 263
The Welcome Table (short fiction). Exum
234

WALKER, DAVID, 1785-1830. Essayist,
Orator
Appeal in Four Articles . . . (excerpt:
Preamble—essay). Barksdale 154, Braw-
ley 125, Long 26, Miller, R. 70
Appeal In Four Articles . . . (excerpt: Art.
1: Our Wretchedness in Consequence
of Slavery—essay). Baker 55, Barksdale
156, Brawley 128, Davis 43, Miller, R.
71, Rose 44
Appeal in Four Articles . . . (excerpt: Art.
II: Our Wretchedness in Consequence of

(WALKER, DAVID)
Ignorance—essay). Baker 55, Brawley 130, Brown 588, Miller, R. 73
Appeal in Four Articles . . . (excerpt: Art. III: Our Wretchedness in Consequence of the Preachers of the Religion of Christ—essay). Brawley 135, Miller, R. 77
Appeal in Four Articles . . . (excerpt: Art. IV: Our Wretchedness in Consequence of the Colonizing Plan—essay). Brawley 138

WALKER, EVAN K. Playwright, Short Fiction Writer
Harlem Transfer (short fiction). Coombs 2:171, King 2:47

WALKER, JOSEPH A., 1935- . Playwright
Odono (drama). King 349

WALKER, MARGARET ABIGAIL ALEXANDER, 1915- . Critic, Essayist, Fiction Writer, Poet
New Poets (essay). Gayle 2:89
Religion, Poetry and History: Foundations for a New Educational System (essay). Curry 36

Jubilee (excerpt—fiction). Chambers 27, Stanford 35

Ballad of the Free (poetry). Henderson 166
Ballad of the Hoppy Toad (poetry). Chapman 2:203, Henderson 161
Birmingham (poetry). Adoff 3:149
Childhood (poetry). Adoff 3:148, Bell 77, Black 39, Hayden 2:145, Long 522
Dark Blood (poetry). Black 41
Delta (excerpts—poetry). Kerlin 330
For Andy Goodman, Michael Scheverner and James Chaney (poetry). Brooks 152, Randall 2:158
For Malcolm X (poetry). Adoff 3:150, Exum 117, Ford 98, Henderson 165, Randall 20, Randall 2:157
For Mary McLeod Bethune (poetry). Breman 155, Hughes 2:326, Pool 2:148
For My People (poetry). Adams 3:2, Adoff 2:107, Adoff 3:144, Baker 261, Barksdale 635, Bell 73, Black 39, Bontemps 2:128, Breman 153, Brown 409, Chambers 22, 303, Chapman 459, Davis 527, Davis, C. 271, Emanuel 495, Freedman 271, Ford 95, Hayden 137, Hayden 2:138, Henderson 163, Hughes 2:314, Kearns 498, Kearns 2:271, Kendricks 344, Patterson 3:219, Rose 63, Turner 3:254, Turner 4:98
For My People (excerpt—poetry). Kerlin 329
Girl Held Without Bail (poetry). Adoff 3:148, Randall 2:156
Harriet Tubman (poetry). Hughes 2:320, Stanford 45, Troupe 28, Weisman 19
Iowa Farmer (poetry). Hayden 144
Jackson, Mississippi (poetry). Brooks 151

Lineage (poetry). Adoff 3:148, Bell 77, Hayden 2:141
Memory (poetry). Long 521
Micah (poetry). Exum 120, Henderson 166
Molly Means (poetry). Bell 74, Bontemps 2:130, Emanuel 496, Hayden 2:142, Hughes 2:309
Now (poetry). Williams 155
October Journey (poetry). Adoff 2:28, Adoff 3:146, Bontemps 2:132, Ford 96, Hughes 2:317, Pool 180
Ode (poetry). Ford 98
Poppa Chicken (poetry). Davis 529
Prophets for a New Day (poetry). Brooks 150, Exum 118, Randall 2:160
Southern Song (poetry). Black 41, Long 520
Street Demonstration (poetry). Randall 2:156
We Have Been Believers (poetry). Adoff 3:145, Bell 76, Davis 530, Ford 96, Hayden 139, Hughes 2:312, Jordan 130, Long 523, Pool 179, Singh 15

WALKER, MIKE. Essayist
The Hip Teacher (essay). Bookers 42

WALKER, VICTOR STEVEN, 1947- . Short Fiction Writer
The Long Sell (short fiction). Chapman 2:190

WALLACE, MICHELE. Autobiographer
Sixth Grade (autobiography). Exum 194

WALROND, ERIC, 1898-1966. Editor, Essayist, Fiction Writer
The Palm Porch (short fiction). Locke 2:115
Subjection (short fiction). Barksdale 600
The Wharf Rats (short fiction). Hughes 3:48
The Yellow One (short fiction). Calverton 39, Davis, C. 121, Emanuel 126, James 93

WALTER, NINA WILLIS. Poet
Shallow Pools (poetry). Weisman 57

WALTON, BRUCE. Poet
Black Consciousness (poetry). Brown, P. 96

WANDICK, W. D. Poet
For the Honeybee and Her Poets (poetry). Brown, P. 97

WANGARA, HARUN KOFI. See LAWRENCE, HAROLD G.

WANGARA, MALAIKA AYO. See LAWRENCE, JOYCE WHITSITT.

WARD, DOUGLAS TURNER, 1931- . Critic, Editor, Playwright
Brotherhood (drama). King 229

(WARD, DOUGLAS TURNER)
Day of Absence (drama). Brasmer 179, Couch 25, Hatch 695, Hayden 161, Miller, R. 492, Oliver 340
Happy Ending (drama). Brasmer 221, Couch 3, Oliver 324

WARD, FRANCIS, 1935- . Critic, Editor, Essayist, Playwright
Home Has Always Been Blackness (poetry). Brown, P. 131

WARD, SAMUEL RINGGOLD, 1817-c.1864. Autobiographer, Orator
Autobiography of a Fugitive Negro (excerpt—autobiography). Long 88

Speech on the Fugitive Slave Bill (speech). Brown 622

WARD, THEODORE, 1902- . Critic, Playwright
Big White Fog (drama). Brown 561, Hatch 278
Our Lan' (drama). Turner 5:115

WARD, VAL GRAY. Critic, Poet
Gwen Brooks, a Pyramid (poetry). Brown, P. 99

WARREN, LLOYD. Poet
Leviticus Tate (poetry). Murphy 150

WASHINGTON, AUSTIN D. Poet
To Be Black Is To Suffer (poetry). Murphy 2:132

WASHINGTON, BOOKER TALIAFERRO, 1856-1915. Educator, Autobiographer, Orator, Essayist, Historian
Story of My Life and Work (excerpts—autobiography). Brown 742
Up from Slavery (excerpt—autobiography). Freedman 100
Up from Slavery (excerpt: Address to the Atlanta Exposition—autobiography). Kendricks 140
Up from Slavery (excerpt: Helping Others—autobiography). Dreer 122
Up from Slavery (excerpt: The Negro in Political Life—autobiography). Kendricks 144
Up From Slavery (excerpt: Ch. 1. A Slave Among Slaves—autobiography). Calverton 471, Long 134, Patterson 3:66, Stanford 57, Turner 6:14
Up From Slavery (excerpt: Ch. II—autobiography). Calverton 484
Up From Slavery (excerpt: Ch. 3: Struggle for an Education—autobiography). Davis 153
Up From Slavery (excerpt: Chap. III: Excerpt—autobiography). Turner 6:15
Up From Slavery (excerpt: Ch. 7: Early Days at Tuskegee—autobiography). Barksdale 412, Miller, R. 137
Up From Slavery (excerpt: Ch. 8: Teaching School in a Stable and a Hen-House—

autobiography). Barksdale 415, Stanford 59
Up From Slavery (excerpt: Ch. 13: Two Thousand Miles for a Five-Minute Speech—autobiography). Barksdale 419
Working with the Hands (excerpt: Moral Values of Hand Work—autobiography). Kendricks 146

The Masses of Us Are To Live by the Production of Our Hands (essay). Gayle 47

Atlanta Exposition Address (1895) (speech). Adams 4:11, Baker 87, Barksdale 424, Brown 673, Curry 5, Davis 158, Dreer 193, Ford 15, Long 145, Stanford 61
Educational Outlook in the South (speech). Davis, C. 67
Harvard Alumni Dinner Address, 1896 (speech). Davis 161, Ford 17
The "Shaw Monument Speech" (speech). Cromwell 285
Some of the Qualities Essential to the Most Successful School Life (speech). Cromwell 289

WASHINGTON, DELL. Poet
Learning Family (poetry). Coombs 213

WASHINGTON, HAZEL L. (Poet
Loud Jazz Horns (poetry). Murphy 154
Mother America (poetry). Murphy 151
A Woman At War (poetry). Murphy 152

WASHINGTON, J. E. Biographer
William de Fleurville (biography). Watkins 440

WASHINGTON, RAYMOND, 1942- . Poet
Freedom Hair (poetry). Chapman 2:388
Moon Bound (poetry). Chapman 2:389
Vision from the Ghetto (poetry). Chapman 2:387

WASHINGTON, THOMAS, JR. Poet
Funk (poetry). Shuman 414
In Memory of Freedom Marchers (poetry). Shuman 415
Man Made Winter (poetry). Shuman 415

WATKINS, FRANCES ELLEN. See HARPER, FRANCES ELLEN WATKINS.

WATKINS, LUCIAN BOTTOW, 1879-1921. Poet
Ebon Maid and Girl of Mine (poetry). Kerlin 306
A Message to the Modern Pharaohs (poetry). Kerlin 271
My fallen star has spent its light (first line—poetry). Kerlin 269
The New Negro (poetry). Kerlin 270
A Prayer of the Race That God Made Black (poetry). Kendricks 197, Kerlin 59
Star of Ethiopia (poetry). Johnson 211

(WATKINS, LUCIAN BOTTOW)
To Our Friends (poetry). Johnson 212
Two Points of View (poetry). Johnson 212

WATKINS, WILLIAM. Orator
Address delivered before the Moral Reform Society in Philadelphia, August 8, 1836 (speech). Porter 155

WATSON, ADELINE CARTER. Poet
Shall Race Hatred Prevail (excerpt—poetry). Kerlin 264

WATSON, EVELYN. Poet
Dream World (poetry). Dreer 78

WATSON, HARMON C., 1943- . Playwright
Those Golden Gates Fall Down (drama). Ford 289

WATTS, DANIEL H. Essayist
The Sickness of America (essay). Gayle 126

WEATHERLY, TOM, 1942- . Editor, Poet
Arroyo (poetry). Adoff 3:399, Wilentz 143
Autobiography (poetry). Chapman 2:351
Blue for Franks Wooten (poetry). Chapman 2:353, Wilentz 146
Canto 4 (Gullfish) (poetry). Adoff 3:397
Canto 5 (Coon fire) (poetry). Adoff 3:398
Canto 7 (first thesis) (poetry). Adoff 3:398
Crazy What She Calls (poetry). Wilentz 143
first monday scottsboro alabama (poetry). Adoff 3:399
imperial thumbprint (poetry). Adoff 3:399
mud water shago (poetry). Chapman 2:353
Red and Yellow Fooles Coat (poetry). Wilentz 146
Speculum Oris (poetry). Wilentz 147
Your eyes are mith (poetry). Chapman 2:352

WEAVER, ELEANOR. Poet
in Higher Places (poetry). Murphy 3:161
Mulatto (poetry). Murphy 3:162

WEBSTER, CARTER. Poet
Creation (poetry). Murphy 153
Crucifixion (poetry). Murphy 154

WEEDEN, LULA LOWE. Poet
Dance (poetry). Cullen 229
Have You Seen It (poetry). Cullen 228
The Little Dandelion (poetry). Cullen 229
Me Alone (poetry). Cullen 227
Robin Red Breast (poetry). Cullen 228
The Stream (poetry). Cullen 228

WEEKS, ALAN. Poet
Some Brothers Cry (poetry). Coombs 217

WEEKS, RICARDO, 1917- . Poet
Fallacy (poetry). Murphy 157

Flotsam (poetry). Murphy 155
Fugitive (poetry). Murphy 157
I Dream a War (poetry). Murphy 156
Window Washer (poetry). Murphy 156

WELBURN, RON, 1944- . Critic, Editor, Essayist, Poet, Short Fiction Writer
and universal (poetry). Chapman 2:358
Avoidances (poetry). Adoff 3:466
black is beautiful (poetry). Chapman 2:355
Cecil County (poetry). Adoff 3:467
Condition Blue/Dress (poetry). Chapman 2:357
Eulogy for Population (poetry). Adoff 3:467, Jones 262
First Essay on the Art of the U.S. (poetry). Jones 263
it is overdue time (poetry). Chapman 2:356
lyrics shimmy like (poetry). Chapman 2:356
Percussions (poetry). Troupe 237
put u red-eye in (poetry). Chapman 2:357
Regenesis (poetry). Major 131
Tu (poetry). Major 131
Wayman, As a Driven Star (poetry). Breman 493
Which way (poetry). Chapman 2:354

WELCH, JAMES. Poet
Verifying the Dead (poetry). Troupe 428
Why I Didn't Go to Delphi (poetry). Troupe 428

WELLS, BERNICE YOUNG MITCHELL. Essayist, Biographer
A Versatile Relative of Mine: Colonel Charles Young (essay). Dreer 179

WELLS, JACK CALVERT. Poet, Fiction Writer
Then I Met You (poetry). Murphy 158

WESLEY, CHARLES HARRIS, 1891- . Essayist, Educator, Minister, Historian
Collapse of the Confederacy (excerpt—essay). Brown 872
The Pursuit of Things (speech). Dreer 205

WESLEY, JOHN. Essayist
Jimmy South (essay). Bookers 158

WESLEY, RICHARD, 1945- . Playwright, Critic
Black Terror (drama). Bullins 219

WESS, DEBORAH FULLER. Poet
My Sea of Tears (poetry). Murphy 159
Sergeant Jerk (poetry). Murphy 159

WEST, DOROTHY, 1910- . Critic, Editor, Fiction Writer
The Living Is Easy (excerpt—fiction). Hill 2:480
Jack in the Pot (short fiction). Clarke 3:53
The Richer, the Poorer (short fiction). Hughes 3:130

WHALEY, JUNE D., 1952- . Poet
Friends (poetry). Lane 81
Granny (poetry). Lane 80
Last Rites for the City (poetry). Lane 84
Mornings Don't Never Change With Us (poetry). Lane 82
Old Negroes (poetry). Lane 78
The Other Side (poetry). Lane 77
Relating to the People (poetry). Lane 78
Viet Nam—Away from Viet Nam (poetry). Lane 79

WHEATLEY, PHILLIS, 1753-1784. Poet
To Arbour Tanner, 7/19/1772 (letter). Dreer 94

A Farewell to America (To Mrs. S. W.) (poetry). Barksdale 42, Dreer 22
Goliath of Gath (poetry). Turner 3:167, Turner 4:11
His Excellency, General Washington (poetry). Dreer 24, Kendricks 28
An Hymn To The Evening (poetry). Brawley 41, Cromwell 5, Davis 13, Dreer 26
An Hymn to the Morning (poetry). Barksdale 42, Brawley 40, Cromwell 5, Davis 12, Ford 4, Haslam 253
Imagination (poetry). Calverton 175
Isaiah (poetry). Miller, R. 10
Liberty and Peace (poetry). Brawley 53, Brown 286, White 31
Niobe in Distress . . . (poetry). Brawley 44
Ode on the Birthday of Pompey Stockbridge (poetry). Robinson 111
On Being Brought from Africa to America (poetry). Barksdale 41, Davis 11, Dreer 22, Ford 3, Hayden 2:7, Kendricks 28, Lomax 205, Long 18, Miller, R. 10, Robinson 100, Stanford 13, Turner 3:166, Turner 4:10
On Freedom (poetry). Stanford 13
On Friendship (poetry). Robinson 111
On Imagination (poetry). Brawley 42, Davis 13, Ford 4, Hughes 2:9, Long 15, Robinson 107, White 28
On Recollection (poetry). Robinson 105
On the Death of a Young Lady Five Years Old (poetry). Patterson 3:28
On the Death of the Rev. Mr. George Whitefield (poetry). Barksdale 40, Brawley 37, Davis 11, Ford 3, Porter 532, Robinson 100
On Virtue (poetry). Barksdale 41
Thoughts on the work of Providence (poetry). Robinson 101
To a Gentleman and Lady on the death of the Lady's brother, etc. (poetry). White 30
To a Gentleman on His Voyage to Great Britain For the Recovery of his Health (poetry). Johnson, C. 78
To His Excellency, General Washington (poetry). Barksdale 43, Brawley 52, Brown 285, Davis 15, Ford 4, Hayden 2:5, Hughes 2:7, Miller, R. 11, Robinson 108

To S. M., A Young African Painter, on Seeing His Work (poetry). Brawley 51, Ford 4, Patterson 3:29, Robinson 110
To The Right Honorable William, Earl of Dartmouth . . . (poetry). Brawley 39, Brown 283, Chambers 43
To The Right Honorable William, Earl of Dartmouth (excerpt—poetry). Cromwell 6, Hayden 2:4, Lomax 204, Randall 2:38
To the University of Cambridge in New England (poetry). Barksdale 41, Brawley 36, Davis 10, Long 17, Robinson 99, Turner 3:166, Turner 4:10

WHEELER, CHARLES ENOCH, 1909- . Poet
Adjuration (poetry). Bontemps 2:105, Hughes 2:272
Tumult (poetry). Hughes 2:273

WHIPPER, WILLIAM, 1801-1885. Orator, Essayist
An address delivered in Wesley Church on the evening of June 12, before the Coloured Reading Society of Philadelphia, for Mental Improvement, 1828 (speech). Porter 105
Address on Non-Resistance to Offensive Aggression (speech). Barksdale 133
To the American People (speech). Porter 204

WHITAKER, PATRICK W., 1946- . Poet
The Godmakers (poetry). Shuman 417
I Black (poetry). Shuman 418
No Man Can Touch (poetry). Shuman 419
Speakers of the House (poetry). Shuman 420
The Women (poetry). Shuman 422

WHITAKER, TOMMY. Poet
After Depression Came Soul (poetry). Murphy 2:134
One Way (poetry). Murphy 2:135

WHITE, CLARENCE CAMERON, 1880- . Essayist
The Negro's Gift to American Music (essay). Calverton 267

WHITE, EDGAR. Playwright, Short Fiction Writer
Loimos (short fiction). King 2:361
Sursum Corda (Lift Up Your Hearts) (short fiction). Coombs 2:189

WHITE, GEORGE H., 1852-1918. Orator
Defense of the Negro Race (speech). Brown 660

WHITE, JOSEPH, 1933- . Playwright, Poet, Short Fiction Writer
The Leader (drama). Jones 605
Old Judge Mose Is Dead (drama). Singh 175

(WHITE, JOSEPH)
Black Is a Soul (poetry). Adoff 2:94, Adoff 3:261

WHITE, LUCY. Playwright
The Bird Child (drama). Locke 253

WHITE, MICHYLE. Poet
"I prepare for night changes" (poetry). Coombs 218

WHITE, WALLACE. Short Fiction Writer
Kiss the Girls for Me (short fiction). Coombs 2:199

WHITE, WALTER, 1893-1955. Fiction Writer, Essayist
I Investigate Lynchings (essay). Adoff 4:35, Barksdale 583, Brown 1005, Watkins 210
The Paradox of Color (essay). Locke 2:361

Fire in the Flint (excerpt: a Negro Doctor in the South—fiction). Brown 181, Calverton 73

WHITFIELD, JAMES M., 1822-1878. Poet
America (poetry). Brawley 228, Brown 290
America (excerpt—poetry). Barksdale 223, Randall 2:35, Robinson 40
America (excerpt: The Forerunners—poetry). Randall 2:35
How Long? (poetry). Brawley 233
Lines on the Death of John Quincy Adams (poetry). Brawley 246
The Misanthropist (poetry). Brawley 241, Robinson 43
The North Star (poetry). Brawley 248
Prayer of the Oppressed (poetry). Brawley 240
Stanzas for the First of August (poetry). Robinson 48
To Cinque (poetry). Robinson 49

WHITMAN, ALBERY ALLSON, 1851-1901. Poet
Custer's Last Ride (poetry). Patterson 3:94, Robinson 230
Hymn to the Nation (poetry). Robinson 226
An Idyl of the South (excerpt—poetry). Kerlin 36
Leelah Misled (excerpt—poetry). Robinson 207
The Lute of Afric's Tribe (poetry). Robinson 228
Rape of Florida (excerpt—poetry). Barksdale 447, Calverton 175
The Southland's Charms (excerpt—poetry). Robinson 224
Stonewall Jackson, 1886 (poetry). Robinson 233
To The Student (poetry). White 50
Twasinta's Seminoles (excerpt—poetry). Brown 297, Robinson 222
Ye Bards of England (poetry). Robinson 232, White 50

WHITSITT, JOYCE. See LAWRENCE, JOYCE WHITSITT

WIGGINS, BERNICE LOVE, 1897- . Poet
Church Folks (poetry). Brewer 42

WIGGINS, LIDA KECK. Poet
Life's lowly were laureled with verses (first line—poetry). Kerlin 41

WILLIAMS, CHARLES P. Poet
The Steps (poetry). Demarest 102

WILLIAMS, COLLEEN. Short Fiction Writer
There Will Always Be Hope (short fiction). Dreer 242

WILLIAMS, DELORES S. Poet
Little Girl Talk (poetry). Exum 121

WILLIAMS, EDWARD G., 1929- . Essayist, Fiction Writer
Great Day for a Funeral (short fiction). Shuman 171
Nightmare (short fiction). Shuman 211
Remembrance of a Lost Dream (short fiction). Shuman 219

WILLIAMS, ERNEST K., JR. Poet
Ain't It a Drag, Baby!! (poetry). Bookers 65

WILLIAMS, GEORGE WASHINGTON, 1849-1891. Essayist, Clergyman
History of the Negro Race in America (excerpt—essay). Barksdale 391
History of the Negro Troops in the War of the Rebellion (excerpt—essay). Barksdale 260, Brown 863, Davis 143
A History of the Negro Troops in the War of the Rebellion (excerpt: Ch. 14—essay). Kendricks 126

WILLIAMS, JOHN ALFRED, 1925- . Fiction Writer, Critic, Essayist, Editor
Literary Ghetto (essay). Hemenway 227
The Manipulation of History and of Fact . . . (essay). Clarke 2:45
This Is My Country, Too (excerpt—essay). Adoff 4:146

Captain Blackman (excerpt — fiction). Troupe 103
The Man Who Cried I Am (excerpt—fiction). Baker 677, Davis 677, Reed 313
Navy Black (excerpt—fiction). Singh 121, Williams 157
Night Song (excerpt: Ch. 5—fiction). Ford 341

Safari West (poetry). Breman 204, Major 132

A Good Season (short fiction). King 2:107
Son in the Afternoon (short fiction). Baker 343, Emanuel 394, Hughes 3:288, Kearns 2:197, Margolies 230, Patterson 3:192

WILLIAMS, JOHN M. Poet
Carmen ad Classem (poetry). Cuney 55

WILLIAMS, LUCY ARIEL. See HOLLO-
WAY, LUCY ARIEL WILLIAMS.

WILLIAMS, MANCE. Poet
For Lover Man, and All the Other Young
Men Who Failed to Return from World
War II (poetry). Hughes 56
A Year Without Seasons (poetry). Hughes
68

WILLIAMS, PATRICIA. Essayist
A Quiet Place Observed (essay). Bookers
62

WILLIAMS, PETER, 1780?-1840. Orator
Anthems and Hymns, 1808-1814 (poetry).
Porter 562

A Discourse Delivered in St. Philip's
Church for the Benefit of the Coloured
Community of Wilberforce in Upper Canada, on the Fourth of July 1830 (sermon). Porter 294

Discourse Delivered on the Death of Captain Paul Cuffe (excerpt—speech).
Brawly 101
An Oration on the Abolition of the Slave
Trade: Delivered in the African Church,
in the city of N. Y., Jan. 1, 1808, With
an introductory Essay by Henry Sipkins
(speech). Porter 343

WILLIAMS, RENE, 1951- . Poet
Daddy (poetry). Shuman 423
Now (poetry). Shuman 424

WILLIAMS, ROBERT F. Essayist
Negroes with Guns (excerpt: From Exile—
essay). Adoff 4:193
U.S.A.: the Potential of a Minority Revolution (excerpt—essay). Adoff 4:196

WILLIAMS, SHERLEY ANNE. Short Fiction
Writer
Tell Martha Not to Moan (short fiction).
Exum 239, Stadler 114

WILLIAMS, VINCENT. Poet
My Boy (poetry). Murphy 3:163
Remember (poetry). Murphy 3:163
Yas Suh! (poetry). Murphy 3:164
Youth (poetry). Murphy 3:164

WILLIAMS, VIRGINIA. Editor, Journalist.
Teacher
Black Man from Atlanta (poetry). Shuman
425
So Tired (poetry). Shuman 427

WILLIAMSON, D. T. Poet
While April Breezes Blow (poetry). Kerlin
314

WILLIAMSON, HARVEY M., 1908- .
Critic, Poet, Short Fiction Writer
Cicero Jones (poetry). Murphy 164
From the Delta's Unmarked Graves (po-
etry). Murphy 3:165
Gospi Anderson (poetry). Murphy 3:165
I Shall Remember These (poetry). Kerlin
320, Murphy 3:167
Lily Baines (poetry). Murphy 3:167
Nostalgia (poetry). Murphy 3:167

WILLMAN, EUGENE B. Poet
Lament of the Farm (poetry). Murphy
3:169
Song of the Maimed Soldier (poetry). Murphy 3:170

WILSON, ART. Poet
Black Sunrise (poetry). Coombs 222
Treasure Hunt (poetry). Coombs 219

WILSON, AUGUST, 1945- . Poet
Theme One: the Variations (poetry). Adoff
3:491

WILSON, CHARLES E., 1932- . Essayist
The Screens (essay). Jones 133

WILSON, CHARLES P., 1885-?. Poet
Somebody's Child (poetry). Kerlin 179

WILSON, ERNEST J., JR., 1920- . Poet
Mae's Rent Party (poetry). Hughes 2:371
Paternal (poetry). Hughes 2:370

WILSON, FRANK H. Playwright
Sugar Cane (drama). Locke 165

WILSON, TED, 1943- . Poet
Count Basie's (poetry). Jones 199
Music of the Other World (poetry). Jones
198
S. C. M. (poetry). Jones 200

WIMBERLI, SIGMONDE KHARLOS,
1938- . Poet
Drum Song Sister (poetry). Brown, P. 100

Fear Came Early (short fiction). Brooks
2:13

WIMS, WARNER B. Poet
The Painful Question (poetry). Murphy
2:137

WINSTON, HARRY. Short Fiction Writer
Greater Love (short fiction). Ford 2:155
Life Begins at Forty (short fiction).
Ford 2:248

WITHERSPOON, JILL, 1947- . Poet
Anniversary (poetry). Lane 86
For My Friends at the Boy's Training
School (poetry). Lane 90
King Still/Lives (poetry). Lane 89
The Nam (poetry). Lane 89
Riding the Bus Home (poetry). Lane 85

(WITHERSPOON, JILL)
Sambas and Things (poetry). Lane 88
Thieves Give More To Blue (poetry). Lane 88
Two Countries (poetry). Lane 86
We Could Take (poetry). Lane 87
Without Your Lean Brown Back (poetry). Lane 87

WITHERSPOON, NAOMI CORNELIA LONG. See **MADGETT, NAOMI CORNELIA LONG WITHERSPOON.**

WOODSON, CARTER G., 1875-1950. Essayist, Historian, Fiction Writer
Fifty Years of Negro Citizenship (essay). Watkins 224
History Made to Order (essay). Brown 839
The Negro In Our History (excerpt: Ch. 9: The Negro and The Right of Man—essay). Turner 6:46

History and Propaganda (speech). Cromwell 303

WOODSON, JON, 1944- . Poet
Saturday (poetry). Davis 775

WOOTEN, CHARLES R., 1949- . Poet
Dying (poetry). Shuman 429
Stream of Consciousness on Ahmed's Last Drink (poetry). Shuman 429

WORK, J. D. (pseudonym?). Teacher, Poet
It's Great to Be a Problem (poetry). Kendricks 198

WRIGHT, BRUCE MCMARION, 1918- . Critic, Editor, Poet
The African Affair (poetry). Adams 3:59, Adoff 3:171, Bontemps 2:144, Cuney 60, Hughes 2:357
And Always (poetry). Cuney 60
Four Old Bodkins for My Analyst (poetry). Pool 183
I Shall Build a Music Box (poetry). Cuney 64
Journey to a Parallel (poetry). Cuney 56, Hughes 2:355
Madam, You Are Astonished (poetry). Cuney 58
Memoriam (poetry). Cuney 59
My Lady of the Cloisters (poetry). Cuney 63
Quest and Quarry (poetry). Cuney 57
A Recollection for Madrigals (poetry). Cuney 61
Sarcasmes (poetry). Cuney 59
To Be Dazzled by the Racing of Her Blood (poetry). Singh 20
To Be Set to Sad Music (poetry). Cuney 58
When You Have Gone From Rooms (poetry). Pool 183

WRIGHT, CHARLES STEVENSON, 1932- . Critic, Essayist, Playwright, Fiction Writer

The Wig (excerpt: Ch. 4—fiction). Reed 331
A New Day (short fiction). Hughes 3:341, Patterson 3:235, Robinson 2:404

WRIGHT, JAY, 1935- . Playwright, Poet
Benjamin Banneker Helps to Build a City (poetry). Troupe 173
Death As History (poetry). Adoff 3:280, Henderson 286
The End of the Ethnic Dream (poetry). Jones 365
The Frightened Lover's Sleep (poetry). Jones 367
The Homecoming Singer (poetry). Adoff 3:279
The Invention of a Garden (poetry). Wilentz 163
An Invitation to Madison County (poetry). Adoff 3:275, Breman 346, Wilentz 150
Jalapeñā Gypsies (poetry). Chapman 2:361
Moving To Wake at Six (poetry). Wilentz 155
The Neighborhood House (poetry). Chapman 2:360
Plea for the Politic Man (poetry). Henderson 289
This Morning (poetry). Hughes 17, Jordan 99, Patterson 3:273
Wednesday Night Prayer Meeting (poetry). Adoff 3:272

WRIGHT, NATHAN, JR. Essayist, Poet
The Question of Power (essay). Curry 229

WRIGHT, RICHARD, 1908-1960. Autobiographer, Essayist, Playwright, Poet, Fiction Writer
Black Boy (excerpt—autobiography). Adoff 4:51, Hayden 189, Rose 64, 263
Black Boy (excerpt: Valedictorian—autobiography). Stanford 120
Black Boy (excerpt: The Wages of Humility—autobiography). Davis 460, Demarest 138
The Ethics of Living Jim Crow; an Autobiographical Sketch—autobiography). Baker 297, Barksdale 542, Brown 1050, Chapman 288, Emanuel 238, Kearns 2:247, Watkins 390
Native Son (drama with Paul Green). Hatch 393
How Bigger Was Born (essay). Burnett 215, Chapman 538, Hemenway 166
Introduction: Blueprint for Negro Writing (essay). Gayle 3:315
Literature of the Negro in the U. S. (essay). Gayle 2:198
Our Strange Birth (essay). Kearns 2:5
Psychological Reactions of Oppressed People (essay). Adoff 4:64, Curry 58

Five Episodes (excerpt from Unfinished Novel—fiction). Hill 2:139
Native Son (excerpt—fiction). Freedman 155, Rose 83, 136

(WRIGHT, RICHARD)

Native Son (excerpt: Fate and Bigger Thomas—fiction). Patterson 3:162

Native Son (excerpt: Fear—fiction). Davis, C. 187

Uncle Tom's Children (excerpts—fiction). Kendricks 243

I Was in the South When Neither Law nor Tradition Was on My Side (narrative). Gayle 82

Between the World and Me (poetry). Adams 3:63, Adoff 2:70, Adoff 3:107, Bontemps 2:103, Breman 109, Chapman 436, Long 483, Singh 13

Hokku: In the Falling Snow (poetry). Adoff 2:87, Breman 111

Hokku Poems (poetry). Adoff 3:108, Bontemps 2:104

I Have Seen Black Hands (poetry). Adoff 3:105, Brown 401, Jordan 112

Almos' a Man (short fiction). Hughes 3:91, James 189, Singh 61, Watkins 3

Big Black Good Man (short fiction). Ford 171

Big Boy Leaves Home (short fiction). Barksdale 548, Chambers 52, James 139, Margolies 19

Bright and Morning Star (short fiction). Baker 270, Brown 105, Clarke 75, Long 485

Down by the Riverside (short fiction). Miller, R. 264

Long Black Song (short fiction). Haslam 289

Man Who Killed a Shadow (short fiction). Emanuel 227

Man Who Lived Underground (short fiction). Chapman 114, Hayden 19, Rose 190

The Man Who Saw The Flood (short fiction). Gibson 60

The Man Who Was Almost A Man (short fiction). Davis 470, Ford 166, Turner 72, Turner 3:362

The Man Who Went to Chicago (short fiction). Adams 4:65, Kearns 452, Margolies 143

The Plea (short fiction). Williams 173

WRIGHT, SARAH. E. Critic, Fiction Writer, Poet

Roadblocks To the Development of Negro Writers (essay). Conference 61

This Child's Gonna Live (excerpt—fiction). Exum 256

The Negro Woman in American Literature (panel discussion). Exum 9

To Some Millions Who Survive Joseph E. Mander, Senior (poetry). Adoff 3:212

Until They Have Stopped (poetry). Adoff 3:215

Urgency (poetry). Hughes 2:270, Pool 185, Pool 2:143

Window Pictures (poetry). Pool 184

WRIGHT, STEPHEN J. Essayist

Promise of Equality (essay). Curry 16

WRIGHT, THEODORE S. 1797-1847. Orator, Clergyman, Abolitionist, Essayist

Letter to Rev. Archibald Alexander, D.D. (letter). Barksdale 128

A Pastoral Letter, Addressed to the Colored Presbyterian Church in the City of New York, June 20th, 1832 (sermon). Porter 472

Proceedings of the New York Anti-Slavery Society, 1837 (excerpt—speech). Kendricks 59

WYCHE, MARVIN, JR., 1951- . Poet

And She Was Bad (poetry). Bontemps 2:210

Five Senses (poetry). Bontemps 2:213

Leslie (poetry). Bontemps 2:212

We Rainclouds (poetry). Bontemps 2:211

YANCY, BESSIE WOODSON. Poet

Knee-Deep (poetry). Murphy 3:170

The Price (poetry). Weisman 7

Where Do You Live? (poetry). Weisman 54

YELDELL, JOYCE. Poet

Why, Mahalia? (poetry). Pool 2:206

YERBY, FRANK, 1916- . Fiction Writer, Poet

Calm After Storm (poetry). Bontemps 2:138

The Fishes and the Poet's Hands (poetry). Bontemps 2:134, Hughes 2:332

Weltschmerz (poetry). Bontemps 2:136

Wisdom (poetry). Bontemps 2:136

You Are a Part of Me (poetry). Bontemps 2:137

Health Card (short fiction). Hughes 3:192, Patterson 3:181, Singh 100

The Homecoming (short fiction). Clarke 147, James 219

My Brother Went to College (short fiction). Turner 86, Turner 3:376

YOUNG, ALEXANDER, 1939- . Essayist, Fiction Writer, Poet

Statement on Aesthetics, Poetics, Kinetics (essay). Chapman 2:533

Snakes (excerpt—fiction). Reed 347

Who Is Angelina? (excerpt—fiction). Troupe 237

Before a Monument (poetry). Murphy 161

Birthday Poem (poetry). Breman 414, Miller, A. 16

The Curative Powers of Silence (poetry). Wilentz 177

A Dance for LiPo (poetry). Miller, A. 3

A Dance for Ma Rainey (poetry). Chapman 2:366, Major 134

A Dance for Militant Dilettantes (poetry). Adoff 3:362, Chapman 2:367, Coombs 234, Miller, A. 1

(YOUNG, ALEXANDER)
Dance of the Infidels (poetry). Adoff 3:363, Chapman 2:368
Dancer (poetry). Adoff 3:364, Miller, A. 14
Dancing All Alone (poetry). Coombs 233
Dancing in the Laundromat (poetry). Miller, A. 6
Dancing on The Shore (poetry). Coombs 231
Dear Old Stockholm (poetry). Wilentz 175
Everywhere (poetry). Wilentz 169
For Joanne in Poland (poetry). Miller, A. 8
For Poets (poetry). Adoff 3:361, Coombs 231, Miller, A. 17
Friday the Twelfth (poetry). Wilentz 178
Hey Boy (poetry). Murphy 160
I Arrive in Madrid (poetry). Coombs 228
The Kiss (poetry). Adoff 3:367, Wilentz 172
Lemons, Lemons (poetry). Miller, A. 5
A Little More Traveling Music (poetry). Chapman 2:365
Loneliness (poetry). Adoff 3:368
Lonesome in the Country (poetry). Wilentz 168
Love's Helplessness (poetry). Murphy 162
Malaguina Saluosa (poetry). Wilentz 171
Moon-Watching by Lake Chapala (poetry). Coombs 231, Miller, A. 12
The Move Continuing (poetry). Adoff 3:365, Coombs 236, Miller, A. 7
Myself When I Am Real (poetry). Adoff 3:365
The Offering (excerpt—poetry). Miller, A. 9
Pachuta/a Memoir (poetry). Miller, A. 11
Poetry (poetry). Miller, A. 2
Ponce DeLeon/a Morning Walk (poetry). Wilentz 174
The Prestidigitator [1] (poetry). Chapman 2:369
The Prestidigitator [2] (poetry). Chapman 2:370
The Song Turning Back into Itself (poetry). Miller, A. 13, Troupe 195, Wilentz 167
There Is a Sadness (poetry). Wilentz 173
Yes, the Secret Mind Whispers (poetry). Adoff 3:367
Chicken Hawk's Dream (short fiction). Chapman 2:146

YOUNG, CARRIE A. Poet, Short Fiction Writer
Adjo Means Goodbye (poetry). Williams 191

YOUNG, FRANK A. Poet
Flame of Green (poetry). Murphy 3:172
A Fool's Wisdom (poetry). Murphy 3:171

YOUNG, NATHAN BEN. Essayist, Fiction Writer, Historian, Journalist
Eighteenth Street (essay). Johnson, C. 37
The Genealogy of an American Champion (essay). Dreer 162

YOUNG, SUSAN. Poet
The Life of a Slum Child (poetry). Bookers 13

YOUNG BEAR, RAY A. Poet
In Dream: The Privacy of Sequence (poetry). Troupe 350

ZEALY, YOLANDE. Poet
A Prayer (poetry). Bookers 51

ZUBENA, SISTER. See CONLEY, CYNTHIA M.

ZUBER, RON. Playwright
Three X Love (drama). King 429

INDEX BY TITLE

Aardvark
Fields, Julia
An ABC of Color
Dubois, William Edward Burghardt
Abraham Lincoln
Fentress, John W.
Abraham Lincoln of Rock Spring Farm
Tolson, Melvin Beaunorus
The Abrogation of the Seventh Commandment, by the American Churches, 1835. Signed—a Puritan
Ruggles, David
Absence
McKay, Claude
Abu
Randall, Dudley
The Accident
Patterson, Raymond Richard
Accident: Edgecomb General Hospital, May 16, 1968
Fields, Julia
Accountability
Dunbar, Paul Laurence
An Acrostic for Julia Shepard
Horton, George Moses
An Act of Prostitution
McPherson, James Alan
An Ad in the Times
Harris, William J.
An address delivered at Bethel Church, Pennsylvania; on the 30th of September, 1818. Before the Pennsylvania Augustine Society, for the education of People of Colour
Saunders, Prince
An address delivered before the American Moral Reform Society, Philadelphia, Aug. 17th, 1837
Forten, James, Jr.
Address delivered before the Humane Mechanics' Society, on the 4th of July, 1834
Corr, Joseph M. (Rev.)
Address delivered before the Moral Reform Society in Philadelphia, August 8, 1836
Watkins, William
An address delivered in Wesley Church on the evening of June 12, before the Coloured Reading Society of Philadelphia for Mental Improvment, 1828
Whipper, William

An Address Delivered on the Celebration of the Abolition of Slavery in the State of New York, July 5, 1827
Paul, Nathaniel
Address on Non-Resistance to Offensive Aggression
Whipper, William
An Address on the Condemnation of John Joyce.
Tighlman, Chief Justice
An Address to the Negroes of the State of New York
Hammon, Jupiter
An Address to Miss Phillis Wheatley, Ethiopian Poetess
Hammon, Jupiter
An Address to the New York African Society, for Mutual Relief
Hamilton, William
Address to the Paris Antislavery Conference
Martin, J. Sella
An Address to the Public and People of Colour
Allen, Richard
Address to the Slaves of the United States of America
Garnet, Henry Highland
An Address to the Wyandotte Nation and Accompanying Letter to William Walker dated May 25, 1817.
Stewart, John
Adieu
Riley, Constantea E.
Adjo Means Goodbye
Young, Carrie A.
Adjuration
Wheeler, Charles Enoch
Admonition
Morris, Stanley, Jr.
Admonitions
Clifton, Lucille
Adulthood
Giovanni, Nikki
Advice
Bennett, Gwendolyn B.
Advice To The Girls
Harper, Frances Ellen Watkins
Affirmation
Collins, Helen Armstead Johnson

117

Africa
Alexander, Lewis Grandison
Africa
McKay, Claude
Africa
Rivers, Conrad Kent
Africa–Guyana
Carew, Jan
Africa: Return and Turnabout
Henry, Lois-Allison
The Africa Thing
Miller, Adam David
Africa to Me
Allen, Samuel W.
Africa II
Long, Doughtry
The African
Courlander, Harold
The African
Kelley, William Melvin
The African Affair
Wright, Bruce McMarion
African Beauty Rose
Cumbo, Kattie M.
African China
Tolson, Melvin Beaunorus
African Dream
Kaufman, Bob
African Love History
Jones, LeRoi
African Madness
Tate, Eleanora E.
African question mark
Hughes, Langston
African Responses to Malcolm X
Lacy, Leslie Alexander
Afrique Accidentale
Joans, Ted
Afro-American Fragment
Hughes, Langston
Afro-American Literary Critics: An Introduction
Turner, Dawin T.
Afroamerican literature: the Conscience of Man
Jeffers, Lance
The Afro-American Playwright in the New York Professional Theatre, 1923–1959
Turner, Darwin T.
After
Madgett, Naomi Cornelia Long Witherspoon
After All
Hayes, Donald Jeffrey
After Depression Came Soul
Whitaker, Tommy
After Hearing a Radio Announcement . . .
Troupe, Quincy
After Kent State
Clifton, Lucille
After MLK: The Marksman Marked Leftover Kill
Addison, Lloyd
After Saturday Nite Comes Sunday
Sanchez, Sonia
After the Killing
Randall, Dudley

After the Quarrel
Dunbar, Paul Laurence
After the Rain
Crouch, Stanley
After the Record Is Broken
Emanuel, James A., Sr.
After the Winter
McKay, Claude
After Winter
Brown, Sterling A.
Aftermath
Harper, Michael S.
Afternoon into Night
Dunham, Katherine
An Afternoon of a Young Poet
Holman, Moses Carl
Afternoon off
Pitts, Lucia Mae
Afterwards They Shall Dance
Kaufman, Bob
An Afterword: for Gwen Brooks
Lee, Don L.
Again the Summoning
Cumberbatch, Lawrence S.
Against Segregation in Schools
Cain, Richard H.
Age
Cumbo, Kattie M.
An Agony as Now
Jones, LeRoi
Ain't It a Drag, Baby!!
Williams, Ernest K., Jr.
Ain't that a Groove
Cobb, Charlie
Air
Major, Clarence
The Air is Dirty
Thompson, Glen
Al asil suddi—the origin of blackness
Jackman, Marvin
Al Fitnah Mukajri
Jackman, Marvin
Al Fitnah Muhajir
Nazzam Al Sudan
Alabama
Fields, Julia
Alabama Centennial
Madgett, Naomi Cornelia Long Witherspoon
Alafia
Odaro
Alan Paton Will Die
Scott, Johnie H.
The Alarm Clock
Evans, Mari
Albert Ayler: Eulogy for a Decomposed Saxophone Player
Crouch, Stanley
Alcoved Agonies
Pritchard, Norman Henry, II
Alexander Hamilton
Pickens, William
Algiers 1969: A Report on the Pan-American Cultural Festival
Hare, Nathan

Ali
  Corbin, Lloyd
Alien
  Hayes, Donald Jeffrey
The Alien Land of Richard Wright
  Redding, Jay Saunders
The Alienated Richard Wright: a Native Son Remembered
  Bush, Joseph Bevans
The Alienation of James Baldwin
  Clarke, John Henrik
The Alienation of Negro Litreature
  Glicksberg, Charles I.
All Behind the Line Is Mine
  Johnson, Bradlon
All Day Long
  Angelou, Maya
All Day We've Longed for Night
  Fabio, Sarah Webster
All Hung Up
  Cumbo, Kattie M.
All Night Visitors
  Major, Clarence
All Praise
  Crouch, Stanley
All that Glitters
  Propes, Arthur
All the Clacks
  Rodgers, Carolyn M.
All the Rain Long It Was Daying
  Redmond, Eugene B.
All The World Moved
  Jordan, June Meyer
All White Cast
  Caldwell, Ben
Allegory in Black
  Clark, Carl
The Alley Cat Brushed His Whiskers
  Cuney, Waring
Alma Mater
  Bibb, A. Denee
Almos' a Man
  Wright, Richard
The Almost Revolutionist
  Lockett, Tena L.
The Almost White Boy
  Motley, Willard
Alone
  Giovanni, Nikki
Along This Way
  Johnson, James Weldon
Alpha and Omega
  Smith, Abram G. F.
The Alternative
  Jones, LeRoi
The Alternative
  Owens, Rev. John Henry
Always the Same
  Hughes, Langston
Am Driven Mad
  Polite, Allen
Am I a Man?
  Manning, Pamela
Amandla
  Kgositsile, Keorapetse William

Amateur Night in Harlem
  Davis, Gene
Ambivalence
  Bush, Joseph Bevans
Ambrosia
  Fields, Julia
Amen
  Thomas, Richard W.
Amen Corner
  Baldwin, James
America
  Clarke, John Henrik
America
  Dumas, Henry L.
America
  Jones, James Arlington
America
  Kellum-Rose, Matthew
America
  McKay, Claude
America
  Whitfield, James M.
America Bleeds
  Lewis, Angelo
The American Cancer Society or There Is More Than One Way to Skin a Coon
  Lorde, Audre
The American Dream
  Scott, Johnie H.
American Folk Literature
  Brewer, J. Mason
American Gothic (or To Satch)
  Allen, Samuel W.
American Heartbreak
  Hughes, Langston
American History
  Harper, Michael S.
American Ideals
  Conley, Malcolm Christian
American Negro
  Coleman, Anita Scott
American Negro Folk Literature
  Fauset, Arthur Huff
American Negro Literature
  Redding, Jay Saunders
American Race Problem as Reflected in American Literature
  Brown, Sterling A.
American Setup
  Major, Clarence
American Slavery
  Douglass, Frederick
Analysands
  Randall, Dudley
Anatomy of Frustration
  Cumbo, Kattie M.
Ancestors
  Randall, Dudley
And Always
  Wright, Bruce McMarion
And Aren't I a Woman?
  Truth, Sojourner
And Beauty's All Around
  Fields, Julia
And bury the dog that does not bark
  Bell, George R.

And Death Went Down
  Berry, Josie Craig
And Fall Shall Sit in Judgment
  Lorde, Audre
And Hickman Arrives
  Ellison, Ralph Waldo
And I can remember still your first lies
America
  Hand, Q. R.
And I passed by
  Andrew, Joseph Maree
And If I Die Before I Wake
  Goss, Clay
And Now Irrevocably
  Pitts, Lucia Mae
And on This Shore
  Holman, Moses Carl
And Once Again: Pain
  Browne, William
And One Shall Live In Two
  Brooks, Jonathan Henderson
And/or
  Brown, Sterling A.
And She Was Bad
  Wyche, Marvin Jr.
And Shine Swam On
  Neal, Larry
And So Tomorrow
  Boyd, Samuel E.
And the Heart Speaks
  Geary, Bruce C.
And the Old Women Gathered
  Evans, Mari
And Then We Heard the Thunder
  Killens, John Oliver
And There Are Those
  Thompson, James W.
And Through the Caribbean Sea
  Danner, Margaret
and universal
  Welburn, Ron
And Was Not Improved
  Bennett, Lerone, Jr.
And we conquered
  Penny, Rob
And What about the Children
  Lorde, Audre
And What Shall You Say
  Cotter, Joseph Seamon, Jr.
And Where Can I Go Now Except Away
  Randall, Jon
And Where, My Love, Are You?
  Peace, Jerry
And While We Are Waiting
  Rodgers, Carolyn M.
And Why the Softness?
  Randall, Dudley
Angelina
  Dunbar, Paul Laurence
An Angel's Prayer
  Sims, Lefty
Angling up from the wheeling feet of fire
  Gardner, Carl
Angola Question Mark
  Hughes, Langston

Anne-Marie Duvall
  Gaines, Ernest J.
Anner' Lizer's Stumblin' Block
  Dunbar, Paul Laurence
The Anniversary
  Anthony, Florence
Anniversary
  Murphy, Beatrice M.
Anniversary
  Witherspoon, Jill
Announcement
  Stewart, James T.
Anonymous
  Jones, James Arlington
Another Consumes
  Jones, James Arlington
Another Country
  Baldwin, James
Another Day
  Brown, Isabella Maria
Another Day
  Kennedy, Vallejo Ryan
Another Man Has Died
  Franklin, Charles
Another Time, Another Place
  Cumbo, Kattie M.
Another Season
  Harper, Michael S.
An Answer
  Jones, James Arlington
The Answer
  Owens, Rev. John Henry
The Answer
  Simmons, Judy Dothard
Answer to a Perplexing Question
  King, Martin Luther, Jr.
Answer to Dunbar's "A Choice"
  Cotter, Joseph Seamon, Sr.
Answer to Dunbar's "After a Visit"
  Cotter, Joseph Seamon, Sr.
Answer to Prayer
  Johnson, James Weldon
—answer to yr question of am i not yr
woman even if u went on shit again
  Sanchez, Sonia
Antar of Araby
  Cuney-Hare, Maud
An Ante-Bellum Sermon
  Dunbar, Paul Laurence
Anthems and Hymns, 1808–1814
  Fortune, Michael
Anthems and Hymns, 1808–1814
  Hamilton, William
Anthems and Hymns, 1808-1814
  Sidney, Robert Y.
Anthems and Hymns, 1808-1814
  Williams, Peter
Anticipation
  Tinsley, Tomi Carolyn
Antigone I
  Martin, Herbert Woodward
Antigone VI
  Martin, Herbert Woodward
Antigone XI
  Martin, Herbert Woodward

Antigone XII
Martin, Herbert Woodward
Antigone XV
Martin, Herbert Woodward
Antigone and Oedipus
Ray, Henrietta Cordelia
The Anti-Semanticist
Hoagland, Everett
Antonio Maceo
Richardson, Willis
Anxiety
Goodwin, Ruby Berkley
Any Human to Another
Cullen, Countee Porter
Apology
Durem, Ray
Apology for Apostasy?
Knight, Etheridge
Apology for Wayward Jim
Hughes, James C.
Apology to Leopold Sedar Senghor
Johnston, Percy Edward
Apology (To the Panthers)
Clifton, Lucille
The Apostle
Fuller, Hoyt W.
Apostolic
Brewer, J. Mason
Appeal of Forty Thousand Citizens, Threatened With Disenfranchisement, to the People of Pennsylvania
Purvis, Robert
Appeal in Four Articles . . .
Walker, David
Appeal to the Colored Citizens of New York and Elsewhere in Behalf of the Press, 1835
Ruggles, David
An Appeal to the Conscience of the Black Race to See Itself
Garvey, Marcus
Appearances
Anderson, Garland
Appoggiatura
Hayes, Donald Jeffrey
Approximations
Hayden, Robert Earl
April Crucifix, To: Dr. Martin Luther King
Thomas, Richard W.
An April Day
Cotter, Joseph Seamon, Jr.
April 4, 1968
Goode, Michael
April 5th
Graham, Donald L.
April Longing
Cleaves, Mary Wilkerson
April Is On the Way
Dunbar-Nelson, Alice
The April of Alabama
McClellan, George Marion
Apropos of Africa
Locke, Alain Leroy
Arabesque
Horne, Frank M.
Arabesque
Johnson, Fred

Area
Clemmons, Carole Gregory
Aren't We All?
Stateman, Norman Hills
Areytos
Brierre, Jean
Arise, Ye Garvey Nation
Guinn, I. E. (Bishop)
An Aristotelian Elegy
Bogle, Donald E.
Ark of Bones
Dumas, Henry L.
Armageddon
Hill, Leslie Pinckney
Armour
Johnson, Georgia Douglas
Arms & Exit
Thompson, James W.
Arroyo
Weatherly, Tom
Arson and Cold Lace
Long, Worth
Art of a Poet
Horton, George Moses
The Art of Fiction
Ellison, Ralph Waldo
Arctic Tern in a Museum
Newsome, Mary Effie Lee
Arrangement in Black
O'Donnell, E. P.
Arthur Ridgewood, M. D.
Davis, Frank Marshall
Artists' and Models' Ball
Brooks, Gwendolyn
As
Pritchard, Norman Henry, II
As a Basic
Porter, Linda
As a Possible Lover
Jones, LeRoi
As Bald as She Could Be
Sherman, Jimmie
As Critic
Danner, Margaret
As I Grew Older
Hughes, Langston
As the Old Year Passed
Moore, William H. A.
As to the Leopard's Spots
Miller, Kelly
As When Emotion Too Far Exceeds Its Cause
Oden, Gloria Catherine
As You Leave Me
Knight, Etheridge
Ascendancy
Simmons, Herbert Alfred
Ask Me Why I Love You
Hawkins, Walter Everette
Ask Your Mama
Hughes, Langston
An Aspect of Love, Alive in the Ice and Fire
Brooks, Gwendolyn
Aspiration
Hughes, James C.

Assailant
Raven, John
The Assassin
Redmond, Eugene B.
Assassination
Lee, Don L.
assassination
Moreland, Charles King, Jr.
Assassination
Parker, Patricia
Aswelay
Pritchard, Norman Henry II
At Candle-Lightin' Time
Dunbar, Paul Laurence
At Early Morn
Dismond, Henry Binga
At Life's End
Luke, Allen
At Long Last
Patterson, Lindsay
At Niagara
Dett, Robert Nathaniel
At Sea
Guerard, Vera E.
At Sea
Toomer, Jean
At that Moment
Patterson, Raymond Richard
At the Carnival
Spencer, Anne
At the Closed Gate of Justice
Corrothers, James David
At the Ebony Circle
Quigless, Helen G.
At the Golden Day
Ellison, Ralph Waldo
At The Inn
Pritchard, Sheila
At the Spring Dawn
Grimke, Angelina Weld
At War
Atkins, Russell
At Will
Jones, James Arlington
Atlanta Exposition Address
Washington, Booker Taliaferro
Atlantic City Waiter
Cullen, Countee Porter
Atman
Saxon, Dan
Atrocities
Giovanni, Nikki
Attention
Scott, Johnie H.
Attic Romance
Harmon, Florence Marion
The Attitude of the American Mind Toward
the Negro Intellect
Crummell, Alexander
Attucks, The Martyr
Richardson, Willis
The Auction
Tolson, M. Beaunorus
Auditions
Saunders, Ruby Constance X.

Audubon Drafted
Jones, LeRoi
Auf Wiedersehen
Hayes, Donald Jeffrey
August 2
Jordan, Norman
August 10, 1969
Thomas, Richard W.
Aunt Chloe's Lullaby
Davis, Daniel Webster
Aunt Clo
Gaines, Ernest J.
Aunt Jane Allen
Johnson, Fenton
Aunt Jemima of the Ocean Waves
Hayden, Robert Earl
Aunt Lou
Gainest, Ernest J.
Aunt Sue's Stories
Hughes, Langston
Author of an Attitude
Major, Clarence
Autobiography
Davis, Arthur P.
Autobiography
DuBois, William Edward Burghardt
Autobiography
Henson, Josiah
Autobiography
Little, Malcolm
Autobiography
Vassa, Gustavus
Autobiography
Weatherly, Tom
Autobiography of a Fugitive Negro
Ward, Samuel Ringgold
Autobiography of an Ex-colored Man
Johnson, James Weldon
Autobiography of Miss Jane Pittman
Gaines, Ernest J.
Autobiography of Malcolm X
Little, Malcolm
Autumn God
Redmond, Eugene B.
Autumn Rain
Harris, Helen C.
Autumn Sadness
Braithwaite, William Stanley Beaumont
Autumn Song
Hill, William Allyn
Avey
Toomer, Jean
Avoidances
Welburn, Ron
Awakened by a Woman's Cedared Thighs
Jeffers, Lance
The Awakening
Collazo, Jamie
The Awakening
Kgositsile, Keorapetse William
The Awakening: a Memoir
Bontemps, Arna
The Awakening of American Negro Literature,
1619–1900
Haslam, Gerald W.

Award
Durem, Ray
Awareness
Lee, Don L.
Away
Harris, Marla V.
The Award
Monn, Albert
Azikiwe in Jail
Hughes, Langston

The Babies of Biafra
Dunham, Katherine
Baby Cobina
Hayford, Gladys May Casely
Baby Hair
Nichols, Constance
Babylon Revisited
Jones, LeRoi
Bacchanal
Hayden, Robert Earl
Back Again, Home
Lee, Don L.
Back into the Garden
Fabio, Sarah Webster
Back With the Wind: Mr. Styron and the
Reverend Turner
Thelwell, Mike
Backlash Blues
Hughes, Langston
Bad Man
Edmonds, Randolph
Bad News
Scott, Johnie H.
Badman of the Guest Professor
Reed, Ishmael
Bahamas I
Cumbo, Kattie M.
Bahamas II
Cumbo, Kattie M.
Baha 'u'llah in Garden of Ridivan
Hayden, Robert Earl
The Baker's Boy
Newsome, Mary Effie Lee
Balance
Giovanni, Nikki
Baldwin and the Problem of Being
Kent, George E.
A Ballad for Stirling Street
Sanchez, Sonia
Ballad for the Brother
Saunders, Ruby Constance X.
Ballad of a Man that's Gone
Hughes, Langston
Ballad of Birmingham
Randall, Dudley
The ballad of chocolate Mabbie
Brooks, Gwendolyn
Ballad of Joe Meek
Brown, Sterling A.
Ballad of Nat Turner
Hayden, Robert Earl
Ballad of Remembrance
Hayden, Robert Earl
The Ballad of Rudolph Read
Brooks, Gwendolyn

The Ballad of Sue Ellen Westerfield
Hayden, Robert Earl
Ballad of the Free
Walker, Margaret Abigail
Ballad of the Hoppy Toad
Walker, Margaret Abigail
Ballad of the Lame Man and the Blind Man
Cuney, Waring
Ballad of the Landlord
Hughes, Langston
Ballad of the Morning Street
Jones, LeRoi
Ballad of the Students' Sit-ins
Merriam, Eve
Ballad Of The True Beast
Hayden, Robert Earl
Ballad of Uncle Tom
Harrell, Dennis
Ballade of One That Died Before His Time
Brawley, Benjamin Griffith
Balm in Gilead—a Christmas jingle, played
with trumpets and muffled drums
Horne, Frank M.
Balo
Toomer, Jean
The Band of Gideon
Cotter, Joseph Seamon, Jr.
The Banjo Player
Johnson, Fenton
Banjo Song
Dunbar, Paul Laurence
Banking Coal
Toomer, Jean
Baptism
Lomax, Pearl Cleage
Baptism
McKay, Claude
Baraka as Poet
Taylor, Clyde
Barbados
Marshall, Paule
Barbecued Cong: or We Laid Mai Lai Low
Redmond, Eugene B.
Baroness and the Black Musician
Neal, Larry
Barred
Vaughn, Naomi Evans
Barricades
Harper, Michael S.
The Barrier
McKay, Claude
Bars Fight
Terry, Lucy
Basic
Durem, Ray
Basic Unity Program, Organization of Afro-
American Unity
Little, Malcolm
Bassy
Loftin, Elouise
Bathed Is My Blood
La Grone, Oliver
The Battle
Jones, James Arlington
Battle Report
Kaufman, Bob

Baxter's Procrustes
  Chesnutt, Charles Waddell
Bayou Legend
  Dodson, Owen
be cool, baby
  Penny, Rob
Be Daedalus
  Alba, Nanina
Be Natural, Baby
  Saunders, Ruby Constance X.
Be You
  Jordan, Norman
The Beach Umbrella
  Colter, Cyrus
Beale Street
  Cuney, Waring
Beale Street, Memphis
  Snyder, Thurmond L.
Bean Eaters
  Brooks, Gwendolyn
The Beast Section
  Smith, Welton
The Beast With Chrome Teeth
  Snyder, Thurmond L.
The Beat
  Lucas, James R.
The Beat
  Seese, Ethel Gray
Beating hearts
  Balagon, Kuwasi
Beating That Boy
  Ellison, Ralph Waldo
Beautiful Bathtub
  Harris, William J.
Beautiful Black Me
  Rodgers, Loretta
Beautiful Black Men
  Giovanni, Nikki
Beautiful Black Women
  Jones, LeRoi
The beautiful day
  Spellman, Alfred B.
The Beautiful Day #2
  Spellman, Alfred B.
Beautiful Light and Black Our Dreams
  King, Woodie, Jr.
Beauty and The Diamond Ring
  Moore, John P.
The Beauty of Living
  Kellum-Rose, Matthew
Beauty Then Is Being
  Thompson, James W.
Because I Have Wandered Long
  Burroughs, Margaret Taylor Goss
Because Is Why
  Randall, Jon
Bedtime Story
  Malcom, Barbara
Beetlecreek
  Demby, William
Beehive
  Toomer, Jean
Before a Monument
  Young, Alexander
Before / and After
  Latimore, Jewel Christine

Before Autumn Leaves Turn Gold
  Shaed, Dorothy Lee Louise
Before the Feast of Shushan
  Spencer, Anne
Before the Mayflower: A History of Black
America (excerpt: The African Past)
  Bennett, Lerone, Jr.
Beginning And End
  Madgett, Naomi Cornelia Long Wither-spoon
The Beginning of a Long Poem on Why I
Burned the City
  Benford, Lawrence
Behind the Scenes
  Keckley, Elizabeth
Behold the Bride
  Lytle, Corinne
Being Different
  Major, Clarence
A Being Exit in the World
  Hernton, Calvin C.
being property once myself
  Clifton, Lucille
A Belated Oriole
  McClellan, George Marion
Believe, Believe
  Kaufman, Bob
The Bells of Notre Dame
  Brawley, Benjamin Griffith
Belly Song
  Knight, Etheridge
Belsen, Liberation Day
  Hayden, Robert Earl
Ben O
  Gaines, Ernest J.
The Bench
  Rive, Richard
Benediction
  Hayes, Donald Jeffrey
Benediction
  Kaufman, Bob
Benediction
  Lomax, Pearl Cleage
Benign Neglect / Mississippi, 1970
  St. John, Primus
Benjamin Banneker Helps to Build a City
  Wright, Jay
Bent-back Jim
  Harris, William J.
Best Loved of Africa
  Danner, Margaret
The Best of Simple
  Hughes, Langston
Between Me and Anyone Who Can Under-stand
  Scott, Sharon
Between the World and Me
  Wright, Richard
Beverly Hills, Chicago
  Brooks, Gwendolyn
Beware: Do Not Read This Poem
  Reed, Ishmael
Beyond the Nigger
  Plumpp, Sterling Dominic
Biafra
  Mack, L. V.

The Big Bell In Zion
   Shackelford, Theodore Henry
Big Black Good Man
   Wright, Richard
Big Boy Leaves Home
   Wright, Richard
Big Momma
   Fields, Julia
Big Momma
   Lee, Don L.
The Big Sea
   Hughes, Langston
Big White Fog
   Ward, Theodore
Biographical Sketch of Archibald H. Grimké
   Grimke, Angelina Weld
Biography
   Jones, LeRoi
The Bird Child
   White, Lucy
A Bird in the City
   Bryant, Frederick James, Jr.
A Bird is Singing
   Turner, Lucy Mae
Bird of Passage
   Scott, Dennis
Birmingham
   Fields, Julia
Birmingham
   Walker, Margaret Abigail
Birmingham 1963
   Patterson, Raymond Richard
Birmingham Sunday
   Hughes, Langston
Birth
   Scott, Eddie, Jr.
Birth in a Narrow Room
   Brooks, Gwendolyn
The Birth of John Henry
   Tolson, Melvin Beaunorus
Birthday Poem
   Young, Alexander
Birthday Song to Cleveland
   Sims, Cleveland
Birthplace Revisited
   Corso, Gregory
The Bishop of Atlanta: Ray Charles
   Bond, Horace Julian
Bits and Pieces
   Ford, Gregory J.
The Bitter Cup
   Troup, Cornelius V.
Bitterness
   McLean, Eldon George
The Black Aesthetic in the Thirties, Forties
and Fifties
   Randall, Dudley
Black All Day
   Patterson, Raymond Richard
Black Am I Like the Night
   Scott, Calvin
Black and Full
   Crews, Stella Louise
Black and Lyrical
   Penny, Rob

Black and Tan
   Ragland, J. Farley
Black and White . . .
   Fortune, Timothy Thomas
Black and White
   Rutherford, Tony
The Black Angel
   Harper, Michael S.
Black Angel Child
   Plumpp, Sterling Dominic
Black Art
   Jones, LeRoi
Black Art: Mute Matter Given Force and
Function
   Karenga, Maulana Ron
Black Art Spirits
   Johnson, Alicia Loy
The Black Arts Movement
   Neal, Larry
Black Arts: Notebook
   O'Neal, John
The Black Bird
   Jackman, Marvin
Black Bourgeoisie
   Frazier, E. Franklin
Black Bourgeoisie
   Jeffers, Lance
Black Bourgeoisie
   Jones, LeRoi
Black Boy
   Robinson, Ophelia
Black Boy
   Wright, Richard
Black Boy Singing
   Nichols, Eleanor Graham
Black Cameo on Pink Quartz
   Burton, John W.
Black Can Be Beautiful
   Bohanon, Mary
Black Cargoes
   Mannix, Daniel P. and Malcolm Cowley
Black Children
   Clemmons, Carole Gregory
Black Church On Sunday
   Mosley, Joseph M., Jr.
Black Comedy
   Rusan, Francille
Black Consciousness
   Scott, Johnie H.
Black Consciousness
   Walton, Bruce
A Black Cop's Communion
   Kemp, Arnold
Black Criterion
   Major, Clarence
Black Critic
   Lee, Don L.
Black Cultural Nationalism
   Karenga, Ron
Black Cycle
   Charles, Martha Evans
Black Dada Nihilism
   Jones, LeRoi
The Black Doctor
   Aldridge, Amanda Ira

The Black Draftee from Dixie
  Clifford, Carrie Williams
Black Drama
  Mitchell, Loften
Black Eurydice
  Clemmons, Carole Gregory
Black Faces
  Coleman, Anita Scott
The Black Finger
  Grimke, Angelina Weld
Black Fire
  Bethune, Lebert
The Black Folk Arrest Their Blackness
  Jeffers, Lance
Black for Dinner
  Colter, Cyrus
Black Future
  Cumbo, Kattie M.
Black Gauntlet
  Cousins, William
Black Goddess
  Cumbo, Kattie M.
Black Henry
  Ologboni, Tejumola
The Black Horseman
  Richardson, Willis
Black humor
  Emanuel, James A., Sr.
Black Ice
  Patterson, Charles
Black Is
  Grosvenor, Verta Mae
Black Is . . .
  Stevens, Sandra E.
Black Is a Soul
  White, Joseph
Black Is Beautiful
  Brewster, Townsend T.
Black Is Best
  Thompson, Larry E.
Black Is Good
  Carmichael, Stokely
Black Jam for Dr. Negro
  Evans, Mari
Black Judgment
  Giovanni, Nikki
Black Judgements
  Giovanni, Nikki
Black Lady in an Afro Hairdo Cheers for
Cassius
  Holmes, R. Ernest
Black Lady's Inspiration
  Diggs, Alfred
Black Lotus / a Prayer
  Johnson, Alicia Loy
The Black Madonna
  Rice, Albert
Black Magdalens
  Cullen, Countee Porter
Black Magic
  Randall, Dudley
Black Magic
  Sanchez, Sonia
Black Magic, Black Art
  Milner, Ronald

Black Majesty
  Cullen, Countee Porter
Black Mammies
  Holloway, John Wesley
The Black Mammy
  Johnson, James Weldon
A Black Man
  Cornish, Sam
Black Man from Atlanta
  Williams, Virginia
Black Man's Burden
  Grit, Bruce
A Black Man Talks of Reaping
  Bontemps, Arna W.
Black Man, 13th Floor
  Emanuel, James A., Sr.
Black Manhattan
  Johnson, James Weldon
The Black Man's Burden
  Holtzclaw, William H.
Black Man's Burden
  Killens, John Oliver
The Black Man Must Leave the South
  Greener, Richard T.
Black Man's Feast
  Fabio, Sarah Webster
The Black Man's Soul
  Corrothers, James D.
Black Moses, Black Moses Black Moses
Black
  Conyus
A Black Mother's Plea
  Moore, Birdell Chew
Black Mother Praying
  Dodson, Owen
Black Music / A Beginning
  Lee, Don L.
Black Music Man
  Gee, Lethonia
Black Muslim Boy in a Hospital
  Emanuel, James A., Sr.
Black No More
  Schuyler, George Samuel
Black Music: New Black Revolutionary Art
  Graves, Milford
Black Narcissus
  Barrax, Gerald William
Black Narrator
  Alhamisi, Ahmed Akinwole
Black on White
  Littlejohn, David
Black Orpheus
  Bryant, Frederick James, Jr.
Black Panther
  Hughes, Langston
Black Pawns in a White Game
  Lester, Julius
Black People
  Jones, LeRoi
Black Phoenix
  Powe, Blossom
The Black Playwright in the Professional
Theatre of the United States of America 1859–
1959
  Turner, Darwin T.

A Black Poet to Saint Exupery
  Clemmons, Carole Gregory
Black Poet, White Critic
  Randall, Dudley
A Black Poetry Day
  Johnson, Alicia Loy
Black Poetry
  Randall, Dudley
Black Politics: a Brief Summary Beginning
the New Revolution in the 1950s
  Curry, Gladys J.
Black Power
  Carmichael, Stokely and C. V. Hamilton
Black Power
  Giovanni, Nikki
Black Power
  Patterson, Raymond Richard
Black Power
  Saxon, Alvin A.
Black Power
  Spriggs, Edward S.
Black Power—A Scientic Concept Whose
Time Has Come
  Boggs, James
black power poem
  Reed, Ishmael
Black Proclamation
  Jeffrey, Robert
The Black Psyche
  Killens, John Oliver
Black Recruit
  Johnson, Georgia Douglas
Black Reflections
  Carter, Loleta
The Black revolution is passing you by
  Giovanni, Nikki
Black Samson of Brandywine
  Dunbar, Paul Laurence
Black Seasons—Haiku
  Randall, Jon
Black Sister
  Cumbo, Kattie M.
A Black Social Statement on the Occasion
of . . .
  Bradford, Walter
Black Soldier
  Cleaves, Mary Wilkerson
Black Sons of Bitches
  Davidson, John Allen, Jr.
Black Soul of the Land
  Jeffers, Lance
Black Star Line
  Dumas, Henry L.
A Black Stick with a Ball of Cotton for a
Head and a Running Machine for a Mouth
  Hernton, Calvin C.
Black Students
  Fields, Julia
Black Studies: International Dimensions
  Long, Richard A.
Black Study
  Harper, Michael S.
Black Sunrise
  Wilson, Art
Black Taffy
  Kenner, Peggy Susberry

Black Terror
  Wesley, Richard
Black Theatre—Go Home
  Milner, Ronald
Black Thoughts
  Ogilvie, D. T.
Black Thunder
  Bontemps, Arna W.
Black Is Black: A Letter To Africa
  Berry, Faith
Black Theatre
  Bambara, Toni Cade
Black Tornado
  Hardnett, Linda G.
Black Trumpeter
  Dumas, Henry L.
Black Tuesday
  Kellum-Rose, Matthew
Black Vignettes
  Bohanon, Mary
The Black Violinist
  Allen, Winston
Black Warrior
  Jordan, Norman
Black Warriors
  Schuyler, George Samuel
Black Weariness
  Davis, Frank Marshall
Black Woman
  Amerson, Rich
Black Woman
  Holmes, R. Ernest
Black Woman
  Johnson, Georgia Douglas
Black Woman
  **Madgett, Naomi Cornelia Long Wither-
spoon**
The Black Woman of the South: Her Neglects
and Her Needs
  Crummell, Alexander
Black Woman Throws a Tantrum
  Malcom, Barbara
The Black Writer and His Role
  Gerald, Carolyn Fowler
The Black Writer Vis-à-Vis His Country
  Killens, John Oliver
Black Writing
  Lee, Don L.
Black Writing
  Neal, Larry
Blackberry Sweet
  Randall, Dudley
The Blackbird
  Graham, Linda B.
The Blacker the Berry
  Thurman, Wallace
blackgoldblueswoman
  Hall, Kirkwood M.
Blackie Speaks on Campus: A Valentine for
Vachel Lindsay
  Crouch, Stanley
Blackie Thinks of His Brothers
  Crouch, Stanley
Blackman / an unfinished history
  Lee, Don L.

Blacklove / East
  Snellings, Rolland
Blackness Can: A Quest for Aesthetics
  Emanuel, James A., Sr.
Blacksinging
  Randall, Jon
Blackstone Rangers
  Brooks, Gwendolyn
Blackwoman
  Lee, Don L.
Blades of Steel
  Fisher, Rudolph
Blake, or The Huts of America
  Delany, Martin R.
Blend
  Lee, Ed
Blight
  Bontemps, Arna W.
Blind and Deaf Old Woman
  Major, Clarence
Blind Old Woman
  Major, Clarence
Blind Street
  Oliver, Georgiana
Blood on the Forge
  Attaway, William
Blood-Burning Moon
  Toomer, Jean
Bloodbirth
  Lorde, Audre
Bloodrites
  Jones, LeRoi
Bloodsmiles
  Lee, Don L.
Bloodsonnet LIV
  Randall, James A., Jr.
Bloodsonnet XLIX
  Randall, James A., Jr.
Bloodsonnet XXI
  Randall, James A., Jr.
Bloodsonnet XVI
  Randall, James A., Jr.
Bloodsonnet XXXV
  Randall, James A., Jr.
Blow Man, Blow . . .
  Anderson, Charles
Bludoo Baby, Want Money, and Got Alligator to Give
  Jones, LeRoi
Blue
  Auburt, Alvin
Blue / Black Poems
  Johnson, Alicia Loy
A Blue Day for a Black Woman
  Donegan, Pamela
Blue Eyes Were the Foundry
  Jeffers, Lance
Blue for Franks Wooten
  Weatherly, Tom
blue horses
  Roberson, Charles Edwin
Blue Jean Wearin Women???
  Henderson, Sharon
Blue Melody
  Powell, William I.

Blue Meridian
  Toomer, Jean
The Blue of Madness
  Kemp, Arnold
Blue Ruth: America
  Harper, Michael S.
Blue Tanganyika
  Bethune, Lebert
Blue Texarkana
  Stokes, Glenn
Blueprint
  Tinsley, Tomi Carolyn
Blueprint for Negro Authors
  Ford, Nick Aaron
The Blues
  Ferdinand, Val
blues
  Maxey, Bob
The Blues
  Sanchez, Sonia
The Blues
  Morris, James Cliftonne
Blues Ain't No Mockin Bird
  Bambara, Toni Cade
Blues and Bitterness
  Bennett, Lerone, Jr.
The Blues Begins
  Leaks, Sylvester
Blues chorus
  Rodgers, Peter T.
Blues for Bessie
  O'Higgins, Myron
Blues for Lucifer
  Jackman, Marvin
Blues for Mister Charlie
  Baldwin, James
Blues, for Sallie
  Crouch, Stanley
Blues in Stereo
  Hughes, Langston
Blues Note
  Kaufman, Bob
Blues Spiritual
  Hernton, Calvin C.
The Blues Today
  Jackson, Mae
The Bluest Eye
  Morrison, Toni
Blk Love Song
  Ferdinand, Val
blk/Rhtoric
  Sanchez, Sonia
BLKARTSOUTH get on up
  Ferdinand, Val
Boats in Winter
  Fields, Julia
Bombardment and Aftermath
  Clarke, John Henrik
Bombs in Barcelona
  Hughes, Langston
Bombs on Asian Flesh Descending
  Jeffers, Lance
The Bomb Thrower
  Sexton, Will
Book of American Negro Poetry
  Johnson, James Weldon

The Book of Love
Braithwaite, William Stanley Beaumont
Booker T. and W.E.B.
Randall, Dudley
Booker T. Washington
Fentress, John W.
The Book's Creed
Cotter, Joseph Seamon, Sr.
Bootie Black and the Seven Giants
Cook, Mike
Bop
Hughes, Langston
Bopping
Henderson, David
Border Line
Hughes, Langston
Boredom '67
Rusan, Francille
Borne
Owens, Daniel Walter
Boston Road Blues
Henderson, David
Boston Tea
Cannon, David Wadsworth, Jr.
Bottled
Johnson, Helene Hubbell
Bought and Paid For
Bohanon, Mary
Bound No'th Blues
Hughes, Langston
The Bouquet
Chesnutt, Charles Waddell
Boy
Cumbo, Kattie M.
The Boy and the Ideal
Cotter, Joseph Seamon, Sr.
Boy at the Window
Dodson, Owen
Boy Breaking Glass
Brooks, Gwendolyn
The Boy Who Painted Christ Black
Clarke, John Henrik
A Boy's Need
Johnson, Herbert Clark
Brainwashing Dramatized
Johnson, Don Allen
Brainwashing of Black Men's Minds
Hare, Nathan
Brass Spittoons
Hughes, Langston
Brave Words for a Startling Occasion
Ellison, Ralph Waldo
Bread on the Water
Chapman, Nell
Break Now This Silence
LaGrone, Oliver
Break of Day
Brown, Sterling A.
Breakout
Gordon, Charles F.
Breakthrough
Rodgers, Carolyn M.
Breakthrough
Sinclair, John
Breath in My Nostrils
Jeffers, Lance

A Breath of Life
Lenihan, Andrew
The Bridge
Jones, LeRoi
A Brief Account of the Settlement and Present Situation of the Colony of Sierra Leone, in Africa, 1812
Cuffee, Paul
Brief Thought Before Dawn
De Saavedra, Guadalupe
Bright and Morning Star
Wright, Richard
Bright and Mownin' Star
Thelwell, Mike
Bright Moment
Cantoni, Louis J.
Bring the Soul Blocks
Cruz, Victor Hernandez
Broadminded
Durem, Ray
Broken Banjo
Richardson, Willis
Broken Heart, Broken Machine
Grant, Richard E.
The Bronx Is Next
Sanchez, Sonia
Bronxomania
Cruz, Victor Hernandez
Bronze Queen
McBrown, Gertrude Parthenia
Bronzeville Breakthrough
Fabio, Sarah Webster
Bronzeville Man with a Belt in the Back
Brooks, Gwendolyn
Bronzeville Mother
Brooks, Gwendolyn
Bronzeville Poet
Perkins, Eugene
Brooklyn
Marshall, Paule
Brooks and Stones
Cunningham, James
Brother
Latimore, Jewel Christine
Brother Carlyle
Kelley, William Melvin
Brother Harlem Bedford Watts Tells Mr. Charlie Where It's At
Hamilton, Bobb
Brother Malcolm
Major, Clarence
Brother Malcolm's Echo
Kgositsile, Keorapetse William
Brother Rat
Crews, Stella Louise
Brother . . . The Twilight
Evans, Mari
Brotherhood
Ward, Douglas Turner
Brothers
Johnson, James Weldon
Brothers
Jones, Joshua Henry, Jr.
Brothers at the Bar
Madgett, Naomi Cornelia Long Witherspoon

Brothers, The Struggle Must Go On
(Members don't git weary)
  Jordan, Norman
Brown Boy to Brown Girl
  Cullen, Countee Porter
A Brown Girl Dead
  Cullen, Countee Porter
The Brown Overcoat
  Sejour, Victor
Brown River, Smile
  Toomer, Jean
Buffalo
  Dumas, Henry L.
The Bull
  Clemmons, Carole Gregory
Bull Shit
  Cortez, Jayne
Bumi
  Jones, LeRoi
The Burglar
  Bethune, Lebert
Burial of the Young Love
  Cuney, Waring
Buried Deep
  Gordon, Edythe Mae
Burn, Baby, Burn
  Jackman, Marvin
Burn, Baby, Burn
  Overton, Sharlet
Bursting Bonds
  Pickens, William
Bury Me in a Free Land
  Harper, Frances Ellen Watkins
Bury the Dead
  Pitts, Lucia Mae
Bus Stop
  Morrow, Gloria
Business and Philanthropy
  DuBois, William Edward Burghardt
But Can See Better There, and Laughing
There
  Brooks, Gwendolyn
But for One
  Jones, James Arlington
But He Was Cool (or: He Even Stopped for
a Green Light
  Lee, Don L.
Butterfly
  Holmes, Ethlynne E.
A Butterfly in Church
  McClellan, George Marion
Buttons
  Turner, Raymond
Bwagamoyo
  Bethune, Lebert
By an Inland Lake
  Braithwaite, William Stanley Beaumont
By Glistening, Dancing Seas
  Gee, Lethonia
By Rugged Ways
  Dunbar, Paul Laurence
Byron's Oak at Newstead Abbey
  Fortune, Timothy Thomas

Cabaret
  Brown, Sterling A.

Carbaret
  Hughes, Langston
Cadence
  Lyle, K. Curtis
Cala Vendor's Cry
  Johnson, James Weldon
Caleb the Degenerate
  Cotter, Joseph Seamon, Sr.
Ca'line's Prayer
  Clifton, Lucille
A Call for Black Unity
  Cumbo, Kattie M.
Call to Worship
  Lomax, Pearl Cleage
Calling
  Thomas, Richard W.
Calling the Doctor
  Holloway, John Wesley
Calm After Storm
  Yerby, Frank
Calway Way
  Miller, May
Calypso
  Stone, Leroy O.
Calypso
  Taylor, Mervyn
Cambridge, Mass.
  Bond, Horace Julian
Cameo No. II
  Jordan, June Meyer
Camouflage
  Vaughn, Naomi Evans
Camus: I Want to Know
  Kaufman, Bob
Can an Angry Black Man Write of Laughter
and Love?
  Dolan, Harry
Can I Write You an Anthem
  Harris, William J.
Can You Dig Where I'm Commin' From
  Priestley, Eric John
Can a Metronome Know the Thunder or
Summon a God?
  Reed, Ishmael
Canto #4
  Johnston, Percy Edward
Canto IV
  Boyd, Francis A.
Canto 4
  Weatherly, Tom
Canto V
  Boyd, Francis A.
Canto 5
  Weatherly, Tom
Canto 7
  Weatherly, Tom
Caprice
  Cullen, Countee Porter
Captain Blackman
  Williams, John Alfred
A Captain Returns
  Hill, James H.
Carma
  Toomer, Jean
Carmen
  Cruz, Victor Hernandez

Carmen ad Classem
Williams, John M.
Carnevale
Nottingham, Pat
The Carousel
Oden, Gloria Catherine
Carpentry
Addison, Lloyd
Carry Me Back
Cuney, Waring
Castles in the Air
Jamison, Roscoe Conkling
Cat and the Saxophone
Hughes, Langston
The Catacombs
Demby, William
Catechism of a Neo-American hoodoo Church
Reed, Ishmael
Catechism: Operation Homecoming
Barlow, George
Cathexis
Bryant, Frederick James, Jr.
Catwoman or the Lament of Bruce Wayne
Harris, William J.
Cavalier
Bruce, Richard
C. C. Rider
Rodgers, Carolyn M.
Cecil County
Welburn, Ron
Celebrated Return
Major, Clarence
Cell No. 40, East Cambridge Jail, Cambridge, Massachusetts, July 26, 1910
Jones, Edward Smyth
Cell Song
Knight, Etheridge
Census
Hughes, Langston
Century of Negro Portraiture in American Literature
Brown, Sterling A.
Ceremonies in Dark Old Men
Elder, Lonne III
Chain Waves
Anderson, S. E.
Chained
Johnson, Ruth Brownlee
Challenge
Brown, Sterling A.
The Challenge
Haynes, Samuel A.
Challenge
Pitts, Lucia Mae
The Challenge of a Black Scholar
Hare, Nathan
The Chameleon Is Everywhere
Jones-Quartey, H.A.B.
Change
Cobb, Bessie A.
Change Is Not Always Progress
Lee, Don L.
A Change of Heart
Gray, Darrell M.
Change the Joke and Slip the Yoke
Ellison, Ralph Waldo

Changed Mind
Ologboni, Tejumola
Change-up
Lee, Don L.
The Changing Satus of the Mulatto
Reuter, E. B.
A Chant for young / brothas & sistuhs
Sanchez, Sonia
Chaos in a Ghetto Alley
Scott, Johnie H.
Charades on East Fourth Street
Elder, Lonne III
Charge Delivered to the African Lodge, June 24, 1797 at Metonomy
Hall, Prince
A Charge Delivered to the Brethren of the African Lodge on the 25th of June, 1792
Hall, Prince
Charlie Parker: The Human Condition
Jones, LeRoi
Charles Parker, 1925–1955
Cuney, Waring
Charles S. Johnson: Entrepreneur of the Harlem Renaissance
Gilpin, Patrick J.
Charles W. Chesnutt, Pioneer in the Fiction of Negro Life
Gloster, Hugh Morris
Chase
Dumas, Henry L.
Chatter-Stick Sermon
Faggett, H. L.
Chaucer
Brawley, Benjamin Griffith
The Checkerboard
Anderson, Alston
Cheesy, Baby
Holmes, R. Ernest
Cherries
Braithwaite, Edward
The Cherrybomb Command
Spencer, Wade
The Chicago Defender Sends a Man to Little Rock (Fall, 1957)
Brooks, Gwendolyn
The Chicago Picasso
Brooks, Gwendolyn
Chicken Hawk's Dream
Young, Alexander
The Child Is Found
Este, Charles H.
Childhood
Latimore, Jewel Christine
Childhood
Walker, Margaret Abigail
Children and a Fetus
Jeffers, Lance
Children of the Cosmos
Balagon, Kuwasi
Children of the Mississippi
Brown, Sterling A.
Children of the Poor
Brooks, Gwendolyn
Children of the Sun
Johnson, Fenton

Children's Children
  Brown, Sterling A.
Children's Rhymes
  Hughes, Langston
A Child's Nightmare
  Hamilton, Bobb
A Chill Morning
  Senna, Carl
Chill of the Night
  Finch, Linda
The Chinaberry Tree
  Fauset, Jessie Redmond
Chinese River Prophet Song
  Dancy, Walter K.
The Chip Woman's Fortune
  Richardson, Willis
Choice
  Dunbar, Paul Laurence
A Choice of Weapons
  Parks, Gordon
Choicy
  Tatum, Lawrence Carlyle
Chopin Deciphered
  Fields, Julia
Chops Are Flying
  Crouch, Stanley
Chris
  Gaines, Ernest J.
Chrismus on the Plantation
  Dunbar, Paul Laurence
Christ in Alabama: Religion In the Poetry of
Langston Hughes
  Emanuel, James A., Sr.
Christ in Alabama
  Hughes, Langston
Christmas at Melrose
  Hill, Leslie Pinckney
Christmas Cheer
  Lewis, Corinne E.
Christmas Eve in France
  Fauset, Jessie Redmond
Christmas Folk Song
  Dunbar, Paul Laurence
Christmas in the Ghetto
  Powe, Blossom
Christmas Lullaby for a New-Born Child
  Gregory, Yvonne
Christmas Morning I
  Freeman, Carol S.
Christmas 1959 et cetera
  Barrax, Gerald William
Christmas Song
  Hughes, Langston
Christophe
  Atkins, Russell
Christophe's Daughters
  Miller, May
Chrysis
  Lewis, Leighla
Chuckie
  Gaines, Ernest J.
Church Burning: Mississippi
  Emanuel, James A., Sr.
The Church Fight
  Gaines-Shelton, Ruth

Church Folks
  Wiggins, Bernice Love
Church Lets Out
  Miller, Jeanette V.
Cicero Jones
  Williamson, Harvey M.
Cincophrenicpoet
  Kaufman, Bob
Circle One
  Dodson, Owen
Circled by a Horsefly
  Quigless, Helen G.
Circles
  Grosvenor, Verta Mae
Circles in Sand
  Abrams, Robert J.
Cities
  Harris, Helen C.
Cities and Seas
  Jordan, Norman
The Citizen
  Howard, Vilma
The City Enscriber
  Maxey, Bob
City Night Storm
  Redmond, Eugene B.
City of Harlem
  Jones, LeRoi
The City of Refuge
  Fisher, Rudolph
City Park
  Jemmott, Claudia E.
City Rises
  Cunningham, James
City Thought
  Madgett, Naomi Cornelia Long Witherspoon
The City's Love
  McKay, Claude
Civilized Interiors
  Johns, Vernon S.
Clara's Ole Man
  Bullins, Ed
Classic Blues
  Jones, LeRoi
Classified Ad
  Tinsley, Tomi Carolyn
Claude McKay and the Cult of Primitivism
  Stoff, Michael B.
Clear
  Lewis, Angelo
The Close of Day
  Curtwright, Wesley
Close Your Eyes
  Bontemps, Arna W.
Closed Doors
  Shaw, Margaret Adelaide
Clotel: a Tale of the Southern States
  Brown, William Wells
The Clown
  Graham, Donald L.
A Clown at Ten
  Emanuel, James A., Sr.
Clubwoman
  Smith, Mary Carter
Coal
  Lorde, Audre

Cocoa Morning
  Kaufman, Bob
Coffee Break
  Hughes, Langston
Cold Hurt and Sorrow
  Jones, LeRoi
Cold Term
  Jones, LeRoi
Cold War
  Jones, James Arlington
A Collage for Richard Davis – Two Short Forms
  Harrison, De Leon
Collapse of the Confederacy
  Wesley, Charles Harris
College Formal: Renaissance Casino
  Hughes, Langston
The Colonel's Awakening
  Dunbar, Paul Laurence
Colonized Mind
  Marshall, Barbara
The Color Bane
  McClellan, George Marion
Color, Caste, and Economic Relations in the Deep South
  Davis, Allison
Colored
  Cuney, Waring
Colored American Patriots
  Nell, William Cooper
Colored Band
  Dunbar, Paul Laurence
The Colored People in America
  Harper, Frances Ellen Watkins
Colored Soldiers
  Dunbar, Paul Laurence
The Colorist
  Coleman, Anita Scott
Colors for Mama
  McBain, Barbara Mahone
A / Coltrane / Poem
  Sanchez, Sonia
Come Away, My Love
  Kariuki, Joseph
Come Back Blues
  Harper, Michael S.
Come, Beloved
  Smallwood, Will
Come Dusk
  Jones, James Arlington
Come Home Early, Chile
  Dodson, Owen
Come Not Into My Presence
  McLemore, James H.
Come on Home
  Scott, Sharon
Come Out The Wilderness
  Baldwin, James
Come Soft in the Waking Hours of Morning
  Scott, Calvin
Come Visit My Garden
  Dent, Thomas C.
Come Wednesdays
  Jones, James Arlington
Comedy American Style
  Fauset, Jessie Redmond

Comfort and Joy
  Hill, James H.
Coming of Age in Mississippi
  Moody, Anne
The Coming of Chronos to the House of Nightsong
  Hernton, Calvin C.
The Coming of John
  Moore, David
The Coming of the Hoodlum
  Scott, Johnie H.
Comments
  Kenner, Peggy Susberry
Common Dust
  Johnson, Georgia Douglas
Common Meter
  Fisher, Rudolph
Communication
  Seese, Ethel Gray
Communication in Whi - te
  Lee, Don L.
Communion
  Lomax, Pearl Cleage
Companions
  Cooper, Charles B.
Comparison
  Harris, Helen C.
Compensation
  Campbell, James Edwin
Compensation
  Cotter, Joseph Seamon, Jr.
Compensation
  Dunbar, Paul Laurence
The Compensation
  Sarver, Ruth E. J.
Complete Fulfillment
  Bohanon, Mary
Comprehension
  Hill, William Allyn
Compromise; a Folk Play
  Richardson, Willis
Conception
  Cuney, Waring
Concerning One Responsible Negro with New Power
  Giovanni, Nikki
Concert
  Quigless, Helen G.
Concerto for Girl and Convertible
  Johnston, Percy Edward
Concrete Poems
  Pritchard, Norman Henry II
Condition and Prospects of Haiti
  Russworm, John Browne
Condition Blue / Dress
  Welburn, Ron
Condition, Elevation and Destiny of the Colored People of the United States, Politically Considered
  Delany, Martin R.
Condition of Free Negroes
  Delany, Martin R.
Conditional
  Evans, Mari
Confession
  Clarke, John Henrik

Confession
  Hayes, Donald Jeffrey
Confession
  Hill, William Allyn
Confession
  Lomax, Pearl Cleage
The Confession Stone
  Dodson, Owen
Confession to Malcolm
  Conyus
Confessions of an Unwilling Nordic
  Logan, Rayford W.
Confessions of John Joyce, alias Davis, who
was executed . . .
  Joyce, John
Confessions of Nat Turner
  Bradford, William
The Confessions of Nat Turner and the
Dilemma of William Styron
  Poussaint, Alvin F.
The Confessions of Willie Styron
  Killens, John Oliver
Confession to the Eternal She
  Morse, George Chester
Congenital
  Jackson, Katherine
Conjugation
  Clemmons, Carole Gregory
The Conjure Woman
  Chesnutt, Charles Waddell
Conquest
  Johnson, Georgia Douglas
Consecration
  Cuglar, Lois Augusta
Consequence
  Moody, David Reese
A Constant Labor
  Thompson, James W.
Consultation
  Cortez, Jayne
Consumed (For Brother Leroi)
  Cumbo, Kattie M.
Containing Communism
  Cobb, Charlie
Contemplation for Lovers, 1968
  Simmons, Herbert Alfred
Contemporary Negro Poetry: 1914–1936
  Brown, Sterling A.
Contentment
  Jones, James Arlington
Contraband
  Anderson, S. E.
A Contract for the Destruction and Rebuild-
ing of Paterson
  Jones, LeRoi
Contradiction
  Cotter, Joseph Seamon, Sr.
Contradictions
  Sanders, Glenn C.
Contrapuntal No. 6
  Martin, Herbert Woodward
Contrapuntal No. 7
  Martin, Herbert Woodward
Conundrum
  Clark, Carl

The Conversion of a Young Musician
  Marrant, John
Conservation of Letting
  Kellum-Rose, Matthew
Conversation on V.
  Dodson, Owen
Conversation Overheard the Way They Saw
It
  Troupe, Quincy
Conversion
  Toomer, Jean
The Convert
  Bennett, Lerone, Jr.
The Convert
  Danner, Margaret
Conviction
  Harris, Helen C.
Copy of a letter from Benjamin Banneker,
To the Secretary of State, with his answer,
1792
  Banneker, Benjamin
Cor Cordium
  Cullen, Countee Porter
Cora Unashamed
  Hughes, Langston
Cordelia the Crude
  Thurman, Wallace
Cords
  Johnson, Ruth Brownlee
The Corn Song
  Holloway, John Wesley
The Corner
  Bullins, Ed
Corner Meeting
  Hughes, Langston
Cosa Nostra Economics
  Reed, Clarence
The Cosmic Age
  Hernton, Calvin C.
The Cosmic Age
  Sun-Ra
Cosmic Attack on Poets
  Clemmons, Carole Gregory
The Cotillion
  Killens, John Oliver
Cotton Song
  Toomer, Jean
Count Basie's
  Wilson, Ted
Count Down
  Jones, James Arlington
Countee Cullen
  Dodson, Owen
Counter Mood
  Cullen, Countee Porter
Counterpoint
  Dodson, Owen
Counting
  Johnson, Fenton
Counting Out
  Allen, Junius Mordecai
A Coupla Scalped Indians
  Ellison, Ralph Waldo
Couples
  Cuney, Waring

Couplet
  Houston, Virginia
Courting
  Cornish, Sam
Courtyard Level
  Jones, James Arlington
The Covenant
  Cunningham, James
Covenant
  Johnson, Lemuel
Coventry
  Evans, Mari
Crab Man
  Johnson, James Weldon
Crack in the Wall Holds Flowers
  Miller, Adam David
Cracker Man
  Anderson, Charles
Cracker Prayer
  Hughes, Langston
Cradle Song
  Dodson, Owen
The Craftsman
  Christian, Marcus Bruce
Cranes of Wrath and Other Tragedies
  Richards, Nathan A.
Crazy Pigeon
  Knight, Etheridge
Crazy What She Calls
  Weatherly, Tom
The Crazy Woman
  Brooks, Gwendolyn
Creation
  Davis, Frank Marshall
The Creation
  Johnson, James Weldon
The Creation
  Turner, Claire
Creation
  Webster, Carter
Creditor to his Proud Debtor
  Horton, George Moses
Credo
  Johnson, Georgia Douglas
Credo
  Hawkins, Walter Everette
Creed
  Spencer, Anne
Creole Girl
  Collins, Leslie Morgan
Crescendo
  Blackwell, Dorothy F.
Crime and Lynching
  DuBois, William Edward Burghardt
The Crisis
  Dunbar, Paul Laurence
Crisis
  Snellings, Rolland
Crisis in Black Culture
  Snellings, Rolland
Crisis of the Negro Intellectual
  Cruse, Harold
Crispus Attucks
  Brown, William Wells
Crispus Attucks
  Temple, George Hannibal

Crispus Attucks McCoy
  Brown, Sterling A.
Cromlech: a Tale
  Latimore, Jewel Christine
The Cross
  Clemmons, Francois
Cross
  Hughes, Langston
Cross Buns for Friday
  Johnson, Ruth Brownlee
crossed legs
  Johnson, Charles Bertram
Cross over the River
  Cornish, Sam
Crossing a Creek
  Johnson, Herbert Clark
Crow Jane in High Society
  Jones, LeRoi
Crowns and Garlands
  Hughes, Langston
Crucifixion
  Cuney, Waring
Crucifixion
  Webster, Carter
Cruelty
  Jeffers, Lance
'Cruiter
  Matheus, John Frederick
...Cry at Birth...
  Raye, Jesse Andrew
Cry for Me
  Kelley, William Melvin
Crystal Shreds
  Johnson, Dorothy Vena
Cultural Exchange
  Hughes, Langston
Cultural Integration Through Literature
  Ford, Nick Aaron
Cultural Strangulation: Black Literature and
the White Aesthetic
  Gayle, Addison, Jr.
Culture: Negro, Black and Nigger
  Cole, John
Cupid Wags His Tail
  Faggett, H. L.
The Curative Powers of Silence
  Young, Alexander
Cure
  Harris, Helen C.
The Cure All
  Lee, Don L.
Curtain Call, Mr. Aldridge, Sir
  Davis, Ossie
Custer's Last Ride
  Whitman, Albery Allson
Cut in Half
  Harris, William J.
Cuttin' Down To Size
  Dumas, Henry L.
Clairvoyance
  Jordan, Norman
The Cycle
  Raullerson, Calvin H.
Cynic
  Tinsley, Tomi Carolyn

D Blues
  Hernton, Calvin C.
Daddy
  Williams, Rene
A Daddy Poem
  Harris, William J.
Daddy Was a Number Runner
  Meriwether, Louise M.
Dago Red
  Snellings, Rolland
Daily Grind
  Johnson, Fenton
Dali Fantasy
  Twitty, Countess W.
Damascus Blade
  Tolson, Melvin Beaunorus
Damn Equal Shit
  Cooper, Charles B.
The Dance
  Jones, LeRoi
Dance
  Weeden, Lula Lowe
Dance Finale
  Boyd, Samuel E.
A Dance for LiPo
  Young, Alexander
A Dance for Ma Rainey
  Young, Alexander
A Dance for Militant Dilettantes
  Young, Alexander
Dance of the Abakweta
  Danner, Margaret
Dance of the Infidels
  Young, Alexander
Dance the Orange
  Hayden, Robert Earl
Dancer
  Fields, Julia
Dancer
  Young, Alexander
Dancing All Alone
  Young, Alexander
Dancing in the Laundromat
  Young, Alexander
Dancing on the Shore
  Young, Alexander
Dandy, or Astride the Funky Finger of Lust
  Bullins, Ed
Daniel Hale Williams—Pioneer and Innovator
  Cobb, W. Montague
The Danse Calinda
  Torrence, Ridgley
Daquiries At Needlepoint
  Pritchard, Sheila
The Dark and Haunted Tower of Richard Wright
  Scott, Nathan Alexander, Jr.
A Dark and Sudden Beauty
  Jeffers, Lance
Dark Blood
  Walker, Margaret Abigail
The Dark Brother
  Alexander, Lewis Grandison
Dark Ghetto
  Clark, Kenneth B.

Dark Hands
  Smith, Nannie Travis
Dark Heritage
  Christian, Marcus Bruce
Dark little mother mistress
  Durem, Ray
Dark Love
  Cannon, David Wadsworth, Jr.
Dark People
  Cumbo, Kattie M.
The Dark Princess
  DuBois, William Edward Burghardt
Dark Prophesy: I Sing of Shine
  Knight, Etheridge
Dark Shadows
  Hall, John E.
Dark Symphony
  Tolson, Melvin Beaunorus
Dark Testament
  Murray, Pauli
Darkness of Terror
  Valentine, Christopher
Darkwater
  DuBois, William Edward Burghardt
David
  Clemmons, Carole Gregory
Dawn
  Dunbar, Paul Laurence
Dawn
  Grimke, Angelina Weld
Dawn Is Eternally
  LaGrone, Oliver
The Dawn of Love
  Ray, Henrietta Cordelia
Dawn Song
  Smith, Linwood D.
The Dawn Swings In
  Jeffers, Lance
The Dawn's Awake
  Bohanon, Otto Leland
Dawn's Carol
  Ray, Henrietta Cordelia
Day
  Dunbar, Paul Laurence
Day
  Jones, James Arlington
The Day a Dancer Learned to Sing of Dreamless Escapades
  Goodwin, LeRoy
Day and Night
  Alexander, Lewis Grandison
The Day and the War
  Bell, James Madison
Day Dreaming
  Jones, James Arlington
A Day in the British Museum
  Brown, William Wells
A Day in the Life of . . .
  Conyus
A Day in the Life of a Poet
  Troupe, Quincy
Day of Absence
  Ward, Douglas Turner
A Day of Peace, a Day of Peace
  Johnson, Alicia Loy

Day Off the Street
  Sirrah, Leumas
The Day the Old Man Joined the Church
  Thomas, Richard W.
The Day the World almost Came to an End
  Crayton, Pearl
Daybreak
  McClellan, George Marion
Daybreak in Alabama
  Hughes, Langston
Day-breakers
  Bontemps, Arna W.
Days
  Dandridge, Raymond Garfield
. . . Days Prior To
  Wakefield, Jacques
A Day's Recreation
  Stevenson, J. C.
De Ballet of de Boll Weevil
  Johnson, James Weldon
De Cunjah Man
  Campbell, James Edwin
De Dicshonary
  Rice, Jo Nell
De Drum Majah
  Dandridge, Raymond Garfield
De Innah Part
  Dandridge, Raymond Garfield
De La Beckwith and the Bombers
  Jeffers, Lance
De Sun Do Move
  Jasper, John J.
De Way T'ings Come
  Dunbar, Paul Laurence
Dead Fires
  Fauset, Jessie Redmond
The Dead Man Dragged from the Sea
  Gardner, Carl
Dear Brother
  Halsey, William
Dear John, Dear Coltrane
  Harper, Michael S.
Dear Mr. Butts
  Hughes, Langston
Death
  Mphahlele, Ezekial
The Death Bed
  Cuney, Waring
The Death Dance
  Duncan, Thelma Myrtle
The Death Dance
  Lee, Don L.
Death in Autumn
  Fields, Julia
Death in Yorkville
  Hughes, Langston
Death Motion
  Giddings, Paula
The Death of a Dream
  Motley, Dennis
Death of a Friend
  Murray, Pauli
Death of a Grandfather
  Ellison, Ralph Waldo
The Death of a Negro Poet
  Rivers, Conrad Kent

Death of a Nigger
  Bradford, Fred
Death of a Squirrel in McKinley Park
  Barrax, Gerald William
Death of Days and Nights of Life
  Franklin, Clarence
Death of Dr. King
  Cornish, Sam
The Death of Justice
  Hawkins, Walter Everette
Death of Kennedy
  Fields, Julia
Death of Love
  Johnson, Fenton
The Death of Malcolm X
  Jones, LeRoi
The Death of Nick Charles
  Jones, LeRoi
Death of the Moonshine Superman
  Lockett, Reginald
Death of the Old Sea King
  Harper, Frances Ellen Watkins
Death of Tommy Grimes
  Meaddough, R. J., III
Death Scene
  McMillan, Joseph
A Death Song
  Dunbar, Paul Laurence
Death Songs
  Mack, L. V.
Death Sows a Seed
  Oxley, Lloyd G.
Deathwatch
  Harper, Michael S.
Debra . . . An Africanese Name . . .
  Davis, Ronda Marie
Debt
  Cox, Ollie H.
The Debt
  Dunbar, Paul Laurence
Debut
  Hunter, Kristin
December 26, 1968
  Conyus
The Decision
  Dodson, Owen
Declaration
  Pitts, Lucia Mae
Declaration of Independence
  Little, Malcolm
Declaration of Principles of the Niagara
Movement
  DuBois, William Edward Burghardt
A Decoration Day
  McClellan, George Marion
Dedicated to the Living Memory of Miss
Gwendolyn Brooks
  Clemmons, Francois
Dedication
  Madgett, Naomi Long Cornelia Wither-
spoon
Dedication to the Final Confrontation
  Corbin, Lloyd
A Deep Blue Feeling
  Gipson, Edna

Deep Ellum and Central Track
  Brewer, J. Mason
Deepest, Darkest Turn
  Harris, Helen C.
Defeat
  Emanuel, James A., Sr.
Defeat
  Twitty, Countess W.
Defense of the Negro Race
  White, George H.
Defiance of Lunch Rules
  Lenihan, Andrew
definition for blk/children
  Sanchez, Sonia
Definition of Nature
  Redmond, Eugene B.
De-Ho-Cho
  Seese, Ethel Gray
Del Cascar
  Braithwaite, William Stanley Beaumont
Delta
  Walker, Margaret Abigail
Delusion
  Johnson, Georgia Douglas
The Dempsey-Liston Fight
  Jones, LeRoi
Denizen of Hell
  Martinez, Carmen
The Dentist's Wife
  Kelley, William Melvin
Departure
  Dubonee, Ylessa
Depression
  Brooks, Jonathan Henderson
Der Rabbit's Foot
  Corrothers, James David
Desert
  Hughes, Langston
Deserted Plantation
  Dunbar, Paul Laurence
Deserted Village
  Clark, Peter Wellington
The Deserter
  Cotter, Joseph Seamon, Jr.
Design
  Major, Clarence
Desire
  Hughes, Langston
Desire
  Nichols, Constance
Desolate
  McKay, Claude
Desolate City
  McKay, Claude
Destiny
  Cotter, Joseph Seamon, Sr.
Destiny
  Madgett, Naomi Cornelia Long Witherspoon
Determination
  Clark, John Henrik
Detroit
  Johnson, James Weldon
DE – troit Summerscene
  Randall, Jon

The Development of the Black Revolutionary Artist
  Stewart, James T.
The Devil and Sis' Viney
  Allen, Junius Mordecai
Dew
  Brewer, J. Mason
DeWitt Williams on His Way to Lincoln Cemetery
  Brooks, Gwendolyn
Dialect Quatrain
  Christian, Marcus Bruce
A Dialogue Entitled the Kind Master and the Dutiful Servant
  Hammon, Jupiter
Diary of a Bronzeville Boy
  Perkins, Eugene
Did John's Music Kill Him?
  Spellman, Alfred B.
Did You Ever Dream Lucky
  Ellison, Ralph Waldo
Did You Vote Nigger
  Jackman, Marvin
"Didn't it come like a tidal wave"
  King, Leyland
Die Black Pervert
  Lockett, Reginald
Differences
  Tarver, Valerie
A Different Drummer
  Kelley, William Melvin
A Different Image
  Randall, Dudley
The Dilemma of the American Negro Scholar
  Franklin, John Hope
Dilemma of the Negro Novelist in the U.S.
  Himes, Chester B.
Dinner at Diop's
  Fuller, Hoyt W.
Dinner Guest: Me
  Hughes, Langston
Direct Action
  Thelwell, Mike
Dirge
  Troupe, Quincy
Dirge for J. A. Rogers
  Bibbs, Hart LeRoi
Discouraged
  Holloway, John Wesley
A Discourse Delivered in St. Philip's Church, for the Benefit of the Coloured Community of Wilberforce in Upper Canada on the Fourth of July, 1830
  Williams, Peter
Discourse Delivered on the Death of Captain Paul Cuffe
  Williams, Peter
Discovering
  Scott, Sharon
The Discovery of What It Means To Be an American
  Baldwin, James
Disfranchisement of the Negro
  Bunche, Ralph J.
Disillusion
  Brown, Lillian

Dismal Moment, Passing
Major, Clarence
Dispossession
Ellison, Ralph Waldo
Dissertation
Parker, Thomas L.
The Distant Drum
Hernton, Calvin C.
District of Columbia
Richards, Stanley
Dive
Hughes, Langston
The Diver
Hayden, Robert Earl
Divers
Harris, Helen C.
Divestment
Allen, Samuel W.
Divine Afflatus
Fauset, Jessie Redmond
Divine Comedy
Dodson, Owen
Divorce
Ragland, J. Farley
Do
Tolson, Melvin Beaunorus
Do Not Be Afraid of No
Brooks, Gwendolyn
Do Not Think
Freeman, Carol S.
Do Nothing Till You Hear from Me
Henderson, David
Do They Miss Me?
Clark, Benjamin P.
Dogwood Blossoms
McClellan, George Marion
Domestic Law and International Order
Cleaver, Eldridge
Domestics
Cumbo, Kattie M.
The Dominicaine
Dismond, Henry Binga
domo's mirror
Shorter, Lynn
Don't Ask Me Who I Am
Randall, James A., Jr.
The Don't-Care Negro
Cotter, Joseph Seamon, Sr.
Don't Cry, Scream
Lee, Don L.
Don't Pay
Saunders, Ruby Constance X.
Don't Say Goodbye to the Pork-Pie Hat
Neal, Larry
Don't Wanna Be
Sanchez, Sonia
Don't You Forget It
Stewart, James T.
Don't You Want to Be Free?
Hughes, Langston
The Door
Levinson, Nick
Doorway at 12 Midnight
Cooper, Charles B.
The Doorway That We Hide Behind
McNeil, Dee Dee

Double Harvest
Cantoni, Louis J.
Double Standard
Harper, Frances Ellen Watkins
The Dougal
Brown, Frank London
The dove
Hughes, Langston
Dowager's Death
Gardner, Carl
Down by the Riverside
Wright, Richard
Down Fish Trap Lane
Love, J. Austin
Down Wind, Against the Highest Peaks
Major, Clarence
A Downed Black Pilot Learns How to Fly
Coleman, Horace Wendell
Downtown-Boy Uptown
Henderson, David
The Dozens
Barrax, Gerald William
Dr. Jekyll and Mr. Hyde, and the Negro
Schuyler, George Samuel
The Draft and the Negro
Lee, Ulysses
Draftees
Hughes, Langston
Dragons at Noon
Redmond, Eugene B.
Dragon's Blood
Reed, Ishmael
Drama of Negro Life
Gregory, Montgomery
The Drama of Negro Life
Locke, Alain Leroy
Dream
Crews, Stella Louise
Dream
Edwards, Solomon
The Dream
Hayden, Robert Earl
The Dream
Parker, Gladys Marie
Dream About Me
Twitt, Nathaniel I.
The Dream and the Song
Corrothers, James David
Dream Boogie
Hughes, Langston
A Dream Deferred
Hughes, Langston
Dream Love
Sarver, Ruth E. J.
Dream Market
Moten, Cora Ball
The Dream of a Southern Governor
Carter, Jimmie
A Dream of Revenge
Gooden, Lauretta Holman
Dream Sequence, Part 9
Madgett, Naomi Cornelia Long Wither-spoon
Dream #6
Harrison, De Leon

Dream Song
  Alexander, Lewis Grandison
Dream Variation
  Hughes, Langston
Dream World
  Watson, Evelyn
The Dreamer
  Hughes, Langston
Dreamin' Town
  Dunbar, Paul Laurence
Dreams
  Cooper, Charles B.
Dreams
  Davis, Frank Marshall
Dreams
  Davis, Gloria
Dreams
  DuBois, William Edward Burghardt
Dreams (1)
  Dunbar, Paul Laurence
Dreams (2)
  Dunbar, Paul Laurence
Dreams
  Giovanni, Nikki
Dreams
  Hughes, Langston
Dreams
  Richards, Elizabeth Davis
Dreams Are Fragile
  Burbridge, Edward Dejoie
Dreams Are So Pale
  Beverly, Katherine
The Dreams of the Dreamer
  Johnson, Georgia Douglas
Drenched in Light
  Hurston, Zora Neale
dress rehearsal paranoia #2
  Reed, Ishmael
The Drinking Gourd
  Hansberry, Lorraine
Drowned Love
  Jones, LeRoi
Drum Song Sister
  Wimberli, Sigmonde Kharlos
Drums at Dusk
  Bontemps, Arna W.
Drunken Lover
  Dodson, Owen
Drums of Africa
  Moreland, Charles King, Jr.
Dry August
  Sebree, Charles
Dry July
  Adoff, Arnold
Dry Spell Blues
  House, Eddie "Son"
Dry Wishing Well
  Ford, Wallace
Duel with the Clock
  Edwards, Junius
Dunbar
  Spencer, Anne
Dunbar and Cotter
  French, James Edgar
Duncanson
  Dabney, Wendell Phillips

The Dunes
  Root, E. Merrill
Dunsfords Travels Everywhere
  Kelley, William Melvin
Durer
  Martin, Herbert Woodward
Durham: Capital of the Black Middle Class
  Frazier, E. Franklin
Dusk
  Cowdery, Mae V.
Dusk
  Grimke, Angelina Weld
Dusk of Dawn
  DuBois, William Edward Burghardt
Dusk Song
  Moore, William H.
Dusk Thoughts
  Twitty, Countess W.
Dust
  Cuney, Waring
Dust
  Overby, Beatris
Dust Bowl
  Davis, Robert A.
Dust Tracks on a Road
  Hurston, Zora Neale
Dutchman
  Jones, LeRoi
Dying
  Wooten, Charles R.
Dying Bondman
  Harper, Frances Ellen Watkins
Dylan, Who Is Dead
  Allen, Samuel W.
Dynamite Growing out of Their Skulls
  Hernton, Calvin C.
Dynamite Transported from Canada to New York City
  Major, Clarence

Each Morning
  Jones, LeRoi
Early Autumn
  Hughes, Langston
Early Jam
  Campbell, E. Simms
Earth
  Snellings, Rolland
Earth and Stars
  Edmonds, Randolph
Earth Bosom
  Bohanon, Mary
An Earth Song
  Hughes, Langston
Earth-quake
  Cuney, Waring
Easter
  Thurman, I. M.
Easter Bunny Blues or All I Want for Christmas Is the Loop
  Dooley, Thomas
The Easter Flower
  McKay, Claude
An Easter Message
  Clifford, Carrie Williams

Easy Way Out
  Malcom, Barbara
Ebon Maid and Girl of Mine
  Watkins, Lucian Bottow
Ebony
  Lyle, K. Curtis
The Ebony Elephant
  Lawson, Edward
Ebony Rhythm
  Butler, Hood C.
Echo
  Blackwell, Dorothy F.
Eclipse
  Haynes, Albert E., Jr.
Eclipse
  Rashidd, Amir
eclipse
  Roberson, Charles Edwin
Economics of the Founding Fathers
  Harris, Abram L.
The Edict
  Jamison, Roscoe Conkling
Editorial from the North Star, Vol.,—No. 1
  Douglass, Frederick
Editorial Poem on an Incident of Effects
Far Reaching
  Atkins, Russell
Edith Mother of Man
  Thomas, Richard W.
The Educated Negro and His Mission
  Scarborough, W. S.
Education
  Lee, Don L.
Education of the Negro in the United States
  Thompson, Charles H.
Educational Outlook in the South
  Washington, Booker Taliaferro
Effendi
  Harper, Michael S.
Efficiency Apartment
  Barrax, Gerald William
Effie
  Brown, Sterling A.
Effigy
  Alexander, Lewis Grandison
Egg-boiler
  Brooks, Gwendolyn
Egotistic Runt
  Davis, Frank Marshall
8 Ball
  Barlow, George
Eighteenth Street
  Young, Nathan Ben
1831: For Vincent Terrell
  Redmond, Eugene B.
18,000 feet
  Roberson, Charles Edwin
El Beso
  Grimke, Angelina Weld
El Hajj Malik
  Davidson, Norbert R., Jr.
El-Hajj Malik El-Shabazz
  Hayden, Robert Earl
The Elder Dumas
  Richardson, Willis

Election Day (Newark, New Jersey)
  Jones, LeRoi
The Electric Cop
  Cruz, Victor Hernandez
Electronic Nigger
  Bullins, Ed
The Elegance of Memory
  Kgositsile, Keorapetse William
Elegy
  Tinsley, Tomi Carolyn
Elegy for a lady
  DeLegall, Walter
Elegy for David Diop
  Kgositsile, Keorapetse William
Elements of Grammar
  Hernton, Calvin C.
Elephant Rock
  St. John, Primus
The Elevator Man Adheres to Form
  Danner, Margaret
Elimination of the Blues
  Anderson, S. E.
Eliza Harris
  Harper, Frances Ellen Watkins
Eloise
  Moreland, Charles King, Jr.
Elvin Jones Gretsch Freak
  Henderson, David
Elvin's Blues
  Harper, Michael S.
Emancipation in the District of Columbia
(April 16, 1862)
  Bell, James Madison
Emancipation of Georg-Hector (a Colored
Turtle)
  Evans, Mari
Embryo
  Troupe, Quincy
Emerson
  Cotter, Joseph Seamon, Sr.
Emerson and the South
  Butcher, Philip
The Emigrant
  Clark, Benjamin P.
Emile
  Gaines, Ernest J.
Emmett Till
  Emanuel, James A., Sr.
Emotions of the Blacks
  Shaw, Doris Ann
Emperor of Haiti
  Hughes, Langston
The Empty Woman
  Brooks, Gwendolyn
The Encampment Choir
  Carr, Clarence F.
Enchantment
  Alexander, Lewis Grandison
Enchantment
  Jones, Georgia Holloway
The End
  Bressack, Gordon
End of a Dream
  Stewart, Ollie
The End of Man Is His Beauty
  Jones, LeRoi

The End of Silence
  Brown, Elaine
End of the Chapter
  Dunbar, Paul Laurence
The End of the Ethnic Dream
  Wright, Jay
The End of the World
  Kemp, Arnold
Ending
  Jordan, Norman
The Enemy
  Franklin, J. E.
Enemy of Man
  Johnson, Alicia Loy
Enemy Territory
  Kelly, William Melvin
Energy
  Cruz, Victor Hernandez
Energy For a New Thing
  Mkalimoto, Ernie
Enigma
  Fauset, Jessie Redmond
The Engagement Party
  Boles, Robert
English Sparrows
  Seese, Ethel Gray
Enough
  Brown, William
Enslaved
  McKay, Claude
Entreaty
  Arnold, Walter G.
Entries: 13, 14, 15, 21
  Nottingham, Pat
Entry
  Tinsley, Tomi Carolyn
Envoi
  Patterson, Raymond Richard
The Ephemera
  McClellan, George Marion
Epigram
  Brister, Iola M.
Epigram
  Lanusse, Armand
Epigram. Poem by Armand Lanusse, trans-
lated by L. Hughes.
  Hughes, Langston
Epilogue
  Hughes, Langston
Epilogue: bewildered souls i've looked upon
condemned
  Kwarther, Stephen
Epiphany
  Dumas, Henry L.
Epistrophe
  Jones, LeRoi
Epitaph for a Bigot
  Johnson, Dorothy Vena
Epitaph for a Lady I Know
  Cullen, Countee Porter
Epitaph for a Negro Woman
  Dodson, Owen
Epitaph for Jimmy
  Davis, Gloria
Epitaph to a Man
  Reedburg, Robert

Epitaphs
  Cullen, Countee Porter
Equality
  McMillan, Herman L.
Equality
  Razafkeriefo, Andrea
Ere Sleep Comes Down to Soothe the
Weary Eyes
  Dunbar, Paul Laurence
Escape
  Alexander, Lewis Grandison
The Escape: Or, A Leap for Freedom
  Brown, William Wells
Escape
  Johnson, Georgia Douglas
Essay, 1828
  DeGrasse, Isaiah G.
Essay in Political Philosophy
  King, Martin Luther, Jr.
Essence
  Cantoni, Louis J.
Essie Mae
  Nelson, David
Esther
  Toomer, Jean
Esthete in Harlem
  Hughes, Langston
Eternal Desire
  Morrison, William Lorenzo
The Eternal Self
  Braithwaite, William Stanley Beaumont
Eternity
  Dandridge, Raymond Garfield
Eternity
  McClellan, George Marion
The Ethics of Living Jim Crow; an Auto-
biographical Sketch
  Wright, Richard
Ethiopia
  Harper, Frances Ellen Watkins
Ethiopia
  Johnson, Fenton
Ethiopia at the Bar of Justice
  McCoo, Edward J.
Ethnic Impact in American Literature
  Kent, George E.
Ethnography of a Downtown Joint
  Thomas, Richard W.
Etienne
  Gaines, Ernest J.
Etta Morten's Attic
  Danner, Margaret
Etta's Mind
  Gant, Lisbeth A.
Eugene McCarthy
  Jones, James Arlington
Eulogy
  Rodgers, Carolyn M.
Eulogy for Philosophers
  Fields, Julia
Eulogy for Population
  Welburn, Ron
Europe
  Forbes, Calvin
Evanescent Love
  Redmond, Eugene B.

Evenin' Air Blues
Hughes, Langston
Evening
Harris, Helen C.
Evening Reverie
Laws, Clarence A.
Evening Song
Toomer, Jean
An Evening Thought
Hammon, Jupiter
Every Harlem Face is Afromanism Surviving
Spriggs, Edward S.
Every Man a King
Fortune, Timothy Thomas
Every Slave Has the Right to Be Free
Remond, Charles Lenox
Everybody's Protest Novel
Baldwin, James
Everyday Use
Walker, Alice
Everything
Gadsden, Janice Marie
Everywhere
Young, Alexander
Evicted
Murphy, Beatrice M.
Evicted Worlds
Thomas, Richard W.
Evil Is No Black Thing
Fabio, Sarah Webster
Evolution
Cox, Thelma Parker
Excerpt
Jones, Joshua Henry, Jr.
Excursion on a Wobbly Rail
Harrison, DeLeon
The Excuse
Greene, Carl H.
Execution
Fields, Julia
Execution
Randall, James A., Jr.
Exhortation: Summer, 1919
McKay, Claude
The Exiles
Hare, Nathan
Existence
DeSaavedra, Guadalupe
Exitus
Smith, Laura E.
An Ex-Judge at the Bar
Tolson, Melvin Beaunorus
Exodus
Baldwin, James
The Exodus
Langston, John Mercer
Expectancy
Moore, William H. A.
Expectation
Dunbar, Paul Laurence
Experience
McLean, Eldon George
Explanation
Tarver, Valerie
Explanation of the Black Psyche
Killens, John Oliver

Exposition
Jones, James Arlington
Express Rider
Myles, Glenn
Extension
Snellings, Rolland
Extenuation to Certain Critics
Cullen, Countee Porter
Extinguisher Extinguished
Ruggles, David
Eye of Love
Horton, George Moses
The Eyes of My Regret
Grimke, Angelina Weld

The Fabulous Miss Marie
Bullins, Ed
Face
Toomer, Jean
Face of Poverty
Smith, Lucy
Face to Face
Jones, James Arlington
Facing the Challenge of a New Age
King, Martin Luther, Jr.
Facts
Dandridge, Raymond Garfield
Fading cadence
Thompson, James W.
The Failure of William Styron
Kaiser, Ernest
A Fairy Story
Day, Caroline Bond
Faith
Lyons, Leona
Faith of the American Negro
Johnson, Mordecai Wyatt
Fake-Out
Cumberbatch, Lawrence S.
Fall Down
Hernton, Calvin C.
Fall/1968
Thomas, Richard W.
Fall To
Jones, Howard
Fallacy
Weeks, Ricardo
The Fallen
Seese, Ethel Gray
Falling
Jemmott, Claudia E.
Falling
Kaufman, Bob
Fallout: a Letter to a Black Boy
Teague, Bob
Falstaff
Evans, Emmery, Jr.
Family Meeting
Mackey, William Wellington
A Family Tree
Parker, Patricia
Fantasy
Bennett, Gwendolyn B.
Fantasy and Conversation
Lorde, Audre

Fantasy in Purple
  Hughes, Langston
Far From Africa: Four Poems
  Danner, Margaret
The Fare to Crown Point
  Myers, Walter D.
A Farewell to America
  Wheatley, Phillis
The Farm—The Negro's Best Chance
  Miller, Kelly
Father, Son, and Holy Ghost
  Lorde, Audre
A Father Tells His Son About the Status
  of Liberty
  Hamilton, Bobb
Father the Year Is Fallen
  Lorde, Audre
Fear
  Richards, Edward
Fear
  Tinsley, Tomi Carolyn
Fear Came Early
  Wimberli, Sigmonde
Fear Not
  Bohanon, Mary
The February Rain Is Falling
  Anderson, William
The Federal Theatre
  Brown, Sterling A.
Feeding the Lions
  Jordan, Norman
Feel Eyes
  Crews, Stella Louise
Feelings of a Very Light Negro as the Con-
  frontation Approaches
  Lomax, Pearl Cleage
Feet Live Their Own Life
  Hughes, Langston
Feet o' Jesus
  Hughes, Langston
The Feet of Judas
  McClellan, George Marion
Felix of the Silent Forest
  Henderson, David
The Fellah, the Chosen Ones, the Guardian
  Llorens, David
Fellow Travelers
  Jones, James Arlington
The Feral Pioneers—for Dancer
  Reed, Ishmael
Fern
  Toomer, Jean
A Festival in Christendom
  Hawkins, Walter Everette
Fifteenth Amendment
  Harper, Frances Ellen Watkins
Fifty Years
  Johnson, James Weldon
Fifty Years of Negro Citizenship
  Woodson, Carter G.
Fighter
  Smith, John Caswell
The Fighting Finnish
  Lacy, March
Figure
  Hayden, Robert Earl

Final Call
  Hughes, Langston
A Final Escape from American Slavery
  Roper, Moses
Finale
  Turner, Darwin T.
Find a Role, Define a Role
  Turner, Raymond
Find the Girl
  Bohanon, Mary
Finding a Way Out
  Moton, Robert Russa
Finer Points
  Grover, Wayne
The Finger Meal
  Pringle, Ronald J.
Finger Poppin'
  Anderson, Charles
Finis
  Cuney, Waring
Fire, Hair, Meat and Bone
  Johnson, Fred
Fire in the Flint
  White, Walter
The Fire Next Time
  Baldwin, James
The Fire That Laid Her Mad
  Jeffers, Lance
The 1st
  Clifton, Lucille
First Claims Poem
  Cruz, Victor Hernandez
First Essay on the Art of the U.S.
  Welburn, Ron
First Fight, Then Fiddle
  Brooks, Gwendolyn
First Kiss
  Pitts, Lucia Mae
First Lady
  Harrison, Edna L.
first monday scottsboro alabama
  Weatherly, Tom
The First One
  Hurston, Zora Neale
First Time I was Sweet Sixteen
  Malcom, Barbara
The Fisherman
  Emanuel, James A., Sr.
The Fisherman
  Thomas, Richard W.
Fisherman's Luck
  Matthews, Ralph
The Fishes and the Poet's Hands
  Yerby, Frank
Fishing
  Cunningham, James
The Fist Party
  Scott, Johnie H.
Five Episodes
  Wright, Richard
Five Senses
  Wyche, Marvin, Jr.
Five Smooth Stones
  Fairbairn, Ann
Five Vignettes
  Toomer, Jean

5 Winos
Rodgers, Carolyn M.
Five Winters Ago
Henderson, David
Friday the Twelfth
Young, Alexander
Flag of the Free
Jones, Edward Smyth
The Flagellants
Polite, Carlene Hatcher
The Flags
Booker, Sue
Flags
Brooks, Gwendolyn
Flame Heart
McKay, Claude
Flame of Green
Young, Frank A.
A Flame Within
Jones, Marte
Flamenco Sketches
Stone, Leroy O.
Flames
Evans, Mari
The Fledgling Bard and the Poetry Society
Margetson, George Reginald
Flesh Line, the Space
Major, Clarence
Flies on Shit
Troupe, Quincy
The Flight
Randall, Dudley
Flight
Vale, Coston
Flight of the Natives
Richardson, Willis
The Flogging
Milner, Ronald
Flood Song
Chappell, Helen F.
Floodtide
Snellings, Rolland
The Florida Cock
Pritchard, Sheila
Florida Road Workers
Hughes, Langston
Flotsam
Weeks, Ricardo
Flower of Love
McKay, Claude
Flowers
Fields, Julia
Flowers for the Trashman
Jackman, Marvin E.
Flowers of Darkness
Davis, Frank Marshall
The flowers take the tears
Cotter, Joseph Seamon, Sr.
Flute Players. Poem by Jean Joseph Rabea-
rivels.
Hughes, Langston
Fly Blackbird
Hatch, James V. and Jackson, C. Bernard
A Fly in Buttermilk
Baldwin, James

The Flyer
Blue, Cecil A.
Flying Home
Ellison, Ralph Waldo
Fo' Want a dat Pot a' Gold
Cooper, Charles B.
Fog
Mattheus, John Frederick
Fogged
Burton, John W.
Foggy
Hall, Douglas
A Folding and Unfolding
Smith, Welton
A Folk Fabel: The Third World Had Hung
the un/ Humans
Latimore, Jewel Christine
Folk Tales
Hurston, Zora Neale
Fon
Dumas, Henry L.
Food for Thought
Ferdinand, Val
Fooling Our White Folks
Hughes, Langston
Fool's Voice
Salgado, Lionel
A Fool's Wisdom
Young, Frank A.
Footnote to a Gray Bird's Pause
Cunningham, James
For a Black Poet
Barrax, Gerald William
For a Certain PH.D I know
Fletcher, T. Thomas Fortune
For a Child
Madgett, Naomi Cornelia Long Wither-
spoon
For a Discontented Soul
Shaed, Dorothy Lee Louise
For a Lady I Know
Cullen, Countee Porter
For a Lady of Pleasure Now Retired
Giovanni, Nikki
For a Mouthy Woman
Cullen, Countee Porter
For a Pessimist
Cullen, Countee Porter
For a Poet
Cullen, Countee Porter
For All Things Black and Beautiful
Rivers, Conrad Kent
For Andy Goodman, Michael Scheverner and
James Chaney
Walker, Margaret Abigail
For Angela
Gilbert, L. Zack
For Ann
Hoagland, Everett
For Bill Hawkins, a Black Militant
Harris, William J.
For Billie Holiday
Hughes, Langston
For black Newark: 1968
Spriggs, Edward S.

For Black People
Lee, Don L.
For Black Poets Who Think of Suicide
Knight, Etheridge
For both of Us at Fisk
Scott, Sharon
For Brother Malcolm
Spriggs, Edward S.
For Cal
Cunningham, James
For Che
Conyus
For Cousin L. B., in Noxapater, Mississippi
Moreland, Charles King, Jr.
For de Lawd
Clifton, Lucille
For Death by Choice
Lomax, Pearl Cleage
For Don and Donna
Crews, Stella Louise
For Dr. Coffin Who Loves
Clemmons, Carole Gregory
For Edwin R. Embrée
Dodson, Owen
For Eusi, Ahy Kwei and Gwen Brooks
Kgositsile, Keorapetse William
For Frantz Fanon
Terrell, Robert L.
For Freckled-Face Gerald
Knight, Etheridge
For Free
Pritchard, Sheila
For God's Sake
Reddy, T. J.
For Gwen
Elliston, Maxine Hall
For Gwen
Scott, Sharon
For Gwendolyn Brooks
Gilbert, L. Zack
For Gwendolyn Brooks
Giovanni, Nikki
For Gwendolyn Brooks
King, Helen H.
For Gwendolyn Brooks—a Whole and Beautiful Spirit
Latimore, Jewel Christine
For H. M. G.
Houston, Virginia
for h. w. fuller
Rodgers, Carolyn M.
For her, The design
Major, Clarence
For Janet
Harris, William J.
For Janice
Harris, William J.
For Jim, Easter Eve
Spencer, Anne
For Joannie in Poland
Young, Alexander
For John Keats, Apostle of Beauty
Cullen, Countee Porter
For Langston Hughes
Knight, Etheridge

For Le Roi Jones
Fleming, Ray
(For Lee)
Nicholas, A. X.
For Leroi Jones
Kgositsile, Keorapetse William
For Lionel Hampton
La Grone, Oliver
For Love to Survive
Snellings, Rolland
For Lover Man, and All the Other Young Men Who Failed to Return from World War II
Williams, Mance
(For Mack)
Nicholas, A. X.
For Mack C. Parker
Murray, Pauli
For Malcolm
Lawrence, Joyce Whitsitt
For Malcolm, a Year After
Knight, Etheridge
For Malcolm: After Mecca
Barrax, Gerald William
For Malcolm, U. S. A.
Emanuel, James A., Sr.
For Malcolm Who Walks in the Eyes of Our Children
Troupe, Quincy
For Malcolm X
Alba, Nanina
For Malcolm X
Fields, Julia
For Malcolm X
Walker, Margaret Abigail
For Mary McLeod Bethune
Walker, Margaret Abigail
For Me Again
Joans, Ted
For Me Who Don't Read Classics
Lawrence, Joyce Whitsitt
For Mother in Paradise
Conley, Malcolm Christian
For Mr. Dudley, a Black Spy
Emanuel, James A., Sr.
For My Brother
Dodson, Owen
For My Brother * * A Big Apple Poet
Randall, Jon
For My Friends at the Boy's Training School
Witherspoon, Jill
For My Grandmother
Cullen, Countee Porter
For My Mama and Hers
Adams, Jeanette
For my unborn son
Abrams, Robert J.
For My People
Walker, Margaret Abigail
For My People's Children
Cumbo, Kattie M.
For My Unborn and Wretched Children
Spellman, Alfred B.
(for Nigareens)
Latimore, Jewel Christine

For Nubian Dudes Steeped Deep in Negritude
  Penny, Rob
For O.—Two Hung-up
  Rodgers, Carolyn M.
For Our Lady
  Sanchez, Sonia
For Our Women
  Neal, Larry
For Paris Review 'Writer at Work'
  Ellison, Ralph Waldo
For Paul Laurence Dunbar
  Cullen, Countee Porter
For Poets
  Young, Alexander
(For Poki)
  Nicholas, A. X.
For Real
  Cortez, Jayne
For Richard Wright
  Rivers, Conrad Kent
For Sammy Younge
  Cobb, Charlie
For Sapphire, My Sister
  Jones, Alice H.
For Saundra
  Giovanni, Nikki
For Some Poets
  Jackson, Mae
For Stephen Dixon
  Gilbert, L. Zack
For the Candle Light
  Grimke, Angelina Weld
For the Defense
  Jones, James Arlington
For the Honeybee and Her Poets
  Wandick, W. D.
For the Lips of One Grown Weary
  Chappell, Helen F.
For the Truth (Because it is necessary)
  Spriggs, Edward S.
For Theresa
  Giovanni, Nikki
For Tom Postell, dead black poet
  Jones, LeRoi
For Unborn Children
  Livingston, Myrtle Smith
For Walter Washington
  Dent, Thomas C.
For William Edward Burghardt DuBois on His Eightieth Birthday
  Lattimer, Bette Darcie
For You
  Tinsley, Tomi Carolyn
For You, Sweetheart
  Fisher, Leland Milton
Foregather
  Johnson, Georgia Douglas
Foreclosure
  Brown, Sterling A.
The Forerunners
  Redding, Jay Saunders
Forest Park
  Brown, William
Forever
  Dunbar, Paul Laurence

Forever
  Todd, Ella
Forget Me Not
  Plato, Ann
Forget to Not
  Kaufman, Bob
Forgiveness
  Smallwood, Will
The Forgotten
  Patterson, Raymond Richard
Forgotten Dreams
  Silvera, Edward S.
Fork of the West River
  Henderson, David
Formula
  Ogletree, Carolyn J.
Foscati
  Braithwaite, William Stanley Beaumont
#4 (Where My Grandmother lived)
  Long, Doughtry
Four epitaphs
  Cullen, Countee Porter
Four Glimpses of Night
  Davis, Frank Marshall
Four lines of a Black Love Letter Between Teachers
  Roberson, Charles Edwin
Four Old Bodkins for My Analyst
  Wright, Bruce McMarion
Four Questions Addressed to His Excellency the Prime Minister
  Vaughn, James P.
Four Sheets to the Wind and a One-Way Ticket to France
  Rivers, Conrad Kent
Four Stations in His Circle
  Clarke, Austin
Four Walls
  Conley, Malcolm Christian
Four Walls
  Dickinson, Blanche Taylor
Fourth Dance Poem
  Barrax, Gerald William
4th Dimension
  Henderson, David
Foxey Lady
  Solomon, Philip
Fragility
  Smith, James Edgar
Fragment
  Fauset, Jessie Redmond
Fragment
  Johnson, James Weldon
Fragment
  Jones-Quartey, H. A. B.
Fragment Reflection I
  Linyatta
Fragments
  Tinsley, Tomi Carolyn
Frank
  Perry, Robert N., Jr.
Frank Horne and the Second Echelon Poets of the Harlem Renaissance
  Primau, Ronald
Frank London Brown
  Stuckey, Sterling

Frank Marshall Davis: Writer
Davis, Frank Marshall
Frank Yerby as Debunker
Turner, Darwin T.
Frankie Mae
Smith, Jean Wheeler
Franklin Delano Roosevelt
Pitts, Lucia Mae
Frederick Douglass
Cornish, Sam
Frederick Douglass
Cotter, Joseph Seamon, Sr.
Frederick Douglass
Dunbar, Paul Laurence
Frederick Douglass
Hayden, Robert Earl
Frederick Douglass
Johnson, Georgia Douglas
Frederick Douglass
Miller, Kelly
Frederick Douglas: 1817–1895
Hughes, Langston
Free Wine on Communion Day
Smith, Linwood D.
The Freedmen's Bureau
DuBois, William Edward Burghardt
Freedom
Hill, Leslie Pinckney
Freedom
Hughes, Langston
Freedom
Newsome, E. Marie
Freedom
Reason, Charles L.
Freedom Hair
Washington, Raymond
Freedom in Mah Soul
Cannon, David Wadsworth, Jr.
Freedom ride
Hughes, Langston
Freedom Rider: Washout
Emanuel, James A., Sr.
Freedom rider
Evans, Mari
Freedom Train
Hughes, Langston
Freedom's Snare
Lee, Ed
Free-Lance Pallbearers
Reed, Ishmael
A Freeman's Flight from the South
Allen, William G.
A Friend For a Season
Harrison, Deloris
Friends
Durem, Ray
Friends
Whaley, June D.
Friends I Am Like You Tied
Spellman, Alfred B.
Friendship
Lalande, Athelstan R.
Frightened Flower
Harris, William J.
The Frightened Lover's Sleep
Wright, Jay

A Frolic
Dunbar, Paul Laurence
From a Brother Dreaming in the Rye
Cunningham, James
From a Bus
Lawrence, Joyce Whitsitt
From an Eighteen Year old poet with a
raggedy face
Taylor, Prentiss, Jr.
From Cavities of Bones
Parker, Patricia
From Dawn to Dusk
Jones, James Arlington
From Generation to Generation
**Madgett, Naomi Cornelia Long Wither-
spoon**
From Poetry by Black Writers to Black
Poetry: a Brief History
Gibson, Donald B.
From Selma
Hughes, Langston
From Sleep, Dark Settles in the Eye
Reddy, T. J.
From Superman to Man
Rogers, Joel Augustus
From the Bleachers
Jones, James Arlington
From the Bone, From the Blood, the Rib
du Cille, Ann
From the Crowd
Braithwaite, William Stanley Beaumont
From the Dark Tower
Cullen, Countee Porter
From the Delta's Unmarked Graves
Williamson, Harvey M.
From the German of Uhland
Johnson, James Weldon
From the Narrator's Trance
Cunningham, James
From the Sidelines
Bates, Myrtle
From 21A
Chandler, Len
Fruit of the Flower
Cullen, Countee Porter
Frustration
Hunter, Eleanor C.
Frustration, a Heritage
Cox, Thelma Parker
Fugit Amor
Houston, Virginia
Fugitive
Weeks, Ricardo
Fulfillment
Johnson, Helene Hubbell
Full Moon
Hayden, Robert Earl
The Function of Black Literature at the
Present Time
Gayle, Addison, Jr.
The Funeral
Perry, Robert N., Jr.
The Funeral
Shockley, Ann Allen
Funeral of Martin Luther King, Jr.
Giovanni, Nikki

Funk
Washington, Thomas, Jr.
The Funny Company (or Why Ain't him and his girls on T. O.?)
Pfister, Arthur
Funnyhouse of a Negro
Kennedy, Adrienne
Future of Negro Poetry
Emanuel, James A., Sr.
The Future of the Negro
Douglass, Frederick

Gabriel
Mason, Clifford
Gabriel—Hanged for leading a slave revolt
Hayden, Robert Earl
Gabriel's Prayer
Baldwin, James
The Gallows
Tolson, Melvin Beaunorus
The Game
King, Woodie, Jr.
Game of Game
Giovanni, Nikki
Games
Bass, George Houston
Gamma
Tolson, Melvin Beaunorus
Gangster's Death
Reed, Ishmael
Garden Ghosts
Haywood, Clara H.
Garnishing the Aviary
Danner, Margaret
Garvey's Ghost
Neal, Larry
A Gathering of Artists
Johnson, Alicia Loy ,
Genealogy
Jones, LeRoi
Genealogy
Phillips, Frank Lamont
The Genealogy of an American Champion
Young, Nathan Ben
Geneology
Kaufman, Bob
General Drums
Matheus, John Frederick
Generation
Lorde, Audre
The Generation Gap
Saunders, Ruby Constance X.
Generations
Fields, Julia
Generations
Simmons, Judy Dothard
Genesis on an Endless Mosaic
Dumas, Henry L.
The Geni in the jar
Giovanni, Nikki
Genifrede
Harris, Helen Webb
Gentleman Caller
Bullins, Ed
George
Randall, Dudley

George Moses Horton, Myself
Horton, George Moses
George Washington and the Negro
Donaldson, Ulysses S.
Georgia Dusk
Toomer, Jean
Georgia—It's the Gospel Truth
Hoagland, Everett
The German Invasion
Smith, James McCune
Get up, Blues
Emanuel, James A., Sr.
"Getting It Together"
Staples, Shirley
Getting Things Together
Kellum-Rose, Matthew
Gethsemane
Bontemps, Arna W.
Getting Down to Get Over
Jordan, June Meyer
Ghana Calls
DuBois, William Edward Burghardt
Ghetto
Johnson, Yvette
Ghetto Love—Song—Migration
Clemmons, Carole Gregory
A Ghetto-torn Fantasy
McGriff, (Miss) T. P.
Ghetto Waif
Felton, B.
Ghost Poem I
Neal, Larry
Ghost Poem 3
Neal, Larry
Ghost Writer
Tinsley, Tomi Carolyn
Gift
Freeman, Carol S.
Gift from Kenya
Miller, Mary
Gift of Horses
Jeffers, Lance
The Gift of Laughter
Fauset, Jessie Redmond
Gift of the Black Tropics
Domingo, W. A.
The Gilded Six-Bits
Hurston, Zora Neale
Giles Johnson, Ph.D.
Davis, Frank Marshall
Gingerbread Mama
Long, Doughtry
Girl from Oklahoma
Cuney, Waring
Girl Held Without Bail
Walker, Margaret Abigail
The Girl with the Afro
Bennett, Bob
Git on Board, Chillun
Henderson, Elliot B.
Gittin' Happy
Ragland, J. Farley
Give Them Grace
Lawrence, Joyce Whitsitt
The Glass Stomach
Thomas, Richard W.

Glimpse
  Lomax, Pearl Cleage
A Glorious Company
  Davis, Allison
The Glory of the Day Was in Her Face
  Johnson, James Weldon
Go Down, Death
  Johnson, James Weldon
Go Down, Moses
  Christian, Marcus Bruce
Go South, Young Man, Go South
  Hughes, Langston
Go Tell It on the Mountain
  Baldwin, James
Go Up For Glory
  Russell, Bill
Go Work in My Vineyard
  Harper, Frances Ellen Watkins
The Goal
  Cotter, Joseph Seamon, Jr.
God Bless America
  Killens, John Oliver
God Bless Our Home
  Evans, Emmery, Jr.
God Gave Me a Son
  Daniel, Portia Bird
God Give To Men
  Bontemps, Arna W.
The Godmakers
  Whitaker, Patrick W.
God's Gift to the Woman
  Stallworth, Robert
God's Trombones
  Johnson, James Weldon
Gods in Vietnam
  Redmond, Eugene B.
Goin' a Buffalo
  Bullins, Ed
Gold Coast
  McPherson, James Alan
Gold Is the Shade Esperanto
  Danner, Margaret
A Gold Watch Hung in the Sky
  Conyus
A Golden Afternoon in Germany
  Delany, Clarissa Scott
The Golden Age. Time Past
  Ellison, Ralph Waldo
Golden Moonrise
  Braithwaite, William Stanley Beaumont
The Golden Stool
  Holmes, Glen
Goldfish Bowl
  Faggett, H. L.
The Goldfish Monster
  Crayton, Pearl
Golgotha Is a Mountain
  Bontemps, Arna W.
Golgotha Nihilist
  Salgado, Lionel
Goliath of Gath
  Wheatley, Phillis
Gone
  Bohanon, Mary
A Good Assassination Should Be Quiet
  Evans, Mari

The Good Black Poet and the Good Gray
Poet: The Poetry of Hughes and Whitman
  Gibson, Donald B.
A Good God
  Bohanon, Mary
A Good Long Sidewalk
  Kelley, William Melvin
Good Mornin' Blues
  Johnson, James Weldon
Good Morning
  Hughes, Langston
Good Morning, Captain
  Johnson, James Weldon
Good News for the Underprivileged
  Thurman, Howard
A Good Season
  Williams, John Alfred
Good Times
  Clifton, Lucille
Good to be in you
  Randall, Dudley
Good-bye
  Johnson, Georgia Douglas
Goodbye, Christ
  Hughes, Langston
Goodby David Tamunoemi West
  Danner, Margaret
Goodbye Old Year
  Jones, Joshua Henry, Jr.
The Goophered Grapevine
  Chesnutt, Charles Waddell
Gorilla, My Love
  Bambara, Toni Cade
The Gospel Truth
  Earley, Jacqueline
Gospi Anderson
  Williamson, Harvey M.
Gossip
  Jones, James Arlington
Gotta Keep Butting My Head against the
Wall and Hoping Maybe the Wall Will Break
before I Bust My Brains Out
  Marshall, Lee
Graduating
  Huff, William Henry
Grand Central Station
  Martin, Herbert Woodward
A Grandfather Poem
  Harris, William J.
Grandma
  Hughes, Langston
Granny
  Whaley, June D.
Granny Black Poet
  Pfister, Arthur
Granny Maumee
  Torrence, Ridgley
Grass Fingers
  Grimke, Angelina Weld
Grass Man
  Verano, Maami
Gratitude
  Jones, James Arlington
Graven Images
  Miller, May

Gray Dawn
  Braithwaite, William Stanley Beaumont
The Gray Wolf's Ha'nt
  Chesnutt, Charles Waddell
The Great Civil Rights Law
  Evans, Mari
Great Day for a Funeral
  Williams, Edward G.
Great Goodness of Life
  Jones, LeRoi
The Great Pax Whitie
  Giovanni, Nikki
The Great Santa Barbara Oil Disaster OR:
  Conyus
Greater Love
  Winston, Harry
The Greek Room
  Thompson, James W.
Green Apples
  Randall, Dudley
Green Pears
  Honigman, Robert
Green Valley
  Johnson, Dorothy Vena
Greenness
  Grimke, Angelina Weld
Greetings
  Peace, Jerry
Grief Streams Down My Chest
  Jeffers, Lance
Grill Room
  Patterson, Jesse F.
Grist in the Mill
  Thurman, Wallace
Groove, Bang and Jive Around
  Cannon, Steve
Grow in Hope and Grace
  Baker, Barbara Anne
Growin' Into Blackness
  Salimu
Growing Clean
  Green, Donald
Growing Up
  Redmond, Eugene B.
The Growth of Negro Literature
  Calverton, Virgil F.
Guadalajara
  Major, Clarence
Guadalupe W. I.
  Guillen, Nicholas
The Guerrilla—Cong
  Harper, Michael S.
A Guerrilla Handbook
  Jones, LeRoi
The Guest
  Murphy, Beatrice M.
Guest Lecturer
  Turner, Darwin T.
Guiding Light
  Jones, James Arlington
Guilt Redeemed
  Kemp, Arnold
Guilty
  Goodwin, Ruby Berkley
Guitar
  Dodson, Owen

Guitar Music
  Cuney, Waring
Gullah
  Peterkin, Julia
Gumption
  Hughes, Langston
A Gust of Wind
  Hill, James H.
Gutter Rats
  McLean, Eldon George
Gwen Brooks, a Pyramid
  Ward, Val Gray
Gwen Brooks—Our Inspirer
  Murapa, Rukudzo
Gwen; words pretty or precise
  Bradford, William
Gwendoln Brooks
  Lee, Don L.
The Gypsies
  Banks, Barbara
Gyre's Galax
  Pritchard, Norman Henry II

Habana
  Bond, Horace Julian
Habitual
  Harris, William J.
Haiku
  Knight, Etheridge
Hail, Dionysus
  Randall, Dudley
Haiti
  DuBois, William Edward Burghardt
Half Black, Half Blacker
  Plumpp, Sterling Dominic
A Hamlet Rives Us
  Tolson, Melvin Beaunorus
Hampton-Tuskegee: Missioners of the Mass
  Moton, Robert Russa
Hands
  Coleman, Anita Scott
Hands
  Overby, Beatris
Hands
  Thompson, Glen
Hands of a Brown Woman
  Davis, Frank Marshall
Hanging Out in the Music
  Henderson, David
Hangman
  Ai
A Happening in Barbados
  Meriwether, Louise M.
Happiness
  Burvick, Karen
Happiness
  Holmes, Ethlynne E.
Happy Day
  Cunningham, James
Happy Ending
  Ward, Douglas Turner
Happy Fairies
  McBrown, Gertrude Parthenia
Hard Daddy
  Hughes, Langston

Hard Rock Returns to Prison from the Hospital for the Criminal Insane
  Knight, Etheridge
Hard Time Blues
  Cuney, Waring
Harlem
  Brierre, Jean
Harlem
  Hughes, Langston
Harlem Anthropology
  Henderson, David
The Harlem Dancer
  McKay, Claude
Harlem Freeze Frame
  Bethune, Lebert
Harlem Gallery: From the Inside
  Neal, Larry
Harlem Gallery
  Tolson, Melvin Beaunorus
Harlem in January
  Fields, Julia
The Harlem of Langston Hughes' Poetry
  Davis, Arthur P.
Harlem on the Rocks
  Hairston, Loyle
Harlem Quest
  Kelley, William Melvin
Harlem Riot, 1943
  Murray, Pauli
Harlem Shadows
  McKay, Claude
Harlem; Sidewalk Icons
  Pitcher, Oliver
Harlem '67
  Reed, Clarance
Harlem Sounds: Hallelujah Corner
  Browne, William
Harlem Sweeties
  Hughes, Langston
Harlem Teacher
  Freeman, Lorraine
Harlem, the Beautiful Years
  Bontemps, Arna W.
Harlem: the Cultural Capital
  Johnson, James Weldon
Harlem Transfer
  Walker, Evan K.
Harlem Wine
  Cullen, Countee Porter
Harriet Beecher-Stowe
  Dunbar, Paul Laurence
Harriet Tubman
  Cornish, Sam
Harriet Tubman
  Miller, May
Harriet Tubman
  Walker, Margaret Abigail
A Harsh Greeting
  Gray, Darrell M.
Harvard Alumni Dinner Address, 1896
  Washington, Booker Taliaferro
Harvard Law School Forum Speech of March 24, 1961
  Little, Malcolm
Harvest Song
  Toomer, Jean

Hatred
  Bennett, Gwendolyn B.
Hatred
  Murphy, Beatrice M.
The Haunted Oak
  Dunbar, Paul Laurence
Havana Dreams
  Hughes, Langston
Have You Seen It
  Weeden, Lula Lowe
Haven
  Hayes, Donald Jeffrey
! ! ! He ! ! !
  Newsome, E. Marie
He Also Loved
  McKay, Claude
He Came In Silvern Armor Trimmed In Black
  Bennett, Gwendolyn B.
He Keeps Company with What He Knows
  Booker, Sue
He Said She Said She Said He Said
  Jones, Jymi
He Sees Through Stone
  Knight, Etheridge
He Was a Man
  Brown, Sterling A.
Health Card
  Yerby, Frank
Hear Those Tambourines
  Greene, Carl H.
Hearing James Brown at the Café des Nattes
  Long, Richard A.
Heart at the Woods
  Curtwright, Wesley
The Heart of a Woman
  Johnson, Georgia Douglas
Heart of Black Ghetto
  Perkins, Eugene
The Heart of the World
  Jones, Joshua Henry, Jr.
The Heart Toasts
  Burbridge, Edward Dejoie
Heaven
  Hughes, Langston
Heavy Water Blues
  Kaufman, Bob
Hegiria
  Johnson, Herschell
Hell, Mary
  Eckels, Jon B.
The Hell-bound Train
  Brown, Landa Loretta
Hello Blackness
  Kemp, Arnold
Hemlock for the Artist: Karenga Style
  Cunningham, James
Henry Ossawa Tanner
  Fauset, Jessie Redmond
Henry Ossawa Tanner
  Porter, James A.
Her Story
  Madgett, Naomi Cornelia Long Witherspoon
Her Sweet Jerome
  Walker, Alice

Her Wedding Day
  Thomas, Richard W.
Herbert III
  Shine, Ted
Here and Now
  Cater, Catherine
Here—Hold My Hand
  Evans, Mari
Here Is the Sea
  Bontemps, Arna W.
Here Where Coltrane Is
  Harper, Michael S.
Heritage
  Bennett, Gwendolyn B.
Heritage
  Buford, Naomi E.
Heritage
  Clinton, Dolores
Heritage
  Cullen, Countee Porter
Heritage for Harold Jackman
  Cullen, Countee Porter
Heritage
  McKay, Claude
Hero of the Road
  Hawkins, Walter Everette
Heroes
  Carter, Karl
The Heroic Slave
  Douglass, Frederick
He's Coming Home At Last
  Greene, Emily Jane
He's Doing Natural Life
  Conyus
Hey Boy
  Young, Alexander
Hidden Name and Complex Fate
  Ellison, Ralph Waldo
Hide My Face? On Pan-Africanism and Negritude
  Drake, John Gibbs St. Clair, Jr.
High-cool/2
  Cunningham, James
High Modes: Vision As Ritual: Confirmation
  Harper, Michael S.
High on Life
  Kaufman, Bob
High on the Hog
  Fields, Julia
High Tide
  Twitty, Countess W.
High to Low
  Hughes, Langston
High Yaller
  Fisher, Rudolph
The Hill
  Stevens, Ruby
The Hills of Sewanee
  McClellan, George Marion
The Hindered Hand
  Griggs, Sutton Elbert
The Hireling and the Slave
  Grayson, William John
The Hip Teacher
  Walker, Mike

His Answer
  Thompson, Clara Ann
His Body Is an Eloquence
  Lane, Pinkie Gordon
His Excellency, General Washington
  Wheatley, Phillis
His First Step
  Gordon, Charles F.
His Hera Mourned
  Geran, Juliana
His Own Maniac Self
  Hope, Lezli
Historic Episodes
  Clark, Peter Wellington
An Historic Moment
  Harris, William J
History and Propaganda
  Woodson, Carter G.
History Made to Order
  Woodson, Carter G.
History of the Negro Race in America
  Williams, George Washington
History of the Negro Troops in the War of the Rebellion
  Williams, George Washington
History of the Poet As a Whore
  Lee, Don L.
The History of the Spiritual
  Johnson, James Weldon
Hog Meat
  Davis, Daniel Webster
Hokku
  Hoagland, Everett
Hokku: In the Falling Snow
  Wright, Richard
A Hokku Poem
  Alexander, Lewis Grandison
Hokku Poems
  Wright, Richard
The Hole
  Thomas, Richard W.
Hollerin' the Blues
  Broonzy, Big Bill
Holy Days
  Neal, Larry
Holyghost Woman
  Major, Clarence
Homage to the Empress of the Blues
  Hayden, Robert Earl
Home
  Brown, Sterling A.
Home
  Jones, LeRoi
Home Has Always Been Blackness
  Ward, Francis
Home Thoughts
  McKay, Claude
Home to Harlem
  McKay, Claude
Homeboy
  Little, Malcolm
homecoming
  Sanchez, Sonia
The Homecoming
  Yerby, Frank

The Homecoming Singer
  Wright, Jay
Homesick Blues
  Hugnes, Langston
Homing
  Bontemps, Arna W.
Homing Swallows
  McKay, Claude
Honkey
  Cooper, Charles B.
Hope
  Burton, John W.
Hope
  Cooper, Charles B.
Hope
  Johnson, Georgia Douglas
Hope for Africa
  Crummell, Alexander
Hope of Liberty
  Horton, George Moses
Hope was faced alone
  Mizell, Don A.
Hopelessness
  Jamison, Roscoe Conkling
hospital/poem
  Sanchez, Sonia
Hot Blood/Bad Blood
  Luciano, Felipe
Hot-Foot Hannibal
  Chesnutt, Charles Waddell
Hot Lunch
  Crouch, Stanley
A House Divided
  Taylor, Jeanne A.
A House in Taos
  Hughes, Langston
House in the World
  Hughes, Langston
House Made of Dawn
  Momaday, N. Scott
House of Falling Leaves
  Braithwaite, William Stanley Beaumont
The House of Sham
  Richardson, Willis
The House of Time
  Cousins, William
The House on Mettler Street
  Taylor, Jeanne A.
House Under Arcturus
  Braithwaite, William Stanley Beaumont
Housecleaning
  Giovanni, Nikki
How Are You Gonna Keep 'Em from the Fiery Pits after They've Seen Me Toetap?
  Rusan, Francille
How Bigger Was Born
  Wright, Richard
How can I love . . .
  Lorde, Audre
How Do You Do
  Bullins, Ed
How He Went
  Hyde, Evans
How High the Moon
  Jeffers, Lance

how i got ovah
  Rodgers, Carolyn M.
How John Boscoe Outsung the Devil
  Davis, Arthur P.
How Long?
  Whitfield, James M.
How long Blues
  Johnson, James Weldon
How Long Has Trane Been Gone?
  Cortez, Jayne
How Lucy Backslid
  Dunbar, Paul Laurence
How Many Poets Scrub the River's Back?
  Jeffers, Lance
How to Change the USA
  Edwards, Harry
How to Describe Fall from Now on
  Major, Clarence
How To See Angels
  Pritchard, Sheila
How to Succeed
  Kemp, Arnold
How We Must Teach the Children
  Thomas, Richard W.
Howard Street
  Heard, Nathan C.
Howard: the National Negro University
  Miller, Kelly
However Small a Deed
  Jones, James Arlington
The Huey Newton Trial
  Anderson, William
The Huge Dull Night Under the Stars
  Tannenbaum, Sheldon
Human Life
  Jeffers, Lance
Humanistic Protest in Recent Black Poetry
  Barksdale, Richard K.
Humiliation
  Jeffers, Lance
Humility
  Coleman, Anita Scott
Humoresque
  Christian, Marcus Bruce
Hunchback Girl: She Thinks of Heaven
  Brooks, Gwendolyn
Hunger
  Foster, Francis M.
Hunger
  Harris, Helen C.
Hungry Black Child
  Miller, Adam David
The Hunters
  Kellum-Rose, Matthew
Hush
  Scott, Johnie H.
Hush Now
  Parrish, Dorothy C.
Hushed by the Hands of Sleep
  Grimke, Angelina Weld
A Hymn
  Dunbar, Paul Laurence
Hymn
  Lomax, Pearl Cleage
Hymn
  Randall, Dudley

Hymn
  Walker, Alice
Hymn for the Slain in Battle
  Braithwaite, William Stanley Beaumont
Hymn of Thanksgiving
  Brown, Henry "Box"
A Hymn To The Evening
  Wheatley, Phillis
An Hymn to the Morning
  Wheatley, Phillis
Hymn to the Nation
  Whitman, Albery Allson
Hymn Written After Jeremiah Preached to
Me in a Dream
  Dodson, Owen
Hypocrisy in Black
  Cooper, Charles B.

i
  Thomas, Beverly
I—
  Moryck, Brenda Ray
i aint seen no poems stop a .38
  Lee, Don L.
I Am
  Abramson, Dolores
I Am a Black Woman
  Evans, Mari
I Am a Cowboy in the Boat of Ra
  Reed, Ishmael
I Am a Man
  Hunt, Ted
I Am Here to Announce
  Davis, Ronda Marie
I Am Man
  Tinsley, Tomi Carolyn
I Am Mother's Gentle Pet
  Folly, Dennis Wilson
I Am Not Lazy . . .
  Evans, Mari
I Am Speaking of Future Good-ness and
Social Philosophy
  Jones, LeRoi
I Am the Record of Man
  Jeffers, Lance
I Am Too Much Loved
  Haywood, Clara H.
I Am Waiting
  Goode, Michael
I Arrive in Madrid
  Young, Alexander
Ibe
  Shorter, Lynn
I Black
  Whitaker, Patrick W.
I Break the Sky
  Dodson, Owen
I Can Get It for You Wholesale
  Lyle, K. Curtis
i can luv Blkman
  Cousins, Linda
I Closed My Shutters Fast Last Night
  Johnson, Georgia Douglas
"I could never ask you"
  King, Leyland

I Could Not Know
  Hughes, Lois Royal
I Died One Night
  Hannah, George
I do not know the power of my hand
  Jeffers, Lance
I Do Not Marvel, Countee Cullen
  Collier, Eugenia N.
I Do not Want to Turn Away
  Abrams, Robert J.
I Dream a War
  Weeks, Ricardo
I Dream a World
  Hughes, Langston
I Dream Alone Again
  Goodwin, Ruby Berkley
I Dream You Harlem
  Martin, Herbert Woodward
I Followed a Path
  Parker, Patricia
I Had No Thought of Violets of Late
  Dunbar-Nelson, Alice
I-Hate-Love Poem N.3
  Berry, Chantal Sandre
I Have a Dream
  King, Martin Luther, Jr.
I Have a Friend
  Spencer, Anne
I Have a Rendezvous with Life
  Cullen, Countee Porter
I Have a Song
  Hill, Leslie Pinckney
I Have Always Wanted Black Power
  Gayle, Addison, Jr.
I Have Folded My Sorrows
  Kaufman, Bob
I Have Seen Black Hand
  Tolson, Melvin Beaunorus
I Have Seen Black Hands
  Wright, Richard
I Have Seen Them
  Jordan, Norman
I Have Spent My Life
  Burroughs, Margaret Taylor Goss
I Hear The Soul Of A Murderer Tonight
  Honigman, Robert
I Heard a Young Man Saying
  Fields, Julia
I Heard Your Heart's Soft Tears
  Harris, Helen C.
I Investigate Lynchings
  White, Walter
I Killed One
  Greene, Carl H.
I Knew You Better
  Randall, Jon
I Know a Lady
  Thomas, Joyce Carol
I Know I'm Not Sufficiently Obscure
  Durem, Ray
I Know Jesus Heard Me
  Anderson, Charles
I Know My Soul
  McKay, Claude
I Know She Will Pray For Me
  Bourke, Sharon

I Know Why the Caged Bird Sings
Angelou, Maya
I Laugh Talk Joke
Dumas, Henry L.
I Looked and Saw History Caught
Spellman, Alfred B.
I Love Those Little Booths at Benvenuti's
Brooks, Gwendolyn
I Love You, What More Can I Say?
Gray, Jocelyn
I Loved You Once
Randall, Dudley
I Make a Nation
Jeffers, Lance
I never saw him before—a Mississippi Folk Song
Horne, Frank M.
I Offer You Wine
Pitts, Lucia Mae
I Own a Dream
Smallwood, Will
I Pass
Smith, Abram G. F.
I Played on David's Harp
Johnson, Fenton
I Pledge Allegiance
Tarver, Valerie
"I prepare for night changes"
White, Michyle
i remember
Jackson, Mae
i remember how she sang
Penny, Rob
I Remember Papa
Dolan, Harry
I Remember That Day
Bourke, Sharon
i rode with geronimo
Conyus
I, Satan
Harris, William J.
I Saw Beauty
Haywood, Clara H.
I Saw Them Lynch
Freeman, Carol S.
I See and Am Satisfied
Miller, Kelly
I See You Standing, Toothpick Lady
Harris, William J.
I Seek
Cuestas, Katherine L.
I Shall Build a Music Box
Wright, Bruce McMarion
I Shall Not Be Moved
Stewart, Ollie
I Shall Remember These
Williamson, Harvey M.
I Share Your Presence
Harris, Helen C.
I Sing
Goodwin, Ruby Berkley
I Sing My People
Jeffers, Lance
I Sing No New Songs
Davis, Frank Marshall

I Sing of Shine
Knight, Etheridge
I Sit and Sew
Dunber-Nelson, Alice
I Spread These Flaps of Flesh and Fly
Jeffers, Lance
I Strongly Sweep
Jeffers, Lance
I Substitute for the Dead Lecturer
Jones, LeRoi
I Swear to You, That Ship Never Sunk in Middle-Passage!
Cumberbatch, Lawrence S.
I Think I See Him There
Cuney, Waring
I Think I Thought a Lie
Thomas, D. Gatewood
I Thought It Was Tangiers I Wanted
Hughes, Langston
I Thought of My True Love
Cuney, Waring
I Told Jesus
Plumpp, Sterling Dominic
I, Too, Hear America Singing
Bond, Horace Julian
I, Too, Know What I Am Not
Kaufman, Bob
I, Too, Sing America
Hughes, Langston
I Touch the Past
Jeffers, Lance
I Touched the hand of a soldier dead
Emanuel, James A., Sr.
i used to wrap my white doll up in
Jackson, Mae
I Wake Up Screaming
Hall, Carlyle B.
I Want to Die While You Love Me
Johnson, Georgia Douglas
"I Want You To Hear Me"
Mizell, Don A.
I Was in the South When Neither Law nor Tradition Was on My Side
Wright, Richard
I watched little black boys
Malcom, Barbara
I Weep
Grimke, Angelina Weld
I will hide my soul and its mighty love
McClellan, George Marion
I will sit now
Polite, Allen
I will suppose that fate is just
Cotter, Joseph Seamon, Sr.
I, Woman
Fields, Julia
I Wonder
Blanton, Lorenzo D.
I Wonder
Hand, Q. R.
I / Wonder . . .
Poole, Tom
I Wonder
Ragland, J. Farley
I Wonder As I Wander
Hughes, Langston

I Wonta Thank Ya
  Ologboni, Tejumola
I Work Here to Please You
  Mitchell, Loften
I Would Be a Painter Most of All
  Chandler, Len
I would like to be Serene
  Cortez, Jayne
Icicles on Trees
  Finley, Catherine L.
I'd Rapp
  Giovanni, Nikki
The Idea of Ancestry
  Knight, Etheridge
Identity
  Latimore, Jewel Christine
Ideological Forces in the Work of the Negro
Writer
  Cayton, Horace R.
The Idiot
  Randall, Dudley
Idle Chatter
  Cooper, Charles B.
The Idle Head
  Richardson, Willis
Idolatry
  Bontemps, Arna W.
Idyl
  Ray, Henrietta Cordelia
An Idyl of the South
  Whitman, Albery Allson
Idyll
  Jameson, Gladys M.
If Beer Cans Were Bullets
  Pfister, Arthur
If Blood Is Black, Then Spirit Neglects My
Unborn Son
  Rivers, Conrad Kent
If Ever You Should Walk Away
  Pitts, Lucia Mae
If Hair Makes Me Black, I Must Be Purple
  Hardnett, Linda G.
If I Could Touch
  Braithwaite, William Stanley Beaumont
If I Knock You Down, Don't You Blame
It On Me
  Cook, Mike
If I Ride This Train
  Johnson, Joe
If I Stand in My Window
  Clifton, Lucille
If I Tell You That
  Rusan, Francille
If in reverse
  Bell, George R.
If Love Be Staunch
  Cullen, Countee Porter
If Love Dies
  Fields, Julia
If Not In Summer
  Madgett, Naomi Cornelia Long Wither-
  spoon
If She Bees
  Pfister, Arthur
if the black frog will not ring
  Roberson, Charles Edwin

If the Stars Should Fall
  Allen, Samuel W.
If There Be Sorrow
  Evans, Mari
If This Be Good-bye
  Goodwin, Ruby Berkley
If We Cannot Live as People
  Lynch, Charles Henry
If We Could See
  Meschi, Howard
If We Must Die
  Edwards, Junius
If We Must Die
  McKay, Claude
If Winter Comes
  Gullins, D. Edna
If You Come Softly
  Lorde, Audre
If You Forget
  McDuffie, Eleanor
If You Love Them, Wouldn't You Like to
See Them Better Off?
  Balagon, Kuwasi
If You Saw a Negro Lady
  Jordan, June Meyer
I'll Never Escape the Ghetto
  Sanders, Stanley
I'll Remember Lincoln
  Dawley, Jack H.
I'll Walk the Tightrope
  Danner, Margaret
Illusions
  Hall, Kirkwood M.
I'm A Worker
  Cortez, Jayne
I'm Going To Make Time My Master
  Folly, Dennis Wilson
I'm Here
  Sherman, Jimmie
I'm Just a Little Penny
  Harrell, Dennis
I'm Just a Stranger Here, Heaven Is My
Home
  Clemmons, Carole Gregory
I'm Just an Idealist
  Martinez, Lydia
I'm No Martian
  Harris, William J.
I'm Not Lonely
  Giovanni, Nikki
Image in the Mirror
  Kenner, Peggy Susberry
The Image of Man as Portrayed by Ralph
Ellison
  O'Daniel, Therman B.
The Image Reach
  Sun-Ra
Imagination
  Wheatley, Phillis
Imamu Amiri Baraka: The Quest for Moral
Order
  Jacobus, Lee A.
Immediate Program of the American Negro
  DuBois, William Edward Burghardt
Immortality
  Horne, Frank M.

Impasse
  Hughes, Langston
imperial thumbprint
  Weatherly, Tom
Impossibility
  Coleman, Jamye H.
Impressions
  Hall, Kirkwood M.
Impressions of Chicago: For Howlin' Wolf
  Troupe, Quincy
In A Graveyard
  Braithwaite, William Stanley Beaumont
In a Harlem Storefront Church
  Reed, Clarence
In a Lifetime
  Jones, James Arlington
In Abraham's Bosom
  Green, Paul
In All The Days Of The Dunes
  Pritchard, Sheila
In between
  Moore, Willard
In Between Time
  Jackson, Marsha Ann
In Black
  DuBois, William Edward Burghardt
In Black Turf
  Rivera, Edward
In Bondage
  McKay, Claude
In Chapala, Jal
  Major, Clarence
In Darkness and Confusion
  Petry, Ann Lane
In Defense of Black Poet
  Rivers, Conrad Kent
In Defense of the Negro Male
  Bullock, Doris Powers
In Dream: The Privacy of Sequence
  Young Bear, Ray A.
In Finality Where to Go Is What to Do
  Barrett, Lindsay
in Higher Places
  Weaver, Eleanor
In Homage to Heavy Loaded Trane, J. C.
  Joans, Ted
In Light Half Nightmare and Half Vision
  Hayden, Robert Earl
In Love With Harlem
  Hughes, Langston
In Memoriam
  Jones-Quartey, H.A.B.
In Memoriam: Rev. Martin Luther King, Jr.
  Jordan, June Meyer
In Memory of Colonel Charles Young
  Cullen, Countee Porter
In Memory of Freedom Marchers
  Washington, Thomas, Jr.
In Memory of Katie Reynolds, Dying
  McClellan, George Marion
In Memory of Martin Luther King
  Randall, James A., Jr.
In Menelek's Court
  Richardson, Willis
In My Father's House: A Reverie
  Allen, Samuel W.

In Need Of A Catullus To Adore
  Geran, Juliana
In New England Winter
  Bullins, Ed
In One Battle
  Jones, Le Roi
in orangeburg my brothers did
  Spellman, Alfred B.
In Reverse
  Porter, Linda
In Search of a God
  Thomas, Charles Cyrus
In Some Time Hence
  Taylor, Isabelle McClellan
In Spite of All This Much Needed Thunder
  Gilbert, L. Zack
In Spite of Death
  Hawkins, Walter Everette
In Spite of Handicaps
  Bullock, Ralph W.
In Splendid Error
  Branch, William Blackwell
In Texas Grass
  Troupe, Quincy
In the Early Morning Breeze
  Cumberbatch, Lawrence S.
In the End Let All White Racists Thank the
Holy Jackass
  Fields, Julia
In the Evening
  Johnson, Fenton
In the Faculty Room
  Barlow, George
In The Heart of a Rose
  McClellan, George Marion
In the Inner City
  Clifton, Lucille
In the Interest of Black Salvation
  Lee, Don L.
In The Line Of Duty
  Troupe, Quincy
In the Matter of Two Men
  Corrothers, James David
In the Mecca
  Brooks, Gwendolyn
In the Morning
  Dunbar, Paul Laurence
In the Mourning Time
  Hayden, Robert Earl
In the Name of God
  Evans, Mari
In The Silence
  Fuller, Stephany
In the Time of Revolution
  Lester, Julius
In the Wine Time
  Bullins, Ed
In These Dissenting Times
  Walker, Alice
In This House There Shall Be No Idols
  Rodgers, Carolyn M.
In Time of Crisis
  Patterson, Raymond Richard
Inauguration
  Thomas, Lorenzo

Incense of the Lucky Virgin
  Hayden, Robert Earl
Incest for Brothers: a Criticism
  Cunningham, James
Incident
  Cullen, Countee Porter
Incidental Pieces to a Walk: For Conrad
  Cunningham, James
Incidentally
  Lewis, Leighla
An Inconvenience
  Raven, John
Incurable
  Tinsley, Tomi Carolyn
Index to a Black Catharsis
  Thomas, Richard W.
India
  Scott, Johnie H.
indianapolis / summer / 1969 / poem
  Sanchez, Sonia
Indictment
  Bush, Joseph Bevans
Indictment
  Parrish, Dorothy C.
Indictment
  Saxon, Alvin A.
Indifference
  Cumbo, Kattie M.
An Indignation Dinner
  Corrothers, James David
Inevitability
  Perry, Robert N., Jr.
The Inevitable Road
  McLean, Eldon George
Infants of Summer
  Raphael, Lennox
Infants of the Spring
  Thurman, Wallace
Infelicia
  Menken, Adah Isaaks
Infinite
  Sirrah, Leumas
The Ingrate
  Dunbar, Paul Laurence
The Inhumanity of Slavery
  Douglass, Frederick
Initiation
  Cortez, Jayne
Inner-city Slums
  Gilbert, Willie
Innocence
  Spencer, Anne
Inquiry
  Clarke, John Henrik
Inquiry
  Clarke, LeRoy
Insanity, the Question
  Sirrah, Leumas
Inscription
  Hayes, Donald Jeffrey
The Insidious Dr. Fu Man Chu
  Jones, LeRoi
Insight
  Cannon, David Wadsworth, Jr.
Instant Revolution
  Major, Clarence

Instantaneous
  Ayers, Vivian
Instructions to a Princess
  Reed, Ishmael
Integration and Race Literature
  Davis, Arthur P.
The Intellectuals
  Randall, Dudley
Intent
  Scott, Johnie H.
The Interesting Narrative of the Life of Olaudah Equiano, or Gustavus Vassa the African. Written by Himself.
  Vassa, Gustavus
An Interesting Social Study
  Hunter, Kristin
Interim
  Delany, Clarissa Scott
Interim
  Houston, Virginia
Interlude
  Smith, Welton
Intermission
  Brooks, Gwendolyn
Interracial
  Johnson, Georgia Douglas
Interrogation
  Arnold, Walter G.
An Interview with Clarence Major and Victor Hernandez Cruz
  Shepperd, Walt
Interview with Ralph Ellison
  Chester, Alfred and Vilma Howard
Intimacy
  Seese, Ethel Gray
Into Blackness Softly
  Evans, Mari
Into the Mainstream and Oblivion
  Mayfield, Julian
Intoxication
  Holman, Moses Carl
Introduction
  Bennett, Lerone, Jr.
Introduction
  Johnson, Charles S.
Introduction
  Lee, Don L.
Introduction: Blueprint for Negro Writing
  Wright, Richard
Introduction from *The Book of Negro Folklore*
  Bontemps, Arna W.
Introduction to Negro Biography
  Brawley, Benjamin Griffith
The Invaders
  Reed, Clarence
The Invention of a Garden
  Wright, Jay
The Invention of Comics
  Jones, LeRoi
Invisible Man
  Ellison, Ralph Waldo
The Invisible Man
  Rivers, Conrad Kent
"Invisible People"
  Lee, Roger B.

Invitation
  Davis, Ronda Marie
Invitation
  Patterson, Raymond Richard
An Invitation to Madison County
  Wright, Jay
Invocation
  Dinkins, Rev. Charles R.
Invocation
  Johnson, Helene Hubbell
Iowa Farmer
  Walker, Margaret Abigail
Iron Years: for Money
  Major, Clarence
Ironic: LLD
  Braithwaite, William Stanley Beaumont
Irritable Song
  Atkins, Russell
Irving
  Marshall, Lee
Is It Because I Am Black?
  Cotter, Joseph Seamon, Jr.
Is Natural, Takes Me In
  Major, Clarence
Is That Really What Little Girls Are Made Of?
  Cumbo, Kattie M.
Isaiah
  Wheatley, Phillis
Islam and The Black Arts: an Interview with Amiri Baraka
  Faruk
Island
  Hughes, Langston
Isolation
  Johnson, Georgia Douglas
It
  Thomas, Richard W.
"It ain't no jive"
  Wakefield, Jacques
It Has Come To Black Beauty
  Randall, Jon
It Is Again
  Burroughs, Margaret Taylor Goss
It Is Deep
  Rodgers, Carolyn M.
It Is in Shadows
  Crews, Stella Louise
it is overdue time
  Welburn, Ron
It Is Time
  Joans, Ted
It Is Time for Action
  Bennett, Bob
It May Be Bad
  Taylor, Jerry
It Seems To Me
  Anderson, Edna L.
It shall flash through coming ages
  Harper, Frances Ellen Watkins
It Was a Funky Deal
  Knight, Etheridge
It Was a Hot Day
  Mason, Leo J.
It Was Here
  Powe, Blossom

It was Knife
  Polite, Allen
It Was Not Fate
  Moore, William H. A.
Itching Heels
  Dunbar, Paul Laurence
It's a Long Way
  Braithwaite, William Stanley Beaumont
It's a Long Way to Saint Louis
  Miller, Adam David
It's a Terrible Thing!
  Hoagland, Everett
It's All Complicated Up
  Redding, Jay Saunders
It's All Through Life
  Carmichael, Waverly Turner
It's Curtains
  Joans, Ted
It's Great To Be a Problem
  Work, J. D.
It's Here in the
  Atkins, Russell
It's Time (Repatriation . . . Africa?)
  Cumbo, Kattie M.
'Ittle Touzle Head
  Dandridge, Raymond Garfield
I've Got a Home in that Rock
  Patterson, Raymond Richard
I've Learned to Sing
  Johnson, Georgia Douglas
Ivory Musks in Orbit
  Kgositsile, Keorapetse William
Ivory Tusks
  Allen, Samuel W.

Jack Frost
  McBrown, Gertrude Parthenia
Jack in the Pot
  West, Dorothy
The Jackal-Headed Cowboy
  Reed, Ishmael
Jackson, Mississippi
  Walker, Margaret Abigail
Jalapenã Gypsies
  Wright, Jay
James
  Gaines, Ernest J.
James Baldwin . . . in Conversation
  Georgakas, Dan
James Powell on Imagination
  Neal, Larry
A January Dandelion
  McClellan, George Marion
January 3, 1970
  Jackson, Mae
Japanese Hokku
  Alexander, Lewis Grandison
Jasmine
  McKay, Claude
Jazz
  Brown, Frank London
Jazz
  Rodgers, Carolyn M.
Jazz and the Jazz Age: 1918–1926
  Locke, Alain Leroy

Jazz at Home
  Rogers, Joel Augustus
Jazz Band
  Davis, Frank Marshall
Jazz Band in a Parisian Cabaret
  Hughes, Langston
Jazz Coltrane Sings
  Dancy, Walter K.
Jazz, Jive, and Jam
  Hughes, Langston
Jazz Must be a Woman
  Joans, Ted
Jazzonia
  Hughes, Langston
Jazz poem
  Hines, Carl Wendell, Jr.
Jazzy Vanity
  Thomas, Richard W.
Jazztet Muted
  Hughes, Langston
Je Suis un homme
  Joans, Ted
Jealous
  Dunbar, Paul Laurence
Jealousy
  De Saavedra, Guadalupe
Jean
  Jackson, James Thomas
Jean Toomer: As Modern Man
  Thompson, Larry E.
Jedgement Day
  Pawley, Thomas D., Jr.
Jefferson in a Tight Place
  Horton, George Moses
Jelly Wrote
  Spellman, Alfred B.
Jeremy
  Scott, Johnie H.
Jerked to God
  Johnson, Dorothy Vena
Jessie Mitchell's Mother
  Brooks, Gwendolyn
Jesus Was Crucified or: It Must Be Deep
  Rodgers, Carolyn M.
Jew
  Randall, James A., Jr.
The Jewel
  De Saavedra, Guadalupe
Jill Made It With a Goat
  Harris, William J.
Jim
  Perry, Robert N., Jr.
Jimmy South
  Wesley, John
Jim's Probation
  Dunbar, Paul Laurence
Jimsella
  Dunbar, Paul Laurence
Jitterbugging in the Streets
  Hernton, Calvin C.
Jitterbugs
  Jones, LeRoi
The Job
  Caldwell, Ben

The job
  Moore, Willard
Job Hunters
  Edward, H. F. V.
Job Security
  Charles, Martha Evans
The Joel blues
  Spellman, Alfred B.
John Coltrane / an impartial review
  Spellman, Alfred B.
John Henry
  Johnson, James Weldon
John Henry in Harlem
  Tolson, Melvin Beaunorus
John Henry, a Negro Legend
  Johnson, Guy B.
Jonathan's Song
  Dodson, Owen
Journal of Charlotte Forten
  Forten, Charlotte L.
Journey from The Night
  Thompson, James W.
Journey to a Parallel
  Wright, Bruce McMarion
Journey to Atlanta
  Baldwin, James
Joy
  Delany, Clarissa Scott
Joy
  Hughes, Langston
Joy or Sorrow
  Johnson, Leanna F.
Juan de Pareja
  Long, Richard A.
Juan Latino, Magister Latinus
  Schomberg, Arthur A.
Jubilee
  Walker, Margaret Abigail
Judas Iscariot
  Cullen, Countee Porter
Judas Iscariot
  Holman, Moses Carl
Judeebug's Country
  Johnson, Joe
Judge Lynch
  Rodgers, John W., Jr.
Judgement Day
  Foreman, Kent
The Judgment Day
  Johnson, James Weldon
Judgment Marked by a Cellar: The American Negro Writer and the Dialect of Despair
  Scott, Nathan Alexander, Jr.
JuJu
  Snellings, Rolland
A Juju of My Own
  Bethune, Lebert
Juke Box Love Song
  Hughes, Langston
July 31
  Jordan, Norman
July 27
  Jordan, Norman
Jumby
  Fauset, Arthur Huff

Jump Bad
  Rodgers, Carolyn M.
Jumpstreet for a Black Man
  Brown, Daryl
Juncos
  Cantoni, Louis J.
A June Song
  Grimke, Angelina Weld
Junebug Graduates Tonight
  Shepp, Archie
Jungle
  Smith, Mary Carter
Jungle Fever
  Mack, L. V.
Jungle Taste
  Silvera, Edward S.
Junglegrave
  Anderson, S. E.
Junior Addict
  Hughes, Langston
Junkee-Joe Had Some Money
  Milner, Ronald
Junkies Are Full of (Shhh . . .)
  Jones, LeRoi
Just Like a Tree
  Gaines, Ernest J.
Just Making It
  Thomas, Richard W.
Just One in a Series
  Jackson, Mae
Jus. Taking Note
  Scott, Sharon
Justice
  Hall, John E.
Justice
  Hughes, Langston
Justice
  Perry, Peggy

KaBa
  Jones, LeRoi
Kabnis
  Toomer, Jean
Karintha
  Toomer, Jean
Keep Me, Jesus, Keep Me
  Carmichael, Waverly Turner
Keep on Pushing
  Henderson, David
Keep the Faith Blues
  Dumas, Henry L.
Kid
  Hayden, Robert Earl
Kid Stuff
  Horne, Frank M.
Kids
  Thomas, Richard W.
Kidnap Poem
  Giovanni, Nikki
The Killer
  Coggins, Frank
The Kind of Man He Is
  Clifton, Lucille
Kinds of Blue
  McCurine, William

The King of Soul, or, The Devil and Otis Reading
  Caldwell, Ben
King of the Bingo Game
  Ellison, Ralph Waldo
King Still/Lives
  Witherspoon, Jill
The King's Dilemma
  Richardson, Willis
The Kiss
  Young, Alexander
Kiss the Girls for Me
  White, Wallace
Kitchenette Building
  Brooks, Gwendolyn
Klactoviedsedstene
  Russell, Charles L.
Knee-Deep
  Yancy, Bessie Woodson
Knock on Wood
  Dumas, Henry L.
Know This Is True
  Bonahon, Mary
Knowledge
  Tinsley, Tomi Carolyn
Knoxville, Tennessee
  Giovanni, Nikki
Ku Klux
  Hughes, Langston
Kunter
  Neal, Larry

L. A.: the order of Things
  Cobb, Charlie
La Perla Negra
  Underwood, Edna Worthley
La Trinidad
  Lambert, Calvin S.
La Vie C'est La Vie
  Fauset, Jessie Redmond
Lacrimae Aethiopiae
  Johnson, Charles Bertram
Lacrimas or There Is a Need to Scream
  Lyle, K. Curtis
Ladies In Waiting
  De Anda, Peter
Lady in Waiting
  du Cille, Ann
Lady, Lady
  Spencer, Anne
Lady Leo: Miss T.
  Crouch, Stanley
Lady's Days
  Neal, Larry
Lamda
  Tolson, Melvin Beaunorus
Lament
  Daniel, Portia Bird
Lament
  Dodson, Owen
Lament of the Farm
  Willman, Eugene B.
Lancelot
  Bontemps, Arna W.
A Land Beyond the River
  Mitchell, Loften

Land of Make Believe
  Reddy, T. J.
Langston Hughes
  Bond, Horace Julian
Langston Hughes
  Brooks, Gwendolyn
Langston Hughes
  Fields, Julia
Langston Hughes and the Harlem Renaissance, 1921–1931: Major Events & Publications
  Taylor, Patricia E.
The Languages We Are
  Bryant, Frederick James
Last Days of the American Empire (including Some Instructions for Black People)
  Jones, LeRoi
Last Evening with a Lady
  Thomas, Richard W.
Last Letter to the Western Civilization
  Ogilvie, D. T.
The Last M. F.
  Rodgers, Carolyn M.
Last Message to the World
  DuBois, William Edward Burghardt
The Last Mile
  Slay, Johnnie Bea
Last Night I Died
  Harrison, DeLeon
last poem i'm gonna write about us
  Sanchez, Sonia
The Last Quarter Moon of the Dying Year
  Brooks, Jonathan Henderson
Last Quatrain of the Ballad of Emmett Till
  Brooks, Gwendolyn
Last Rites for the City
  Whaley, June D.
The Last Thing of Beauty
  Bressack, Gordon
last week my mother died
  Lee, Don L.
The Last Warehouse
  Miller, May
Last Whipping
  Hughes, Langston
Late
  Madgett, Naomi Cornelia Long Witherspoon
Late Corner
  Hughes, Langston
Late Dream
  Salgado, Lionel
Late Lesson
  Haywood, Clara H.
Late Visitor
  Tinsley, Tomi Carolyn
later i'll say
  Clifton, Lucille
Laughers
  Hughes, Langston
The Law
  De Saavedra, Guadalupe
The Law
  Haynes, Albert E., Jr.
Lawd, Dese Colored Chillum
  Saunders, Ruby Constance X.

Lawrence of the River
  Hurston, Zora Neale
Lazy
  Johnson, James Weldon
Lead
  Cortez, Jayne
Lead Belly Gives an Autograph
  Jones, LeRoi
The Leader
  White, Joseph
The Leaders
  Randall, Dudley
Learning Family
  Washington, Dell
Learning To Dance
  Graham, Ruby Bee
Learning to Read
  Harper, Frances Ellen Watkins
Leaves
  Cullen, Countee Porter
Lecture on Slavery No. 2
  Douglass, Frederick
Lee-ers of Hew
  Cunningham, James
Leelah Misled
  Whitman, Albery Allson
Leg Man
  Stewart, Ollie
Legacy
  Jones, LeRoi
Legacy
  Patterson, Charles
Legacy: My South
  Randall, Dudley
Legacy of a Blue Capricorn
  Cunningham, James
legacy of a brother
  Fernandez, Renaldo
Legacy of Malcolm X and the Coming Black Nation
  Jones, LeRoi
The Legacy of the Ancestral Arts
  Locke, Alain Leroy
Legacy of the Word
  Saxon, Alvin A.
The Legend of Tannhauser and Elizabeth
  McClellan, George Marion
Legend of Versailles
  Tolson, Melvin Beaunorus
Legion, the Demoniac
  Huntley, Elizabeth Maddox
Lemme Tell You What My Black Is All About
  Reed, Clarence
Lemons, Lemons
  Young, Alexander
Length of Moon
  Bontemps, Arna W.
Lennox Avenue Bar
  Hughes, Langston
Lennox Avenue Mural
  Hughes, Langston
L'Envoi
  Hill, Leslie Pinckney
Leola
  Gaines, Ernest J.

Le Retour au Village aux Perles
    Debrosses, Nelson
Le Retour de Napoléon
    Sejour, Victor
LeRoi Jones and Contemporary Black Drama
    Phillips, Louis
Leroi jones talking
    Jones, LeRoi
leroy
    Jones, LeRoi
Leslie
    Wyche, Marvin, Jr.
The Lesson
    Dunham, Katherine
Lester Young
    Joans, Ted
Let America Be American Again
    Hughes, Langston
Let Me Be Held When the Longing Comes
    Fuller, Stephany
Let Me Live
    Herndon, Angelo
Let My Last Breath Be Immortal
    Jeffers, Lance
Let None Ignobly Halt
    Cotter, Joseph Seamon, Sr.
Let the Book Close
    Pitts, Lucia Mae
Let the Church Roll on
    Ford, Nick Aaron
Let the Light Enter
    Harper, Frances Ellen Watkins
Let Them Come to Us
    Pitts, Lucia Mae
Let There Be Three of Us
    Hughes, Lois Royal
Let Us Begin the Real Work
    Sanchez, Sonia
Lethe
    Johnson, Georgia Douglas
The Letter
    Burbridge, Edward Dejoie
Letter
    Hughes, Langston
The Letter
    Murphy, Beatrice M.
Letter across Doubt and Distance
    Holman, Moses Carl
Letter addressed to the Honourable George
Thatcher, Member of Congress 1799
    Forten, James, Jr.
Letter XI
    Brown, William Wells
Letter from a Wife
    Reese, Sarah Carolyn
Letter from Benjamin Banneker to Thomas
Jefferson, August 19, 1791
    Banneker, Benjamin
Letter in 'Crisis,' March, 1928, to Roland A.
Barton
    DuBois, William Edward Burghardt
Letter in Winter
    Patterson, Raymond Richard
Letter Relative to Conditions in Hayti, July
1, 1824, Written to the Editor of the Colum-

bian Sentinel
    Paul, Thomas
Letter to a White Colleague
    Gayle, Addison, Jr.
Letter to E. Franklin Frazier
    Jones, LeRoi
Letter to Garrison
    Nell, William Cooper
Letter to His Master
    Douglass, Frederick
Letter to Mr. Horace Greeley
    Horton, George Moses
A Letter to Mrs. Stowe
    Douglass, Frederick
Letter to My Nephew
    Baldwin, James
Letter to My Nephew
    Bontemps, Arna W.
Letter to My Sister
    Spencer, Anne
Letter to Rev. Archibald Alexander, D.D.
    Wright Theodore S.
Letter to the Chronicle
    Kaufman, Bob
Letter to Thomas Becket . . .
    Harris, William J.
Letters
    Cravat, John A.
Letters Found Near a Suicide
    Horne, Frank M.
Letters From A Journey
    Baldwin, James
Letters from a Man of Color; on a late
Bill before the Senate of Pennsylvania
    Forten, James, Jr.
Letters to a Black Boy
    Teague, Bob
Letters to Garrison
    Brown, William Wells
Letters to Samuel May, Jr.
    Brown, Josephine
Leverett House Forum
    Little, Malcolm
Leviticus Tate
    Warren, Lloyd
The Leviathan
    Simpson, Juanita
Liars Don't Qualify
    Edwards, Junius
liberation/poem
    Sanchez, Sonia
Liberty and Peace
    Wheatley, Phillis
Libretto for the Republic of Liberia
    Tolson, Melvin Beaunorus
Life
    Dunbar, Paul Laurence
Life
    Jefferson, Richard
Life
    Jones, James Arlington
Life
    Madgett, Naomi Cornelia Long Wither-
spoon
Life
    Sanchez, Sonia

The Life and Confession of Johnson Green, who is to be executed this day, Aug. 17th, 1786 for the Atrocious Crime of Burglary; Together with his last and dying words, a broadside.
  Green, Johnson
Life and loves of Mr. Jiveass Nigger
  Brown, Cecil
Life and Religious Experience of Jarena Lee . . . 1836
  Lee, Jarena
Life and Times of Frederick Douglass
  Douglass, Frederick
Life after Death
  Thomas, Richard W.
Life, a Gamble
  Mayhand, Ernest A., Jr.
Life as Reflected off an Onyx Stone
  Parker, Thomas L.
Life Begins at Forty
  Winston, Harry
Life centered by this last obsession
  Bell, George R.
The Life Experience and Gospel Labors of the Rt. Reverend Richard Allen
  Jones, Absalom and Richard Allen
Life for My Child Is Simple
  Brooks, Gwendolyn
Life in My Own Dust
  Kenner, Peggy Susberry
Life Is Fine
  Hughes, Langston
Life Is the Art of Drawing
  Ogletree, Carolyn J.
The Life of a Slum Child
  Young, Susan
The Life of Josiah Henson
  Henson, Josiah
Life of Lincoln West
  Brooks, Gwendolyn
The Life of the Spirit in the Natural World
  Conner, Charles H.
Life on the Sea Islands
  Forten, Charlotte L.
Life With Red Top
  Fair, Ronald L.
The Life You Save
  Kelley, William Melvin
A Life-Day
  Vashon, George B.
Life-long, Poor Browning
  Spencer, Anne
Life's Like the Wind
  Burton, John W.
Life's lowly were laureled with verses
  Wiggins, Lida Keck
Life's Tragedy
  Dunbar, Paul Laurence
Lifetime
  Oliver, Georgiana
Lift every voice and sing
  Johnson, James Weldon
Light
  Jordan, Norman
Light, Light, Light
  Christmas, Edward

The Light of the Women
  Gunner, Frances
The Light of Victory
  Margetson, George Reginald
The Lights at Carney's Point
  Dunbar-Nelson, Alice
Like a Piece of Blues
  Davis, Gloria
Like a Strong Tree
  Mc Kay, Claude
Like a Winding Sheet
  Petry, Ann Lane
Like Brothers We Meet
  Horton, George Moses
Like Me
  Halsey, William
Like the tide: Cloudward
  Kgositsile, Keorapetse William
Like Unto a Rose
  Hughes, Lois Royal
Lilacs
  McBrown, Gertrude Parthenia
Lilies
  Graham, Linda B.
Lily Baines
  Williamson, Harvey M.
Limitations of Life
  Hughes, Langston
Lincoln
  Dunbar, Paul Laurence
Lincoln
  Fortune, Timothy Thomas
Lincoln University 1954
  Hughes, Langston
Line of Duty
  Olsen, Paul
Lineage
  Walker, Margaret Abigail
Lines
  Martin, Herbert Woodward
Lines on Leadership
  Hill, Leslie Pinckney
Lines on the Death of John Quincy Adams
  Whitfield, James M.
Lines to a Nasturtium
  Spencer, Anne
Lines to Garcia Lorca
  Jones, LeRoi
Lines to Our Elders
  Cullen, Countee Porter
Lines to the Black Oak
  La Grone, Oliver
Lines Written at the Grave of Alexander Dumas
  Bennett, Gwendolyn B.
Linked between Two obscurities
  Bell, George R.
Lip Service
  Quigless, Helen G.
Listen
  Patterson, Charles
Listen, America, Ebony Middle-Class Is Talking
  Taylor, Jeanne A.
Listen, Children
  Clifton, Lucille

Listen Lord—A Prayer
  Johnson, James Weldon
Listen to the Big Black at S. F. State
  Sanchez, Sonia
Listening to Bach
  Jeffers, Lance
A Litany at Atlanta
  DuBois, William Edward Burghardt
The Litany of the Dark People
  Cullen, Countee Porter
Literary Ghetto
  Williams, John Alfred
Literary Poetry
  Randall, Dudley
The Literature of Harlem
  Kaiser, Ernest
Literature of the Negro in the U.S.
  Wright, Richard
Little Birches
  Newsome, Mary Effie Lee
Little Black Boy
  Marshall, Barbara
Little Boy's Prayer
  Blessitt, Bernadine
Little Brown Baby
  Dunbar, Paul Laurence
A Little Cabin
  Johnson, Charles Bertram
Little Café
  Pitts, Lucia Mae
The Little Dandelion
  Weeden, Lula Lowe
Little Dark Girl
  Thomas, Richard W.
Little Dog
  Hughes, Langston
Little Girl Talk
  Williams, Delores S.
Little Grey Leaves
  Popel, Esther
Little Ham
  Hughes, Langston
Little Helper
  Shaw, Edna
A Little More about the Brothers and Sisters
  Scott, Sharon
A Little More Traveling Music
  Young, Alexander
A Little Poem
  Brooks, Gwendolyn
A Little Poem
  Brown, Linda
Little Son
  Johnson, Georgia Douglas
A Little Song
  Braithwaite, William Stanley Beaumont
Little Song on Housing
  Hughes, Langston
Little Sonnet to Little Friends
  Cullen, Countee Porter
The Little Things of Life
  Ezell, Doris Amurr
Little white schoolhouse blues
  Lennon, Florence Becker
Live Celebration
  Fabio, Sarah Webster

A Live Eschatology
  Neal, Larry
Liveralissimo
  Bibbs, Hart Leroi
Living in a Slum—What Slums Need
  Shepherd, Gerald
The Living Is Easy
  West, Dorothy
Living through the Senses Is Living in Love
  Pyne, A. Warnyeneh
The Living Truth
  Plumpp, Sterling Dominic
Living With Music
  Ellison, Ralph Waldo
Loam Norton
  Brooks, Gwendolyn
Loch Lomond
  Lambert, Calvin S.
Locus
  Hayden, Robert Earl
Locust of Satan
  Vallejo
Loimos
  White, Edgar
Loneliness
  Jordon, Winifred Virginia
Loneliness
  Young, Alexander
Loneliness and Madness
  Jeffers, Lance
Loneliness Is a Movie Theatre
  Harris, William J.
Lonely Crusade
  Himes, Chester B.
Lonely Mother
  Johnson, Fenton
Lonely, Thou
  Thomas, Richard W.
Lonely Tulip Grower
  Alvarez, Julia
Lonely Woman
  Cortez, Jayne
Lonesome in the Country
  Young, Alexander
Lonesome Road
  Redding, Jay Saunders
The Long, Black Line
  Gilbert, L. Zack
Long Black Song
  Wright, Richard
A Long Day in November
  Gaines, Ernest J.
Long de Cool o' Night
  Johnson, Fenton
Long Distance
  Clemmons, Carole Gregory
Long Gone
  Brown, Sterling A.
Long Live the Peace Corps of America
  Scott, Johnie H.
The Long March
  Johnson, Alicia Loy
The Long Night Home
  Gordon, Charles F.
The Long Sell
  Walker, Victor Steven

A Long Way from Home
  Mc Kay, Claude
Longing
  Lewis, Lillian Tucker
Longlegs
  Major, Clarence
Look at My Face, a collage
  Rodgers, Carolyn M.
Look At that Gal
  Bond, Horace Julian
Look for Me, Dear Mother
  Alhamisi, Ahmed Akinwole
Look For You Yesterday, Here You Come Today
  Jones, LeRoi
Looking for Equality
  McMillan, Herman L.
A Loop In The Day
  Seese, Ethel Gray
Lord
  Cornish, Sam
Lord, Girl She Dance, She Dance
  Reed, Clarence
Lord, While I Sow Earth
  Cornish, Sam
Lorraine Hansberry
  Miller, Jordan H.
Losers Weepers
  Dolan, Harry
The lost baby poem
  Clifton, Lucille
Lost Dancer
  Toomer, Jean
Lost Illusions
  Johnson, Georgia Douglas
Lost Love
  McMillan, Herman L.
Lost Moment
  Fuller, Hoyt W.
Loud Jazz Horns
  Washington, Hazel L.
The Loudest Voice
  Paley, Grace
The Louisiana Weekly #4
  Henderson, David
Love
  Clark, Benjamin P.
Love
  Clarke, John Henrik
Love
  Cooper, Charles B.
Love
  Dent, Thomas C.
Love
  Higgins, Dewey
Love
  Horton, George Moses
Love
  Jennings, Kevin
Love
  Parks, Valerie
Love
  Pritchard, Norman Henry II
Love
  Turner, Darwin T.

Love Ain't Hip
  Royster, Sandra H.
love child—a black aesthetic
  Hoagland, Everett
Love Despoiled
  Dunbar, Paul Laurence
A Love Dirge to the Whitehouse (or: it Soots You Right)
  Fletcher, Bob
Love from My Father
  Clemmons, Carole Gregory
Love Has Two
  Clemmons, Carole Gregory
Love Is a Flame
  McClellan, George Marion
Love Is a Purple Toothpick
  Booker, Sue
Love Light
  Joans, Ted
Love Me Black Woman
  Kemp, Arnold
Love Note
  Brooks, Gwendolyn
Love of a Woman
  Kennedy, Vallejo Ryan
Love of Life
  Evans, Emmery, Jr.
Love Poem
  Clemmons, Carole Gregory
A Love Poem
  Knight, Etheridge
Love Poem
  Randall, Dudley
Love Rejected
  Clifton, Lucille
Love Song
  Allen, Samuel W.
Love Song for Seven Little Boys Called; Sam
  Fuller, Charles H., Jr.
Love Song for Willa Mae
  Fuller, Charles H., Jr.
A Love Song for Wing
  Fuller, Charles H., Jr.
Love Song in Middle Passage
  Neal, Larry
Love Story Black
  Demby, William
Love, The Exotic Maiden
  Lambert, Calvin S.
Love Your Enemy
  Iman, Kasisi Yusef
Lovelight
  Johnson, Georgia Douglas
A Lovely Love
  Brooks, Gwendolyn
The Lovely Red Color of Feelings
  Evans, Emmery, Jr.
Lover's Farewell
  Horton, George Moses
A Lover's Lament
  Foster, Francis M.
Lovers' Lane
  Dunbar, Paul Laurence
The Lovers of the Poor
  Brooks, Gwendolyn

Love's Good-Night
  Johnson, Fenton
Love's Helplessness
  Young, Alexander
Love's Phases
  Dunbar, Paul Laurence
Love's Way
  Cullen, Countee Porter
Lovesigns
  Hope, Lezli
Loving Beauty is Loving God
  Taylor, Isabelle McClellan
Loving Blues
  Danner, Deborah
Low to High
  Hughes, Langston
Low Wages
  Thomas, Richard W.
The Lower Rungs of the Ladder
  Brawley, Benjamin Griffith
Lullaby
  Moten, Cara Ball
Lullaby for Ann-Lucian
  Forbes, Calvin
Lullaby, My Son
  Brown, Fannie Carole
Lullaby to a Dream
  Christopher, James (Nakisaki)
The Luminous Darkness
  Thurman, Howard
Lumumba Section
  Kgositsile, Keorapetse William
Lumumba's Grave
  Hughes, Langston
The Lute of Afric's Tribe
  Whitman, Albery Allson
The Lynching
  Govan, Oswald
The Lynching
  Mc Kay, Claude
The Lynching
  Taylor, Isabelle McClellan
Lynching and Burning
  St. John, Primus
A Lynching for Skip James
  Graham, Ruby Bee
Lynching of Jube Benson
  Dunbar, Paul Laurence
The Lynching Tree
  Peace, Jerry
lyrics shimmy like
  Welburn, Ron
Lyrics to the Well-Beloved
  Jones-Quartey, H. A. B.

Ma Honey
  Reason, Arthur W.
Ma Rainey
  Brown, Sterling A.
Machines Can Do It Too
  Dumas, Henry L.
Mad Man's Blues
  Mack, L. V.
Madam and Her Madam
  Hughes, Langston

Madam, You Are Astonished
  Wright, Bruce McMarion
Made
  Halsey, William
Madheart
  Jones, LeRoi
Madhouse
  Hernton, Calvin C.
Madimba: Gwendolyn Brooks
  Harper, Michael S.
Madness one Monday evening
  Fields, Julia
Madrigal
  Guillen, Nicholas
Mae's Rent Party
  Wilson, Ernest J., Jr.
Magalu
  Johnson, Helene Hubbell
Magnets
  Cullen, Countee Porter
Maid and Violinist
  Butler, James Alpheus
The Maiden Who Always Refused
  Ellis, Alfred B.
Maine Morning
  Pritchard, Sheila
The Mainstream of Society
  Lee, Don L.
The Majesty of the Law
  Ford, Nick Aaron
Major Themes in the Poetry of Countee
Cullen
  Canaday, Nicholas, Jr.
Make me a grave wher'er you will
  Harper, Frances Ellen Watkins
Making It, or Black Corruption
  Green, Donald
Making of a Militant
  Bey, Yillie
The Making of Mamma Harris
  Poston, Ted
Making Poetry Pay
  Hughes, Langston
Malaguina Saluosa
  Young, Alexander
Malcolm
  Cumbo, Kattie M.
Malcolm
  Sanchez, Sonia
Malcolm
  Smith, Welton
Malcolm Spoke/Who Listened?
  Lee, Don L.
Malcolm Was a Man
  Davis, Ossie
Malcolm X
  Brooks, Gwendolyn
Malcolm X
  Hite, Vernoy E.
Malcolm X—an Autobiography
  Neal, Larry
The Malcontents
  Lewis, Dio
Malevolence
  Hall, Carlyle B.

Mama
  Blakeley, Nora
Mama
  Horne, Frank M.
Mama Hazel Takes to Her Bed
  Bambara, Toni Cade
Mama Knows
  Scott, Sharon
Mama Too Tight
  Conyus
Mama's Missionary Money
  Himes, Chester B.
Mamma Settles the Drop-out Problem
  Gates, Betty
Mammy's Baby Scared
  Carmichael, Waverly Turner
Man
  Lee, Ed
Man and Maid
  Morris, Myra Estelle
The Man Child
  Baldwin, James
Man Made Winter
  Washington, Thomas, Jr.
Man Thinking About Woman
  Lee, Don L.
Man to Man
  Goss, William Thompson
Man White, Brown Girl, etc.
  Oden, Gloria Catherine
The man who complains
  Hawkins, Walter Everette
The Man Who Cried I Am
  Williams, John Alfred
The Man Who Cried I Am: a Critique
  Henderson, David
Man Who Killed a Shadow
  Wright, Richard
Man Who Lived Underground
  Wright, Richard
The Man Who Saw The Flood
  Wright, Richard
The Man Who Trusted the Devil Twice
  Stokes, Herbert
The Man Who Was Almost A Man
  Wright, Richard
The Man Who Went to Chicago
  Wright, Richard
Man with a Furnace in his Hand
  Jeffers, Lance
The Man With The Horn Is Not Just
Blowing
  Seese, Ethel Gray
Man Woman
  Martin, Herbert Woodward
Manchild In a Promised Land
  Brown, Claude
Mandela's Sermon
  Kgositsile, Keorapetse William
The Manipulation of History and of Fact . . .
  Williams, John Alfred
Many Die Here
  Jones, Gayle
Many Sing Songs
  Greene, Carl H.

Many Thousands Gone: Richard Wright's
Native Son
  Baldwin, James
The Map
  Oden, Gloria Catherine
The Marathon Runner
  Johnson, Fenton
Marihuana and a Pistol
  Himes, Chester B.
Market
  Hayden, Robert Earl
Marketing the Products of American Negro
Writers
  Branch, William Blackwell
The Marriage
  Greaves, Donald
Marrow of My Bone
  Evans, Mari
The Marrow of Tradition
  Chesnutt, Charles Waddell
Martin County, North Carolina
  Mebane, Mary Elizabeth
Martin Luther King
  Brooks, Gwendolyn
Martin Luther King
  Patterson, Raymond Richard
Martin's Blues
  Harper, Michael S.
Martyrdom
  Thomas, Richard W.
Martyrs (February 21, 1965)
  Simmons, Herbert Alfred
Martyrs (April 4, 1968)
  Simmons, Herbert Alfred
Mary
  Clifton, Lucille
Mary, May I
  Cooper, Charles B.
Mary Passed this Morning
  Dodson, Owen
Mary's Convent
  Colter, Cyrus
Maryuma
  Phillips, Frank Lamont
The Mask
  Delany, Clarissa Scott
Masks
  Fields, Julia
Masque
  Latimore, Jewel Christine
The Masses of Us Are To Live by the Pro-
duction of Our Hands
  Washington, Booker Taliaferro
The Master of a Slave
  Sanders, Glenn C.
Mater Dolorosa
  Hill, Leslie Pinckney
Mathematical Problem in Verse
  Banneker, Benjamin
Mathematics
  Dunham, Katherine
Matter of Fact
  Jones, James Arlington
A Matter of Principle
  Chesnutt, Charles Waddell

A Matter of Time
  Brown, Frank London
A Matter of Vocabulary
  McPherson, James Alan
Maud Martha
  Brooks, Gwendolyn
The Maudlin Mist of Morning
  Lee, Audrey
May I Not Love
  Payne, Rev. Daniel A.
Mayday
  Roberson, Charles Edwin
McDonogh Day in New Orleans
  Christian, Marcus Bruce
Me Alone
  Weeden, Lula Lowe
Me and the Mule
  Hughes, Langston
Me—I'm black
  Sirrah, Leumas
Me, In Kulu Se & Karma
  Rodgers, Carolyn M.
The Me Nobody Knows: Children's Voices
from the Ghetto
  Joseph, Stephen M., ed.
Mea Culpa
  Cuestas, Katherine L.
Measurements
  Harris, Helen C.
A Medal for Willie
  Branch, William Blackwell
Medger Evers
  Brooks, Gwendolyn
Meditation on a Cold, Dark and Rainy Night
  Horton, George Moses
Meditations of a European Farmer
  Clarke, John Henrik
The Meeting
  Brown, Elaine
The Meeting after the Saviour Gone
  Clifton, Lucille
Mellow
  Cruz, Victor Hernandez
Mellow
  Hughes, Langston
The Melting Pot
  Gibson, Donald B.
Melting Pot
  Randall, Dudley
Memo
  Lynch, Charles Henry
A Memoir Presented to the American Con-
vention for Promoting the Abolition of
Slavery, and Improving the Condition of the
African Race, December 11, 1818
  Saunders, Prince
Memoirs of a Shoeshine Boy
  Mims, Harley
Memorandum
  Graham, Ruby Bee
Memorial
  McKay, Claude
Memorial Discourse Delivered in the Hall
of the House of Representatives, Feb. 12, 1865
  Garnet, Henry Highland

Memorial Wreath
  Randall, Dudley
Memoriam
  Wright, Bruce McMarion
Memories of the Long Seat
  Kenner, Peggy Susberry
Memory
  Walker, Margaret Abigail
Memory of June
  McKay, Claude
Memphis Blues
  Brown, Sterling A.
Men
  Echols, Carl
The Men Are All Away
  Malcom, Barbara
Mental Man
  Davis, Frank Marshall
Mentors
  Brooks, Gwendolyn
Merry-Go-Round
  Hughes, Langston
Message
  Harris, Helen C
A Message All Black People Can Dig
  Lee, Don L.
A Message for Langston
  Dent, Thomas C.
Message from the Atlanta Prison
  Garvey, Marcus
Message to the Grass Roots
  Little, Malcolm
A Message to the Modern Pharoahs
  Watkins, Lucian Bottow
Metagnomy
  Pritchard, Norman Henry II
The Metal Was Stuck Deep
  Greene, Carl H.
Metamorphism
  Johnson, Helene Hubbell
Metaphorical Egress
  Dancy, Walter K.
Micah
  Walker, Margaret Abigail
Michael
  Lewis, Jaceylin
Middle Passage
  Cox, Sandra
Middle Passage
  Hayden, Robert Earl
The Middle Passage and After
  Miller, Adam David
Midway
  Madgett, Naomi Cornelia Long Wither-
  spoon
Migration
  Clemmons, Carole Gregory
Mike 65
  Raphael, Lennox
Miles' Delight
  Joans, Ted
Miltant
  Hughes, Langston
Milton
  Ray, Henrietta Cordelia

Mind and Soul After Dark
 Jordan, Norman
Mine Eyes Have Seen
 Dunbar-Nelson, Alice
Mingus
 Kaufman, Bob
The Minister
 Johnson, Fenton
Minstrel Man
 Hughes, Langston
Miracle
 Blackman, Louise
The Miracle
 Clemmons, Francois
Miracles
 Bontemps, Arna W.
Mirage
 Pritchard, Sheila
The Mirages
 Hayden, Robert Earl
The Misanthropist
 Whitfield, James M.
Misapprehension
 Dunbar, Paul Laurence
Misfit
 Turner, Clare
Miss Cynthie
 Fisher, Rudolph
Miss Liza's Banjer
 Davis, Daniel Webster
Miss Luhester Gives a Party
 Fair, Ronald L.
Miss Melerlee
 Holloway, John Wesley
Miss Muriel
 Petry, Ann Lane
Miss Nora
 Patterson, Lindsay
Miss Packard and Miss Giles
 Dodson, Owen
Miss Rosie
 Clifton, Lucille
Miss Samantha Wilson
 Davis, Frank Marshall
Missed You
 Adams, Jeanette
Missing Beat
 Rodgers, Carolyn M.
Mississippi Concerto
 Snellings, Rolland
Mistakes
 Vaughn, Naomi Evans
Mister Toussan
 Ellison, Ralph Waldo
Mixed Sketches
 Lee, Don. L.
Mock Pop Forsooth: a Tale of life and death
 Thompson, James W.
Mockery
 Tinsley, Tomi Carolyn
Modern Moses, or 'My Policy' Man
 Bell, James Madison
Mojo Mike's Beer Garden
 Davis, Frank Marshall
Molly Means
 Walker, Margaret Abigail

Moment in Paradise
 Pitts, Lucia Mae
A Moment in the White
 Jones, James Arlington
A Moment Please
 Allen, Samuel W.
A Mona Lisa
 Grimke, Angelina Weld
Monday
 Thomas, Richard W.
Monody
 Geran, Juliana
Monologue
 Johnson, Alicia Loy
The Monster
 Milner, Ronald
Montgomery
 Cornish, Sam
Montgomery, Alabama
 Merriam, Eve
The Months
 Ray, Henrietta Cordelia
Montmartre
 Hughes, Langston
Monument in Black
 Howard, Vanessa
Mood
 Cullen, Countee Porter
The Mood
 Prettyman, Quandra
Moon Bound
 Washington, Raymond
Moonlight
 Harris, Helen C.
Moonlight, Moonlight
 Major, Clarence
Moon-minded The Sun . . .
 Lorde, Audre
Moon-Watching by Lake Chapala
 Young, Alexander
Morality
 Madgett, Naomi Cornelia Long Wither-
 spoon
Morality
 Saxon, Alvin A.
More Letters Found Near a Suicide
 Horne, Frank M.
Morning
 Golden, Bernette
The Morning After
 Himes, Chester B.
Morning Light
 Newsome, Mary Effie Lee
Morning Meditation
 Lomax, Pearl Cleage
Morning, Noon and Night
 Shine, Ted
Morning Poem for the Queen of Sunday
 Hayden, Robert Earl
Morning Raga for Malcolm
 Neal, Larry
Morning Star
 St. John, Primus
Mornings Don't Never Change With Us
 Whaley, June D.

Mortality
  Dunbar, Paul Laurence
Mortgaged
  Richardson, Willis
The Mortification of the Flesh
  Dunbar, Paul Laurence
Mosaic Harlem
  Dumas, Henry L.
Moscow
  Hughes, Langston
Mose
  Brown, Sterling A.
Moses Miles
  Maxey, Bob
Moses Mitchell
  Davis, Frank Marshall
The Mother
  Brooks, Gwendolyn
Mother
  Clemmons, Francois
The Mother
  Johnson, Georgia Douglas
Mother America
  Washington, Hazel L.
Mother and Child
  Hughes, Langston
Mother Dear and Daddy
  Edwards, Junius
Mother Nature
  Jones, James Arlington
Mother Night
  Johnson, James Weldon
A Mother Speaks: the Algiers Motel Incident, Detroit
  Harper, Michael S.
Mother to Son
  Hughes, Langston
Mother to Son
  Rivers, Conrad Kent
The Mothers
  Cuney, Waring
Moths
  Fields, Julia
Motto
  Hughes, Langston
Mountain in a Storm
  Carter, Herman, J. D.
Mountains
  Cannon, David Wadsworth, Jr.
Mountains
  Hayden, Robert Earl
The Mournful Lute
  Payne, Rev. Daniel A.
A Mourning Letter from Paris
  Rivers, Conrad Kent
Move
  Jones, LeRoi
The Move Continuing
  Young, Alexander
Move Un-Noticed to Be Noticed: a Nationhood Poem
  Lee, Don L.
Move Up
  Tinsley, Tomi Carolyn
Movie Queen
  Vaughn, James P.

Moving Deep
  Burroughs, Margaret Taylor Goss
Moving to Wake at Six
  Wright, Jay
Mr. Cornelius Johnson, Office Seeker
  Dunbar, Paul Laurence
Mr. Roosevelt Regrets
  Murray, Pauli
Mr. Z
  Holman, Moses Carl
Mrs. Bailey Pays the Rent
  Reid, Ira De Augustine
Mrs. Johnson Objects
  Thompson, Clara Ann
Mud in Vietnam
  Lester, Julius
mud water shago
  Weatherly, Tom
The Muhammad Ali-Patterson Fight
  Cleaver, Eldridge
Mulatto
  Hughes, Langston
Mulatto
  Weaver, Eleanor
Mulatto Flair
  Spencer, Gilmore
The Mulatto to His Critics
  Cotter, Joseph Seamon, Jr.
The Mulatto's Song
  Johnson, Fenton
Mulch
  Miller, Adam David
The Mules of Caesar
  Allen, Samuel W.
Mumbo Jumbo
  Reed, Ishmael
A Murderer Awaiting Sentence
  Stevens, Ruby
Muse in Late November
  Brooks, Jonathan Henderson
Music of the Other World
  Wilson, Ted
Music Screams in the Mind
  Hope, Lezli
Musical Comedy
  Cuney-Hare, Maud
MWilu / or Poem for the Living
  Lee, Don L.
My Ace of Spades
  Joans, Ted
My America
  La Grone, Oliver
My Angel
  Brooks, Jonathan Henderson
My Aunt Clara
  Clemmons, Francois
My baby
  Harris, William J.
My Beard
  Sherman, Jimmie
My Beige Mom
  Spriggs, Edward S.
My Birthright, Too
  Danner, Margaret

My Black Man's Togetherness Was Called Revolt
Kennedy, Vallejo Ryan
My Blackness Is the Beauty of This Land
Jeffers, Lance
My Blue Angel
Harris, William J.
My Bondage and My Freedom
Douglass, Frederick
My Boy
Williams, Vincent
My Brother
Danner, James
My Brother and Me
Reed, Clarence
My Brother Went to College
Yerby, Frank
My Childhood
Randall, Dudley
My City
Johnson, James Weldon
My Dungeon Shook
Baldwin, James
My Epitaph
Alexander, Lewis Grandison
My Face
Davis, Gloria
My fallen star has spent its light
Watkins, Lucian Bottow
My Father
Jeffers, Lance
My Friend
Allen, Samuel W.
My Friend, Wendell Berry
Harris, William J.
My Girl Wants To Leave Ohio
Harris, William J.
My Hate
Lewis, Leighla
My Heart Has Known Its Winter
Bontemps, Arna W.
My Heritage
Menken, Adah Isaaks
My Hero
Brawley, Benjamin Griffith
My House
Giovanni, Nikki
My House
Mc Kay, Claude
My Lady of the Cloisters
Wright, Bruce McMarion
My Lady's Lips Am Like De Honey
Johnson, James Weldon
My Lai as Related to No. Vietnam Alabama
Rodgers, Carolyn M.
My Life
Parks, Henrietta C.
My life were lost if I should keep
Hill, Leslie Pinckney
My Little Dreams
Johnson, Georgia Douglas
My Lord, What a Morning
Cuney, Waring
My Love When This Is Past
Burroughs, Margaret Taylor Goss

My Mama Moved Among the Days
Clifton, Lucille
My Man Bovanne
Bambara, Toni Cade
My Man Let Me Pull Your Coat
Evans, Mari
My Man Was Here Today
Saunders, Ruby Constance X.
My Mother
Mc Kay, Claude
My Mother Was a Black Woman
Porter, Linda
My Mother's Child
Simmons, Carmel
My Music, My Music!
Jeffers, Lance
My Name Is Afrika
Kgositsile, Keorapetse William
My Own Hallelujahs
Gilbert, L. Zack
My People
Hughes, Langston
My people laugh and sing
Johnson, Charles Bertram
My people no longer sing
Kgositsile, Keorapetse William
My Plant and I
Thomas, Richard W.
My Poem
Giovanni, Nikki
My Portion
Tinsley, Tomi Carolyn
My Poverty and Wealth
Cotter, Joseph Seamon, Sr.
My Rainy Day
Jeffrey, Maurine L.
My Sadness Sits Around Me
Jordan, June Meyer
My Sea of Tears
Wess, Deborah Fuller
My Sort o' Man
Dunbar, Paul Laurence
My Soul
Alexandre, Marie E.
My Soul and I
Tolson, Melvin Beaunorus
My Southern Home
Brown, William Wells
My Spring Thing
Hoagland, Everett
My Storm-Shook Belly Must Hide a Prodigy
Jeffers, Lance
My Street Is Kind of Dead
Campbell, Josie
Myrtle Avenue
Mc Kay, Claude
Myself
Jeffers, Lance
Myself When I Am Real
Young, Alexander
The Mystery
Braithwaite, William Stanley Beaumont
Myth
Greenlee, Sam
Mythe of a Negro Literature
Jones, LeRoi

Naked
  Bohanon, Mary
The Nam
  Witherspoon, Jill
Name In Print
  Hughes, Langston
Names on a Monument at Oberlin, Ohio
  Ackerson, John
Nanette Neely / wherever you are
  Coleman, Horace Wendell
Narrative
  Atkins, Russell
A Narrative of Some Remarkable Incidents, in the Life of Solomon Bayley 1825
  Bayley, Solomon
Narrative of the Adventures and Escape of Moses Roper from American Slavery
  Roper, Moses
Narrative of the Black Magicians
  Neal, Larry
Narrative of the first schoolday
  Eckford, Elizabeth
Narrative of the Life and Adventures of Henry Bibb
  Bibb, Henry
A Narrative of the Life and Adventures of Venture, A Native of Africa: But Resident above sixty years in the United States of America, 1798
  Smith, Venture
Narrative of the Life of Frederick Douglass
  Douglass, Frederick
Narrative of the Life of Henry "Box" Brown
  Brown, Henry "Box"
A Narrative of the Lord's Wonderful Dealings with John Marrant, a Black, 1802
  Marrant, John
Narrative of the Proceedings of the Black People During the Late Awful Calamity in Philadelphia (with Absalom Jones)
  Allen, Richard
Narratives of the Sufferings of Lewis and Milton Clarke . . .
  Clarke, Milton
A Narrative of the Uncommon Sufferings and Surprising Deliverance of Briton Hammon, Negro Man Servant to General Winslow of Marshfield, in New England, 1760
  Hammon, Briton
Nat Turner
  Allen, Samuel W.
Nat Turner
  Edmonds, Randolph
Nat Turner
  Robinson, Ophelia
Nat Turner's Confession
  Turner, Nat
Nation
  Cobb, Charlie
The Nation Is Like Ourselves
  Jones, LeRoi
The Nation of Islam—Is This a True Religion?
  Lomax, Louis Emanuel
Nationalism
  Simmons, Dan

Nationalism vs. Pimp Art
  Jones, LeRoi
Nation's Blood
  Cooper, Charles B
A Nation's Greatness
  Riley, Edwin Garnett
The Nation's Neglected Child
  Cotter, Joseph Seamon, Sr.
Native Ascension
  Cooper, Charles B.
Native Son
  Wright, Richard and Paul Green
Nativity
  Hayford, Gladys May Casely
Nat's Last White Man
  Bennett, Lerone, Jr.
Natural Black Beauty
  Goncalves, Joe
Natural History of Race Prejudice
  Faris, Ellsworth
Natural Man
  Brown, Theodore
Naturally
  Lorde, Audre
The Nature of . . .
  Bethune, Lebert
Navy Black
  Williams, John Alfred
Near Calvary
  Richardson, Willis
A Needed Poem for My Salvation
  Sanchez, Sonia
Negritude
  Emanuel, James A., Sr.
Negritude and Its Relevance to the American Negro Writer
  Allen, Samuel W.
The Negro
  Emanuel, James A., Sr.
The Negro
  Hughes, Langston
The Negro
  Kellum-Rose, Matthew
The Negro
  Lee, Don L.
The Negro
  McKay, Claude
The Negro Actor's Deficit
  Lewis, Theophilus
The Negro: An Essay on Definition
  Gibson, Donald B.
The Negro and the American Stage
  Locke, Alain Leroy
The Negro and the American Theatre
  Locke, Alain Leroy
The Negro and World War II
  DuBois, William Edward Burghardt
Negro Art and America
  Barnes, Albert C.
The Negro Artist and the Racial Mountain
  Hughes, Langston
The Negro As Artist And In American Art
  Butcher, Margaret Just
Negro Audience
  Carter, Herman J. D.

Negro Builders and Heroes
   Brawley, Benjamin Griffith
Negro Character As Seen By White Authors
   Brown, Sterling A.
The Negro Child
   Cotter, Joseph Seamon, Sr.
The Negro Church
   Razafkeriefo, Andrea
The Negro Dance
   Dunham, Katherine
Negro Dancers
   Hughes, Langston
Negro Dancers
   McKay, Claude
The Negro Digs Up His Past
   Schomberg, Arthur A.
The Negro Dramatist's Image of the Universe
   Turner, Darwin T.
Negro Dreams
   Long, Doughtry
The Negro Family in the United States
   Frazier, E. Franklin
Negro Folk Expression
   Brown, Sterling A.
The Negro Genius
   Neal, Larry
A Negro Girl: Echo of that Older Mother's Moan
   Jeffers, Lance
Negro Hero
   Brooks, Gwendolyn
Negro History
   Sherman, Jimmie
Negro History Week
   Harris, Ernestine
The Negro in American Culture
   Locke, Alain Leroy
The Negro in American History
   Cromwell, John W.
The Negro In American Literature
   Braithwaite, William Stanley Beaumont
The Negro in Colonial New England, 1620–1776
   Greene, Lorenzo Johnston
The Negro In Literature
   Brawley, Benjamin Griffith
The Negro in the American Rebellion: His Heroism and His Fidelity
   Brown, William Wells
The Negro In Our History
   Woodson, Carter G.
The Negro in the Literature of the Reconstruction
   Gross, Theodore
The Negro In Virginia
   Lewis, Roscoe E.
Negro Life in Washington
   Dunbar, Paul Laurence
A Negro Looks at His South
   Bond, Horace Mann
A Negro Love Song
   Dunbar, Paul Laurence
The Negro Mind Reaches Out
   DuBois, William Edward Burghardt

The Negro Mother
   Hughes, Langston
Negro Mother's Lullaby
   Cullen, Countee Porter
The Negro of the Jazz Band
   Peterson, Dorothy
Negro Patriotism and Devotion
   Miller, Kelly
Negro Peddler's Song
   Johnson, Fenton
The Negro Pioneers
   Kellogg, Paul U.
Negro Poets
   Johnson, Charles Bertram
Negro Poets and Their Poetry
   Thurman, Wallace
Negro Poets, Then and Now
   Bontemps, Arna W.
The Negro Problem
   DuBois, William Edward Burghardt
The Negro Race Not Under a Curse
   Crummell, Alexander
The Negro Renaissance: Jean Toomer and the Harlem Writers of the 1920s
   Bontemps, Arna W.
The Negro Revolt
   Lomax, Louis Emanuel
Negro Serenade
   Campbell, James Edwin
The Negro Singer
   Corrothers, James David
The Negro Soldiers
   Jamison, Roscoe Conkling
A Negro Soldier's Vietnam Diary
   Martin, Herbert Woodward
A Negro Speaks of Night
   Brister, Iola M.
The Negro Speaks of Rivers
   Hughes, Langston
Negro: The Word and the Meaning
   Pearson, Bernard
The Negro Theatre and the Harlem Community
   Mitchell, Loften
Negro Woman
   Alexander, Lewis Grandison
The Negro Woman in American Literature
   Lincoln, Abbey
The Negro Woman in American Literature
   Marshall, Paule
The Negro Woman in American Literature
   Wright, Sarah E.
The Negro Woman in American Literature
   Childress, Alice
The Negro Writer and American Literature
   Redding, Jay Saunders
The Negro Writer and His Materials
   Mitchell, Loften
The Negro Writer and His Relationship To His Roots
   Redding, Jay Saunders
The Negro Writer—Pitfalls and Compensations
   Smith, William Gardner
The Negro Writer— Shadow and Substance
   Redding, Jay Saunders

Negro Youth Speaks
  Locke, Alain Leroy
Negroes Have a Right to Fight Back
  Killens, John Oliver
Negroes' Tragedy
  McKay, Claude
Negroes with Guns
  Williams, Robert F.
The Negro's Americanism
  Herskovits, Melville J.
The Negro's Armageddon
  Vaughn, George L.
The Negro's Contribution
  Locke, Alain Leroy
The Negro's Educational Creed
  Cotter, Joseph Seamon, Sr.
The Negro's Gift to American Music
  White, Clarence Cameron
The Negro's Image of the Universe, as Reflected in His Fiction
  Jackson, Blyden
The Negro's Negro in Negro Literature
  Jackson, Blyden
The Negro's Plea
  Cooley, Katherine
A Negro's Prayer
  Hamilton, Richard T.
The Neighborhood House
  Wright, Jay
Neighbors
  Spencer, Anne
The Neighbors Stood on the Corner
  Cuney, Waring
Nemesis
  Douglass, Frederick
Neon Diaspora
  Henderson, David
The New Black Literature: Protest or Affirmation
  Fuller, Hoyt W.
New Blues from a Brown Baby
  Sharp, Saundra
The New Breed
  Labrie, Peter
A New Dance
  Anderson, S. E.
New Dawn
  Kgositsile, Keorapetse William
The New Day
  Johnson, Fenton
A New Day
  Wright, Charles Stevenson
New England Spinster
  Braithwaite, William Stanley Beaumont
The New Frontage on American Life
  Johnson, Charles S.
The New Integrationist
  Lee, Don L.
New Lights on an Old Song
  Scarborough, Dorothy
The New Mirror
  Petry, Ann Lane
The New Negro
  Garvey, Marcus
The New Negro
  McCall, James Edward

The New Negro
  McKay, Claude
The New Negro
  Sexton, Will
The New Negro
  Watkins, Lucian Bottow
The New Negro: An Interpretation
  Locke, Alain Leroy
The New Negro in Literature
  Brown, William Wells
The New Negro Poet in the Twenties
  Redding, Jay Saunders
The New Pietá: for the Mothers and Children of Detroit
  Jordan, June Meyer
The New Poetry of Black Hate
  Davis, Arthur P.
New Poets
  Walker, Margaret Abigail
New Season
  Harper, Michael S.
The New Sheriff
  Jones, LeRoi
A New Surge in Literature
  Morrison, Allan
New Year's Anthem
  Fortune, Michael
New Year's Prayer
  Goodwin, Ruby Berkley
New York City 1970
  Lorde, Audre
New York In The Spring
  Budbell, David
New York the Nine Million
  Martin, Herbert Woodward
Newark, For Now
  Rodgers, Carolyn M.
The Newark Public Library Reading Room
  Torregian, Sotere
The News
  Dunbar, Paul Laurence
Newsletter from My Mother
  Harper, Michael S.
Nexus
  Harris, Helen C.
Ngoma
  Dumas, Henry L.
Nice Colored Man
  Joans, Ted
A Nickle Bet
  Knight Etheridge
Nigerian Unity, or: Little Niggers Killing Little Niggers
  Lee, Don L.
The Nigga Section
  Smith, Welton
Nigger
  Barlow, George
Nigger
  Gregory, Dick
Nigger
  Horne, Frank M.
Nigger
  Sanchez, Sonia
Nigger Crazy
  Dolan, Harry

Nigh) Th' cry, pT
  Atkins, Russell
The Night
  Cumbo, Kattie M.
Night
  Dunbar, Paul Laurence
Night
  Fletcher, T. Thomas Fortune
Night
  Gardner, Benjamin Franklin
Night
  Hayes, Donald Jeffrey
Night
  Jackson, Mae
Night
  Peace, Ernest E.
Night
  Ransom, Birdelle Wycoff
Night and a Distant Church
  Atkins, Russell
Night and Morn
  Hughes, Langston
Night Club Entrance
  Brister, Iola M.
Night Funeral in Harlem
  Hughes, Langston
Night Interpreted
  Hoagland, Everett
Night of the Ol' Plantashun
  Davis, Daniel Webster
Night Piece
  Patterson, Raymond Richard
The Night Rains Hot Tar
  Jeffers, Lance
Night Slivers
  Turner, Darwin T.
Night Song
  Beverly, Katherine
Night Song
  Williams, John Alfred
Night Sung Sailor's Prayer
  Kaufman, Bob
Night Walks Down the Mountain
  Hill, William Allyn
Nightmare
  Emanuel, James A., Sr.
Nightmare
  Williams, Edward G.
Nighttime
  Raphael, Lennox
The Night's For Cryin'
  Himes, Chester B.
Nikki-Rosa
  Giovanni, Nikki
Nina Simone
  Clemmons, Carole Gregory
19 Necromancers from Now
  Reed, Ishmael
The Ninth Savior
  Thomas, Richard W.
Niobe in Distress . . .
  Wheatley, Phillis
Nittygritty
  Bush, Joseph Bevans
No Bargains Today
  Kenner, Peggy Susberry

The No 'Count Boy
  Green, Paul
no dawns
  Perry, Julianne
No Day of Triumph
  Redding, Jay Saunders
No End to the Limit
  Jackson, Maurice Shelley
No Enemies
  Clark, Benjamin P.
No Fools, No Fun
  Lacy, March
No Greater Love
  Stewart, Ollie
No Images
  Cuney, Waring
No Man Can Touch
  Whitaker, Patrick W.
No More
  Clark, Carl
No More Marching
  Lee, Don L.
No New Music
  Crouch, Stanley
No Place to Be Somebody
  Gordone, Charles
No Poem Because Time Is Not a Name
  Jordan, June Meyer
No Reservations
  Giovanni, Nikki
No Room in the Inn
  Ford, Nick Aaron
No Tears
  Clarke, John Henrik
No Time for Poetry
  Fields, Julia
No Way Out
  Curry, Linda
Noah: a Cold Cold Man
  Crouch, Stanley
Noblesse Oblige
  Fauset, Jessie Redmond
Nobody Knows My Name (excerpt: A Letter from the South
  Baldwin, James
Nobody Rides the Roads Today
  Jordan, June Meyer
Nocturnal
  McMillan, Herman L.
Nocturnal Sounds
  Cumbo, Kattie M.
Nocturne
  Bennett, Gwendolyn B.
Nocturne
  Blackwell, Dorothy F.
Nocturne
  Cullen, Countee Porter
Nocturne
  Dubonee, Ylessa
Nocturne
  Hayes, Donald Jeffrey
Nocturne
  Madgett, Naomi Cornelia Long Witherspoon
Nocturne at Bethesda
  Bontemps, Arna W.

Nocturne of the Wharves
  Bontemps, Arna W.
Nocturne on the Rhine
  Drayton, Ronald
Nocturne Varial
  Alexander, Lewis Grandison
A Non Poem about Vietnam or (Try Black)
  Rodgers, Carolyn M.
The Noonday April Sun
  Love, George
. . . Nor Do I Expect
  Harris, William J.
North and South
  McKay, Claude
The North Star
  Whitfield, James M.
North to Hell
  Attaway, William
Northboun'
  Holloway, Lucy Ariel Williams
Nostalgia
  Lee, Audrey
Nostalgia
  Williamson, Harvey M.
Not Blue
  Cumbo, Kattie M.
Not for Gold
  Echols, Carl
Not I Alone
  Madgett, Naomi Cornelia Long Wither-spoon
Not Just Whistling Dixie
  Spellman, Alfred B.
Not They Who Soar
  Dunbar, Paul Laurence
Not Wanted
  Brooks, Rosa Paul
Not We Many
  Cooper, Clarence L., Jr.
Not Without Laughter
  Hughes, Langston
Not Your Singing, Dancing Spade
  Fields, Julia
A Note for Music Lovers
  Rusan, Francille
A Note of Humility
  Bontemps, Arna W.
Notes for a Movie Script
  Holman, Moses Carl
Notes Found Near a Suicide
  Horne, Frank M.
Notes for a Speech
  Jones, LeRoi
Notes from a Guerilla Diary
  Snellings, Rolland
Notes from a Savage God
  Drayton, Ronald
Notes of a Native Son
  Baldwin, James
Notes on a Native Son
  Cleaver, Eldridge
Nothing and Something
  Harper, Frances Ellen Watkins
Nothing Endures
  Cullen, Countee Porter

Nothing Is
  Sun-Ra
Nothing Lovely As a Tree
  Bryant, Frederick James, Jr.
The Novels of James Baldwin
  Bone, Robert
Novels of Jessie Fauset
  Braithwaite, William Stanley Beaumont
November Cotton Flower
  Toomer, Jean
November/December (Echoing Voices of Remembrances
  Cumbo, Kattie M.
Now
  Bogle, Donald E.
Now
  Walker, Margaret Abigail
Now
  Williams, Rene
Now Ain't that Love?
  Rodgers, Carolyn M.
Now, All You Children
  Durem, Ray
Now and Then
  Jones, James Arlington
Now I Understand
  Cumbo, Kattie M.
Now in the black
  Porter, Timothy L.
Now poem. for us
  Sanchez, Sonia
Now that he is safely dead
  Hines, Carl Wendell, Jr.
Now that Henry Is Gone
  Riley, Clayton
Now That I Am Forever with Child
  Lorde, Audre
Now the Time Is Ripe To Be
  Goncalves, Joe
Nude Young Dancer
  Hughes, Langston
Nullo
  Toomer, Jean
Number Eight Apollo
  Barlow, George
Number Five Cooper Square
  Johnston, Percy Edward
Number 5—December
  Henderson, David
Number Please?
  Pearson, Bernard
Numbers, Letters
  Jones, LeRoi
The Numbers Writer
  Pharr, Robert Dean
Nura
  Crews, Stella Louise
NYC Love Poem
  Clemmons, Carole Gregory
Nymph
  Lorde, Audre

O
  Pritchard, Norman Henry II
O Black and Unknown Bards
  Johnson, James Weldon

O Daedalus, Fly Away Home
  Hayden, Robert Earl
O Great Black Mosque
  Joans, Ted
O-Jazz-O
  Kaufman, Bob
O Southland!
  Johnson, James Weldon
O White Mistress
  Johnson, Don Allen
Oaxaca
  Lorde, Audre
Obituary
  Hayden, Robert Earl
Oblivion
  Fauset, Jessie Redmond
Ocean
  Boyd, John
October 5th, 1963
  Kaufman, Bob
October Journey
  Walker, Margaret Abigail
October 16
  Hughes, Langston
October XXIX, 1795
  Braithwaite, William Stanley Beaumont
The Octoroon
  Johnson, Georgia Douglas
Ode
  Hope, Lezli
Ode
  Walker, Margaret Abigail
Ode on the Birthday of Pompey Stockbridge
  Wheatley, Phillis
Ode to a Beautiful Woman
  Clark, Carl
Ode to a Dying Sun
  Simmons, Herbert Alfred
Ode to Booker T. Washington
  Dungee, Roscoe Riley
Ode to Ethiopia
  Dunbar, Paul Laurence
Ode to John Coltrane
  Troupe, Quincy
Ode to Justice
  Johnson, Dorothy Vena
Ode to Leslie Parham
  Moreland, Charles King, Jr.
Ode to Lonachtitlan
  Harper, Michael S.
Ode To the Idiots
  Pfister, Arthur
Ode to the Smiths: Bessie, Mamie, Laura, Clara and Trixie
  Thomas, Charles Cyrus
Odono
  Walker, Joseph A.
Odyssey of Big Boy
  Brown, Sterling A.
Of a Woman Who Turns Rivers
  Llorens, David
Of Alexander Crummell
  DuBois, William Edward Burghardt
Of Bread and Wine
  La Grone, Oliver

Of Course We Will Not Accept One Jot or Tittle Less Than Full Manhood Rights
  DuBois, William Edward Burghardt
Of Dictators
  Perry, Robert N., Jr.
of faith: confessional
  Jordan, June Meyer
Of Love
  Harris, Helen C.
Of the Cosmic-Blueprints
  Sun-Ra
Off d pig
  Reed, Ishmael
The Offering
  Young, Alexander
Offertory
  Lomax, Pearl Cleage
Oh Banana Man
  Harris, William J.
Oh, Lord
  Payne, Antoinette T.
Oh My, Oh Yes
  Cuney, Waring
Oh, my way and thy way
  Cotter, Joseph Seamon, Sr.
Oh, Yeah!
  Scott, Sharon
O. K.
  Cruz, Victor Hernandez
OKay
  Scott, Sharon
OKay Negroes
  Jordan, June Meyer
Ol' Doc' Hyar
  Campbell, James Edwin
Old Black Men
  Johnson, Georgia Douglas
Old Black Men Say
  Emanuel, James A., Sr.
Old Blues Singers Never Die
  johnson, Clifford Vincent
The Old Deserted Cabin
  Means, Sterling M.
Old Friends
  Johnson, Charles Bertram
The Old Glory
  Barrax, Gerald William
Old Jim Crow
  Allen, Winston
Old Jonah
  Daniels, Ionie
Old Judge Mose Is Dead
  White, Joseph
Old Lang Hughes
  Jackson, Maurice Shelley
Old Laughter
  Brooks, Gwendolyn
Old Lecture Notes
  Cantoni, Louis J.
Old Lem
  Brown, Sterling A.
Old Love Butchered
  Jeffers, Lance
Old Maid
  Silvera, Edward S.

Old Man Pete
  Edmonds, Randolph
Old-Marrieds
  Brooks, Gwendolyn
Old Negroes
  Whaley, June D.
The Old Order
  Cox, Ollie H.
The Old Plantation Grave
  Means, Sterling M.
The Old Repair Man
  Johnson, Fenton
Old Things
  Johnson, Charles Bertram
Old Witherington
  Randall, Dudley
Old Workman
  Cuney, Waring
Old Workman's Song
  Cuney, Waring
An Old Woman Remembers
  Brown, Sterling A.
Olduvai Gorge: Homo Sacrificus
  Hawkins, Darnell
Ole Sis Goose
  Bontemps, Arna W.
Oliver Wendell Holmes
  Cotter, Joseph Seamon, Sr.
Ollie Miss
  Henderson, George Wylie
On a Birthday
  Bennett, Gwendolyn B.
On a Colored Doll
  Howard, Floretta
On a Letter I Received
  Shaed, Dorothy Lee Louise
On a Proud Man
  Cotter, Joseph Seamon, Sr.
On Apathy
  Greene, Carl H.
On Becoming
  Cleaver, Eldridge
On Becoming a Writer
  Ellison, Ralph Waldo
On Being Brought from Africa to America
  Wheatley, Phillis
On Being Crazy
  DuBois, William Edward Burghardt
On Being Hit
  Goss, Clay
On Being Negro in America
  Redding, Jay Saunders
On Black Theater
  Riley, Clayton
On Broadway
  Engel, Tim
On Calvary's Lonely Hill
  Johnson, Herbert Clark
On Contemporary Issues
  Ridhiana
On Evergreen Street
  Blackman, Sherry
On Freedom, 1828
  Sidney, Thomas S.
On Freedom
  Wheatley, Phillis

On Friendship
  Wheatley, Phillis
On Getting a Natural
  Randall, Dudley
On Getting an Afro
  Randall, Dudley
On Gossip Behind My Back
  Conyus
On Having a Young Mistress
  Randall, Dudley
On Hearing James W. Riley Read
  Cotter, Joseph Seamon, Sr.
On Hearing of the Intention of a Gentleman
to Purchase the Poet's Freedom
  Horton, George Moses
On Imagination
  Wheatley, Phillis
On Liberty and Slavery
  Horton, George Moses
On Listening to the Spirituals
  Jeffers, Lance
On My Blk/ness
  Johnson, Alicia Loy
On My Strand
  Scott, Sharon
On Passing Two Negroes on a Dark Country
Road Somewhere in Georgia
  Rivers, Conrad Kent
On Philosophy
  Marshall, Barbara
On Philosophy
  Marshall, Lee
On Reaching My Twenty-fourth Year
  Tinsley, Tomi Carolyn
On Recollection
  Wheatley, Phillis
On Revolutionary Culture
  Douglas, Emery
On Riots
  Leslie, Cy
On Seeing an Old Friend
  Royster, Sandra H.
On Seeing Diana Go MaDDDDDDDDD
  Lee, Don L.
On Seeing Two Brown Boys in a Catholic
Church
  Horne, Frank M.
On Slavery
  Allen, George R.
On Snobbery
  Clemmons, Carole Gregory
On Spring
  Horton, George Moses
On the Birth of My Son, Malcolm Coltrane
  Lester, Julius
On the Coast of Maine
  Hayden, Robert Earl
On the Death of a Child
  Silvera, Edward S.
On the Death of a Young Lady Five Years
Old
  Wheatley, Phillis
On the Death of the Rev. Mr. George
Whitefield
  Wheatley, Phillis

On the Death of William Edward Burghardt Dubois by African Moonlight and Forgotten Shores
  Rivers, Conrad Kent
On the Dedication of Dorothy Hall
  Dunbar, Paul Laurence
On the Emerging Playwright
  Mitchell, Loften
On the Fine Arts Garden, Cleveland
  Atkins, Russell
On the First Day of Summer in the Twenty-fifth Year of Our Lives
  Adams, Jeanette
On the Fugivite Slave Law
  Rogers, Elymas Payson
On the Ledge
  Marshall, Lee
On the Rainstorm After Sonia Sanchez
  Moreland, Charles King, Jr.
On Request
  Marshall, Barbara
On the Road ˅
  Hughes, Langston
On the Road One Day, Lord
  Green, Paul
On the Truth of the Savior
  Horton, George Moses
On the Way Home
  Hughes, Langston
On Trains
  McPherson, James Alan
On Universalism
  Knight, Etheridge
On Virtue
  Wheatley, Phillis
On Visiting a Dead Man on a Summer Day
  Piercy, Marge
On Watching a World Series Game
  Sanchez, Sonia
On Wearing Ears
  Harris, William J.
Once
  Walker, Alice
Once Upon a Time
  Jones, James Arlington
The One
  Pitcher, Oliver
One
  Rodgers, Carolyn M.
1½ Seasons
  Spellman, Alfred B.
One April
  Pitts, Lucia Mae
One Day
  Pitts, Lucia Mae
One Day We Played a Game
  Cullen, Countee Porter
One-eyed Black Man in Nebraska
  Cornish, Sam
One Friday Morning
  Hughes, Langston
One Last Word
  Turner, Darwin T.
One Sided Shoot-Out
  Lee, Don L.

One Spark Can Light a Prairie Fire
  Neal, Larry
One Thousand Nine Hundred and Sixty-Eight Winters . . .
  Earley, Jacqueline
One Time Henry Dreamed the Number 47
  Long, Doughtry
One, Two, Three
  Sirrah, Leumas
One Way
  Whitaker, Tommy
One Way to Heaven
  Cullen, Countee Porter
One Way to Victory
  Ford, Nick Aaron
One-Way Ticket
  Hughes, Langston
One Year Ago
  Llorens, David
Onion Bucket
  Thomas, Lorenzo
The Only Man on Liberty Street
  Kelley, William Melvin
Only My Words
  Davis, Frank Marshall
The Only One
  Lee, Don L.
O-o-oo-ld Miss Liza
  Powell, Leslie
Open Letter
  Dodson, Owen
An Open Letter to Thomas Dixon, Jr.
  Miller, Kelly
The Optimist
  Hammond, Mrs. J. W.
The Optimist
  Lewis, Ethyl
Opportunities for Development of Negro Talent
  Killens, John Oliver
Oppression
  Hughes, Langston
Opus 7
  Harris, Helen C.
Orange
  Graham, Linda B.
Orange Soda and Chocolate Cupcakes
  Bush, Joseph Bevans
An Oration Commemorative of the Abolition of the Slave Trade; Delivered Before the Wilberforce Philanthropic Association, January, 1809
  Sidney, Joseph
Oration Delivered in Corinthian Hall, Rochester, July 5, 1852
  Douglass, Frederick
An oration delivered in the African Zion Church on July 4, 1827, in Commemoration of the Abolition of Domestic Slavery in this State, 1827.
  Hamilton, William
Oration on the Abolition of the Slave Trade
  Eagans, Peter Malachi
An Oration on the Abolition of the Slave Trade: Delivered in the African Church, in the

city of N.Y., Jan. 1, 1808, With an introductory Essay by Henry Sipkins
Williams, Peter
An Oration on the Abolition of the Slave Trade; Delivered in the African Church, in the Ctiy of N.Y., January 2, 1809.
Sipkins, Henry
An oration on the Abolition of the Slave Trade, Delievered in the Episcopal Asbury African Church, in Elizabeth Street, New York, January 2, 1815
Hamilton, William
Oration on the Abolition of the Slave Trade, Delivered on the First Day of January, 1813 in the African Methodist-Episcopal Church, 1813
Lawrence, George
An oration on the abolition of the slave trade delivered on the first of January, 1814, at the African Church of St. Thomas.
Parrott, Russell
Orators and Oratory
Allen, William G.
The Ordeal
Johnson, Georgia Douglas
The Ordeal of Richard Wright
Ford, Nick Aaron
The Organizer
Thelwell, Michael
Oriflamme
Fauset, Jessie Redmond
Origin and Growth of Afro-American Literature
Clarke, John Henrik
The Origin, Horrors and Results of Slavery, 1834–
Quinn, William Paul
Origins
Kgositsile, Keorapetse William
Orishas
Neal, Larry
Orison
Rivers, Conrad Kent
Ostriches and Grandmothers
Jones, LeRoi
othello jones dresses for dinner
Roberson, Charles Edwin
Other Nat Turners
Cornish, Sam
The Other Side
Whaley, June D.
The Other Side of Christmas
Meaddough, Ray J., III
Our Country
Monn, Albert
Our Days Are Numbered
Johnson, Alicia Loy
Our Greatest Gift to America
Schuyler, George Samuel
Our Lan'
Ward, Theodore
Our Land
Hughes, Langston
Our Little Renaissance
Locke, Alain Leroy

Our Lives
Scott, Sharon
Our Love Was a War Baby
Tinsley, Tomi Carolyn
Our Meeting
Joseph, Raymond A.
Our Mission
Brooks, William F.
Our Nat Turner and William Styron's Creation
Hamilton, Charles V.
Our Strange Birth
Wright, Richard
Our Task
Ray, Henrietta Cordelia
"our world is"
Wakefield, Jacques
Out in the Still Wet Night
Love, J. Austin
Out of Heaven
Madgett, Naomi Cornelia Long Witherspoon
Out of the Dark
Guinn, Dorothy
The Outcast
Carter, Loleta
The Outcast
McKay, Claude
The Outing
Baldwin, James
Over a Glass of Wine
Mack, L. V.
Over the Line
Stevenson, C. Leigh
The Overcoat
Davis, John Preston
Ovo
Pritchard, Norman Henry II
The Owl Answer
Kennedy, Adrienne
The Owl Killer
Dean, Philip Hayes
Oyster Man's Cry
Johnson, James Weldon

Pa
Smart, Alice McGee
Pa Sees Again
Dixon, Edwina S.
Pachuta /a Memoir
Young, Alexander
Packey
Culbertson, Ernest H.
Paean
Brooks, Jonathan Henderson
The Pagan Isms
McKay, Claude
Pagan Prayer
Cullen, Countee Porter
Pain in One
Hughes, Langston
The Painful Question
Wims, Warner B.
Pains With a Light Touch
Lee, Don L.

The Painted Lady
  Danner, Margaret
The Painter
  McBrown, Gertrude Parthenia
The Pale Blue Casket
  Pitcher, Oliver
The Palm Porch
  Walrond, Eric
The Palm Wine Seller
  Hayford, Gladys May Casely
Pansy
  Newsome, Mary Effie Lee
Panther
  Cornish, Sam
The Panther
  Ray, Irvin
Panther Man
  Emanuel, James A., Sr.
The Paper Boy
  Hiner, Edna
paper route
  Moreland, Charles King, Jr.
Pappy's Last Song
  Jeffrey, Maurine L.
Parade
  Hughes, Langston
Paradox
  Clark, Peter Willington
The Paradox
  Dunbar, Paul Laurence
Paradox
  Grimke, Angelina Weld
The Paradox of Color
  White, Walter
Parapoetics
  Redmond, Eugene B.
Parasitosis
  Davis, Ronda Marie
Parcy Jutridge
  Pritchard, Norman Henry II
Pardon me while I pretend
  Bell, George R.
The Park in Milan
  Smith, William Jay
the parking lot world of sergeant pepper
  Johnson, Charles Bertram
The Party
  Dunbar, Paul Laurence
Party Solicitor
  Jones, James Arlington
Passage
  Pritchard, Norman Henry II
Passing
  Hughes, Langston
Passing
  Stevens, Ruby
The Passing of Grandison
  Chesnutt, Charles Waddell
Passive Resistance
  Danner, Margaret
Pastels
  Fields, Julia
Pastourelle
  Hayes, Donald Jeffrey
Paternal
  Wilson, Ernest J., Jr.

The Path of Dreams
  McClellan, George Marion
Pathology of Race Prejudice
  Frazier, E. Franklin
Paths to the Future
  Kgositsile, Keorapetse William
Patience
  Horne, Frank M.
Patience of a People
  Bryant, Frederick James, Jr.
The Patient: Rockland County Sanitarium
  Hernton, Calvin C.
Patriotic Ode on the Fourteenth Anniversary
of the Persecution of Charlie Chaplin
  Kaufman, Bob
Patroness
  Barrax, Gerald William
Pattern
  Hughes, Langston
Patterns of the Harlem Renaissance
  Kent, George E.
Paul Laurence Dunbar
  Corrothers, James David
Paul Laurence Dunbar: The Rejected Symbol
  Turner, Darwin T.
Paul Robeson
  Brooks, Gwendolyn
Paul Robeson and the Provincetowners
  Robeson, Eslanda Goode
Paul Robeson, Negro
  Robeson, Eslanda Goode
The Pauper's Grave
  Clark, Benjamin P.
A Pause for a Fine Phrase
  Emanuel, James A., Sr.
Pavlov
  Madgett, Naomi Cornelia Long Wither-
  spoon
Paying Dues
  Golden, Bernette
Peace
  Hughes, Langston
Peace
  Johnson, Georgia Douglas
Peace
  Miller, Larry A.
Peace
  Morris, James Cliftonne
Peace and Principle
  Taylor, Isabelle McClellan
Peace Is a Fragile Cup
  Davis, Frank Marshall
Peace, the Lot Left Over from Justice
  Reddy, T. J.
Peaches
  Thigpen, William A., Jr.
Peaches
  Musu Ber
Pellets of May 2, 1960
  Browne, Roscoe Lee
Pending Solemnization
  Spriggs, Edward S.
Pennsylvania Station
  Hughes, Langston
Pentecostal Sunday/A Song of Power
  Henderson, David

People
  Clemmons, Carole Gregory
The People Did Not Choose Mr. Washington as a Leader
  Miller, Kelly
People of Gleaming Cities, and of the Lion's and the Leopard's Brood
  Bourke, Sharon
People Who Have No Children Can Be Hard
  Brooks, Gwendolyn
Perception
  Finley, Catherine L.
Perchance
  Tinsley, Tomi Carolyn
Percussions
  Welburn, Ron
Percy
  Myles, Glenn
Percy / 68
  Myles, Glenn
Perhaps
  Kaufman, Bob
Perhaps Not So Soon One Morning
  Gayle, Addison, Jr.
Persecuted, Betrayal, Volkswagon Blues
  Harris, William J.
Personal
  Hughes, Langston
Personal Jihad
  Neal, Gaston
Personal Prayer of Millions
  Taylor, D.
Personality Sketch: Bill
  Davis, Ronda Marie
Perspectives
  Randall, Dudley
The Petition of the People of Colour, Free Men, within the city and suburbs of Philadelphia. To the President, Senate and House of Representatives, December 30, 1799.
  Jones, Absalom
Peut-être
  Jones, James Arlington
Phantom Color Lines
  Hill, Timothy Arnold
Philistinism and the Negro Writer
  Jones, LeRoi
Philodendron
  Collins, Helen Armstead Johnson
Philosophy
  Dunbar, Paul Laurence
Philosophy and Opinions of Marcus Garvey or Africa for the Africans
  Garvey, Marcus
Philosophy for Street Folk
  Thomas, Richard W.
Phoenix
  Rodgers, Carolyn M.
Photograph
  Prettyman, Quandra
Photographs: a Vision of Massacre
  Harper, Michael S.
Piano After War
  Brooks, Gwendolyn
Pick a Bale of Cotton
  Johnson, James Weldon

Picnic: The Liberated
  Holman, Moses Carl
A Picnic with Sinclair Lewis
  Cayton, Horace R.
Picture for Her Dresser
  Hughes, Langston
Pictures
  Major, Clarence
Piece
  Mack, L. V.
Pilate In Modern America
  Allen, George Leonard
The Pilgrims
  McCluskey, John
Pimp: Story of My Life
  Beck, Robert
Pimp's Last March: Death REQuest
  Crouch, Stanley
Pink Toes
  Himes, Chester B.
Pirouette
  Lorde, Audre
Pity Me
  Haywood, Clara H.
Plagiarism for a Trite Love Poem
  Rodgers, Carolyn M.
The Plaint of the Factory Child
  Johnson, Fenton
The Plan
  Brawley, Benjamin Griffith
A Plan of Peace—Office for the United States
  Banneker, Benjamin
The Plane: Earth
  Sun-Ra
Plans
  Brooks, Helen Morgan
Play a Blues for Louise
  Cuney, Waring
A Plea
  Bohanon, Mary
Plea
  Harris, Helen C.
Plea
  Hill, Edna White
The Plea
  Wright, Richard
Plea for the Politic Man
  Wright, Jay
Plea to My Sister Carolyn Cunningham: the Artist
  Cunningham, James
Please
  Jackson, Mae
The Pleasures
  Payne, Rev. Daniel A.
Pledge
  Smallwood, Will
The Plight—Theme variation fugue and coda
  Thompson, James W.
Plowin' Cane
  Holloway, John Wesley
Plumes
  Johnson, Georgia Douglas
Po' Boy Blues
  Hughes, Langston

Po' Sandy
  Chesnutt, Charles Waddell
The Pocketbook Game
  Childress, Alice
Poem
  Cuestas, Katherine L.
Poem
  Dickinson, Blanche Taylor
Poem
  House, G. L.
Poem
  Hughes, Langston
Poem
  Oliver, Georgiana
Poem
  Stewart, James T.
Poem: a Negro in Two Parts
  Scott, Johnie H.
Poem: A Piece
  Stewart, James T.
Poem Addressed to Women
  Harper, Frances Ellen Watkins
Poem and ½ for Blackwoman
  Pfister, Arthur
Poem at Thirty
  Sanchez, Sonia
Poem By a Slave
  Horton, George Moses
Poem Composed for the Soirée of the Vigilant
Committee of Philadelphia
  Payne, Rev. Daniel A.
Poem/Ditty-Bop
  Rodgers, Carolyn M.
A Poem for a Poet
  Lorde, Audre
Poem for Aretha
  Giovanni, Nikki
Poem for Black Boys
  Giovanni, Nikki
A Poem for Black Hearts
  Jones, LeRoi
Poem for B.M.C. No. 1
  Giovanni, Nikki
A Poem for Children, with Thoughts on
Death
  Hammon, Jupiter
Poem (for d c's 8th graders—1966–67)
  Sanchez, Sonia
A Poem for Democrats
  Jones, LeRoi
Poem For E. J. Summer '71
  Crews, Stella Louise
Poem for Eric Dolphy
  Graham, Donald L.
poem for ethridge
  Sanchez, Sonia
Poem for Flora
  Giovanni, Nikki
A Poem for Heroes
  Fields, Julia
A Poem for Integration
  Saxon, Alvin A.
A Poem for Jill / 68
  Myles, Glenn
Poem for Joyce
  Scott, Johnie H.

Poem for Larry Ridley
  Simmons, Judy Dothard
Poem for My Children
  Sanchez, Sonia
Poem for my family: Hazel Griffin and
Victor Hernandez Cruz
  Jordan, June Meyer
A Poem for My Father
  Sanchez, Sonia
Poem for Painters
  Henderson, David
Poem For Pearl Primus' Dancers
  Dodson, Owen
a poem for positive thinkers
  McBain, Barbara Mahone
Poem from the Empire State
  Jordan, June Meyer
Poem: Let us Poets put away our pens
  Fields, Julia
Poem: Little Brown Boy
  Johnson, Helene Hubbell
A Poem Looking for a Reader
  Lee, Don L.
Poem (No Name N. 3) (The Black Revo-
lution Is Passing You By)
  Giovanni, Nikki
Poem of Angela Yvonne Davis
  Giovanni, Nikki
Poem: On My Happy/Matrimonial Condition
  Jordan, June Meyer
Poem: The night is beautiful
  Hughes, Langston
Poem to a Nigger Cop
  Hamilton, Bobb
Poem To Americans
  Jackson, Gerald
A Poem to Complement Other Poems
  Lee, Don L.
Poem to the Hip Generation
  Moore, David
Poem: "You said. don't write me a love
poem . . ."
  Lomax, Pearl Cleage
Poem: You Went Away
  Jefferson, Richard
Poem for Friends
  Troupe, Quincy
Poem for Herbie Nichols
  Harrison, DeLeon
Poem for the Birthday of Huey Newton
  Torregian, Sotere
A Poem Some People Will Have to Under-
stand
  Jones, LeRoi
Poem to American Poets
  Cullen, Countee Porter
Poems
  Lester, Julius
Poems About Playmates
  Davis, Ronda Marie
Poems: Birmingham 1962–1964
  Fields, Julia
Poems for Half White College Students
  Jones, LeRoi
Poems for Malcolm
  Rodgers, Carolyn M.

Poems for My Brother Kenneth, VII
  Dodson, Owen
Poems for the Lonely
  Jackson, Mae
Poems for Thel—The Very Tops of Trees
  Major, Joseph
Poems for two cities
  Fields, Julia
Poems Modern
  Greene, Carl H.
The Poet
  Anderson, Alice D.
The Poet
  Brooks, Jonathan Henderson
Poet
  Cotter, Joseph Seamon, Sr.
The Poet
  Cullen, Countee Porter
The Poet
  Dandridge, Raymond Garfield
The Poet
  Dunbar, Paul Laurence
Poet
  Hayes, Donald Jeffrey
The Poet and Dreamer
  Jordan, Norman
The Poet and the Baby
  Dunbar, Paul Laurence
The Poet Deserts His Ivory Tower
  Madgett, Naomi Cornelia Long Wither-
  spoon
A Poet Questions His Immortality
  Turner, Claire
The Poet Speaks
  Johnson, Georgia Douglas
Poet to Bigot
  Hughes, Langston
A Poetess
  Carter, Herman J. D.
Poetic Reflections Enroute to and during the
Funeral and Burial of Henry Dumas, Poet
  Redmond, Eugene B.
Poetic Themes
  Cantoni, Louis J.
Poetry
  Martinez, Lydia
Poetry
  Priestley, Eric John
Poetry
  Young, Alexander
Poetry in the Harlem Renaissance
  Moore, Gerald
Poetry Lesson
  Cruz, Victor Hernandez
The Poetry of Three Revolutionists: Don L.
Lee, Sonia Sanchez, and Nikki Giovanni
  Palmer, R. Roderick
Poets
  Pitts, Lucia Mae
The Poet's Fable Petition
  Horton, George Moses
The Poet's Guilt
  Pfister, Arthur
A Poet's Odyssey
  Tolson, Melvin Beaunorus

Point of Departure: Fire Dance Fire Song
  Kgositsile, Keorapetse William
Point of No Return
  Evans, Mari
Poker Party
  Kelley, William Melvin
Polarity
  Cooper, Charles B.
The Policeman
  Fields, Julia
The Politics of Ellison's Booker: Invisible
Man As Symbolic History
  Kostelanetz, Richard
The Politics of Rich Painters
  Jones, LeRoi
poll
  Roberson, Charles Edwin
Pome for Dionne Warwick aboard the air-
craft carrier U. S. S. Enterprise
  Snellings, Rolland
Pome For Weird Hearts and All You Mothers
  Alhamisi, Ahmed Akinwole
Pomp's Case Argued
  Davis, Daniel Webster
Ponce DeLeon/a Morning Walk
  Young, Alexander
Pool Hall
  MBembe
Poor Boy Blues
  Thomas, Ramblin'
Poor Renaldo
  Madgett, Naomi Cornelia Long Wither-
  spoon
The Poor Wife and the Rich Wife
  Ellis, Alfred B.
Poppa Chicken
  Walker, Margaret Abigail
Poppa's Come Home
  Brown, Elaine
Poppa's Story
  Meaddough, Ray J. III
Popsicle Cold
  Jordan, Norman
Porky
  Clemmons, Carole Gregory
Portrait
  Adams, Jeanette
Portrait
  Allen, George Leonard
Portrait
  Rodgers, Carolyn M.
Portrait in Black Soul
  Cousins, Linda
Portrait in Georgia
  Toomer, Jean
Portrait: Jimmy Mack
  Taylor, Prentiss, Jr.
Portrait Number One
  Crews, Stella Louise
Portrait Number Two
  Crews, Stella Louise
Portrait of a Poet
  Butler, James Alpheus
Portrait of a White Nigger
  Rodgers, Carolyn M.

Portrait of Johnny Doller
  Graham, Donald L.
Portrait of Malcolm X
  Knight, Etheridge
Portrait of Wallace Thurman
  Henderson, Mae Gwendolyn
Portrait Philippines
  Duckett, Alfred A.
Positive for Sterling Plumpp
  Lee, Don L.
positives
  Latimore, Jewel Christine
Possum
  Dunbar, Paul Laurence
Post War Ballad
  Johnson, Dorothy Vena
Postscript
  Rivers, Conrad Kent
Power and Racism
  Carmichael, Stokely
Powers of Love
  Horton, George Moses
Practical Concerns
  Harris, William J.
Praise Due to Gwen Brooks
  Conley, Cynthia M.
Praise of Creation
  Horton, George Moses
Pray For The Lovers
  Cortez, Jayne
Prayer
  Brown, Isabella Maria
A Prayer
  Cotter, Joseph Seamon, Jr.
Prayer
  Cuney, Waring
Prayer
  Hughes, Langston
Prayer
  Margetson, George Reginald
Prayer
  Toomer, Jean
A Prayer
  Zealy, Yolande
Prayer/15
  Thomas, Richard W.
Prayer for a Hill
  Beverly, Katherine
Prayer Meeting, or, The First Militant Minister
  Caldwell, Ben
Prayer of the Oppressed
  Whitfield, James M.
A Prayer of the Race That God Made Black
  Watkins, Lucian Bottow
Prayer to the Muse of Song
  Mitchell, Matthew
Prayer To The White Man's God
  Anderson, Charles
Prayers of God
  DuBois, William Edward Burghardt
The Preacher: Ruminates Behind the Sermon
  Brooks, Gwendolyn
Precocious Curiosity
  Brown, Linda
Preface to a 20 Volume Suicide Note
  Jones, LeRoi

Prejudice
  Johnson, Georgia Douglas
Prelude
  Braithwaite, Edward
Prelude
  Rivers, Conrad Kent
Prelude for Dixie
  Rivers, Conrad Kent
Premonition
  Rodaniche, Arcadeo
Prescience
  Hayes, Donald Jeffrey
present
  Sanchez, Sonia
President Lincoln's Proclamation of Freedom
  Harper, Frances Ellen Watkins
Presidential Press Parley
  Dooley, Thomas
The Pressures
  Jones, LeRoi
The Prestidigitator [1]
  Young, Alexander
The Prestidigitator [2]
  Young, Alexander
A Pretender
  Graham, Ernestine
Previous Condition
  Baldwin, James
The Price
  Yancey, Bessie Woodson
Pride
  Burton, John W.
Pride and Prejudice
  Smith, Linwood D.
Primary Lesson: the Second Class Citizen
  Sun-Ra
Prime
  Hughes, Langston
A Primer for Today
  Tolson, Melvin Beaunorus
Primeval Mitosis
  Cleaver, Eldridge
The Primitive
  Lee, Don L.
Primitives
  Randall, Dudley
Primrose and Thistle
  Butler, James Alpheus
Princeling
  Evans, Mari
The Principles of the Universal Negro Improvement Association
  Garvey, Marcus
Prison
  Jeffers, Lance
Prisons, prisons
  Durem, Ray
Private Letter to Brazil
  Oden, Gloria Catherine
Pro Patria America, 1861
  Menken, Adah Isaaks
Problem in Social Geometry—the Inverted Square
  Durem, Ray

Proceedings of the New York Anti-Slavery Society, 1837
  Wright, Theodore S.
Procession
  Miller, May
Processional
  Lomax, Pearl Cleage
Proclamation/From Sleep Arise
  Rodgers, Carolyn M.
The Prodigal Son
  Johnson, James Weldon
The Profile on the Pillow
  Randall, Dudley
Progress
  Mebane, Mary Elizabeth
The Progress of Liberty
  Bell, James Madison
Prologue
  Hoagland, Everett
Prologue to a Supposed Play
  Cotter, Joseph Seamon, Sr.
Promenade
  Cornish, Sam
Promise
  Pitts, Lucia Mae
Promise of Equality
  Wright, Stephen J.
The Promise of Strangers
  Moore, Birdell Chew
Promulgations
  Hughes, Langston
Prophecy
  Hayden, Robert Earl
Prophets for a New Day
  Walker, Margaret Abigail
The Prophet's Warning or Shoot to Kill
  Dooley, Thomas
Proposition 15
  Harper, Michael S.
The Prospects of Black Bourgeoisie
  Harris, Abram L.
The Protective Grigri
  Joans, Ted
Protest
  Cullen, Countee Porter
Proud Shoes
  Murray, Pauli
Proverbs
  Jackman, Marvin
Proving
  Johnson, Georgia Douglas
The Pruning
  Miller, Adam David
Psalm for Sonny Rollens
  DeLegall, Walter
The Psalm of the Uplift
  Allen, Junius Mordecai
Psychedelic Fireman
  Henderson, David
Psychological Reactions of Oppressed People
  Wright, Richard
Psychology: The Black Bible
  Cleaver, Eldridge
Puck Goes to Court
  Johnson, Fenton

Pulkha
  Dickerson, Juanita M.
Punctuation Suite
  Pitts, Lucia Mae
Puppet-Player
  Grimke, Angelina Weld
The Puppets Have a New King
  Dumas, Henry L.
Purlie Victorious
  Davis, Ossie
Purple
  Graham, Linda B.
The Purple Flower
  Bonner, Marita
The Pursuit of Things
  Wesley, Charles Harris
put u red-eye in
  Welburn, Ron
Puzzle
  Dunbar, Paul Laurence
Puzzled
  Hughes, Langston
Pygmalion
  Hamilton, Bobb
Pygmies Are Pygmies Still, Though Percht on Alps
  Brooks, Gwendolyn

The Quarrel
  Jeffers, Lance
Quatrains
  Bennett, Gwendolyn B.
Queens of the Universe
  Sanchez, Sonia
Query
  Dooley, Thomas
Query
  Houston, Virginia
Quest
  Madgett, Naomi Cornelia Long Witherspoon
Quest and Quarry
  Wright, Bruce McMarion
Questing
  Spencer, Anne
Question
  Anderson, Charles
Question
  Clarke, John Henrik
Question
  Harris, Helen C.
Question and Answer
  Hughes, Langston
The Question Is
  Evans, Emmery, Jr.
The Question of Power
  Wright, Nathan, Jr.
Question to a Mob
  Gooden, Lauretta Holman
Quicksand
  Larsen, Nella
Quiet Has a Hidden Sound
  Braithwaite, William Stanley Beaumont
A Quiet Place Observed
  Williams, Patricia

A Quiet Talk with Myself
  Gordone, Charles
Quietus
  Russell, Charles L.
The Quilt
  Newsome, Mary Effie Lee
Quo Vadis
  Twitty, Countess W.
A Quoi Bon?
  Smith, Jules Wynn
Quoits
  Newsome, Mary Effie Lee

The Rabbi
  Hayden, Robert Earl
Rabbit Boss
  Sanchez, Thomas
Race
  Davis, Frank Marshall
Race and the Negro Writer
  Gloster, Hugh Morris
Race Compliments
  Sherman, Jimmie
Race Prejudice in America
  Goodwin, Ruby Berkley
The Race Question
  Madgett, Naomi Cornelia Long Wither-
  spoon
Race Results, U.S.A. 1966
  Fabio, Sarah Webster
Rachel
  Grimke, Angelina Weld
Racial Integrity
  Schomburg, Arthur A.
Racial Self-Expression
  Frazier, E. Franklin
Racism and the White Backlash
  King, Martin Luther, Jr.
Racist Psychotherapy
  Black, Isaac J.
The Radical
  Cuney, Waring
Radicals and Conservatives
  Miller, Kelly
Rag Doll and Summer Birds
  Dodson, Owen
Railroad Avenue
  Hughes, Langston
Rain
  Brown, William
Rain
  Brown, William
Rain
  Burton, John W.
Rain
  Turner, John Adolph
The Rain Is in Our Heads
  Rodgers, Carolyn M.
Rain Music
  Cotter, Joseph Seamon, Jr.
Rain Rain on the Splintered Girl
  Reed, Ishmael
A Rain Song
  Johnson, Charles Bertram
The Rain Song
  Rogers, Alex

Rain Wish
  Blackman, Louise
Raindrop
  Tinsley, Tomi Carolyn
Rainy Day
  Lewis, Harry Wythe, Jr.
Rainy Days
  Razafkeriefo, Andrea
Rainy Season Love Song
  Hayford, Gladys May Casely
A Raisin in the Sun
  Hansberry, Lorraine
Raison d'etre
  Pitcher, Oliver
Ralph Ellison: a Critical Study
  Christian, Barbara
Ralph Ellison and the Uses of Imagination
  Bone, Robert
Rape of a Man
  Scott, Eddie, Jr.
Rape of Florida
  Whitman, Albery Allson
Rapping along with Rhonda Davis
  Cunningham, James
Rap's Poem
  Brown, H. Rap
Rat Joiner Routs the Klan
  Poston, Ted
A Rat's Mass
  Kennedy, Adrienne
The Ray
  Milner, Ronald
Ray Charles at Mississippi State
  Dent, Thomas C.
Rays
  Geran, Juliana
"Reach Out"
  Flynn, Javita G.
Reaching Back
  Sharp, Saundra
Re-Act for Action
  Lee, Don L.
Reading from the Record
  Lomax, Pearl Cleage
Reading Walt Whitman
  Forbes, Calvin
The real people loves one another
  Penny, Rob
The Real Question
  Dunbar, Paul Laurence
The Realist
  Greene, Carl H.
Reality
  Clark, Peter Wellington
Reality
  Johnson, Yvette
Reality
  Pitts, Herbert Lee
Realization
  Lankin, Mattie T.
The Realization of a Dream Deferred
  Brown, Fannie Carole
The Reapers
  Toomer, Jean
The Reasons for This State of Mind
  Randolph, A. Philip

Rebel
   Boyd, Samuel E.
Rebel
   England, Jay Raymond
The Rebel
   Evans, Mari
Rebirth
   Giddings, Paula
Recapitulation
   Houston, Virginia
Recessional
   Johnson, Georgia Douglas
The Reckoning
   Madgett, Naomi Cornelia Long Wither-spoon
Reckoning A.M. Thursday After an Encounter
   Linyatta
Reclaiming the Lost African Heritage
   Clarke, John Henrik
Recollection
   Govan, Donald D.
A Recollection for Madrigals
   Wright, Bruce McMarion
Recollections of Seventy Years
   Payne, Rev. Daniel A.
Reconnaissance
   Bontemps, Arna W.
Recreation
   Priestley, Eric John
Red
   Cullen, Countee Porter
Red Bonnet
   Patterson, Lindsay
Red and Yellow Fooles Coat
   Weatherly, Tom
The Red Hat
   Brown, Martha
The Red, the Black and the Green
   Anderson, S. E.
Red-Bone Hound
   Ford, Heywood
Reena
   Marshall, Paule
Reflection
   Scott, Eddie, Jr.
Reflection of a Peace Marcher
   Dorsey, David
Reflections
   Gardner, Carl
Reflections
   Howard, Vanessa
Reflections on a Lost Love
   Lee, Don L.
Reflections on April 4, 1968
   Giovanni, Nikki
Reflections on Richard Wright: a Symposium on an Exiled Native Son
   Bontemps, Arna W.
Reflections on Richard Wright: a Symposium on an Exiled Native Son
   Cayton, Horace R.
Reflections on Richard Wright; a Symposium on an Exiled Native Son
   Hill, Herbert

Reflections on Richard Wright: a Symposium on an Exiled Native Son
   Redding, Jay Saunders
Reflections Written on Visiting the Grave of a Venerated Friend
   Plato, Ann
The Reformer
   Thomas, Richard W.
Refugee
   Madgett, Naomi Cornelia Long Wither-spoon
Refugee in America
   Hughes, Langston
The Regal
   Mebane, Mary Elizabeth
Regenesis
   Welburn, Ron
Rehabilitation and Treatment
   Martinez, Joe
reincarnation
   Jackson, Mae
Rejoice
   Clorox
Relating to the People
   Whaley, June D.
Relations and Duties of Free Colored Men in America to Africa
   Crummell, Alexander
Release
   Lambert, Calvin S.
Release
   Murphy, Beatrice M.
Religion and the Pure Principles of Morality, the Sure Foundation on Which We Must Build, Oct. 1831
   Stewart, Marie
Religion, Poetry and History: Foundations for a New Educational System
   Walker, Margaret Abigail
Remarks at the American Academy of Arts and Sciences Conference on the Negro American, 1965.
   Ellison, Ralph Waldo
Remarks on the subject of Temperance, delivered before the American Moral Reform Society, in St. Thomas Church, Pa. Aug. 16th, 1837.
   Cook, John Francis
Remember
   Johnson, Georgia Douglas
Remember
   Williams, Vincent
Remember Not
   Johnson, Helene Hubbell
Remember Times For Sandy
   Rodgers, Carolyn M.
Remember: when the door closes you in
   Graham, Donald L.
Remembering Nat Turner
   Brown, Sterling A.
Remembrance
   Burbridge, Edward Dejoie
Remembrance of a Lost Dream
   Williams, Edward G.
Remigrant
   Hernton, Calvin C.

Remnant Ghosts at Dawn
LaGrone, Oliver
The Renaissance Re-examined
Hadlin, Warrington
Rencontre
Fauset, Jessie Redmond
Rendezvous
Hughes, Lois Royal
Rendezvous with God
Goodwin, Ruby Berkley
The Repeal of the Missouri Compromise Considered
Rogers, Elymas Payson
Reply to His Old Mistress
Loguen, Jermain W.
Report
Harper, Frances Ellen Watkins
Reprobate
Shaed, Dorothy Lee Louise
Reptile
Raven, John
Requiem
Chapman, Nell
Requiem
Johnson, Georgia Douglas
Requiem
Matheus, John Frederick
Requiem
Pitts, Lucia Mae
Requiem for Brother X
Mackey, William Wellington
Requiem for Tomorrow
Conyus
Requiescat in Pace
Clark, Benjamin P.
Resignation
Beverly, Katherine
Resolutions at Harper's Ferry, 1906
DuBois, William Edward Burghardt
Resolutions of the People of Color, at a meeting held on the 25th of January, 1831. with an address to the Citizens of New York, 1831, in answer to those of the New York Colonization Society
Bell, Philip
Resolutions of the people of Color, at a Meeting held on the 25th of January, 1831, With an address to the Citizens of New York, 1831 In answer to those of the New York Colonization Society
Ennals, Samuel
A Resonant Silence
Llorens, David
Response
Kaufman, Bob
A Response to the Visiting Poet's Name
Clemmons, Carole Gregory
Responsive Reading
Lomax, Pearl Cleage
Resurrection
Giddings, Paula
Resurrection
Horne, Frank M.
Resurrection
Margetson, George Reginald

Retaliation
Tinsley, Tomi Carolyn
Retrospect
Lomax, Pearl Cleage
Retrospection
Johnson, Georgia Douglas
Retrospection
McLean, Eldon George
Retrospection of a Black Woman
Vaughn, Naomi Evans
The Return
Bontemps, Arna W.
Return
Brown, Sterling A.
Return of the Native
Jones, LeRoi
The Reunion
Dodson, Owen
Reveille
Jackson, James Thomas
The Revelation
Crouch, Stanley
Revelation
Dickinson, Blanche Taylor
Revelation
Lawrence, Joyce Whitsitt
Revelations
Brown, Sterling A.
Review from Staten Island
Oden, Gloria Catherine
Revolt in the South
Dismond, Henry Binga
Revolt of the Angels
Clarke, John Henrik
The Revolt of the Evil Fairies
Poston, Ted
Revolution Man Black
Goss, Linda
Revolution
Thomas, Richard W.
Revolution?/Illusion?
Randall, Jon
Revolutionary Music
Giovanni, Nikki
Revolutionary Nationalism and the Afro-American
Cruse, Harold
The Revolutionary Screw
Lee, Don L.
The Revolutionary Theatre
Jones, LeRoi
A Revolutionary Tale
Giovanni, Nikki
Reward Ungiven
Jones, James Arlington
Rhapsody
Braithwaite, William Stanley Beaumont
Rhythm Is a Groove (#2)
Neal, Larry
Rhythm Section/Part One
Cruz, Victor Hernandez
Richard Hunt's Arachne
Hayden, Robert Earl
Richard Wright's Blues
Ellison, Ralph Waldo

The Richer, the Poorer
  West, Dorothy
The Riddle
  Johnson, Georgia Douglas
Riddle of the Sphinx
  DuBois, William Edward Burghardt
The Rider of Dreams
  Torrence, Ridgley
Riders to the Blood-Red Wrath
  Brooks, Gwendolyn
Riding Across John Lee's Finger
  Crouch, Stanley
Riding the Bus Home
  Witherspoon, Jill
Riding the Goat
  Miller, May
Right-Mindedness
  Crummell, Alexander
Right Now
  Crouch, Stanley
Right on: White America
  Sanchez, Sonia
A Right Proper Burial
  Richardson, Alice I.
The Right Thing
  Lacy, Ed
The Right to Criticize American Institutions
  Douglass, Frederick
Ring-around-the-Rosy
  Cumbo, Kattie M.
Riot
  Brooks, Gwendolyn
Riot Laugh and I Talk
  Henderson, David
Riot Rimes: U.S.A.
  Patterson, Raymond Richard
Riots and Rituals
  Thomas, Richard W.
Rip-off
  Davis, Ronda Marie
Rippling Shadows
  Cunningham, James
The Rise
  Fuller, Charles H., Jr.
Rise! Young Negro—Rise!
  Fenner, John J., Jr.
The Rising
  Cortez, Jayne
The Rite
  Randall, Dudley
Rites for Cousin Vit
  Brooks, Gwendolyn
Rites Fraternal
  Barber, John
Rites of Passage
  Lorde, Audre
The Rivals
  Dunbar, Paul Laurence
Riven Quarry
  Oden, Gloria Catherine
The River
  Cornish, Sam
River George
  Lee, George Washington
River Voices
  Cunningham, James

Rivers of Bones and Flesh and Blood
  Redmond, Eugene B.
The Roach
  Raven, John
The Road
  Johnson, Helene Hubbell
Road to Anywhere
  Johnson, Dorothy Vena
The Road to the Bow
  Corrothers, James David
Roadblocks to the Development of Negro Writers
  Wright, Sarah E.
Roaring Third
  Johnson, Helen Aurelia
Robert G. Shaw
  Ray, Henrietta Cordelia
Robert Gould Shaw
  Dunbar, Paul Laurence
Robert Hayden's Use of History
  Davis, Charles T.
Robert Whitmore
  Davis, Frank Marshall
Robin Red Breast
  Weeden, Lula Lowe
A Robin's Poem
  Giovanni, Nikki
Robin's Strange Assignment
  Cannon, Steve
Robobuchinary X-mas/Eastuh julie 4/etc etc etc etc
  Rodgers, Carolyn M.
Rock, Church
  Hughes, Langston
Rock, Church, Rock!
  Bontemps, Arna W.
The Rock Pile
  Baldwin, James
Rocks
  Barrett, Lindsay
Roland Hayes
  Brown, Sterling A.
Roland Hayes
  Tolson, Melvin Beaunorus
Roland Hayes Beaten
  Hughes, Langston
Role of the Negro Writer in an Era of Struggle
  Fuller, Hoyt W.
Romance
  McKay, Claude
Rome Is Dying
  Johnson, Fenton
Rondeau
  Fauset, Jessie Redmond
Rondeau Redoublé
  Riquet, Nicol
The Room
  Harrison, DeLeon
Roosevelt Smith
  Davis, Frank Marshall
Roots
  Carter, Karl
Rosalie Pritchett
  Molette, Barbara J. and Carlton W.

Rose Petals
Harris, Helen C.
Rosedale Street
Cox, Walter
Roses and Revolutions
Randall, Dudley
Rotation
Bond, Horace Julian
Rough Diamond
Killens, John Oliver
'Round 'Bout Midnight, Opus 17
Johnston, Percy Edward
Round Table
Kenner, Peggy Susberry
'Round the Neighborhood
Howard, Floretta
Round Trip Ticket
Harris, Helen C.
The royal palms
Walcott, Derek
Roy's Wound
Baldwin, James
Rubin
Cooper, Charles B.
The Rubinstein Staccato Etude
Dett, Robert Nathaniel
Ruby Brown
Hughes, Langston
Ruby-Jane, Mother-Wife
Morris, James Cliftonne
Rude Awakening
Grant, Micki
Rudolph Is Tired of the City
Brooks, Gwendolyn
Rulers
Johnson, Fenton
Runagate Runagate
Hayden, Robert Earl
Runner Mack
Beckham, Barry
Rush City—The Hale
Redmond, Eugene B.
Russian Cathedral
McKay, Claude
Rustic Love
Brown, Joe C.
Ruth's Story
VanDyke, Henry
Rye Bread
Braithwaite, William Stanley Beaumont

S. C. M.
Wilson, Ted
S. C. Threw S. C. into the Railroad Yard
Joans, Ted
Sacred Chant for the Return of Black Spirit and Power
Jones, LeRoi
The Sacrifice
Barrax, Gerald William
Sacrifice
Duncan, Thelma Myrtle
The Sacrifice
Jordan, Norman
Sacrificial Ritual
Alhamisi, Ahmed Akinwole

Sad and Blue
Harris, Howard
The Saddest Tears
Durem, Ray
Sadie and Maud
Brooks, Gwendolyn
Sadie's Playhouse
Danner, Margaret
Safeguard
Murphy, Beatrice M.
Safari
Long, Worth
Safari West
Williams, John Alfred
Saga of Resistance
Sun-Ra
Sahdji
Nugent, Bruce
Sailors on Leave
Dodson, Owen
Saint Francis of Assisi
DuBois, William Edward Burghardt
Saint Is a Soul Brother
Bush, Joseph Bevans
Saint Isaac's Church, Petrograd
McKay, Claude
Saint Julien's Eve: for Dennis Cross
Cunningham, James
Saint Louis Blues and Solvent Bank
Handy, W. C.
Saint Louis Woman
Bontemps, Arna W., and C. Cullen
Saint Louis Woman
Cullen, Countee Porter and Arna Botemps
Saint Malcolm
Latimore, Jewel Christine
Saint Paul and the Monkeys
Kelley, William Melvin
Saint Peter Relates an Incident of the Resurrection Day
Johnson, James Weldon
Sallie Jewel
Crouch, Stanley
Sally: Twelfth Street
Madgett, Naomi Cornelia Long Witherspoon
Salt Water
Stokes, Deborah
Salutamus
Brown, Sterling A.
Salute
Pitcher, Oliver
Salute to the Passing
Himes, Chester B.
Salute to the Tan Yanks
Griffin, Amos J.
Salvation
Jones, Gayle
Samantha Is My Negro Cat
Harris, William J.
Sambas and Things
Witherspoon, Jill
Same in Blues
Hughes, Langston
Sammy Lee
Sherman, Jimmie

Samory
  Miller, May
Sam's World
  Cornish, Sam
San Francisco
  Roberts, Walter Adolphe
san francisco county jail cell b-6
  Conyus
Sanctuary
  Dumas, Henry L.
Sanctuary
  Randall, Dudley
Sandals
  Jeffers, Lance
The Sand-Clock Day
  Dolan, Harry
Sandy Star
  Braithwaite, William Stanley Beaumont
Santa Claus Is a White Man
  Clarke, John Henrik
Santa Claws
  Joans, Ted
Sapling
  Johnson, Yvette
Sarah
  Hamer, Martin J.
Sarcasmes
  Wright, Bruce McMarion
Sassafras Memories
  Spriggs, Edward S.
Sassafras Tea
  Newsome, Mary Effie Lee
Satchmo
  Tolson, Melvin Beaunorus
Satori
  Jones, Gayle
Saturday
  Woodson, Jon
Saturday Night in Harlem
  Browne, William
Saturday's Child
  Cullen, Countee Porter
The Savage Dreamer
  Fortune, Timothy Thomas
Say It Loud, I'm Black and I'm Proud
  Brown, James
Scamp
  Dunbar, Paul Laurence
Scapegoat
  Dunbar, Paul Laurence
Scarlet Woman
  Johnson, Fenton
Scarecrow People
  Hernton, Calvin C.
Scenery
  Joans, Ted
Schemin'
  Lomax, Pearl Cleage
A Scholar Looks at an Oak
  Tolson, Melvin Beaunorus
School integration riot
  Hayden, Robert Earl
Schwerner, Chaney, Goodman
  Patterson, Raymond Richard
Scintilla
  Braithwaite, William Stanley Beaumont

Sciplinin' Sister Brown
  Campbell, James Edwin
Scotsboro, Too, Is Worth Its Song
  Cullen, Countee Porter
The Screamers
  Jones, LeRoi
The Screens
  Wilson, Charles E.
The Scuba Diver Recovers the Body of a
Drowned Child
  Barrax, Gerald William
Sea Charm
  Hughes, Langston
Searching
  Clorox
Search for a new land
  Lester, Julius
Seascape
  Randall, James A., Jr.
Seasonal
  Tinsley, Tomi Carolyn
The Seasons
  Perry, Robert N., Jr.
The Sea-Turtle and the Shark
  Tolson, Melvin Beaunorus
Secon' Pickin'
  Brewer, J. Mason
Second Avenue Encounter
  Patterson, Raymond Richard
The Second Coming
  Clark, Carl
Second Line/Cutting the Body Loose
  Ferdinand, Val
The Second Plane
  Jordan, Norman
2nd Solo
  Thomas, Richard W.
The Second Unveiling
  Scott, Eddie, Jr.
Secret
  Bennett, Gwendolyn B.
The Secrets II
  Cruz, Victor Hernandez
Sectional Touchstone
  Benitez, Lillie Kate Walker
Seduction
  Giovanni, Nikki
See How They Run
  Vroman, Mary Elizabeth
See What Tomorrow Brings
  Thompson, James W.
The Seed of a Slum's Eternity
  Priestley, Eric John
Seed of Nimrod
  Harrison, DeLeon
Seeds
  Snyder, Thurmond L.
A Seeing Eye-Dog
  Sharp, Saundra
Seizin
  Fields, Julia
The Seer
  Butcher, James W., Jr.
Selassie at Geneva
  Christian, Marcus Bruce

Self
  Pritchard, Norman Henry II
Self
  Skeeter, Sharyn Jeanne
Self-criticism
  Cullen, Countee Porter
Self-determination (The Philosophy of the American Negro)
  Hill, Leslie Pinckney
The Self-Hatred of Don L. Lee
  Lee, Don L.
Self World
  Major, Clarence
The Seminole
  Clark, Benjamin P.
Sence You Went Away
  Johnson, James Weldon
The Senegalese
  Fuller, Hoyt W.
A Sense of Coolness
  Troupe, Quincy
A September Night
  McClellan, George Marion
Sept. 26, 1967
  Thomas, Richard W.
Sequel to the Above
  Spellman, Alfred B.
Sequel to the Pied Piper of Hamlin
  Cotter, Joseph Seamon, Sr.
A Sequence from the Roach Rider, a play
  Smith, Welton
Sergeant Jerk
  Wess, Deborah Fuller
The Sermon
  Sister Bernadine
Sermon From the Thirteenth Floor of a Tomb
  Thomas, Richard W.
Sermon on the Warpland
  Brooks, Gwendolyn
Sermonette
  Reed, Ishmael
A Serpent Smiles
  Evans, Mari
Serraveza
  Fuller, Hoyt W.
Service
  Johnson, Georgia Douglas
Service, Please
  Gorham, Myrtle Campbell
The Serving Girl
  Hayford, Gladys May Casely
Setting/Slow Drag
  Rodgers, Carolyn M.
The Setting Sun
  Horton, George Moses
Seventh Avenue Poem
  Bullins, Ed
seventh son
  Roberson, Charles Edwin
Seventh Street
  Toomer, Jean
Shade of Darkness
  Jackson, James Thomas
Shades of Pharoh Sanders Blues for My Baby
  O'Neal, John

Shadji, an African Ballet
  Bruce, Richard
Shadow
  Bruce, Richard
Shadow and Sun
  Brown, William
Shadow of the Plantation
  Johnson, Charles S.
Shadows
  Clarke, Helen F.
Shadows
  Smith, James Edgar
Shakespeare
  Ray, Henrietta Cordelia
Shall Race Hatred Prevail
  Watson, Adeline Carter
Shallow Pools
  Walter, Nina Willis
Sharon Will Be No/Where on Nobody's Best Selling List
  Scott, Sharon
The "Shaw Monument Speech"
  Washington, Booker Taliaferro
She Left Herself One Evening. Poem by Leon Damas
  Hughes, Langston
She Never Knew?
  Booker, Simeon, Jr.
She of the Dancing Feet Sings
  Cullen, Countee Porter
She Said . . .
  Brooks, Jonathan Henderson
She Walked Alone
  Bates, Daisy
She Wears a Dress
  Jeffers, Lance
She'll Speak To Generations Yet To Come
  Burroughs, Margaret Taylor Goss
Shelter
  Fields, Julia
The Shepherd
  Hyman, Mark
The Sheriff's Children
  Chesnutt, Charles Waddell
Shine On, Mr. Sun
  Allen, Junius Mordecai
Ships that Pass in the Night
  Dunbar, Paul Laurence
A Shit a Riot
  Wakefield, Jacques
The Shoe Shine
  De Saavedra, Guadalupe
Shoe, Tell Me What You Know
  Collazo, Jamie
Shoplifter
  Edwards, Solomon
Shopping for Light
  Thomas, Richard W.
A Short Poem for Frustrated Poets
  Scott, Johnie H.
shorty blue
  Moreland, Charles King, Jr.
Show Me, Lord, Show Me
  Iman, Kasasi Yusef
Shrine To What Should Be
  Evans, Mari

Sic Vita
   Braithwaite, William Stanley Beaumont
Sickle Pears
   Dodson, Owen
The Sickness of America
   Watts, Daniel H.
Sid down Chillun
   Ragland, J. Farley
Sidewalk Blues
   Raphael, Lennox
Sidi' Ahmed Bada: Portrait of a Black Intel-
lectual
   Lawrence, Harold G.
Sight
   Moten, Cora Ball
A Significant Other
   Todd, Joe
The Signs
   Pritchard, Norman Henry II
Signs of Sleep
   Brown, Joe C.
Signs of Spring
   Pickett, Herbert
Signs of the Times
   Dunbar, Paul Laurence
Signals
   Latimore, Jewel Christine
Silent music
   Thompson, James W.
The Silent Prophet
   Jordan, Norman
Silhouette
   Hughes, Langston
Simon the Cyrenian Speaks
   Cullen, Countee Porter
Simple
   **Madgett, Naomi Cornelia Long Wither-
spoon**
Simple Prays a Prayer
   Hughes, Langston
Simple Stakes a Claim
   Hughes, Langston
Simple's Uncle Sam
   Hughes, Langston
Simply Heavenly
   Hughes, Langston
Sing Me a New Song
   Clarke, John Henrik
The Singer
   Danner, James
The Singer
   Jessye, Eva Alberta
Singing Dinah's Song
   Brown, Frank London
Sinner
   Jordan, Norman
Sinner Man, Where You Gonna Run To?
   Neal, Larry
'Sippi
   Killens, John Oliver
Sister Brother
   Goncalves, Joe
A Sister Crosses Over
   Thomas, Richard W.
Sister Lou
   Brown, Sterling A.

Sister Mandy Attends the Business League
   Hamilton, Richard T.
Sister Son/ji
   Sanchez, Sonia
A Sister Speaks of Rapping
   Staples, Shirley
The Sit-In
   Turner, Darwin T.
Sitinner
   Jeffers, Lance
Sitting on the Side of the Bed With My Un-
derwear on . . . Thinking
   Thomas, Richard W.
6:00 A. M.
   Thomas, Richard W.
Six O'Clock
   Dodson, Owen
Six Sunday
   Bibbs, Hart Leroi
six ten sixty-nine
   Conyus
Sixteen
   Cooper, Charles B.
Sixteen, Yeah
   Emanuel, James A., Sr.
Sixth Grade
   Wallace, Michele
Sketch of a Varying Evening Sky
   Boyd, John
Sketches of a Trip Home
   Bradford, William
Sketches of Harlem
   Henderson, David
Skillet Love on Flame
   Cooper, Charles B.
The Sky Is Gray
   Gaines, Ernest J.
Sky Pictures
   Newsome, Mary Effie Lee
The Slave
   Jones, LeRoi
Slave and the Iron Lace
   Danner, Margaret
Slave Auction
   Harper, Frances Ellen Watkins
Slave Days
   Cooper, Charles B.
Slave Life in Georgia
   Brown, John
Slave Mother
   Harper, Frances Ellen Watkins
Slave Narrative
   Steward, Austin
Slave on the Block
   Hughes, Langston
The Slave Raid
   Porter, Kenneth W.
Slavery
   Horton, George Moses
Slave's Complaint
   Horton, George Moses
Sleep Is a Blanket over the Eye
   Jones, Pamela
Slim Greer
   Brown, Sterling A.

Slim in Atlanta
  Brown, Sterling A.
Slim in Hell
  Brown, Sterling A.
Slow Riff for Billy
  Cunningham, James
Slow through the Dark
  Dunbar, Paul Laurence
The Slum
  Campbell, Frank
The Slum
  Danner, Deborah
Slum Dreams
  Hughes, Langston
The Slump
  Bailey, William Edgar
Sly and the Family Stone
  Henderson, David
The Small Bells of Benin
  Danner, Margaret
Small Comment
  Sanchez, Sonia
Smelt Fishing
  Hayden, Robert Earl
No Smiles
  Phillips, Frank Lamont
The Smoking Sixties
  Killens, John Oliver
Smothered Fires
  Johnson, Georgia Douglas
Snake Eyes
  Jones, LeRoi
Snakes
  Young, Alexander
Snapshots of the Cotton South
  Davis, Frank Marshall
Snow
  Shaed, Dorothy Lee Louise
Snow in October
  Dunbar-Nelson, Alice
Snowflakes
  Burton, John W.
So?
  Vaughn, James P.
So Deep in Rivers of That Stromsberg Time
  Jeffers, Lance
So Much
  Johnson, Charles Bertram
So Peaceful in the Country
  Offord, Carl Ruthven
So Quietly
  Hill, Leslie Pinckney
So Softly Smiling
  Himes, Chester B.
So This Is Our Revolution
  Sanchez, Sonia
So Tired
  Williams, Virginia
So We Went to Harlem
  Henderson, David
So We've Come At Last To Freud
  Walker, Alice
The So-Called Western Avant-Garde Drama
  Bullins, Ed
Social Comment
  Fishberg, Lawrence

Social Realism in Charles W. Chesnutt
  Ames, Russell
Social Worker
  Cantoni, Louis J.
Society and Self in Recent American Literature,—for Ralph Ellison
  Scott, Nathan Alexander, Jr.
Soft Birmingham Sunday
  Parker, Thomas L.
Soft Boiled
  Stewart, Ollie
Sojourner Truth
  Fauset, Arthur Huff
Sojourner Truth
  Miller, May
Solace
  Delany, Clarissa Scott
Solar Flight
  Carpenter, Howard
Soldiers of the Dusk
  Johnson, Fenton
Soledad
  Hayden, Robert Earl
Soliloqui
  Collins, Leslie Morgan
Soliloquy
  Parrish, Dorothy C.
Soliloquy of a Turkey
  Dunbar, Paul Laurence
Solitary Visions of a Kaufmanoid
  Cunningham, James
Solitude
  Hall, Carlyle B.
Solo
  Cortez, Jayne
Solo on the Drums
  Petry, Ann Lane
A Solo Song: for Doc
  McPherson, James Alan
Some Aspects of the Negro in Contemporary Literature
  Matheus, John Frederick
Some Brothers Cry
  Weeks, Alan
Some Children Are . . .
  Oslo, Jo Tenjford
Some Day
  Edmonds, Randolph
Some Days! Out Walking Above
  Harrison, DeLeon
Some Get Wasted
  Marshall, Paule
Some Hop-Scotching
  Spriggs, Edward S.
Some Notes on Frederick Douglass . . .
  Jackson, James Thomas
Some Observations on a Black Aesthetic
  Miller, Adam David
Some Observations on the American Race Problem
  Jones, Eugene Kinckle
Some of the Qualities Essential to the Most Successful School Life
  Washington, Booker Taliaferro

Some Personal Reminiscences of Paul Laurence Dunbar
 Arnold, Edward
Some Pseudo Philanthropist
 Harrison, DeLeon
Some Reflections on the Black Aesthetic
 Neal, Larry
Some Smooth Lyrics for a Natural People
 Johnson, Alicia Loy
Some Things Are Very Dear To Me
 Bennett, Gwendolyn B.
Somebody Call (for help)
 Rodgers, Carolyn M.
Somebody's Child
 Wilson, Charles P.
Somebody's Slow Is Another Body's Fast
 Jones, LeRoi
Something Different, Something More
 Murray, Albert
Something Old, Something New
 Greene, Carl H.
Something to Think about and Dig Jazz
 Butler, Reginald
Sometimes I Go to Camarillo and Sit in the Lounge
 Lyle, K. Curtis
Sometimes I Wonder If You
 Crews, Stella Louise
Sometimes My Husband
 Parker, Patricia
Son
 Emanuel, James A., Sr.
Son in the Afternoon
 Williams, John Alfred
Son of lightning
 Cesaire, Aime
The Son of My Father
 Gayle, Addison, Jr.
Son, You Really Can't Laugh About It
 Ellison, Ralph Waldo
Song
 du Cille, Ann
Song
 Dumas, Henry L.
Song
 Dunbar, Paul Laurence
Song
 Holman, Moses Carl
Song
 Hughes, Langston
A Song
 Jamison, Roscoe Conkling
Song
 Jeffers, Lance
Song for a Banjo Dance
 Hughes, Langston
Song for a Dark Girl
 Hughes, Langston
Song for a Negro Wash-woman
 Hughes, Langston
Song for a Suicide
 Hughes, Langston
Song for Aimé Césaire
 Kgositsile, Keorapetse William
The Song (for Kevin)
 Jackson, Gerald

Song for Kwame
 Cortez, Jayne
Song For the First of August
 Bell, James Madison
Song for the Sisters
 Spellman, Alfred B.
Song from Brooklyn
 Cumbo, Kattie M.
Song in Spite of Myself
 Cullen, Countee Porter
A Song No Gentleman Would Sing to Any Lady
 Cullen, Countee Porter
Song of a Goat
 Clark, John Pepper
Song of a Syrian Lace Seller
 Braithwaite, William Stanley Beaumont
Song of Ditta
 Kain, Gylan
The Song of Fire
 Snellings, Rolland
Song of Hannibal
 Christian, Marcus Bruce
A Song of Living
 Braithwaite, William Stanley Beaumont
A Song of Praise
 Cullen, Countee Porter
Song of Sour Grapes
 Cullen, Countee Porter
A Song of Thanks
 Jones, Edward Smyth
Song of the Awakened Negro
 Brown, Ruby Berkeley
Song of the Maimed Soldier
 Willman, Eugene B.
Song of the Moon
 McKay, Claude
Song of the Negro
 Ford, Nick Aaron
Song of the Smoke
 DuBois, William Edward Burghardt
Song of the Son
 Toomer, Jean
Song of Tom
 Hall, Kirkwood M.
Song to X and Son Yet to Be Born
 Tinsley, Tomi Carolyn
Song: Today and Tomorrow
 Braithwaite, William Stanley Beaumont
The Song Turning Back into Itself
 Young, Alexander
Songs for the Cisco Kid #2
 Lyle, K. Curtis
Songs for the People
 Harper, Frances Ellen Watkins
Sonnet for a writer
 Emanuel, James A., Sr.
Sonnet for June
 Gordon, Edythe Mae
Sonnet I (He Came In Silvern Armour Trimmed In Black)
 Bennett, Gwendolyn B.
Sonnet Sequence I
 Turner, Darwin T.
Sonnet Spiritual
 Luper, Luther George, Jr.

Sonnet: These Are No Wind Blown Rumors
  Cullen, Countee Porter
Sonnet to a Negro in Harlem
  Johnson, Helene Hubbell
Sonnet to Negro Soldiers
  Cotter, Joseph Seamon, Jr.
Sonnet II (Some Things Are Very Dear To Me)
  Bennett, Gwendolyn B.
Sonnet: What Am I Saying Now
  Cullen, Countee Porter
Sonnet (Where Are We to Go When This Is Done?)
  Duckett, Alfred A.
The Sonnet—Ballad
  Brooks, Gwendolyn
Sonny's Blues
  Baldwin, James
Sonny's Not Blue
  Greenlee, Sam
Sons
  Clemmons, Francois
Sophisticated Postscript for a Five-Page Letter
  Chappell, Helen F.
Sopranosound, Memory of John
  Bourke, Sharon
Sorrow Is the Only Faithful One
  Dodson, Owen
The Sorrow Songs: the Spirituals
  Locke, Alain Leroy
SOS
  Jones, LeRoi
The Soudan
  Buyson, Clarence F.
Soul
  Black, Austin
Soul
  Graham, Donald L.
Soul
  Lino
Soul
  Simmons, Barbara
Soul and Star
  Johnson, Charles Bertram
Soul Clap Hands and Sing
  Marshall, Paule
Soul Food
  Cleaver, Eldridge
Soul Food
  Hughes, Langston
Soul Food
  Jones, LeRoi
Soul Gone Home
  Hughes, Langston
Soul of Christ
  Cooper, Charles B.
Soul on Ice
  Cleaver, Eldridge
Soul-Smiles
  Anderson, S. E.
Souls of Black Men
  Vaughn, Naomi Evans
Soul on ice
  Jackman, Marvin

Soul Suffering
  Gullins, D. Edna
The Souls of Black Folk
  DuBois, William Edward Burghardt
Sound Flowers
  Johnson, Herschell
Sound of Afro-American History Chapter II
  Anderson, S. E.
Sound of Afro-American Music
  Anderson, S. E.
The Sound of Allah's Horn
  Snellings, Rolland
South African Bloodstone
  Troupe, Quincy
South State Street Profile
  Davis, Frank Marshall
South Street
  Silvera, Edward S.
Southern blues
  Johnson, James Weldon
Southern Colonel
  Edmonds, Randolph
Southern Cop
  Brown, Sterling A.
Southern Justice
  Lee, Ed
A Southern Love Song
  Jones, Joshua Henry, Jr.
Southern Mansion
  Bontemps, Arna W.
Southern Negro Heart Cry
  Parks, Valerie
Southern Road
  Brown, Sterling A.
Southern Road
  Randall, Dudley
Southern Song
  Walker, Margaret Abigail
A Southern Tale
  Farmer, James
Southland
  Alexander, Lewis Grandison
The Southland's Charms
  Whitman, Albery Allson
Souvenir
  Madgett, Naomi Cornelia Long Witherspoon
Souvenirs
  Randall, Dudley
Spacin'
  Davis, Ronda Marie
A Spade Is Just a Spade
  Hawkins, Walter Everette
Spain
  Chittick, Conrad
Spanish Blues
  Black, Lewis
A Sparrow Is a Bird
  Danner, Margaret
The spawn of slums
  Thompson, James W.
Speak Neither of Turning Memory around
  Jones, James Arlington
Speak the Truth to the People
  Evans, Mari

Speakers of the House
  Whitaker, Patrick W.
Speakin' at de Cou'thouse
  Dunbar, Paul Laurence
Spearo's Blues
  Redmond, Eugene B.
Special Assignment
  Patterson, Thomas C.
Special Bulletin
  Hughes, Langston
Special Section for Niggas on the Lower
East side or: Divert the Division and Multiply
  Smith, Welton
Spectrum
  Evans, Mari
Speculum Oris
  Weatherly, Tom
Speech
  Hayden, Robert Earl
Speech at a reception for Mr. Douglass in
England 1846
  Douglass, Frederick
Speech before Sentence
  Langston, Charles
Speech delivered at the Anti-Colonization
Meeting, London, 1833
  Paul, Nathaniel
Speech in Faneuil Hall June 8, 1849
  Douglass, Frederick
Speech on the Death of William Lloyd Gar-
rison
  Douglass, Frederick
Speech on the Fugitive Slave Bill
  Ward, Samuel Ringgold
Speech to the Young . . .
  Brooks, Gwendolyn
Spell It with a Capital
  Barnet, ————
Spin Me a Dream
  Harris, Helen C.
Spinster: Old
  Davis, Frank Marshall
Spirit Enchantment
  Bullins, Ed
The Spirit of Creation Is Blackness
  Jones, LeRoi
The Spirit Voice
  Reason, Charles L.
Spirits
  Cruz, Victor Hernandez
Spirits Unchained
  Kgositsile, Keorapetse William
A Spiritual
  Dunbar, Paul Laurence
Spiritual Cleanliness
  Alhamisi, Ahmed Akinwole
Spiritual Song
  Allen, Richard
Spirituals
  Dunbar, Paul Laurence
Spirituals
  Hughes, Langston
A Splib Odyssey
  Troupe, Quincy
Split Standard
  Bibbs, Hart Leroi

Sporting Beasley
  Brown, Sterling A.
Sprin' Fevah
  Dandridge, Raymond Garfield
Spring
  Clemmons, Carole Gregory
Spring
  Hill, Leslie Pinckney
Spring
  Jones, James Arlington
Spring
  Moore, Willard
Spring Dawn
  McClellan, George Marion
Spring in New Hampshire
  McKay, Claude
Spring in the Jungle
  Redmond, Eugene B.
Spring in the South
  Christian, Marcus Bruce
Spring of Joy
  Guerard, Vera E.
Spring with the Teacher
  Jessye, Eva Alberta
Springtime
  Miller, Clifford Leonard
Springtime, Ghetto, U.S.A.
  Allen, Samuel W.
Spunk
  Hurston, Zora Neale
Square Business
  Penny, Rob
The Squared Circle
  Killebrew, Carol
Stack O'Lee Blues
  Hurt, Mississippi John
The Staircase
  Allen, Samuel W.
The Stake-Out
  Taylor, Jeanne
The Stamper of Life
  Booker, Sue
Stanzas for the First of August
  Whitfield, James M.
Star Journey
  **Madgett, Naomi Cornelia Long Wither-
  spoon**
Star of Ethiopia
  Watkins, Lucian Bottow
Star of the Morning
  Mitchell, Loften
The Starter
  Spence, Eulalie
State/Ment
  Jones, LeRoi
Statement on Aesthetics, Poetics, Kinetics
  Young, Alexander
Statement on Basic Aims and Objectives of the
Organization of Afro-American Unity
  Little, Malcolm
Statement on Black Arts
  Lee, Don L.
Statement on Poetics
  Davis, Frank Marshall
Statement on Poetics
  Fields, Julia

Statement on Poetics
Hayden, Robert Earl
Statement on Poetics
Jones, LeRoi
Statement on Poetics
Lee, Don L.
Statement on Poetics
Madgett, Naomi Cornelia Long Witherspoon
Statement on Poetics
Major, Clarence
Statement on Poetics
Randall, Dudley
Statement on Poetics
Rivers, Conrad Kent
Statement on Poetics
Sanchez, Sonia
Status Quo
Dismond, Henry Binga
Status Symbol
Evans, Mari
The Steel Makers
Harris, Leon R.
The Steps
Williams, Charles P.
Stereo
Lee, Don L.
Stereotype to Archetype: the Negro in American Literary Criticism
Gross, Theodore
Sterling Brown: The New Negro Folk-Poet
Locke, Alain Leroy
Stevedore
Collins, Leslie Morgan
The Stick Up
Killens, John Oliver
Stickin' To de Hoe
Davis, Daniel Webster
Still
Lawrence, Joyce Whitsitt
Still Hue
Hughes, Langston
Still Life: Lady with Birds
Prettyman, Quandra
The Still Soaring Black Angel
Redmond, Eugene B.
The Still Voice of Harlem
Rivers, Conrad Kent
Still with Me, Ghost?
Tinsley, Tomi Carolyn
Stonewall Jackson, 1886
Whitman, Albery Allson
Stonewall Jackson's Waterloo
Murray, Albert
Stopped
Polite, Allen
Storm at Evening
Perry, Robert N., Jr.
Storm Ending
Toomer, Jean
Story of My Life and Work
Washington, Booker Taliaferro
The Story of the Zeros
Cruz, Victor Hernandez
Story/Riff
Rodgers, Carolyn M.

Strange
Fields, Julia
Strange
Harris, William J.
Strange Legacies
Brown, Sterling A.
Strange Ways
Pitts, Lucia Mae
Strategies
Smith, Welton
The Stream
Weeden, Lula Lowe
Stream of Consciousness on Ahmed's Last Drink
Wooten, Charles R.
The Street
Morris, James Cliftonne
The Street
Petry, Ann Lane
The Street Called Petticoat Lane
Smart, Alice McGee
Street Demonstration
Walker, Margaret Abigail
A Street in Kaufman-ville
Cunningham, James
Street scene
Anderson, Charles
The Streets Are Small
Thomas, Edward
Streetscene
Troupe, Quincy
The Strength of Gideon
Dunbar, Paul Laurence
Strictly Matrimony
Hill, Errol
Strictly Speaking
Ragland, J. Farley
Striking the Economic Balance
Johnson, Charles S.
The Strong-Backed Whore
Jeffers, Lance
Strong Horse Tea
Walker, Alice
Strong Men
Brown, Sterling A.
Strong Men, Riding Horses
Brooks, Gwendolyn
Student
Harris, William J.
Study Peace
Jones, LeRoi
Subjection
Walrond, Eric
Substitution
Spencer, Anne
Subterfuge
Twitty, Countess W.
Suburbia
Martinez, Maurice
The Subway
Rivers, Conrad Kent
Subway Rush Hour
Hughes, Langston
Subway Wind
McKay, Claude

Subway Witnesses
  Thomas, Lorenzo
Success
  Johnson, Dorothy Vena
Sudden Flight
  Harris, Helen C.
A Sudden Trip Home In the Spring
  Walker, Alice
Suffer the Children
  Lorde, Audre
Suffrage
  Pickens, William
Sugar Cane
  Wilson, Frank H.
Sugarfields
  McBain, Barbara Mahone
Suicide
  Burton, John W.
Suicide
  Freeman, Carol S.
The Suicide
  Hughes, Langston
The Suicide Note
  Scott, Johnie H.
Suicides
  Jones, James Arlington
Suicide's Note
  Hughes, Langston
Sukardri
  Saxon, Alvin A.
Sula
  Morrison, Toni
Summary
  Sanchez, Sonia
Summer
  Cuney, Waring
The Summer After Malcolm
  Neal, Larry
Summer Magic
  Hill, Leslie Pinckney
Summer Matures
  Johnson, Helene Hubbell
Summer Morn in New Hampshire
  McKay, Claude
Summer Oracle
  Lorde, Audre
Summer's End
  Curtwright, Wesley
Summer Street
  Skeeter, Sharyn Jeanne
A Summer Tragedy
  Bontemps, Arna W.
Summer Words for a Sistuh Addict
  Sanchez, Sonia
Summertime and the Living
  Hayden, Robert Earl
The Sun
  Dunbar, Paul Laurence
The Sun Came
  Knight, Etheridge
A Sun Heals
  Latimore, Jewel Christine
Sun Ritual
  Redmond, Eugene B.
The Sun Went Down in Beauty
  McClellan, George Marion

Suncoming
  LaGrone, Oliver
Sunday Evening at Gwen's
  Sanchez, Sonia
Sunday Morning
  Moreland, Wayne
A Sunday Morning in the South
  Johnson, Georgia Douglas
Sundays Are Special
  Sharp, Saundra
Sundays of Satin-legs Smith
  Brooks, Gwendolyn
Sunglasses
  Silber, Fred
Sunni's Unveiling
  Loftin, Elouise
Sunny
  Madgett, Naomi Cornelia Long Wither-
    spoon
Sunrise
  Snellings, Rolland
Sunrise on the Sunset
  Ford, Wallace
Sunset
  Caution, Ethel
Sunset
  Dunbar, Paul Laurence
Sunset
  Lee, Mary Effie
Sunset Horn
  O'Higgins, Myron
Sunset Thoughts
  Cuney, Waring
Sunsets
  Cantoni, Louis J.
The Suppliant
  Johnson, Georgia Douglas
Supplication
  Cotter, Joseph Seamon, Jr.
Suppression
  Cortez, Jayne
Suppression
  De Saavedra, Guadalupe
Suppression
  Marshall, Lee
Supremacy
  Gillison, Lenora
Supremacy
  Johnson, Leanna F.
Surrender
  Grimke, Angelina Weld
Sursum Corda
  White, Edgar
Survivor: One
  Jones, James Arlington
Suspended
  Bohanon, Mary
Suspension
  Lorde, Audre
The Suttee
  Oxley, Lloyd G.
Sutton E. Griggs: Novelist of the New
Negro
  Gloster, Hugh Morris
Swallow the Lake
  Major, Clarence

Swamp Moccasin
  Matheus, John Frederick
The Swan-Vain Pleasures
  Horton, George Moses
Sweat
  Hurston, Zora Neale
Sweat
  Jones, James Arlington
Sweet Diane
  Barlow, George
Sweet Digestion
  Jones, James Arlington
Sweet Dreams of Comradeship
  Harris, William J.
Sweet Home
  Taylor, Sandra
Sweet Potato Man
  Johnson, James Weldon
Sweet Rough Man
  Rainey, Gertrude "Ma"
A Sweet Thing/Last Thoughts
  Fenner, Lanon A., Jr.
Sweeten 'Tatahs
  Corrothers, James David
Sweethearts in a Mulberry Tree
  Knight, Etheridge
The Swing of Life
  Coleman, Jamye H.
Sybil Warns Her Sister
  Spencer, Anne
Sylvester's Dying Bed
  Hughes, Langston
Symbiosis
  Harris, William J.
Symbol of Courage
  Hamilton, Roland T.
Sympathy
  Dunbar, Paul Laurence
Sympathy
  Durem, Ray
Sympathy
  Jones, Tilford
Symphonies
  Popel, Esther
The Symphony
  Hill, Leslie Pinckney
Symphony
  Horne, Frank M.
Synonym for Selective History
  Reddy, T. J.
The Syntax of the Mind Grips
  Troupe, Quincy
System of Dante's Hell
  Jones, LeRoi

T. C.
  Bradford, William
Table of Wishes Come True
  Demby, William
Tableau
  Cullen, Countee Porter
Tableau vivant
  Thompson, James W.
Take a Giant Step
  Peterson, Louis

Take four
  Evans, Mari
Take Tools Our Strength
  Simmons, Gerald L., Jr.
Takes Time
  Brooks, Gwendolyn
Tales
  Jones, LeRoi
Tales of Simple
  Hughes, Langston
Tales of Poor Ulysses
  Raphael, Lennox
A Talk with George
  Polite, Allen
Tally
  Miller, May
Tambourine
  Cunningham, James
Tampa Red's Contemporary Blues
  Lyle, K. Curtis
Tanka I—VIII
  Alexander, Lewis Grandison
T'Appin
  Fauset, Arthur Huff
Taps
  Johnson, Georgia Douglas
The Task of Negro Womanhood
  McDougald, Elise Johnson
Tauhid
  Snellings, Rolland
The Teacher
  Hill, Leslie Pinckney
Teaching English as a Foreign Language to Students with Sub-Standard Dialects
  Musgrave, Marian E.
The Teaching of Afro-American Literature
  Turner, Darwin T.
Tears
  Bates, Myrtle
Tears and a Dream
  Jackson, Marsha Ann
Tearsplotches for My Children
  Jeffers, Lance
Tell Martha Not to Moan
  Williams, Sherley Anne
Tell Me, Ye Sad Winds
  Fortune, Timothy Thomas
Tell Pharoh
  Mitchell, Loften
Tell Rachel, He Whispered
  Dodson, Owen
Tell Yo' Ma I Said So
  Turner, Ezra W.
Temperate Belt
  Collins, Durward, Jr.
Temptation
  Beverly, Katherine
Temptation
  Dunbar, Paul Laurence
Temptation
  Hughes, Langston
10-9-8-7-6-5-4-3-2 Death
  Browne, Roscoe Lee
Tenebris
  Grimke, Angelina Weld

Tenement Room: Chicago
  Davis, Frank Marshall
Termination
  Ford, Wallace
Terra Cotta
  Lyle, K. Curtis
Testimonial
  Hankins, Paula
Testimonials
  Fields, Julia
Testimony
  Rodgers, Carolyn M.
Thank you, M'am
  Hughes, Langston
Thanking God
  Braithwaite, William Stanley Beaumont
Thanksgiving
  Braithwaite, William Stanley Beaumont
Thanksgiving
  Clemmons, Francois
A Thanksgiving Sermon
  Jones, Absalom
That Bright Chimeric Beast
  Cullen, Countee Porter
That Hill
  Dickinson, Blanche Taylor
That House
  Rashidd, Amir
That Hunger Beyond Our Physical Shapes
  Thomas, Richard W.
That Old Time Religion
  Jackman, Marvin
That Other Golgotha
  Fletcher, T. Thomas Fortune
That Same Pain, That Same Pleasure: an
Interview with Ralph Ellison
  Stern, Richard G.
That She Would Dance No More
  Smith, Jean Wheeler
That Vengeance Gathers
  Stanford, Theodore
That We Head Towards
  Fuller, Stephany
That's a Summer Storm
  Cumbo, Kattie M.
That's Mighty Fine
  Allen, Samuel W.
Theatre: The Negro In And Out Of It
  Baldwin, James
Theft
  Popel, Esther
Their blood cries out
  Beecher, John
Their Eyes Were Watching God
  Hurston, Zora Neale
Theme Brown Girl
  Hill, Elton
Then It Was
  Jordan, June Meyer
Theme for English B
  Hughes, Langston
Theme One: the Variations
  Wilson, August
Theme with Variations
  Coleman, Anita Scott

Then I Met You
  Wells, Jack Calvert
Theophilus Lewis and the Theatre of the
Harlem Renaissance
  Kornweibel, Theodore, Jr.
There Are No Tears
  Allen, Samuel W.
There Are Seeds to Sow
  Golden, Bernette
There Are Times
  Jemmott, Claudia E.
There is a nation
  Jeffers, Lance
There Is a Sadness
  Young, Alexander
There Is a Tree More Ancient than Egypt
  Forrest, Leon
There Is Confusion
  Fauset, Jessie Redmond
There Must Be Words
  Cullen, Countee Porter
There Should Be Time
  Bates, Myrtle
There Will Always Be Hope
  Williams, Colleen
Therefore, Adieu
  Cullen, Countee Porter
There's Not a Friend Like the Lowly Jesus
  Anderson, William
These Are My People
  Johnson, Fenton
These Beasts and the Benin Bronze
  Danner, Margaret
These Low Grounds
  Turpin, Waters Edward
These Poems
  Jordan, June Meyer
These Things I Love
  Mitchell, Matthew
These Words
  Harris, Helen C.
Thespian
  Hernton, Calvin C.
They already dance to our drums
  House, G. L.
They Are Calling Me
  McBrown, Gertrude Parthenia
They Are Killing All the Young Men
  Henderson, David
They That Sit In Darkness
  Burrill, Mary
They've lynched a man in Dixie
  Jones, Joshua Henry, Jr.
Thief
  Hernton, Calvin C.
Thieves Give More To Blue
  Witherspoon, Jill
A Thing Born of Darkness
  Lyons, Martha E.
Things Said When He Was Gone
  Dickinson, Blanche Taylor
Things Too Beautiful
  Butler, James Alpheus
Think Black
  Lee, Don L.

Think Twice and Be Nice
  Joans, Ted
Third Degree
  Hughes, Langston
Third Generation
  Himes, Chester B.
Third Sermon on the Warpland
  Brooks, Gwendolyn
The 38
  Joans, Ted
This Age
  Patterson, Raymond Richard
This ain't no mass thing
  Evans, Mari
This Baptism with Fire . . .
  Nicholas, A. X.
This Child's Gonna Live
  Wright, Sarah E.
This Damn Earth
  Cooper, Charles B.
This Day
  Douglas, Elroy
This Hour
  LaGrone, Oliver
This Is an African Worm
  Danner, Margaret
This Is for Freedom, My Son
  Stewart, Charles
This Is For You
  Smith, Linwood D.
This Is My Country, Too
  Williams, John Alfred
This Is My Life
  Braithwaite, William Stanley Beaumont
This Is My Vow
  Pitts, Lucia Mae
This Is the City
  Johnson, Yvette
This Is the Home of My Fathers
  Sherman, Jimmie
This Is the Thing We Ask
  Pitts, Lucia Mae
This Island Now (Jamaica)
  Cumbo, Kattie M.
This Man Is Full
  Emmons, Ronald
This Morning
  Wright, Jay
This Morning, this Evening
  Baldwin, James
This Night of Peace
  Tinsley, Tomi Carolyn
This Place
  Graves, Conrad
This Place
  Hayes, Donald Jeffrey
This Poem for Black Women
  Lockett, Reginald
This Temple
  Major, Clarence
This the Poet as I See
  Dancy, Walter K.
This Way to the Flea Market
  Fauset, Jessie Redmond
A Thorn Forever in the Breast
  Cullen, Countee Porter

Those Boys that Ran Together
  Clifton, Lucille
Those Golden Gates Fall Down
  Watson, Harmon C.
Those Winter Sundays
  Hayden, Robert Earl
Thought
  Echols, Carl
Thoughts from a Fillmore
  Cooper, Charles B.
Thoughts in a Zoo
  Cullen, Countee Porter
Thoughts of a Lawyer Out of Work
  Cooper, Charles B.
Thoughts of Death
  Brown, Sterling A.
Thoughts of the Girl He Left Behind
  Brister, Iola M.
Thoughts on the work of Providence
  Wheatley, Phillis
Three Black Playwrights: Loften Mitchell, Ossie Davis, Douglas Turner Ward
  Bigsby, C.W.E.
Three Brown Girls Singing
  Holman, Moses Carl
Three Kings
  Vaughn, James P.
Three Men
  Gaines, Ernest J.
Three Movements and a Coda
  Jones, LeRoi
Three Poems for Gwendolyn Brooks
  Kendrick, Delores
Three Poems for Nat Nakasa
  Cumbo, Kattie M.
Three Poems On War
  Honigman, Robert
3 Serendipitous Poems
  Exum, Pat Crutchfield
3 Units Single Cycle
  Linyatta
Three Up None Down
  Crouch, Stanley
Three Views of dawn
  Patterson, Raymond Richard
Three X Love
  Zuber, Ron
Threnody
  Cuney, Waring
Threnody
  Hayes, Donald Jeffrey
Threnody for a Brown Girl
  Cullen, Countee Porter
The Threshing Floor
  Cotter, Joseph Seamon, Sr.
A Thrift of Wishes
  Spellman, Alfred B.
Through the Prism of Folklore: The Black Ethos in Slavery
  Stuckey, Sterling
Through the Varied Patterned Lace
  Danner, Margaret
Thunder at Dawn
  Brown, Benjamin A.
Thunder Storm
  Randall, Dudley

Thus Speaks Africa
  Hawkins, Walter Everette
The Works Shall Praise Thee
  Dinkins, Rev. Charles R.
Tla, Tla
  Patterson, Raymond Richard
Ti Yette
  Matheus, John Frederick
Tid-Bit
  Burton, John W.
The Tide Inside, It Rages
  Barrett, Lindsay
The Tiger
  McKay, Claude
'Til the End of the World
  Ezell, Doris Amurr
Till the Sun Goes Down
  Jackman, Marvin
Time
  Jones, James Arlington
Time
  Lewis, Dio
Time
  Margetson, George Reginald
A Time In The Bosom Of Scar
  Mays, Clyde E.
A Time to Mourn
  Knight, Etheridge
Timely Message
  Jones, James Arlington
Timid Lover
  Cullen, Countee Porter
Time and Tide
  LaMarre, Hazel L.
Time In The City
  LaGrone, Oliver
Time Poem
  Hill, Quentin
Time to Die
  Dandridge, Raymond Garfield
Tina
  Thomas, Richard W.
Tired
  Dandridge, Raymond Garfield
Tired
  Johnson, Fenton
Tired Poem / Slightly Negative / More
Positive!
  Rodgers, Carolyn M.
The Tired Worker
  McKay, Claude
Titanic
  Ledbetter, Huddie
Title
  Bennett, Bob
To ——
  Braithwaite, William Stanley Beaumont
To
  Cook, Gwendolyn
To ——
  Dandridge, Raymond Garfield
To ——
  Monroe, Isabelle H.
To a Brown Boy
  Cullen, Countee Porter

To a Brown Girl
  Cullen, Countee Porter
To a Brown Girl
  Davis, Ossie
To a Caged Canary in a Negro Restaurant
  Hill, Leslie Pinckney
To a Captious Critic
  Dunbar, Paul Laurence
To a Certain Lady in Her Garden
  Brown, Sterling A.
To a cold caucasian on a bus
  Danner, Margaret
To a Dark Girl
  Bennett, Gwendolyn B.
To a Departing Favorite
  Horton, George Moses
To a Gentleman and Lady on the death of
the Lady's brother, etc.
  Wheatley, Phillis
To a Gentleman on His Voyage to Great
Britain For the Recovery of his Health
  Wheatley, Phillis
To a girl who knew what side her bread
was buttered on
  Lorde, Audre
To a Mocking Bird
  Fields, Herman E.
To a Negro Mother
  Burrell, Benjamin Ebenezer
To a Negro Preacher
  Emanuel, James A., Sr.
To a Nobly-gifted Singer
  Hill, Leslie Pinckney
To a Note from a Rainy Day
  Crouch, Stanley
To a Persistent Phantom
  Horne, Frank M.
To a Poet
  McKay, Claude
to a poet i knew
  Latimore, Jewel Christine
To a Rosebud
  Jessye, Eva Alberta
To a Schoolgirl, 1905
  DuBois, William Edward Burghardt
To a Skull
  Jones, Joshua Henry, Jr.
To a Single Shadow without Pity
  Cornish, Sam
To A Stolen Flute
  Cantoni, Louis J.
To a Whippoorwill
  Bond, Frederick W.
To a Wild Rose
  Bailey, William Edgar
To a Wite Boy
  Latimore, Jewel Christine
To a Woman Who Wants Darkness and
Time
  Barrax, Gerald William
To A Young Blood
  Powe, Blossom
To a Young Girl Leaving the Hill Country
  Bontemps, Arna W.
To a Young Poet
  Morse, George Chester

To a Young Suicide
  Hill, William Allyn
To All Black Women from All Black Men
  Cleaver, Eldridge
To All Brothers
  Sanchez, Sonia
To All Sisters
  Sanchez, Sonia
To All the Nice White People
  Durem, Ray
To America
  Johnson, James Weldon
To An Avenue Sport
  Collins, Helen Armstead Johnson
To an Ecclesiast I Know
  Hill, William Allyn
To an Icicle
  Dickinson, Blanche Taylor
To Anita
  Sanchez, Sonia
To Arbour Tanner
  Wheatley, Phillis
To be . . .
  Abramson, Dolores
. . . to be a woman
  Earley, Jacqueline
To Be Black Is To Suffer
  Washington, Austin D.
To Be Dazzled by the Racing of Her Blood
  Wright, Bruce McMarion
To Be in Love
  Brooks, Gwendolyn
To Be On . . .
  Cooper, Charles B.
To Be Quicker
  Lee, Don L.
To Be Set to Sad Music
  Wright, Bruce McMarion
To Be the Invisible Man
  Harris, William J.
To Blk / Record / Buyers
  Sanchez, Sonia
To Bobby Seale
  Clifton, Lucille
To Certain Critics
  Cullen, Countee Porter
To Certain Negro Leaders
  Hughes, Langston
To Chessman and Associates
  Allen, Samuel W.
To Chick
  Horne, Frank M.
To Children
  McGaugh, Lawrence
To Chuck
  Sanchez, Sonia
To Cinque
  Whitfield, James M.
To Clarissa Scott Delany
  Grimke, Angelina Weld
To Crack That Nut Were a Seeker Task
  Jeffers, Lance
To Da-duh, in Memoriam
  Marshall, Paule
To Death
  Hughes, Lois Royal

To Dinah Washington
  Knight, Etheridge
To Egypt
  Davis, Gloria
To Eliza
  Horton, George Moses
To End Nuttery
  Cooper, Charles B.
To Endymion
  Cullen, Countee Porter
To F. S. 1.
  Turner, Claire
To Fanon
  Kgositsile, Keorapetse William
To France
  Cullen, Countee Porter
To Gwen
  Ologboni, Tejumola
To Gwen Brooks
  Chenault, John
To Gwen, mo luve
  Rodgers, Carolyn M.
To Gwen with Love
  Eckels, Jon B.
To Gwendolyn Brooks
  Dennis, R. M.
To Gwendolyn Brooks
  Knight, Etheridge
To Gwendolyn Brooks the Creator In the
  Beginning—Words
  Reynolds, B. A.
To Hell With Dying
  Walker, Alice
to his children
  Taylor, Alrutheus Ambush
To His Excellency, General Washington
  Wheatley, Phillis
To Hollyhocks
  McClellan, George Marion
To James Brown
  Harper, Michael S.
To James Weldon Johnson
  Jones, Georgia Holloway
To John Keats, Poet, At Springtime
  Cullen, Countee Porter
To Join or Not to Join
  McFarlane, Milton
To Keep the Memory of Charlotte Forten
  Grimké
  Grimke, Angelina Weld
To Koala, Who Will Be Extinct
  Clemmons, Carole Gregory
to L.
  Perry, Julianne
To Lincoln
  Azikiwe, Ben N.
To Lincoln at Graduation
  Silvera, Edward S.
To Lincoln University 1923–1924
  Gordon, Barefield
To Lovers
  Harris, Helen C.
To Lovers
  Thomas, Richard W.
To Lovers of Earth: Fair Warning
  Cullen, Countee Porter

To Make a Poem in Prison
  Knight, Etheridge
To Mareta
  Johnson, Herschell
To Maria Callas
  Clemmons, Francois
To Martin Luther King Jr.
  Seese, Ethel Gray
To Melody
  Allen, George Leonard
To Midnight Nan at Leroy's
  Hughes, Langston
To Mississippi Youth
  Little, Malcolm
To Morani/Munger
  Sanchez, Sonia
To Mother and Steve
  Evans, Mari
To Mr. Charles and Sister Annie
  Saxon, Alvin A.
To My Contemporaries in the Great American Universities
  Hill, Elton
To My Father
  Ray, Henrietta Cordelia
To My Grandmother
  Johnson, Mae Smith
To My Lost Child
  Sexton, Will
To My Neighbor Boy
  Hammond, Mrs. J. W.
To My Old Master
  Anderson, Jourdon
To My Son
  Johnson, Georgia Douglas
To My Son Parker, Asleep in the Next Room
  Kaufman, Bob
To Nancy
  Kellum-Rose, Matthew
To Nita
  Cannon, David Wadsworth, Jr.
To O. E. A.
  McKay, Claude
To Our Boys
  Underhill, Irvin W.
To Our First Born
  Dooley, Thomas
To Our Friends
  Watkins, Lucian Bottow
To Paul Robeson
  Brierre, Jean
To Paul Robeson, Opus No. 3
  Johnston, Percy Edward
To Prometheus
  Hawkins, Walter Everette
To Richard Wright
  Rivers, Conrad Kent
To S.M., A Young African Painter, on Seeing His Work
  Wheatley, Phillis
To Samuel Coleridge Taylor, Upon Hearing His (Song)
  Johnson, Georgia Douglas
To Satch
  Allen, Samuel W.

To Save a Tear
  De Saavedra, Guadalupe
To Some Millions Who Survive Joseph E. Mander, Senior
  Wright, Sarah E.
To Some Who Are Prone to Criticize
  Turner, Claire
(To Someone I Met on 125th Street, 1966)
  Jackson, Mae
To Strike for Night
  Bethune, Lebert
To the American Convention for promoting the Abolition of Slavery . . .
  Allen, George R.
To the American People
  Whipper, William
To the Bright Bystanders
  Reddy, T. J.
To the Dunbar High School—A Sonnet
  Grimke, Angelina Weld
To the First of August
  Plato, Ann
To the Humane and Benevolent Inhabitants of the city and County of Philadelphia, Address delivered Dec. 10, 1818
  Forten, James, Jr.
To the J.F.K. Quintet
  Fraser, W. Alfred
To the Men in 350th Hdg Co.
  Harris, Helen C.
To the Men of the Soviet Army
  Dismond, Henry Binga
To the Mercy Killers
  Randall, Dudley
To the Muse
  Harris, Helen C.
To the New Annex to the Detroit County Jail
  Thomas, Richard W.
To the Pale Poets
  Durem, Ray
To the Peoples of Earth
  Sun-Ra
To the Right Honorable William, Earl of Dartmouth . . .
  Wheatley, Phillis
To the Sea
  Braithwaite, William Stanley Beaumont
To the Singer
  Harris, Helen C.
To the Singular Arrival of Chris and Julie Ruke
  Thomas, Richard W.
To the Sisters
  Rodgers, Loretta
To the Smartweed
  Hill, Leslie Pinckney
To the South
  Dunbar, Paul Laurence
To the Student
  Whitman, Albery Allson
To the Survivors of Hiroshima and Nagasaki
  Thomas, Richard W.
To the University of Cambridge in New England
  Wheatley, Phillis

To the White Friends
  McKay, Claude
To the White Man
  Tarver, Valerie
To Turn from Love
  Fabio, Sarah Webster
To Vanity
  Turner, Darwin T.
To Vietnam
  Cobb, Charlie
To William Stanley Braithwaite
  Johnson, Georgia Douglas
To You
  Hardnett, Linda G.
To You
  Horne, Frank M.
To You
  Stevens, Ruby
To You Who Read My Book
  Cullen, Countee Porter
Toast
  Horne, Frank M.
A Toast to Harlem
  Hughes, Langston
Today
  Neal, Gaston
Today is a day of great joy
  Cruz, Victor Hernandez
today is not like they said . . .
  Hall, Kirkwood M.
Today is sun
  Adoff, Arnold
Today: The Idea Market
  Nicholas, Michael
Toe Jam
  Jackson, Elaine
Together
  Rodgers, Carolyn M.
The Toilet
  Jones, LeRoi
Tokenism: 300 Years for Five Cents
  Jones, LeRoi
Tokens
  Bennett, Gwendolyn B.
Toleration
  Vale, Coston
Tombs
  Thomas, Richard W.
Tomorrow
  Powe, Blossom
Tomorrow the Heroes
  Spellman, Alfred B.
Tomorrow's for remembering
  Thompson, James W.
Tomorrow's Winds
  Boyd, Samuel E.
Tom-tom
  Cesaire, Aime
Tony get the boys
  Graham, Donald L.
Torches
  Chittick, Conrad
The Tortoise and the Elephant
  Ellis, Alfred B.
The Touch
  Cullen, Countee Porter

A Touch of Innocence
  Dunham, Katherine
Touché
  Fauset, Jessie Redmond
Tour 5
  Hayden, Robert Earl
Toward a Definition: Black Poetry of the Sixties
  Lee, Don L.
Toward Black Liberation
  Carmichael, Stokely
Towards a Black Aesthetic
  Fuller, Hoyt W.
Towards a Walk in the Sun
  Kgositsile, Keorapetse William
Towards Our Theatre: a Definitive Act
  Kgositsile, Keorapetse William
The Town Fathers
  Tolson, Melvin Beaunorus
Toy Poem
  Giovanni, Nikki
Tracin' Tales
  Dandridge, Raymond Garfield
Traffic Signs
  Troup, Cornelius V.
Tragedy
  Lee, Ed
Tragedy at Hampton
  Hughes, Langston
The Tragedy of Pete
  Cotter, Joseph Seamon, Sr.
The Tragic Mulatto Theme in Six Works of Langston Hughes
  Davis, Arthur P.
The Train Ride
  Browne, George B.
The Train Runs Late to Harlem
  Rivers, Conrad Kent
Train Whistle Guitar
  Murray, Albert
The Traitor
  Lee, Don L.
'Trane
  Reed, Clarence
Transcendental Blues
  Rahman, Yusef
Transformation
  Alexander, Lewis Grandison
Transformation
  Troupe, Quincy
Transient
  Pitts, Lucia Mae
Translation
  Spencer, Anne
Trapped
  Hite, Vernoy E.
Travelling Through Fog
  Hayden, Robert Earl
Travels in the South: a Cold Night in Alabama
  Mahoney, William
Travois of the Nameless
  Torregian, Sotere
Treasure Hunt
  Wilson, Art
A Tree Design
  Bontemps, Arna W.

Tree of Heaven
  Madgett, Naomi Cornelia Long Witherspoon
Tree Poem
  Jones, Paulette
Treehouse
  Emanuel, James A. Sr.
Trellie
  Jeffers, Lance
Trends in Negro American Literature (1940–1965)
  Davis, Arthur P.
Triangle
  Greer, Roslyn
Tribute
  Cullen, Countee Porter
Tribute to Countee Cullen, 1928
  McCall, James Edward
Tribute to Duke
  Fabio, Sarah Webster
Tricked Again
  Ridhiana
Trifle
  Johnson, Georgia Douglas
Tripart
  Jones, Gayle
The Triple Benison
  Ray, Henrietta Cordelia
Tripping With Black Writing
  Fabio, Sarah Webster
Trivia
  Murphy, Beatrice M.
A Triviality
  Cuney, Waring
Tropics in New York
  McKay, Claude
Trouble in Mind
  Childress, Alice
The Trouble With Intellectuals
  Randall, Dudley
Trouble with the Angels
  Hughes, Langston
Troubled Jesus
  Cuney, Waring
Troubled Woman
  Hughes, Langston
Truant
  McKay, Claude
True Import of Present Dialogue; Black vs. Negro
  Giovanni, Nikki
True Love
  Cuney, Waring
Trumpet Player—52nd Street
  Hughes, Langston
Trussey's Visit
  Henderson, Elliot B.
Truth
  Brooks, Gwendolyn
Truth
  Clarke, John Henrik
Truth
  Green, Donald
Truth
  Harper, Frances Ellen Watkins

The Truth
  Joans, Ted
Truth
  McKay, Claude
Truth Is Quite Messy
  Harris, William J.
Truth Stranger than Fiction
  Henson, Josiah
Tu
  Welburn, Ron
Tud
  Major, Clarence
Tulips from their Blood
  Brooks, Edwin
Tumult
  Wheeler, Charles Enoch
The Tumult and the Shouting
  Pawley, Thomas D., Jr.
Tunk
  Johnson, James Weldon
Turk
  Cornish, Sam
Turn Me to My Yellow Leaves
  Braithwaite, William Stanley Beaumont
Turn Out the Light
  Jones, Joshua Henry, Jr.
The Turncoat
  Jones, LeRoi
Tuskegee
  Hill, Leslie Pinckney
Twang
  Robinson, T. L.
Twasinta's Seminoles
  Whitman, Albery Allson
Twelve Gates
  Thomas, Lorenzo
12 Gates to the City
  Giovanni, Nikki
Twelve Proverbs of the Ewe
  Ellis, Alfred B.
Twelve Years a Slave
  Northup, Solomon
Twentieth-Century Fiction and the Black Mask of Humanity
  Ellison, Ralph Waldo
#20 (From the Window)
  Long, Doughtry
#28 (Black people)
  Long, Doughtry
#25 (If 'Trane had only seen her body)
  Long, Doughtry
Twenty fifth Birthday, 1893
  DuBois, William Edward Burghardt
The Twenty Grand
  Madgett, Naomi Cornelia Long Witherspoon
Twenty Six Ways of Looking at a Blackman
  Patterson, Raymond Richard
Two
  DuBois, William Edward Burghardt
Two-an'-Six
  McKay, Claude
2 B Blk
  Ferdinand, Val
Two Countries
  Witherspoon, Jill

Two Dedications
  Brooks, Gwendolyn
Two Dreams
  Franklin, Clarence
Two From the Country
  Holmes, R. Ernest
Two Jazz Poems
  Hines, Carl Wendell, Jr.
Two Ladies Bidding us 'Good Morning'
  Vaughn, James P.
Two Lean Cats
  O'Higgins, Myron
Two Little Boots
  Dunbar, Paul Laurence
Two Mornings
  McGaugh, Lawrence
The Two Offers
  Harper, Frances Ellen Watkins
Two Poems
  Lee, Don L.
Two Poems for Black Relocation Centers
  Knight, Etheridge
Two Poems from 'Trinity: a Dream Sequence'
  Madgett, Naomi Cornelia Long Witherspoon
Two Points of View
  Watkins, Lucian Bottow
Two Quartets
  Cuney, Waring
Two Questions
  Braithwaite, William Stanley Beaumont
Two Races
  Burke, Inez M.
Two Somewhat Different Epigrams
  Hughes, Langston
Two Songs of Love
  Heath, Gordon
Two Way
  Cruz, Victor Hernandez
Two Who Crossed a Line
  Cullen, Countee Porter
The Two Worlds
  Lyman, James C.
Tyson's Corner
  St. John, Primus

U Name This One
  Rodgers, Carolyn M.
The Ubiquitous Lions
  Joans, Ted
Uh, Uh; But How Do It Free Us?
  Sanchez, Sonia
Uhuru
  Alhamisi, Ahmed Akinwole
Ultimate Equality
  Durem, Ray
Ultimatum
  Cousins, William
Un Frère au Tombeau de son Frère
  Lanusse, Armand
Un-American Invesitgators
  Hughes, Langston
The Uncalled
  Dunbar, Paul Laurence
Uncertainty
  Parks, Henrietta C.

Uncle Bull-boy
  Jordan, June Meyer
Uncle Eph-Epicure
  Campbell, James Edwin
Uncle Eph's Banjo Song
  Campbell, James Edwin
Uncle Jesse
  Barlow, George
Uncle Jim
  Cullen, Countee Porter
Uncle Ned an' de Mockin' Bird
  Henderson, Elliot B.
Uncle Tom
  Ragland, J. Farley
Uncle Tom's Cabin. Alternate Ending
  Jones, LeRoi
Uncle Tom's Children
  Wright, Richard
Undefeated
  Jones, James Arlington
Under the Harlem Shadow: a Study of Jessie Fauset and Nella Larsen
  Sato, Hiroko
Underground Railroad. A Record . . .
  Still, William
The Underlying Strife
  Hernton, Calvin C.
Undertow
  Hughes, Langston
Undertow
  Spence, Eulalie
Underway
  McCoy, Fleetwood M., Jr.
An Unexpurgated communiqué to David Henderson: London—1966
  Hernton, Calvin C.
Unfinished
  Jones, LeRoi
Unhistorical events
  Kaufman, Bob
Unholy Missions
  Kaufman, Bob
Universal Salvation—A Very Ancient Doctrine
  Haynes, Lemuel B.
The Unknown
  Jeffers, Lance
Unknowns
  Cumbo, Kattie M.
The Unknown Soldier
  Silvera, Edward S.
Unnameable Objects, Unspeakable Crimes
  Baldwin, James
Underground
  Rivers, Conrad Kent
An Unofficial Eulogy
  Harris, William J.
Unrepentant
  Twitty, Countess W.
Unrewarded
  Jones, James Arlington
The Unsung Heroes
  Dunbar, Paul Laurence
Until
  Roker, Myntora J.
Until They Have Stopped
  Wright, Sarah E.

Untitled
  Balagon, Kuwasi
Untitled
  Bradford, William
Untitled (Angling up from the wheeling feet of fire)
  Gardner, Carl
Untitled (Remember: when the door closes you in)
  Graham, Donald L.
Untitled (You Walk Like Bells)
  Hannibal, Gregor
Untitled [To Smell the stink of rotting / brownstones]
  Hill, Pamela Woodruff
Untitled (We Will Be No Generashuns to Cum)
  Latimore, Jewel Christine
Untitled
  Lomax, Pearl Cleage
Untitled (I Take / My War Machine)
  Page, Daphne Diane
Untitled (So / I've found me / at last
  Page, Daphne Diane
Untitled (Why should I be eaten by love?)
  Randall, James A., Jr.
Untitled (fish is)
  Scott, Sharon
Untitled (Hi Ronda)
  Scott, Sharon
Untitled
  Spellman, Alfred B.
Untitled (in orangeburg my brothers did)
  Spellman, Alfred B.
Untitled Novel
  Lofty, Paul
Untitled Poem
  Grant, Otto
Untitled Poem
  Hand, Q. R.
Untitled Poem
  Koven, Diva Goodfriend
untitled: requiem for tomorrow
  Conyus
Unveiled
  Jones, James Arlington
Up Alone And Late
  Pritchard, Sheila
Up from Slavery
  Washington, Booker Taliaferro
Up on the Spoon
  Crouch, Stanley
Upon Being Black One Friday Night in July
  Latimore, Jewel Christine
Upon Finding a False Friend
  Alee, Lycurgus J.
Upon leaving the parole board hearing
  Conyus
Upon Looking at Love
  Brown, Delores A.
Urban Dream
  Cruz, Victor Hernandez
Urgency
  Wright, Sarah E.
Us
  Johnson, Herschell

Us
  Lester, Julius
U.S.A.: the Potential of a Minority Revolution
  Williams, Robert F.
Utopia
  Latimore, Jewel Christine

The Vacant Lot
  Brooks, Gwendolyn
Vacant Lot
  Randall, Dudley
Valediction
  Banks, Barbara
Values
  Johnson, Georgia Douglas
Vanity
  Jones, James Arlington
Variation
  Hughes, Langston
Variations on a Theme
  Cullen, Countee Porter
Variety
  Goss, William Thompson
Vashti
  Harper, Frances Ellen Watkins
Vaticide
  O'Higgins, Myron
The Veil
  Hughes, Lois Royal
Veracruz
  Hayden, Robert Earl
Verifying the Dead
  Welch, James
Verisimilitude
  Davis, John Preston
Verse Written In the Album of Mademoiselle
  Dalcour, Pierre
A Versatile Relative of Mine: Colonel Charles Young
  Wells, Bernice Young Mitchell
Very Black Man
  Brown, Elaine
Vestiges: Harlem Sketches
  Fisher, Rudolph
Vet's Rehabilitation
  Durem, Ray
Vice
  Jones, LeRoi
A Victim of Microbes
  Allen, Junius Mordecai
Victor or Legacy
  Kgositsile, Keorapetse William
Viet Nam—Away from Viet Nam
  Whaley, June D.
Vietnam: I Need More Than This Crust of Salt
  Jeffers, Lance
Vieux Carré
  Roberts, Walter Adolphe
View from the Corner
  Allen, Samuel W.
Vietnam #4
  Major, Clarence
Vignette
  Burton, John W.

Villanelle of Washington Square
  Roberts, Walter Adolphe
Vincent Ogé
  Vashon, George B.
The Violent Space
  Knight, Etheridge
Violets
  Dunbar-Nelson, Alice
Virginalis
  Geran, Juliana
Virginia
  Loftin, Elouise
Virgin Field
  Braziel, Arthur
A Vision
  Fernandis, Sarah Collins
The Vision / a Poem in Blank Verse
  Boyd, John
Vision from the Ghetto
  Washington, Raymond
The Vision of Lazarus
  Johnson, Fenton
Visions . . . Leaders . . . Shaky Leaders . . .
Parasitical Leaders . .
  Franklin, Clarence
A Visit
  Randall, James A., Jr.
Visit of a Fugitive Slave To The Grave of
Wilberforce
  Brown, William Wells
Visit of the Professor of Aesthetics
  Danner, Margaret
Visit to Dunbar's Tomb
  Dabney, Wendell Phillips
The Visitation
  Sun-Ra
Vive Noir!
  Evans, Mari
A Voice Above the Wind
  Bertha, Gus
Voice in the Crowd
  Joans, Ted
The Voice of the Hill
  Carter, Herman J. D.
The Volcano
  Walcott, Derek
Voodoo
  Coleman, Ethel
Voodoo On the Un-assing of janis joplin
  Rodgers, Carolyn M.
Voyage of Jimmy Poo
  Emanuel, James A., Sr.

The Wait
  Troupe, Quincy
Waiting for Her Train
  Lee, Audrey
Wake Cry
  Cuney, Waring
Wake-Up Niggers
  Lee, Don L.
Walk
  Horne, Frank M.
Walk Down My Street
  Dorsett, Vincent

Walk Hard
  Hill, Abram
Walk with de Mayor of Harlem
  Henderson, David
Walking Among the Benches
  Greene, Carl H.
Walking East on 125th Street
  Johnson, Ray
Walking Parker Home
  Kaufman, Bob
The Wall
  Brooks, Gwendolyn
The Wall
  Lee, Don L.
The Walls of Jericho
  Dickinson, Blanche Taylor
The Walls of Jericho
  Fisher, Rudolph
Walu, the Antelope
  Kellum-Rose, Matthew
The Want of You
  Grimke, Angelina Weld
War
  Patterson, Jesse F.
War
  Thomas, Richard W.
War Babies
  Franklin, Charles
The Warden Said to Me the Other Day
  Knight, Etheridge
Warning
  Haynes, Samuel A.
Warning
  Hughes, Langston
The Warning—A Theme for Linda
  Milner, Ronald
Warning to Brothers
  Thomas, Richard W.
Warren
  Clemmons, Francois
Warriors Prancing
  Rashidd, Niema
Warrior's Prayer
  Dunbar, Paul Laurence
Warwick Castle
  Pitts, Lucia Mae
Was That Really How Her Garden Grew?
  Cumbo, Kattie M.
The Washer-Woman
  Bohanon, Otto Leland
Washiri Poet
  Cumbo, Kattie M.
A WASP Woman Visits a Black Junkie in
Prison
  Knight, Etheridge
Waste
  Murphy, Beatrice M.
Wasted
  Thomas, Richard W.
The Watchers
  Braithwaite, William Stanley Beaumont
Watermelon
  Smith, G. T.
Watermelon Vendor's Cry
  Johnson, James Weldon

Watts
  Rivers, Conrad Kent
Watts
  Saxon, Alvin A.
Watts, 1966
  Scott, Johnie H.
Watts—Little Rome
  McKeller, Sonora
The Way It Is
  Goncalves, Joe
The Way It Went Down
  Neal, Larry
Way Out West
  Jones, LeRoi
Way-out Morgan
  Brooks, Gwendolyn
Wayman, As a Driven Star
  Welburn, Ron
The Ways of Men
  Grimke, Angelina Weld
The Wayside Well
  Cotter, Joseph Seamon, Sr.
A Wayward Child
  Llorens, David
We a Ba-a-d People
  Sanchez, Sonia
. . . We Ain't Got No Time
  Graham, Donald L.
We Are an Embryo People
  Simpson, Juanita
We Are Black But We Are Men
  Dinkins, Rev. Charles R.
We Are No One
  Thomas, Richard W.
"We Are Not Mantan"
  Johnson, Herschell
We Assume
  Harper, Michael S.
We Can't Breathe
  Fair, Ronald L.
We Could Take
  Witherspoon, Jill
We Dance Like Ella Riffs
  Rodgers, Carolyn M.
We Don't Need No Music
  Gadsden, Janice Marie
We Exist Living Dead
  Wakefield, Jacques
We Had to Occupy a Seat Apart
  Brown, Josephine
We Have a Tryst
  Tinsley, Tomi Carolyn
We Have Been Believers
  Walker, Margaret Abigail
We have fashioned laughter
  Johnson, Charles Bertram
We Have Passed the Point of No Return
  Robeson, Eslanda Goode
We Know No More
  Fortune, Timothy Thomas
We Launched a Ship
  Goodwin, Ruby Berkley
We Live in a Cage
  Harris, William J.
We Must Lead
  Pitts, Herbert Lee

We Own the Night
  Jones, LeRoi
We Own the Night—A Play of Blackness
  Garrett, Jimmy
We Pass
  Murphy, Beatrice M.
We Rainclouds
  Wyche, Marvin, Jr.
We Real Cool
  Brooks, Gwendolyn
We Righteous Bombers
  Bass, Kingsley B., Jr.
We the Black Woman
  Micou, Regina
We The People
  Taylor, D.
We travel a common road, Brother
  Harris, Leon R.
We Used To Really / Be Up-tight
  Thomas, Richard W.
We Waiting on You
  Spriggs, Edward S.
We Walk the Way of the New World
  Lee, Don L.
We Wear the Mask
  Dunbar, Paul Laurence
We Who Came After
  Fair, Ronald L.
We Who Would Die
  Dismond, Henry Binga
Weak Dynamite
  Major, Clarence
The Weary Blues
  Hughes, Langston
Wedding Procession, from a Window
  Emanuel, James A., Sr.
Wednesday Night Prayer Meeting
  Wright, Jay
Wednesday Night Prayer Meeting or Rappin'
to My Boy
  Dooley, Thomas
Weeds in My Garden
  Pitts, Lucia Mae
Weeksville Women
  Loftin, Elouise
Weh Down Souf
  Davis, Daniel Webster
Welcome for Etheridge
  Cunningham, James
The Welcome Table
  Walker, Alice
Welcomed Exit
  Jones, James Arlington
Welfare
  Mungen, Horace
Well, After Freedom
  Guidon, Henry
"well well"
  Wakefield, Jacques
Welt
  Johnson, Georgia Douglas
Weltschmerz
  Yerby, Frank
We're Still a Proud Race
  Owens, I. L.

We're the Only Colored People Here
  Brooks, Gwendolyn
West at bay
  Hernton, Calvin C.
West India Emancipation Speech
  Douglass, Frederick
West Ridge Is Menthol-Cool
  Graham, Donald L.
Western Town
  Cannon, David Wadsworth, Jr.
Westward Flight
  Seese, Ethel Gray
We've Got to Live before We Die
  Jones-Quartey, H.A.B.
The Wharf Rats
  Walrond, Eric
What Bright Push button?
  Allen, Samuel W.
What Can I Say?
  Powe, Blossom
What Color Is Lonely?
  Rodgers, Carolyn M.
What deeds have sprung from plow and pick
  Cotter, Joseph Seamon, Sr.
What Do I Care?
  Curtwright, Wesley
What Do I Care For Morning
  Johnson, Helene Hubbell
What do you want, America?
  Davis, Frank Marshall
What Does Negro Youth Think of Present-Day Negro Leaders?
  Davis, Allison
What Good Are Words
  Smith, Linwood D.
What Happens
  Jordan, June Meyer
What Am I Really Like Inside
  Douglass, Rudolph
What I Need, Is a Dark Woman
  Anderson, Charles
What If It Had Turned Up Heads
  Gaines, Ernest J.
What Is
  De Saavedra, Guadalupe
What Is a Slave?
  Clark, Benjamin P.
What is Africa to me
  Cullen, Countee Porter
What Is God?
  Robinson, Etholia Arthur
What Is It
  Spellman, Alfred B.
What Is Love?
  Morris, Myra Estelle
What is to be done: The role of an Authentic Black Intelligensia
  Snellings, Rolland
What Is the Negro Doing?
  Jordan, W. Clarence
What marked the river's flow
  Burroughs, Margaret Taylor Goss
What Moor Has Placed His Body in My Throat
  Jeffers, Lance

What My Child Learns of the Sea
  Lorde, Audre
What Need Have I for Memory?
  Johnson, Georgia Douglas
What Order
  Clemmons, Carole Gregory
What Poetry is for Me
  Scott, Johnie H.
What Shall I Give My Children
  Brooks, Gwendolyn
What The Black Man Wants
  Douglass, Frederick
What the Negro Thinks of the South
  Schuyler, George Samuel
What the Negro Wants
  Hughes, Langston
What We Know
  Patterson, Raymond Richard
What's Happening to the Heroes
  Grosvenor, Verta Mae
The Wheel
  Hayden, Robert Earl
When a Woman Gets Blue
  Jordan, Norman
When a Feller's Itchin' to Be Spanked
  Dunbar, Paul Laurence
When All Is Done
  Dunbar, Paul Laurence
When back people are
  Spellman, Alfred B.
When Brown Is Black
  Kgositsile, Keorapetse William
When Dawn Comes to the City
  McKay, Claude
When de Co'n Pone's Hot
  Dunbar, Paul Laurence
When De Saints Go Ma'ching Home
  Brown, Sterling A.
When Dey 'Listed Colored Soldiers
  Dunbar, Paul Laurence
When I Am Dead
  Dodson, Owen
When I Am Dead
  Johnson, Georgia Douglas
When I Awoke
  Patterson, Raymond Richard
When I Die
  Johnson, Fenton
When I Have Wrung the Last Tear
  Jeffers, Lance
When I Heard Dat White Man Say
  Gilbert, L. Zack
When I'm Alone
  Thomas, Richard W.
When in Rome
  Evans, Mari
When Mahalia Sings
  Prettyman, Quandra
When Malindy Sings
  Dunbar, Paul Laurence
When New Green Tales
  Myles, Glenn
When Night Comes
  Lawrence, Joyce Whitsitt
When Ol' Sis' Judy Pray
  Campbell, James Edwin

When She Spoke of God
  Jeffers, Lance
When Slavery Seems Sweet
  Bullins, Ed
When Something Happens
  Randall, James A., Jr.
When State Magicians Fail
  Reed, Ishmael
When Sue Wears Red
  Hughes, Langston
When Summer Comes
  Cantoni, Louis J.
When My Uncle Willie Saw
  Freeman, Carol S.
When the Black Mule Kicked
  Randall, Jon
When the Fish Begin to Bite
  Allen, Junius Mordecai
When the Green Lies over the Earth
  Grimke, Angelina Weld
When thy king is a boy
  Roberson, Charles Edwin
When We Hear the Eye Open
  Kaufman, Bob
When You Have Forgotten Sunday: The
Love Story
  Brooks, Gwendolyn
When You Have Gone From Rooms
  Wright, Bruce McMarion
Where Do We Go From Here?
  Strickland, William
Where Do You Live?
  Yancy, Bessie Woodson
Where Else?
  Jones, James Arlington
Where Have You Gone
  Evans, Mari
Where Is My Woman Now
  Harper, Michael S.
Where To
  Cooper, Charles B.
Where, When, Which?
  Hughes, Langston
Which way
  Welburn, Ron
While at Good Old Cornell
  Martinez, Lydia
While April Breezes Blow
  Williamson, D. T.
While Cecil Snores: Mom Drinks Cold Milk
  Cunningham, James
While Sitting Here in Class
  Martinez, Lydia
Whimsey
  Brown, William
The Whipping
  Hayden, Robert Earl
White
  Mungen, Horace
The White City
  McKay, Claude
Whi/te boys gone
  Ferdinand, Val
White Collar Job
  Morris, Myra Estelle

White Dresses
  Green, Paul
White Fear
  Smith, Nannie Travis
White God
  Fletcher, T. Thomas Fortune
White hope
  Reed, Ishmael
White Horses
  McKay, Claude
The White House
  McKay, Claude
White Houses
  McKay, Claude
A White Loaf of Bread
  Killens, John Oliver
White Magic: An Ode
  Braithwaite, William Stanley Beaumont
White Mice at the Parcel Post Window
  Cuney, Waring
White people
  Henderson, David
White People got Trouble, Too
  Durem, Ray
White Powder
  Cruz, Victor Hernandez
The White Problem In America
  Bennett, Lerone, Jr.
The White Race and Its Heroes
  Cleaver, Eldridge
White Rat
  Jones, Gayle
A White Road
  Braithwaite, William Stanley Beaumont
The White Troops Had Their Orders But The
Negroes Looked Like Men
  Brooks, Gwendolyn
White Weekend
  Troupe, Quincy
The White Witch
  Johnson, James Weldon
Whitey, Baby
  Emanuel, James A., Sr.
Who But the Lord
  Hughes, Langston
Who Collects the Pain
  Burroughs, Margaret Taylor Goss
Who Has Seen the Wind?
  Kaufman, Bob
Who Is Angelina?
  Young, Alexander
Who Is Not a Stranger Still
  Burroughs, Margaret Taylor Goss
Who Is That A-Walking in the Corn?
  Johnson, Fenton
Who Shall Die?
  Randall, James A., Jr.
Who's Got His Own
  Milner, Ronald
Who's Life?
  Sirrah, Leumas
Who's Passing for Who?
  Hughes, Langston
Who Speaks Negro?
  Fabio, Sarah Webster

Who's the Man Asleep?
  Sirrah, Leumas
Whut a Dawn
  Bohanon, Mary
Why
  Brown, William
Why
  Clorox
Why Adam Sinned
  Rodgers, Alex
Why Be Silent
  Trotter, William Monroe
Why Do I Love This Country
  Cleaves, Mary Wilkerson
Why Fades a Dream?
  Dunbar, Paul Laurence
Why I Didn't Go to Delphi
  Welch, James
Why I Eulogized Malcolm X
  Davis, Ossie
Why I Left America
  Baldwin, James
Why I Rebel
  Sye, Robert J.
Why I Returned
  Bontemps, Arna W.
Why, Mahalia?
  Yeldell, Joyce
Why Me?
  Sharon
Why Should We March?
  Randolph, A. Philip
Why Try
  Joans, Ted
Why We Can't Wait
  King, Martin Luther, Jr.
Why Worry?
  Reason, Arthur W.
Why Would I Want to Be in the Distant Hills?
  Harris, William J.
Why, you Reckon?
  Hughes, Langston
Widow
  Major, Clarence
Widow Walk
  Dodson, Owen
The Wife of His Youth
  Chesnutt, Charles Waddell
The Wife-Woman
  Spencer, Anne
Wig
  Hall, Kirkwood M.
The Wig
  Wright, Charles Stevenson
The Wild Goat
  McKay, Claude
Wild Roses
  Newsome, Mary Effie Lee
Will The Real Black People Please Stand
  Barnwell, Desiree A.
Will There Be Another Riot in Watts?
  Dolan, Harry
William and Ellen Craft
  Johnson, Georgia Douglas

William Styron's Nat Turner—Rogue—Nigger
  Hairston, Loyle
Williebelle
  Jeffers, Lance
Willow Bend and Weep
  Johnson, Herbert Clark
Wilmington, Delaware
  Giovanni, Nikki
Wind from all Compass Points
  Paz, Octavio
Wind Goddess: Sound of Sculpture
  Redmond, Eugene B.
Window Pictures
  Wright, Sarah E.
Window Washer
  Weeks, Ricardo
Window Washers
  Anthony, James K.
Winds of Change
  Hairston, Loyle
Wine in the Wilderness
  Childress, Alice
The Wine of Ecstacy
  Tolson, Melvin Beaunorus
Wings
  Smith, Laura E.
Wings of Oppression
  Hill, Leslie Pinckney
Winter
  Scott, Eddie, Jr.
A Winter Death
  Randall, James A., Jr.
Winter Is Coming
  Carmichael, Waverly Turner
A Winter Song
  Harris, William J.
A Winter Twilight
  Grimke, Angelina Weld
Winter Weather Forecast
  Anthony, James K.
Winter's Morn
  Brooks, Rosa Paul
Wintertime in the Ghetto
  Thigpen, William A., Jr.
Wintry Child-Burial
  Geran, Juliana
Wisdom
  Yerby, Frank
Wisdom and War
  Hughes, Langston
Wisdom Cometh With the Years
  Cullen, Countee Porter
The Wisdom of Silence
  Dunbar, Paul Laurence
The Wise
  Cullen, Countee Porter
Witch Doctor
  Hayden, Robert Earl
With All Deliberate Speed
  Lee, Don L.
With My Napalm Six Shooters
  Harris, William J.
With the Lark
  Dunbar, Paul Laurence
Witherspoon
  Jeffers, Lance

Without Benefit of Declaration
  Hughes, Langston
Without Name
  Murray, Pauli
Without Your Lean Brown Back
  Witherspoon, Jill
Woman
  House, G. L.
Woman
  Loftin, Elouise
The Woman
  Thomas, Richard W.
A Woman At War
  Washington, Hazel L.
The Woman Thing
  Lorde, Audre
Woman with Flower
  Madgett, Naomi Cornelia Long Witherspoon
The Womanhood
  Brooks, Gwendolyn
The Women
  Whitaker, Patrick W.
Women and Kitchens
  Cuney, Waring
Women in Politics
  Morris, Myra Estelle
Women Suffrage Movement
  Douglass, Frederick
The Wonder of the Modern Age
  Miller, Clifford Leonard
The Wonderful World of Law and Order
  Davis, Ossie
Woodrow Wilson and the Negro
  Miller, Kelly
The Wooing
  Dunbar, Paul Laurence
A Word About Justice
  Muller-Thym, Thomas
A Word About Simple
  Jackson, Blyden
Word Poem
  Giovanni, Nikki
A Word To the Wise Is Enough
  Patterson, Raymond Richard
Words
  Brooks, Helen Morgan
Words
  Golden, Bernette
Words
  Goncalves, Joe
Words Like Freedom
  Hughes, Langston
Words! Words!
  Fauset, Jessie Redmond
Work It Out
  Fabio, Sarah Webster
The Worker
  Lilly, Octave, Jr.
The Worker
  Thomas, Richard W.
The Workin' Machine
  Sherman, Jimmie
Working with the Hands
  Washington, Booker Taliaferro

The World and the Jug
  Ellison, Ralph Waldo
World House
  King, Martin Luther, Jr.
The World I See
  Evans, Mari
The World Is a Mighty Ogre
  Johnson, Fenton
World Is Full of Remarkable Things
  Jones, LeRoi
The World Is Ready to Explode
  Sherman, Jimmie
World Weariness
  Cannon, David Wadsworth, Jr.
The World Wonders
  Miller, Clifford Leonard
The Worms
  Merriweather, Angela
Would I for All That Were
  Sun-Ra
The Wounds of Jesus
  Lovelace, C. C.
The Wreath
  Allen, Samuel W.
Writers: Black and White
  Hughes, Langston
The Writing of Essays
  Brawley, Benjamin Griffith
Written for Love of an Ascension—Coltrane
  Rodgers, Carolyn M.
The Wrong Side of the Morning
  Miller, May
Wrong's Reward
  Hawkins, Walter Everette
W. W.
  Jones, LeRoi

Y'all Forgit
  Bowen, Robert
Yardbird's Skull
  Dodson, Owen
Yas Suh!
  Williams, Vincent
Ye Bards of England
  Whitman, Albery Allson
A Year Without Seasons
  Williams, Mance
Yellow
  Harrison, DeLeon
The Yellow Bird
  Thompson, James W.
The Yellow One
  Walrond, Eric
Yes, I am lynched. Is it that I
  Dandridge, Raymond Garfield
Yes, Jesus Loves Me
  Johnson, Joe
Yessuh
  Cooper, Charles B.
Yes, the Secret Mind Whispers
  Young, Alexander
Yesterday's Child
  Reedburg, Robert
Yesterday's Hero
  Marshall, Lee

Yet Do I Marvel
  Cullen, Countee Porter
You
  Silvera, Edward S.
You and I
  Sirrah, Leumas
You and Me
  Rice, Jo Nell
You Are a Part of Me
  Yerby, Frank
You Are Alms
  Thompson, James W.
You Are Black
  Clarke, Helen F.
You Are Instantly Enfolded
  Burroughs, Margaret Taylor Goss
You Are Stolen Kisses in My Unsuspecting
Sleep
  Jones, Marte
You Are The Brave
  Patterson, Raymond Richard
You Ask
  Seese, Ethel Gray
You Because
  Sharon
You come to me
  Troupe, Quincy
You Finished It
  Lee, Don L.
You Gonna Let Me Take You Out Tonight,
Baby?
  Bullins, Ed
You know, Joe
  Durem, Ray
You Taught Me Love
  Bunton, Frederica Katheryne
You Tell Me
  Harris, William J.
You Touch My Black Aesthetic and I'll
Touch Yours
  Mayfield, Julian
You Walk Like Bells
  Hannibal, Gregor
You Wear Black Plastic Sunglasses
  Harris, William J.
Young Africans
  Brooks, Gwendolyn
A Young David: Birmingham
  Brooks, Helen Morgan
Young Gal's Blues
  Hughes, Langston
Young Hermit Speaks
  Harris, Helen C.
Young Heroes
  Brooks, Gwendolyn
Young Negro Poet
  Hernton, Calvin C.
The Young Ones
  Brown, Sterling A.
The Young Ones, Flip Side
  Emanuel, James A., Sr.
Young Poet
  O'Higgins, Myron
Young Soul
  Jones, LeRoi

Young Trainings
  McGaugh, Lawrence
The Young Warrior
  Johnson, James Weldon
Your eyes are mith
  Weatherly, Tom
Your Eyes Have Their Silence
  Barrax, Gerald William
Your Hands
  Grimke, Angelina Weld
Your Presence
  Beier, Ulli
Your promise
  Davis, Gloria
Your Songs
  Bennett, Gwendolyn B.
Your World
  Johnson, Georgia Douglas
You're Nothing but a Spanish Colored Kid
  Luciano, Felipe
You're The One
  Taylor, Mervyn
Youth
  Horne, Frank M.
Youth
  Hughes, Langston
Youth
  Johnson, Georgia Douglas
Youth
  Williams, Vincent
Youth of Twenty Contemplates Suicide
  Fletcher, T. Thomas Fortune
Youth Sings a Song of Rosebuds
  Cullen, Countee Porter
You've Taken My Nat and Gone
  Harding, Vincent
Yuh Lookin' Good
  Rodgers, Carolyn M.

Zalka Peetruza
  Dandridge, Raymond Garfield
Zalka Peetruza
  McKay, Claude
Zapata and the Landlord
  Spellman, Alfred B.
Zeus in August
  Mack, L. V.
Zion
  Geran, Juliana
Zocalo
  Harper, Michael S.
Zora Neale Hurston
  Bone, Robert
Zora Neale Hurston and the Eatonville
Anthropology
  Hemenway, Robert